AF678642

Transforming Politics and Policy in the Digital Age

Jonathan Bishop
Centre for Research into Online Communities and E-Learning Systems, Belgium

A volume in the Advances in Public Policy and Administration (APPA) Book Series

Information Science REFERENCE
An Imprint of IGI Global

Managing Director:	Lindsay Johnston
Production Editor:	Jennifer Yoder
Development Editor:	Allison McGinniss
Acquisitions Editor:	Kayla Wolfe
Typesetter:	Justin North
Cover Design:	Jason Mull

Published in the United States of America by
Information Science Reference (an imprint of IGI Global)
701 E. Chocolate Avenue
Hershey PA 17033
Tel: 717-533-8845
Fax: 717-533-8661
E-mail: cust@igi-global.com
Web site: http://www.igi-global.com

Copyright © 2014 by IGI Global. All rights reserved. No part of this publication may be reproduced, stored or distributed in any form or by any means, electronic or mechanical, including photocopying, without written permission from the publisher. Product or company names used in this set are for identification purposes only. Inclusion of the names of the products or companies does not indicate a claim of ownership by IGI Global of the trademark or registered trademark.

Library of Congress Cataloging-in-Publication Data

Transforming politics and policy in the digital age / Jonathan Bishop, editor.
pages cm
Includes bibliographical references and index.
ISBN 978-1-4666-6038-0 (hardcover) -- ISBN 978-1-4666-6039-7 (ebook) -- ISBN 978-1-4666-6041-0 (print & perpetual access) 1. Information technology--Social aspects. 2. Information technology--Political aspects. 3. Information society. 4. Political participation--Technological innovations. 5. Internet in public administration. I. Bishop, Jonathan, 1979-
HM851.T734 2014
303.48'33--dc23

2014013117

This book is published in the IGI Global book series Advances in Public Policy and Administration (APPA) (ISSN: pending; eISSN: pending)

British Cataloguing in Publication Data
A Cataloguing in Publication record for this book is available from the British Library.

All work contributed to this book is new, previously-unpublished material. The views expressed in this book are those of the authors, but not necessarily of the publisher.

For electronic access to this publication, please contact: eresources@igi-global.com.

Advances in Public Policy and Administration (APPA) Book Series

ISSN: pending
EISSN: pending

MISSION

Proper management of the public sphere is necessary in order to maintain order in modern society. Research developments in the field of public policy and administration can assist in uncovering the latest tools, practices, and methodologies for governing societies around the world.

The **Advances in Public Policy and Administration (APPA) Book Series** aims to publish scholarly publications focused on topics pertaining to the governance of the public domain. APPA's focus on timely topics relating to government, public funding, politics, public safety, policy, and law enforcement is particularly relevant to academicians, government officials, and upper-level students seeking the most up-to-date research in their field.

COVERAGE

- Government
- Law Enforcement
- Political Economy
- Politics
- Public Administration
- Public Funding
- Public Policy
- Resource Allocation
- Urban Planning

IGI Global is currently accepting manuscripts for publication within this series. To submit a proposal for a volume in this series, please contact our Acquisition Editors at Acquisitions@igi-global.com or visit: http://www.igi-global.com/publish/.

The Advances in Public Policy and Administration (APPA) Book Series (ISSN pending) is published by IGI Global, 701 E. Chocolate Avenue, Hershey, PA 17033-1240, USA, www.igi-global.com. This series is composed of titles available for purchase individually; each title is edited to be contextually exclusive from any other title within the series. For pricing and ordering information please visit http://www.igi-global.com/book-series/advances-public-policy-administration/97862. Postmaster: Send all address changes to above address. Copyright © 2014 IGI Global. All rights, including translation in other languages reserved by the publisher. No part of this series may be reproduced or used in any form or by any means – graphics, electronic, or mechanical, including photocopying, recording, taping, or information and retrieval systems – without written permission from the publisher, except for non commercial, educational use, including classroom teaching purposes. The views expressed in this series are those of the authors, but not necessarily of IGI Global.

Editorial Advisory Board

Anas Malik Alahmed, *Indiana University, USA*
Mohamad Alkhouja, *University of Maryland, USA*
Gado Alzouma, *American University of Nigeria, Nigeria*
Spyros Angelopoulos, *University of Warwick, UK*
Hamid R. Arabnia, *University of Georgia, USA*
Nelli Babayan, *Freie Universität Berlin, Germany*
Romain Badouard, *Mines ParisTech, France*
Mohd. Zaini Abu Bakar, *Universiti Sains Malaysia, Malaysia*
Marco Bani, *Scuola Superiore Sant'Anna Pisa, Italy*
Ilona Biernacka-Ligieza, *University of Opole, Poland*
Stansilas Bigirimana, *Africa University, Zimbabwe*
G. R. Boynton, *University of Iowa, USA*
Stefano Braghiroli, *University of Tartu, Estonia*
Yana Breindl, *Göttingen Centre for Digital Humanities, Germany*
Ivo Bukovsky, *Czech Technical University in Prague, Czech Republic*
Tom Carlson, *Åbo Akademi University, Finland*
Raphael Cohen-Almagor, *University of Hull, UK*
Massimo Cuono, *University of Torino, Italy*
Primavera De Filippi, *CERSA/CNRS, France*
Kamil Demirhan, *Hacettepe University, Turkey*
Jon Dron, *Athabasca University, Canada*
Kevin Fernandez, *Universiti Sains Malaysia, Malaysia*
Mary Francoli, *Carleton University, Canada*
Alison Freeman, *University of Wollongong, Australia*
Johannes Fritz, *Friedrich-Alexander-Universität Erlangen-Nürnberg, Germany*
Nuhu Gapsiso, *University of Maiduguri, Nigeria*
D. Elisabeth Glassco, *Rutgers, USA*
Ramakrishna Gokaraju, *University of Saskatchewan, Canada*
Cédric Gossart, *Telecom Business School, France*
M. V. Rajeev Gowda, *Indian Institute of Management Bangalore, India*
Amit Gupta, *Solido Design Automation Inc., Canada*
Madan M. Gupta, *University of Saskatchewan, Canada*

Raza Hasan, *Pop Currency, USA*
Rugayah Gy Hashim, *Universiti Teknologi MARA, Malaysia*
Noriyasu Homma, *Tohoku University, Japan*
Satheesh Ka, *Accenture Services Ltd., India*
Nikos Kaplantzis, *University of Athens, Greece*
Argyro P. Karanasiou, *University of Leeds, UK & Bournemouth University, UK*
Elitza Katzarova, *University of Trento, Italy*
Bert-Jaap Koops, *Tilburg University, The Netherlands*
Joanna Kulesza, *University of Lodz, Poland*
Georgios Lappas, *Technological Institute (TEI) of Western Macedonia, Macedonia*
Jun Liu, *University of Copenhagen, Denmark*
Cecilia G. Manrique, *University of Wisconsin – La Crosse, USA*
Shannon E. Martin, *Indiana University, USA*
Larry Martinez, *California State University, USA*
Eldred Masunungure, *University of Zimbabwe, Zimbabwe*
Samuel Mungai Mbuguah, *Masinde Muliro University of Science and Technology, Kenya*
Norbert Merkovity, *University of Szeged, Hungary*
Patricia Mindus, *Uppsala University, Sweden*
Gary Moats, *Lee University, USA*
Adam Monteith, *Independent Researcher, USA*
Colin Morgan, Univ*ersity of South Wales, UK*
Shepherd Mpofu, *University of the Witwatersrand, South Africa*
Geoffrey Muchiri Muketha, *Masinde Muliro University of Science and Technology, Kenya*
Francesca Musiani, *MINES ParisTech, France*
Rui Alexandre Novais, *University of Porto, Portugal & University of Minho, Portugal & University of Liverpool, UK*
Alison N. Novak, *Drexel University, USA*
Sivamurugan Pandian, *Universiti Sains Malaysia, Malaysia*
Bogdan Pătruţ, *Vasile Alecsandri University of Bacau, Romania*
Purnima Prakash, *Indian Institute of Management Bangalore, India*
Mohammad Reza Rajati, *University of Southern California, USA*
Valentina Reda, *University of Naples Federico II, Italy*
Torsten Reiners, *Curtin Business School, Australia*
Rosália Rodrigues, *Universidade da Beira Interior, Portugal*
António Rosas, *Universidade Aberta, Portugal & Universidade Técnica de Lisboa, Portugal*
Steven Sams, *Brunel University, UK*
Robert J. Sarfi, *Boreas Group LLC, USA*
Valérie Schafer, *French National Research Council (CNRS), France*
Sónia Pedro Sebastião, *Technical University of Lisbon, Portugal*
Keren Sereno, *Independent Researcher, Israel*
Bill Sherman, *Seattle University, USA*
Bhupesh Kumar Singh, *G. B. Pant University of Agriculture and Technology, India*
Jakob Svensson, *Karlstad University, Sweden*
Sam Takavarasha, Jr., *Computer Science University of Zimbabwe, Zimbabwe*

Holly Tootell, *University of Wollongong, Australia*
Cristian Vaccari, *University of Bologna, Italy*
Andreas Veglis, *Aristotle University of Thessaloniki, Greece*
Nicole Velasco, *Lee University, USA*
Gyanendra Kumar Verma, *Indian Institute of Information Technology Allahabad, India*
Lucia Vesnic-Alujevic, *Ghent University, Belgium*
Shefali Virkar, *University of Oxford, UK*
Timothy D. Webster, *Genist Systems Inc., Canada*
Joseph Wilson, *University of Maiduguri, Nigeria*
Lincoln C. Wood, *Auckland University of Technology, New Zealand*
Prodromos Yannas, *Technological Institute (TEI) of Western Macedonia, Macedonia*

Table of Contents

Detailed Table of Contents

This chapter addresses the relation community-society in the case of Web-based constellations; how is society represented if we meet Web-based communities? Why are Web-based societies kept invisible while Web-communities emerge as a quasi-natural consequence of Web presence? Did Web-communities flourish because society is absent on the Web? How can we expect the equivalent of societies to penetrate life on the Web? Will there be rules on pre-emptive strike of cyber hackers? etc.

Information Seeking Behaviour (ISB) is becoming an interesting topic, especially with the advancement of the World Wide Web and technologically enhanced data collection techniques. Differences between generations, such as the Net Generation and Baby Boomers are becoming more and more evident. The Net Generation have shown they are enjoying more public policy participation than ever before through the use of the Internet. Finding an overall methodology that takes into account this generation is therefore a challenge. This chapter applies a heuristic framework to a number of research papers on the Net Generation and ISBs in order to critically analyse and evaluate the information within it in order to gain an insight into the most effective approach to ISB research. Through interpreting these research papers, this chapter attempts to gauge the scope and develop an understanding of ISB research in relation to the Net Generation and discover the most effective methodological approach for the emerging discipline.

Beyond the likes of a purely technical issue, situated at the heart of the transport layer of the TCP/IP protocol, net neutrality takes the form of a complex political debate. This chapter's endeavour is to study the set of dimensions that make it possible for net neutrality to be read as a global political issue. The chapter follows the constantly evolving notion of net neutrality as it interrogates the Internet as a laboratory of governance, the actors and dynamics involved in the establishment of a "technical democracy" and the dialectic between the Internet's universal, egalitarian ideal and the techno-political measures shaping the "network of networks."

While the concept of Classroom 2.0 has been around for over a decade, the concept of electronic and distance learning as a mode to improve education outcomes has existed ever since the first broadcast of television programs carrying educational content. The governments in the United Kingdom have always sought to intervene in education, whether this has been allowing schools to opt-out of local authority control with grant-maintained schools under Margaret Thatcher, co-operative trusts under Tony Blair, or free schools under David Cameron. Not all government interventions are as successful. Homogenized one-size-fits-all education based on catchment areas such as Comprehensive Schools and state-run projects like the UK e-University have been shown to lack the return on investment of Specialist and Independent Schools and the Open University. This chapter reviews some of the microeconomic models used by governments to intervene in the market for instructional services, including e-participation in education, namely Classroom 2.0. It also looks at some of the possibilities of Classroom 2.0 in education systems that have been affected by UK and respective devolved government's education policy.

Wales is the "land of the poets so soothing to me," according to its national anthem. The political and economic landscape does not on the whole provide for the many creative people that are in Welsh communities. Social media Websites like MySpace and YouTube as well as Websites like MTV.com, eJay, and PeopleSound, whilst providing space for artists to share their works, but do not usually consider the needs of local markets, such as in relation to Welsh language provision through to acknowledgement of Welsh place names and Wales's status as a country. The chapter finds that there are distinct issues in relation to presenting information via the Web- or Tablet-based devises and suggests some of the considerations needed when designing multi-platform environments.

How has the Internet come about in Europe? How did the "network of networks" and ICTs become political stakes for EU Institutions? This chapter sheds light on facts, limits, and tensions of the building of a political union in the ICT regulation field. It analyses the role of various stakeholders, from technical experts to ordinary citizens, according to a historical approach structured around three key notions: appropriating, governing, and using the Internet. By studying a relatively long period (from the 1970s to the early 2010s) and by observing the Internet as a tool for both internal consolidation and for asserting the EU on the international stage, the authors map the main features and trends that structure the European relationship to the "network of networks." They, thus, show that the Internet's political dimension encompasses numerous and heterogeneous issues in the European context.

Alternative news Websites are a fascinating arena for studying the dynamics between politics, media, and activism. This chapter presents a comparison of news framing in Israeli mainstream news Websites versus Israeli alternative news Websites. To achieve this, 342 items which were published over the course of 14 months (November 2007-December 2008) in 8 Israeli media originations were coded. These items covered the demonstrations and direct actions against the Separation Fence near the Palestinian village of Ni'lin in which Israeli radical left activists took part. The items were coded by qualitative content analysis according to the principles of the Grounded Theory Method. The findings show considerable differences concerning the characters of quoted sources, media frames, coverage patterns, and linking strategies between the mainstream Websites (and print newspaper) and the alternative Websites. Out of those differences, 4 potential political functions that alternative news Websites can fulfill in radical political protests are identified: recruiting activists, consolidating a subversive political consciousness and strengthening the collective identity, building online network between colleague organizations, and distributing and storing controversial information. This research shows that in order to develop a deeper understanding of the role of new media in social protests, it is necessary to simultaneously rely on alternative media, theories, and studies in addition to the emerging knowledge regarding the characters and uses of the Internet in general.

The coal fields communities in Wales were once one of the most prosperous places to live in the British Isles. Many people flocked to Wales in search of a new life and opportunities for their family. Coal became known as "Black Gold" and the industrialized coal fields became centres of productivity. Media use in Welsh households has generally been controlled by dominating men who saw and in many cases still see themselves as the "heads of the household." Such control over the media consumption of women was not out of place in the UK as a whole, where men have assumed a place as a de facto media institution who force choices of what to watch on their households. This chapter presents a longitudinal study of three women in Wales conducted between 2000 and 2013 that shows how the media consumption and audience styles have changed over time so that power structures from both men and traditional media institutions have all but eroded.

Section 4
E-Government, E-Voting, and E-Democracy

In the Internet age, the increasing prevalence of online voting regularly sparks controversy regarding security. This chapter addresses the topic of Internet voting by describing the characteristics of a democratic election and placing this new mode of voting within the context of the entire family of electronic voting systems. The link between transparency of the electoral system, voter confidence, and legitimacy is then reiterated, and the components of reliability and safety requirements of security are detailed. This analysis and the overview of several real implementations of Internet voting systems in this chapter show that transparency vanishes due to the combination of anonymity and virtualization of the votes while absolute security seems out of reach. Finally, it appears that the search for procedures for verifying the proper operation of the procedures should be accompanied by a strong evolution of the electorate legal rules.

Technologies carry politics since they embed values. It is therefore surprising that mainstream political and legal theory have taken the issue so lightly. Compared to what has been going on over the past few decades in the other branches of practical thought, namely ethics, economics, and the law, political theory lags behind. Yet the current emphasis on Internet politics that polarizes the apologists holding the Web to overcome the one-to-many architecture of opinion building in traditional representative democracy, and the critics who warn that cyber-optimism entails authoritarian technocracy has acted as a wake up call. This chapter sets the problem, "What is it about ICTs, as opposed to previous technical devices, that impact on politics and determine uncertainty about democratic matters?," into the broad context of practical philosophy by offering a conceptual map of clusters of micro-problems and concrete examples relating to "e-democracy." The point is to highlight when and why the hyphen of e-democracy has a conjunctive or a disjunctive function in respect to stocktaking from past experiences and settled democratic theories. The chapter's claim is that there is considerable scope to analyse how and why online politics fail or succeed. The field needs both further empirical and theoretical work.

Local governments, and particularly local public officials, have adopted online social networking tools en masse in an effort to communicate with constituents. As this chapter shows, the resulting information flow consists of communication from the public official to constituents, from constituents to the public official, and among constituents, but in the context of the public official's social network. This environment constitutes a "civic social network," which operates as the new public square. Many local governments, however, are attempting to bar officials' use of civic social networks because they risk violation of open government laws, such as open meeting and open records laws. This effort to stifle valuable civic communication harms norms of transparency and accountability – the very values that open government laws should promote. These laws should be revised or reinterpreted to allow civic social networks to fulfill their promise as the new public square.

Preface

The word "politics" may conjure different things in different people. For me, as a former town councilor, it refers to all the unnecessary shenanigans that take place in elections and elected institutions by those seeking to be elected by the popular vote. Politics, I, therefore, find undesirable, and the aim of this book is to show how different strategies and technologies can be used so that public policy—which elected representatives are supposed to implement—is achieved without the unwanted position taking of politics.

I, therefore, introduce the concept of Polnetics – derived from the first three letters of politics and policy, the last three letters of Internet, and the "ics" to signify the link with politics. The title of this book, *Transforming Politics and Policy in the Digital Age*, perfectly sets up the aim of Polnetics – to achieve public policy by transforming political systems so that the partisanism and tribalism are removed so that problems are dealt with without reinforcing the positions of political parties.

Polnetics as a field of study is distinct from other concepts I have worked on, such as network politics and e-politics. Network politics focuses mainly on technology, whether mobile phone networks, engineering, or the Internet. E-politics mainly focuses on government systems and politicians, such as the ways the elected representatives try to "engage" with the public. Whilst e-politics will investigate the relationships between politicians and government in relation to technology, the field of Polnetics looks more at the social aspects of current affairs and online debate shifts, where policymaking is the focus and party politics, and other political issues are seen as getting in the way of policy creation and implementation.

This book is split into four sections. The first section, "Digital Divide and Equality of Access," seeks to look at the barriers to policy-making by people in minority and other social groups. The first chapter in this section is by Piet Kommers, titled "Sense of Community." This chapter importantly looks at the issue of the digital divide and equality of access, the perfect chapter to start this section, which features both terms. The chapter argues that a lot is needed to advance past social media in order to have a "Web society," where tests of emulation, variation, and transformation will allow true 3D environments to exist to alter the way the Internet is imagined as an environment for community and change.

The second chapter in the first section is by me and looks into the information seeking behaviour of a range of people who were born over a 20-year period known as the Net Generation. Whilst many academics have tried to put a date range on the Net Generation, it is clear that in different societies the extent that teenagers have grown up with technology to be the first group of digital teens is different for each country and maybe even each locality. This chapter, therefore, makes an important contribution in understanding the difference between younger generations like this and the older ones (e.g. Baby Boomers) who will have different approaches to using the Internet. The chapter takes a comparative document analysis approach by comparing four relevant research papers and discussing the consequences for understanding the Net Generation.

The third chapter in section one is by Valérie Schafer, Francesca Musiani, and Hervé Le Crosnier. The chapter attempts to look beyond the technical issue surrounding network neutrality. This chapter's endeavour is to study the set of dimensions that make it possible for net neutrality to be read as a global political issue. The chapter follows the constantly evolving notion of net neutrality as it interrogates the Internet as a laboratory of governance, the actors and dynamics involved in the establishment of a "technical democracy," and the dialectic between the Internet's universal, egalitarian ideal and the techno-political measures shaping the "network of networks." The final chapter in section one is by me and explores the various issues arising out of macroeconomics for education. It looks at the various models of school, from monopolies to perfect competition and discusses their implications in England and Wales, where education policies are quite different.

Section two looks at international, national, and regional issues. The first chapter, by me and Lisa Mannay, looks at the Welsh music scene and how Welsh musician are at a disadvantage, as the political and economic landscape does not on the whole provide for the many creative people that are in Welsh communities. The chapter discusses how, despite social media Websites like MySpace and YouTube as well as Websites like MTV.com, eJay, and PeopleSound providing space for artists to share their works, they do not usually consider the needs of local markets, such as in relation to Welsh language provision through to acknowledgement of Welsh place names and Wales's status as a country. The second chapter, by Valérie Schafer and Romain Badouard, looks at how the Internet has come about in Europe. How did the "network of networks" and ICTs become political stakes for EU institutions? This chapter proposes to shed light on facts, limits, and tensions of the building of a political union in the ICT regulation field. It analyses the role of various stakeholders, from technical experts to ordinary citizens, according to a historical approach structured around three key notions: appropriating, governing, and using the Internet. Both of these chapters show how the consideration of issues at a local level, and indeed an international level, will impact how people take an interest with others in their communities.

Keren Sereno's chapter, the third in this section, presents a comparison of news framing in the Holy Land, such as the difference between the mainstream news approved of by the Zionist leadership in the Israelian Authority compared to alternative news Websites, often expressing non-Zionist opinion. This chapter explores the demonstration at the Separation Fence near the Palestinian village of Ni'lin in which Zionist activists took part. The chapter argues that in order to develop a deeper understanding of the role of new media in social protests it is necessary to simultaneously rely on alternative media, theories, and studies in addition to the emerging knowledge regarding the characters and uses of the Internet in general. The final chapter in this section, by me, presents a longitudinal study of three women in Wales conducted between 2000 and 2013, which by using genre theory shows how the media consumption and audience styles have changed over time so that power structures from both men and traditional media institutions have all but eroded. Both of these final chapters show that the targeting of media at different audiences is a key part of multimedia studies and the extent to which technology can appeal to different audiences.

Section three opens with a chapter by Mary Francoli, which explores the concept of the "Social Media Campaign." Mary uses the example of the May 2011 election dubbed "Canada's First Social Media Election." The chapter asks "What makes a campaign social?" as well as whether the term "social media campaign" adequately describes current campaign practices. Ultimately, the chapter argues we have limited evidence that social media has led to increased sociality when it comes to electoral politics, which calls the appropriateness of the term "social media campaign" into question. The second chapter, by Cédric Gossarw, builds on those in the previous section by examining the extent to which digital technologies can threaten democracy by creating "information cocoons," within which information is filtered and tailored to individual tastes and prevailing opinions. The chapter suggests a methodology to evaluate that risk, as well as ways to mitigate it. Various methods have been used to analyse the polarisation of opinions in human societies, such as the ones analysing the traces left by Internet users in blogs or hypertext links. The chapter, therefore, provides a review of these methods after having explained the main factor conducive to the creation of information closure. Both these chapters provide a clear message that public policy and political campaigns need to understand their audience to be effective.

The third and final chapter of the section is by me and looks at using media and genre theories to understand the impact of Internet trolling in the area of current affairs. My chapter tries to distinguish the 1990s kind of trolling from the 2010s kind by referring to the former as classical trolling and the latter anonymous trolling. It concludes by presenting a model for understanding which genres of online community are at risk for particular types of trolling. I would hope that my final chapter in this section extends the discussion on the public sphere through making it possible to see how different types of online media change based on the medium.

The first chapter in section four is from Chantal Enguehard. Chantal's chapter addresses the topic of Internet voting by describing the characteristics of a democratic election and placing this new mode of voting within the context of the entire family of electronic voting systems. The link between transparency of the electoral system, voter confidence, and legitimacy is then reiterated and the components of reliability and safety requirements of security are detailed. The second chapter by Patricia Mindus raises the concern that an emphasis on Internet politics polarizes the "apologists" that attempt to overcome the one-to-many architecture of opinion-building in traditional representative democracy. The main theme is that there is considerable scope to analyse how and why online politics fail or succeed. The field needs both further empirical and theoretical work. Both of these chapters show that there is a clear fragmentation in how policymaking is done online, showing that there are a number of issues that need to be resolved before the Internet forms a core part of policymaking and problem-sharing.

William R. Sherman, in the third chapter in this section, argues that local governments, and particularly local public officials, have adopted online social networking tools en masse in an effort to communicate with constituents. William argues that the environment constitutes a "civic social network," which operates as the new public square and efforts by governments to stifle valuable civic communication harms norms of transparency and accountability. The fourth and final chapter by Bert-Jaap Koops and Bibi van den Berg argues that identity information is a major factor in people's willingness to participate in online applications, but that it is a double-edged sword. The chapter triangulates findings from a survey among Government 2.0 users and quantitative and qualitative analyses of Dutch Government 2.0 Websites. This reveals the identity information Web 2.0 users want to have of other participants and are willing to provide about themselves, the importance of the role of information of civil servants, and the relationship of identity information with the interaction level on Government 2.0 applications. It is clear from these final two chapters that the politicians have a lot to gain from social media and so-called Web 2.0 as applied to party politics.

Through the compilation of chapters in this book, I hope to have shown that there is an alternative to the representative democracy that exists in the West, where decisions are made by politicians, even if they can be made by the people they represent amicably. Politicians, I would argue, should only need to make decisions on two occasions – when the issue is so divisive that the only way to resolve it is through an independent person who carries the legitimacy of being elected or where an essential service or provision that would not be provided without government intervention needs to have the backing of those who are responsible for a constituency where such service or provision is needed.

Jonathan Bishop
Centre for Research into Online Communities and E-Learning Systems, Belgium

Section 1
Digital Divide and Equality of Access

Chapter 1
Sense of Community:
Perceptions of Individual and Group Members of Online Communities

Piet Kommers
University of Twente, The Netherlands

ABSTRACT

This chapter addresses the relation community-society in the case of Web-based constellations; how is society represented if we meet Web-based communities? Why are Web-based societies kept invisible while Web-communities emerge as a quasi-natural consequence of Web presence? Did Web-communities flourish because society is absent on the Web? How can we expect the equivalent of societies to penetrate life on the Web? Will there be rules on pre-emptive strike of cyber hackers? etc.

INTRODUCTION

The "Digital Divide" and "Equality of Access" can be seen as the top agenda for the full societal integration of Web-applications. Any other efforts to make social networking and social media integrative seem to be obsolete if not citizens have a fair access and mindset for Web presence. Web communities may already resonate the ideals from for instance Emile Durkheimer's concern on how societies could maintain their integrity and coherence in modernity. Durkheimer's early idea on sociology developed in the late 19th and early 20th century. One hundred year later, the murky perspectives of segregated societies are intimidating; even for those who fought for anti-monarchy and lifting religious barriers; they would hesitate to welcome the so-called networked society.

At the arrival of Web-based communities the question arose in how far the attribute "community" is at stake. Traditionally, community sense is based upon "membership" and "relational patterns." Being in a "central position" would legitimate that a member has a crucial position. Dropping out when being in a central position causes the community structure to fall apart. However the targeted "sense" goes beyond structure and status; Faith, commitment, consensus, mutual belonging and a shared sense of purpose. As the essence of community gets in focus, the clearer it distinguishes from society, especially as the notion of community grew on the evolv-

DOI: 10.4018/978-1-4666-6038-0.ch001

Copyright © 2014, IGI Global. Copying or distributing in print or electronic forms without written permission of IGI Global is prohibited.

ing individualism (Etzioni, 1993). The answer to the question "Can communities develop without societal context?" seems to be affirmative, as we the answer to the question "if societies essentially need communities?"

BACKGROUND

"Community" refers back to "commune" (in common) and thus contrasts with "Society" that is closer associated with urban aggregations: Divisions of labor, class awareness and the invention of "collective consciousness" (Durkheim, 1997). Sarason (1974) declares sense of community as the willingness to comply with what others expect from them; being a member of a larger structure. Gusfield (1975) discerns the territorial and the relational. We can say that through the Web and its virtuality, the relational aspect of communities have conquered the territorial; even the superimposed topology on relationship patterns seems to fail. Besides family relationships, proximity and adjacency have ruled community membership. "Close friendship" was often misunderstood and led to the notion of "real friendship." Its basis was that despite a community contours two persons found mutual affinity. It leads to suppose communities as intermediate stage between society and friendship. The "networked society" characterizes as escaping from spatial of ideological proximity; any momentary criterion for making a relationship is valid, as long as there is a mutual sense of sharing or trusting. The fascination was that 2nd and 3rd order relationships developed so well in SNSs (Social Network Sites). Transient networks derive power from its "you, me, here and now." It is like meeting a person at the bus station, who asks you to share a taxi; the conversation and affinity develops just around this shared need to arrive at another location, without any obligation to ask "why" or "what if." In a certain way this transient togetherness could be seen as the most pure format for joining as the legitimation to sit together is completely in the incident of location and time; no question on history or ambition.

SHARING SPACE AND TIME ON THE WEB

Place and space: Web presence allows closeness without further obligation. In terms of browsing and anchoring, Web-meetings are sharing a transition: meeting and farewell are destined by earlier meetings with those who were linked to those of one contact before. Social media add to the traditional face-to-face meetings as it allows to see the longer chains of episodes; who were meeting just before and just after my meeting? What remarkable events typically happen at a certain fragment of the week? Time and duration: what episodes are good candidates to organize a party? Which group suffers from a long time-out? Etc. Sharing space and time means: invest in common awareness; the fact that both you and one of you community members spend efforts in (re)defining values, means that you both recognize each other in later plans. In other words: increase the chance that you mention each other in future project plans. So: sharing is more than common ownership. It implies mutual advocacy for each other's potential. The notion of space seems to be convertible with attentional salience. In terms of marketing potential this is a seed for curiosity and recognition in case of parallel candidates. In terms of sense of community it is an early step towards altruistic attitude: those who

LOOKING GOOD: THE ROLE OF BEAUTY IN WEB COMMUNITIES

Recently a study in social networking revealed that users tend to make new connections via attractive friends (Jaschinski & Kommers, 2012). The experiment intended to understand better how relationships develop online. "Social network sites have become essential for managing relationships in today's life," they explain. "Therefore, it is increasingly important for scientists to understand how impressions are formed and connections develop in the virtual world." People meet in online communities while using their profile and its photo. Community members can only control their photo, not how it is perceived. Also they cannot control the profiles of other users. Newcomers judge a new member based on his/her company. In face-to-face settings a person has the opportunity to project him/herself in a variety of modes and overrule an earlier photographic impression via the Web. 78 Students participated to see how the attractiveness of Facebook friends affects the impressions formed of friends of friends by users. The photos of "friends" were mocked up as if they were Facebook friends. Students were asked to carry out a "hot or not" type assessment based purely on the visual appearance of the user's profile photo within the page. The results showed that persons were considered as more likeable and were seen as a potential friend when they are associated with good-looking friends. In essence the results can be exploited by job seekers and early artists, who need the attractiveness of the public. Similar effects of attractiveness on the Web can be expected for other modalities as soon as they appear on network sites. It implies that Web communities may suffer from the more narrow channels where "friends are attracted because of friends, friends' friends and beyond.

MOTIVES AND RELEVANCE OF ONLINE FRIENDSHIPS

Similar to the role of beauty, a next study traced different motives why persons establish online friendships, for example via Facebook (Damaschke & Kommers, 2012). Via a focus group this study also looked into the differences in importance that profile owners attach to different (groups of) online friends. The study resulted in four categories of factors that influenced the number of friendships that a person establishes online; person–focused, online–friends, purpose and dedication. The awareness of these categories may serve as a tool for potential employers who can then easily assess an applicant based on his/her number of online friends. But also it might work as attractor for those who search community members and those who want to evaluate a community's effectiveness.

IMPLICATIONS AND FUTURE RESEARCH DIRECTIONS

We have seen that the manifestations of Web-based communities has stimulated the lust in liaising with groups and mentalities that would be too subtle in the era of face-to-face meetings only. We could say that by sacrificing the endurance and trust criterion we allowed ourselves to explore human nature of being multi-facetted. We have seen that Web-based gatherings brought a milder criterion for perceiving a sense of community. However the same factors of virtuality and transience in Web communities make us cautious about deceiving factors like the facial- rather than the voice expression. Also the epistemic- ("relationship pattern on Facebook") rather than the episodic parameters (what did you and me experience together in a face-to-face situation?). The big difference is that in real face-to-face situations the proportion of shared attention is much higher than in mediated presence like social media or teleconferences. Future research should therefore focus on the differential effects of unilateral versus multiplexed social attention. It seems inevitable that the direct face-to-face experience provokes a much deeper impact on both partners. The slightest distraction via intermittent social media access will hamper this basic mutual trust of readiness and dedication.

DISCUSSION

If the current trend towards social life on the Web follows the traditional sequence of innovative development, then we can expect some interesting processes to see the coming years. The traditional sequence is that a new medium like for instance "Computer Aided Design" typically goes through the next stages:

1. Emulation; copy the pencil-based drawing table as literally as possible.
2. Variation; bring new elements in the tools and procedures for sketching and 2D layout.
3. Transformation from 2D representation into 3D spatial modelling, skipping the stage of "drawing."

Similarly we may ask ourselves where we are now in building and imagining Web-communities. If you believe we are now in Stage1, it means that we just try to copy mechanisms that we already know from face-to-face, letter-based correspondence and mass media a long time before.

If you estimate social media already arrived in Stage 2, it implies that we managed to make substantial contributions to the traditional way people meet and maintain social relationships.

It is not likely that you adopt the opinion that social media already essentially "changed" social life. More likely is that we expect one of the coming social media to supplant some of the social contact mechanisms nowadays and add completely new add new ways to find new friendships and social environments really.

Based on my chapter you may already guess that my opinion is that with the current generation of social media we still are in Stage 1: We just try to mimic what is between people in circles of interest. It can be seen as an early step towards Web-community. However it is still a way to go before we arrive at "Web-society"; it would imply that, similar to the transition from rural to urban, citizens in Web communities can intermingle and cooperate based their various levels of professionalism while still the overall societal etiquette stays intact. We are still far away from this. One of the first steps is that Web-communities reach the level of normative formation like for instance uncontrived attention during sessions. Please make up your mind what is your criterion for the next generation of Web-based communities.

REFERENCES

Damaschke, K. C., & Kommers, P. (2012). Motives and relevance of online friendships. *IJWBC*, *8*(2), 266–280.

Durkheim, E. (1997). *The division of labor in society* (L. A. Coser, Trans.). New York: Free Press.

Etzioni, A. (1993). *The spirit of community: Rights, responsibilities and the communitarian agenda*. New York: Crown.

Jaschinski, C., & Kommers, P. (2012). Does beauty matter? The role of friends' attractiveness and gender on social attractiveness ratings of individuals on Facebook. *IJWBC*, *8*(3), 389–401. doi:10.1504/IJWBC.2012.048060

Sarason, S. B. (1974). *The psychological sense of community: Prospects for a community psychology*. San Francisco: Jossey-Bass.

KEY TERMS AND DEFINITIONS

Mediated Communication: Human communication that uses intermediate steps like "distance media" in order to bridge space and even time-zones (a-synchronous communication).

Multiplexed Attention: Attention that is spread along several goals like listening to the radio while driving a car or cooking diner. Media like smart phones and tablet PCs penetrate in settings that do not allow scattered attention. Complex tasks like aircraft battles or brain surgery prescribe our attention to rotate along the many dimensions so that finally no criterion is "overlooked."

Networked Society: The awareness that nowadays (postmodern society) the traditional dimensions like religion, class society, hierarchic authority etc. get less and less impact on what we strive at, are afraid of, etc. Transport, distance media (TV, telephone and the Internet) have worked as a catalyst for the notion that we are member in many social networks at the same time. Social media have sped up this process even more; there are no limits in terms of 'social presence' or the number of 'friends' that we allow to see our more intimate messages.

Online Friendship: Both 1) the situation of sustaining friendships that evolved during face-to-face relationships before, and 2) also the creation of completely new friendship relationships are part of "Online Friendship." In case of 2 we might question when "real friendship" is at stake, while this question might be appropriate in case of 1 as well.

Sense of Community: The extent to which the members of a Web community feel the circumstance of a real social binding like in natural social groupings: the amount of altruism, trust, recognition of identity and authenticity, etc.

Virtuality: The trend to accept models and the more indirect representations of our reality as real enough in order to explore them and use them for our imagination and decision making.

Web-Based Communities: Social gathering via social media and social networking. Its members feel a certain amount of social cohesion: The so-called amount of Sense of Community.

Chapter 2
We Don't Do Politics:
An Analysis and Discussion of Information Seeking Behaviour Research in Relation to the Net Generation

Jonathan Bishop
Centre for Research into Online Communities and E-Learning Systems, Belgium

ABSTRACT

Information Seeking Behaviour (ISB) is becoming an interesting topic, especially with the advancement of the World Wide Web and technologically enhanced data collection techniques. Differences between generations, such as the Net Generation and Baby Boomers are becoming more and more evident. The Net Generation have shown they are enjoying more public policy participation than ever before through the use of the Internet. Finding an overall methodology that takes into account this generation is therefore a challenge. This chapter applies a heuristic framework to a number of research papers on the Net Generation and ISBs in order to critically analyse and evaluate the information within it in order to gain an insight into the most effective approach to ISB research. Through interpreting these research papers, this chapter attempts to gauge the scope and develop an understanding of ISB research in relation to the Net Generation and discover the most effective methodological approach for the emerging discipline.

INTRODUCTION

The world is under the influence of three major trends: the revolutionary development of information and communication technologies; the transition to a knowledge society; and the new learning mode of the Net Generation (Lee, 2013). Online communities have the potential to radically transform social interaction and community formation (Lutters & Ackerman, 2003). Research into online communities draws on methods, theories and practices from many disciplines, making this an exciting and challenging field (Preece & Maloney-Krichmar, 2005). One group that has taken full advantage of Internet systems is the Net Generation. Online technologies such as network gaming are highly effective at influencing not just the perspective of N-Geners but their view of being citizens (Oblinger, 2004). As voters the Net Generation have shown they are enjoying

DOI: 10.4018/978-1-4666-6038-0.ch002

Copyright © 2014, IGI Global. Copying or distributing in print or electronic forms without written permission of IGI Global is prohibited.

more public policy participation than ever before through the use of the Internet (Tak, 2006). It is therefore important to have an understanding of how literature on the Net Generation inter-relates with other literature.

Net Generation's experiences in engaging and interacting in electronic communications, particularly in games, means low level interactivity in a learning management system is of little interest to them (Oliver & Goerke, 2007). Investigations into the use of online communities have used a range of these methods from the theoretical, based on literature reviews (Bishop, 2007c) to empirical studies using quantitative research methods such as questionnaires (Leung, 2003). There are those based on qualitative methods using interviewing to develop detailed narratives about Internet use (Choi & Ross, 2006). And there are those which combine interviewing with questionnaires (Choo, Detlor, & Turnbull, 2000). The latter three of these three studies will be investigated in detail and critically evaluated.

BACKGROUND

Much research into information seeking behaviour (ISB) has focused on a small number of factors identified before the empirical investigation has begun (Berryman, 2006). Traditional locations for information seeking, like libraries, no longer have a monopoly on information sources, but such sources can apply classic marketing principles to attract and better serve new generations of users, such as the Net Generation (Barnes, Marateo, & Ferris, 2007). Indeed, students from the Net Generation are generally interested in having online multimedia resources at their fingertips and one of the driving factors in the creation of Web-based educational resources is on-going student demand (Krzic et al., 2013).

Research has found that both the Net Generation and Baby boomers identify Google and human sources as the first sources they use for quick searches (Connaway, Radford, Dickey, De Angelis Williams, & Confer, 2008). This showed that young N-Geners mentioned consulting parents most frequently, while the older N-Geners consult friends and professors. Connaway et al. (2008) found that Baby Boomers indicate that they consult their personal libraries and colleagues.

There have been a number of models that have attempted to understand online communities. de Souza and Preece (2004) developed the Online Community Framework and later Bishop (2007c) proposed the Ecological Cognition Framework (ECF). The later of these two models provides a useful basis for analysing what motivates actors to participate in online communities and the specific elements of their mind and body and the world that could affect their political behaviour. Bishop's framework (2007a) was developed through drawing from the literature on online communities the factors that influence behaviour in these systems. The ECF, which is illustrated on the left in the diagram in Figure 2, is made up of four layers containing quantifiable elements connected by process arrows with specific qualities. As explored in more detail by Bishop (2007a) the Environment is the base of the model, which contains actors who can be measured by factors such as age, height, and others, artefacts, which can be measured by size, texture and others, structures and other external representations. The Environment is connected upwards by the Stimuli process to Level 3, which contains the sensory preceptors. Level 3 is connected to Level 2 by the 'impetus', which converts the stimulus from the environment into something understandable by the mind. Level 2 contains the cognitions that are evoked by the particular impetus, such as a resonance from a social stimulus from someone speaking may provoke a remembered belief or remind someone of a plan. These 'cognitions' can also be measured using various quantifiable measures. The next process is the 'intent', which is based on the cognition evoked and leads to one of the five binary opposition forces being provoked at Level 1. The selected binary opposition forces then create a new cognition which interacts with other cognitions between Level 1 and 2, then the process between Level 2 and 3 is where the actor makes a judgement as to whether they want to accept this cognition or change it, and the final process is where the cognition creates a response, be it something internal such as a new belief or a specific change in the external environment.

Research Methods for Understanding Online Participation

Methodologies and methods have often been thought of in terms of quantitative and qualitative, though the distinction between method and methodology is crucial to designing a research study. According to Silverman (2006) methodology identifies a general approach to studying research topics, whereas method refers to a specific research technique. Much research into the online information seeking follows a 'hypothetico-deductive' approach. According to the hypothetico-deductive (HD) method of theory testing, a hypothesis is confirmed on the basis of its observational consequences (Grimes, 1990). The hypothetico-deductive method is considered to be the principal means by which causal relationships are established and the most effective means of modelling known phenomena (Henwood & Pidgeon, 1993, p.14).

Surveying the research into information seeking behaviour, suggests that the hypothetico-deductive approach is indeed the dominant methodology in researching online information seeking behaviour, even if not explicitly stated, with studies as early in the World-wide Web's development as 1998 adopting the method (Gorman, 1998). Mansourian and Madden (2007) identify a range of other approaches used to research information seeking behaviour, such as inductive research from a phenomenological perspective.

Mansourian and Madden (2007) also state that, 'Web searching is a multifaceted exercise, so the appropriateness of a research method is dependent on the focus of the study,' suggesting that there is room for a range of research methods for investigating the topic. They do however cite Martzoukou (2004) who argues for an overall methodology for researching information seeking behaviour, which gives researchers a framework for a consistent approach to studying the subject, perhaps much in the same way case studies have been used for studying organisations and ethnography has been used for studying human cultures.

METHODOLOGY

Some of the most widely used methods for researching online are interviewing, observation and document analysis (Mann & Stewart, 2000). Interviewing is the most widely applied technique for conducting systematic social inquiry in academic, clinical, business, political and media life with qualitative research being well established in this area and observational techniques are also widely used in conventional qualitative research, frequently used in conjunction with some form of interviewing (*ibid.*). Choi and Ross (2006) clearly stated that they adopted a qualitative approach. Henn, Weinstein, and Foard (2006) argue that a definition of qualitative research could be that which is associated with interpretative investigations with the aim to develop and appreciation of the underlying motivations that people have for doing what they do as opposed to simply test out theories.

The overall question therefore is whether there is a specific approach to studying information seeking behaviour. It could be possible to study this question through a systematic literature review of ISB research. However, this study will take three research papers on information seeking behaviour and the Net Generation and assess them against a range of heuristic questions. The papers chosen were not selected from a probability sample, meaning that generalising this study may not be appropriate. It was however selected from a list provided by the Information Studies department of Aberystwyth University and the Faculty of Business and Law at Kingston University. The former also provided the heuristics for the investigation. One of the selected papers, Choo et al. (2000), is titled 'Information seeking on the Web: an integrated model of browsing and searching'. Girden (2001, p.1) indicates that one of the first stages to evaluating a research article is investigating what the research is about, the problem and purposes proposed. With this in mind it can be seen that the study by Choi and Ross (2006), can also be seen as qualitative using the above definition as it attempts to understand the motivations for young people using the Internet without any preconceptions. It also considers the changing power relationships of the use of online communities by young people in South Korea who meet the definition of being part of the Net Generation and discusses the policy and practice changes required to ensure what they consider a more balanced use of the Internet. It can also be seen that the study by Leung (2003), appears quantitative using the above definition as it uses specific variables to test a particular worldview, and also investigates the seductive properties of the Internet and its use by the Net Generation.

McNiff, Lomax, and Whitehead (2003, p.10) argue that all research sets out to generate valid evidence to support a claim to new knowledge, and an important part of explaining this new knowledge is to state the research aims, objectives, and questions. With this in mind, it can be seen that Leung's study sets out to identify attributes that can distinctly characterise the Net-generation and examines how these attributes, together with perceived seductive properties of the Internet and gratifications-obtained from Internet use, can predict N-geners use of popular Internet activities, such as online communities. Choi and Ross (2006) set out to consider the effect the Internet has had within Korean families and society and in particular how shifts in power relationships between the key players within the Korean family and wider society have implications for government policy.

Steger (2005, p.20) argues that a sound investigation requires a clearly defined terminological and conceptual framework. Leung's paper used as its conceptual framework the understanding of the Net Generation developed by (Tapscott, 1998), whereas Choi & Ross used the concept of 'Internet Addiction' as their conceptual framework, which defines it as a pathological Internet use pattern that goes from enchantment, or 'obsession', by way of disillusionment, or 'avoidance', back to balance, or 'normal'.

Marczyk, DeMatteo, and Festinger (2005) indicate that in order for a study to produce both valid and reliable results the measurement approach chosen has to be appropriate so that it accurately assesses and represents what it is intended to measure. The measurement used by Leung is well considered as it draws on examples from (Tapscott, 1998), who pioneered the understanding of the Net Generation, whereas Choi & Ross's assumes an unproven belief that there is such a thing as Internet Addiction, as they state "According to the CIPC measuring tool, two of the respondents were in the 'dangerous user group', seven had the potential to become dangerous users and the remainder were 'normal' users." Choi and Ross (2006) by using this instrument are assuming it as valid, but have not described it in any way to allow people to make judgements about its validity.

Leung collected data from a telephone survey after drawing numbers from a telephone directory with all calls being made from a central location during the evening hours using a computer-assisted telephone interviewing system. Choi and Ross

(2006) on the other hand used interviewing techniques to generate narratives about the N-Geners of which there were 25 compared to Leung's 976. While Leung's measurement tool of variables associated with the Net Generation is appropriate for attempting to understand the significance of their motives for using the Internet, Choi and Ross's (2006) fails to measure what the research aimed to measure.

Cohen, Manion, and Morrison (2000) argue that an important element of a research article is that the researchers pay sufficient attention to validity and reliability, bearing in mind that reliability is a necessary but insufficient condition for validity in research and that reliability is a necessary precondition of validity. The three papers possibly did not pay as much attention to the questions of validity and reliability as they could have done. According to Walliman (2006) the selection of participants can affect the result of a study. In Choi & Ross's study the researchers selected actors from a school where the individuals were of mixed ability in Internet use and aged between 13 and 18 years old and at the time making them part of the Net Generation. Leung (2003) on the other hand used a probability sample of 976 actors who were also part of the Net Generation, aged 16-24 years old, which were selected from a telephone directory by first selecting randomly a page, then selecting randomly a column within the page, and finally selecting randomly a name with a phone number in the column. Walliman (2006) argues that the probability sampling method used by Leung gives the most reliable representation of the whole population, while non-probability techniques such as that used by Choi and Ross (2006) rely on the judgement of the researcher and cannot be used to make generalisations about the whole population.

Studies like these two attempt to make generalisations about specific groups of individuals that fit into segments of the population rather than being representative of the whole population. Drowning, Nichols, and MacAdam (1993) indicate that while it is important to understand how young people compare with each other inside an institution the activity of the wider community should be considered also. This would seem to suggest that the population to be investigated should be everyone in a society as opposed to a small segment of the whole population. This appears to create a problem for researchers as on the one hand Leung chooses a method that allows for the proposing of generalisations, but at the same time needs to restrict the sample to a specific age group, which means that the study becomes based on a quasi-non-probability design, which restricts the ability to generalise the results. Conversely, Choi and Ross (2006) openly choose a non-probabilistic design restricting the sample to the Net Generation and while the study does not technically allow for generalisations it provides insights into the 25 actors interviewed.

The issue of sample size also affects the extent to which a study can make generalisations. Walliman (2006) argues that if a population is homogenous then a small sample size will give a fairly representative view of the whole. However, Tapscott (1998) argues that the Net Generation actors that are explored in these two studies are not homogenous, so this may require a bigger sample size. That said, as most qualitative studies cannot arguably give generalisations, this should be less of an issue. Furthermore as the purpose of these studies is to investigate a segment of the population there will be an inherent bias in the data that excludes those who are not part of the Net Generation, suggesting that the most suitable method for making generalisations would be to collect data from a probability sample of the population as a whole and then compare the results of those that fit into the Net Generation with the others. The problem with this is that whilst it would allow for clear generalisations it would not have the benefits of the qualitative approach of finding out detailed information about the investigated group and their motivations for using online communities.

Research Questions (Heuristics)

The following research questions were identified as part of the study and formed heuristics during the investigation:

1. Has the author set out a research question and what do they appear to be attempting to discover?
2. What where the research methods chosen to answer the research question(s)?
3. How appropriate are these methods to answering the research question(s)?
4. How convincing are the findings from a methodological standpoint?

RESULTS

The abstract of this paper clearly sets out that the aim of the paper is to present '*findings from a study of how knowledge workers use the Web to seek external information as part of their daily work*'. The exact nature of this research problem and the other objectives are explored below under Heuristic 1. The study by Choo et al. (2000) study could be considered empirical as it is guided by a scientific process involving the systematic collection, processing and interpretation of data in order to resolve the research problem (Leedy & Ormrod, 2009). According to Girden (2001, p.2) there are three concepts associated with empirical research, which are controlled observation, reliability and validity. These will be explored in more detail in the analysis of Heuristic 4, after firstly exploring Heuristic 2, the research methods used, and Heuristic 3, the appropriateness of these methods to understanding the research question.

Heuristic 1: The Research Questions

(Choo et al., 2000) set out three clear research objectives:

1. To develop a behavioural model of information seeking on the Web based on modes of browsing and searching differentiated by information needs and information seeking activity;
2. To develop operational methods for measuring information seeking on the Web by analysing browser-based actions and events; and,
3. To combine the use of multiple, complementary methods of collecting qualitative and quantitative data on how people seek and use Web-based information in their natural work settings.

The authors seem to be quite clear about what they want to achieve, which is usually more implied in academic papers rather than explicitly stated. From these objectives, it appears that Choo et al. (2000) are trying to develop a conceptual framework for understanding online information seeking behaviour through an empirical inquiry using a range of methods. According to Reed (2004) understanding the behaviour of biological entities such as humans through trying to construct useful conceptual frameworks is not an easy task. This is because conceptual frameworks are not easy to propose or validate, as 'one must have ideas about how the structure of (or behaviour of) the whole is related to the assumptions about the parts'. This seems to suggest, in keeping with the findings of Berryman (2006), that to develop a model, as appeared to be the intention of Choo et al. (2000), requires some a priori specification to the data analysis in keeping with current theory. This is in fact what happened with Choo et al. (2000), who used the model of Ellis and Haugan (1997) as a starting point for their conceptual framework.

Heuristic 2: The Research Methods

It is argued that using more than one research strategy enables researchers to triangulate data by using a variety of methods to test the validly and reliability of their findings (Aldridge & Levine, 2001). The definition by Henn et al. (2006) argues that qualitative research is that which is associated with interpretative investigations with the aim to develop an appreciation of the underlying motivations that people have for doing what they do as opposed to simply test out theories appears to be a more appropriate definition. To this regard we can see that Leung's study, which attempted to understand the motivations for Internet use by online community users, chose a numerical-based method that may not have been appropriate for the purpose. Choi and Ross (2006) on the other hand had the same intention, but chose interviewing, which could be seen as more appropriate for discovering the underlying motivations for a specific behaviour, whereas Leung's approach was more appropriate for exploring what affects the nature of the behaviour and what cognitions and other factors influence it and the values of those elements.

The diagram in Figure 1 suggests that the process arrows in the ECF (Bishop, 2007a; 2007c) can be related to an actor's behaviour through qualitative methods such as interviewing (i.e. thought processes) and quantitative measures such as brain imaging (i.e. cognitions. As the purpose of the two studies investigated in this paper were to explore the motivations for using

Figure 1. Choosing between qualitative and quantitative in the ECF

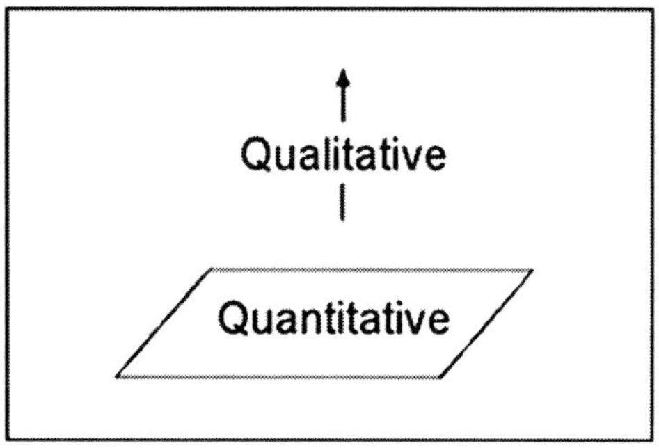

the Internet then a qualitative approach such as that used by Choi & Ross may have been more appropriate. However, this alone would miss out understand the individual actor completely and how they compare with others in the sample and the population. Leung's attempt to understand what beliefs have that influenced the behaviour of the Net Generation participants would have been more suited to understanding the elements of the individual's mental states that the motivations that lead them to participate. In any case if Tapscott (1998) is right and the Net Generation are made up of heterogeneous individuals then this makes them more difficult to investigate as a group and what may apply to one N-gener may not apply to another, suggesting that while these groups are segments of the population they are not necessarily a stratum. This seems to suggest this group of people should be studied on an individual level such as by their attitudes, which would require a more quantitative approach to measuring their cognitions in addition to a qualitative approach for exploring the cause of their behaviour or change.

Figure 2 suggests some of the quantitative methods that can be used to explore individuals at each of the layers of the ECF. As depicted, Leung's study collecting numerical information on the beliefs N-geners have about their behaviour fits into the analysis of Level 2 of the ECF. This means that Leung's methodology was not fit for the purpose of investigating the underlying motives for N-geners contributing to online communities, but was more suited to discovering the individual differences of participants, which would have been more useful if Leung had compared them against a sample of the whole population. Choi & Ross's study on the other hand developed detailed narratives about the N-geners' motivations, which appeared to cover the six processes of the ECF, including the areas of the environment and elements within themselves that motivate them to act in the environment and change their own beliefs, values and other cognitions.

Figure 2. Possible quantitative methods for investigating activity in online and organic communities based on the ECF

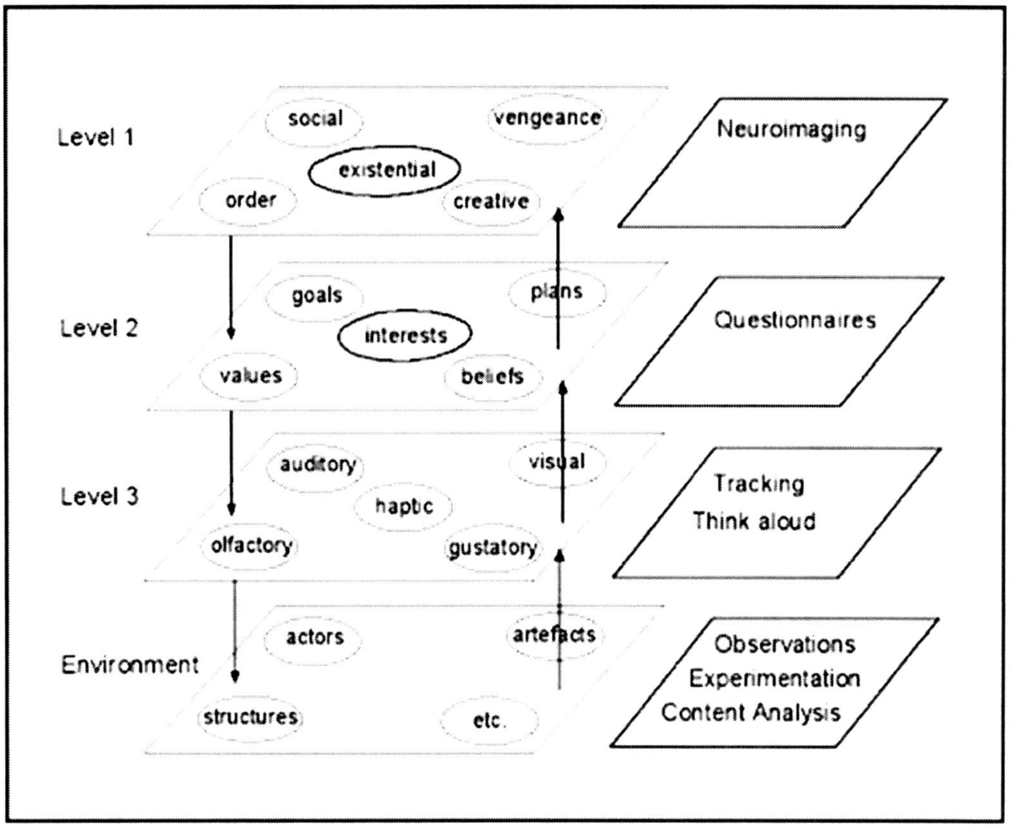

Leung's study could have been improved to greater explore the differences between the Net Generation and other groups by investigating more than just Level 2 of the ECF. He could have, for example, used a quantitative content analysis to investigate the occurrence of specific terms in the online communities used by N-geners in addition to looking at their cognitions. Document analysis, such as content and narrative analysis can provide information that may or may not be accessible by other methods as sometimes qualitative material can best reveal innermost thoughts, frames of reference, reactions to situations and cultural conventions for the reason that language often tells more about people than they want to disclose, or than they know about themselves, and it can bring to light things that a researcher might not think to ask about (Smith, 2000). Narrative analysis was used by Choi and Ross (2006), which proved useful in understanding N-geners, though a content analysis of the online communities they use could have provided even more insights into the specific aspects of the environment that motivate them.

Another method that could have been used in place of or in addition to the content analysis would be an observational method such as the structured observation. This could have been done in a physical environment such as a school or college, which could have looked at how N-geners use online communities and e-learning systems during educational activities. Structured observation is a technique that allows researchers using explicitly formulated rules to observe specific aspects of behaviour that can be recorded in specific variables for a quantitative analysis (Bryman & Bell, 2003).

The study by Choo et al. (2000) used a variety of data collection methods; questionnaires, interviews, and observations recorded using 'WebTracker logs'. The questionnaires used in the study could be considered to be quantitative, as could the observation data, whereas the interviews could be considered qualitative. According to Jones (1997), a quantitative research design allows flexibility in the treatment of data, in terms of comparative analyses, statistical analyses, and repeatability of data collection in order to verify reliability. Jones indicates that on the other hand, qualitative research design allows understandings of the topic to be investigated from the participants' perspectives. Despite the claimed objectivity of quantitative research, the direction and outcome of research is heavily based on the characteristics and experience of the researcher and the individual interpretation they give to the data (Williamson, 2002).

Questionnaires are one of the most widely used data collection techniques as they are an efficient way of collecting data from a large number of people, which is necessary to have the necessary normal distribution to generalise the findings to the wider population (Saunders, Thornhill, & Lewis, 2009).

Heuristic 3: The Appropriateness of the Research Methods

According to Holzinger (2005) questionnaires are useful for studying how end users use a particular system and their preferred features, but need some experience to design. Harwood & Hutchinson (2009) argues that self-administered questionnaires are usually standardised so that '*everyone sees the same questions, worded in exactly the same way with exactly the same instructions*'. This approach, which was adopted by Choo et al. (2000), provides an objective means of administering a questionnaire, however those that complete the questionnaire may not fully understand each question in the same way, which is something that can be adjusted with alternative approaches, such as the use of computer-assisted quantitative interviewing (CAQI). Indeed, Sapsford (2006) indicates that choosing between these two methods is often based on the same goal, which is standardisation, in order to create 'precise and unambiguous' understandings of the questions or statements.

Choi and Ross (2006) using their sample of 25, which Nielsen (1993) argues is enough for most user-based studies, could have also used a method such as the think-aloud technique to gather quantitative data on the sensory capabilities of the Net Generation in addition to the narrative analysis method they used which can be used to look at the processes that transform what individuals perceive into what they do. The think aloud technique according to Lewis (1982) involves having the actor participating in the study use a system such as a virtual community while verbalising their experience for the researcher to record. According to Nielsen (1993) this allows the researcher to get a very direct understanding of the aspects of a system that the user perceives that helps them achieve their goals or get in the way of their goals, meaning that the researcher can record quantitative data such as the number of times an actor looks at or clicks on a particular link. A more natural, but possibly more expensive alternative to the think-aloud technique would be to use sensory tracking devices. Kuniavsky (2003) indicates that sensory tracking methods such as eye-tracking allow the researcher to create a map of where an actor looked and for how long revealing information on how they perceive a system such as an online community and the aspects of the environment that dominated their thought process.

With a sample of 25, Choi & Ross could have also explored the motivating factors behind N-geners' Internet behaviour through a focus group, a qualitative method that supports spontaneous reactions and group dynamics according to Nielsen (1993), giving greater insights into how this segment of the population relate to each other and how their experiences of online communities may be similar. According to Kuniavsky (2003) focus groups allow the participants to share their view of issues and assumptions that lie at the core of their experiences and relate them to specific situations.

Both Choi and Ross (2006) and Leung could have explored in detail the response process of the ECF to look at the specific behaviours of N-geners in online communities by logging actual use. According to Nielsen (1993) logging actors' actual use of a system is particularly useful because it shows how users perform their work and also because it is easy to automatically collect data from a large number of users working under different circumstances.

Choi & Ross could have opted to do case studies of N-Geners at different schools and adult colleges to see whether there are distinctive similarities between the way N-Geners use online communities and differences between them and older generations, possibly using a variety of the above methods. The basic case study entails the detailed and intensive analysis of a single case with some of the best known studies in business and management research being based on this method, which can be an investigation of a single organisation, a single location, a person, or an event (Bryman & Bell, 2003). Some case studies investigating an organisation have provided insights into the types of problems usability studies are likely to encounter, as well as some valuable lessons learned along the way in the organisation (Rowley, 1994) and others looking at the development of online learning communities over a number of years have managed to refine design methodologies (Bishop, 2007b).

According to Schechter, Krishnan, and Smith (1998), using server logs as an observation of user actions can allow for the quick generation of profiles using records of a large number of accesses to the system. O'Leary (2005, p.174) points out that the difficulty with some observational studies is that the observers often record everything then look for patterns later. However Choo et al. (2000) appear to have set the system up to record very specific things.

According to Voida, Mynatt, Erickson, and Kellogg (2004) interviews are a cornerstone of human-computer interaction research and, as a research method, they can both be deeply valuable and distinctly challenging. The reasoning of Choo et al. (2000) for using interviews was to gain an insight into the reasoning behind the particular drives for a type of information seeking behaviour. The fact-finding nature of it was particularly suited to an empirical study and allowed the researchers to give some context to the quantitative data.

An alternative to the structured observation is the observer-as-participant method, or 'ethnography', which could have investigated the characteristics of N-geners' behaviour in online communities. Ethnography offers a rigorous approach to the analysis of information systems practices using observational techniques, with the notion of context being one of the social construction of meaningful frameworks and as a research method, ethnography is well suited to providing information systems researchers with rich insights into the human, social and organizational aspects of information systems development and application. This is because because ethnography deals with actual practices in real world situations, it allows for relevant issues to be explored and frameworks to be developed which can be used by both practitioners and researchers and also means that researchers can deal with real situations instead of having to contrive artificial situations for the purpose of quasi-experimental investigations (Harvey & Myers, 1995).

Heuristic 4: Methodological Issues

This heuristic attempts to discover how the conduct of the research, and the methodological approaches used, affect confidence in the findings.

Controlled Observation

Controlled observation of empirical research attempts to control the conditions of the research to eliminate 'noise' which would otherwise adversely affect the data so that the reader can replicate the study (Girden, 2001, p.2).

In terms of the questionnaire, Choo et al. (2000) indicate that it was '*administered at the participants' work places, during the first site visit.*' This is a reasonable approach to controlling the observation by contemporary standards. While in the past a controlled observation would have meant each participant attending a laboratory of some sort with identical settings, it has become acceptable to use different locations providing they provide the same situated context, as Choo et al. (2000) did through selecting workplaces.

The observation carried out by Choo et al. (2000) also seemed to satisfy this criterion of controlled observation. The study collected data from the participants' Web browser on their browsing behaviour. Again the study was situated in their workplaces providing a similar context for each subject. An alternative approach, which would have met the controlled observation criterion better, but perhaps not the validity one below would have been a laboratory-based eye-tracking system. However, this would not have assessed browsing behaviour in the 'workplace'.

Reliability

Reliability refers to a broad range of phenomena that indicates that studies should allow for repeatability and consistency (Girden, 2001, p.2).

Reliability can refer to the precision of the instruments used to collect the data. Therefore for instance the WebTracker software used by Choo et al. (2000) would have to be consistently applied to all the cases where the data was collected. They indicate that the software ran of participants' computers continuously for two weeks and 'recorded all URL calls and requests, as well as most browser menu selections, and wrote these events into a local log file on each participant's hard disk.' This appears to suggest that there was consistency in the collection of data from subjects, meaning the data was probably valid.

The questionnaires, through being the same for each participant, appeared to also have consistency, and as they were collected in the same context should have been equally applied to each subject. However, Choo et al. (2000) did not provide any measure of reliability, such as Cronbach's alpha, meaning the reader cannot be sure of the questionnaire's reliability as an instrument.

The interviews were conducted using a 'critical incident technique'. There are risks in exploratory interviews that reliability can be compromised through questions not being applied equally. Choo et al. (2000) appeared to conduct the interviews as a fact-finding exercise from a positivist paradigm rather than one to determine meaning, which means it was more likely to produce consistent results.

Validity

Validity is the part of empirical research that is concerned with appropriateness, meaningfulness and usefulness (Girden, 2001, p.3). Considering the study by Choo et al. (2000), they did not discuss any confounds in the browsing behaviour, such as experience of participants, age, or education level beyond noting that prior experience with a Website may affect differentiation in the browsing behaviour.

Choo et al. (2000) also did not discuss whether participants were selected as a probability or non-probability sample, meaning the generalizability of their results is uncertain. This could leave the study open to selection bias where the performance of the subjects is more characteristic with what the researcher is looking for than typical of the general population. The authors did not discuss any case of or the lack of selective loss, whereby participants leave the study due to factions such as mortality or attrition. Furthermore Choo et al. (2000) did not discuss either interaction effects or the Hawthorn effect. That is, with regard to the former, they did not appear to control for any workplace events that would affect the performance of participants in completing the task over the two-week period. Also with regard to the latter, they did not state what effect participants' awareness that they were being monitored had on the approach and frequency of their browsing behaviour.

Secondly, this investigation has evaluated the coherence of the research designs of the two aforementioned research papers. Bearing in mind the view of Steger (2005, p.20) that a sound investigation requires a clearly defined terminological and conceptual framework this was explored showing that Leung's paper used as its conceptual framework the understanding of the Net Generation developed by Tapscott (1998), whereas Choi & Ross used the concept of 'Internet Addiction' as their conceptual framework. Using the premise of Marczyk et al. (2005) that in order for a study to produce both valid and reliable results the measurement approach chosen has to be appropriate so that it accurately assesses and represents what it is intended to measure it was shown that the measurement used by Leung was well considered as it draws on examples from Tapscott (1998), whereas Choi & Ross's assumed an unproven belief that there is such a thing as Internet Addiction.

Thirdly, this investigation has considered the design alternatives that could have been used by the authors of the two studies. In line with the ethos of the programme a seminal work proposing a model for understanding online communities (Bishop, 2007a; 2007c) was utilised to evaluate the papers and propose a framework for deciding the most appropriate methodology for investigating these virtual environments and their impact on individuals.

IMPLICATIONS AND FUTURE RESEARCH DIRECTIONS

Considering the findings of this paper would suggest that an empirical approach is necessary to justify any theoretical or conceptual model of information seeking behaviour on the Web. Investigating other similar research, such as Cutrell and Guan (2007), in addition to this paper, it might be suggested that an experimental design using an observation approach is the most effective methodology for investigating information seeking behaviour. This would differentiate the field from ethnography, where observations are also used, but which are not in controlled settings. It would also differentiate it from the action research and case study approaches, where particular behaviours are understood through exploring and controlling for behavioural differences, of which the findings of are not generalizable.

CONCLUSION

The Net Generation is one of the most complex groups in terms of their information seeking behaviour (ISB). Much research into ISBs has focused on a small number of factors identified before the empirical investigation has begun. Finding an overall methodology for understanding the unique aspects of the Net Generation, while taking into account other generations is a challenge. The relevance of the discipline could be considered comparable to ethnography and organisational case studies. This study applied a heuristic framework to three research papers in order to critically analyse and evaluate the information within it in order to gain an insight into the most effective approach to ISB research, especially in relation to politics and N-Geners.

This investigation has explored three elements of the design and implementation of three papers that utilise qualitative or quantitative methodologies. Firstly the investigation has identified and described the research design and data collection strategies of three papers that attempt to explore the motives behind the group of people. Following the rule of Girden (2001, p.1), which states a first step to evaluating a research article is investigating what the research is about, both of the research papers appear to clearly outline the problem and purposes of their research with the study by Choi and Ross (2006) considering the changing power relationships the use of online communities by young people in South Korea who meet the definition of being part of the Net Generation and discusses the policy and practice changes required to ensure what they consider a more balanced use of the Internet, and the study by Leung (2003) investigating the seductive properties of the Internet and its use by the Net Generation, which is defined as a group of people born between 1977 and 1997. The third and final paper, Choo et al. (2000), used a range of research methods to explore ISB in an online context.

ACKNOWLEDGMENT

The author would like to acknowledge all those who provided advice and recommendations on this chapter. Earlier versions of this chapter were presented in part fulfilment of the MScEcon in Information Systems degree at Aberystwyth University as (Bishop, 2011, 2009), with some of the research being carried out at Kingston University.

REFERENCES

Aldridge, A., & Levine, K. (2001). *Surveying the social world: Principles and practice in survey research*. Buckingham, UK: Open University Press.

Barnes, K., Marateo, R., & Ferris, S. P. (2007). Teaching and learning with the net generation. *Innovate Journal of Online Education, 3*(4), 771–772.

Berryman, J. (2006). What defines 'enough' information? How policy workers make judgements and decisions during information seeking: Preliminary results from an exploratory study. *Information Research, 11*(4), 11–14.

Bishop, J. (2007a). Ecological cognition: A new dynamic for human-computer interaction. In B. Wallace, A. Ross, J. Davies, & T. Anderson (Eds.), *The mind, the body and the world: Psychology after cognitivism* (pp. 327–345). Exeter, UK: Imprint Academic.

Bishop, J. (2007b). Evaluation-centred design of E-learning communities: A case study and review. In V. Grout, D. Oram & R. Picking (Eds.), *Proceedings of the Second International Conference on Internet Technologies and Applications* (ITA07 ed., pp. 1-9). Wrexham, UK: University of Wales Press.

Bishop, J. (2007c). Increasing participation in online communities: A framework for human–computer interaction. *Computers in Human Behavior, 23*(4), 1881–1893. doi:10.1016/j.chb.2005.11.004

Bishop, J. (2009). *Developing a holistic approach for investigating online communities: A critical evaluation of two research articles (No. BHM802)*. Swansea, UK: The Crocels Press.

Bishop, J. (2011). *An analysis and discussion of an investigation of online information seeking behaviour research: The case of 'information seeking on the web: An integrated model of browsing and searching' (No. DSM1810).* Swansea, UK: The Crocels Press.

Bryman, A., & Bell, E. (2003). *Business research methods.* Oxford, UK: Oxford University Press.

Choi, Y. S., & Ross, L. (2006). Policy and power: The impact of the internet on the younger generation in South Korea. *Social Policy and Society, 5*(3), 421–429. doi:10.1017/S1474746406003095

Choo, C. W., Detlor, B., & Turnbull, D. (2000). Information seeking on the web: An integrated model of browsing and searching. *First Monday, 5*, 2–7. doi:10.5210/fm.v5i2.729

Cohen, L., Manion, L., & Morrison, K. (2000). *Research methods in education* (5th ed.). London: Routledge Falmer. doi:10.4324/9780203224342

Connaway, L. S., Radford, M. L., Dickey, T. J., De Angelis Williams, J., & Confer, P. (2008). Sense-making and synchronicity: Information-seeking behaviors of millennials and baby boomers. *Libri, 58*(2), 123–135. doi:10.1515/libr.2008.014

Cutrell, E., & Guan, Z. (2007). What are you looking for? An eye-tracking study of information usage in web search. In *Proceedings of the SIGCHI Conference on Human Factors in Computing Systems.* ACM.

de Souza, C. S., & Preece, J. (2004). A framework for analyzing and understanding online communities. *Interacting with Computers, 16*(3), 579–610. doi:10.1016/j.intcom.2003.12.006

Drowning, K. E., Nichols, D. P., & MacAdam, B. (1993). *Reaching a multicultural student community: A handbook for academic librarians.* Westport, CT: Greenwood Publishing Group, Inc.

Ellis, D., & Haugan, M. (1997). Modelling the information seeking patterns of engineers and research scientists in an industrial environment. *The Journal of Documentation, 53*(4), 384–403. doi:10.1108/EUM0000000007204

Girden, E. R. (2001). *Evaluating research articles from start to finish* (2nd ed.). Thousand Oaks, CA: Sage Publications, Inc.

Gorman, P. (1998). Information seeking of primary care physicians: Conceptual models and empirical studies. In *Proceedings of the Second International Conference on Research in Information Needs, Seeking and use in Different Contexts.* Academic Press.

Grimes, T. R. (1990). Truth, content, and the hypothetico-deductive method. *Philosophy of Science, 57*(3), 514–522. doi:10.1086/289571

Harvey, L. J., & Myers, M. D. (1995). Scholarship and practice: The contribution of ethnographic research methods to bridging the gap. *Information Technology & People, 8*(3), 13–27. doi:10.1108/09593849510098244

Harwood, E. M., & Hutchinson, E. (2009). Data collection methods series: Part 2: Select the most feasible data collection mode. *Journal of Wound, Ostomy, and Continence Nursing, 36*(2), 129. doi:10.1097/01.WON.0000347654.49228.44 PMID:19287261

Henn, M., Weinstein, M., & Foard, N. (2006). *Social research.* London: Sage Publications Ltd.

Henwood, K., & Pidgeon, N. (1993). *Qualitative research and psychological theorizing.* London, UK: Sage Publications.

Holzinger, A. (2005). Usability engineering methods for software developers. *Communications of the ACM, 48*(1), 71–74. doi:10.1145/1039539.1039541

Jones, I. (1997). Mixing qualitative and quantitative methods in sports fan research. *Qualitative Report, 3*(4), 1–6.

Krzic, M., Strivelli, R. A., Holmes, E., Grand, S., Dyanatkar, S., & Lavkulich, L. M. et al. (2013). Virtual soil monoliths: Blending traditional and web-based educational approaches. *Journal of Natural Resources and Life Sciences Education, 42*(1), 1–8.

Kuniavsky, M. (2003). *Observing the user experience: A practitioner's guide to user research.* London: Morgan Kaufmann Publishers.

Lee, A. Y. (2013). Literacy and competencies required to participate in knowledge societies. *Conceptual Relationship of Information Literacy and Media Literacy in Knowledge Societies,* 3.

Leedy, P. D., & Ormrod, J. E. (2009). *Practical research: Planning and design.* Academic Press.

Leung, L. (2003). Impacts of net-generation attributes, seductive properties of the internet, and gratifications-obtained on internet use. *Telematics and Informatics, 20*(2), 107–129. doi:10.1016/S0736-5853(02)00019-9

Lewis, C. (1982). Using the 'thinking-aloud' method in cognitive interface design (No. Research report RC9265). Yorktown Heights, NY: IBM T.J. Watson Research Centre.

Lutters, W. G., & Ackerman, M. S. (2003). Joining the backstage: Locality and centrality in an online community. *Information Technology & People, 16*(2), 157–182. doi:10.1108/09593840310478676

Mann, C., & Stewart, F. (2000). *Internet communication and qualitative research: A handbook for research online.* London: Sage Publications.

Mansourian, Y., & Madden, A. D. (2007). Methodological approaches in web search research. *The Electronic Library, 25*(1), 90–101. doi:10.1108/02640470710729146

Marczyk, G. R., DeMatteo, D., & Festinger, D. (2005). *Essentials of research design and methodology.* Hoboken, NJ: John Wiley & Sons.

Martzoukou, K. (2004). A review of web information seeking research: Considerations of method and foci of interest. *Information Research, 10*(2), 10–12.

McNiff, J., Lomax, P., & Whitehead, J. (2003). *You and your action research project.* London: Routledge.

Nielsen, J. (1993). *Usability engineering.* San Francisco, CA: Morgan Kaufman.

O'Leary, Z. (2005). *The essential guide to doing research.* Thousand Oaks, CA: SAGE Publications Inc.

Oblinger, D. G. (2004). The next generation of educational engagement. *Journal of Interactive Media in Education,* 1.

Oliver, B., & Goerke, V. (2007). Australian undergraduates' use and ownership of emerging technologies: Implications and opportunities for creating engaging learning experiences for the net generation. *Australasian Journal of Educational Technology, 23*(2), 171.

Preece, J., & Maloney-Krichmar, D. (2005). Online communities: Design, theory, and practice. *Journal of Computer-Mediated Communication, 10*(4).

Reed, M. C. (2004). Why is mathematical biology so hard? *Notices of the American Mathematical Society, 51*(3), 338–342.

Rowley, D. E. (1994). *Usability testing in the field: Bridging the laboratory to the user.* Boston, MA: Academic Press. doi:10.1145/259963.260374

Sapsford, R. (2006). *Survey research.* Thousand Oaks, CA: Sage Publications Ltd.

Saunders, M., Thornhill, A., & Lewis, P. (2009). *Research methods for business students.* New York: Financial Times/Prentice Hall.

Schechter, S., Krishnan, M., & Smith, M. D. (1998). Using path profiles to predict HTTP requests. *Computer Networks and ISDN Systems, 30*(1-7), 457-467.

Silverman, D. (2006). *Interpreting qualitative data: Methods for analyzing talk, text and interaction* (3rd ed.). London, UK: Sage Publications.

Smith, C. P. (2000). Content analysis and narrative analysis. In H. T. Reis, & C. M. Judd (Eds.), *Handbook of research methods in social and personal psychology.* Cambridge, UK: Cambridge University Press.

Steger, U. (2005). *Sustainable development and innovation in the energy sector.* London: Springer.

Tak, J. (2006). Political advertising in Japan, South Korea, and Taiwan. In *The SAGE handbook of political advertising*. Thousand Oaks, CA: Sage Publications, Incorporated. doi:10.4135/9781412973403.n17

Tapscott, D. (1998). *Growing up digital: The rise of the net generation.* London: McGraw-Hill.

Voida, A., Mynatt, E. D., Erickson, T., & Kellogg, W. A. (2004). Interviewing over instant messaging. In *Proceedings of Conference on Human Factors in Computing Systems,* (pp. 1344-1347). Academic Press.

Walliman, N. (2006). *Social research methods.* London: Sage Publicaitons Ltd. doi:10.4135/9781849209939

Williamson, K. (2002). *Research methods for students and professionals: Information management and systems.* Wagga Wagga, Australia: Centre for Information Studies, Charles Sturt University. doi:10.1533/9781780634203

KEY TERMS AND DEFINITIONS

Document Analysis: Document analysis, such as content and narrative analysis can provide information that may or may not be accessible by other methods as sometimes qualitative material can best reveal innermost thoughts, frames of reference, reactions to situations and cultural conventions for the reason that language often tells more about people that they want to disclose.

Ethnography: Ethnography is research method that in terms information systems can provide researchers with rich insights into the human, social and organizational aspects of information systems development and application.

Information Seeking Behaviour: The searching for particular information online, or searching on an escapism basis.

Interviews: Interviews are a cornerstone of human-computer interaction research and, as a research method, they can both be deeply valuable and distinctly challenging.

Net Generation: The Net Generation is a group of people born over a 20 year period who have grown up with digital technologies such as the Internet for which is essential to their way of life, including as digital teens.

Think-Aloud Technique: This involves having an actor participating in a study use a system such as a virtual community while verbalising their experience for the researcher to record.

Chapter 3
Net Neutrality:
An Issue of Democracy

Valérie Schafer
National Center for Scientific Research (CNRS), France

Francesca Musiani
Georgetown University, USA & MINES ParisTech, France

Hervé Le Crosnier
University of Caen-Basse Normandie, France & National Center for Scientific Research (CNRS), France

ABSTRACT

Beyond the likes of a purely technical issue, situated at the heart of the transport layer of the TCP/IP protocol, net neutrality takes the form of a complex political debate. This chapter's endeavour is to study the set of dimensions that make it possible for net neutrality to be read as a global political issue. The chapter follows the constantly evolving notion of net neutrality as it interrogates the Internet as a laboratory of governance, the actors and dynamics involved in the establishment of a "technical democracy" and the dialectic between the Internet's universal, egalitarian ideal and the techno-political measures shaping the "network of networks."

INTRODUCTION

Introduced by Tim Wu in 2003, the concept of neutrality of the Internet – or, more briefly, net neutrality – first became a source of debate in the United States, reaching Europe only slightly later. At its core is the idea that all packets of information that circulate within the "network of networks" should be treated equally, regardless of their source and recipient. This principle's preservation, and alternatively its violations, occur against a backdrop of complex issues concerning the relationships between Internet access providers, content and service, operators (including transit operators), content delivery networks, consumers, and governance stakeholders (Schafer, Le Crosnier, & Musiani, 2011).

The issue is primarily an economic one. Network operators emphasize the possible alternatives for infrastructure funding, at a time when band-

DOI: 10.4018/978-1-4666-6038-0.ch003

Copyright © 2014, IGI Global. Copying or distributing in print or electronic forms without written permission of IGI Global is prohibited.

width is increasingly used for consumer content, as well as the strategies for improving "Quality of Service," enabling improved transit of certain types of information. But behind and alongside economics, the issue is also deeply political.

Within this analysis, this chapter seeks to outline powerful and divergent values and imaginaries, and to invite a (re)thinking of each actor's role on the Internet chain, from ISPs to users, from states and regulators to citizens, in an ecosystem in fragile equilibrium and perpetual motion. First, the chapter addresses the ways in which, during the past ten years, the notion of net neutrality has acquired an important political dimension. This process is grounded in legal precedents, both in the United States and the European Union; it is also shaped by the democratisation of Internet uses, the technological evolutions of the "network of networks," the evolution of power relations between the different actors of the Internet value chain. The second part of the chapter locates net neutrality in a more general and highly political context, that of Internet governance. It does so not only from a theoretical point of view, but a very practical one, showing the variety of actors that take part in the debate, as well as the variety of national declinations of the controversy. The global nature of the net neutrality controversies does not erase the national specificities of debates, regulations and norm-making processes – demonstrating how this controversy, while overcoming boundaries and frontiers, does not obliterate them.

BACKGROUND

In *Protocol Politics*, Laura DeNardis showed to what extent protocol adoption, particularly of IPv6, is the site where "markets meet protocols" (DeNardis, 2009, p. 227). She argues that changes in architecture imply changes in power arrangements; one could add that changing power arrangements repeatedly engender changes in architecture.

To analyze information and communication technologies and the so-called "new media," particularly those that are based on the Internet, software studies, critical code studies and cyber-infrastructure studies have recently responded to the challenge of inter-disciplinarity (Fuller, 2008), drawing on past studies in the sociology of technology and science that have explored the social and political qualities of infrastructure (Star, 1999). Elsewhere, some authors operating at the crossroads of computer science, sociology, law, and Science and Technology Studies (STS), have shown that innovative methodological approaches and studies on network architectures, integrating the connection between these and networked practices, are possible (Agre, 2003; Braman, 2011; Elkin-Koren, 2006; Star & Bowker, 2002). Modifications in architecture have not only causes, but also consequences, that are economic, political and social, and it is the constant interaction between these issues that is put into question in any discussion of net neutrality. These considerations cannot be separated from those of the uses and practices taking place daily on the Web, and from the power relations at work in the Internet economy.

FROM A SEEMINGLY TECHNICAL ISSUE TO A POLITICAL CONCEPT

An Evolving Concept

The concept of net neutrality has been evolving ever since Tim Wu's 2003 article. Its appropriation by numerous actors with divergent goals helped to make it polysemic.

Debating an Increasingly Mobile Internet

At the end of 2002, cable operators in the United States, accustomed to managing relationships on a two-sided market (financing by users; negotiations with producers to create "packages"), asked the Federal Communications Commission (FCC) for authorization to conduct specific negotiations with producers on broadband networks, thereby refusing to extend the neutrality rule that had been the signature of narrowband Internet. In response, in a letter to the FCC in 2003, Tim Wu and Lawrence Lessig pointed out the dangers that such a violation of neutrality to the transport layer would pose to innovation, and to the non-discriminatory treatment of users.

Four years later, the FCC opposed the cable operator Comcast's restriction of user access to BitTorrent, citing network neutrality. On December 21, 2010, by three votes against two, it adopted a text on net neutrality, which received mixed reactions because although it put into place explicit rules regarding cable Internet, those for mobile networks are still considered insufficient.

Mobile Internet brings the issues of 2003 back into play, under the cover of a new technology. Access restrictions to certain protocols, such as Voice over IP, and other limits are officially justified by weak allocation of band frequency, but they owe much to industrial battles, partially conducted under the cover of political debates.

The FCC's intervention in the Comcast affair was hardly appreciated by industry giants. Comcast appealed in court, and in April 2010 obtained a victory: the FCC ruling was disallowed, following the liberal economic logic that a federal authority cannot intervene in the technical decisions of a private actor. According to this logic, provided that the original model of a symmetrical Internet is no longer implemented, and "pure" neutrality does not exist, some consider any political intervention aimed at limiting the increase of violations to be premature, stressing that pragmatism and the laws of the market must prevail and decide. This is the approach endorsed by advocacy groups like *Hands Off the Internet*, for example, which is supported by operators and equipment manufacturers including AT&T and Alcatel. However, court cases are increasing – they have passed the frontiers of the United States and have now acquired a more international dimension, not unlike the Internet itself. The French ISP and telecom operators Cogent and Orange were called before the French Competition Authority in August 2011, the former accusing the latter of curbing flow, especially that which came from the site Megaupload.

The Polysemy of the Neutrality Notion

The concept of net neutrality convenes an entire vocabulary imbued with a strong symbolic charge (neutrality, discrimination, equity, etc.). Yet, the criticisms and concerns that arise are not based on words alone. The debate may have real consequences on the "network of networks," depending on whether a *laissez-faire* approach is adopted, or, in contrast, a regulation or a law favouring net neutrality.

Other sensitive issues also come into play. In France, they concern Hadopi (the Creation and Internet Law) and Loppsi 2 (an orientation and planning law for the improvement of national security); these two law projects have led to enflamed debates on copyright protection and security respectively. In the United States, similar issues were raised in early 2012 around the (aborted) adoption of the Stop Online Piracy Act (SOPA) and the Preventing Real Online Threats to Economic Creativity and Theft of Intellectual Property Act (PIPA). The global debate around the Anti-Counterfeiting Trade Agreement (ACTA), rejected by the European parliament on July 4, 2012, has also heavily mobilized Internet users. The issue of the transport layer's neutrality is part of the growing awareness of the political issues that surround the Internet; even if the application layer and the issues concerning services are more often at the centre of users' claims, and demands, than Internet architecture and the "lower layers" – despite the close link existing between the two levels.

Indeed, modifications in the transportation of data over the Internet entail changes in the access to services and applications. Tim Berners-Lee, founder of the Web in the early 1990s, underscores how their futures are tied, since every Web user is by default an Internet user: "A good ISP will often manage traffic so that when bandwidth is short, less crucial traffic is dropped, in a transparent way, so users are aware of it. An important line exists between that action and using the same power to discriminate. This distinction highlights the principle of net neutrality [...]. A neutral communications medium is the basis of a fair, competitive market economy, of democracy, and of science" (Berners-Lee, 2010).

This is why considering the boundaries of the net neutrality question is essential (e.g., should it encompass the entire Internet value chain, or only the routing of data?) and why many prefer the term "open Internet" over that of "neutral Internet." "Open Internet refers to an open space that is not under the control of any single actor, where everyone can freely create and initiate, and have their expression, creation, and work accessible to the entire Internet" (French Secretary of State for Strategic Studies and the Development of the Digital Economy, 2010). The term is vested with broader values (freedom of enterprise, of expression, and so on); David Clark, who received a Sigcomm Award[1] in 1990 for his contributions to the Internet, highlights how the idea of openness is consubstantial to the net (Clark, 2007). Moreover, he notes that many supporters of openness, like the major industrial players, aren't necessarily defending "social" values: above all, the industry's future and revenues are under consideration. By promoting openness, they are promoting the "800-pound gorillas."[2]

Tensions in the Internet Ecosystem

The very idea of the rupture of neutrality harbours the seeds of specific trade agreements between content producers, and access services and networks, as can be seen with cable and satellite TV packages. At stake behind these issues are potential modifications of the entire Internet value chain, starting with changes in its architecture.

A Gradual Erosion of the Founding Principles

At the Internet's inception, decentralization governed traffic transmissions. In addition, a fundamental principle of packet circulation was that of "best effort": the network would do its best; there was no complete guarantee of packet delivery, for example, at times of high traffic. However, this model would not withstand mainstream development.

In particular, the introduction of the World Wide Web in 1990 led to the dissemination of asymmetrical architectures, based on "clients" and "servers." Services like social networks, messaging tools, applications, and digital content storage were also based on technical and economic models in which users requested services from powerful servers that stored information and/or managed traffic.

The Internet's commercial explosion rapidly shifted the large majority of its traffic to a "downstream" paradigm of television and traditional media. The growth of spam, and the constantly increasing presence of bandwidth-intensive protocols, jeopardized the Internet's proper functioning as a "common good" (Hess & Ostrom, 2006). This led to questions on the net's cooperative character, as management measures eroded symmetry: the deployment of firewalls, the increase in dynamic IP addresses, the popularity of Network Address Translation (NAT), and a desire to enhance service quality—a euphemism for privileged traffic.

In the logic of responding to congestion and service quality, paradoxical solutions appear. Such is the case for the development of Content Delivery Networks (CDN) like Akamai. CDNs build a dedicated network of servers that store in-demand content close to Internet users to facilitate delivery:

if they can solve congestion problems, they may also pose a threat to the Internet model, "since it is the biggest players, or the most profitable, that may have better access, both in latency and in speed, to the end consumer" (CGIET, 2010). When we know that people refuse to wait for pages to load, or when the Google search engine uses response time as a quality criterion for an information page, the economic imbalance introduced by CDNs becomes a preview of what might happen if overall neutrality were threatened.

The Recomposition of the Internet Value Chain: Towards "Vectoralism"?

As a central node of both technical and economic architecture, telecommunications companies negotiate in their own best interests to share Internet-generated value. Because they are in direct contact with users, they also try to follow, or even anticipate (as with the so-called "ultra-broadband"), the public's desire for constantly more access, reliability, and speed. To keep pace with innovation, they must continually improve network quality, which represents a heavy investment compounded by the risk of rapid obsolescence.

Are the evolutions of the Internet's economic model, and the distribution of revenues between various service and access providers, permanent issues? Is the development of applications that consume evermore bandwidth (video, immersion games, and so on), along with the desire to invest in more efficient infrastructure, making the relationship between Internet service providers and application providers obsolete? Who should pay: should operators alone bear the cost of network expansion and evolution, bringing about exponential growth of network-related use? Should we regulate the share of the bandwidth reserved for managed services like Internet TV? Should some contents receive priority treatment over others, and according to what criteria (profitability, payment by content providers, utility)?

Telecommunications companies don't want to remain confined to a provider role for content and service providers, assuming the industrial risks and user discontent in times of congestion. The arrogant financial health of the Internet's "pure players" makes them appear as actors that should take part in telecom operators' investment efforts. This brings with it a will to introduce private commercial negotiations between network operators and content/service providers. Telecommunications, which can modulate the speed of access to services, is in a strong position to negotiate kickbacks for rapid content delivery. It is around this central point that the issue of net neutrality comes into play. If a carrier can identify the type of protocol used in each information packet of (video, peer-to-peer, etc.), and apply specific rules according to its sender, it then becomes *the* central player, able to impose its models and interests throughout the Internet.

The long-term risk of this scenario could be the strengthening of "vectoralism" (Le Crosnier, 2008), i.e., the consolidation of metering industries (which have access to user consumption habits) with media industries (which have the means to influence that user). This concept designates new models, through the transformation of search engines into media, or more precisely "vectors," which, like Google, include at once advertising revenue, content control, and autonomous infrastructure (servers, networks, etc.). Vectors are also beginning to fill administrative roles (for example, electronic medical records), which reinforces user dependence and calls into question the role of government.

The Internet's Imaginaries and Values in Question

Behind the question of neutrality, values are up for debate—values of liberalism and the trajectories of innovation—and so are imaginaries. For this reason, questioning the neutrality of the transport layer goes beyond infrastructure issues and traffic equilibrium, to touch on the Internet's evolution more generally, its logic of support that is open to technical and social innovation.

Innovation: Stimulated or Paralyzed?

Proper management of information flow, based on service quality to the end user of a now fully globalized network, occurs both through information flow control procedures, and through the amount and relevance of necessary software and hardware. However, Internet traffic modelling using classical statistical laws is fraught with difficulties: Internet has expanded to interconnect billions of machines, and today, its behaviour as a whole is no longer fully understood. These difficulties in measuring serve those who stand to profit from the vagueness, by highlighting the risks of network congestion, a problem clearly linked with mobile phones, because of the limited allocation of wireless resources, still less proved for fixed Internet, which is above all not inevitable. Among the alternatives considered, cloud computing and the peer-to-peer model are two serious alternatives. The choice—between an increasingly ubiquitous unknown (the cloud), and the "evergreen" qualities of the P2P model, which revisits the topology of pre-commercial Internet, building on the "margins" of the Net—are not without consequences for the Internet.

Above all, under the guise of protecting the entire Internet ecosystem from congestion, the "net hog" has been stigmatized. The argument against these high bandwidth consumers has been used in France to push forward *à la carte* Internet using the model of "big consumer, big payer." But experience shows that early adopters often stimulate innovation and open the way to new practices. Fragmenting the Internet and opening the door to neutrality violations may destabilize a process of innovation that has been at work since its inception.

Indeed, by choosing to place intelligence not at the heart of the network but at its periphery, at both ends of communication ("end-to-end"), its designers ensured an ongoing development of innovations; thus, when new forms of information coding are developed (for example, when the company Real Networks created the first audio stream protocol in 1995), the inventors only need to distribute the player supporting it (in this case, RealAudio Player). Thus, they can experiment with and develop their product, whose longevity would be arbitrated by public success (Schafer, Le Crosnier, & Musiani, 2011, p. 40).

This end-to-end architecture is one of the Internet's founding pillars (Saltzer, Reed, & Clark, 1981). The telecommunications players saw this as a "heresy": they imagined their technical and economic future still relied on maintaining processing capabilities at the network's core (Huston, 2008). They pursued this vision with what they now call "Next Generation Networks." With capacity for "Deep Packet Inspection," these networks can discriminate between information packets according to origin, protocol, and user, and can provide interception capabilities, for example for cybersecurity[3]. The end-to-end principle and the idea of placing the intelligence of the network, instead of its centre, at its periphery – the vision of the Internet's founding fathers – can be eroded; but other founding elements of the Internet, in particular its distributed and symmetrical character, have been affected – not only by the development of several applications based on a client/server model, but also by the restrictions imposed by operators. For example, VoIP or P2P have been throttled on mobiles in France, but it was not the case for the cabled Internet. A document from the French Federation of Telecoms, disclosed in summer 2011, proposed both the end of unlimited Internet – a French specificity initiated in the early 2000s and preserved to this day – and a discrimination option on selected protocols, specifically P2P and newsgroups. Both distributed architecture and founding practices become optional, in favour of a model reminiscent of traditional media.

Restrictions related to attempts at discriminating against certain packets or even certain protocols, and the potential for agreements between operators and content providers, could create an entry ticket into the network of networks, preventing new players from entering the market. In addition, a variety of recent laws aimed at strengthening intellectual property (the above-mentioned Hadopi, SOPA, PIPA, that have given network operators a central role in system surveillance), or wiretapping (per the U.S. Patriot Act of 2001, destined to "fight terrorism"), allegedly pose a danger to the "democratic Internet" efforts put forward by proponents of neutrality (Free Press, *La Quadrature du Net*, Association for the Advancement of Free Software, the Foundation for a Free Information Infrastructure, and others), carrying the debate into the fields of rights, citizenship, and equality.

Internet: Between "Common Good" and "Gated Communities"

The Internet protocols were designed in a model of openness and collaboration. We can consider the Internet at its beginning as a common good, which then, as a result of being disseminated to the public, became a "semi-common good." It is in the same spirit that Tim Berners-Lee founded the World Wide Web Consortium for Web protocols in the mid-1990s, and obtained from CERN (the European Council for Nuclear Research), the liberty to develop the Web as we know it today.

While Alcatel-Lucent, Orange and others do not exclude agreements with the "giants" of the Web, and as the idea of an *à la carte* Internet gains ground, Tim Berners-Lee is also concerned about several trends affecting the Web he originally created. In particular, socio-digital networks leverage users' personal data to provide added-value services, but only on their own sites. They thus create "sealed silos" that lock users into their system and do not allow them to easily export or retrieve data.

The trend by mega-corporations to lock users into their services is also evident on the side of terminal manufacturers: Apple's private model prohibits content and media providers from directly providing their applications to users, or from buying goods (music, digital books, etc.) outside the Apple ecosystem. This commercial force even allows Apple to break away from collectively developed norms, as with its digital book format iBooks, which withdraws from the ePub V3 standard, and whose software only allows books to be commercially diffused on Apple's iTunes service.

This balkanization of the Internet is reinforced by a new trend in Internet-based services: cloud computing. Each cloud operator tries to keep its users, the cloud acting as a "second network" over and above the communication network itself. Apart from the short-term profits made by advertising or paid services, the lifetime value (the estimated value a user can produce for a company) is also coveted.

Neutrality violations propagate all the way to the application layer: search engines determine responses based on advertising revenue. Value systems ("Like" on Facebook, "+1" on Google), and social networks associated with services (for example Ping, "a social network made for music," but also tailored to iTunes and Apple), form a set of competing systems, which extend along the entire Internet value chain. Here again, they are not without impact on access to information: with Search Plus Your World, users can have access to the results of a Google search engine influenced by their friends' +1s. On Facebook, automatic recommendations are commonplace. The issue of "exclusivities," particularly for mobile Internet, and the mergers between communication operators and other actors (Orange's acquisition of the Deezer music distribution system; the merger between Spotify and Google) are symptomatic of the emergence of vertical conglomerates. Google, for example, has been subject to investigations in the U.S. and Europe for abuse of its dominant position on the market: at stake was whether the company had prevented Android mobile phone manufacturers from using competitors, or if it gave preferential placement to its own products. The FCC is also interested in Google's practices with respect to Google+, whose results are incorporated into search results, which may give it an advantage over other social networks.

AN ISSUE OF GOVERNANCE

Content and Internet service providers, justice and politics, users: all actors in the Internet chain confront these issues. The net neutrality debate is a multi-stakeholder debate, and reflects changes in Internet governance.

Towards Open Debates for Open Networks

Although the network of networks escapes centralized government in the classical sense, power relations are not absent from its management, which raises issues much broader than "mere" technical evolution and the specialized debates that have led to the creation of the Internet Engineering Task Force.

A Multi-Stakeholder Debate

An initial phase of the Internet corresponded to a more informal mode of operation, illustrated by the creation of the Network Working Group in 1968, in the early days of Arpanet, and the Request for Comments (RFCs) in 1969. The Internet's development led to a progressive structuring of technical bodies, gathered in 1992 within the Internet Society, while the World Wide Web Consortium (W3C) was formed in 1994 to establish technical exchange and Web technology standardization.

This structure, outside the traditional standardization and normalization bodies for telecommunications (for example, the International Telegraph and Telephone Consultative Committee), and data processing (the International Organization for Standardization), is highly original and continues today. It responds to two concerns of the Internet's "founding fathers": ensure open technical debate, and freely disseminate specifications to promote their adoption, while allowing many ideas to be born as needed and to emanate from multiple actors. The process of filing technical documents, their subjection to debate, and eventual transformation into norms, in this way remains in the hands of engineers.

A major shift took place in 1998, with the creation of ICANN (Internet Corporation for Assigned Names and Numbers), a private not-for-profit organization based on Californian private law and bound by a Memorandum of Understanding with the U.S. Department of Commerce. ICANN's management of Internet naming was strongly criticized. It became a symbol of U.S. domination over the Internet, and unilateral governance of its resources—a specifically geopolitical issue.

Internet governance saw another important development in the early 2000s, with the World Summit on the Information Society, held in Geneva in 2003 and in Tunis in 2005. Initiated by the UN and organized by the International Telecommunication Union, WSIS was an opportunity to test a deliberately "multi-stakeholder" form (Massit-Folléa, Méadel & Monnoyer-Smith 2012; Raboy, Landry & Shtern 2010; Malcolm 2008). No comprehensive multilateral framework was forged; it took the bursting of the "dot-com bubble" to bring about a rather cautious declaration and the creation of the Working Group on Internet Governance. This Working Group defines Internet governance as "the development and application by Governments, the private sector and civil society, in their respective roles, of shared principles, norms, rules, decision-making procedures, and programmes that shape the evolution and use of the Internet," adding that "it also includes other significant public policy issues, such as critical

Internet resources, the security and safety of the Internet, and developmental aspects and issues pertaining to the use of the Internet" (WGIG 2005).

The net neutrality debate can thus be understood as a microcosm of wider debates about Internet governance: it displays the confrontations of private sector actors in the Internet economy (operators, application providers, CDN, etc.), states (interventions by the United States President Barack Obama, the European Commissioner for the Digital Agenda Neelie Kroes, the French Parliament, the Dutch government, among others), national regulatory authorities, and finally civil society (American Civil Liberties Union, Free Press, April, etc.), even in its most radical forms (Anonymous). The stances of the "founding fathers" – to name but two, the creator of the World Wide Web Tim Berners-Lee and Creative Commons founder Lawrence Lessig – are also relevant in these debates. However, the results of a public consultation conducted by the French Government in 2010 testify to the fact that actors are involved in many different ways, and do not all carry the same weight in discussions. Few responded (361 actors, predominantly belonging to the private sector); and those more heavily involved in the day-to-day technical and economic operations of the Internet tend to "naturalize" the debate, using arguments that tend to marginalize other voices (academics, engineers, Internet developers, and civil society organizations).

Several Visions for Governance

As the debate plays out in several domains (the courts, regulatory powers, Congress and Parliament, the European Commission, citizen consulting, etc.), at times it encounters reluctance from certain actors to move to a broad consultation model. In the United States, for example, the FCC faces strong opposition by companies that refuse to recognize its decision-making authority, a position reinforced by the ruling of Comcast Corp. v. FCC.

The question of the FCC's status, and its legitimacy in imposing neutrality rules, lies at the heart of current controversies in the United States. The debate was revived in November 2011, when the Senate rejected, by 52 votes to 46, a resolution proposed by Republicans and passed by the House of Representatives on "Internet deregulation," which the President had threatened to veto. Issues of powers and competencies are determined by legislation, at times skilfully used; thus, Akamai, acting as a Content Delivery Network (CDN), seeks to evade neutrality rules by arguing that it does not qualify by statute as a telecommunications operator.

Issues of power and legitimacy underlie several different visions of governance, of which Bing and Bygrave (2009) have developed a typology.

The first is *spontaneous scheduling*, such as that proposed by Johnson and Post in *Law and Borders* (1996), which places trust in the internal laws of cyberspace, "disconnecting" them from those of "real" world. This idea is a bit difficult to follow, since the issues affecting the Internet have been profoundly social, economic and political ever since its transition to a commercial and public system.

Another governance model promotes an *international* or *transnational approach*. While both approaches share the idea that governance can only be conducted within a framework that transcends national borders, the transnational approach can be illustrated by bodies such as W3C and ICANN, and finds its legitimacy in heavily technically-oriented institutions.

A third path is that of *government regulation*, criticized by opponents to the FCC position, who accuse it and the U.S. government of overstepping their prerogative. They also consider such a measure to be premature and denounce *a priori* interventionism, even though very few cases have been raised. Thus, the Body of European Regulators for Electronic Communications (BEREC) has found that neutrality violations remain rare in Europe, and closely supervised by regulators. This is also the position of several European countries, like Sweden.

Market governance is a fourth trend advocated by operators and opponents of net neutrality, who assert that legislation halts innovation, positing economic liberalism as the main source of competition and innovation. However, liberalism and *laissez-faire* are not synonyms, and in recent years, regulatory authorities have often been the main guarantors of competition. It is also in the name of innovation and liberalism that some neutrality proponents demand action, warning against the risk of a *laissez-faire* approach that could penalize smaller and newer entrants in favour of well-established companies.

Finally, a fifth possible route is *governing by technique*, which refers to Lawrence Lessig's expression, "Code is Law." The "founding fathers" themselves don't hesitate to speak out, and Vinton Cerf joined Lessig when, in a letter to the US Congress on November 8, 2010, he expressed his support for neutrality-ensuring measures... speaking in the name of Google, for which he is Chief "Internet Evangelist."

All these actors defend positions that reflect divergent values and imaginaries that are quite challenging to bring together. The neutrality of the Internet is thus crossed with the same tensions as its governance. Its redefinition, and the willingness of some actors to orient it towards processes of reflection and multi-stakeholder decisions, should not erase the hesitations and reluctance to openness displayed by others. Integrating members of civil society into the discussion, and providing them with a venue in which they may be listened, does not necessarily mean they are fully heard. Above all, it is the weight of Internet companies and communication giants, whether service providers or operators, that currently seems to dominate the game. However, notwithstanding the global, powerful reach of such communication empires, states have not relinquished their privilege of outlining national solutions.

Global Issue, National Trends

Over the past two years, nearly all democratic countries have engaged with the issue of net neutrality.

Different Contexts

The situations of the United States and European states are distinguished by their economic context. Landline telephony is more concentrated in the U.S., around a handful of operators: Verizon, AT&T, Qwest and Sprint. But internal differences distinguish countries in the European Union, France being an exception with its landline-Internet packages, whose prices are well below those of its neighbours. This situation stems from the offensive initiative of the operator Free, which in 2002 adopted an unlimited plan, offering "Triple Play." But differences in infrastructure and pricing are not the only issues involved in the various national trajectories.

Comparing media treatment of net neutrality in France and the U.S. also reflects the desire to carry out the debate in different contexts. The press in the United States places more emphasis on questions of liberalism and innovation: how to protect competition and consumers best? In France, the debate is centred on rights and freedom, and has been deeply informed by discussions around the Creation and Internet Law that led to the creation of Hadopi, and by discussions of Loppsi 2. A United Nations report in June 2011 "is alarmed by proposals to disconnect users from Internet access if they violate intellectual property rights. This also includes legislation based on the concept of 'graduated response', which imposes a series of penalties on copyright infringers that could lead to suspension of Internet service, such as the so-called "three-strikes-law" in France and the Digital Economy Act 2010 of the United Kingdom" (La Rue, 2011). In the view of an important part of the public opinion, the danger to civil liberties caused by excessive intervention into network access is connected to net neutrality, especially insofar as placing controls on the activities of Internet users requires the participation (imposed by law in France) of service providers.

The interim report on the neutrality of the Internet and of networks, filed by two French deputies, Laure de la Raudière and Corinne Ehrel, opens with a reference to the Declaration of the Rights of Man and Citizen, affirmed in decision 2009-580 of 10 June 2009, by the Constitutional Council, which notes: "12. Considering that under Article 11 of the Declaration of the Rights of Man and of the Citizen of 1789: 'The free communication of ideas and opinions is one of the most precious of the rights of man. Every citizen may, accordingly, speak, write, and print with freedom, but shall be responsible for abuses of this freedom as shall be defined by law'; that with the current means of communication and given the generalized development of online communication services for the public, as well as the importance of these principles for participation in democratic life and the expression of ideas and opinions, this right includes the freedom to access these services" (French National Assembly, 2011).

France is politicizing a debate that other countries seek to keep within the boundaries of economics. With the interim report, Laure de la Raudière stresses the need to respond to the inadequacies of current and future legislation, while other countries prefer a more pragmatic, wait-and-see, or juridical doctrine-based path; and in doing so, she underlines the implication in net neutrality issues of a variety of legal and political cultures, originated by different stakeholders.

Trends at Work In the Debate

National governments are taking part in the debate on net neutrality to varying degrees: the Obama administration has engaged forcefully in the discussion, and the FCC decisions have revealed the divergent viewpoints between Republicans and Democrats on an issue that affects liberalism, competition, consumer rights and the regulatory role of government. Member countries of the European Union are able to interpret the measures taken at Community level in a more or less binding fashion. These measures are imposing new obligations of transparency, with clear, comprehensive and easily accessible explanations in contracts regarding traffic management procedures, restrictions on access to services or equipment, anticipated reactions to ensure network security and integrity (Article L. 121-83, modified from the Consumer Code). This takes us right to the centre of the net neutrality question. In addition, the "third telecom package" (a decision taken at the European level in 2011) extends the regulatory power of national regulators and allows them to impose minimum requirements for network service quality to avoid congestion. European countries must take into account these measures, structures of competition, and relationships between their countries' economic actors, power relations, but also a political and legal culture that can engage reflection in different directions.

In several countries, the question of net neutrality is not acutely posed. This is the case of Australia, where the competition authority (ACCC) refused to impose a form of neutrality in 2004. It assessed volumetric pricing, in particular, to be a guarantee in itself of the unwillingness on the part of ISPs to block content, encouraging them instead to discover new uses. Rather than discrimination, ISPs practice "affirmative action," allowing unlimited access to certain content. But this is also the country that put forward a national monitoring system in the name of fighting against child pornography.

The Swedish position is also unfavourable to neutrality legislation, highlighting the fact that customers are rarely limited to a single operator, and can switch if unsatisfied. Moreover, the country's regulatory authority, arguing that net neutrality breaches have not yet arisen in the country, emphasizes transparency and competition over enacting legislation for a still uncertain problem.

Other countries are more invested in the debate: as the Italian case shows, a peculiar, highly polarised media context and the pervasive presence of political issues in the communication sector – two dynamics that have taken hold during the twenty years of on-and-off Silvio Berlusconi government of the country – can be sources of deliberation and politicisation for the debate. Concrete neutrality violations may also accelerate the discussion's development, as in the case of Norway, that faced such an incident in 2006, when a Norwegian operator limited bandwidth access to the National Public Broadcasting Website (CGIET, 2010). The national regulatory authority responded by defining guidelines on how economic actors should reach consensus. South Korea also experienced a neutrality violation that year, when several operators slowed down or blocked the Hanaro Telecom IPTV service, which they felt consumed excessive bandwidth. The KCC forced the companies involved to negotiate, but without taking any special precautions. The Japanese government, on the other hand, affirmed the principles of neutrality in a 2007 report produced by the Ministry of Internal Affairs and Communications. And finally, the Netherlands adopted a law to protect net neutrality in May 2012, becoming the first country to do so.

FUTURE RESEARCH DIRECTIONS

The net neutrality debates are far from being concluded, and so is the related research. In France, the Digital National Council (*Conseil national du numérique*) has released, in 2013, a document outlining its favorable opinion vis-à-vis a law safeguarding net neutrality. Worldwide, the core issues related to net neutrality are regularly put forward, whether the notion is explicitly used or not. They demand attention by researchers according to several lines of inquiry:

- Methodical comparisons between different national ways of addressing the issue in the media, in politics, in legal venues, would shed further light on the current state of power balances among the different actors of the Internet, at the national and international levels.
- The European Union's stand on net neutrality is also particularly interesting to follow: its capacity to produce and propose unified solutions will determine its credibility in the definition of a unified digital strategy.
- The United States has been leading the debates for a long time. It will be interesting to observe the extent to which it will be able to maintain this "defining" role; or, inversely, whether the specific national and regional ways will increasingly take hold, perhaps to the extent of defining the notion differently.
- The recent evolutions in the significance of terms such as neutrality, openness, transparency, call for a detailed follow-up of the semantic – and legal – evolutions they determine, or contribute to shape.

CONCLUSION

Despite its entirely technical appearance, the debate on Internet neutrality is shaped today just as importantly by dynamics including economic power relations, and the political translation of these relationships into laws and institutions; new practices of communication, and the mobilisation of different imaginaries. In this chapter, we have sought to show how technical issues, by affecting Internet architectures and models, may organize the political future of tools that are as essential to our daily lives as the network of networks. Some attributes of the technology, which often escape users' attention and knowledge, influence critical issues of Internet policy and uses, such as data processing and physical storage, computational resources management, and search engine query forms and results.

Moreover, political democracy brings about technical democracy, and not the other way around. The Internet's political, economic and social stakes remind us that technology is not an inherent carrier of values, which originate with people.

While some of the Internet's founders demanded that the "network of networks" transcend laws and state boundaries, which they viewed as a guarantee of its development and future, the preservation of these very foundations of openness is increasingly becoming a political issue, in which states are sometimes held as guarantors against autarchic tendencies by large conglomerates. If the Internet's first architecture fostered freedom of expression, innovation, and the construction of a digital commons, another architecture is currently being built, based on filtering, packet inspection, differentiated services and a break with the concept of transport layer neutrality, which allows for the emergence of trade agreements between access and content providers. New entrants in the network economy, together with citizens, will be drawn into a process of Internet balkanization, in the image of what currently exists in the world of traditional media and telephony. States and national regulatory authorities have a definite role to play, to preserve an Internet that allows for the expression of the diverse trends and viewpoints that cross it – by "dreamers" and "merchants" (Faucilhon, 2010) alike.

REFERENCES

Agre, P. (2003). Peer-to-peer and the promise of internet equality. *Communications of the ACM*, *46*(2), 39–42. doi:10.1145/606272.606298

Benkler, Y. (2006). *The wealth of networks: How social production transforms markets and freedom*. New Haven, CT: Yale University Press.

Berners-Lee, T. (2010, November 22). Long live the web: A call for continued open standards and neutrality. *Scientific American*. Retrieved July 27, 2013, from http://www.scientificamerican.com/article.cfm?id=long-live-the-Web

Braman, S. (2011). Designing for instability: Internet architecture and constant change. In *Media in transition 7 (MIT7) unstable platforms: The promise and peril of transition*. Cambridge, MA: Academic Press.

Bygrave, L., & Bing, J. (2009). *Internet governance: Infrastructure and institutions*. Oxford, UK: Oxford University Press. doi:10.1093/acprof:oso/9780199561131.001.0001

Callon, M. (1991). Techno-economic networks and irreversibility. In *A sociology of monsters: Essays on power, technology, and domination* (pp. 132–161). London: Routledge.

Clark, D. (2007). Network neutrality: Words of power and 800-pound gorillas. *International Journal of Communication*, *1*, 701–708.

DeNardis, L. (2009). *Protocol politics: The globalization of internet governance*. Cambridge, MA: The MIT Press. doi:10.7551/mitpress/9780262042574.001.0001

Elkin-Koren, N. (2006). Making technology visible: Liability of internet service providers for peer-to-peer traffic. *New York University Journal of Legislation and Public Policy*, *9*(15), 15–76.

Faucilhon, J. (2010). *Rêveurs, marchands et pirates: Que reste-t-il du rêve de l'internet* [Dreamers, Merchants and Pirates: What remains of the Internet dream?]. Lekti.

French General Council on Industry. Energy and Technology (CGIET). (2010). *La neutralité dans le réseau internet*. [Neutrality in the Internet Network]. Retrieved July 27, 2013, from http://www.cgiet.org/documents/2010_05_31_2009_31_CGIET_Neutralite-rapportfinal.pdf

French National Assembly. (2011). *Rapport d'information sur la neutralité de l'internet et des réseaux*. [Information Report on the Neutrality of the Internet and of networks]. Retrieved July 27, 2013, from http://www.scribd.com/doc/52921570/Rapport-provisoire-de-la-mission-d-information-sur-la-neutralite-du-net.

Fuller, M. (Ed.). (2008). *Software studies: A lexicon*. Cambridge, MA: The MIT Press. doi:10.7551/mitpress/9780262062749.001.0001

Goldsmith, J., & Wu, T. (2006). *Who controls the internet? Illusions of a borderless world*. Oxford, UK: Oxford University Press.

Helfrich, S., Kuhlen, R., Sachs, W., & Siefkes, C. (2009). *Gemeingüter – Wohlstand durch teilen* [Common Goods: Prosperity by Sharing]. Berlin: Heinrich Böll Stiftung.

Hess, C., & Ostrom, E. (2006). *Understanding knowledge as a commons: From theory to practice*. Cambridge, MA: The MIT Press.

Huston, G. (2008). *The end of end to end?* The ISP Column.

La Rue, F. (2011). *Report of the special rapporteur on the promotion and protection of the right to freedom of opinion and expression*. United Nations General Assembly. Retrieved July 27, 2013, from http://www.ohchr.org/Documents/HRBodies/HRCouncil/RegularSession/Session20/A-HRC-20-17_en.pdf

Le Crosnier, H. (2008). Tentative de définition du vectorialisme. [Attempting to Define Vectoralism]. In *Traitements et pratiques documentaires: vers un changement de paradigme? Actes de la deuxième conférence document numérique et société*. [Documentary Processing and Practices: Towards a Paradigm Shift? Second Conference on the Digital Document and Society]. ADBS, Sciences et techniques de l'information.

Lessig, L. (2002). *The future of ideas: The fate of the commons in a connected world*. New York: Vintage.

Malcolm, J. (2008). *Multi-stakeholder governance and the internet governance forum*. Wembley, WA: Terminus Press.

Massit-Folléa, F., Méadel, C., & Monnoyer-Smith, L. (Eds.). (2012). *Normative experience in internet politics*. Paris: Presses de l'Ecole des Mines.

Minar, N., & Hedlund, P. (2001). A network of peers – Peer-to-peer models through the history of the Internet. In *Peer-to-peer: Harnessing the power of disruptive technologies*. Sebastopol, CA: O'Reilly.

Moglen, E. (2010). Freedom in the cloud: Software freedom, privacy and security for web 2.0 and cloud computing. In *Proceedings of ISOC Meeting*. New York: ISOC.

Musiani, F. (2010). When social links are network links: The dawn of peer-to-peer social networks and its implications for privacy. *Observatorio*, *4*(3), 185–207.

Raboy, M., Landry, M., & Shtern, J. (2010). *Digital solidarities, communication policy and multi-stakeholder global governance*. New York: Peter Lang.

Saltzer, J., Reed, D., & Clark, D. (1981). End-to-end arguments in system design. In *Proceedings of Second International Conference on Distributed Computing Systems* (pp. 509-512). Academic Press.

Schafer, V. (2012). Internet, l'illusion démocratique: De la république des ingénieurs à la gouvernance (1968-2011). [Internet, the Democratic Illusion. From Engineers' Republic to Governance]. In Internet et politique. Paris: CNRS Ed.s/Les Essentiels d'Hermès.

Schafer, V., Le Crosnier, H., & Musiani, F. (Eds.). (2011). La neutralité de l'internet, un enjeu de communication. [Net Neutrality, an Issue of Communication]. CNRS Ed.s/Les Essentiels d'Hermès, Paris.

Secretary of State for Strategic Studies and the Development of the Digital Economy. (2010). *Consultation publique sur la 'neutralité du net', synthèse des réponses* [Public Consultation on 'Net Neutrality', Summary of Responses]. French Republic: Academic Press.

Star, S. L. (1999). The ethnography of infrastructure. *The American Behavioral Scientist, 43*(3), 377–391. doi:10.1177/00027649921955326

Star, S. L., & Bowker, G. (2002). How to infrastructure. In *Handbook of new media* (pp. 151–162). London: Sage.

Van Schewick, B. (2010). *Internet architecture and innovation*. Cambridge, MA: The MIT Press.

Working Group on Internet Governance. (2005). *Report of the working group on internet governance at the world summit on the information society* (Document WSIS-II/PC-3/DOC/5-E). Retrieved July 27, 2013, from http://www.itu.int/wsis/docs2/pc3/off5.pdf

Wu, T. (2003). Network neutrality, broadband discrimination. *Journal on Telecommunications & High Technology Law, 2*, 141.

ADDITIONAL READING

Abbate, J. (2000). *Inventing the Internet*. Cambridge, MA: The MIT Press.

Barratt, N., & Shade, L. R. (2007). Net neutrality: Telecom policy and the public interest. *Canadian Journal of Communication, 32*, 295–305.

Bendrath, R., & Mueller, M. (2011). The end of the net as we know it? Deep packet inspection and Internet governance. *New Media & Society, 13*, 1142–1160. doi:10.1177/1461444811398031

Blevins, J., & Barrow, S. (2009). The political economy of free speech and network neutrality: A critical analysis. *Journal of Media Law & Ethics, 1*(1/2), 27–48.

Brito, J., & Ellig, J. (2007). A tale of two commissions: Net neutrality and regulatory analysis. *CommLaw Conspectus: Journal of Communications Law and Policy, 16*, 1–52.

Cherry, B. (2007). Analyzing the net neutrality debate through awareness of agenda denial. *International Journal of Communication, 1*, 580–595.

Crocioni, P. (2011). Net neutrality in Europe: Desperately seeking a market failure. *Telecommunications Policy, 35*(1), 1–11. doi:10.1016/j.telpol.2010.12.007

Curien, N., & Maxwell, W. (2011). *La neutralité d'Internet* [Net Neutrality]. Paris: La Découverte.

DeNardis, L. (2009). *Protocol Politics: The Globalization of Internet Governance*. Cambridge, MA: The MIT Press. doi:10.7551/mitpress/9780262042574.001.0001

Faulhaber, G. (2007). Network neutrality: The debate evolves. *International Journal of Communication, 1*, 680–700.

Flichy, P. (2001) *L'imaginaire d'Internet* [The Internet Imaginaire]. Paris: La découverte.

Hahn, R., Litan, R., & Singer, H. (2007). The economics of wireless net neutrality. *Journal of Competition Law & Economics*, *3*(3), 399–451. doi:10.1093/joclec/nhm015

Hart, J. (2011). The net neutrality debate in the United States. *Journal of Information Technology & Politics*, *8*(4), 418–443. doi:10.1080/19331681.2011.577650

Kim, M., Chung, C. J., & Kim, J. H. (2011). Who shapes network neutrality policy debate? An examination of information subsidizers in the mainstream media and at Congressional and FCC hearings. *Telecommunications Policy*, *35*, 314–324. doi:10.1016/j.telpol.2011.02.005

McKelvey, F. (2010). Ends and ways: The algorithmic politics of network neutrality. Global Media Journal: Canadian Ed., 3(1), 51-73.

Meinrath, S. D., & Pickard, V. W. (2008). Transcending net neutrality: Ten steps toward an open Internet. *Journal of Internet Law*, *12*(6), 11–21.

Mueller, M., & Asghari, H. (2012). Deep packet inspection and bandwidth management: Battles over BitTorrent in Canada and the United States. *Telecommunications Policy*, *36*, 462–475. doi:10.1016/j.telpol.2012.04.003

Nunziato, D. (2009). *Virtual Freedom: Net neutrality and free speech in the Internet Age*. Stanford: Stanford University Press.

Powell, A., & Cooper, A. (2011). Net neutrality discourses: Comparing advocacy and regulatory arguments in the US and the UK. *The Information Society*, *27*(5), 311–325. doi:10.1080/01972243.2011.607034

Serres, A. (2003) *Aux sources d'Internet: l'émergence d'Arpanet d'Arpanet* [The Internet's Wellsprings: The Emergence of Arpanet]. Villeneuve d'Ascq: Presses Universitaires du Septentrion.

Storsul, T. (2010). Television in cyberspace: The net neutrality tussle in Norway. In J. Gripsrud, & H. Moe (Eds.), *The Digital Public Sphere. Challenges for Media Policy* (pp. 83–96). Göteborg: Nordicom.

Wu, T., & Yoo, C. (2007). Keeping the Internet Neutral?: Tim Wu and Christopher Yoo Debate. *Federal Communications Law Journal*, *59*(3), 575–592.

Yoo, C. S. (2005). Beyond network neutrality. *Harvard Journal of Law & Technology*, *19*(1), 1–77.

Yoo, C. S. (2012). Network neutrality and the need for a technological turn in Internet scholarship. In M. E. Price, S. G. Verhulst, & L. Morgan (Eds.), *Routledge handbook of media law* (pp. 539–555). New York, Abingdon: Routledge.

KEY TERMS AND DEFINITIONS

Deep Packet Inspection (DPI): A form of computer network data filtering that examines a packet as it passes an inspection point, searching for protocol non-compliance, intrusions, viruses, spam, criteria to decide whether the packet needs to be routed to a different destination, or for the purpose of collecting statistical information.

End-to-End Principle: A classic design principle of computer networking, stating that application-specific functions should reside in the end hosts of a network rather than in intermediary nodes.

Internet Governance: As defined by the Working Group on Internet Governance (after the World Summit on the Information Society, WSIS, in 2005), the development and application by Governments, the private sector and civil society, in their respective roles, of shared principles, norms, rules, decision-making procedures, and programmes that shape the evolution and use of the Internet.

Internet Service Provider (also ISP or Internet Access Provider): A business or organization that offers users access to the Internet and related services. Usually a telephone company or other communication provider.

Net Neutrality (also Network Neutrality or Internet Neutrality): The principle according to which all packets of information that circulate within the "network of networks" should be treated equally, regardless of their source and recipient.

Packet Switching: A digital networking communications method that groups all transmitted data – regardless of content, type, or structure – into suitably sized blocks, called packets.

Peer-to-Peer (P2P) Network: A computer network organized according to a decentralized and distributed architecture, in which nodes act as both suppliers and consumers of resources.

Protocol: In computer science, a (communications) protocol is a system of digital rules for message exchange within or between computers.

ENDNOTES

1. Initiated in 1989, the award honors IT professionals who have made a significant contribution to the field of data networks and computer communications.
2. A reference to the American riddle, "Where do 800-pound gorillas sit? Anywhere they want," intended to illustrate the omnipotence of major IT companies.
3. The closing of Megaupload in January 2012 by the American authorities was based on legislation that punishes illegal downloading (the *Digital Millennium Copyright Act*), but also and above all on anti-mafia legislation (RICO, or the *Racketeer Influenced and Corrupt Organizations Act*).

Chapter 4
Microeconomics of Education and the Effect of Government Intervention:
The Role of Classroom 2.0 in Facilitating the UK Government's Schools Policies

Jonathan Bishop
Centre for Research into Online Communities and E-Learning Systems, Belgium

ABSTRACT

While the concept of Classroom 2.0 has been around for over a decade, the concept of electronic and distance learning as a mode to improve education outcomes has existed ever since the first broadcast of television programs carrying educational content. The governments in the United Kingdom have always sought to intervene in education, whether this has been allowing schools to opt-out of local authority control with grant-maintained schools under Margaret Thatcher, co-operative trusts under Tony Blair, or free schools under David Cameron. Not all government interventions are as successful. Homogenized one-size-fits-all education based on catchment areas such as Comprehensive Schools and state-run projects like the UK e-University have been shown to lack the return on investment of Specialist and Independent Schools and the Open University. This chapter reviews some of the microeconomic models used by governments to intervene in the market for instructional services, including e-participation in education, namely Classroom 2.0. It also looks at some of the possibilities of Classroom 2.0 in education systems that have been affected by UK and respective devolved government's education policy.

INTRODUCTION

The education market, particularly with regards to schools has been intended to be driven by self-interest, by both parents and education providers. The self-interest of parents, as consumers is in choosing schools that will provide maximum advantage to their children and the self-interest of schools or their senior managers, as producers is in making policy decisions that are based upon ensur-

DOI: 10.4018/978-1-4666-6038-0.ch004

Copyright © 2014, IGI Global. Copying or distributing in print or electronic forms without written permission of IGI Global is prohibited.

ing that their institutions thrive, or at least survive in the market (Gewirtz, Ball, & Bowe, 1995). The educational e-participation market as a whole has similarly been driven by self-interest, from that of the shareholders who want a high return on their investment to that of the senior workers who see an increase in profits as a way of furthering their own objectives. Schools could be considered to be part of the educational e-participation market where they use any form of electronic equipment to enhance participation in the learning process (Bishop, 2007). This could include a primary classroom that teaches word-processing using computers, to a high school where lecture-like lessons are delivered using Microsoft Powerpoint presentations (ibid).

BACKGROUND

A number of economic models for regulating education activities are at the disposal of governments. UK Government policies on education have in recent decades been about removing control over education provision from central government. Whether this was the New Labour Government devolving authority to Scotland, Wales and Northern Ireland legislators, or the Coalition Government encouraging the opt-out from local authority control in England, this has been an aspect of education policy in the UK since 1997.

Legal Issues in Market-Based Education

It has been argued that education should go beyond the bricks and mortar of school buildings, including into the home and community venues (Bishop, 2012b). The types of business models to do this are extensive. Some of the more effective models in relation to education, such as those with limited liability are discussed in Table 1.

Other than the charitable incorporated organisations, there are no references to charities in Table 1, but for a very good reason. Charities, including charitable trust can exist alongside or as part of these organisations. Other organisation types, such as companies limited by shares and

Table 1. Types of organisational structure suited to education

Company Type	Description
Company Limited by Guarantee	A company limited by guarantee is a type of private limited typically used for not-for-profit organisations that want to fulfill charitable objects but with greater freedoms.
Community Interest Company	A Community Interest Company (CIC) is a limited company, with special additional features, created for the use of people who want to conduct a business or other activity for community benefit, and not purely for private advantage.
Charitable Incorporated Organisation	A charitable incorporated organisation, or CIO, is a new legal form for a charity that is an incorporated form of charity which is not a company as it only has to register with the Charity Commission and not Companies House. A CIO is only created once it is registered by the Commission can enter into contracts in its own right and its trustees will normally have limited or no liability for the debts of the CIO.
Co-operative Trusts	Co-operative Trusts are free-standing education co-operatives with a social mission, owned by their local school communities. The rationale behind this initiative was to use the framework of 'Co-operative values' to encourage autonomy for schools, but based on a much closer relationship between schools and their local communities.
Academies	Academies are publicly funded independent schools that are not managed by a local authority. They can set pay and conditions for their staff and also change the length of their terms. Academies do not have to follow the national curriculum.

Source: UK Government

other for-profit companies, such as those created through Private Finance Initiatives (PFI), Public Private Partnerships (PPP) and through outsourcing will be considered alongside these in this chapter, but the focus will be on those capable of being charities and/or trusts.

A common theme among all charitable and other trusts is that there must be a public benefit to its operations (Atiyah, 1958). Any of the organisational structures in Table 1 cannot be used to benefit a group of individuals connected in some way to the organisation, such as children of its employees, as proven in Gilmour v Coats [1949] A.C. 426. This was cemented into law by the New Labour Government with the Charities Act 2006 (Geessink, 2013). The "personal nexus test," introduced by Oppenheim v Tobacco Securities Trust Co Ltd [1951] A.C. 297 [1951] 1 All E.R. 31 HL, established that there should be little connection between those who fund a charitable trust and those who benefit from it. Whilst on the one hand this might deal with tax avoidance opportunities, it makes it difficult to develop educational cooperatives, or commune like organisations where those whom benefit from it also work for it. Such a problem was in part addressed by New Labour with the establishment of Co-operative Trusts in the [Education Act 2005], and extended by the Coalition Government with Free Schools and Academies with the [Act].

One of the first schools to be awarded Co-operative Trust status was Reddish Vale Technology College in Stockport (Humphreys, 2011; Thorpe, 2011). As part of its public benefit outlook it established a further organisation outside of its compulsory education remit to bring local stakeholders, including schools, churches, businesses, community groups and charities together in order to establish a co-operative named "re:dish." The complex legal structures, including the need to navigate rules like the "personal nexus test" when it comes to charitable trusts, and the restrictions on certain type of organisations not being able to service all markets, makes achieving the charitable purpose of 'advancement of education,' for people from all backgrounds that much more difficult (Iwobi, 2009). The remainder of this chapter will focus on the issues arising out of the restrictions and otherwise put on the formation of schools and other establishments by the UK Government, particularly focusing on the developments made by the Coalition Government in improving on the work of the New Labour Government. The next section importantly discusses the impacts of the devolved administrations on the education market, who face the same challenges as in England, which might need the same solutions.

A BRIEF HISTORY OF UK AND DEVOLVED GOVERNMENT INTERVENTION IN EDUCATION MARKETS

In the UK, the role of providing education has been provided by Local Education Authorities (LEAs) since the enactment of the Education Act 1902. The 1988 Education Act removed the management responsibilities for schools from LEAs and imposed a role of being responsible for strategic planning. Local authorities were required to devise a formula to determine how it would distribute funds to local schools, which had to be approved by central government.

The Conservative Government further restricted LEAs by making it possible for parents to call a referendum to opt-out of local authority control, which may have been extended to removing education from the remit of local authority responsibility had there not been a change of Government in 1997 (Chandler, 2001). This may be the case as there has been a push by the Coalition Government in this direction since taking power in 2010. Maynard (1975) argued that in a system of allocating places to schools based on a catchment area, parents have the right to move house, and some can opt-out of the LEA-funded school and send their child to a fee-paying school. Each of these choice strategies requires finance, and so the catchment system provides choice only to those who can afford it. Despite this depiction of choice and competition, it is difficult to describe school markets as free markets (Gewirtz et al., 1995). Through its attempts to control the information system of the education market via national testing, local league tables and other performance indicators, central government asserts a planning function while pursuing the rhetoric of autonomy and choice.

The introduction of the National Curriculum by the Conservative Government in 1988 saw a homogenising of the education being provided across the United Kingdom. This meant that a parent living in the North East of England could move their family to Wales, knowing that their children could resume their education from the same point they were at in their previous school. The Labour Government that came to power in 1997 decided to continue with the LEA structure and brought many of the schools that opted-out back into the control of local authorities. This had the effect of removing the market created by the previous administration with a move towards providing education based solely on catchment areas and not the ability to pay or other selection mechanisms. New Labour's abolition of the Assisted Places scheme in 1997 which previously allowed low-income parents to send their children to private school further limited choice of parents in the marketplace, meaning state-provision of education became a norm for most parents, even if it was not in the interests of their child. The regional governments that came out of the devolution settlements for Scotland and Wales in 1998 continued the drive towards state-controlled education by recognising the LEAs as responsible for the funding and direction of individual schools.

Through maintaining the LEA structure, the abolition of league tables and the continuation of the National Curriculum, the regional governments originally adopted a quasi-market approach to perfect competition in which both parents and schools have limited influence in the market and where all consumers have perfect information about a homogeneous product determined by a directly elected government. This was broadened to some extent in Wales with the introduction of the 'skills-based curriculum', where the objectives of schools was no longer to provide state-sanctioned knowledge, but to provide a broad and localised curriculum that provided the skills to enable effective learning and community participation beyond compulsory education. Since the resignation of the unpopular education minister for Wales, Jane Davidson, the Welsh Government has taken a more choice-based approach to schools more typical of the New Labour Governments. This has included the introduction of a Website to aid parents in choosing schools by comparing school statistics (My Local School: http://mylocalschool.wales.gov.uk), as well as introducing 'banding,' which like league tables allows parents to compare the outcomes of a particular school. Its introduction of a similar Website for healthcare (My Local Health Service: mylocalhealthservice.wales.gov.uk) and making food outlets display their hygiene ratings suggests the Welsh Government is starting to move unpopular decisions in public service cuts to the people (i.e. the market), who though people power will reject underperforming services in favour of ones more suited to their needs.

The Coalition Government of Conservative and Liberal Democrats that came to power in 2010 took steps to reverse the forced opt-in of LEA control of schools in England by bringing forward plans to allow greater financial freedom so they become 'Academies' if they were to opt-out. This was distinctly different from the devolved administrations' approaches, which were committed to state controlled education, and laid the foundation for more market-led approaches to education. Perhaps unfortunately, in 2012 the Coalition Government proposed the re-introduction of 'grammar schools,' which educate children of different abilities in different schools based on their ability. The problem with this is that programmes such as Classroom 2.0, which tailor information for each child, would not have the benefits it would have in a mixed ability setting where it adjusts the challenge of learning materials based on the ability of the child using it.

A REVIEW OF THE MICROECONOMIC MODELS IN EDUCATION MARKETS

There are a number of clearly identifiable models in terms of school legal and economic structures, even though the schools may not actually consider themselves in this way, which can be quite academic. The types of school in the UK can be thought of in terms of there being a perfect competition model, a monopolist competition model, monopolies, and oligopolies.

Perfect Competition Model

The perfect competition model assumes the existence of numerous consumers unable to significantly influence market price as well as numerous small firms unable to significantly influence market supply and who all produce a homogeneous product. Consequently, each firm is a price taker regarding the demand curve for its product as being perfectly elastic at the going market price, perfect information is available in the form of the price of the homogeneous product and there is freedom to enter to leave the market at any time (Griffiths & Wall, 2000). To some degree this may in theory match the system in England where there is a subject based national curriculum, even if the schools have different legal structures. Indeed, governments can more generally intervene in perfect competition markets to control the specifications of the homogeneous products being offered to ensure they comply with government objectives or to increase the influence of the consumers or firms in the market. The national curriculum is one aspect of this, and school management is another. For instance in the case of management structure it is the Coalition Government's policy to force weak schools to become academies, run by sponsors and head-teachers of strong schools (Dimmock, 2011). In terms of the national curriculum the coalition can be seen to have moved it back towards the subject-based curriculum it originally was (Young, 2011).

Governments may also want to influence product price either directly or indirectly through introducing tax or incentive schemes, such as vouchers or allowing firms to charge tuition fees. The Conservative Government tried to introduce such quasi-market approaches with the introduction of City Technology Colleges and sponsored grant-maintained schools (Walford, 2000). Concepts such as 'pupil led formulas' that can mean schools get more money for accepting children with disabilities or from low income backgrounds, something that was envisaged in the creation of grant maintained schools (Conway & Lawrence, 2013). Not only were City Technology Colleges a significant part of resolving the problems associated with the perfect-competition failures of earlier education models, but the introduction of the 'assisted places scheme' also challenged its furtherance (Selwyn, 2013). This policy was reversed by the subsequent New Labour Government when it first came to power, which attempted to return to the perfect competition model by focusing funds on ensuring homogeneity of class sizes (i.e. no more than 30) to provide the same provision to all (Heath, Sullivan, Boliver, & Zimdars, 2013).

The perfect competition model would perhaps fit best with a state-sponsored home education programme. Home education is the education of children in and around the house by their parents or by those appointed by the parents and can be seen as a temporary or permanent alternative to the education provided by the state or by private schooling (Taylor, 2000). Central Government policy in the UK has since the 1980s been accepting of the right of parents to 'home-ed' their children with Education Acts requiring local education authority to facilitate parents in using such a right while maintaining statutory obligations. New Labour's drive to provide childcare entitlement to parents so they can 'go back to work' somewhat limited the extent to which public perception warmed to home education and the Coalition Government's focus on large Academies in England further diminished any drive towards home education.

Monopolistic Competition Model

The monopolistic competition model assumes the existence of a large number of firms in the market who each act independently of each other, freedom to enter and leave the market at any time, and where each firm produces non-homogeneous products (Griffiths & Wall, 2000). An example of monopolistic competition in education is a locality where several schools are trying to attract the same student population, and where some schools may want to attract some parents in preference to others. The Co-operative Trusts model introduced by the New Labour Government provided the freedoms associated with the monopolistic competition model, allowing schools to make more decisions and provide education not restricted by a homogenised national curriculum. In these markets, schools can identify these parent niches in the market by specifics or by descriptors. Indeed the Coalition Government's free school initiative has been conceptualized as 'start-up schools' because of the ease with which groups of people can enter the market (Hatcher, 2011). Specifics include such items as the rate at which clients purchase services, the range of products available (e.g. the range of courses or extracurricular activities) and media exposure. Descriptors cover variables such as age, gender, geo-demographics (e.g. social structure of a school's catchment area) and people's preferred lifestyle (Harvey & Busher, 1996). This model of competition is perfectly suited to privately run schools, such as by parents. Indeed, it has been argued since the dawn of New Labour that if parents were put in control of schools then school curricula and programs would be designed to accommodate their concerns, and government intervention would only need to be limited to allow families the greatest possible freedom in educating their children (Ebeling, 1994).

Online participation in education has the potential to give parents, who may not be educators, access to the latest knowledge on any subject. This means that with the help of firms providing e-participation in education technology they can give their children access to authentic information that has potentially been through strict quality tests within an environment in which they feel comfortable and in which their parents can trust. The 'Free Schools' plan presented by the Coalition Government in 2010 means that the potential for parent run schools is a reality, and e-participation in education could play and important part in the process. Free schools can provide education in most parts of the community, whereas under the Comprehensive system they were constrained to buildings that had planning permission. This model has the potential to lead to a marketplace of multiple firms offering distinctly different products to each other, meaning the self-interest of parents will be harnessed to provide a tailored education based on a whole community approach.

In a market based on monopolist competition, central government may want to intervene to limit the number of firms, impose regulations relating to the standards and range of products, the customer base and set conditions for entering or leaving the market. Governments face continued pressure from the electorate and lobby groups to ensure certain, such as individuals from low socio-economic backgrounds or minority groups, have access to essential services. This could lead to the imposition of quota systems, where firms are required to accept certain consumers in place of their desired customers to meet government policy.

In markets where firms can enter and exit easily, governments may want to impose restrictions to ensure that consumers continue to receive educational services, even at times when the market would normally require cutbacks or the cessation of certain products. This could materialize in the form of a policy where a school is required to register all students for a particular examination when it is likely the school will drop in the league table as a result.

Monopolies and Oligopolies

A monopoly is a market that is served only by one supplier, known as a monopolist. A monopolist can typically increase its profits by charging a price higher than the competitive equilibrium price and selling less of its product than would be supplied in a competitive market. Where a monopoly exists in the case of schools, it is most likely to be controlled by the government itself or a firm that the government approves to provide education in a particular locality. Governments may also wish to restrict the freedoms of monopolists in these markets through imposing price restrictions, imposing catchment areas, or through making it possible for more firms to enter the market. Indeed, it has been argued that post-1988 markets in education, as a result of the introduction of catchment areas, can be compared with the status ante, which has been variously referred to as state monopoly schooling or selection by mortgage (Gorard & Fitz, 1998). In terms of charitable trusts, one might question whether a trust school that serves a market that has been partitioned in such a way that it covers only those from privileged backgrounds would meet the definition of charitable. The law relating to charitable trusts has been formed in such a way that the wealthy should not benefit from such education set-ups at the expense of the taxpayer.

Free schools are perhaps less likely to produce monopolies as they can be set up regardless of catchment areas. However their ability to become charitable trusts might be challengeable. In the cases of IRC v Educational Grants Association [1967] 2 All E.R. 893 and Re Koettgen's Will Trust [1954] 2 W.L.R. 166 it was determined that where the vast majority of spending is targeted at those with a direct interest in the organisation it is not charitable. This may be problematic for the free schools policy, as if it is owned and/run by the parents of the children in the school it might fall foul of the "personal nexus test." Indeed the case of Re Compton [1945] 1 All E.R. 198 says that where there is not a sufficient benefit to the community a charitable trust does not exist. However a school based on a Cooperative Trust model, where parents and their children can join voluntarily regardless of geography, if the judgement in Re Koettgen was applied, it might mean that if the trust is directed at those without the means to pay then this may override the personal nexus test prohibiting persons connecting with those running an organisation to benefit from it.

The provision of education on the basis of franchises, where a private firm has a monopoly on a specific area, has no more benefits that what a public sector monopoly without competitors can offer.

An oligopoly is a market structure in which a few firms dominate the industry. Crucially these few firms recognize their rivalry and interdependence, fully aware that any action on their part is likely to induce counter-actions by their rivals (Griffiths & Wall, 2000). In these markets, governments may believe that firms are not doing enough to improve standards or attract a greater number of consumers to the market. Governments may wish to intervene through imposing growth targets or imposing penalties if certain standards are not met. This would be done on the premise that it would stimulate competition between firms in the belief that this would increase growth in the sector and improve standards. In fact, the Welsh Government has created 'virtual' oligopolies of schools in order to improve standards – called 'family schools.' The term family refers to a group of schools put together to encourage them to improve their standards through an artificial form of competition. The schools that fit within a family are selected according to the proportion of pupils entitled to free school meals, the number of pupils living in the 20% most deprived areas of Wales. Also included is the number of pupils with special education and those with English as an additional language. If Wales were to move away from its more homogenised policy on school ownership and management then schools may be more likely to gain a charitable status on the basis of the funding framework put in place by the Welsh Government, which not only focuses on education, but relief of poverty also. Whilst it is often thought that there is not 'public benefit' test in the case of relief of poverty, Re Scarisbrick's Will Trusts [1951] 1 All E.R. 822 found that where those who are to benefit from a trust, such as those from the same family, then they cannot be considered charitable.

BRIDGING THE GAP: THE ROLE OF CLASSROOM 2.0 FOR MARKET-DRIVEN EDUCATION

The complexity of policy formation with respect to e-participation in education funding in schools is further compounded by the requirement to address the needs of a range of stakeholders in the state and commercial sectors (Mee, 2006). E-participation in education has a role to play in the modernization process of economies, societies and education systems. The Digital Classroom of Tomorrow Figure 1 is envisaged as not simply consisting of educators and learners or indeed only hard-wired personal computers, but also accessible at a distance through many forms of new media, including mobile phones, personal digital assistants (PDAs), tablet computing, and interactive television (iTV) as demonstrated by (Bishop, 2004). Indeed, the classroom of tomorrow may consist mainly of these ubiquitous systems, not tied to any geographical location or boundary. Portable technology could enable people to learn anywhere; on the bus or on the train, while at home or while on the plane.

Indeed, Kanamori and Kobayashi (2004) has described an e-participation in education system with a mobile videophone for home education of learners with severe physical impairments and Bishop (2009) investigated a mobile system in which both home and school-based learners could interact with an educator-set learning program through a persuasive mobile agent.

The Role of eTwinning

The concept of eTwinning is one that is essential to the realization of Classroom 2.0. It involved schools and other community venues, including home-educated children, linking up through the Cloud or other Internet system so that the learners can interact regardless of frontiers. There has been an eTwinning project as part of the Digital Classroom of Tomorrow Project, linking a Welsh Medium High School and an English Medium (Bishop, 2004, 2012a). Rolled out across Europe as part of the Classroom 2.0 initiative, it has become clear than linking schools, even after the novelty factor has worn off, can have wide ranging benefits in terms of choice and satisfaction with learning programs.

The Role of Learning Objects

Learning objects are reusable pieces of educational material intended to be strung together to form larger educational units such as activities, lessons, or whole courses (Brooks, Cooke, & Vassileva, 2003). Learning objects are typically relatively small content components that are meant to be reusable in different contexts, associated with 'metadata', so that they can be managed, searched (Neven & Duval, 2002). The availability of Open Source learning management systems such as Moodle means that it is now possible for even the smallest of schools to make use of e-participation in education facilities and achieve the same high

Figure 1. The digital classroom of tomorrow

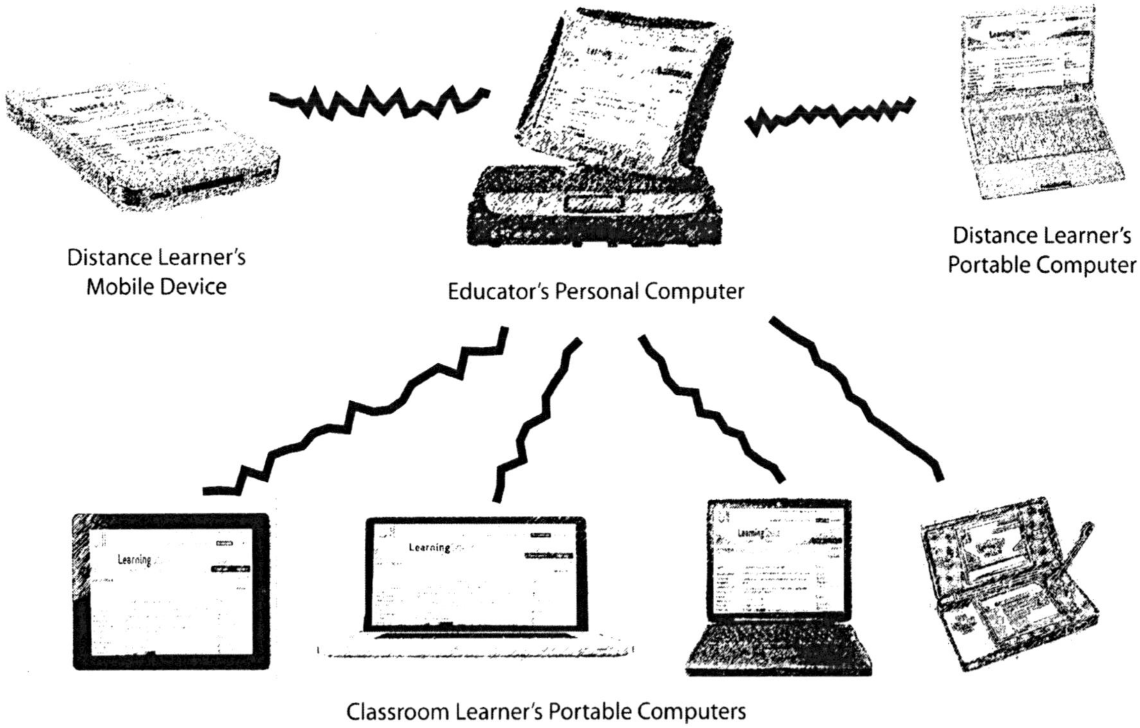

standards as even the biggest of educational establishments. The Faculty of Health at Birmingham City University uses Moodle and because of its policy towards re-using learning materials through learning objects, use of their managed learning environment has increased dramatically (MacKenzie & Walsh, 2009). Learning objects, if their depositaries are accessible, could mean that a parent educating their child from home could give that learner the same breadth and depth of knowledge as someone with an individual learning plan at an elite private school. Open learning objects could do for compulsory education what the Open University has done for Higher Education – provide high quality learning materials accessible to all whatever their level of attainment.

The Role of Computer Assisted Marking

As early as the 1970s computers were being spoken of as having the potential to speed up the marking of student assignments to assist educators and allow them to get on with the job of teaching (Rushby, 1979), something referred to as Computer Assisted Marking (CAM). A more egalitarian cause may also benefit from such an approach, which is greater social mobility through fairer assessment based on standardized questions and criteria. Like learning objects computerized tests could be developed by leading education providers and made available to those whose reputations are still being developed. Standardized marking of this kind across schools, colleges and universities could bring some legitimacy to league tables, whether published widely as is the case in England, or only available to officials, as has been the case in Wales in terms of schools since education policy in this area was devolved. Standardized assessment would mean the 'best' students would get the 'best' grades, irrespective of the individual marking schemes of educational establishment they attended. Universities with high entry criteria and a lot of formative assessment and individual tuition such as the Oxford and Cambridge colleges may still produce the best results, but the average grades would be a truer reflection of individual student performance based on the objective criteria fed into the CAM software, rather than inflated grades which currently mean a degree from one university is not perceived to be as good as a degree from another.

IMPLICATIONS AND FUTURE RESEARCH DIRECTIONS

In 2009 the Emotivate Project proved the '*Excellence in Transforming Understanding through Distributed Independent Education Resources*' (ETUDIER) approach to education. By giving 11 young people in Treforest the opportunity to learn new skills in Photoshop using Moodle and classroom support, Emotivate gave these young people the chance, through designing collages of ideas on what they knew about Treforest's past and what hopes they had for its future, the chance to make a difference. These were then designed as a mural by an artist and the young people then painted it before it was installed. This ETUDIER approach to education involved using existing and sometimes under-used buildings in the community for the project. By using existing these buildings in the community, it showed a community education provider needs a maximum of three core staff. The remainder staffing and support can be 'contingent workers', as happened with sub-contractors in the construction industry before the Labour Government acted on the demands of the trade unions.

DISCUSSION

The education market, particularly compulsory education is driven by self-interest. Parents will always want the best for *their* child whatever the market conditions imposed by the government of the day and often regardless of the needs of other parents. Government policies in the UK, especially in relation to schools in England have tried to harness parent power more effectively through various models of school that are not dictated to by government. Many of these school constitutions have been driven by making use of charitable principles such as the advancement of education and the relief of poverty. The extent to which schools are charitable by this means often affects those parents who will participate in them. It has been found for instance that it is not possible for an employer to have a charitable trust to provide education to their employees, unless it is directed at staff in poverty, or another related group that can benefit from charitable assistance. The choice of model for a school usually places it into a particular market theory, such as a monopoly, a form of monopolistic competition or a perfect competition model. Conceptualising school models on this basis can assist the government in determining what policies to use so that those schools can provide maximum advantage to their pupils. Regardless of a school's constitution it is clearly that they can benefit from information and communications technologies to allow pupils to connect with those at other schools who might be from a different background to them, and who they might otherwise never meet.

E-participation in education has the potential to give each learning access to the best quality knowledge tailored to their individual needs. Government policy in the UK has fluctuated between schools being controlled by local authorities, as under Labour, to being independent of the State as has been the drive under successive Conservative governments. Under both governments there have been providers outside the general market, which have mainly provided specialist education to either disadvantaged groups or elite education for the children of wealthy parents, in both cases providing individual education plans to learners. E-participation in education has the potential to bridge the gap so that all pupils regardless of advantage or disadvantage can have access to education programs tailored to them. Legislation currently allows parents to opt-out of the traditional education system and educate their children from home. Further drives in the use of open 'learning objects' and standardized assessment could mean that home education could become a realistic option. The development of 'free schools' run independently of State education could lead to greater demands for ubiquitous e-participation in education that can be accessed anywhere in the community. This would lead to a marketplace with many 'firms' providing 'non-homogeneous' products, with many others seeking support from other parents to increase revenues from State funds. The need for collaboration between parents and schools to ensure their children have effective social interaction may mean the Digital Classroom of Tomorrow will not simply consist of a single building housing many pupils, but a network of computers and mobile devices operating across the community in people's homes and premises in the community.

REFERENCES

Atiyah, P. S. (1958). Public benefit in charities. *The Modern Law Review*, *21*(2), 138–154. doi:10.1111/j.1468-2230.1958.tb00465.x

Bishop, J. (2004). *The potential of persuasive technology for educating heterogeneous user groups*. (Unpublished MSc Thesis). Univeristy of Glamorgan, Pontypridd, UK.

Bishop, J. (2007). *An investigation into how the European Union affects the development and provision of e-learning services*. (Unpublished LLM Thesis). University of Glamorgan, Pontypridd, UK.

Bishop, J. (2009). The role of multi-agent social networking systems in ubiquitous education: Enhancing peer-supported reflective learning. In T. T. Goh (Ed.), *Multiplatform e-learning systems and technologies: Mobile devices for ubiquitous ICT-based education* (pp. 72–88). Hershey, PA: IGI Global. doi:10.4018/978-1-60566-703-4.ch005

Bishop, J. (2012a). Co-operative e-learning in the multilingual and multicultural school: The role of 'classroom 2.0' for increasing participation in education. In P. M. Pumilia-Gnarini, E. Favaron, E. Pacetti, J. Bishop, & L. Guerra (Eds.), *Didactic strategies and technologies for education: Incorporating advancements* (pp. 137–150). Hershey, PA: IGI Global. doi:10.4018/978-1-4666-2122-0.ch013

Bishop, J. (2012b). Lessons from the emotivate project for increasing take-up of big society and responsible capitalism initiatives. In P. M. Pumilia-Gnarini, E. Favaron, E. Pacetti, J. Bishop, & L. Guerra (Eds.), *Didactic strategies and technologies for education: Incorporating advancements* (pp. 208–217). Hershey, PA: IGI Global. doi:10.4018/978-1-4666-2122-0.ch019

Brooks, C., Cooke, J., & Vassileva, J. (2003). Versioning of learning objects. In *Proceedings of the Advanced Learning Technologies,* (pp. 296-297). IEEE.

Chandler, J. A. (2001). *Local government today*. Manchester, UK: Manchester University Press.

Conway, J., & Lawrence, M. (2013). Competition between schools. In *Equality and diversity in education 1: Experiences of learning, teaching and managing schools*. Academic Press.

Dimmock, C. (2011). Diversifying schools and leveraging school improvement: A comparative analysis of the English radical, and Singapore conservative, specialist schools' policies. *British Journal of Educational Studies*, *59*(4), 439–458. doi:10.1080/00071005.2011.636732

Ebeling, E. R. (1994). Building community through education. *Building a Community of Citizens: Civil Society in the 21st Century,* 119-132.

Geessink, L. (2013). *Segmenting and targeting new charity donors. (Bachelor of Business AdministrationThesis).* Twente, The Netherlands: University of Twente.

Gewirtz, S., Ball, S. J., & Bowe, R. (1995). *Markets, choice, and equity in education*. Buckingham, UK: Open University.

Gorard, S., & Fitz, J. (1998). Under starters orders: The established market, the Cardiff study and the Smithfield project. *International Studies in Sociology of Education*, *8*(3), 299–316. doi:10.1080/0962021980020030

Griffiths, A., & Wall, S. (2000). *Intermediate microeconomics: Theory and applications*. Reading, MA: Addison-Wesley Longman Ltd.

Harvey, J. A., & Busher, H. (1996). Marketing schools and consumer choice. *International Journal of Educational Management*, *10*(4), 26–32. doi:10.1108/09513549610122165

Hatcher, R. (2011). The conservative-liberal democrat coalition government's free schools in england. *Educational Review*, *63*(4), 485–503. doi:10.1080/00131911.2011.616635

Heath, A., Sullivan, A., Boliver, V., & Zimdars, A. (2013). Education under new labour, 1997–2010. *Oxford Review of Economic Policy*, *29*(1), 227–247. doi:10.1093/oxrep/grt003

Humphreys, P. (2011). Personalised education and co-operation—Connections. *Journal of Cooperative Studies*, *44*(3), 52.

Iwobi, A. (2009). Out with the old, in with the new: Religion, charitable status and the charities act 2006. *Legal Studies*, *29*(4), 619–650. doi:10.1111/j.1748-121X.2009.00129.x

Kanamori, K., & Kobayashi, I. (2004). Mobile videophone and e-learning for students with physical impairments. In *Proceedings of the 2nd IEEE International Workshop on Wireless and Mobile Technologies in Education (WMTE'04),* (pp. 203-204). IEEE.

MacKenzie, N., & Walsh, A. (2009). Enhancing the curriculum: Shareable multimedia learning objects. *Journal of Systems and Information Technology*, *11*(1), 71–83. doi:10.1108/13287260910932421

Maynard, A. (1975). *Experiment with choice in education*. London, UK: Institute of Economic Affairs.

Mee, A. (2006). E-learning funding for schools: A policy paradox? *British Journal of Educational Technology*, *38*(1), 63–71. doi:10.1111/j.1467-8535.2006.00596.x

Neven, F., & Duval, E. (2002). Reusable learning objects: A survey of LOM-based repositories. In *Proceedings of the Tenth ACM International Conference on Multimedia,* (pp. 291-294). ACM.

Rushby, N. J. (1979). *Computers in the teaching process*. New York: John Wiley & Sons, Inc.

Selwyn, N. (2013). Researching the once-powerful in education: The value of retrospective elite interviewing in education policy research. *Journal of Education Policy*, *28*(3), 339–352. doi:10.1080/02680939.2012.728630

Taylor, L. A. (2000). Home education regulations in europe and recent UK research. *Peabody Journal of Education*, *75*(1), 49–70. doi:10.1207/S15327930PJE751&2_5

Thorpe, J. (2011). Co-operative schools in the UK. *Journal of Co-Operative Studies*, *44*(3), 57–62.

Walford, G. (2000). From city technology colleges to sponsored grant-maintained schools. *Oxford Review of Education*, *26*(2), 145–158. doi:10.1080/03054980050031363

Young, M. (2011). The return to subjects: A sociological perspective on the UK coalition government's approach to the 14–19 curriculum. *Curriculum Journal*, *22*(2), 265–278. doi:10.1080/09585176.2011.574994

KEY TERMS AND DEFINITIONS

Classroom 2.0: Classroom 2.0 refers to a form of learning instruction that involves using the personal computers of pupils – either remotely or in class – to allow them to enjoy education that is personalised to them and their needs.

Education Policy: Education policy is influenced by a number of factors, including the government of the day, academics and school staff.

eTwinning: The concept of eTwinning refers to a situation where one school is partnered with another so that pupils can use information and communications technologies to work with pupils at a different school to them.

Home Education: Home education is education that is not provided at a school but in the home of a pupil of compulsory education age. It might rely on distance learning approaches and Classroom 2.0 environments with eTwinning can also pupils to collaborate with other learners who are in schools.

Microeconomics: Microeconomics is a discipline within economics which studies the actions of individual members of the public and the impact of their actions on institutions and other organisations.

Monopolist Competition: The monopolistic competition model assumes the existence of a large number of firms in the market who each act independently of each other, freedom to enter and leave the market at any time, and where each firm produces non-homogeneous products.

Monopoly: A monopoly is a market that is served only by one supplier, known as a monopolist. A monopolist can typically increase its profits by charging a price higher than the competitive equilibrium price and selling less of its product than would be supplied in a competitive market.

Oligopoly: An oligopoly is a market structure in which a few firms dominate the industry. Crucially these few firms recognize their rivalry and interdependence, fully aware that any action on their part is likely to induce counter-actions by their rivals.

Perfect Competition: The perfect competition model assumes the existence of numerous consumers unable to significantly influence market price as well as numerous small firms unable to significantly influence market supply and who all produce a homogeneous product.

UK Government: Those elected or appointed to the UK Parliament whom form part of the executive either through the cabinet or as ministers accountable to that cabinet, whom have a degree of control over instruments of government, such as the civil service.

Section 2

International, National, and Regional Issues

Chapter 5
Using the Internet to Make Local Music More Available to the South Wales Community

Jonathan Bishop
Centre for Research into Online Communities and E-Learning Systems, Belgium

Lisa Mannay
Centre for Research into Online Communities and E-Learning Systems, UK

ABSTRACT

Wales is the "land of the poets so soothing to me," according to its national anthem. The political and economic landscape does not on the whole provide for the many creative people that are in Welsh communities. Social media Websites like MySpace and YouTube as well as Websites like MTV.com, eJay, and PeopleSound, whilst providing space for artists to share their works, but do not usually consider the needs of local markets, such as in relation to Welsh language provision through to acknowledgement of Welsh place names and Wales's status as a country. The chapter finds that there are distinct issues in relation to presenting information via the Web- or Tablet-based devises and suggests some of the considerations needed when designing multi-platform environments.

INTRODUCTION

There are literally thousands of people that want to make it in the music industry, as highlighted by the recent success of television programmes such as Pop Stars, Pop Idol and the X-Factor. Wales is a country known for its love of music in English or Welsh. Founders of Wales' two biggest Welsh language record labels are, however established in the Welsh language live music scene, which is not easily accessible to all (Edwards, 2011).

DOI: 10.4018/978-1-4666-6038-0.ch005

Since the creation of the World Wide Web, many Websites claiming to give musicians a better chance of getting a record deal have come online. In addition to these hundreds of commercial sites, the availability of Web site creation software has meant that musicians can create their own Web sites to showcase their work, though these often look unprofessional. The popular commercial Websites allow musicians to promote themselves to a large audience. However, these sites appear to be targeted mainly at artists of music, with the

Copyright © 2014, IGI Global. Copying or distributing in print or electronic forms without written permission of IGI Global is prohibited.

consumer facing a complicated and difficult task to navigate each interface. Indeed, the number of people educated in Wales taking part in the music scene is a lot less than Scotland and England (Sturman, Rowe, Sainsbury, Wheater, & Kerr, 2012).

There are perhaps two main issues that put a barrier between people and information; access to it and the ability to access it. Information inequality is not a new phenomenon. This type of inequality has existed ever since the development of writing – and it will probably remain. Perhaps we will even have to accept that the fact that information inequality will increase in the network society (van Deursen & van Dijk, 2011; Van Dijk, 2005). An easy answer to removing this relatively new form of information inequality would be to give everyone access to an Internet-enabled device, but would people necessarily have the skills to use this technology? In the age of the iPad, iPhone, and affordable yet usable Android-based systems the answer is probably yes.

Minority Cultures and the Internet

Minority cultures are not often considered in relation to Website design, where are often unable to consider the individual needs or others. This can include misrepresentation such as when stereotypical, misleading or incorrect information is provided about a minority culture (Cunliffe, 2007). However, social network services such as Facebook might be important environments for minority language maintenance, as networks of strong ties may help speakers resist pressures towards language shift (Honeycutt & Cunliffe, 2010). Even so, it has been found that almost 90 per cent of the young people interviewed used Social networking services regularly, and the language they used on these sites reflected to a large extent the language they used with contacts in the real world (Morris, Cunliffe, & Prys, 2012).

Music and the Internet

The MP3 (MPEG-3) file format has become the standard for distributing near-CD quality music in a compact format (Brandenburg, 1999). The use of the format probably became more widespread due to the introduction of the free music sharing software know as Napster which was developed by Shawn Fanning in 1999 during his 'freshman' year at the North-eastern University (Fox, 2001). Napster's software application enables users to locate and share media files from one convenient, easy-to-use interface. It also provides media fans a forum to communicate their interests and tastes with one another via instant messaging, chat rooms, and Hot List user bookmarks. Although Napster provided an ideal way to distribute music, it caused problems as its users were exploiting the file-sharing facility to distribute music to those without licences. Had the system been used responsibly, it would have allowed holders of a legal CD to easily obtain an electronic version from anywhere in the world without having to take their CD with them.

PCs, Tablets and Other Audio-Visual Media Services

The Internet has great potential for providing more exciting Interactive entertainment services, especially in relation to music accessed by using a tablet (Koskela, Julkunen, Keranen, Kostamo, & Ylianttila, 2009). Existing services such as Peoplesound.com demonstrate how easy it can be to find a piece of music from a particular genre to download. These services are often designed for access from PCs, which require a lot of experience to get used to using. Tablet devices, such as the Apple iPad, offer an ideal means to reduce the digital-divide, as the hardware is much easier to use than a personal computer meaning low skilled users can participate in what many take for granted (Lee et al., 2013). The iPhone and iPad provide even more effective means to access music services, as do other smartphones and tablets, such as those based around Android or Windows Mobile. These technologies are often free, providing an Internet or telephone subscription is purchased. This is a big difference to the cost of PCs, which are sold for around €799 (£500) making tablet a more affordable way to access online content.

Innovation in Web and App Development

Innovation is perhaps an over-used and misunderstood term, meaning different things to different people. In the graphics design sector, it has come to mean new designs that inspire people into new forms of creative thinking. In the computing sector it generally refers to new applications or techniques in order to complete a task. In the past, many people have concentrated on one form of innovation over the other, believing them to be mutually exclusive. However, the Web offers a new opportunity to bring the two together to form applications that not only feel and look good, but working in such a way that they are also usable by their target group. Perhaps this unified approach to Web design is what will make a Web application 'innovative'.

As everyone knows the Internet is far from a new concept and with over 25 years of fine-tuning having taken place the world's giant network of networks has now become accepted as a medium for business delivery, both to consumers and within supply chains (Fawcett, 2000). Edison said that genius is 10 percent inspiration and 90 percent perspiration and thus the way to get appropriate and innovative design ideas (and not just ideas for cool designs that nobody can use) is to watch users and see what they like, what they find easy, and where they stumble (Nielsen, 2000). As a result the innovation taking place within the Internet arena is amazing, with leading computer companies rolling out new products on a daily basis (Fawcett, 2000). There is plenty of scope for creating innovative applications for the Internet. However, in order to develop an innovative application it is important to look at existing services and how users interact with them. The way to get good design ideas is quite often to follow usability engineering methodology and steep yourself in user reactions and data (Nielsen, 2000). Web developers from a graphic design background, with limited knowledge of human-computer-interaction tend to design Web sites that they would like to use, as illustrated in the early nineties when the Web was in its infancy. It could be argued that designs that current Web users do not find usable is innovative and that once people adapt they will find this 'innovative' design acceptable.

Usability counts for a lot in any encounter with a new product and is what allows people to explore the product and discover what it has to offer (Buchanan, 2000). Whether one wants to explore a product goes beyond the utility of the product and beyond issues of usability as we all have choices in the marketplace and have to decide why one should select one product or another (Buchanan, 2000). Buchanan suggests that if a user wants to use a site, they may be willing to put up with poor usability. Perhaps the best way to decide this is to use existing methods for testing the acceptability of Web applications.

Figure 1 sets out the requirements of system acceptability, which include parameters applicable to Web site design, including key areas such as usability and utility (that form part of practical acceptability) and social acceptability (Nielsen, 1993).

Interestingly, 'Subjectively Pleasing' forms only a small part of the 'Usability' parameter. When developing a Web site, graphic designers tend to concentrate on its visual appearance more

Figure 1. Nielsen's (1993) parameters for system acceptability

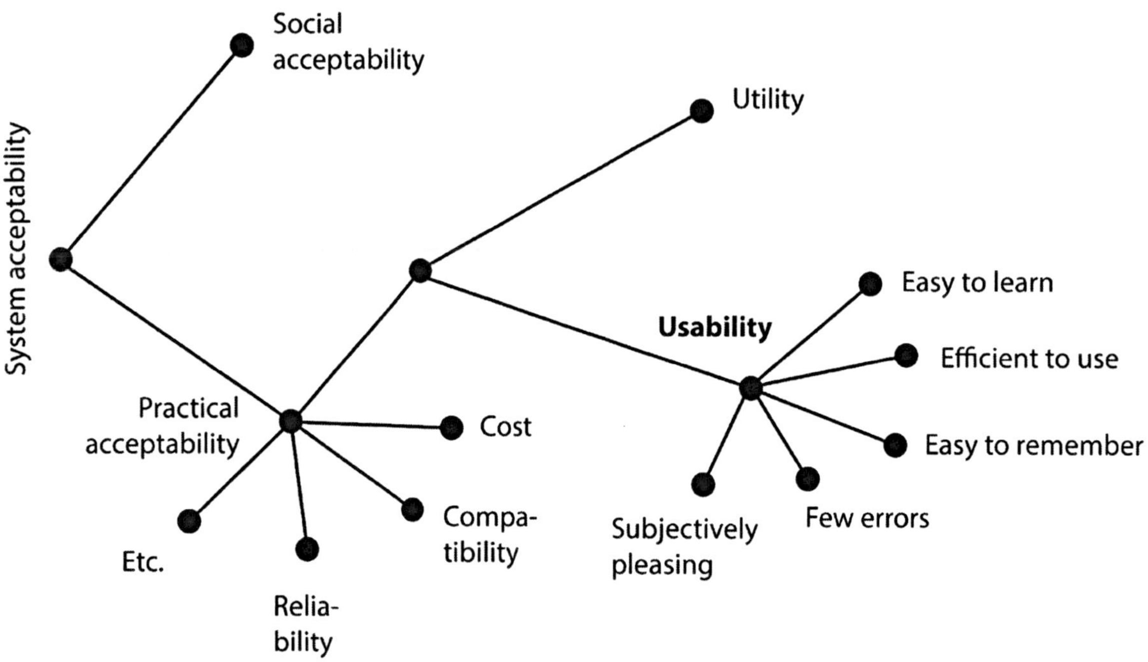

than how usable it is. Using usability engineering as a basis, it should be possible to decide whether a cool design or 'innovative' application is usable. It is possible for an application to not meet the 'System Acceptability' criteria in Figure 1 if it is not socially acceptable, even if it meets all the requirements to make it practically acceptable. This is the challenge facing graphic designers and programmers alike, to develop applications that its potential users want to use as well as be able to use.

BACKGROUND

Wales is well known for its music talents, but it is rare that the best of local talent is played on 'South Wales's Number One Radio Station' – whichever that happens to be these days. Even so, a growing confidence and interest in the Welsh language and contemporary Welsh music is only matched by a corresponding lack of interest in Welsh politics (Phillips, Lawton, Cairns, & Gardner, 2000). Indeed, there are sometimes opposing political, commercial and nationalistic pressures on Welsh musicians to sustain a living in difficult circumstances (Carr, 2012).

The Internet provides an ideal platform for making this music more available and accessible to the South Wales community. Whilst access to the Internet within Wales has decreased, from 93 per cent in 2002 to 88 per cent in 2004 (Jones, Packham, Beynon-Davies, & Pickernell, 2011), mobile broadband is now the fastest growing means of accessing the Internet in Wales and this trend is likely to continue (Davies, 2012). The necessity for a unified industry that facilitates musicians to exploit their intellectual property rights inside and outside of Wales is also emphasized as an important factor regarding the capacity of the Welsh music industry to propagate employment for its workforce (Carr, 2012).

Local colleges in Wales offer starter courses to introduce people to computers, tablets and the Internet more generally. For younger people who are eager to and capable of adapting to what is a very complicated technology, these courses have been useful. Even with these centres, the PC could be considered to be the barrier between unskilled people and the Internet as personal computers are difficult to use. Welsh music educators have began discussions about a national music curriculum; basic issues such as the value of passive versus active music making (Rohwer & Rohwer, 2012).

The user has to first get used to using a mouse, a device that is in no way similar to anything they have used previously, then they have to get to grips with the operating system. As an information and entertainment delivery method, the television has many key benefits over the personal computer to the people with low skills in the Objective One areas in Wales. They are likely to already know how to use a remote control for their TV and using the Internet could be considered similar to using Teletext.

Providing people with the skills to access the Internet alone will not allow people to access these services. Few people in South Wales have a PC connected to the Internet, and although schools and libraries are being connected, the number of PCs available is still too low to provide access to everyone who would want to use them. On October 24, 2001 the Welsh Assembly Government announced an £18.4m investment to speed up the roll out of high-speed broadband Internet services throughout schools, libraries and lifelong learning centres in Wales. It announced the same thing over 10 years later in relation to optic-fibre-based high speed broadband. This should have increased the Internet access across Wales, but how will this affect consumers that want to use the Internet for entertainment and multimedia services?

AN INVESTIGATION INTO THE ISSUES AFFECTING THE PROVISION OF MUSIC SHARING SERVICES IN WALES AND BEYOND

The purpose of this study was to interview participants in Wales and design a social media platform for Wales – called 'Welsh Tunes' – that would take account of the needs of musicians in Wales. The study was conducted in a similar style to a software development plan.

Participants

Nearly twenty-five of the thirty participants wanted to be able to upload music, even though only twenty of them produce music. This suggests that the concept of being able to listen to music uploaded by others is popular with consumers. The features that all of those surveyed wanted were charts, to be able to download music, links to resources and to listen to music. Forums, chat and news were the least wanted features, though opinion polls and reviews were wanted by most.

Methodology

The development of the Welsh Tunes music service followed the approach in the revised star lifecycle (Bishop, 2007).points of the star are not ordered in or connected in a sequence, meaning a development activity can be started at any stage. However, the various activities are highly interconnected, through the evaluation process in the centre. Thus, this lifecycle is evaluation-centred; results of each activity are evaluated before going on to the next activity (Bishop, 2007; Hix & Hartson, 1993).

Figure 2. Bishop's (2007) adaptation of the star lifecycle

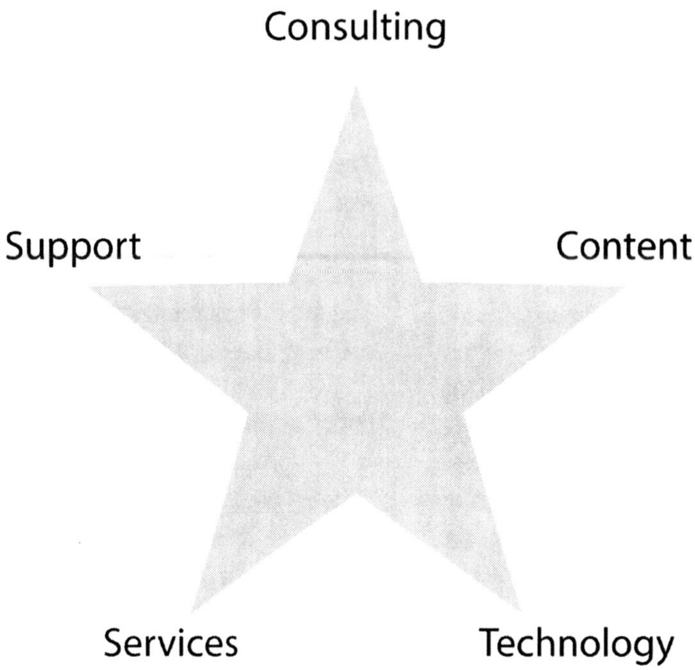

Results

This study involved looking at existing Web sites that offered similar features or a similar user base to the Welsh Tunes music service being developed. The supplement to this report contains all the sites looked at in this study, but three of the most influential are described in detail. The aim is to assess what the potential users of the Welsh Tunes music service want from an application of this kind. It identifies the interests they have, the things they like to do on such a site and the features that are important to them.

Consulting

The applications will be database-driven, which influences the way the sites are designed. It is important to ensure that both the Tablet and Web versions integrate well with the database. The applications will target different user groups, so it is important to design the user interfaces differently to suit the target group.

User Groups

The study identified two main types of user. The artist is someone who has media to provide. The consumer is the person that listens to the music, the person that wants the product. These two users are almost completely different; they have different needs and expectations of the Internet. The research showed that 67% of those that took part listened to and/or bought music, with 33% of participants producing their own music.

These two groups can also be sub-divided into four groups, each with their own specific needs. The artists are either musicians that are signed to a record company or seeking a record deal or performance opportunity. The consumers are either representatives from the music industry searching for these musicians or music listeners, accessing the site for entertainment.

Business Planning

The failure of many innovative Internet ventures is believed to have been down to a lack of consideration of the business and marketing issues that

Figure 3. A banner advert to promote the Welsh Tunes music service

are used in the formation of offline enterprises. It is important to investigate these to ensure the sustainability of the Web application. Projects that are not backed by a sponsor, such as a large media organisation have to consider ways to generate revenue. This can be difficult as there are limited ways to do this with a brand that is not well known. Figure 3 presents a banner advert that uses branding in the form of the 'Welsh Tunes' logo to ignite interest in the application.

The steepness of revenue growth over time and the magnitude of revenue generation are likely to be underestimated using conventional financial analysis techniques (Hagel & Armstrong, 1997). Organisers who use those conventional techniques may end up vastly underestimating the potential of their virtual community investment and therefore either foregoing investment entirely or under-investing and thereby increasing the risk of pre-emption and business failure (Hagel & Armstrong, 1997). The model proposed by Hagel and Armstrong (1997) in Figure 4 is a useful model for looking a virtual community from a commercial point of view. However, the model is limiting as it suggests that revenue should be gained through targeted advertising and vendors who participate in the site.

Content

This research looks at existing music Web sites from both a design and content angle. It looks at the style and layout that is currently being used by music Web sites and the look and feel, which users accept as well as what services are currently available. The content is probably the most important consideration in the user's mind. However, there are issues such as limited screen space and the need for rich multimedia.

Music Genre

The study also looked at the genre of music that users listen to and those that they produce. Out of the thirty users surveyed, the majority listened to pop, rock, R&B and alternative music. The majority of those that produced music also preferred the same genre, suggesting that pop, rock and R&B is the music that should be concentrated on when choosing content for the site.

The classical and dance genres were the least popular amongst both those who listened to music and produced it. Knowing this will be important when implementing features, as these genres could be filtered out, so the content that users are most interested in are focused on.

All of the sites looked at in the study (see Table 1) have clearly been designed to provide content to consumers, with little thought to the music producer's requirements. This is possibly because the sites are trying to target the music at the consumers, who listen to the music rather than a site for music artists to upload their music to. With the exception of eJay.co.uk, the sites investigated do very little to encourage user interaction. Even though some have a community area, this is a section of the site as opposed to a site that has user-generated-content techniques applied throughout.

The study indicated that users have little interest in forums and chat rooms, but liked the idea of opinion polls and reviews. In the design stage, these are the issues that must be taken into account, as it is not just the content from music artists and the media companies that consumers are interested in, but their opinion as well.

Figure 4. Hagel & Armstrong's (1997) overview of the dynamics of increasing returns

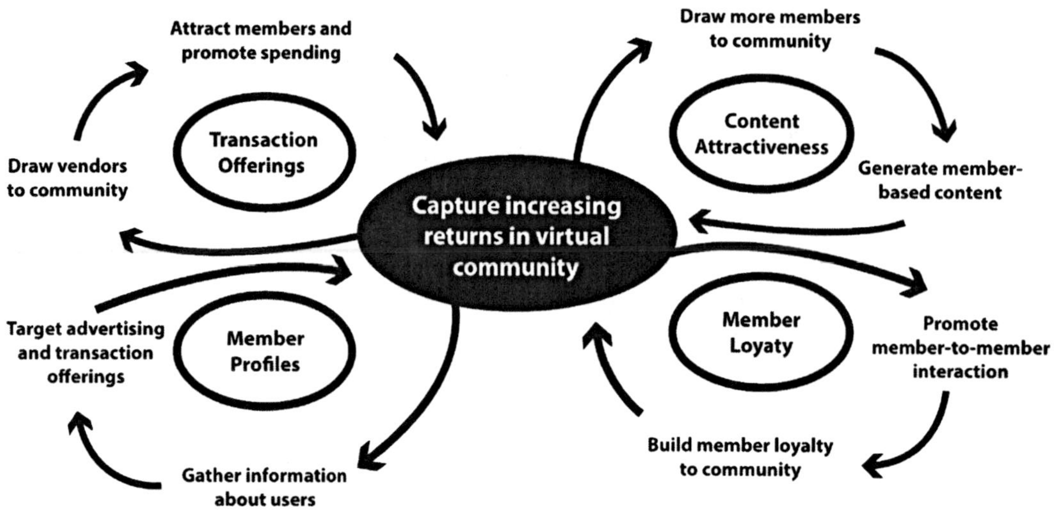

Technology

This stage investigates the available technologies that can be used to implement the service. Issues such as the compatibility with the hardware currently being used by consumers and the level of functionality are looked at. The main issue in deciding the right technologies to implement Websites and apps with is whether they will be compatible with all current Web browsers and Tablet devices. Table 2 outlines the implementation methods and their main advantages and disadvantages.

Table 1. Internet-based music services investigated

Website	Description
eJay.com	The eJay Website allows music artists to upload their music for consumers to download and vote on. The chart position of a particular track an artist has uploaded is affected by a number of factors; the number of times it is downloaded, how it is rated by the consumer and the number of times it is listened to. Although this site does not exploit user generated content techniques to their fullest, it provides artists and consumers with useful information on what is the most popular music.
Peoplesound.com	Peoplesound.com is targeted at consumers more than music artists. When the users visit the site they are provided with links to different genre, competitions and featured bands. The design of the site is very clear, making it easy to find the required content. Peoplesound.com provides users with a extensive selection of charts from the top twenty songs on the site, to the official singles and albums charts.
MTV.com	The first page of the MTV Website is quite complex and does not display at all well on a television. However, despite the technical problems with the site, it offers a number of useful features and contains a lot of content. Users are able to listen to music using the "MTV Player" and view detailed profiles of artists; read interviews, reviews; and download music.
YouTube	YouTube is a video sharing Website owned by Google, which allows artists to set up 'Channels' to make their music videos available to the Website's users. Whilst it can help artists create fan-bases, it can also mean that artists are targeted for abuse by so-called trolls, as happened in the case of Isobel Fay.
MySpace	MySpace is a long-standing social media platform for musicians and their fans. It allows artists to create customised profiles and share news with their followers.

Table 2. Types of technology for developing Web-services

Technology	Description
Server-side Scripting	Server-side scripting methods, such as Microsoft's ASP.NET and Macromedia's ColdFusion allows Web developers create dynamic Web sites linked to databases. It offers many advantages over traditional programming techniques as the site can be made to automatically display the most recent data, without the code being changed. Server-side scripting is only dependent on the platform it is being run on, making it compatible with any Web Browser or Tablet so long as it outputs the correct version of HTML.
Flash	Adobe Flash is a medium to deliver dynamic content via the Web and smartphones. The slowness and poor user-interface design of many Flash animations has lead many professional Web developers and casual surfers to avoid it. The first Web sites were tagged with the name 'brochureware' because of how they were made to resemble magazines and had no unique design of their own.
Java	Java is a high-level programming language developed my Sun Microsystems. Java is an object-orientated language similar to C++, but simplified to eliminate language features that cause common programming errors. Webopedia says that Java is a general-purpose language with a number of features that make the language suited for use on the World Wide Web. Java has an advantage over programming languages like Visual Basic because it can be run on nearly all current desktop platforms.
JavaScript	JavaScript is a scripting language developed by Netscape to enable Web authors to design interactive sites. Although it shares many of the features and structures of the full Java language, it was developed independently.

Metaphors

Metaphors, such as mediating artefacts have been used in operating systems and desktop applications effectively for years, but their use on the World Wide Web have still not been put to effective use in the majority of cases (Bishop, 2005). The greatest weakness of metaphors is that they seem to entice designers to be overly clever and push the site in directions that seem fun and appropriate within the metaphor but leave users' real goals behind (Nielsen, 2000). However, metaphor can provide unifying framework for the design that will make it feel more than a collection of individual items. Second, metaphor can facilitate learning by allowing users to draw upon the knowledge they already have about the reference system (Nielsen, 2000)

Using metaphors to represent information would not be appropriate for the Welsh Tunes media service as the screen size on Tablets is limited and the use of large graphics would limit the amount of information that could be made available to consumers. In the Task Analysis, consumers clearly indicated that accessing content was what they most wanted. Using text-based buttons seems more appropriate as a wider range of content can be made available. However, in some cases, such as audio player controls, using metaphors such as the play button symbol would be appropriate to create simplicity.

Alpha Testing

Alpha testing is usually done by expert users of the application when it is in an incomplete state. This allows technical issues with the application to be identified at an early stage and dealt with before it is tested with real users. A cost effective method for conducting this is a usability engineering approached called Heuristic Evaluation (Nielsen, 1993).

Services

A brand consists of a range of different parameters, which all together create total consumer perception of the product. The five categories in Figure 5 indicate the key elements, which create the basic brand platform or the brand 'DNA'. It is essential that the questions in each category have been thought through before the brand establishes an online presence, as a weak brand platform will be clearly reflected as a weak Web site (Lindstrom, 1999).

Figure 5. The sign-up page for new artists

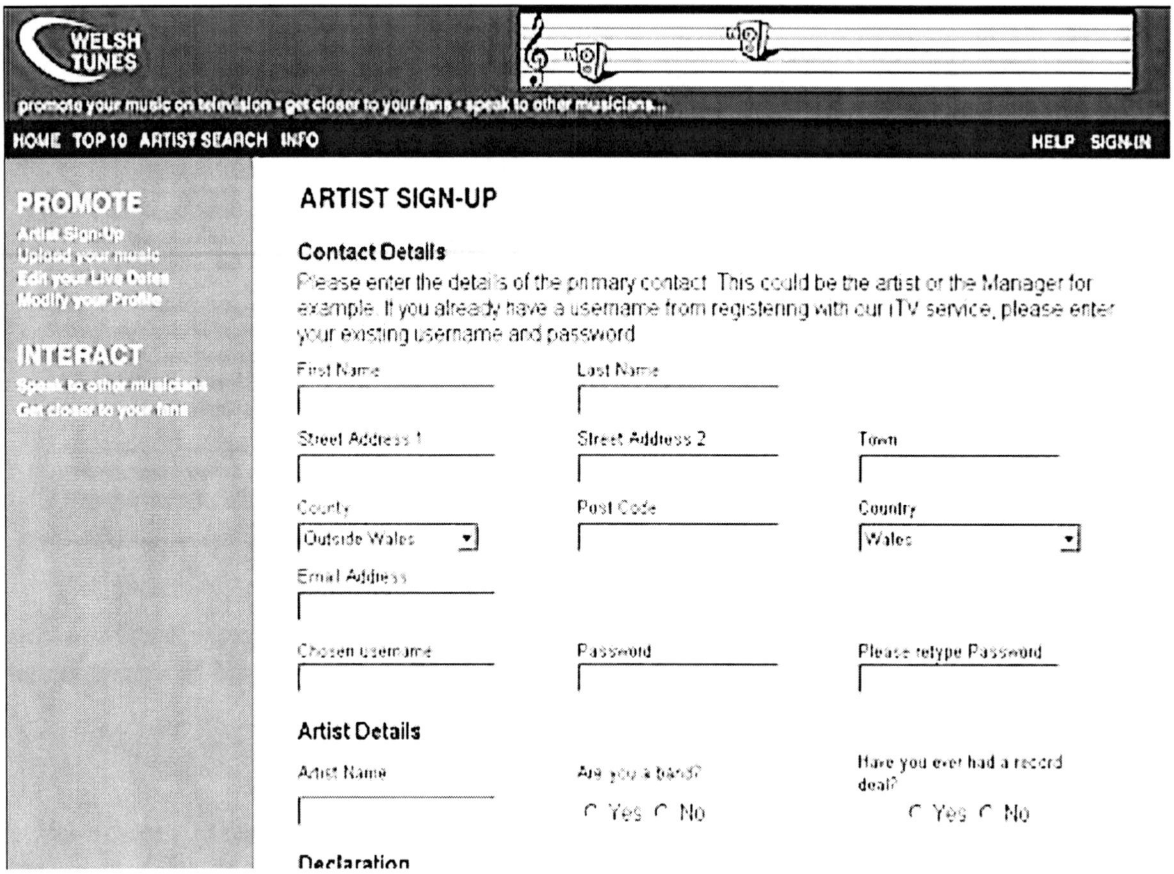

Lindstrom's model provides a basis for identifying the parameters that make up a successful brand. It demonstrates that building a strong brand is not just about having an innovative product or 'cool' logo, but involves a process of maintaining a relationship with consumers and gaining their trust. The build a brand, one needs to think about what one wants customers to see by paying attention to what one is providing that satisfies the emotional part of their experience in dealing with your community (Bressler & Grantham, 2000). Answering these questions requires something beyond simply going through a set of steps to build an electronic community, as it entails a rethink of what one wants one's community to be, and providing the right support to build and maintain the application (Bressler & Grantham, 2000). As Bressler suggests, a brand can only grow if the application meets the needs of its users. When developing the brand based on Lindstrom's model, the users have to be considered as each parameter is developed.

Support

The implementation is possibly the most complex part of the project. After the application has been designed and all the innovative ideas generated, programming them into a usable application is a difficult task.

Beta Testing

Software companies use beta testing, where a forthcoming product is released to a small number of selected individuals for their comments. Beta testing can provide user feedback that arrives in time to improve the first full release of the product, so it is highly recommended not just to view beta testing as a debugging method to find programming errors but also to set up a systematic method for collecting and analysing user comments regarding mismatches between the software and their needs (Nielsen, 1993).The Beta Testing takes the form of a quantitative questionnaire in which the user is asked to indicate their experiences in using the application by selecting the appropriate number on a semantic differential scale.

LESSONS FOR DESIGNING ADAPTIVE MULTIMEDIA SYSTEMS FOR SOCIAL MOBILITY

The main characteristics of multimedia are the integration of several types of data and high-level interactivity caused by the relatively high control the user has over interaction (Van Dijk, 2005). The Welsh Tunes music service's design is based on a four-tier structure. The Tablet user interface and the Web user interface, both have a universal branding. These modules present the user with a usable interface over the lower modules. User Generated Content is the content that users produce. The Revenue generation is the model for gaining income to sustaining the site.

Content Management System

The Welsh Tunes music service is designed to give artists complete control over the content they provide for the Tablet version. Artists are able to add, remove and edit their records and the tracks associated with them. This means that they will be able to add the different segments (e.g. record cover, audio files) of the record at the times they feel appropriate. In addition, artists are also able to update the details about themselves (e.g. description, musical influences), the dates they will be performing live as well as access the messages and comments posted to them from consumers.

Web sites that are personalised assist in allowing the consumer to achieve their goals. When a user informs a Web site what he or she wants, he or she now has an investment in the service. If the service a Web site provides the consumer with value, he or she will use the service more often and think long and hard before switching to a competing service (Allen, Yaeckel, & Kania, 1998). Personalisation forms an important part of the user interface for the Tablet version. Consumers are more likely to want these features than the artists, whose main goal is to promote themselves by making their content available.

Adaptive Recommendation Options

The Welsh Tunes music service recommends particular records to the consumer based on the genres they access most often on the popularity of particular records. For example if a consumer listens to Pop music 50% of the time, then half their recommendations will be for Pop music. The popularity of records with other consumers determines whether they appear in the recommendations.

Integrated Playlist Manager

Consumers have the option to 'bookmark' their favourite music tracks, reorder them and listen to them at any time they choose. This feature should encourage users to use the system more often as they would use it more like they would a 'Juke Box' as opposed to a Web site that allows them to download free music.

Universal Branding and Marketing for Multi-Modal Multimedia Systems

In the traditional brand relationship, communication flows between the vendor and the consumer. Brand-based on-line communities have demonstrated the potential benefits of dialogue flowing between consumers via two utilities: real-time chat taking place in chat rooms and asynchronous discussions. The popularity of interactive communication gives the brand Web site an abundance of free content from the consumer community (Brynjolfsson & Urban, 2001). Both the Tablet and Web versions have a similar look and feel to them so that the user knows that they are from the same provider - having a unique logo in a prominent position is the most obvious way of doing this. The different user interfaces use the same fonts and have similar colour schemes.

Tablet User Interface

The main purpose of the tablet version is optimised for consumers to access the music and information made available to them by artists who use the Web version in a more usable format. The user interface of the tablet version is designed in a completely different way to the Web version as it is mainly targeted at consumers who may have limited skills in using information technology. A number of important design issues have been looked at to decide how best to design the interface.

Navigation and Node Layout

Internet sites designed for the Web have historically only allowed their users to display a node by selecting an item from a list of hyperlinks. This method often makes it difficult for the low-skilled consumer to make an accurate decision as to what hyperlink to click on. This problem can be addressed through graphical representation of information, by using metaphors or icons.

Graphical Navigation System

Metaphors are not the only way of representing a hyperlink in graphical form, less obscure methods can be very effective and helping the consumer in decision making. A Graphical Navigation System, based on the images from the covers of the record allows the consumer to select a record based on recognition of the graphic as opposed to having to recall specific details. This form of representing hyperlinks also makes it easier for Tablet users to navigate the interface using a remote control, which can be more difficult than a mouse.

Web User Interface

The target user group for the Web version of the Welsh Tunes music service are the artists of music (signed and unsigned artists). Their primary use of the application is to make samples of their music and video clips available to the consumers who use the Tablet version. The Web version also targets representatives from the music industry who may be looking to form a relationship with the artists.

Navigation and Node Layout

The interface will follow a similar design style to a 'framed' interface, but will be based on HTML tables. This is to make it work on all Web browsers and so that the user can scroll down the page, without being forced to see the links and advertising. The section navigation is located in the top frame and the sub-section links are located in the left frame. This is consistent with most Web sites and should therefore be a familiar yet distinctive interface.

Figure 6. The tablet version of the Welsh Tunes music service

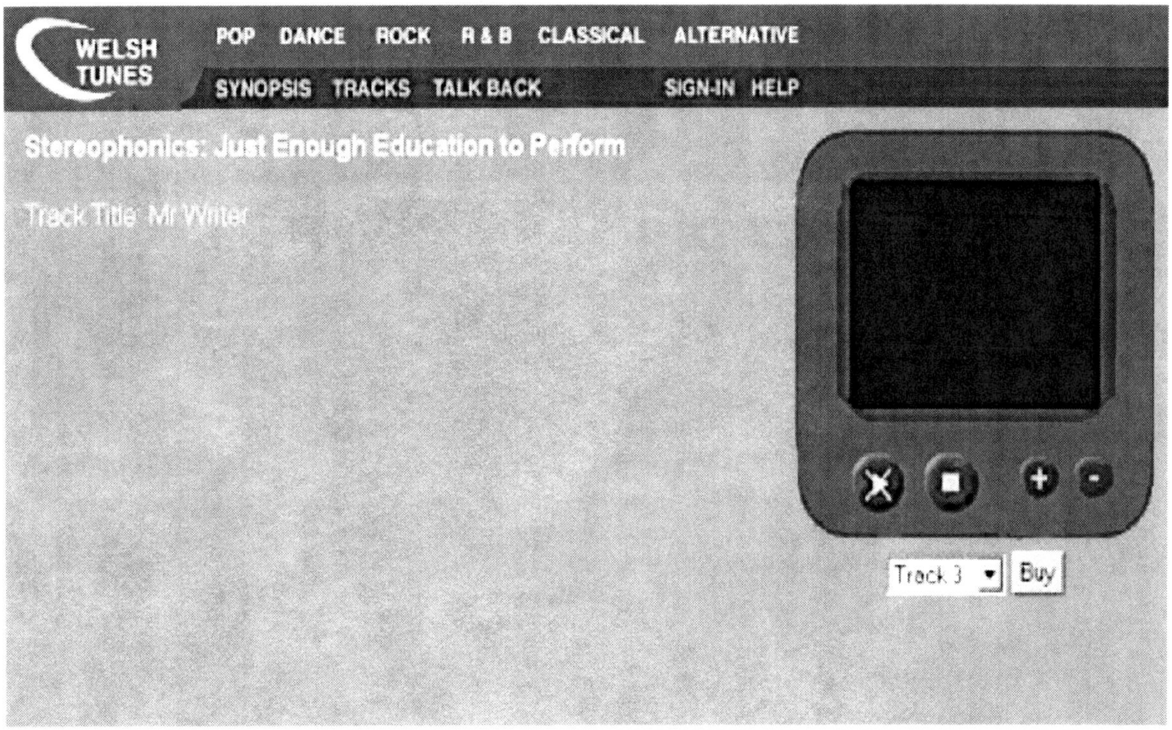

IMPLICATIONS AND FUTURE RESEARCH DIRECTIONS

This project demonstrates that by basing the design of a Web application on an Adaptive Multimedia System, Web sites can meet the needs of diverse user groups by proving an engaging and personalised user interface. The project identifies that successful Web applications are not those that have 'cool' designs, but are those that use innovative methods to create and maintain a brand that the users of a Web application can associate themselves with. Multimedia is the links between several devices in one interactive medium, or links between several media in one interactive device. Applications with sound, text, data and images can be integrated in a combination of several devices or in a single device.

DISCUSSION

When the Welsh Tunes project first began, the Websites reviewed within this study were not aimed towards the actual user or consumer, therefore the language and navigation within them was too complex. This is even more so the case when you consider using them on a smaller device such as a tablet or smartphone. Due to the lack of airplay for Welsh local talent on regional radio stations, especially since 'Red Dragon FM' was subsumed into 'Capital Radio,' the Internet provides the platform needed to allow accessibility for the whole of the South Wales community. This is where the implementation of 'Welsh Tunes' began.

Participants helped to identify the features they wanted from the service and research into existing Websites that offered similar features was

Figure 7. The Website version of the Welsh Tunes music service

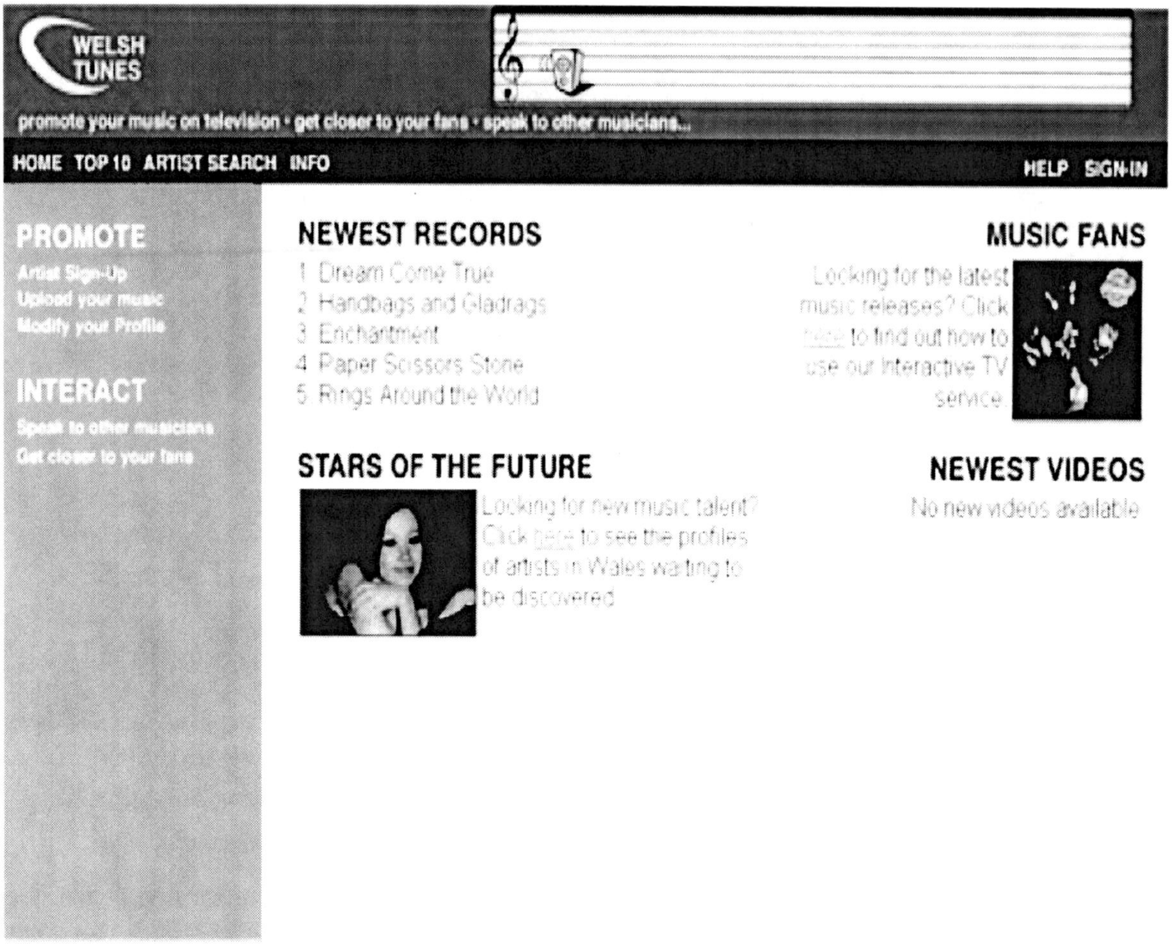

undertaken, taking both content and design into consideration. With regards to design, the target group had to be identified for both the Web and tablet version. Also the genre of music to be included in the site was identified through the study.

The research on other Websites indicated that they were designed to provide actual content so that the user can listen to and download music, rather than also allowing an artist to upload their music and allow user interaction.

When implementing the service, hardware compatibility with current Web browsers, tablet devices and the level of functionality were investigated. Through alpha testing by the authors and then beta testing by carefully selected individuals, valuable feedback with regards to design and usability was gained.

Both the tablet and Web user interfaces have universal branding. They both have a similar look and feel and are obliviously from the same provider, due to the prominent 'Welsh Tunes' logo. In the tablet version, the artist has control of content and it is fully updateable. This personalisation is an important part of the user interface.

The service recommends songs based on the users most popular record choices and their most accessed genre. The user can also bookmark and reorder tracks, much like a jukebox. The tablet version is targeted at people who may have limited IT skills. It does this by using metaphors or icons, rather than the usual hyperlinks found on Internet sites. Using graphics such as album covers, makes it easy for consumers of all levels to navigate the interface.

The Web version of the music service is targeted at the actual artists of the music, allowing them to upload samples of their work and making them available to the consumers of the tablet version. It will be in an interface that appears framed, allowing users to scroll down the page, avoiding the links and advertising. As is the case with many Websites, the section navigation is at the top and sub-sections are on the left.

Through extensive research and the differing test methods conducted through this study, the implementation of a Website that allows adaptability and a recognisable brand, would indeed make local music more available to the South Wales Community.

REFERENCES

Allen, C., Yaeckel, B., & Kania, D. (1998). *Internet world guide to one-to-one web marketing*. Hoboken, NJ: John Wiley & Sons, Inc.

Bishop, J. (2005). The role of mediating artifacts in the design of persuasive e-learning systems. In *Proceedings of the First International Conferences on Internet Technologies and Applications,* (pp. 54-62). University of Wales.

Bishop, J. (2007). Evaluation-centred design of e-learning communities: A case study and review. In V. Grout, D. Oram & R. Picking (Eds.), *Proceedings of the Second International Conference on Internet Technologies and Applications* (pp. 1-9). Wrexham, UK: University of Wales Press.

Brandenburg, K. (1999). *MP3 and AAC explained*. Paper presented at the Audio Engineering Society Conference: 17th International Conference: High-Quality Audio Coding. New York, NY.

Bressler, S. E., & Grantham, C. (2000). *Communities of commerce: Building internet business communities to accelerate growth, minimize risk, and increase customer loyalty*. New York: McGraw-Hill Professional.

Brynjolfsson, E., & Urban, G. L. (2001). *Strategies for e-business success*. Hoboken, NJ: John Wiley & Sons, Inc.

Buchanan, R. (2000). Good design in the digital age. *AIGA Journal of Design for the Network Economy*, *1*(1), 1–5.

Carr, P. (2012). National identity versus commerce: An analysis of opportunities and limitations within the Welsh music scene for composers and performing musicians. *Popular Music History*, *5*(3), 265–285. doi:10.1558/pomh.v5i3.265

Cunliffe, D. (2007). Minority languages and the internet: New threats, new opportunities. *Multilingual Matters*, *138*, 133.

Davies, D. T. (2012). *Broadband services in Wales: First report of session 2012-13, report, together with formal minutes, oral and written evidence.* The Stationery Office.

Edwards, R. (2011). *Sarah Hill, 'Blewytirhwng?' The place of welsh pop music*. Burlington, VT: Ashgate.

Fawcett, N. (2000). Just what is innovation? *Technology Review*, (4): 1–7.

Fox, G. (2001). Peer-to-peer networks. *Computing in Science & Engineering*, *3*(3), 75–77. doi:10.1109/5992.919270

Hagel, J., & Armstrong, A. (1997). *Net gain: Expanding markets through virtual communities*. Boston, MA: Harvard University Press.

Hix, D., & Hartson, H. R. (1993). *Developing user interfaces: Ensuring usability through product & process*. New York: John Wiley & Sons, Inc.

Honeycutt, C., & Cunliffe, D. (2010). The use of the welsh language on Facebook: An initial investigation. *Information Communication and Society*, *13*(2), 226–248. doi:10.1080/13691180902914628

Jones, P., Packham, G., Beynon-Davies, P., & Pickernell, D. (2011). False promises: E-business deployment in Wales' SME community. *Journal of Systems and Information Technology*, *13*(2), 163–178. doi:10.1108/13287261111135990

Koskela, T., Julkunen, J., Keranen, V., Kostamo, N., & Ylianttila, M. (2009). *User experiences on a community-based music voting service*. Paper presented at the Services-I. New York, NY.

Lee, A., Lang, R., Davenport, K., Moore, M., Rispoli, M., & van der Meer, L. et al. (2013). Comparison of therapist implemented and iPad-assisted interventions for children with autism. *Developmental Neurorehabilitation*, (0): 1–7. doi:10.3109/17518423.2013.830231 PMID:23030702

Lindstrom, M. (1999). *Brand building on the Internet*. London: Kogan Page Publishing.

Morris, D., Cunliffe, D., & Prys, C. (2012). Social networks and minority languages speakers: The use of social networking sites among young people. *Sociolinguistic Studies*, *6*(1), 1–20. doi:10.1558/sols.v6i1.1

Nielsen, J. (1993). *Usability engineering*. San Francisco: Morgan Kaufman.

Nielsen, J. (2000). *Designing web usability*. New York, NY: New Riders.

Phillips, R., Lawton, D., Cairns, J., & Gardner, R. (2000). *Culture, community and curriculum in Wales: Citizenship education for the new democracy?* Education for Citizenship.

Rohwer, D., & Rohwer, M. (2012). How participants envision community music in Welsh men's choirs. *Research and Issues in Music Education, 10*(1).

Sturman, L., Rowe, N., Sainsbury, M., Wheater, R., & Kerr, D. (2012). Citizens in transition in England, Wales and Scotland: Young citizens at 18-25. Academic Press.

van Deursen, A., & van Dijk, J. (2011). Internet skills and the digital divide. *New Media & Society*, *13*(6), 893–911. doi:10.1177/1461444810386774

Van Dijk, J. A. G. M. (2005). *The network society: Social aspects of new media* (2nd ed.). London: Sage Publications Ltd.

KEY TERMS AND DEFINITIONS

Adaptive Hypermedia: Adaptive hypermedia refers to those systems that can change, through personalisation or customisation, to the needs of the users.

Customisation: Customisation is distinct from personalisation in that it is controlled by the user and not the system they are using.

Multi-Modal Multimedia System: A multi-modal multimedia system is one that can operate across platforms such as through a Web Browser, a tablet and mobile phones.

Personalisation: Personalisation is distinct from customisation in that it is controlled by the system and not the user that is operating it.

Tablet: A tablet computer is a portable multi-media system that can be held in one's hands and is usually operated by touch, such as with one's fingers or a stylus.

Web Browser: A Web-browser is an application run on a PC or similar device for accessing Websites on the Internet.

Chapter 6
Internet:
A Political Issue for Europe (1970s - 2010s)

Romain Badouard
University of Cergy-Pontoise, France

Valérie Schafer
French National Center for Scientific Research (ISCC, CNRS), France

ABSTRACT

How has the Internet come about in Europe? How did the "network of networks" and ICTs become political stakes for EU Institutions? This chapter sheds light on facts, limits, and tensions of the building of a political union in the ICT regulation field. It analyses the role of various stakeholders, from technical experts to ordinary citizens, according to a historical approach structured around three key notions: appropriating, governing, and using the Internet. By studying a relatively long period (from the 1970s to the early 2010s) and by observing the Internet as a tool for both internal consolidation and for asserting the EU on the international stage, the authors map the main features and trends that structure the European relationship to the "network of networks." They, thus, show that the Internet's political dimension encompasses numerous and heterogeneous issues in the European context.

INTRODUCTION

The European Union has often been seen as a secondary player in Internet governance. The development of its protocols in major American universities, and then the management of its technical resources by American law organisations, could have relegated European players to mere spectators. Nonetheless, the Europeans did not wait for the Internet to enter network history; and parallel to major American inventions, various projects were supported on the "old continent" to develop alternative technical solutions.

The role of the European stakeholders was not limited to the appropriation of the Internet, and the success of the TCP/IP protocol has not always been obvious: technical choices were open to discussion and "technical rationality" was not the only criteria for decision-taking. Industrial and diplomatic stakes have rapidly come to overtake

DOI: 10.4018/978-1-4666-6038-0.ch006

Copyright © 2014, IGI Global. Copying or distributing in print or electronic forms without written permission of IGI Global is prohibited.

the infrastructure issue. In the specific ideological context of the "information highways" and the "knowledge society," social and political uses have mattered more than the governance of technical resources.

In this chapter, we address the political issues surrounding the development of the Internet in the European Union, using three different angles. According to the first one, we give a description of the early European projects in data network deployment that allows us to analyze how the Internet was integrated into an already complex technical and political context ("Appropriating the Internet"). The second one relies on the study of the role that European experts and engineers groups, along with European institutions, played in the international governance of the Internet during the 1990s. We thus discuss the political challenges of building an "information society" at the time ("Governing the Internet"). The third angle explores the institutional strategies underpinning the development of mechanisms and measures for e-Government and e-Participation at the European level during the 2000s. What was at stake here was the uses of participatory tools to involve citizens in decision-making processes, in order for the institutions to have access to new sources of legitimation of their action, in the framework of an overall internal consolidation strategy ("Using the Internet").

By studying a relatively long period (from the 1970s to the early 2010s), and by observing the Internet as a tool for both internal consolidation, and for asserting the EU on the international stage, we intend to map out the main features and trends that structure the European relationship to the "network of networks." We thus show that the Internet's political dimension encompasses numerous and heterogeneous issues and actors in the European context.

BACKGROUND

At the crossroads of History of Innovation, Political Science and Communication studies, this chapter puts into perspective several political stakes of data networks and their uses, according to a diachronic perspective. It relies on fieldworks analysed by the authors during their PhD: the development of e-government and e-participation mechanisms by the European Commission for Romain Badouard, the development of data networks according to an historical perspective for Valérie Schafer (Schafer, 2012). This paper thus intends to contribute to two main research fields.

The first one is related to the birth of a "Europe of technologies," i.e. the study of the role of technologies in the European construction history. Technologies developments indeed appear to have played a major role in the European construction (Bouneau, Burigana, & Varsori, 2010) to such an extent that we could talk of an "Infrastructural Europeanism" (Schot & Schipper, 2011). Researches dedicated to the development of European data networks have paid a specific attention to the academic actors involved in this history (Davies & Bressan, 2010). We would like this paper to contribute to this field through the analysis of several archival materials: official publications of the European Commission, technical reports from experts, and archives from INRIA, RENATER, CNRS, W3C or ERCIM.

The second one deals with governance issues related to the promotion of an information society at the European scale. If the study of e-governance mechanisms can be considered as a research field in itself (Dawes, 2008; Coleman, 2008), that gives rise to numerous publications in various academic discipline (Scholl, 2009), the European scale has been mainly tackled through the capacity of such technologies to fill the democratic gap between

European decision-makers and citizens. The democratic aspect of e-government has thus been an issue that matters in the European context, through the study of e-participation platforms (Macintosh, 2008; Smith & Dalakiouridou, 2009; Badouard, 2010). We would like this paper to contribute to this field by providing a more broad and institutional overview of the development of e-participation mechanisms, by showing how European institutions have perceived these technologies as major stakes in terms of democratic legitimacy.

APPROPRIATING THE INTERNET

In the 1970s, the British and the French began to conduct pioneering experiments on packet-switching networks—the technical foundations for the TCP protocol in 1974, and then for the TCP/IP one. There was the British National Physical Laboratory (NPL) with Donald Davies at the helm;[1] while the French National Institute for Research in Computer Science and Control (INRIA) conducted researches over conceptual aspects similar to those of ARPANET (whose first nodes were in service in 1969), and developed the CYCLADES network between 1971 and 1979 (Schafer, 2012).

European telecommunications administrations were also developing solutions. Connected to the market and being experts on phone infrastructures, they were in a leading position to take part to the development of networks as they benefited from a monopoly on the transmission lines. Following the British NPL project, the British Post Office created EPSS (the Experimental Packet Switching Network), while the Transpac network opened in France in 1978 and supported from the 1980s to the 2010s the Minitel traffic.

Europe-wide networks were also created, reproducing to a large extent the national approaches carried out by computer scientists and telecommunications experts. From the 1970s until the mid-1990s, Europe witnessed a battle of protocols, whose virulence was based not only on technical aspects, but also on political stakes.

EIN and Euronet: Two European Network Pioneers

In the 1970s, the European Economic Community was quite interested in the national attempts that were put in place to develop data networks. In 1971, it launched COST (Scientific and Technical Cooperation), the first European data network project. The COST 11 project, which was related to telecomputing, was established in November 1971 by the agreement of eight European governments[2] and Euratom (European Atomic Energy Community). The Netherlands joined the team in August 1974. One aim of the project, led by NPL's Derek Barber, was to build a computer network. Negotiations were laborious, because the participants disagreed on technical specifications: whether building a network based on existing techniques (circuit- and message-switching), or experimenting with the promising packet-switching approaches pursued by CYCLADES at INRIA, the NPL, and the network developed in the United States by the Advanced Research Projects Agency, ARPANET. The latter approach was finally adopted in the network that was called EIN (European Informatics Network).

Another project related to telecommunications issues, Euronet, a European computer documentation network, was launched a few years after EIN. Indeed, in March 1975, the Council of European Communities adopted a three-year action plan for the development of scientific and technical information. The action plan aimed at enabling any computer terminal located in the European Community to access the various Member States' scientific, technical, socio-economic and legislative databases and databanks. It also aimed at promoting inter-European cooperation in agriculture, medicine, and other fields. The first European direct information access network opened in March 1980 with nearly 500 databases and databanks. The fifty largest database servers were gathered within a single entity called DIANE (Direct Information Access Network for Europe). In 1975, its realisation was delegated to the telecommunications administrations, thus giving a central place to those who held the lines of transmission throughout Europe[3], while EIN was developed toward computer sciences teams.

While the European Commission initially declared its willingness to cooperate with COST 11, the PTT administrations gradually pushed the EIN solution aside. This decision must be placed in perspective. Indeed, opinions differed on the technical approach to adopt: the common carriers advocated a solution based on virtual circuits (a message circulating in the network is divided into packets that take an identical path, through a virtual communication, prior to the information transfer), while computer scientists, such as those in France's INRIA or in EIN, favoured datagrams (packets with headings allowing a message to be reconstructed at its arrival, crossing the network through an adapted route, each packet choosing the most favourable way to reach its goal). The disagreement on how to move data within the network, and on the qualities of virtual circuits versus datagrams (in terms of congestion, safety, billing, resource allocation, etc.) went on, both at the European and the international levels. Meanwhile, telecommunications officials carried out a policy of standardizing their solution via the X.25 protocol, which they submitted to the International Telegraph and Telephone Consultative Committee in 1976. Inside the Euronet project, telecommunications administrations converged on the common and standardised alternative of X.25.

In both EIN and EURONET cases, the debates credited the Franco-English partnership with a central place, and revealed the initial ambiguity of data network development: if telecomputing requires a mix of telecommunications and computer science, each field keeps its own logic and technical solutions. Moreover, the European Union was confronted with the monopoly of the telecommunications organisations... These oppositions went on through the 1980s and the beginning of the 1990s, and were then complicated by divergent national paths and industrial strategies.

Turning to the "Network of Networks": A Political and Industrial Issue

The landscape of networks in the 1980s was fragmented between telecommunications initiatives on the one hand, which were directed to the general public, and universities and research centres on the other hand, which were involved in the development of national networks (Janet in Britain, DFN in Germany, and so on). A meeting organised in Oslo in July 1983 was the occasion to witness the wide diversity of technological options, while at the same time it enabled to establish a consensus about the need to develop a transnational network (Fluckiger, 2000). The European Commission and a majority of Member States chose to work on the creation of the Open Systems Interconnection, an open layered networks architecture developed by computer scientists' standards body (the International Organization for Standardization). The OSI was indeed seen as a source of independence, while IBM was supporting the creation of EARN (European Academic and Research Network), equivalent to the American university network Bitnet. This "Big Blue" initiative accelerated the decision to create RARE (European Research Associates Network) in 1986. This group of experts proposed an ambitious project of an OSI network to the European Commission, a network that would be supported by COSINE (Cooperation for Open Systems Interconnection Networking in Europe).

While some fears were expressed about the domination of IBM and EARN, another network was experimented in American universities and started to be popular enough to enter the European academic networks: Internet penetration was also an issue of importance for communities of computer scientists. Most of them used UNIX and were readers of the Newsgroups (thematic discussion groups from the Usenet community, often dedicated to computing at the beginning). Yet, the meeting of UNIX and TCP/IP in 1983 promoted Internet penetration in American and later in European universities, particularly via EUnet (the European UNIX Network), which announced its conversion to Internet technology in 1988. Some national networks, such as the Dutch SURFnet, were early adopters of Internet technology. INRIA also made this choice, while simultaneously taking part in the OSI and European game, which could be considered as a "politically correct" strategy.

However, on February 1st 1990, RARE adopted a famous resolution, ie a historical revision, painful for some (Fluckiger, 2000): RARE recognised that Internet protocols were well suited to scientific applications, and that they provided services not supported by OSI norms. But, this resolution did not end the fragmentation of the European networks landscape. For instance, the telecommunication sector did not want to give up IXI (International X.25 Infrastructure), while research communities went on with their own initiatives. In 1992 Ebone, a European TCP/IP network, was created by different European stakeholders, from academic partners such as the members of SURFNET to common carriers or industrial players.[4] Then there was the development of the EMPB Network (European Multi-Protocol Backbone) supported by the European Commission and RARE and the merger between EARN and RARE in 1994, which came through the birth of Terena and the operational structure Dante[5] (Davies & Bressan, 2010).

IP solutions gradually won out, but not without struggles and fierce discussions between the advocates of the different approaches (Martin, 2011).

The period studied in this section (mid 70s, mid 90s) corresponds to the early stage of the Internet development in Europe. At a time where the Web did not exist yet, and the Internet is far from being popular, research and academic net-works are predominant actors. However, the infrastructure building, which appears to be the main stake, is considered according to an industrial perspective. The stormy debates over technical choices do not prevent the emergence of a Europe of ICT, which relies on academic networks. Technical resources and infrastructures are issues around which transnational alliances can be built, and are thus political stakes for European actors and Institutions that try to push the European project forward. This political dimension of ICT will become more manifest in the next period, where the Internet governance will become an opportunity for Europe to make its voice heard on the international stage.

GOVERNING THE INTERNET

Since the 1970s, the wave of interest in European networks was palpable. People began to consider data networks not only as an infrastructure project or a research theme, but also as an information tool (Euronet). In the 1980s and the 1990s, the awareness of the social and political dimensions of ICT policies grew. The popular notion of "information society" raised the issue of the governance of networks that took another dimension in the early 2000's with the World Summit on the Information Society.

Finding a Place in Internet Governance

Development and technical debates outside of standards bodies is part of the Internet's originality, which responds to two concerns of the "founding fathers": to ensure open technical debate and to freely disseminate technical specifications in order to encourage their adoption; and to allow various ideas, coming from different actors, to emerge according to the needs. However they created technical bodies: David Clark's IAB (Internet Advisory/Activities/Architecture Board),

Jon Postel's IANA (Internet Assigned Numbers Authority) for naming, and from 1992, ISoC (Internet Society). These organisations bore a rationale similar to Tim Berners-Lee's one, the founder of the Web in the early 1990s. In 1993, he obtained permission from the European Centre for Nuclear Research, where he developed the system, to make the protocols freely available. This choice was crucial for the future of the Web, and for the W3C structure (World Wide Web Consortium), an international non-profit organisation founded to ensure the Web's proper evolution, and to invent and promote universal languages and protocols.

In the early 1990s, TCP/IP questioned the conditions of Internet reception in Europe: governance bodies (ISoC, ICANN) were born in the margins of standards bodies. They were dominated by US actors and Europe, whose strategy had been to rely on recognised standards bodies, was confronted with an object that disrupted traditional modes of regulation.

Even if during the 1990s and the early 2000s, well-known European scientists obtained good positions in the Internet governance realm[6], the European approach remained poorly defined.

There was the birth of RIPE (European IP Networks) in 1989. In this collaborative group, Internet technical actors exchanged experience deploying and coordinating IP networks in Europe, and discussed the allocation policies of RIPE NCC (European IP Networks -Network Coordination Centre, a private legal organisation founded in the early 1990s and headquartered in Amsterdam).

However, this initiative came from engineers and stakeholders, and not from the European Commission itself. It was less related to a political will than to the assertion of the "computer scientists republic," to take up the words of Patrice Flichy (Flichy, 2001).

The establishment of the W3C was an opportunity for Europeans to become leading actors on the Web governance stage, alongside with MIT. The British Web founder, Tim Berners-Lee, went from CERN to MIT to create the W3C but also proposed the creation of a W3C European host. Since 1995, INRIA first, ERCIM then, host this European part of the W3C.

On the other side, the ISoC-ECC did not held its first meeting before 2001 and the ETSI (the European Telecommunications Standards Institute) met some difficulties being involved in ICANN (Internet Corporation for Assigned Names and Numbers): "IAB's hostile reaction to ETSI's request to be admitted to ICANN as a technical support organisation in August 1999 was quite characteristic. Not only did this manifest itself in renewed opposition by the Internet's leading bodies (IETF and IAB) against official standardisation institutions [...] but we could see equally explicitly the concern within the Internet community at seeing the industrial world's key players acquire 'a capacity of real influence within ICANN'"[7] (Warufsel, 2000).

Even if engineers were aware of the political stakes of Internet governance, it was more through the naming issue that politics takes the leading role. Indeed, the birth of ICANN highlighted the role of the United States Department of Commerce in its organisation. If Europeans first asked for some limitations of the federal government's position within the ICANN, they finally approved its creation in 1998, but could no more ignore the soft power conferred by allocation of resources.

Moreover, the European institutions were disposed to share governance mechanisms, as they benefit from policy instruments that carried out such approaches. For instance, since 2001, the Open Method of Coordination (OMC) suggested in the European Commission's White Paper on the European Governance was "the strongest sign of the questioning of traditional instruments, and the search for governance systems that can maintain a regulation of economic activities and the goals of social solidarity" (Bourcier, 2006). The will for open and transparent governance and a less US centric organization was vigorously echoed by WSIS in Geneva in 2003 and Tunis in 2005.

In November 2011, the U.S. authorities decided to launch a bid for root management. This was meant to signal its independence from ICANN, even if chances were low that a competitor would prevail. For the European Commissioner for the Digital Agenda (since 2009), this was a step forward. "The contract, however, is not yet perfect," wrote Ms. Kroes. "For example, it is reserved for U.S. firms, which is a shame since the Internet is a resource for the whole world."[8]

Parallel to the growing awareness of the soft power conferred by the Internet's resources, Europeans also apprehended its political stakes for the "information highways" and later the "information society." In this context, the question was less about Europe finding its place in international Internet governance, than facilitating the deployment of networks across the European continent, and their appropriation by a large part of the population.

From the Information Society to the Lisbon Strategy

The issues tackled were primarily economic. The Commission had to adopt a prospective approach, and prepared the ground for the advent of the "information society," by building technical infrastructures and identifying possible legal obstacles. In 1987, the "Green Paper on Telecommunications" kicked off a shared policy on the issue.

A turning point occurred in the mid-1990s. In 1994, Al Gore delivered his speech on the "National Information Infrastructure," in which he developed the idea of "information highways." This concept became very successful, and had a particular strategic dimension: in the context of accelerating globalisation, the deployment of an "information society" would require deregulating the telecommunications market, generating higher competition between different economic actors, and lowering entry costs for consumers on these "highways."

During the same period, the Commission adopted a similar strategy. The "information society" became part of a grand narrative in which it would reinvigorate European integration: it was identified as both the objective and the condition for the advent of a common market, a new step towards community building (Dacheux, 2004; Lenk, 2009). The Delors Commission's goal, that were outlined in a report on "growth, competitiveness and employment" (1993), was to find a place for the European economy in a global "information society." The following year, the Bangemann Report identified the terms of this inclusion: the ICT boom was a *sine qua non* for the advent of a "knowledge economy"[9]. The liberalisation of the telecommunications sector, as in the American case, was considered necessary to break the state monopoly that hampered free market competition. The action plan "Towards a European Information Society" was adopted for this purpose in July 1994.

In this second phase, the legal conditions for market development were put in place through a "harmonisation" of national rules and sector-wide liberalisation. However, European countries did not engage in full and complete cooperation. During the same period, each country launched its own action plan to enter the "information society," including the Théry Report in France, the Information Society Initiative in the United Kingdom, and Info 2000 in Germany (Mattelart, 2006). While different countries' plans converged under the Commission's authority, this convergence took on different forms, which came as much from imitation and harmonisation as it did from imposition. In no case this logic was exempted from national issues (Vedel, 1996).

At the time, the political and social dimensions of ICTs were highly underestimated. European public policy evinced a kind of determinism, postulating that merely providing ICTs would produce economic growth. The question of their uses and learning was in many senses obscured (Monnoyer-Smith, 2003).

A third wave came with the Lisbon Strategy (2000), which intended to make the EU "to become the most competitive and dynamic knowledge-based economy in thc world capable of sustainable economic growth with more and better jobs and greater social cohesion."[10] At the time, the U.S.

had a significant advantage. Its Internet penetration rate was three times higher, and its Internet users spent 400% as much time in front of their screens.[11] The EU strove to accelerate Europe's entry in the "information society" by continuing to liberalise its economy and harmonise legislation. But now, the user was taken into account, in an approach that included encouraging use beginning in elementary schools, and making public services available online.

European institutions began to speak of the "knowledge society." The Commission defined the concept as a "society whose processes and practices are based on the production, dissemination, and use of knowledge."[12] The action plan succeeded: Europeans were now seen as consumers first, but also citizens. The inclusion imperative became a gateway to the "information society." The 2002 and 2005 eEurope action plans aimed to build "an information society for all."[13] The priority was to close the "digital divide" that was leaving a large swath of the European population out of the promise of this new society. The gap was addressed, primarily through infrastructure, but the deep inequalities in ICT access only grew as the EU grew larger.

The i2010 initiative, created in 2005, accentuated this dimension without losing sight of economics. Above all, it promoted use in order to bring about "a better use of Europe's main economic asset, namely the largest consumer market in the developed world."[14] With this new action plan, the question of democracy emerged as an issue of European public policy.

In the 1990s and the 2000s, the Internet governance issue and the strategic action plans related to the "information highways" and the "knowledge society" give to the Internet a new political dimension. The economic stakes are predominant, and do not only rely on technical infra-structures: uses and Internet penetration are the conditions for the development of the Internet in Europe, and the European Institutions assert that its promotion implies a liberalization of the telecommunication market in order to break up national monopolies. A new shift happens when the political dimension of the Internet is seen through a more social lens (Internet stakes for education and social integration), and the institutions adapt their discourses, starting to talk about a "knowledge society." A third step is the recognition of the Internet as a tool for internal consolidation, that can serve democratic purposes by involving citizens in decision-making processes, and provide new sources of legitimation for the institutions.

USING THE INTERNET FOR DEMOCRATIC PURPOSES

In the 2000s, the Commission's policies underwent a trend in which the user-consumer was considered through the lens of citizenship, via the development of e-government and e-participation mechanisms. Internet uses had changed, beginning with the Web development of the late 1990s, and its popularisation via the Mosaic browser in 1993. The project of building a "European information society" had to adapt, and online governance appeared as a way to take into consideration the democratic potential of the Internet.

E-Government, for "Europe's Future"

The European Commission's conception of e-government was a junction where the values of the "knowledge society" met the principles of "European governance." The Commission stated in its communications that e-government's primary concern was to "maintain and strengthen good governance in the knowledge society."[15] The Commission saw this foremost as "the use of ICT *combined with* organisational change and new skills in order to improve public services, democratic processes and public policies" (Bradier, 2004, p, 337).

This notion put forward a relatively consumerist vision of the European citizenship. The EU should provide "services" to meet the needs of "clients." Concepts inherited from "new public management" were disseminated through the commercial dimension of a citizen-consumer who, as a user of a service provided by an institutional manager, had certain rights. As action plans progressed, the term took on a social and democratic dimension via e-participation, whereby ICT use facilitated the integration of citizens into decision-making processes.

In 2003, the Commission published its first and stake-setting communication, devoted entirely to e-government: *The Role of eGovernment For Europe's Future*. The communication detailed that ICTs must enable more efficient public services and support democratic processes. Three dimensions were identified: openness and transparency, inclusion, and productivity.

In these documents, the Commission sought not only to define guiding principles for Member States, but also to apply these principles to itself. The eCommission initiative, implemented in the wake of the European governance reform of 2001, meant endowing the institution itself with such tools.

"Primitive" e-government mechanisms were put online: the *Europa* portal was redesigned, and the Eur-Lex online platform went live; the Websites *Dialogue With Businesses* and *Dialogue With Citizens* were created, and reports and meeting minutes were posted to the Parliament and Commission Websites.[16] In parallel, a database was established listing the various civil society organisations able to constitute appropriate interlocutors. This database, CONECCS (Consultation, the European Commission and Civil Society), was created through the free and voluntary registration of the organisations. General principles and minimum standards for consultation were also drawn up in 2002, supplementing the movement towards the regulation and formalisation of the relationship between civil society and European institutions (Obradovic, 2008). In 2008, CONECCS became the Register for Interest Representatives, which had registered over 4,300 organisations at the beginning of 2012.

One of the most notable initiatives may be the April 2001 launch of Interactive Policy Making (IPM), a digital platform to hold public consultations. It was intended not only to inform and to foster debate, but also to involve "stakeholders" in decision-making processes. All consultations conducted by the various branches of the EU Commission could thus be centralised within a unique format, the *Your Voice in Europe* platform.

Towards e-Participation: Acts and Limits of a European ICT-Driven Democracy

The Commission's dealings with e-government went in two directions. On the one hand, it had its own measures for opening the decision-making process to new audiences, and regularising its relations with interest groups. On the other hand, it produced action plans to accelerate the adoption of similar tools by Member States. In this context, questions on public service efficiency and profitability increasing allowed room for citizen participation.

This trend accelerated in 2005, with the launch of the i2010 initiative, led by the Information Society and Media branch, including an eGovernment Action Plan with a five objectives, one of which was to encourage citizen participation in the decision-making process by developing new tools.[17] An eParticipation Preparatory Action Plan was launched. Between 2006 and 2008, 21 projects were selected based on the goal of using the latest Web technologies to enable more effective citizen involvement in decision-making processes. In parallel, e-participation best practices exchange platform, *epratice.eu*, went live. The site allowed e-government practitioners and professionals to exchange ideas and methods for e-participation.

As for e-government, the Commission has its own tools for e-participation. Under "Plan D for Democracy, Dialogue and Debate," established in 2006 following French and Dutch "No's" to referendums on the European Constitutional Treaty, it intended to experiment with innovative consultation methods. Different projects were conducted within this framework, some of them using collaborative Web technologies.

Other participatory devices emerged in the second half of the 2000s. On *EU Tube*, the Commission posted videos on policy conduct and the functioning of Europe. Users could register and load their own videos. On *Debate Europe*, European Internet users could discuss important community issues. Commissioners' personal blogs (*Commissioners' Corner* on the Commission Website), provided information on each member's particular area of expertise, and allowed users to leave comments and write directly to the Commissioner concerned. The Council and Parliament broadcasted their meetings live (*Open Sessions* for the Council and *Europarl TV*), and Parliament offered a multimedia library with many archived documents relating to European public policies.

Unlike the e-government measures, online platforms did not implicate citizens and organisations in the decision-making process (Badouard, 2010), and they were not legally recognised as "policy instruments" (Kassim & Le Gales, 2010), or associated with policy preparation, with rare exceptions. They played a primarily "transformative" role (Smith & Dalakiouridou, 2009), and were intended to raise awareness about community issues among European Internet users. They hoped to stimulate a sense of belonging to the Union through participatory activities. As the results of these experiments were difficult to translate into public policy, the measures were sometimes counter-productive. Indeed, as many studies on citizen participation practices have shown, the absence of links with decision-making only deepens a sense of participant distrust vis-à-vis public authority (Blondiaux, 2008; Blondiaux & Fourniau, 2011). Furthermore, these experiments were expensive, so much so that in the Union's current budget, at the end of *Plan D* and the *eParticipation Preparatory Action Plan*, they were suspended.

A new turning point came in 2011, with the publication of a new e-government action plan. It focuses on "green government," meaning ICT use in government practices to facilitate the transition towards a "green economy" and "open data." Concerns are evolving through action plans: it is no longer a question of democratization, but of "empowerment": "increasing the capacity of citizens, businesses and other organisations to be pro-active in society through the use of new technological tools." The term's use suggests a refocusing on actors rather than mechanisms. A specific priority is given to e-participation, which is directed towards service design (meaning citizen participation in the procedure configuration of public services). Above all, e-government's democratic challenges are directed towards the European Citizens' Initiative, a new European law that allows citizens to "invite" the Commission to legislate on a given theme by gaining a million signatures on a related petition.

While the Internet becomes a political issue, which allow the European Union to adopt a strong posture on the international stage, it appears to be a tool for internal consolidation. First, the "information highways" and the "information society" provide economic opportunities to build a single European market. European citizens, who were away from the debates over technical infrastructures, started to be considered as consumers. Later, when the reform of the European governance meets the action plans related to the information society, the European Commission starts to use the Internet as a channel to communicate with citizens and make them participate at the European level. In this context, the Internet is a gate that allows the institutions to reconsider the democratic deficit of the EU, and to build online mechanisms that could involve citizens in European politics. If this specific strategy is related to communication stakes that imply to highlight the democratic potential of the EU, it shows that the Internet political dimensions overtake the governance issues to infiltrate the very core of democratic system: the legitimacy that citizens participation gives to public authorities.

FUTURE RESEARCH DIRECTIONS

This paper has described several key evolutions of the European Union understanding of data networks stakes since the 1970s. While the Internet has appeared as the best technical solution, its penetration has came with discourses and political agendas that promoted liberalization and globalization. The "information highways," followed by the information and then the knowledge societies, have thus borne a strategic dimension as a lever for economic growth and political cohesion. The overview given in this paper raise several points that will need further investigations:

- The relevance of the European scale to address issues related to data networks. Major contributions in this field will be published within a few months (while we are writing), as the book "Hacking Europe," edited by Gerard Alberts and Ruth Oldenziel, or the six volumes of "Making Europe: Technology and Transformation, 1850-2000" edited by Johan Schot and Phil Scranton. Within these six volumes, two will be dedicated to governance and media issues, and will contribute to demonstrate the relevance of the European scale for the social studies of technologies, and furthermore ICTs. In this perspective, technologies provide a new insight to tackle the European construction, while the transnational scale gives a broad panorama of our technological environment. Several issues raised in this paper would thus need to be deepen: the evolution of the actors of the Internet governance and their values, the European position faced with material suppliers and American contents, the peering agreements, the rates issue, the evolution of European legislations with regards to technologies.
- Future challenges for the European institutions will also need future researches: net neutrality, the unification of the European space with regards to the Internet both in terms of legislation and industrial stakes. Such major evolutions as the Internet of things, cloud computing, big data or open data raise new issues that challenge the European Union capability to define a common strategy in order to not become a "colony of the digital" to take up the expression of the Morin-Desailly report (2013).

CONCLUSION

The Internet is a multi-dimensional political stake for Europe. It primarily constitutes a domain of international public policy in which its difference and unity can be asserted. Technology takes on a strong political dimension, and the internal struggles to impose particular protocols in the 70s and 80s carry a true vision of the Union's position on the international stage. Consequently, the Internet is also becoming a political tool for the EU to strengthen its internal construction: starting with the Lisbon strategy, policies promoting e-government across Europe will be charged with improving European public services and creating new interfaces between policy makers and citizens.

The consciousness of the Internet political stakes went through several steps, from industrial policies and technical standardization, to new modes of governance and legitimation processes. These steps follow the own history of the Internet, which is first developed within closed scientific networks before being opened to the general public. The infrastructure issue is thus overtaken by applications and uses. They also follow the

European construction history, from the epistemic networks to the transnational democracy, passing by the building of a common market. In this context, the Internet highlights the needs for common regulation and for the coordination of national strategies. It builds its own "technological zone," to take up the words of Andrew Barry (2001), that succeeds in linking actors, organisations, technical resources, legislations and public policies in a same European network. But it also highlights that the Internet cannot alone build a European public sphere where the general publics of the various Member States could exchange and participate to the common construction.

The Internet's development in Europe invites one to consider the European construction as an in-between technocracy, transnational culture, and the power of infrastructure and socio-technological ideologies. Negotiations, controversies, ruptures and continuities in the Internet regulation field show a need to study the role of technology as both an issue and a instrument for governance and as a tool and a crystalliser for the aspirations, successes and failures of European politics. This history thus requires a reading of European construction as a dialectically model and a complex co-constructed phenomena.

REFERENCES

Badouard, R. (2010). Pathways and obstacles to e-participation at the European level. *Journal of eDemocracy and Open Government, 2*(2), 99-110.

Barry, A. (2001). *Political machines: Governing a technological society*. London: Athlone Press.

Blondiaux, L. (2008). *Le nouvel esprit de la démocratie: Actualité de la démocratie participative* [The New Spirit of Democracy: Update on Participative Democracy]. Paris: Le Seuil.

Blondiaux, L., & Fourniau, J.-M. (2011). Un bilan des recherches sur la participation du public en démocratie: beaucoup de bruit pour rien? [Review of Research on Public Participation in Democracy: Much Ado about Nothing?]. *Participations, 1*, 10–35. doi:10.3917/parti.001.0008

Bouneau, C., Burigana, D., & Varsori, A. (2010). *Trends in technological innovation and the European construction*. New York: Peter Lang.

Bourcier, D. (2006). Comment s'accorder sur les normes ? Le droit et la gouvernance face à internet. [How to Agree on Norms? Law and Governance Take On the Internet]. *Lex Electronica, 10*(3).

Bradier, A. (2004). Le gouvernement électronique: Une priorité européenne. [E-Government: A European Priority]. *Revue Française d'Administration Publique, 2*(110), 337–347. doi:10.3917/rfap.110.0337

Coleman, S. (2008). Foundations of digital government. In *Digital government: E-government research, case studies, and implementation*. New York: Springer. doi:10.1007/978-0-387-71611-4_1

Dacheux, E. (2004). *L'impossible défi: La politique de communication de l'Union Européenne*. [An Impossible Challenge: The Communication Policy of the European Union]. Paris: CNRS Ed.s.

Davies, H., & Bressan, B. (2010). *A history of international research networking*. Hoboken, NJ: Wiley-VCH. doi:10.1002/9783527629336

Dawes, S. (2008). The evolution and continuing challenges of e-governance. *Public Administration Review*, 86–102. doi:10.1111/j.1540-6210.2008.00981.x

Flichy, P. (2001). *L'imaginaire d'Internet* [The Internet Imaginaire]. Paris: La Découverte.

Fluckiger, F. (2000). Le réseau des chercheurs Européens. [The Network of European Researchers]. *La Recherche*, 328.

Kassim, H., & Le Galès, P. (Eds.). (2010). Exploring governance in a multilevel polity: A policy instrument approach. *West European Politics*, *33*(1). doi:10.1080/01402380903354031

Lenk, K. (2009). *Une théorie politique de l'eGovernment est-elle possible?* [Is a Political Theory of eGovernment Possible?]. Paris: CERSA.

Macintosh, A. (2008). e-Democracy and e-Participation research in Europe. In *Digital governement: E-government research, case studies, and implementation.* New York: Springer.

Martin, O. (2011). *The hidden prehistory of European research networking*. Retrieved July 27, 2013, from http://ictconsulting.ch/reports/EuropeanInternetHistory-draft-B.pdf

Mattelard, A. (2006). *Histoire de la société de l'information* [History of the Information Society]. Paris: La Découverte.

Schafer, V. (2012). *La France en réseaux, années 1960-1980* (Vol. 1). Paris: Cigref and Nuvis. [France in Networks, 1960-1980, Volume 1]

Schipper, F., & Schot, J. (2009). Infrastructural Europeanism, or the project of building Europe on infrastructures. *History and Technology*, *27*(3), 245–264. doi:10.1080/07341512.2011.604166

Scholl, J. H. (2009). *Electronic government: A study domain beyond its infancy*. AMIS Volume on Electronic Government.

Smith, S., & Dalakiouridou, E. (2009). Contextualising public (e)participation in the governance of the European Union. *European Journal of ePractice*, *7*, 1-11.

Vedel, T. (1996). Les politiques des autoroutes de l'information dans les pays industrialisés: Une analyse comparative. [The Politics of Information Highways in Industrialised Countries: A Comparative Analysis]. *Reseaux*, *78*, 11–28.

Warusfel, B. (2000). La gestion de l'internet entre autorégulation et rivalités institutionnelles: Un phénomène mondial à la recherche de son modèle de gouvernance. [Internet Management between Self-Regulation and Institutional Rivalries: A Global Phenomenon in Search of a Governance Model]. *Annuaire Français de Relations Internationales*, *1*, 595–617.

ADDITIONAL READING

European Commission, Towards the Information Society in Europe: An Action Plan, COM(94) 0347, 1994.

European Commission, Green Paper on the Convergence of the Telecommunications, Media And Information Technology Sectors, and the Implications for Regulation: Towards an Information Society Approach, COM(97) 623 final, 1997.

European Commission. Growth, competitiveness, employment. The challenges and ways forward into the 21st century. White Paper, COM(93) 700 Final, 1993. Council of the European Union, Presidency Conclusions. Lisbon, 23/24 March 2000.

European Commission, Realising a European Space for Education and Training Throughout Life, Commission Communication, COM(2001) 678 final, 2001.

European Commission. eEurope 2005: An information society for all. An Action Plan to be presented in view of the Sevilla European Council, 21/22 June 2002, COM (2002) 263 final, Brussels, 2002.

European Commission. The Role of eGovernment for Europe's Future, SEC(2003) 1038, Brussels, 2003.

European Commission. The Commission's Contribution to the Period of Reflection and Beyond: Plan-D for Democracy, Dialogue and Debate, COM (2005) 494 final, Brussels, 2005.

European Commission. i2010 eGovernment Action Plan: Accelerating eGovernment in Europe for the Benefit of All, COM (2006) 173 final, Brussels, 2006.

European Commission. The European eGovernment Action Plan 2011-2015: Harnessing ICT to Promote Smart, Sustainable & Innovative Government, COM(2010) 743, Brussels, 2010.

KEY TERMS AND DEFINITIONS

e-Government: Use of ICTs in public administrations- combined with organisational change - to improve public services and democratic processes and to strengthen support to public.

e-Participation: Use of ICTs in democratic processes that intend to involve citizens in decision-taking procedures.

Information Highways: Term used through the 1990s to refer to digital communication systems and the Internet network.

Information Society: Used as a political issue in the 2000s, this notion refers to a society where information plays a significant economic, political, and cultural role and favours to gain competitive advantage through using information technologies.

Internet Governance: As defined by the Working Group on Internet Governance (after the World Summit on the Information Society, WSIS, in 2005), the development and application by Governments, the private sector and civil society, in their respective roles, of shared principles, norms, rules, decision-making procedures, and programs that shape the evolution and use of the Internet.

ENDNOTES

1 Retrieved July 27, 2013, from http://www.livingInternet.com/i/ii_npl.htm

2 France, Italy, Yougoslavia, Norway, Portugal, Switzerland, Sweden, and the United Kingdom.

3 Nearly 35% of initial investments were funded by PTT (Postal Telephone and Telegraph) administrations.

4 This organization became a company and a society in 1996, supporting both academic and research traffic and also commercial uses.

5 Supporting today the pan-European network dedicated to the research and education community GÉANT.

6 For instance, Christian Huitema and Jean-François Abramatic were appointed respectively as the heads of the Internet Architecture Board in 1993, and the W3C (World Wide Web Consortium) in 1996.

7 Our translation.

8 La "racine" du Net soumise à un appel d'offre [The "Root" of the Net Subject to Bidding]. *Le Monde*, 14 November 2011. Our translation.

9 During the 1990's, one could talk about an inflation of termes related to the "information society", the "knowledge society" or the "knowledge economy". Here, the definition given in the Bangemann Report bore a different meaning than the notions used by the UNESCO or the ITU, and focused more on economic stakes than social or technical ones.

10 Presidency Conclusions, Council of the European Union, 23/24 March 2000. Retrieved July 27, 2013, from http://www.europarl.europa.eu/summits/lis1_en.htm

11 Source: *Le Monde*, 24 March 2000.

12 *Réaliser un espace européen de l'éducation et de formation tout au long de la vie* [Realising a European Space for Education and

Training Throughout Life], Commission Communication, COM(2001) 678 final, 2001: 41. Our translation.

13 *eEurope 2005: An information society for all. An Action Plan to be presented in view of the Sevilla European Council, 21/22 June 2002*, COM(2002) 263 final, Brussels, 2002.

14 Ibid.

15 The Role of eGovernment for Europe's Future. [SEC(2003) 1038], Brussels, 2003: 9.

16 Report of the Commission on European Governance, op. cit.

17 Plan d'action i2010 pour l'e-gouvernement: accélérer l'instauration de l'administration en ligne en Europe dans l'intérêt de tous [i2010 eGovernment Action Plan: Accelerating eGovernment in Europe for the Benefit of All] COM(2006) 173 final, Brussels, 2006.

APPENDIX

Acronyms

- **BPO:** British Post Office
- **COSINE:** Cooperation for Open Systems Interconnection Networking in Europe
- **CONECCS:** Consultation, the European Commission and Civil Society
- **COST:** Scientific and Technical Cooperation
- **DFN:** Deutsche Forschungsnetz
- **DIANE:** Direct Information Access Network for Europe
- **EIN:** European Informatics Network
- **EPSS:** Experimental Packet Switching Network
- **ERCIM:** European Research Consortium for Informatics and Mathematics
- **ETSI:** European Telecommunications Standards Institute
- **EU:** European Union
- **EUNet:** European UNIX Network
- **Euratom:** European Atomic Energy Community
- **GÉANT:** Gigabit European Academic Network Technology
- **IAB:** Internet Advisory/Activities/Architecture Board
- **IANA:** Internet Assigned Numbers Authority
- **ICANN:** Internet Corporation for Assigned Names and Numbers
- **IETF:** Internet Engineering Task Force
- **IMP:** Interactive Policy Making
- **INRIA:** National Institute for Research in Computer Science and Control
- **ISoC:** Internet Society
- **IXI:** International X.25 Infrastructure
- **JANET:** Joint Academic Network
- **NPL:** National Physical Laboratory
- **OMC:** Open Method of Coordination
- **PTT:** Postal Telephone and Telegraph
- **RARE:** European Research Associates Network
- **RIPE:** European IP Networks
- **RIPE NCC:** European IP Networks -Network Coordination Centre
- **W3C:** World Wide Web Consortium

Chapter 7
Whose Voice is Heard? West Bank News Framing in Israeli Mainstream and Alternative News Websites:
Ni'lin 2008 as a Case Study

Keren Sereno
Independent Researcher, Israel

ABSTRACT

Alternative news Websites are a fascinating arena for studying the dynamics between politics, media, and activism. This chapter presents a comparison of news framing in Israeli mainstream news Websites versus Israeli alternative news Websites. To achieve this, 342 items which were published over the course of 14 months (November 2007-December 2008) in 8 Israeli media originations were coded. These items covered the demonstrations and direct actions against the Separation Fence near the Palestinian village of Ni'lin in which Israeli radical left activists took part. The items were coded by qualitative content analysis according to the principles of the Grounded Theory Method. The findings show considerable differences concerning the characters of quoted sources, media frames, coverage patterns, and linking strategies between the mainstream Websites (and print newspaper) and the alternative Websites. Out of those differences, 4 potential political functions that alternative news Websites can fulfill in radical political protests are identified: recruiting activists, consolidating a subversive political consciousness and strengthening the collective identity, building online network between colleague organizations, and distributing and storing controversial information. This research shows that in order to develop a deeper understanding of the role of new media in social protests, it is necessary to simultaneously rely on alternative media, theories, and studies in addition to the emerging knowledge regarding the characters and uses of the Internet in general

DOI: 10.4018/978-1-4666-6038-0.ch007

Copyright © 2014, IGI Global. Copying or distributing in print or electronic forms without written permission of IGI Global is prohibited.

INTRODUCTION

The alternative media tradition is rooted in history; small radical publications have been identified as far back as 16th century Britain. Since then, and to this day, many counter-cultures, -communities, and -groups which possess subversive ideologies publicly criticize accepted ways of life and directly challenge mainstream media organizations. In the middle of the 1980s, the typewriter was described as a Kalashnikov in the hands of the guerilla journalists (Harcup, 2003). If this was indeed so, one must now, at the onset of the 21st century, ask: what are the roles of the computer keyboard, mouse and Webcam in this war for public opinion and support?

The case study of the protest against the Separation Fence near the Palestinian village of Ni'lin, which was built by the state of Israel, is interesting and important in a theoretical sense, and constitutes an example of a visceral and controversial issue in Israeli politics. This subject was also brought before the Israeli Supreme Court, which ruled, to the disapproval of the Israeli government and the Israeli army (Israel Defense Force -IDF), that the fence's design was to be altered in certain areas in order to avoid impinging on Palestinian lives. (The most notable consequence of this ruling is in the Palestinian village of Bil'in). Similar to many previous cases, due to the radical character of the struggle in Ni'lin, the organizations and protestors do not receive favorable media exposure, insomuch as they receive any media exposure at all, which subsequently leads them to use alternative media outlets.

The current research will present a systematic comparison of the sources, media frames and coverage patterns of 342 items which were published at four alternative news Websites, three mainstream news Websites and the most popular print newspaper in Israel. The aim of this chapter is to answer the following research questions:

1. What are the differences between mainstream news Websites (and one print newspaper) and alternative news Websites in covering the protest-related events that took place near village of Ni'lin during 2008?
2. What can be learned from the above differences about the potential political functions of alternative news Websites for radical protest?

Ni'lin is a Palestinian village located three kilometers east of the "Green Line," and is a part of the Ramallah district. The village has a population of approximately 5,000 people, most of which were previously employed in Israel and now subsist on agriculture. In 2008, the state of Israel began expropriating agricultural lands belonging to the people of Ni'lin for the purpose of building the separation fence. Protests against these actions began occurring in June 2008, and continue to occur to this day (December 2012) Palestinian, Israeli and international protestors have actively opposed the construction, using direct actions and demonstrations several times a week each week since construction began.

The majority of the Israeli protesters belong to a well-known anarchic group called Anarchists against the Wall (http://www.awalls.org). This group stands for radical anarchist principles covering a variety of issues (i.e., animal rights, LGBTQ rights, etc.), and presents itself as radically politically-left with respect to the Israeli-Palestinian conflict. The group's members give top priority to the joint (Israeli and Palestinian) struggle against Israeli military and political establishments. They adopt tactics of direct action following a sense of solidarity with the Palestinian people. This organization was literally born on the ground, in a joint protest camp in the village of Mas'ha in April 2003, and has included a few dozen activists. Most of the members are in their 20s and did not serve in the Israeli army (IDF).

It is very important to note that these activists are perceived by most other Israelis as traitors, as Anti-Zionists, as violent and as a real threat to the state of Israel as a Jewish country (Gordon, 2010).

In spite of the protesters' intent to carry out non-violent actions (see Gordon, 2010 for a detailed description of typical weekly demonstrations), during the confrontations throughout the years, these confrontations often turned violent. Protesters were killed and injured by rubber bullets and stun grenades targeted at them by the IDF; the casualties include two Palestinian children, aged 10- and 18-years old, who did not take part in the resistance. Soldiers were often injured by rocks thrown at them. Heavy financial damage was caused to engineering equipment as a result of sabotage, which often led to a halt in construction and the loss of working days. Moreover, during the examined timeframe, the confrontations escalated and exacerbated the struggle over the competing media frames. In July 2008, a video filmed by a Palestinian girl from her home window was broadcast by all of the major Israeli media organizations. The video shows an IDF soldier shooting a cuffed and blindfolded Palestinian man at point-blank range, as a regiment commander is holding the detainee.1 This young woman was able to capture this particular event using a video camera given to her by B'Tselem (http://www.btselem.org), the human rights center in the occupied territories, as part of their "Shooting Back" Project. The sensational images incurred a public outrage.

This event, in conjunction with the tragic killing of three Palestinians by the IDF during those weeks, constitutes another research opportunity for examining two news coverage patterns simultaneously. The first pattern, which receives media prominence during routine times, is the one in which Israel perceives itself as a victim of Palestinian violence. In contrast, the second coverage pattern, which is less prevalent in the Israeli mainstream media, includes defensive coverage (which is apologetic in a small number of cases) in which Israel is perceived as treating the Palestinians unjustly. These patterns make the coverage of the Ni'lin events in the examined year a very productive research platform from which important theoretical insights may be drawn and which can later be used to generalize protest activities by other radical organizations throughout the world.

LITERATURE REVIEW

Alternative Media as the Home of the Excluded

The term "alternative media" has been defined in many ways over the years; however, its prominent characteristics are identified here. First, an independent or alternative media organization is an organization that is not published by a commercial group and is not motivated by profit. Furthermore, alternative media organizations, in their essence, deal with subjects and expose opinions that do not receive continuous coverage in the mainstream media. They express the agendas, opinions, intents and problems of minority groups (either political or social) in that have been shunned, and sometimes even mistreated, by most of the public. The motivation for the formation of many alternative media organizations is dissatisfaction with mainstream media products – their blunt disregard for dissenting views and their symbolic annihilation of opposing views in the dominant public discourse (Atton, 1999, 2002, 2003).

Beyond the mere juxtaposition of alternative media with mainstream media, it is extremely important to note the political and social goals of alternative media organizations - they seek to raise critical awareness and to develop subversive consciousness with regard to the current social order; hence their high significance and their power to affect the readings of hegemonic texts and messages. This media emphasizes the democratic empowerment of the man in the street and the sources that do not belong or closely associate with various societal elites. Positioning the man in the street at the center is twofold: as a dominant source in news coverage and as a force which creates and produces the news in practice; hence there is a call for direct involvement in the political process as well as in the media process. Therefore, it can be said that the alternative media provides its audience and producers with a public voice and an organizational foundation. In order to understand the operational methods of alternative media organizations, as well as the secret to their power and their success, one must remember that these organizations are always an inseparable part of wider and more substantive alternative spaces, meaning that they are rooted in certain social networks and in certain political and ideological contexts (Atton, 1999, 2002, 2003; Downing, 1984, 1988; Downing et al., 2001; Rodriguez, 2001; Hartley, 1982; Harcup, 2003).

The practices of alternative media organizations are very different from the practices of the mainstream media organizations; because these practices are embedded and part of everyday lives of civilians, and due the fact that the "alternative" content is written and produced by non-professionals people. Alternative media organizations are characterized by their communal, egalitarian, decentralized, and non-hierarchical structure. They do not encourage expertise or exclusion; on the contrary, they are as inclusive as possible. Hence, this media can be perceived as a radical challenge to the mainstream media's professional and institutional norms. Still, it is important to remember the alternative media's weakness and faults: lack of journalism professionalization, lack of expertise, and a low level of obligation to principles of neutrality and balance coverage. All of these faults may lead to biased and one-sided media products.

Furthermore, the alternative media prioritizes the kind of journalism that stands for the socially responsible approach, journalism that replaces the objective ideology of the gatekeeper model for the advocate model and its reversed practices. These practices emphasize reliance on unauthorized sources, other than authoritarian elites, and on blurring the classic and mythological boundary between the journalist and the source through first person testimony and writing. The "activist- journalist" / "native reporter" is a common practice in alternative journalism, and this kind of reporting is preferable when compared to the traditional journalist model, which tends to produce more streamlined, "distanced" news items. Indeed, this pattern can sometimes be found among professional journalists who write personal notes (commentary or human interest stories) but in its pure and radical application, it is unique to alternative journalism. These are activists who authorize themselves to give the public their commentary on the political events they take part in themselves (Atton, 1999, 2002, 2003; Downing et al., 2001; Rodriguez, 2001; Harcup, 2003). This reporting practice is in line with the findings that point to the small number of sources in articles appearing in the independent media compared to articles found in the mainstream media (Reich, 2008).

Due to these claims, it is very easy to see the tight connection between social change non-governmental organizations (NGOs) and alternative media, especially during times of social strife and unrest (Atton, 2003; Harcup, 2003), and to understand why this connection can constitute an important political tool for social change. Producing content is not necessarily the main goal of the alternative media, since at many times the recruitment, organization and cultural empowerment of the community are perceived as more important than the content itself, and the alternative media facilitates the occurrence of these processes. The journalists who operate in these media organizations can both produce and maintain a community's culture. In addition, contemporary practices in the alternative media have been found to be capable of creating and empowering local and critical public spheres (Forde et al., 2003; Harcup, 2003; Atton, 1999, 2002). Understanding these practices, through which alternative media organizations fulfill the functions described above, and the establishment of counter public spheres has been considered essential for the understanding of their roles (Downing, 1988; Hamilton & Atton, 2001).

The means available to the alternative media are the same means available to the mainstream media – handpicking interviewees, editing headlines and quotes, providing visual and textual prominence to a certain player/side, siding and accepting the arguments of the actor and his terminology, and presenting the source in a respectable and proper manner. In short, this is the framing process, which includes the entire linguistic, rhetorical and visual means which provide meaning to the event, action, and political actors. Although the means are the same, their use is very different, and in order to understand this difference one must examine news conventions and professional routines within the journalism profession which actually pose an obstacle for anyone who is not a member of the societal elite.

The Mainstream Media as a Tool to Cultivate Social Hierarchies

There are two ways to get into the media – by the respectable way designed for the elites, and by the alternative route of deviation or misery, for anyone outside of the elite. The lower a person's status, the more negative his actions need to be in order to pass the threshold of newsworthiness and penetrate the media with "dangerous" or "miserable" frames. Wolfsfeld defines this interaction between the actors and the media as "competitive symbiosis," a competitive relationship which also includes cooperation, with each side having something to give and take – information or publicity as resources for exchange. The more dependent the actor is on the media in order to gain political profit, the lower his news value. Furthermore, as the event becomes more remote, both geographically and culturally, or describes a complicated social process (rather than personal story) so too will the event become more negative, simplified or ethnocentric for the sake of pertinence (Galtung & Ruge, 1965; Wolfsfeld, 1991; Gamson & Wolfsfeld, 1993; Ryan, 1991; Van Dijk, 1996).

The competition between actors for media success must be examined according to three criteria in determining newsworthiness: structural (prominence), cultural (valence), and dominance. The structural dimension examines the quantitative aspect (the amount of the coverage) of a news story and the level of the actors' accessibility to the media. The cultural dimension examines the meaning given to the events, namely, the extent to which is the event is framed as positive or negative to the actors. This dimension is closely linked to the values and narratives which exist in society (Wolfsfeld, 1997). The level of congruence between the values and goals of the political actor and those of the majority in society – the accepted values and norms at the time and place in which the actor is active – directly impact the amount of media success that an actor may find. It is very difficult to convey a frame of meaning which does not exist or is not accepted in a given society. This factor has far-reaching consequences since most social change organizations express some kind of criticism of the existing social order, and here the importance of the ideological distance between the actor and his contemporary social consensus is most prominent: the more extreme the organization is, the lower its chances are to receive high-quality coverage which adapts its status definition and terminology (Kampf, 1993; Wolfsfeld, 1991; Gamson & Wolfsfeld, 1993; Wolfsfeld, 1997; Paletz & Entman, 1981; Van Zoonen, 1996, Van Dijk, 1996; Hertog & McLeod, 1995; Giltlin, 1980).

Yoon adds an additional measure for examining media success: dominance - how much an actor is presented as an important source. When examining framings, it is important to relate to the journalists' levels of acceptance of the claims and messages authored by the actor, and to what extent they have conformed to his status definition and terminology. The level of legitimacy of the organizations and their sources in the eyes of the journalists is important since these levels have the power to explain the number of times the journalists present them in a dignified manner. When the source is perceived as more legitimate, the quantity and quality of the coverage will increase (Yoon, 2005; Van Dijk, 1996). 2

In addition to the definition of newsworthiness as a mechanism for gatekeeping, there is another filtering mechanism which affects a news story's media coverage - journalists' reliance on authorized sources. This reliance asymmetrically blocks media exposure for sources that are perceived as illegitimate. Studies show that most sources in the media, whether organizations or individuals, belong to some kind of a societal elite (i.e., political, financial, etc.). There is a markedly higher demand for official bureaucratic representatives and spokespeople (sources from institutions such as the police, the military, or government bureaus) to provide the public with a status definition which is agreed upon by the authorities. These reliable sources become the sources who define an event, and the status definition that they put forth actually marks the boundaries of the entire discourse on the subject. In this manner, rhetorical imperviousness is achieved and dominant ideologies are reproduced in the mainstream media (Manning, 2001; Hall et al., 1978; Ericson et al., 1989; Ryan, 1991; Van Dijk, 1996; Harcup, 2003).

A study that examined the coverage patterns of the anarchists' protests in Minneapolis across a wide range of media organizations points to the importance of the following factors in determining coverage patterns: working values and norms which exist in the media organization itself; the values of the reporters who cover the news event; the type of medium in which the news event is covered; and the writing genre (i.e., commentary, personal column, or news report) (Hertog & McLeod, 1995). As a result, it is clear that the number of resources available to the actor, as high as they may be, cannot be the sole factor in determining media success. One must also examine the ideological distance of the actor from the heart of the consensus, and determine how much of his struggle is considered justified and legitimate within the general public and in the eyes of the media (Kampf, 1993).

Harcup (2003), who compared the violent protest events in a United Kingdom (UK) slum in a mainstream newspaper and an independent newspaper, found significant differences in the framings provided by each newspaper for the events. From this ideological analysis, it appears that the mainstream media in the UK tended to cover these events under the "law and order" framing which emphasizes the protestors' violence and their confrontations with the police. This framing perpetuated existing stereotypes regarding the protesting groups and presented them as a menace to public order and to the entire society. Moreover, there was also wide use of authorized sources from the local government, the police, and the judicial system. These findings are a result of the news practices mentioned above and of the accepted social norms among the societal elites.

On the other hand, Harcup found that the alternative media tended to frame the event with a lot more of a social and thematic focus. It emphasized the economic and social difficulties endured by the protestors, and relied primarily upon non-elite sources – protestors who openly impugned the establishment. Many of the sources were anonymous testimonials and some reports were even written in the first person. It is evident that the alternative media ventured far beyond the ideological discourse boundaries and refused to accept the rhetorical imperviousness which characterized the mainstream media's dominant framing of the events. This study shows that alternative media can and does succeed in challenging the dominant discourse, even if only within a limited audience (Harcup, 2003).

It is seems that in this political reality, where the strongest become even stronger through the mass media and stand in the way of the challengers as a result of the structural and cultural factors described above, the alternative media organizations constitute a cordial and friendly alternative that provides proper (self) representation for those who are typically excluded and silenced in mainstream media. The current research is inspired by Harcup's research and compares the coverage of the same events in mainstream vs. alternative media. This comparison will enable us to assess the above dynamics are universal or not to a large extant. Moreover, this research extends Harcup's research to an evaluation of the Internet, not only comparing the different media organizations' Websites, but also accounting for an additional variable - the medium itself. This research will ensure that whatever medium a specific event is published in has an effect on the nature of the coverage through comparisons between the most popular printed newspaper and the most popular mainstream news Websites. This comparison will help to determine whether or not the Internet as a medium with unique characteristic enables easy penetration of critical messages.

Black and White or Many Shades of Gray?

It is important to note that in contrast to the dichotomous approach of the two journalism categories presented by Harcup, Atton (2002) found that there is a mixed use and endorsement of "deviating" elements in each type of journalism above, starting with the writing style and the news values, and culminating with the media frames. He found that some of the articles simultaneously contained elements from both the mainstream and the alternative media. For this reason, he proposed a continuous spectrum model, which contains clearly-defined extremities. Consequently, media organizations are placed along this spectrum according to their level of proximity to a certain media category. By proposing this model, Atton opted to discard the binary perception which prevents a deep and complex understanding of the interaction between these two types of journalism. Atton also found that mainstream media organizations adopt, on certain conditions3, media frames that sympathize with the protest groups, meaning they do not always demonize or marginalize them; rather, in some cases, the mainstream media criticizes social establishments.

While in alternative journalism the point of view is always from within the movement, the mainstream media maintains a certain distance while reporting. The coverage, as sympathetic as it may be, is still written *about* a certain group and is not authored by it. The protestors' perspectives can explicitly appear in an article, but with no deep commitment to them. To present these perspectives in any other way would be to bluntly disrupt the professional norms of balance and neutrality in mainstream media. This extent of distance and isolation from the alternative journalists cannot be expected; they are not satisfied with merely sympathizing with the agenda but rather express complete solidarity with the protestors in different ways.

Atton also found that in the mainstream media, protestors' testimonies are framed in the expected and standard ways – they are only permitted to discuss their personal experiences which are directly relevant to the article. Any criticism against the establishment remains limited to experts only, whether they are the media organization's experts or the movement's speakers – its official spokespeople or representatives that the media has authorized as such. This situation is completely different than that for alternative journalism in which political criticism is given by the activists themselves, along with their personal reports on the events (Atton, 2002).

Coverage Patterns and Representations of the Second Intifada in the Israeli Mainstream Media

As previously mentioned, this research is centered upon articles related to the events that occurred in the Palestinian village of Ni'lin during 2008 and were subsequently published on Israeli news Websites. In order to better understand these events, this research will also examine and describe the different types of coverage patterns that existed for different kinds of events which were identified in the Israeli mainstream media during the second Intifada. In light of the social and political phenomenon of "rallying around the flag" during a national security crisis, there is an increase in the amount of patriotism and ethnocentrism propagated by the popular media. Moreover, during an asymmetrical military or political conflict, the strong side often tried to promote a frame which presents the struggle as justified by saying it is "only" exhibiting a legitimate reaction to an external threat. On the other hand, the disadvantaged side tried to promote a frame of righteous struggle against imperialist occupation. An example of this type of behavior can be found in the Israeli-Palestinian struggle (Wolfsfeld et al., 2008).

During a security crisis, ethnocentric crisis management occurs, affecting the information flow process. The news that is generated contains a strong emphasis on ethnocentrism and patriotism because the mainstream journalists are being aided by authorized and official sources of the political and military elites of the motherland to such an extent that they are almost completely dependent on these sources and their dependence is reflected through their utter acceptance of the elites' status definition. This leads to a situation in which the large majority of the information that is being generated is coming only from sources originating from the same country (Ibid, Ibid).

Likewise it was also found that, compared with cases that suit the accepted cultural framings, in some cases it is harder to act within the frame of the regular and accepted coverage. This happens when an event is too big to be ignored and has to be explained to the public in order to settle its cognitive dissonance and the damage inflicted on national self-image and pride. In those circumstances, the event itself has more significance than the dominant and fluent media discourse in constructing the coverage, because the event itself limits the range of frames it can generate. Based on this, Wolfsfeld et al. distinguished between two kinds of events during the second Intifada: events in which Israel suffered an assault on its sovereignty and then identified and framed itself as a victim, and events in which Israel was the aggressor and then identified and framed itself as defensive. (Ibid, Ibid).

The "victim" framing includes three characteristics: a high level of emotion (sadness, anger) and drama while personalizing the Israeli dead and injured; demonizing the enemy by describing it in charged negative language;, and creating ethnic solidarity. On the other hand, during the events in which Israel was the aggressor three coverage patterns were identified. The first pattern was intellectualism and rationalism – an effort was made to lower the level of drama and emotion in the event coverage. A cold and distanced reporting style which emphasized a tactical and analytical narration of the events while using military language a technical terminology was adopted. It became very easy for the journalists to turn to military sources in these cases in order to receive information which would help them better understand the course of events. Turning to these experts resulted in a cold and emotionally-distant analysis of the event, and a framing of 'war on terror' was obtained. The second coverage pattern was to present the wider context of the event in order to divert the blame onto the other side, while positioning Israel as having reacted to external acts of aggression. At the same time, Israel attempted to both distance itself from guilt and to extenuate the severity of an event (for instance a framing of 'an unfortunate accident'). The third coverage pattern was denial/ disregard or dedicating only a limited amount of attention to enemy casualties. This pattern was also designed to reduce the significance of the suffering and injuries of the Palestinians.

This theory has, so far, only been examined on a major Israeli television channel. In light of the theoretical overview above, this research will examine whether this distinction is valid for reports created and published on alternative news Websites. Other partially similar findings were found in research that examined the representations of Palestinians in mainstream Israeli newspapers (Liebes & Kampf, 2009). The researchers sampled photos that included Palestinians and were published on the front pages of Yedioth Ahronoth and Haaretz between 2000 to 2005. They compared their results to their previous analyses regard the beginning of the second Intifada (the end of the year 2000) and the first Intifada (the end of the 1980s and the beginning of the 1990s). Their conclusion was that a complex media process of expanding the representation of Palestinians in the Israeli media had been happening. During the first Intifada, six characteristics of these representations were identified. The fundamental characteristics were: excising the Palestinian's suffer, enhancement the threat by demonizing and de-personalizing (Liebes, 1997). During the second Intifada, together with these characteristics, new ways to represent the Palestinians were identified. In the new coverage form the Palestinian were not only included, they were presented in a human and personal way. The Israeli readers who follow those images could feel empathy toward the photographed subjects. This change was manifested in 3 major ways:

1. Presenting many different kinds of Palestinians. Palestinians were not only terrorists that were attacking Israelis but they were also leaders, politicians, and common people (i.e., women, children, aged people, etc.) that were victims of Israeli actions.
2. Presenting Palestinians not only in the hard news sections related to terrorist attacks and riots, but also in the soft news sections related to daily life.
3. Presenting Palestinians in the context of ethical violations on behalf of Israeli soldiers. Between 2000 and 2005, several incidents involving Israeli soldiers behaving in immoral manners were exposed. These controversial acts aroused vigorous public debates.

The incident that took place in 2008 near the village of Ni'lin belongs to the third manifestation that Liebes and Kampf recognized. How did each media organization cover this incident? To what extent was the Palestinians' suffer prominent? This research aims to examine the differences in how this incident and the associated Palestinian suffering were covered between the alternative media and the mainstream media. Based on a review of the literature, it appears as though there are several existing studies which have examined how the mainstream Israeli media has covered the Israeli-Palestinian conflict and how both sides have been represented. However, these studies have failed to examine how the alternative Israeli media has covered the conflict. Moreover, little is known about the political functions of alternative news Websites. All of these are issues that the current research seeks to explore.

Based on the above, the following research question will be explored: What differences exist between mainstream news Websites (and one print newspaper) and alternative news Websites in their coverage of the protest-related events that took place near village of Ni'lin during 2008? The author suggests the following hypotheses regarding this research question:

H1: The examined events in each type of media will have different (and even contradictory) media frames. While the mainstream news organizations will uphold the dominant framing of "law and order," the alternative Websites will present "occupation" and "human rights" framing. These differences will be manifested through the use of different linguistic, rhetorical, and visual means in each Website.

H2: There will be fewer actors who are critical of the authorities and the establishment in the mainstream media as there will be in the alternative media.

H3: A difference will be found in the types of quoted sources in the entries on each of the Websites. While most of the sources in the mainstream media will be authorized sources on behalf of the state and the army, the alternative media will allow more unauthorized sources, namely the Israeli and Palestinian protesters and members of human rights organizations.

H4: While the mainstream media will maintain a hierarchical distinction between the journalist and his sources, the alternative Websites will blur the differences between the two by allowing news reporting in the first person, direct calls for action, etc.

What Makes the Internet Such an Attractive Medium for Social Change Activists?

Before the remainder of the hypotheses regarding the potential political functions of the alternative news Websites are presented, a discussion on how the Internet can assist in mobilization and organization and how it can constitute alternative and critical mini-spaces is required. Indeed, a large part of the alternative media organizations which made their first appearance in Europe in the mid-20th century (local newspapers, fanzines, etc.) disappeared, but the idea of alternative media carried on, evolving and whole-heartedly adopting the Internet. These alternative media outlets take advantage of current information technologies that immensely expand the social and communal possibilities for consciousness-development, political recruitment, and the organization of direct action. Although over time the online sphere has become more strongly ruled by corporations, there are still a good number of subversive autonomous spaces (Harcup, 2003).

The Internet provides many possibilities for its users to become active users, thanks to its unique characteristics. First, the Internet is a network of networks with no hierarchical control centers. Second, the Internet is multimedia since it contains a wide variety of media (i.e., text, sound, and image). Third, the interactivity of the Internet empowers the user and allows him to react to existing content while simultaneously creating new content at minimal cost. This characteristic also has to do with its being generative and open for anyone to develop new applications. Last but not least, the Internet is a mass medium to which hundreds of millions of people all over the world are exposed to. It is a global medium which impacts and is impacted by most of the population of developed countries (Dimaggio et al., 2001; Burnett & Marshall, 2003).

The Internet has lowered the media entrance fees; the user may distribute information independently of any formal media organization using a variety of means (Van de Donk et al., 2004; Pickerill, 2003a; Pickerill, 2003b; Cammaerts, 2006; Vedel, 2003; Harcup, 2003; Owens & Palmer, 2003). This technological independence weakens the actors' dependence on corporate media organizations and increases the number of cases in which these actors choose not to turn to the mainstream media. It is important to note that the Internet as a network, rather than as a medium with a central and hierarchical control structure, enables easier penetration and distribution of subversive and radical messages, messages that do not always successfully pass through the conventional channels of the mainstream media (Peterson, 2001). The technological ability for self-representation on the actors' part with no time or space constraints (on the organization's Website, on an alternative news Website, etc.) enables the direct transfer and distribution of their messages in a non-distorted and non-biased manner in order to recruit activists and supporters. For this reason, the Internet constitutes a media channel which circumvents the necessity of the mainstream media, which does not provide them with a suitable platform. Based on this, one can assume that the Internet has become a preferred alternative media channel for social actors who feel silenced by the mainstream media.

The Internet as a Public Sphere for Fostering Collective Identities

In the postmodern age, an urgent need has arisen to carefully examine both the process of forming collective identities among new protest movements and the Internet's role in this process. According to Cohen (1985), it is essential to examine the identity-consolidating processes in order to research the nature of social movements, since a group identity is the way in which a collective is formed (Melucci, 1996). Three major elements which constitute the group identity in social movements were identified:

1. A sense of "us" – a feeling of unity among the group's members, or solidarity in defining the common characteristics which are deemed important by members;
2. The development of awareness and consciousness among group members – a consensus regarding interpretation framings, goals, and means (eg., political consciousness);
3. The maintenance of a culture of direct opposition to the dominant social order (Tayler & Whittier, 1992).

At first glance, it seems paradoxical that of all things the Internet, which is perceived as an isolated medium, can nurture and inspire collective actions. But on the other hand, one can assume that the Internet's ability to promote direct communication, overcoming the physical limitations that face-to-face meetings require, can improve one's ability to communicate and help to create a collective identity and solidarity among individuals (Ross, 1999). Ross claims that the Internet fulfills a decisive role in bridging the gap between the individual and the community/ society by creating new forms of political and cultural solidarity through communication. Salter also claims that the Internet can be used as an informal public sphere which enables uncensored conversations and thus, the formation of collective identities (Salter, 2003).

A study on a political activists' forum in Hong Kong (Lai-yee Ma, 2005) found that such a forum efficiently fosters and encourages collective identity among its users. It was demonstrated that all of the key elements of group identity in social movements (Taylor and Whittier, 1992) correlate directly with users' willingness to engage politically both online and offline. Users who experienced a greater amount of solidarity - who possessed a common consciousness and a collective identity attributable to the forum - tended to participate more readily in political activity offline. Hence, political consciousness as part of the collective identity is a very strong predictor for political involvement online and offline.

The correlations between the variables which were examined show that forums are an efficient platform for gathering people with similar views and ideas, despite possible physical separation. Even with its anonymous nature, the Internet fulfills a symbolic function of building a collective identity, which provides motivation for protest activity offline. Forums possess the potential to become agents of social movements that act on the conscious-symbolic level, as a sort of indoctrination agent that prepares the ground for political recruitment and substantive political involvement (Lai-yee Ma, 2005). This research argues that the content found on alternative news Websites work in a similar manner – it helps to establish collective identity and formulate a contentious consciousness, both of which then translate into political involvement.

Towards a More Equal Media Environment

The Internet has also affected the mainstream news industry. The information-gathering, production, and distribution methods of mainstream news organizations have changed with the Internet's penetration into the communications arena. The convergence phenomenon enables the simultaneous utilization of several technologies in the same article: text, sound, and visual. Moreover, the ability to provide real-time updates to ongoing news stories has increased the frequency of updates while the increased interactivity has blurred the traditional boundaries between creator/source, journalist/citizen (Lehman-Wilzig, 2007; Pew, 2007; Reich, 2008; Deuze, 2003).

Bruns (2008a, 2008b, 2005) claims that the regular models of the media (i.e., production, distribution, and consumption) are no longer relevant. Society is advancing towards a more equal media environment which enables all of its participants to both receive and distribute information on a nearly-equal basis, even going so far as to allow active involvement on the part of the content user. As a result, a producer-user hybrid has been created - *produser*. This merger is suitable to the alternative media's practices.

Linking as a Mechanism for Gatekeeping and Recognition

In contrast to Bruns's approach, some researchers indicate that the gatekeeping model not dead and buried, but that, for many reasons, it is more alive than ever. These reasons include journalists' fear of losing their jobs; the disillusionment stemming from utopian perceptions of involved citizens; and an enormous abundance of information which requires filtering mechanisms (Domingo et al, 2008; Singer, 2005; Bowman, 2008; Lammbert, 2007). The ability to contain enormous amounts of information may lead to a condition of information overflow, which would cause the Internet to be perceived as a less reliable source of information, and can, in fact, increase citizens' dependency on mediators for filtering needs. The practical implication of this is that most Internet users continue to turn to large mainstream media Websites, meaning that the dependency on journalists and editors is far from disappearing (Vedel, 2003).

These filtering mechanisms can results in new and unique patterns in the medium, such as linking, which attempt to leave most of the power in the hands of the professional journalists (Dimitrova et al, 2003). The link is a reference to an additional online information source which expands and deepens a user's knowledge of a certain subject, and is designed to increase the accessibility of information and to provide the user with a convenient way to navigate through the Internet's plethora of information (Dimitrova et al, 2003; Kovarick, 2002). Therefore, the link, which is a unique advantage of the Internet and does not exist in print media, empowers user to decide for himself whether or not to follow the link. The choice is in the hands of the user, meaning his the level of control within the information environment and the information search process has grown. The freedom to choose instills a more interactive character on the process (Peng et al., 1999; Eveland & Dunwoody, 2001; Althaus & Tewksbury, 2000).

Although links empower the user, it is important to remember that they are still expressions of a selection made by the content manager of a given Website. The decision to include certain links while excluding others turns these links into gatekeeping mechanisms which express power and authority by advancement of particular pages/Websites over all the rest (Dimitrova et al., 2003; McAdams & Berger, 2001). Every link, by definition, indicates a significance granted to a specific page/Website representing a certain idea over others. Therefore, the link not only attaches ideas and organizations, but it also provides other Websites/organizations with legitimacy, visibility, recognition, publicity, significance, trust, and authority (Shumate & Dewitt, 2008). Therefore, the links fulfill an important role in the collective action for two reasons: first, they help to build and define the boundaries of a community online; second, networks of links can raise the online visibility and importance of the certain issue due to search engines' rationales (in many cases, a page's ranking is affected by the numbers of the links the specific page has).

Internet researchers who have developed a unique methodology for link analysis point to these additional functions of links in explaining how they can help in establishing a collective identity, consolidating social capital, and creating coalitions among organizations (Biddix & Park, 2008; Shumate & Lipp, 2008; Shumate & Dewitt, 2008; Rogers & Ben-David, 2008; Park & Thelwall, 2003; Rogers & Marres, 2000; Rogers, 2004). Examining the structural connections of a network can reveal important characteristics of the network which lead to offline action. Through link analysis of protest organizations and Websites, one can identify co-operations, ideological proximities, and recognitions. The existence of a network between certain Websites can constitute evidence for the connectivity characteristic of an organization's community. In a study that examined the links network between Websites among the campus living wage movements, it was found that an Internet Website alone is not enough to guarantee a successful struggle. Links to other Websites from the organization's Website were the factors which improved the activist recruitment for and implementation of a protest. Connecting a Website to a larger protest network and turning it into another online node augments the efficacy of the Website as a catalyst for a movement's operations (Biddix & Park, 2008). Therefore, this research must also examine the links that appear in alternative news Websites versus those on mainstream news Websites, and discuss their potential political functions.

Based on the above, a second research question is presented:

What can be learned from the textual differences between mainstream and alternative news Websites about the potential political functions of alternative news Websites when focusing on radical protest?

The methodology of this research is only content analysis (not depth interviews or survey). As a result, it will be difficult to ascertain precisely what the political functions of the alternative news Websites are. Nevertheless, this qualitative content analysis will enable the researcher to identify the writers' intentions and to deduce the potential functions of the articles.

As per the Grounded Theory Method, this component of the research study does not specify any hypotheses that the researcher wishes to confirm; however, the researcher does maintain these general expectations that the writers' political purposes are:

1. To recruit and mobilize individuals to political action;
2. To reinforce subversive consciousness and to strengthen the activists' collective identity;
3. To recognize online political allies and to provide points of reference to the readers via hyperlinks;
4. To improve the accessibility of critical materials.

METHODOLOGY

The aim of the current research is to create a deep understanding of the linguistic and rhetorical differences that exist between alternative and mainstream news Websites. In order to give the maximum attention to the finest of nuances, qualitative content analysis was produced by the author in two stages. During the first phase of the qualitative content analysis, a special emphasis was placed upon criterions which were recognized in previous studies as follows:

1. Who are the sources and the actors in the article?
   a. Are they Palestinian or Israeli?
   b. Do they belong to a security or military elite?
2. What is the framing of the event?
   a. Does it involve "law and order" or "human rights"?
   b. Who is the victim and who is responsible for the violence?
   c. To what extent is the coverage thematic or episodic?
   d. What is the context of the event?
   e. Which actor's perspective received more prominence and support in the article?
3. Do the coverage patterns identified by Wolfsfeld et al. (2008) exist in the article?
4. What additional meanings do the links contribute to the news item?

The second stage of the qualitative content analysis, which aimed to identify the potential political functions of alternative news Websites during radical protest, was done according to Grounded Theory Method. This is a fundamental method for analyzing data and building theories in qualitative research in social sciences. The method was developed in the 1960s by two sociologists: Barney Glaser and Anselm Strauss. The starting point of this method is the belief that human behaviors have consistent patterns that cannot be described mathematically. It is possible to discover these patterns through a systematic and gradual process, while the gathering and analysis of data happens continuously and simultaneously. During the preliminary phase, the researcher should look for ideas and arguments that are consistently repeated in the data. As the study advances, the researcher must clarify and refine these themes, distinguishing between unique arguments. For each theme and sub-theme, there are criterions that support and confirm it. When the researcher has extracted all of the themes and sub-themes (the utilization phase), he must explain the connections between the different themes and identify the core themes. The third and final phase of this method requires the researcher to combine the identified themes and sub-themes, referring to the existent literature, in order to present a complete and valid theory (Gibton, 2001; Glaser & Strauss, 1967).

During the identification of the potential political functions, special attention was given to the writers' intentions and their extra-textual targets. That is to say that in this part of the analysis the researcher was not satisfied with simply finding a distinction between different kinds of words, terms and actors; rather she sought to identify the political purpose(s) in every single item that was published in alternative news Websites. This identification arose during the first phase of analysis by examining the differences between the mainstream and alternative media; these differences indicate different writing objectives. Publishing technical details related the coming protest activities indicates the writer's intent to recruit (new and veteran) activists and to motivate them into action. Writing in either the first- or second-person following a semantic distinguishing between "us" and "them" indicates the writer's intent to reinforce subversive consciousness and to strengthen the activists' collective identity. Publishing links to specific organizations indicates the writer's intent to provide recognition, support and legitimization to those organizations and a practical attempt to increase traffic to their Websites.

In this research, qualitative content analysis was carried out on *all* of the articles dealing with the events that took place in the Palestinian village of Ni'lin which were published between November 2007 and December 2008 in the most popular printed newspaper in Israel, *Yedioth Ahronoth* (22 articles), and in three major Israeli news Websites and four alternative Israeli news Websites. The mainstream news Websites which were chosen were: *Ynet* (www.ynet.co.il), which is owned by the largest printed newspaper in Israel and from which 240 articles were analyzed; *NRG* (www.nrg.co.il), which is owned by the second largest printed newspaper in Israel and from which 38 articles were analyzed; and *NFC* (www.nfc.co.il), which to the best of the researcher's knowledge is not owned by any Israeli media corporation and from which 21 articles were analyzed.

The alternative news Websites that were chosen were all of the Israeli alternative news Websites that were a) in existence during the research period; and b) had published at least one article during the examined time concerning the events in Ni'lin or related events. This was done in order to include all of the ideological sequences and news formats that exist in Israel. The included Websites were: *Wikinews* (he.wikinews.org), a Website that follows open code and collaborative editing principles and from which one article was analyzed; *Scoop* (scoop.co.il), the largest citizens' news Website in Israel (Reich, 2008) and from which five articles were analyzed; *Social TV* (www.tv.social.org.il), a video news Website of activists that emphasizes social and economic criticism and from which one video article was analyzed; *Indymedia Israel* (israel.indymedia.org), a Website constituting the most radical and critical stance in Israel, as it is a local branch of the international Indymedia network, and from which 16 articles were analyzed. This Website identified with radical left-wing activists and its anarchist and democratic principles of news production has been studied extensively. 4 In all, a total of 342 news items were coded.

One can see a great disparity in the number of the items covering the village of Ni'lin between the media organizations, an interesting (and surprising) finding in and of itself. This evidence not only shows that there are different levels of interest surrounding this issue among the various media organizations, but it also points out that the alternative media has to deal with several challenges and weaknesses. The reason why *Ynet* had so many news items dealing with the events in Ni'lin was that they were the only Website to publish dozens of shorter news breaks. These news breaks were very short (2-3 sentences), several were usually published as a series within a very brief period of time, and were accompanied by longer reports.

FINDINGS

Throughout the content analysis, different media frames were discerned, as well as a notable boundary that distinguishes between the mainstream and alternative news Websites. Moreover, in-group differences were also recognized. In particular, it was noted that NFC leans more to the right compared with the rest of the mainstream media outlets which were mostly situated at the center of the political spectrum with a certain left-wing bias for the commentary sections. These findings demonstrate how media organizations and media professionals with opposing ideological views can construct a story in opposite ways through their choice of words, sources, and different perspectives during the coverage.

Likewise, it was again demonstrated that the mainstream media usually finds it difficult to side with social change organizations and challengers of the status quo in their reports if they are required to rely entirely on authorized sources. The mainstream media organizations prefer to leave the sharp and scathing criticism buried in the in-depth reporting situated far away from the hard news sections in the inner pages of supplementary sections, where criticism is more subtle and inferred, or to keep the criticism for personal columns and commentary only. This finding may support, to a certain degree, the claim that citizens' media are not much more than personal columns; however, it is too early to determine if this is indeed the case and further examination is required.

Through the content analysis of the episode in which a restrained Palestinian was shot, as well as in the analysis of the rest of the concurrent events, two competing media frames were identified. In all of the examined theoretical aspects, each media frame has been consistent in its components throughout all of the many events that took place in the area within the examined period. The first identified framing is the one promoted by the Minister of Defense, the IDF Commander-In-Chief, high-ranking IDF officers, various elements in the Military Advocate General's office, Israelis directly involved in the events, and their close associates. The first official response released by the IDF Spokesperson's Unit following the cuffed detainee incident in Ni'lin was quoted to the letter as an integral part of the news items. This is an excellent and exhaustive example that exemplifies all of the components of the mainstream media frame in the affair's coverage until its end, as well as the framing promoted by the IDF in other shooting incidents in which innocent Palestinians were killed.

The IDF released the following statement in response to the allegations and the documentation: 'This is a severe and unacceptable event, which contradicts the values of the IDF. *During the event, a means of riot control ("non-lethal fire") was used against a Palestinian detainee, who was detained by our forces* after he took *part in a* violent demonstration *against the building of the* security fence *in the vicinity of the village of Ni'lin. The army's orders declare that it is strictly forbidden to harm detainees in any way and obligate that detainees are treated respectfully and carefully. Events in which detainees are maltreated in any form,* in accordance with IDF policy, *are thereby brought to investigation by the Investigating Military Police. In this case, upon viewing the video tape documenting the incident, the Military Advocate General, Brigadier Avichai Mendelblit,, instructed the Investigating Military Police to embark upon a formal investigation of the incident. The IDF noted that the Palestinian was examined by a military physician immediately after the events took place, and was deemed to have suffered very light injuries in his right thumb and was* released to his home without need of medical attention.

(IDF Spokesperson's announcement as published in the Israeli media, July 20, 2008; researcher's emphasis in bold)

From the quote above, the mainstream media frame's components can be drawn out as follows: firstly, the IDF condemns the event and sees it as unacceptable and negative. This condemnation is clearly a part of an attempt to maintain the IDF image of a morally-superior military which adheres to a strict ethical code. Since the reality is so severe, there is only so little that can be done to mitigate the harm inflicted upon the IDF's reputation as a result of this incident. Another recurring theme in the IDF's tactics in repairing its public image during this coverage is the emphasis placed upon the fact that that this event was aberrant and exceptional. The third component is the IDF's attempt to shift at least some of the blame onto the Palestinians and to present Israel as "merely" reacting to the external threats it is facing. This tactic of "shifting the blame" is one of the most common tactics in defensive coverage (Wolfsfeld et al., 2008). Last but not least, it is also important to note that there is an attempt to belittle the severity of the event by emphasizing the detainee's light injury, which was so mild that did not even require any medical treatment.

An important semantic difference is the name used by each side to describe the obstacle. While the IDF insists on calling it the "Security Fence," whereas journalists usually call it the "Separation Fence," and the Palestinians, the rest of the protesters, and consequently also the journalists on the alternative news Websites call it the "Apartheid Wall." The meanings derived from each such choice are clear and necessitate no further elaboration.

An inseparable part of the public image repair strategy of the IDF is the attempt to present the appearance of control and professionalism. IDF was portrayed as an authority which operates according to procedures, meaning that an Investigating Military Police investigation is taking place. By presenting the IDF as a responsible and self-correcting organization, the mainstream media restored order (and justice) and therefore helped the authorities regain the public's trust.

On the part of the IDF, one can see an almost complete disregard to the moral issues, the avoidance of using of terms like "unlawful order" or "war crime" and there was a notable effort to present the event as an "accident," a "mishap" and a "misunderstanding."

In stark contrast to this media frame, one can discern a competing media frame brought to light by human rights organizations (B'Tselem – the organization that revealed the affair, Yesh Din, etc.), Ashraf Abu Rachma - the injured Palestinian, social activists who participate in demonstrations against the wall (mostly Anarchists Against the Wall), Palestinian members of the People's Committee Against the Wall and, generally, the residents of Ni'lin. These organizations and individuals tried to promote a wide context framing and discuss the situation in the West Bank as a whole by describing lives under occupation. Most importantly, human rights violations suffered by Palestinians at the hands of Israeli soldiers were presented as routine rather than exceptional, as a trend and ongoing phenomenon that was derived from a political and military policy that cannot be considered temporary misfortunes or misunderstandings. The Palestinian detainee incident was labeled a number of times as a "war crime" and "aggravated abuse" and as the result of a severe moral deficiency, not the result of the professional incompetence of field commanders or soldiers in the field.

Another very important element in this frame is the explanations of the reasons for the local struggle in the village of Ni'lin. The alternative media sources repeatedly emphasize the fact that the last thousands of acres of the village lands were expropriated in favor of expanding nearby settlements and for the construction of the fence. More than that, it was prominent that the fence's current path critically hurts the Palestinian's lives. The protesters constantly provided a wider picture of the specific events and tried to highlight the connections between their daily lives under the Israeli Occupation and the demonstrations. The protesters and the Palestinians stuck to their status definitions of the events – "a non-violent struggle by the people" or "an act of direct democracy" and, of course, they resisted the IDF status definitions – "disorderly conduct," "violent demonstrations" and "rioting." This also relates to the question of accountability for the violence – determining which party involved in an incident is "the aggressor." We can learn from the next example, taken from Wikinews, about how this framing was manifested:

In a country in which its own army murders unarmed demonstrators day after day, *we are not surprised that* the activists who protest against these murders are beaten and arrested... *Achmed was* killed immediately *and his two brothers took his body back to the village (about 1 km), leaving a trail of blood behind them...* Two rubber bullets were fired from a distance of 10 meters penetrated his skull and caused his death... the protesters were arrested and subjected to violence *despite their claims that* the demonstration was legal *and that they* did not break any law. *The* policewomen were continuing to beat some of the protesters *while* they were arrested and tied inside the police car...

As anticipated, in mainstream news Websites, a dominant framing of "law and order" could be found, while the alternative Websites used framings of "human rights" and "occupation." This was manifested not only in the terminology and semantics chosen by each writer/editor as mentioned above, but it was also apparent in the selection of quoted sources. The number of voices and actors critical of the authorities was certainly higher in the alternative media than in the mainstream media, due to the large difference in the types of sources quoted in the reports. The mainstream press relied mostly on official military sources such as the Military Advocate General and the IDF Spokesperson's Unit. These actors constructed the coverage as an intra-Israeli, ethnocentric and rationalistic narrative. Most of those reports focused on the struggle over the contradictory versions of the officer and the sergeant and the severity/insignificance of the charge and the punishment. On the other hand, the alternative media chose not to use these sources at all. The alternative journalists prefer to use non-authorized and unaccredited sources, forcing them to rely on themselves or to use ordinary civilians as sources, whether they are Israeli demonstrators, Palestinian demonstrators, or members of human rights organizations. These sources presented a different perspective that is aligned with the media frame promoted by the Palestinians.

These findings are compatible with Reich's (2008) findings regarding the limited number of sources in the independent press. Moreover, these findings explain why the mainstream Websites maintained the distinction and hierarchy between the journalist and his sources, whereas the alternative media did not. The alternative media Websites, especially *Indymedia Israel*, blurred the boundary between journalist and sources by using direct appeals to the readers in the second person to take part in the demonstrations, some of which the writer himself reports on, for example:

... *Despite the* brutal oppression *of the demonstrations,* today's action was successful. *Many Ni'lin residents (about 5,000) saw and heard from their homes these expressions of solidarity... Following the intensive resistance against the fence construction in the past weeks, the Israeli army has placed a curfew on the village.* Therefore, your *{apply in Hebrew* both *female and male- K.S}* support and participation in the big demonstration is extremely important... *The rallies toward the bulldozers and the settlements are occurring three to four times a week, every week...*

It was not surprising to find out that in several items which were published in alternative news Websites there was a sharp criticism not only with regard to the political authorities but also with regard to the mainstream media and its framing. The next example is very obvious and was taken from *Scoop* news Website

... *In the weekend edition of* YEDIOTH AHRONOTH, *there is a* long articlc *regarding the "weapon clattering" lieutenant colonel, and his "misunderstood" command that a chained Palestinian demonstrator in the village of Ni'lin be shot in his foot.* The report presented *the lieutenant colonel, Omri Burberg, as a very strict officer, but professionally outstanding. His profession, by the way, is as a commander of armor units, and he does not deal with civilian protesters.* I am not so sure how many you can name "professional" a person who finds a reason to "clatter" a loaded weapon in front of chained detainee. It is not clear to me in which brutish sub-culture this behavior considered to be "professional"... *By the way, the soldier who "did not hear correctly" and because of that,* executed an extremely illegitimate order, *has not been reprimanded in any way nor has there been any indication of any intention to do so, no one want to touch the limp. Has anyone heard otherwise? I guess that we have given up completely on the issue of* refusing the extremely illegitimate order, *ha? If this is the case, so oh boy, it is going to be so much fun to watch CNN soon...*

Similar to Atton's (2002) findings, the establishment's media frame was the *dominant but not sole* frame in the mainstream press, and the protester's media frame was the *only one* that appeared in alternative news Websites. Differences were found in the character of the articles for each mainstream media outlet according to the personality and role of the journalist. In *Ynet* and *Yedioth Ahronoth,* the territories correspondents tended more than all other correspondents to not only present the Palestinian perspective, but also to promote it with a certain degree of sympathy. These journalists have chosen to present an emotional and personal framing that may even create identification among the readers. These findings can be explained quite simply due to the fact that the territories correspondent, as a consequence of his position, has much more access to Palestinian sources, unlike the military correspondent or the legal correspondent, for example. Furthermore, one can assume that the editorial considerations intersect with the ideological baggage of each writer (the *Ynet* territories correspondent, Ali Wakad, is Arab), thus giving the readers a chance to be exposed to a competing media frame. Following are examples that represent these differences.

The first example is taken from an article by Ali Waka, the *Ynet* territories correspondent. It expresses, to a large extent, not only emotions, empathy and personalization but also straightforward criticism against the Israeli establishment.

... *The* women *who stood at the entrance of the house of the child that was killed* could not stop their tears. *'They don't have any red lines, they don't have any red lines' they said over and over...* Achmed's uncle, Husain Yosof Mosa, *told Ynet that he doesn't understand why the soldier shot in the direction of the child.* 'He was a little boy that played with his friends, how can he possible have threatened the soldiers?' He said painfully. 'They are just little boys *who saw a rally against the fence and joined it.* To come back dead without a head points out the soldiers' cruelty'... *He said that he* doesn't believe in any prosecution against the Israelis: 'Prosecution won't help, trial won't help. The best they can do is to make a show, like they did in the case of the shooting soldier. *The judges immediately release; they are the legislatures, they are the prosecutor and they are the judges.* They say that they will go to court, but what they actually do is a one big lie, a show for the media ... the dead child was a little and handsome boy *as can be seen from the posters that are hanging in every corner in Ni'lin...* Achmed Saadat and Machmud Muchsan, both friends of the killed child, are ten years old *and were told that they were in the construction area while their friend who was the top student in his class was shot...*

The second example is taken from an article by Efrat Weiss, the *Ynet* military correspondent. It is easy to recognize the distant and rationalistic framing that Wolfsfeld et al. (2008) discussed.

... *The* IDF *reported that the soldiers shot toward* demonstrators who had sabotaged the fence and had thrown stones toward the soldiers. *The incident is still* under comprehensive investigation by the IDF and the Israeli police... *The IDF press releases stated that* 'The IDF feels sorry for any harm caused to non-involved people' *and that* 'In the past weeks, severe demonstrations *have taken place next to the Security Fence in the village of Ni'lin. In those demonstrations, Israeli citizens and foreigners are taking part in order to prevent the construction of the fence in the area.* So far during those demonstrations, more than 20 officers, soldiers and policeman have been injured. *The IDF will continue to build the* Security Fence *in Ni'lin area until it will be finished...*

The above findings demonstrate as Atton, who relied on Hall, claimed, that the hegemony is neither impervious nor impenetrable, and in case there is a journalist who supports the challengers' agenda, this framing will find its way, in different measures and manners, into the journalistic texts of the writer. This situation brings up the need for an approach that presents the different media on a spectrum, with mainstream media on the one end and alternative media on the other, as a substitute for a dichotomist and binary vision of the different media.

Following the research of Wolfsfeld et al. (2008), the current study also found that the Israeli mainstream media covers events where Israel is perceived as a victim in a very different manner than those in which Israel is perceived as the aggressor. Yet, it was also found that this distinction is less relevant to the Israeli alternative media. The examined alternative Websites continued being critical throughout all the events; they did not take a rationalistic approach when covering an event that threatened Israel's image, they did not ignore it, they did not cast the blame onto the Palestinians, and they insisted on thematic reporting that presented events with a wider context.

From all of the differences that were mentioned in Table 1, it is possible to learn about four potential functions that publishing in alternative news Websites may fulfill for radical protest movements: the first potential function is *to recruit activists* and *to maintain contact with dormant (inactive) and distant activists*. The most prominent textual difference between the mainstream news Websites (and the printed newspaper) and the alternative news Websites relates to the number of languages in which articles are written. While in the printed newspaper and the mainstream news Websites all of the articles were written in only one language – Hebrew (except for one Website in which some of the articles could be read in English) - the alternative news Website *Indymedia Israel* (from which most of the "alternative" articles were taken for sampling) offered a translation to English and Arabic for many of the articles. It is reasonable to claim that the main purpose of this multi-lingualism was to enable all potential activists – Israeli, Palestinians, and foreign – to receive updates and to increase the likelihood of them joining the protest. Hence, it can be inferred that this Website is perceived by protest organizations as a stage for recruitment and as a tool for broadening the activists' circles.

The second prominent textual difference between the Websites is in regard to the amount of technical details included in articles in the alternative media, which in fact turn the articles, or at least part of them, into a call to action. In complete opposition to the mainstream media, many of the articles published in *Indymedia Israel* included technical details about protests, including the following details: the protest's date, time, location, pick-up location, transportation coordinator names and telephone numbers, what to bring, what to wear, etc. In light of the tremendous differences between these articles

Table 1. Summary of Findings of the Qualitative Content Analysis

	Alternative Media	Mainstream Media
Sources	Non-authorized; Activists	Authorized; (Military) Elite
Framing	Human Rights; Thematic	Law & Order; Episodic
Coverage Pattern	Israel as Aggressor	Israel as Victim
Links	External – to protest sites	Internal – within the same Website

and the mainstream articles, one certainly gets the impression that the alternative news Websites sometimes turn into public message boards. This serves an important purpose for every organization – keeping in touch with distant and dormant circles of activists.

Most protest organizations in the Internet era have a distribution lists that includes core cadre members, protest organizers, and the rest of the activists. Publishing in an alternative news Website allows protest organizations to directly reach a target audience that is close to and interested in the subject of the protest and is ready to play an active role in the protest, with little to no cost on the part of the organizations, even if that audience is not on the organization's distribution list. Thus, organizations try to recruit new supporters who have never taken part in the organization's activities and to re-engage with distant or dormant supporters who only rarely take part in the activities and are not included on the distribution lists, thereby increasing the number of its supporters and maintaining minimal contact with them until the day when intensive efforts will be done to recruit them.

The second potential function is *to consolidate a subversive political consciousness* and *to strengthen the collective identity*. Relying on Lai-yee Ma's findings (2005), one can assume that articles that appear on alternative news Websites can affect both the consolidation of a collective identity and the development of critical consciousness. Presenting new information, which is not published the mainstream media, accompanied by a critical interpretation of the existing political order, can strengthen critical attitudes and perceptions among readers, which could be translated into active protest.

This critical framing is carried out through the use of certain words that are aimed to insult the establishment, focusing on Israeli security forces (such as "bestial sub-culture," "the green beast" etc.), and through the use of linguistic means that create a division between "us" and "them." Many times these articles include first-person reports or a personal appeal to readers in the second-person plural (including both appeals for male and female as exists in Hebrew). The following are two examples that demonstrate this point:

... *Following the intense opposition activity against the wall in recent weeks, the Israeli army has been imposing a curfew on the village so* your support *is extremely important in a large demonstration...*

... We will leave *for the demonstration on Thursday morning using an organized transport from Tel Aviv ...*

A fluent cultivation of this consciousness can contribute to the consolidation of a collective identity among the members of the protesting community. A well-maintained online collective identity can be part of a solution for the psychological and social needs of the many activists – a sense of belonging, support and encouragement. The following is an example that demonstrates this point:

... In many cases, the demonstrators succeeded in stopping the construction ... the village residents are interested in continuing to collaborate with the Israelis *(in Hebrew both men and women- K.S)* who have been coming to the village since the beginning of the struggle ... *The fact that there is a* new village that has joined the resistance's circle, despite the severe military oppression *that has been occurring toward the activists in all those struggles,* is another good reason *to come and support Ni'lin this week...*

The third potential function that was found is *to build an online network between colleague organizations*. It was found that the mainstream news Websites maintains traditional practices and conventions and invests a great amount of effort to keep balanced and neutral values in a discernible fashion. However, an eminent effort to maintain their status as the sole information providers is also apparent, and their use of links to internal Webpages only strengthens their gatekeeping mechanism. It was found that out of the hundreds of articles analyzed from the mainstream news Websites, only a few did not link to previous articles on the same subject from the *same* newspaper's Website, as was previously discovered (Dimitrova et al., 2003). This finding is exceptionally outstanding, due to the fact that alternative news Websites offer multiple external links which empower the reader and provide him with additional information from different sources.

By adding links to protest organizations' Websites as well as other alternative media organization's Websites from within the published articles, an infrastructure has been created for an online issue network regarding the struggle against the Separation Wall. Among these links, one can find human rights organizations, peace organizations, and independent media outlets, both Israeli and Palestinian, such as Anarchists Against the Wall, B'Tselem, Parents Circle - Families Forum, The Alternative Information Center, and others. It was not surprising to find that there were no links to mainstream media organizations, government Websites, or any right-wing organizations. Pervious researches (Rogers & Ben-David, 2008, 2010)5 have indicated similar findings.

As mentioned before, these links not only enrich the reader's knowledge and refer him to additional sources; they also recognize the linked organizations and express support for what they stand for. Moreover, these links have the power to contribute to increasing solidarity between organizations, improving their visibility online and their recruitment abilities (Biddix & Park, 2008; Shumate & Lipp, 2008; Shumate & Dewitt, 2008; Rogers & Ben-David, 2008, 2010 Park & Thelwall, 2003; Rogers & Marres, 2000; Rogers, 2004).

The fourth potential function is *to distribute and store controversial information*. Another fundamental function of alternative news Websites is that they have been the first and, in many cases, the only public platform that distributes protest information that is not available in the mainstream media. This distribution by itself has significant political implications in the Internet era, even before the information reaches beyond the protest community and apart from the rest of the functions. Knowledge regarding what is going on around us is power even if it doesn't leverage actions or support. Critically been exposing to new pieces of reality is an essential stage in every process of social change.

In the video report about Ni'lin that was published on *Social TV*, one of the members of the organization "Anarchists Against the Wall" expresses her irritation with the mainstream media. The interviewee explains that one of their roles as documenters of injustice is to fill the role of the mainstream media in informing the public about what is happening in the occupied territories. Moreover, she also mentions another two important aspects of their role which lead to a decrease in the degree of violence used by security forces during the demonstrations: their mere presence, as Israelis, beside the Palestinians and their documentation of the events. When people know they are being filmed and that the documentation and its public storage can be used as evidence against them in court when needed, there is a decrease in the degree of violence used by both sides. It seems as though the Israeli protesters understand this and implement the idea in a variety of individual and organizational initiatives. For example, B'Tselem, a human rights center operating in the occupied territories, has initiated the "Shooting Back" Project in which video cameras are distributed to Palestinian civilians (The Hebrew name's literal meaning is: "Armed with Cameras"). Another example is the anarchist collective "Active Stills" (http://www.activestills.org), which documents photos of incidents within the occupied territories and relays them to the mainstream press.

Some of the visual documentation of protest events and alternative information reach not only the members of the protesting community (who reach the alternative news Websites on their own) but also the mainstream media organizations, who do not miss the opportunity to incorporate provocative images into their outlets, as was the case for the Palestinian detainee incident, and from there, the general public and political elites. It is important to note that in most cases, the alternative organizations are the ones that turn the mainstream media, not the other way around.

The Israeli experience teaches us that documentation of this kind (i.e., videos that document different levels of human rights violations in the occupied territories) places criticism over the existing social order on the public agenda, even if it is in a limited and temporary manner. (Liebes & Kampf, 2009) This documentation is provided almost exclusively by protest organizations and constitutes a relatively good way to penetrate the mainstream media with messages of protest.

FUTURE DIRECTIONS

This research was the first to examine the Israeli alternative news Websites and was also the first to reveal the different and contentious media frames, sources and linking strategies that currently exist. Through qualitative content analysis, not only did the Israeli radical left's attitudes toward the separation fence become visible but so too did the potential political functions of those Websites.

Future research must confirm the validity of the four potential functions that were suggested here through additional methodologies such as link analysis and in-depth interviews with the radical organizations' activists and with the readers. This will deepen our understanding and will provide new insights that were not discovered in this research. Moreover, in order to overcome the faults of the current research, similar studies must be conducted on a wide variety of issues (i.e., the environment, anti-globalization, animal rights, etc.) in more countries, with more encoders and through quantitative methods too.

DISCUSSION

This study demonstrates that the discussion about the role of the Internet in the organization of political protest and its activist recruitment cannot be complete, comprehensive and efficient without relating to the issue of alternative media. As the research findings show, online mainstream news Websites, although they are new media, have the power to reproduce political power mechanisms and social hierarchy, sometimes with even greater force than the traditional media. Examining the subject through the theoretical lenses of alternative media enables a crossing between new media and alternative media which enriches our analysis and deepens our understanding. It is possible to find a direct path linking the independent press, with its origins in the beginning of the 16th century, to the flourishing of radical fanzines in Europe throughout the 20th century and on to the establishment of alternative news Websites in the first decade of the 21st century (Harcup, 2003). This path indicates that the technology in and of itself is not sufficient to attain far-reaching developments, but that their political and social utilizations are the ones that turn the wheels of history.

The comparison between the current study's findings and Harcup's (2003) findings enable us to notice the great similarity among the two cases. This similarity can imply some kind of universal constancy and repetition with regard to the dynamics between alternative and mainstream media when they cover radical protest events that turn violent. In both of the studies, alternative media organizations chosen to give voice to those who are usually not heard – the protesters and the common people, who are not elite or establishment. Moreover, in both cases, alternative media organizations chose to use a thematic framing which presents broad context, sides with the protesters' claims and shows them in positive light, while strongly criticizing the establishment and the authorities. On the other hand, mainstream media organizations which follow the professional conventions chose to give prominence to the political and social elites and adopted their situation definition against the activists.

The findings regarding the Israeli mainstream media during the second Intifada in the current research is consistent with previous studies (Wolfsefeld et al., 2008; Liebes & Kampf, 2009). Yet, this research reveals a new angle, that has not been previously studied, namely the political content that is being published in the Israeli alternative news Websites. This chapter points out how unique this kind of political content is in the present Israeli media climate.

Furthermore, this research moves one step beyond where Hurcup left off and examines not only printed newspapers but also an addition medium- the Internet. The biggest differences between printed mainstream media and online mainstream media are the amount of the coverage and information published with regard to the Ni'lin's incidents. *tYedioth Ahronoth*, the largest Israeli printed newspaper, published a small number (22) of news items about Ni'lin in its print version, particularly when compared with its Web-based counterpart, *Ynet,* (both have the same owner but have different editorial staff) which published *11 times more* news items on the samc topic (240).

It is reasonable to assume that the key explanation for this tremendous gap is the physical limitation of space that forces the printed paper to be much more selective than the Web-based paper. At the time of this research, many other significant political events took place (the resignation of Prime Minister Olmert, his bribe investigation at the police was at its peak; the return to Israel of the bodies of two kidnapped Israeli soldiers; a visit from the future President Obama, etc.). These issues all received headlines and first page write-ups in the printed paper, which pushed back and, most of the time, also completely overshadowed the Ni'lin's issues. This finding is in the line with the claim that it is much easier to receive online media coverage than offline media coverage due to several reasons: no space limitations, enormous and constant demand for new items due to wild competition for online audiences, and rapid updates. The practical meaning of this to the protesters is encouraging.

Moreover, another interesting difference between online and offline media relates to the ways in which each format upholds the professional values of journalism – objectivity and balance between rivals. It was found that, unlike the online media, the printed newspaper did not always maintain the balance between the competing actors and opposing media frames in individual articles but the balance was kept at the level of the entire page. In other words, in the printed newspaper, sometimes there were several small articles which presented only one or two sources. These voices did not get any mention in the main article of the page. These small articles always added relevant information which related to the salient one. Therefore, to the best of the researcher's knowledge, this balancing technique is equivalent to the function that hyperlinks fulfill in the mainstream news Websites.

It is important to note the great variance between the ability of mainstream and alternative media to gain access to official documents; oftentimes these documents are not accessible to the alternative reporters. The best examples are the textual material of the confrontation between the officer and the shooting soldier, and the entire indictment itself as published in *Ynet.* This evidence, together with the differences regarding the amount of articles that each type of media produced, can support the claim that has often been raised, namely that the alternative media cannot be a true substitute to the mainstream media; rather it can only be a valuable and critical complementary.

Both traditional mainstream organizations and mainstream new media organizations played only a small role in organizing political protest, since they do not fill the same social and political functions as the alternative media organizations, traditional and new. These functions serve different circles within the organizations, the protest communities and the general public: keeping in touch with distant and dormant activists, recruiting activists (including new members), strengthening critical political consciousness, consolidating collective identity, creating solidarity among organizations, creating a technological infrastructure for an online issue network among protest organizations and additional alternative media Websites, using it as a preliminary platform for mainstream media and maintaining a stock of testimonies and documentation.

These functions point out that the alternative media, in its current reincarnation, remains rooted in certain social and political community contexts and it leverages the new technology in order to strengthen these ties. The dissatisfaction caused by the mainstream media and a wish to empower citizens continue to be the key motivation for using and maintain the alternative media platforms. All the potential functions that were identified in this research indicate that alternative news Websites can be valuable and beneficial tools for organizing political protest. Moreover, it is worthwhile to pay attention to the added value that exists in the technological development of the Internet, with its many possibilities, for organizing social protest. The Internet makes it much easier and more feasible to establish critical and autonomic mini-public spaces, such as alternative news Websites, blogs, message board etc. The Internet is also helping to overcome time and space gaps, saving time and manpower, and substantially lowering the cost of organization and protest operations. In this research, only one online platform has been examined - alternative news Websites. The simplicity of publishing materials, the remarkable accessibility to a global audience, and the minimal costs of using alternative news Websites make them attractive and worthwhile, especially for radical protest organizations.

From the qualitative content analysis of some of the publications on these Websites, one can learn about the political functions they fulfill throughout the entire protest organization process – from the information provision phase through the consciousness raising phase and up to the documentation phase. These functions are not exclusive for radical organizations, but they are mainly concerned with these organizations, for whom the route to mainstream media, either online or offline, is either blocked entirely or contains many obstacles.

A unique characteristic of the Internet is its ability to provide links between multiple information sources; it is this ability that endows the Internet with much of its unique potential to provide power for the weak actors of society, and especially for social change organizations. The vast difference between the links provided by the mainstream news Websites and the alternative news Websites is quite dramatic. While mainstream journalism zealously maintained its power, alternative journalism created solidarity, recognition, and sharing among many Websites of different nationalities, languages and fields of action (i.e., peace, human rights, media, etc.), and truly empowered the reader; it was not concerned with keeping the reader contained to a certain Website at all costs.

This study raises awareness of the research need for relating to theories that deal with alternative media while examining the roles of new media in organizing political protests in the 21st century. This research contribution is important for clarifying the distinction between the many existing online platforms and for deepening our understanding of this new fertile and fascinating field. The theoretical combination between the alternative media and the characteristics of the Internet medium, and the empirical findings of this research affirm the hypothesis that the Internet has become the ideal alternative media channel of our day. It seems that, in many ways, the computer keyboard, the mouse, and digital cameras have replaced the typewriter of the 1980s, as the "Kalashnikov" in the war for public opinion.

There are a lot of battlefields in the real world, but it seems that, in the 21st century, there is one more additional battlefield deep inside the online realm. Each side is not ready to give up; rather, they are preparing their best weapons for a war on public opinion that will last all the way to the winning scene.

ACKNOWLEDGMENT

The author would like to thank Azi Lev-On, Gadi Wolfsfeld, Karin Barzilai- Nahon, Tamar Plesner- Liebes and David Levin, for their helpful comments on earlier versions of this manuscript.

REFERENCES

Althaus, S. L., & Tewksbury, D. (2000). Patterns of internet and traditional news media use in a networked community. *Political Communication*, *17*, 21–45. doi:10.1080/105846000198495

Atton, C. (1999). A reassessment of the alternative press. *Media Culture & Society*, *21*(1), 51–76. doi:10.1177/016344399021001003

Atton, C. (2002). News cultures and new social movements: Radical journalism and the mainstream media. *Journalism Studies*, *3*(4), 491–505. doi:10.1080/14616700220000019209

Atton, C. (2003). What is `alternative' journalism? *Journalism*, *4*, 267–272. doi:10.1177/14648849030043001

Biddix, J. P., & Park, H. W. (2008). Online networks of student protest: The case of the living wage campaign. *New Media & Society*, *10*(6), 871–891. doi:10.1177/1461444808096249

Bowman, L. (2008). Re-examining gatekeeping. *Journalism Practice*, *2*(1), 99–112. doi:10.1080/17512780701768550

Bruns, A. (2005). *Gatewatching: Collaborative online news production*. New York: Peter Lang.

Bruns, A. (2008a). News blogs and citizen journalism: New directions for e-journalism. In *E-journalism: New directions in electronic news media*. New Delhi: BR Publishing.

Bruns, A. (2008b). The active audience: Transforming journalism from gatekeeping to gatewatching. In *Making online news: The ethnography of new media production*. New York: Peter Lang.

Burnett, R., & Marshall, P. D. (2003). *Web theory: An introduction*. New York: Routledge.

Cammaerts, B. (2006). Media and communication strategies of glocalized activists: Beyond media-centric thinking. In *Reclaiming the media: Communication rights and expanding democratic media roles*. Bristol, UK: Intellect.

Cohen, A. P. (1985). *The symbolic construction of community*. New York: Routledge. doi:10.4324/9780203323373

Deuze, M. (2003). The web and its journalisms: Considering the consequences of different types of newsmedia online. *New Media & Society*, *5*(2), 203–230. doi:10.1177/1461444803005002004

Dimaggio, P., Hargittai, E., Neuman, W. R., & Ronbinson, J. (2001). Social implications of the internet. *Annual Review of Sociology*, *27*, 307–336. doi:10.1146/annurev.soc.27.1.307

Dimitrova, D. V., Connolly-Ahern, C., Williams, A. P., Kaid, L. L., & Reid, A. (2003). Hyperlinking as gatekeeping: Online newspaper coverage of the execution of an American terrorist. *Journalism Studies*, *4*(3), 401–414. doi:10.1080/14616700306488

Domingo, D., Quand, T., Heinonen, A., Paulussen, S., Singer, J. B., & Vujnovic, M. (2008). Participatory journalism practices in the media and beyond. *Journalism Practice*, *2*(3), 326–342. doi:10.1080/17512780802281065

Downing, J. (1984). *Radical media: The political experience of alternative communication*. Boston: South End Press.

Downing, J. (1988). The alternative public realm: The organization of the 1980s anti-nuclear press in West Germany and Britain. *Media Culture & Society, 10*, 163–181. doi:10.1177/016344388010002003

Downing, J., Villarreal Ford, T., Gil, G., & Stein, L. (2001). *Radical media: Rebellious communication and social movements*. Thousand Oaks, CA: Sage.

Ericson, R. V., Baranek, P. M., & Chan, J. B. L. (1989). *Negotiation control: A study of news sources*. Milton Keynes, UK: Open University Press.

Eveland, W. P., & Dunwoody, S. (2001). User control and structural isomorphism or disorientation and cognitive load? Learning from the web versus print. *Communication Research, 28*, 48–78. doi:10.1177/009365001028001002

Forde, S., Foxwell, K., & Meadows, M. (2003). Through the lens of the local: Public arena journalism in the Australian community broadcasting sector. *Journalism, 4*, 314–335. doi:10.1177/14648849030043004

Galtung, J., & Ruge, M. (1965). The structure of foreign news. *Journal of Peace Research, 1*, 64–90. doi:10.1177/002234336500200104

Gamson, W., & Wolfsfeld, G. (1993). Movements and media as interacting system. *The Annals of the American Academy of Political and Social Science, 582*, 114–125. doi:10.1177/0002716293528001009

Gibton, D. (2001). Grounded theory method: The meaning of data analysis process and the theory building in qualitative research. In *Genres and traditions in qualitative research*. Tel-Aviv, Israel: Devir.

Gitlin, T. (1980). *The whole world is watching-Media in the making and the unmaking of the new left*. Berkeley, CA: University of California Press.

Glaser, B., & Strauss, A. L. (1967). *The discovery of grounded theory*. Chicago: Aldine.

Gordon, U. (2010). Against the wall: Anarchist mobilization in the Israeli–Palestinian conflict. *Peace and Change, 35*(3), 412–433. doi:10.1111/j.1468-0130.2010.00641.x

Hall, S., Critcher, C., Jefferson, T., Clarke, J., & Roberts, B. (1978). *Policing the crisis: Mugging the state and law and order*. London: Macmillan.

Hamilton, J., & Atton, C. (2001). Theorizing Anglo-American alternative media: Toward a contextual history and analysis of US and UK scholarship. *Media History, 7*(2), 119–135. doi:10.1080/13688800120092200

Harcup, T. (2003). The unspoken – said: The journalism of alternative media. *Journalism, 4*(3), 356–376. doi:10.1177/14648849030043006

Hartley, J. (1982). *Understanding news*. London: Routledge.

Hertog, J.K., & MecLeod, D.M. (1995). Anarchists wreak havoc in downtown Minneapolis: A multi-level study of media coverage of radical protest. *Journalism & Mass Communication Monographs, 151*.

Kampf, R. (1993). *The searching after the cracks in the wall: The attempts to promote feminist issues in the Israeli media*. (MA Thesis). Hebrew University, Jerusalem, Israel.

Kovarick, B. (2002). *Web design for the mass media*. Boston: Allyn & Bacon.

Lai-Yee Ma, M. (2005). *The internet as a social movement agent: A case study on the youth online forum*. Paper presented at the Digital Content and Technology Conference for the Graduate Students in Asia. Retrieved 28 December 2012 from http://www.docin.com/p-58500323.html

Lambert, S. (2007). To post or not to post: Gatekeeping effects of breaking news on internet newspaper websites. In *Proceedings of International Symposium on Online Journalism*. Retrieved 28 December 2012 from http://online.journalism.utexas.edu/2007/papers/Lambert.pdf

Lehman-Wilzig, S. (2007). The end of the traditional printed newspaper: Factors of online journalism that threaten traditional printed journalism. In *Online newspapers in Israel*. Tel-Aviv, Israel: The Israel Democracy Institute and Burda Center for Innovative Communications.

Liebes, T. (1997). *Reporting the Arab Israeli conflict: How hegemony works*. London: Routledege. doi:10.4324/9780203180457

Liebes, T., & Kampf, Z. (2009). From black and white to shades of gray: Palestinians in the Israeli media during the second intifada. *The International Journal of Press/Politics*, *14*(4), 434–453. doi:10.1177/1940161209336226

Manning, P. (2001). *News and news sources: A critical introduction*. London: Sage.

McAdams, M., & Berger, S. (2001). Hypertext. *Journal of Electronic Publishing*, *6*(3). doi:10.3998/3336451.0006.301

Melucci, A. (1996). *Challenging codes: Collective action in the information age*. Cambridge, UK: Cambridge University Press. doi:10.1017/CBO9780511520891

Owens, L., & Palmer, L. K. (2003). Making the news: Anarchist counter-public relations on the world wide web. *Critical Studies in Media Communication*, *20*(4), 335–361. doi:10.1080/07393180320001 42007

Paletz, D. L., & Entman, R. M. (1981). *Media power politics*. New York: Free Press.

Park, H. W., & Thelwall, M. (2003). Hyperlink analyses of the world wide web: A review. *Journal of Computer-Mediated Communication*, *8*(4).

Peng, F., Yeuh, T., Naphtali, I., & Xiaoming, H. (1999). Trends in online newspapers: A look at the U.S. web. *Newspaper Research Journal*, *20*(2), 52–64.

Peterson, A. (2001). *Contemporary political protester: Essays on political militancy*. Ashgate, UK: Hampshire.

PEW- Project for Excellence in Journalism. (2007). *The latest news headlines—Your vote counts*. Retrieved 28 December 2012 from http://www.journalism.org/sites/journalism.org/files/usernewspdf_0.pdf

Pickard, V. (2006). Assessing the radical democracy of Indymedia: Discursive, technical, and institutional constructions. *Critical Studies in Media Communication*, *23*(1), 19–38. doi:10.1080/07393180600570691

Pickerill, J. (2003a). *Cyberprotest: Environmental activism online*. Manchester, UK: Manchester University Press.

Pickerill, J. (2003b). *Out in the open: Indymedia networks in Australia*. Paper presented at the Information, Communication and Society Symposium. Oxford, UK.

Platon, S., & Deuze, M. (2003). Indymedia journalism a radical way of making, selecting and sharing news? *Journalism*, *4*(3), 336–355. doi:10.1177/14648849030043005

Reich, Z. (2008). How citizens create news stories: The ''news access'' problem reversed. *Journalism Studies*, *9*(5), 739–758. doi:10.1080/14616700802207748

Rodriguez, C. (2001). *Fissures in the mediascape: An international study of citizens' media*. Cresskill, NJ: Hampton.

Rogers, R. (2004). *Information politics on the web*. Cambridge, MA: MIT Press.

Rogers, R., & Ben-David, A. (2008). The Palestinian–Israeli peace process and transnational issue networks: The complicated place of the Israeli NGO. *New Media & Society*, *10*(3), 497–528. doi:10.1177/1461444807085321

Rogers, R., & Marres, N. N. (2000). Landscaping climate change: A mapping technique for understanding science and technology debates on the world wide web. *Public Understanding of Science (Bristol, England)*, *9*(2), 141–163. doi:10.1088/0963-6625/9/2/304

Ross, A. (1999). *No sweat*. New York: Verso.

Ryan, C. (1991). *Prime time activism: Media strategies for grassroots organizing*. Boston: South End Press.

Salter, L. (2003). Democracy, new social movements, and the internet: A Habermasian analysis. In *Cyberactivism: Online activism in theory and practices*. New York: Routledge.

Saunders, B. J. (2007). From indymedia to indyjournalism– How indymedia is evolving. In *Proceedings of Our Media - the 6th International OURMedia Conference (OM6)*. Sydney, Australia. Retrieved 28 December 2012 from http://eprints.qut.edu.au/10902/1/10902.pdf

Shumate, M., & Dewitt, L. (2008). The north/south divide in NGO hyperlink networks. *Journal of Computer-Mediated Communication*, *13*, 405–428. doi:10.1111/j.1083-6101.2008.00402.x

Shumate, M., & Lipp, J. (2008). Connective collective action online: An examination of the hyperlink network structure of an NGO issue network. *Journal of Computer-Mediated Communication*, *14*, 178–201. doi:10.1111/j.1083-6101.2008.01436.x

Singer, J. B. (2005). The political J-blogger. *Journalism*, *6*(2), 173–198. doi:10.1177/1464884905051009

Stengrim, L. (2005). Negotiating postmodern democracy, political activism, and knowledge production: Indymedia's grassroots and e-savvy answer to media oligopoly. *Communication and Critical. Cultural Studies*, *2*(4), 281–304.

Taylor, V., & Whittier, N. E. (1992). Collective identity in social movement communities: Lesbian feminist mobilization. In *Frontiers in social movement theory*. New Haven, CT: Yale University Press.

van de Donk, W., Loader, B. D., Nixon, P. G., & Rucht, D. (2004). Introduction social movements and ICTs. In *Cyberprotest: New media, citizens and social movements*. London: Routledge.

Van Dijk, T. A. (1996). Power and news media. In *Political communication in action- states, institutions, movements, audiences*. Hampton Press.

Van Zoonen, L. (1996). A dance of death: New social movements and mass media. In *Political communication in action- States, institutions, movements, audiences*. Hampton Press.

Vedel, T. (2003). Political communication in the age of the internet. In *Political communication in the new era: A cross national prespective*. London: Routledge.

Wolfsfeld, G. (1991). Media, protest and political violence. *Journalism & Mass Communication Monographs, 127*.

Wolfsfeld, G. (1997). *Media and political conflict: News from the Middle East*. Cambridge, UK: Academic Press.

Wolfsfeld, G., Frosh, P., & Awabdy, T. M. (2008). *Ethnocentric news of violent conflict: Journalistic mechanism for covering the second Intifada on Israeli, Plaestinian and Al-Jazeera television*. Paper presented at the Annual Meeting of the International Communication Association. New York, NY.

Yoon, Y. (2005). Legitimacy, public relation, and media access: Proposing and testing a media access model. *Communication Research*, *32*(6), 762–793. doi:10.1177/0093650205281081

KEY TERMS AND DEFINITIONS

Alternative Media Origination: An organization that is not published by a commercial group and is not motivated by profit. In its essence, it deal with subjects and expose opinions that do not receive continuous coverage in the mainstream media. It expresses the agendas, opinions, intents and problems of minority groups (either political or social).

Anarchists against the Wall: A direct action group that stands for radical anarchist principles covering a variety of issues and presents itself as radically politically-left with respect to the Israeli-Palestinian conflict.

Grounded Theory Method: The method was developed in the 1960s by two sociologists: Barney Glaser and Anselm Strauss. According to this method human behaviors have consistent patterns and it is possible to discover these patterns through a systematic and gradual process, so the researcher should look for ideas and arguments that are consistently repeated in the data.

Media Frame: The overall meaning that the media origination constructs to event, group or a person using linguistic, rhetoric and visual tools.

News Website: Website that presents items related to public affairs, and contains selected information on current events.

Qualitative Content Analysis: A research method that exams linguistic and rhetorical components of texts and which the researcher is the main tool for gathering and analyzing the data.

Second Intifada (also Known as the Al-Aqsa Intifada): Was the second Palestinian uprising – a period of intensified Palestinian–Israeli violence, which began in late September 2000 and ended in 2005.

ENDNOTES

1 On July 7, 2008 an Israeli soldier was filmed by a young Palestinian woman shooting a cuffed and blindfolded Palestinian man with a rubber bullet from point-blank range, as a regiment commander is holding the detainee. The Palestinian - Ashraf Abu Rahchma - was arrested for his participation in a violent demonstration against the construction of the Separation Fence. The bullet hit the ground next to Abu- Rahchma's leg and he was injured slightly from a ricochet in his thumb. On July 19, 2008 the video was distributed by B'Tselem, an Israeli human rights organization, and was broadcast by all of the major Israeli media organizations, evoking a national scandal and a public debate. The military court decided to charge the soldier and the officer with the very moderate offense of "inappropriate behavior" and the punishment for the officer was to move him to a different role. Follow this ruling, several Israeli human rights organizations petitioned the Israeli Supreme Court to change the indictment. On July 1, 2009 the Israeli Supreme Court accepted this petition. In the verdict the Supreme Court announced that there was no correlation between the criminal offense and the subsequent indictment and ordered a new indictment. The Supreme Court also rejected the claim that the video had been manipulated. On September 24, 2009 the

Military Advocate General's Corps submitted a new indictment, as requested. In January 2011 the Supreme Court announced its final verdict. It is important to note that this was the first time that the Israeli Supreme Court had interfered with the judgment of the Military Advocate General's Corps.

2 Yoon (2005) discussed five dimensions which examine the level of legitimacy attributable to any given news source: *the level of legality of the organization* – to what extent does the organization accept the rules, the values and the accepted norms of the society and its' social/political systems. This acceptance endows the organization with the right to exist. *The appreciation dimension* – what level of support and sympathy does the organization receive; *The validity dimension* – can the organization obtain its goals (this dimension includes the expertise aspect, the political influence ability, the ability to gain allies and the financial aspect); *The continuity dimension* – to what extent does the organization survive over time, and how faithful and obligated are its adherents. The fifth dimension is the *reliability dimension* – whether the organization is reliable as a source of information and to what extent does it give real, precise and complete information

3 The conditions are: 1) some ideological proximity of the media organization itself to the protestors' worldview, or at the very least, a lack of opposition to the protestors' worldview; and 2) certain journalists who endorse the political campaign fostered by the protesting organizations (these reporters have a lot of power since, through their selection and presentation of sources from among the protesters as legitimate sources and their provision of relatively high visibility to the protestors' claims, they practically break the rhetorical closure of the dominant meaning frame, and present a more complex reality). Namely, there is importance to both the general agenda of the media organizations as well as to the opinions of the reporter. It is very important to note that even if there is first-hand coverage, or a personal witness by an activist, the viewpoint will not be wholly "native," since the reporter must strike a balance between his commitment to his profession and his sympathy to the protest.

4 The network was founded in 1999 in response to the biased coverage of the protests against the WTO by the mainstream media. It contributed to the development of software, newsrooms' models, revolutionary news practices and the enhancement of independent media. While on the one hand, Indymedia as a *network* was sometimes involved in political and personal disputes and organizational paralyzation, as a *model*, Indymedia, along with its basic values, is successful and has been imitated by many initiatives of independent media around the world (Saunders, 2007; Platon & Deuze, 2003; Stengrim, 2005; Pickard, 2006, Pickerill, 2003a; 2003b).

5 Rogers, Richard and Anat Ben-David. 2010. Coming to Terms: A Conflict Analysis of the Usage, in Official and Unofficial Sources, of 'Security Fence,' 'Apartheid Wall,' and other Terms for the Structure between Israel and the Palestinian Territories. Media, Conflict & War, 2, 3, 2010.

Chapter 8
The Pit Head Baths are Now an Internet Café:
The Role of Technology in Transforming Audience, Institutions, and Power Structures among Women in Wales

Jonathan Bishop
Centre for Research into Online Communities and E-Learning Systems, Belgium

ABSTRACT

The coal fields communities in Wales were once one of the most prosperous places to live in the British Isles. Many people flocked to Wales in search of a new life and opportunities for their family. Coal became known as "Black Gold" and the industrialized coal fields became centres of productivity. Media use in Welsh households has generally been controlled by dominating men who saw and in many cases still see themselves as the "heads of the household." Such control over the media consumption of women was not out of place in the UK as a whole, where men have assumed a place as a de facto media institution who force choices of what to watch on their households. This chapter presents a longitudinal study of three women in Wales conducted between 2000 and 2013 that shows how the media consumption and audience styles have changed over time so that power structures from both men and traditional media institutions have all but eroded.

INTRODUCTION

In its history Wales has experienced two main increases in its product possibility frontier. The first influx of potential labour into Wales was during the Roman conquest of Britain. The native Britons in England fled to Wales for safety, hence the country being named 'Wales' by the invaders with the first three letters 'Wal' coming from German, meaning 'people who knew the Romans'. The next major influx was during the mining revolution, when people came from England and other parts of the world to work in the pits to provide a better life for themselves and their family. Wales might be seen as having a power and ideological structure of a perpetual capitalist

DOI: 10.4018/978-1-4666-6038-0.ch008

Copyright © 2014, IGI Global. Copying or distributing in print or electronic forms without written permission of IGI Global is prohibited.

hegemony in which members of a community are always seeking the power of the bourgeois and yet have only the competence of an unskilled member of the proletariat. Whether it be down to trade union or socialist party branches that have a chairman or president who is in control over members whom they command the attention of at committee or other meetings, there is never a shortage of persons willing to lead so that they can wield. Many people in Wales will identify proudly as being 'working class,' and of being socialist, something which often results in the election of Labour Party politicians who claim to be the party of the working-class, whilst other socialist parties claim the same. Perhaps unfortunately for them, such people do not realize that this form of socialism is seen by media studies scholars as a response to a lack of power and ownership that creates a sense of solidarity in poverty that would not exist if members of that group got the power and ownership they seek ideologically through their calls for nationalization and state-led public ownership in general (Branston & Stafford, 2010).

It has been a generally held view that 'old media' such as television and radio have been far more successful technologies than newspapers in terms of how people in Wales interface with the media (Thomas, 2006). However, the post-credit crunch world has seen many surges in apparent disorder from some of the youngest people in society. Whether they are 'smart-mobs' as envisaged by Rheingold (2003) or the "thugs" as described by the media following the 2010 UK riots, it is clear that there is a lot of discontent among the young in today's world. Threats by young users of Facebook to draw the UK riots to the South Wales cities of Cardiff and Swansea may not have materialized, but shows the impact social networking services and other Internet services can have on law and order in communities beyond the screens on which the messages are displayed. Government investment in former coalfields communities, many of which have severe poverty has however assumed that the Internet is the key to reversing poverty and therefore crime. Estimates of the value of investment in community buildings by the Welsh Government ranges from £150,000 to almost £1.5 million for a new purpose-built community centre that include IT suites, community cafés, and Internet lounges (Holtom, 2007). Internet cafes are widespread, relatively cheap and allow individuals and small businesses access to the Internet without the need to own and maintain a computer (Casany, Alier, Mayol, Conde, & García-Peñalvo, 2013). The common held view that one should not move services online because "what about those who can't afford it" is nonsense as all communities are now connected to the Internet in some form. Those 'poor people' who claim welfare benefits often rely on mobile Internet connectivity as home phones and Internet connections are a low priority due to their often excessive costs. Even with increased access to the Internet, a 'collective memory' of coal mining and its tie with the identity of the working classes (of which many young people in Wales still identify with) act to make poverty acceptable (Housley, Moles, & Smith, 2009). This has included an acceptance that the man in the household somehow has the right to control what was watched on a household's television. As this paper shows, increased access to the Internet has transformed this power structure so that women are able to choose which media to access without interference from controlling men.

CHANGING AUDIENCES AND DISCOURSES AMONG WOMEN

When the study of women is usually engaged there are often comparisons made with men. This is not something this paper intends to do as this would commit what the author calls the 'society fallacy.' The society fallacy dicates that it is abserd to think that a survey of a small sample of people can be generalized to a wider population. In contrast the 'ecological principle' is advocated, which is that studying a group of people is only helpful to the point of identifying commonalities between its members in order to determine the individual aspects of those within that group through eliminating those attributes that are common among them. On this basis the paper sees the women who participated in this study as having their own identity and other factors that separate them – such as age and media consumption – are investigated in place of comparing them with men. The research of women should involve more understanding of the commonalities amoung women as separate from their individual differences as humans, rather than deny that there is more to being a woman than being female.

There can easily be considered to be differences in languages between older and younger generations, whether in women or otherwise, but similarities also exist (Bishop, 2011a). Sometimes there can be a surge in use of shared discourses between the various audiences within generations. For instance, with the advent of the iPad the term 'tablet' is now an accepted term among all generations, whereas prior to this it was expected to mean medication to that point that there would be shock if one said one had lost one's tablet. The power structures relating to the way women use the media in Wales can therefore be expected to change as new technology is adopted, but this is not necessarily a given (Loader, 2004). The main barriers to the Internet penetration in women social life have been found to be employment, education and income (Novo-Corti, Varela-Candamio, & García-Álvarez, 2013), even though the benefits for women of using the Internet for things such as social support are well known (O'Mahen et al., 2013).

The Online Misogynism and Other Abuse of Women in Wales: Considering Flame Trolling

It has been said in many contexts that in order for true equality to exist then incompetent women will be sitting on the same platform as incompetent men – implying that only competent women get into powerful positions whereas this is not the case with men. Social media platforms like Twitter has made the abuse of competent women by incompetent men even more possible. In 2013 a high profile feminist campaigner, Caroline Ciardo Perez, who was not from Wales, faced rape threats from a group of people called 'trolls' following her publicly advocating having more women on banknotes. This is a type of bullying online called 'flame trolling,' which is the posting of provocative messages online in order to offend others. This is carried out by what are called 'flame trollers' who are often referred to in the media as 'trolls', and is becoming more common in Wales (Bishop, 2012). The concept of trolls has typically been understood to reflect a group of young people, and more generally people of other ages, who use the Internet to harass others (Phillips, 2011), but this is now known not to be the case.

The use of the term 'troll' in this context in the mass media probably became popularized by the media in the 2010s (Bishop, 2014), even though it existed much earlier, including with its present meaning (Herring, Job-Sluder, Scheckler, & Barab, 2002). Originally the term referred to people who posted messages online to entertain others in a more friendly way (Jansen & James, 2002). Not everyone appreciated 'the joke', but it was more generally good natured than what the term has come to mean today (Bishop, 2014).

CONSIDERING THE ROLE OF GENRE AND CHARACTER IN THE DIGITAL AGE

Online communities can easily be seen to have unique qualities that make them fit into particular genres, and this can affect how anti-social trajectories and the associated transgressive humour are manifested in them. Bishop (2009) presents a model based on an empirical study of the different genres of online communities (Table 1).

Table 1. Advantages and disadvantages of different types of online community genre

Genre	Advantages/Disadvantages
Personal Homepage	Advantages: Regularly updated, allows people to connect with those that they know through leaving messages and joining circle of friends. Disadvantage: Members often need to re-register for each site and cannot usually take their 'Circle of Friends' with them.
Message Boards	Advantages: Posts can be accessed at any time. Easy to ignore undesirable content. Disadvantages: Threads can become very long and reading through the messages is time consuming.
Email Lists and Newsletters	Advantages: Allows a user to receive a message as soon as it is sent. Disadvantages: Cannot always access an archive of messages.
Chat Groups	Advantages: Synchronous. Users can communicate in real-time. Disadvantages: Posts can be sent simultaneously and the user can become lost in the conversation.
Virtual Worlds	Advantages: 3D metaphors allow a user to get more involved in the community. Disadvantages: Requires certain hardware and software that not all users have.
Weblogs and Directories	Advantages: Easily updated, regular content. Disadvantages: Members can't start topics only respond to them.
Wikis and Hypertext Fiction	Advantages: Can allow for collaborative work on literary projects. Disadvantages: Can bring out the worst in people, such as their destructive natures.

Original genres like the personal homepage have now been transposed into social networking services as 'profile pages' which are linked together more often than not through the circle of friends social networking technology. Message Boards are also a common type of online community, composed of threads of discussions that can often be started by any member of the community. Email lists and newsletters are flexible online communities that people can easily join, leave and participate in using only their email account. Chat groups can take many forms and usually allow the instant sending of a message for others to respond to immediately. Virtual worlds also allow for fluid interactions and users can often fashion a particular character for themselves. Weblogs and directories have a particular structure that makes then distinct from other online community genres. Finally Wikis and Hypertext fiction are unique in that it is often possible for someone to create a new page to add to the existing ones and in the case of Wikis it is often possible for others to edit these pages, even if they have been posted by others.

Personal Homepages

The social networking service Facebook was at the time of writing one of the most popular Website of its kind. MySpace and Friendster used to be one of the most effective implementations of the circle of friends method for linking personal homepages of friends to one another. One can see Facebook as having been no different to a GeoCities Website, except it requires little skill for users to set up a personal home page and link it to their friends. Even Facebook's innovative 'Facebook Apps' platform is little different from what CGI scripts and Java applets were in the day of Geocities, and the Wall little different from a Guestbook.

Wikis and Hypertext Fiction: The Case of Wikipedia

Wikipedia is a social media Website where theoretically anyone can participate. In reality it is mainly a close group of people who control specific pages, locking out anyone with a different opinion to them. It shares similarities with hypertext fiction in that it can be extended and changed by anyone in its various forms. Wikipedia is far from the ideal form of online community due to its editors using pseudonyms to help conceal their conflicts of interest in an article.

Chat Groups: The Case of Twitter

One might think of Twitter as a 'micro-blogging' platform, and in fact this has been suggested by others (Bishop, 2009; Yang & Chen-Burger, 2012). However if one looks at the genre of chat groups, which is the instantaneous exchange of opinions with one or more other people then Twitter starts to look less like a blogging platform. On a blog, as pointed out by Bishop (2009) posts can only be started by the blog owner for others to comment on. On Twitter it is possible for anyone to start a conversation with anyone, simply by typing their user name prefixed with a '@', such as @ Imogen_Thomas, making it more like the typical chat platform (Figallo, 1998; Figallo, 1998; Kim, 2000; Preece, 2000). The freedom to start posts directly at any person has been a particular challenge for women using Twitter. In 2013 a number of feminist campigners were set upon via Twitter by those whom may have felt threatened by the equal voice of women in society. For instance a feminist writer who wanted to see more women on banknotes – Caroline Criado Perez – was sent a number of abusive comments relating to rape. Such comments are common in relation to attacks on women by a group of trolls called 'Haters' (Bishop, 2013; Faye, 2012). Alternatively it could be seen as being part of a wider trend of those who share the characteristic of the persons they are advocating rights for being targeted by 'U r Bias trolls' who dislike such posts. This may be likely as R.I.P Trolling is done by those Haters who despise the insincerity that occupies many memorial Website that have sentiments expressed by persons who never knew the deceased (Walter, Hourizi, Moncur, & Pitsillides, 2011).

Weblogs and Directories

As discussed in the previous section, a Weblog is defined by having a single or small group of people who can initiate a discussion for others to comment on. This is similar to directories, such as e-commerce Websites, where the e-tailer lists products they are offering and invites other to comment on them. An unfortunate fact about women bloggers is that many women use them to stand up for women and women's rights (Antunovic & Hardin, 2013) as opposed to them being a person with worthwhile opinions who is equal to other women and not just in relation to men.

A similar problem exists if one considers Weblogs and directories as a whole. It has been shown how women discover Weblogs as instruments to design care givers' directories, instructing what family members or friends can come to visit, wash, cook or clean at a set day of the week (Altena & Ngwenya, 2012). The sterotyping of women as homemakers, even just within research studies, is seemingly not something that appears to be abating. There is the concept of 'mommy blogs,' which refer to blogs by men or women that relate to family and local community issues (Bishop, 2009; Bishop, 2011b; Powell, 2010).

The directory considered in this section is Yahoo!Answers. This social networking platform allows people to ask and answer questions on any topic for those other users of the Website to answer. As can be seen from the image in the left of the questions asked about Wales are often typical of the stereotype of it being a coal mining country which had a troubled relationship with the Prime Minister Margaret Thatcher.

Equally users of Yahoo!Answers take to more direct forms of transgressive humour, such as making offensive jokes about Welsh people and asking others to join in with suggestions, as can be seen from the image on the right of Figure 1. References to "shagging sheep" the all too common abuse of Welsh people surface often as a normal course of activity. Few complaints are

Figure 1. Transgressive humour on Yahoo!Answers

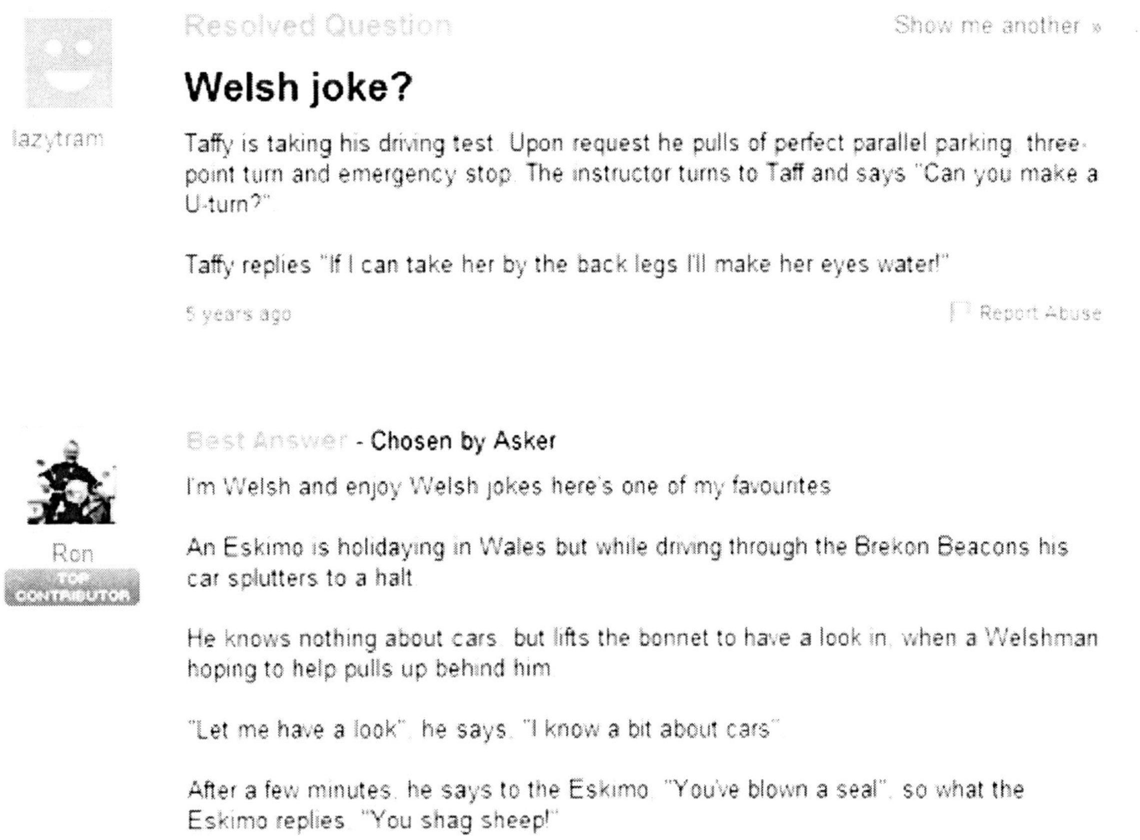

ever made, perhaps legitimizing transgressive humour like this.

Looking at Figure 2, one can see a discussion on teenage suicides in Bridgend, which the responder confirms to the questioner is being whipped up by the media. The answerer then makes a transgressive jibe about the area by saying there must be a virus in the air that is making teens suicidal.

Message Boards

Message boards as a genre of Web-based community characterized by the fact that anyone can start a thread and also anyone can respond (Bishop, 2009). The lack of equality among women in relation to message boards is similar to other platforms. It has been found in particular that many men are querying, correcting and attacking the terms and priorities of these women-organised bulletin boards that many women have complained that the climate is too hostile for them and they have withdrawn as subscribers (McSporran & Young, 2001). It is also unfortunate that those members of message boards that are men tend to receive more messages and messages containing more words and that men control topic discussion even in women-related and bulletin boards (Seward, Harvey, & Carranza, 2009).

One highly spoken about messageboards known for sexism us the 4chan Website (Knuttila, 2011), which is located at www.4chan.org). 4chan is built around a message board format where users are asked to anonymously submit abusive images and others for comment by others

Figure 2. Further transgressive humour on Yahoo!Answers

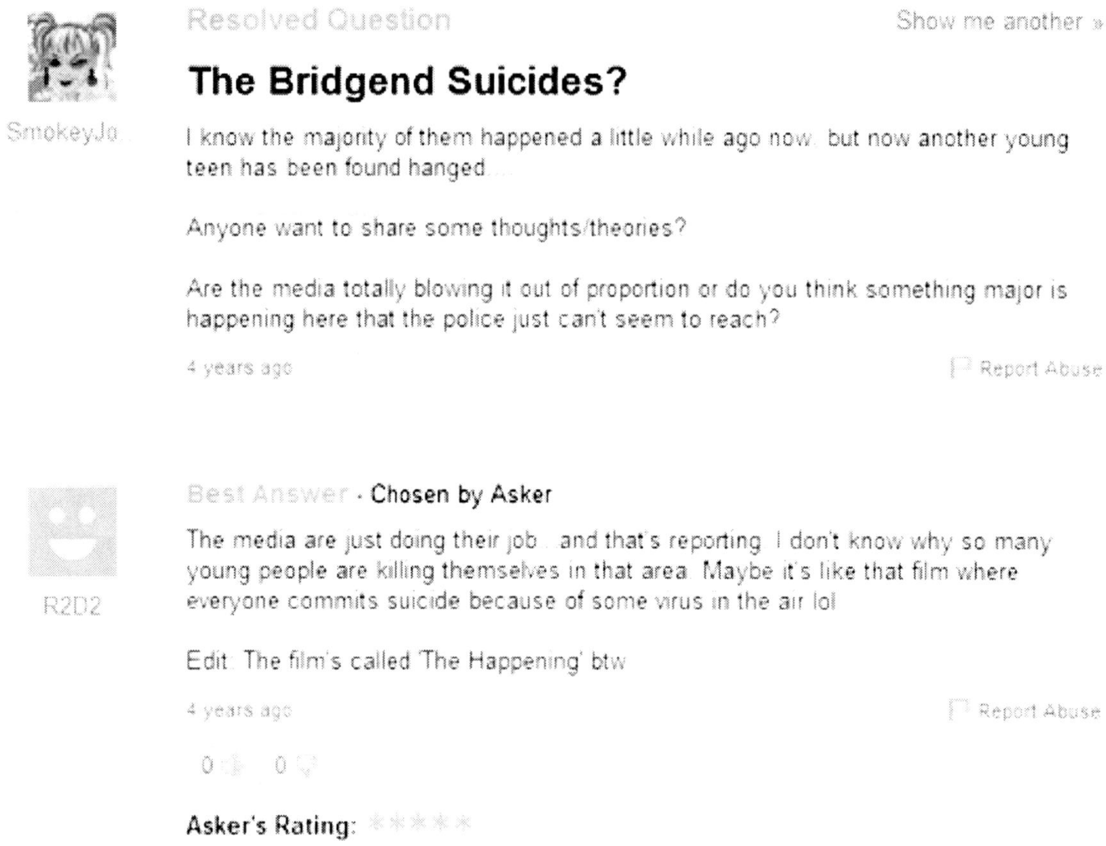

as a kind of anti-social empathy platform. Their abuse was at some of its worst following the death of pop star Michael Jackson, where emotional discussions were the norm on the Website (Schweitzer & Garcia, 2010). In terms of coal mining and people from Wales many of the posts were derogatory. For instance, countries reliant on coal were portrayed as being 'backwards' and Welsh people were treated less favourably. In terms of coal mining and people from Wales in general many of the posts were derogatory. As can be seen from Figure 3, the reactions to the Bridgend suicides discussed in the last section could be considered insensitive at least.

Newsletters and Discussion Lists

Newsletters and Discussion Lists are quite similar and have a shared background. Once it was very common for Websites to keep users up-to-date with what was going on in the online community by sending them emails with summaries of activities. Because of how email was once popular, discussion lists came about where people would send

Figure 3. 4chan reaction to Bridgend suicides

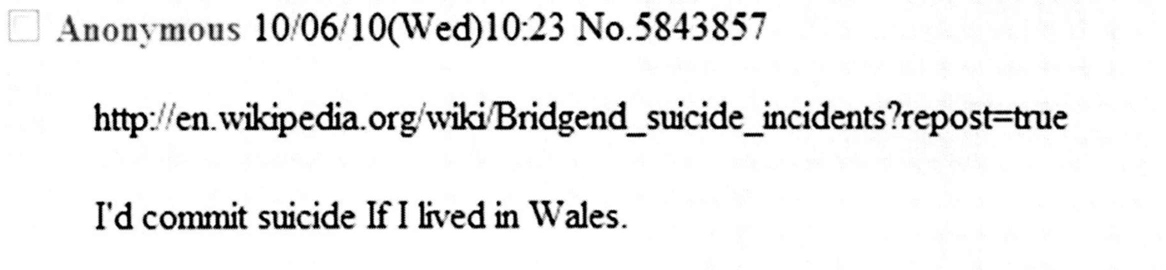

emails to an email address which then sends that email out to a number of other email addresses registered on the server.

Those platforms that are both newsletters and discussion lists – newsgroups – have been somewhat liberating for women who meet with other women from their own and other cultures (Piela, 2013). This is particularly the case in Islamic societies where women are prevented from fully understanding the teachings of Mohammed because of men who oppose the equal treatment advocated him in the Qu'ran (Piela, 2013).

Email Lists, newsletters, and indeed newsgroups, have spawned a degree of flame trolling where with the immediacy of email people can post abusive replies as soon as they receive it. The most popular was at one point Usenet, but with the advent of the Web-based eGroups, later taken over by Yahoo! the accessibility of this platform improved. Today it is possible to access these Usenet groups from Google, and this section will now look at some of the representations of Wales in them.

As can be seen in the thread on the left of Figure 4, the flame troller on this thread is trying to make light of the fact that many Welsh people are on low wages and are having to work hard to obtain them. This type of transgressive humour can cause self-esteem issues, as people are likely to feel a lack of worth and importance essential to motivation (Brown, Jackson, & Cassidy, 2006; Cassidy, Brown, & Jackson, 2013).

In the picture on the right of Figure 4 it is possible to see that on Usenet especially not all narratives are of an abusive nature, especially to the Welsh. The poster in this cases identifies with the plight of the miners who died at Gleision Colliery after their memorial pages were ransacked by flame trollers. This is an emerging response to transgressive humour, where users of the Internet do not always see it as a justifiable form of participation but seek fair and responsible interactions.

A LONGITUDINAL CASE STUDY INTO THREE WOMEN MEDIA USERS LIVING IN WALES

As has been shown in the previous section, different types of online community genre have had different effects on how Wales is represented in new media. The earlier discussion of the discourses in relation to how media consumption in households was once dominated by the decisions of men who see themselves as the 'head of the household,' is relevant when considering the impact of their behaviour on others in a household such as women and young people. This section presents a longitudinal study of women in Wales as media consumers and producers, evaluating the effect of the Internet and various online community genres have on challenging the dominance of men in Welsh households.

Figure 4. A post about Wales in Google Groups (Usenet)

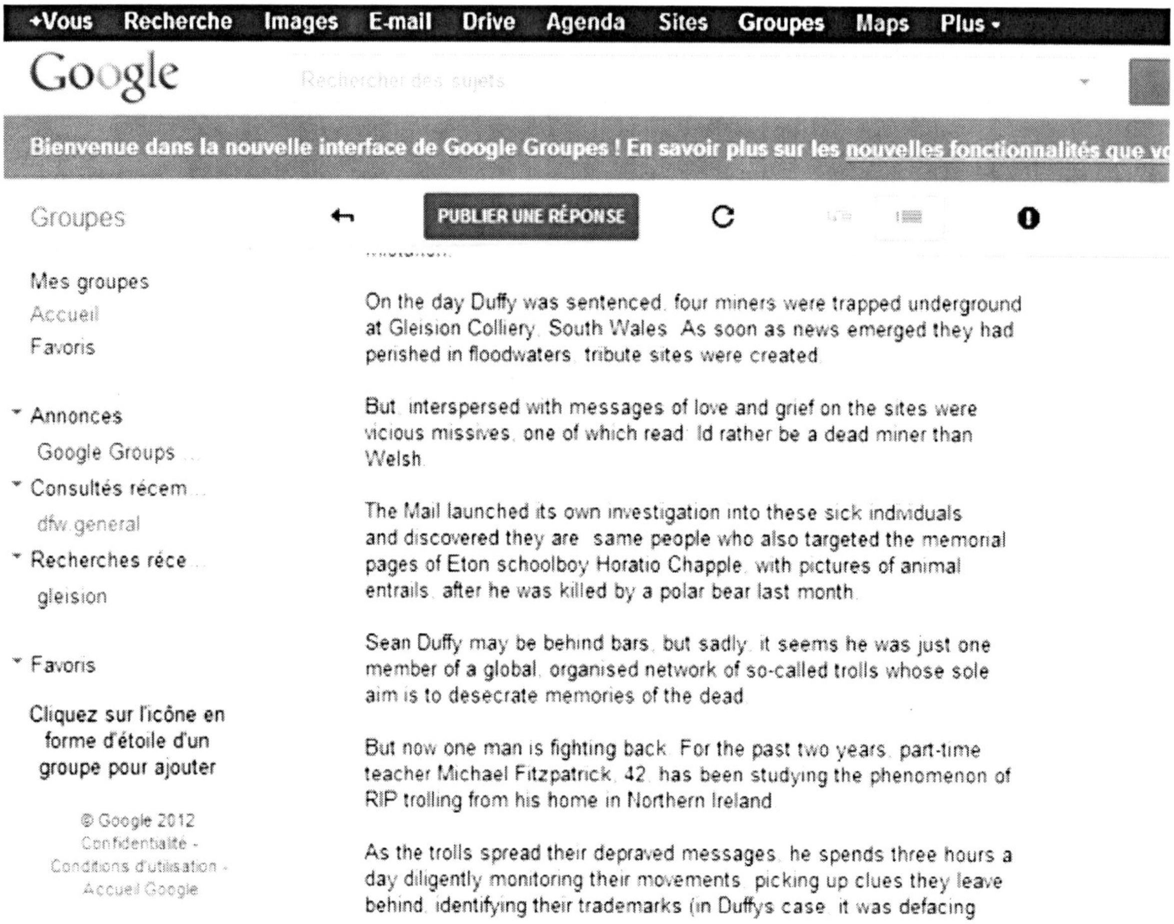

Participants

Three female participants took part in the study, all in different age groups and from different socioeconomic backgrounds. They were selected from a convenience sample of women known to the author. Whilst this might result in a bias on the part of the author and participants, it could be seen as being more likely that evidence could be collected at both stages in the longitudinal study. Choosing only women means gender issues can be excluded on the basis of the ecological principle which is that by finding out what a particular stratum have in common, it is possible to eliminate these to find out their individual differences.

Person G described herself as a "singer/songwriter" who is "influenced by styles like Latin, pop, soul, r'n'b, rock, contemporary, which she has been able to combine on her demo." She said her music "is a mixture of many different styles, which makes the music more outstanding and diverse." Person G was of mixed ethnic origin and was around 20 when she was first interviewed and in her thirties when her media participation was followed up. Person M comes from an Afro-Carribean background and was born in Wales. Following the first study Person M completed a first class honours degree and was successfully admitted onto a funded doctoral programme, which she later withdrew from. Person J was from a middle-class background, who was aged in her 50s during the first part of the study and in her 60s during the second. Her race was of a Caucaisan basis and she identified with being 'White.'

Methodology and Methods

An overall method of narrative and discourse analysis was chosen. A number of data collection methods were used with the three women. These included direct interviews and analysis of documents they produced on the Internet for public consumption. Narrative analysis is a qualitative research strategy that stems from the recognition of the extent to which the stories that people tell provide insight into their experiences (O'Donnell et al., 2013). Narrative analysis is an effective method of recapitulating past experience by matching a verbal sequence of clauses to the sequence of events which (it is implied) actually occurred (Kitto, Nordquist, Peller, Grant, & Reeves, 2013), making it particularly suited to this longitudinal study. The problem with longitudinal studies based on quantitative approaches is that missing data can be common (Twisk, de Boer, de Vente, & Heymans, 2013). On this basis it makes sense to use the interviews and document analysis approach as is done in this study as it is possible to identify (i.e. infer) the links between the first capture of data (i.e. 2000-2004 in this study) against the second capture (i.e. 2010-2013 in this study).

Results

The results of the study have been grouped in the year range the data was created. Interviews that were conducted between 2000 and 2004 were considered separate from data collected from 2010 to 2013. The results discuss how the various online community genres are used between 2010 and 2013 to transform the power structures in households that the three women were subject to prior to 2004.

Media Consumption and Use between 2000 and 2004

The participants were interviewed between 2000 and 2004, which found that in general they had suffered problems with a man in a household dominating the control of the television and choice over news consumption. Some had turned to newspapers to gain some control – which allowed them to switch from one to another. Others spoke of how having televisions in more than one room had given them some control.

Power Structures and Choice of News Source

Even though the male in the household usually controlled the television, the availability of more than one TV in the household has had an impact on the choice of news source. Person G grew up in a generation where there was more than one television in the household. "If I wanted to watch a different channel I would just find another TV," she said.

All three women were able to access a wide range of news sources, with all of them having a television and radio in a private space. They were all able to gain access to the Internet, but none used it as their primary news source. They all seemed to have strong opinions about their preferred source of news. Person M made clear at this stage that if given the choice she would choose Channel 4 News.

I feel that it is important to watch a channel that covers issues other than news and current affairs because social issues are as important as what takes place in Parliament, she said. Since, social issues are the glue of society and the state of our health service, or education system or even class issues are in fact more important for future considerations and awareness than events that have already happened.

Presentation and content were also important factors when choosing between different providers of the same news source. Person J indicated she chose her newspaper because it contained more fashion and health news, and Person M preferred a particular commercial news program as the information was presented in the form of debates. "I prefer the presentation style of Channel 4 News over other channels. Channel 4 provides room for studio debate, which I think enhances quality of the information," she said. "I think that these attributes add value to the news and provided the notion that you are receiving an evaluation rather than just factual news."

News Format and Political Biases

The format of the medium was also an important factor to the participants. Person J found the actual process of purchasing a newspaper formed part of the satisfaction in using it. "I enjoy reading the newspaper. I find that I can get a lot of information. I enjoy buying it," she said. "It gives me pleasure to read it; I like reading the paper and not only that there's a lot of journalists writing for a newspaper – all with different viewpoints."

Although all the participants cited the topical content as a reason for selecting a particular news source, their political persuasion also played an important role. They seemed more likely to choose a particular provider if it agreed with their point of view, as Person J explains. "I changed from the Mail for various reasons; I think they were biased on various issues. [At the time of the death of] Princess Diana," she said. "They had a bad viewpoint of her, and a few other things that I didn't particularly agree with. So I decided to change my paper."

This consumerist reason for changing media source suggests that news providers have to ensure brand loyalty through holding a particular political line. However although Person M was sure of her beliefs, how she arrived at these viewpoints may have been influenced by the amount of choice she had in accessing news media when she was younger. In contrast, when she was younger and her father lived with her, she felt that she was limited to the news she accessed as he made decisions over the use of the television. She said: "I prefer to watch the news in company, I normally suggest a program and see if everyone is in agreement, if there is company, but most times I am alone so I just take over."

Person G was skeptical about the accuracy of the news media and the motives of media institutions. "[I find that the news] informs about things that might be important for the future," she said. "Like that thing with the MMR when people weren't sure if it was safe for their kids, it's useful for like in ten years or so."

The Role of New Media Such as the Internet

They would use the Internet only to follow up a news item they accessed using their primary news source, as Person G explains. "[I use the Internet] for more info on things that I've seen on the news," she said. "When there's something I'm interested in and that's not on the news I look it up on the Internet."

At this point in time, all participants felt they were unlikely to change to the Internet as their primary news source, viewing it as a complementary form of media. "I think I'm of the age where I wouldn't change [to using the Internet]. I'm not saying that I wouldn't find things of interest on there though. I'm not really that up-to-date on the Internet," Person J said. "But, maybe, perhaps when I've got more time, I'd like to learn." She continued by saying: "I would prefer it if someone found it for me and then I could read it, I don't think I'd go on there myself and find it."

Aspirations

What was clear about the two younger women was they were aspirational. Person M aspired to gain a PhD at this stage. "The goal of SESH

(Systematically Engineered Hypermedia Seduction) is towards the development of a framework that supports the evaluation and creation of more engaging and seductive Web based hypermedia products," she said. "At this preliminary stage by no means do we intend to present an example of what we believe to be seductive hypermedia." Person G was also keen to share her ambitions. "I would like to make it as a performer but if that is not possible, I could write songs for other people. I don't just write in one style," she said.

Media Consumption and Use between 2010 and 2013

The media consumption of the three women had changed significantly ten years later. Both Person G and Person M used YouTube in order to enjoy their rights to freedom of expression. As Person M said, YouTube helped her share her aspects of her life with others. "[In one video], I discuss some of the steps I have taken in order enhance my hair journey regarding my product usage," she said. "I am trying to ensure that my journey is holistic rather than just targeted," she continued. "So I am demonstrating what I have been doing to improve my chances of growing long and healthy hair." Person M explained their reason for taking to YouTube to explain their hairstyle journey. "I thought I'd make this little clip because basically, as a result of my journey I've been really stretched psychologically as well as addressing my fitness regime and hair care regime."

Specialist Interests and Aspirations

Person G's interests had not changed, as she was still interested in music and performing as a musician, but had made use of social media like MySpace and YouTube to promote her music and Person M had taken up posting to a blog and YouTube. All participants, Person G, Person J and Person M had signed up to Facebook.

Being creative it is not surprising that Person M and Person G turned to YouTube to get their creative works and experiences out there. In terms of power it is clear that YouTube fits in the Weblog and Directory category as only specific users can post content and replies are invited. This has therefore turned them from being video consumers via the television to video producers via the Internet. This was also the case with regular text-based Weblogs, which both used to express their opinions and ideas,

Person M also explained how Weblogs are now helping her discuss her interests following her withdrawing from her doctoral degree. "At last I have an avenue to air my personal obsessions and fascinations with food," she said. "My aim is share with you some of the culinary delights I have researched, recreated, developed and tweaked over the years in my humble kitchen."

Multicultural and Social Issues

Person M and Person G were both from a minority ethnic background, and Person J lived in a community where such groups were not dominant. Person M explained how cultural issues affected her upbringing. "I was born and raised in the UK, in Wales," she said. "It's socially more of a multicultural society, as you see people all over the world, but it was only in certain areas of the region where I was born and raised that you would see people of colour and lots of different cultures." Person G said how growing up in the Philippines affected her media participation in the form of Latin music where she said she was "influenced by great vocalists with powerful and soulful vocals such as Whitney Houston and Mariah Carey."

Both Person M and Person G said that their social relationships with others had been affected by the introduction of the Internet, which they used to discuss their past in relation to how boyfriends had allegedly treated them. "The place where I'm from is just a small town and even in school if there was something different about you it was a big problem and you had to keep things low key," said Person M. "My ex boyfriend has not accepted my hair. My hair in my relationship, well, I should make a video entitled 'my hair within my relationships,' because that is a whole subject within itself." Person G had a different experience where she alleged a former boyfriend had posted to the Internet about her. "He has posted videos of me singing on YouTube and has set up a Web page about me," she said.

DISCUSSION

This paper has presented the results of a longitudinal study into the media consumption and creation by three women living in Wales. The issues relating to audience, institution and power structures changed dramatically over the two decades covered by the study. Women once relied on media such as newspapers to have independent access to the media it was found, but since the mass take-up of the Internet the opportunities available for this have been more readily available. The women investigated all produced social media including on Facebook. Two of the three women turned to YouTube to express themselves, thus changing the dynamics of the public sphere significantly. It was clear from both instances of the study that media choice was an important thing for the three women investigated. In the case of one she spoke of not being able to watch the BBC youth news programme 'Newsround' because her father instisted on her watching Channel 4 News. The shaping of women through patriarcial power structures and institutions may have taken its toll of the three generations of women in this study.

Limitations and Directions for Future Research

The research has shown that the power structures in Wales have changed and women generally have more command over the media they consumed – and produce for that matter. The study has looked at the different types of flame trolling that can be experienced, but does not look in detail beyond the three women whose media consumption was evaluated. Future research needs to look at the power structures of new media institutions like Twitter and the narrative structures that form part of those. For instance, as most of the women in the study were restricted in their choiceof media by men then further investigation into misogeny in media use could be investigated. For instance future research could look at the context of social media platforms in terms of the way they are used by women, such as whether social media platforms are suitable for the representation of meaning seen from the theory of mind of women as opposed to the men who might be abusive towards them.

REFERENCES

Altena, M., & Ngwenya, N. (2012). Sites that cope, cure and commemorate: Weblogs of terminally ill. *The Presence of the Dead in our Lives, 82*, 55.

Antunovic, D., & Hardin, M. (2013). Women bloggers: Identity and the conceptualization of sports. *New Media & Society*. doi:10.1177/1461444812472323

Bishop, J. (2009). Enhancing the understanding of genres of web-based communities: The role of the ecological cognition framework. *International Journal of Web Based Communities, 5*(1), 4–17. doi:10.1504/IJWBC.2009.021558

Bishop, J. (2011a). *The equatrics of intergenerational knowledge transformation in technocultures: Towards a model for enhancing information management in virtual worlds.* (Unpublished MScEcon Thesis). Aberystwyth University, Aberystwyth, UK.

Bishop, J. (2011b). Mum's the wordpress: A comparative analysis of political and mommy bloggers. In *Proceedings of the 2011 Internet Conference on Internet Computing (ICOMP'2011)*. ICOMP.

Bishop, J. (2012). Scope and limitations in the government of wales act 2006 for tackling internet abuses in the form of 'flame trolling'. *Statute Law Review*, *33*(2), 207–216. doi:10.1093/slr/hms016

Bishop, J. (2013). The effect of deindividuation of the internet troller on criminal procedure implementation: An interview with a hater. *International Journal of Cyber Criminology*, *7*(1), 28–48.

Bishop, J. (2014). Representations of 'trolls' in mass media communication: A review of media-texts and moral panics relating to 'internet trolling'. *International Journal of Web Based Communities*, *10*(1), 7–24. doi:10.1504/IJWBC.2014.058384

Branston, G., & Stafford, R. (2010). *The media student's book*. London: Routledge.

Brown, K., Jackson, M., & Cassidy, W. (2006). Cyber-bullying: Developing policy to direct responses that are equitable and effective in addressing this special form of bullying. *Canadian Journal of Educational Administration and Policy*, *57*(1), 1–36.

Casany, M. J., Alier, M., Mayol, E., Conde, M. A., & García-Peñalvo, F. J. (2013). Mobile learning as an asset for development: Challenges and oportunities. In *Information systems, e-learning, and knowledge management research* (pp. 244–250). Berlin: Springer. doi:10.1007/978-3-642-35879-1_29

Cassidy, W., Brown, K., & Jackson, M. (2013). Moving from cyber-bullying to cyber-kindness: What do students, educators and parents say? In J. Bishop (Ed.), *Examining the concepts, issues and implications of Internet trolling* (pp. 62–83). Hershey, PA: IGI Global. doi:10.4018/978-1-4666-2803-8.ch006

Faye, I. (2012). *Thank you hater.* MAR.

Figallo, C. (1998). *Hosting web communities: Building relationships, increasing customer loyalty, and maintaining a competitive edge*. New York: John Wiley & Sons, Inc.

Herring, S., Job-Sluder, K., Scheckler, R., & Barab, S. (2002). Searching for safety online: Managing trolling in a feminist forum. *The Information Society*, *18*(5), 371–384. doi:10.1080/01972240290108186

Holtom, D. (2007). 10 research note: What are the true costs of community-based learning? *Contemporary Wales*, *20*(1), 159–178.

Housley, W., Moles, K., & Smith, R. (2009). Identity, brand or citizenship? The case of post-devolution wales. *Contemporary Wales*, *22*(1), 196–210.

Jansen, E., & James, V. (2002). *NetLingo: The internet dictionary*. Oxnard, CA: Netlingo Inc.

Kim, A. J. (2000). *Community building on the web: Secret strategies for successful online communities*. Berkeley, CA: Peachpit Press.

Kitto, S., Nordquist, J., Peller, J., Grant, R., & Reeves, S. (2013). The disconnections between space, place and learning in interprofessional education: An overview of key issues. *Journal of Interprofessional Care*, *27*(S2), 5–8. doi:10.3109/13561820.2013.801410 PMID:23930685

Knuttila, L. (2011). User unknown: 4chan, anonymity and contingency. *First Monday*, *16*(10). doi:10.5210/fm.v16i10.3665

Loader, B. D. (2004). *Cyberspace divide: Equality, agency and policy in the information society*. London: Routledge.

McSporran, M., & Young, S. (2001). Does gender matter in online learning?. *Research in Learning Technology, 9*(2).

Novo-Corti, I., Varela-Candamio, L., & García-Álvarez, M. T. (2013). Breaking the walls of social exclusion of women rural by means of ICTs: The case of 'digital divides' in galician. *Computers in Human Behavior*. PMID:24003265

O'Donnell, L., Carson, L., Forciea, M. A., Kinosian, B., Shea, J., & Yudin, J. et al. (2013). What students experienced: A narrative analysis of essays written by first-year medical students participating in a geriatrics home visit. *Journal of the American Geriatrics Society*. doi:10.1111/jgs.12405 PMID:23888907

O'Mahen, H. A., Woodford, J., McGinley, J., Warren, F. C., Richards, D. A., & Lynch, T. R. et al. (2013). Internet-based behavioral activation—Treatment for postnatal depression (netmums): A randomized controlled trial. *Journal of Affective Disorders*. doi:10.1016/j.jad.2013.03.005 PMID:23602514

Phillips, W. (2011). LOLing at tragedy: Facebook trolls, memorial pages and resistance to grief online. *First Monday, 16*(12). doi:10.5210/fm.v16i12.3168

Piela, A. (2013). *Claiming religious authority*. Academic Press.

Powell, R. (2010). Good mothers, bad mothers and mommy bloggers: Rhetorical resistance and fluid subjectivities. *MP: An Online Feminist Journal*, 37-50.

Preece, J. (2000). *Online communities: Designing usability, supporting sociability*. Chichester, UK: John Wiley & Sons.

Rheingold, H. (2003). *Smart mobs: The next social revolution*. New York: Basic Books.

Schweitzer, F., & Garcia, D. (2010). An agent-based model of collective emotions in online communities. *The European Physical Journal B-Condensed Matter and Complex Systems, 77*(4), 533–545. doi:10.1140/epjb/e2010-00292-1

Seward, L., Harvey, V., & Carranza, J. (2009). Computer-mediated communication that brings learning into the present: Gender differences in status differentials and self-disclosure in online peer teaching. *International Journal of Information and Communication Technology Education, 5*(2), 10–20. doi:10.4018/jicte.2009040102

Thomas, J. (2006). The regional and local media in Wales. *Local Journalism and Local Media: Making the Local News*.

Twisk, J., de Boer, M., de Vente, W., & Heymans, M. (2013). Multiple imputation of missing values was not necessary before performing a longitudinal mixed-model analysis. *Journal of Clinical Epidemiology*. doi:10.1016/j.jclinepi.2013.03.017 PMID:23790725

Walter, T., Hourizi, R., Moncur, W., & Pitsillides, S. (2011). Does the internet change how we die and mourn? An overview. *Omega, 64*(4), 12. doi:10.2190/OM.64.4.a PMID:22530294

Yang, C. L., & Chen-Burger, Y. H. (2012). On-line communities making scense: A hybrid micro-blogging platform community analysis framework. *Agent and Multi-Agent Systems. Technologies and Applications*, 134-143.

KEY TERMS AND DEFINITIONS

4chan.org: 4chan is a message board platform for posting images (i.e. an image-board), which is most famously known as being accommodated by a group called Anonymous, who post subversive images on that Website, often following the posting user harming another person on a different Website.

Facebook: Facebook is a social networking platform consisting of various types of Web-based community linked together through the buddy-lists of the users to take part in the Website's services.

Twitter: Twitter is a social networking services that whilst called a 'micro-blog' more resembles a chatroom where anyone can post a message to anyone and reply to a message by anyone.

Yahoo!Answers: Yahoo!Answers is a social media platform resembling a directory and Weblog where a user can start a post for others to comment on. The platform allows users to ask detailed questions and receive answers which they and/or others can vote on.

Section 3
Media, Culture, and Communication

Chapter 9
Exploring the Concept of the "Social Media Campaign"

Mary Francoli
Carleton University, Canada

ABSTRACT

On May 2, 2011, Canadians voted in what the news media dubbed "Canada's First Social Media Election." This allowed Canadians to join their neighbours to the south who, arguably, had gone through one national social media election during the 2008 bid for the presidency. Through a theoretical discussion of what constitutes sociality and networked sociality, and a critical examination of social media as a campaign tool, this chapter asks "What makes a campaign social?" It also asks if the term "social media campaign" adequately describes current campaign practices? In exploring these questions, the chapter draws on the 2011 federal election in Canada and the 2008 American election. Ultimately, the chapter argues we have limited evidence that social media has led to increased sociality when it comes to electoral politics. This calls the appropriateness of the term "social media campaign" into question. Such lack of evidence stems from the dynamism of networked sociality, which renders it difficult to understand, and methodological difficulties when it comes to capturing what it means to be "social."

INTRODUCTION

Political campaigns around the world are increasingly being referred to as 'social media campaigns' in electoral politics. On May 2, 2011 Canadians, for example, voted in what the news media dubbed "Canada's First Social Media Election" (Curry 2011). Britain's first social media election was in 2010 (Arthur 2010). Elections in other parts of the world, such as Singapore and Thailand, are also increasingly being called 'social'. This growing phenomenon has followed Obama's successful use of social media during his 2008 bid for the presidency, which has been described as "the watershed moment for social media in politics" (Curry, 2011). But what makes an election campaign a social media campaign? This concept has been ill defined. Too often it is used to capture the simple presence of a party or political candidate in the social media sphere, or any political activity during an election period that engages with social media. As will be demonstrated, this includes identifying and quantifying parties and candidates with a profile on popular social networking sites,

DOI: 10.4018/978-1-4666-6038-0.ch009

Copyright © 2014, IGI Global. Copying or distributing in print or electronic forms without written permission of IGI Global is prohibited.

such as Facebook or Twitter. The purpose of this chapter is take a step back and to better flush out our understanding of a political social media campaign by asking two main questions. First, what makes a campaign social; is presence on a social networking site sufficient or should they meet additional criteria? Second, does the term social media campaign adequately describe recent election campaigns, such as the 2008 American election or the 2011 Canadian federal election? The answer to this question is more than semantics. Clearly identifying the characteristics of a so called social media campaign has the potential to help us better categorize and discuss the various interactive functions of a campaign as well as the strengths and weaknesses which may be associated with each. Such a nuanced definition or understanding of the concept will be of interest to those studying the intersection between social media and electoral politics as well as those interested in the broader literature related to e-democracy and e-participation which make claims about the potential of technology to enhance democracy and citizen engagement. It also has the potential to help identify gaps in our understanding when it comes to the impact of social media. In doing this it raises interesting questions and issues that might be addressed in the future so that we can have a more concrete understanding of sociality, and networked sociality, which will be discussed below. Perhaps most importantly, having a well-defined understanding of a social media campaign today provides a useful point of departure from which to gauge and discuss future change or deviation.

This chapter is divided into four main sections. The first section starts to explore the above-mentioned questions by building on the concepts of 'social', 'social media' and 'Web 2.0' as well as common understandings political campaigning, to establish criteria for determining what constitutes social media campaigning. The second section offers a brief overview of social media campaigning focusing on the 2008 American election, widely thought of as the first large scale social media election, and the 2011 Canadian federal election as one of the more recent jurisdictions to experience its 'first' social media election. The third section returns to the chapter's original research questions. It explores the elements of the two campaigns discussed here in the context of the definitions offered earlier in the chapter in an effort to construct a better understanding of how a social media campaign might be defined. The fourth, and final, section explores avenues for future research. Ultimately, the chapter argues that we have limited evidence of sociality when it comes to electoral politics, calling the appropriateness of the term social media campaign into question. Such lack of evidence stems from the dynamism of networked sociality, which renders it difficult to understand, and methodological difficulties when it comes to capturing what it means to be social. The goal here is modest. Limitations of length make an in-depth examination of all aspects of the case studies as they relate to Internet technology impossible. They also necessitate the simplifying of the concept of sociality, which has a long, varied and eloquent history. The goal here is to start building a better understanding of social media campaigns and the intersection between the Internet and politics. Future work, building on the discussion offered here, will be both interesting and welcome. It is unlikely to think that social media will cease being a part of the campaign toolbox. Towner and Dulio (2012) forecast continued and growing use of new media, particularly social networking tools, for future campaigns in the United States. Indeed, it wouldn't be farfetched to assume this prediction be fulfilled, not only in the United States, but also much more widely. As such more detailed discussions about what the term means will only continue to gain importance.

BACKGROUND

As an initial step in addressing the chapter's goal to define the term social media campaign, it is useful to take a step back, and first consider what is meant by 'social' and 'social media' and by virtue of that Web 2.0 as it is often use synonymously with the term social media. The concept of social is one that is at the same time inordinately simple, yet tremendously complex. Theorists such as Goffman (1959) and Bourdieu (1977), to just to name a few, focus on the concept of social as it relates to human association. Others still (see Durkheim, 1895 as an example), understand social in terms of structure. Parsons, Turner and Mead explored the idea of social action, which is an interesting point of departure if one thinks of a social media campaign in terms of an action. While the unit of analysis may differ, theorists exploring the social concept share the underlying theme of interactive, or joint, activity. At its simplest it can means association (Dolwick, 2009, p. 21). However, as Dolwick (2009) notes, this might refer to a virtually infinite array of interactions.

The term social media suffers from similarly complicated and varied understandings, but again the idea of interactive or joint activity are key. As noted above, it is not uncommon for social media to be primarily defined as a list of applications or technologies that are considered social. However, some have offered more detailed descriptions of its characteristics and defining features. Danah Boyd (2007), offers one of the early definitions of social networking sites. According to Boyd, they can be defined as "Web-based services that allow individuals to 1) construct a public or semi-public profile within a bounded system, 2) articulate a list of other users with whom they share a connection, and 3) view and traverse their list of connections and those made by others within a system. The nature and nomenclature of these connections may vary from site to site" (2007, p.1).

Boyd's article was written prior to the evolution of the term 'Web 2.0.' However, it is often used interchangeably with the term social media. Social media platforms are a defining feature of Web 2.0. As such, it is interesting to round out our discussion on definitions with one focused on Web 2.0. Here, the work of Matthew Allen is interesting to consider. Allen (2008) builds on aspects of O'Reilly's (2005) original definition of the term Web 2.0. According to Allen, Web 2.0 is "a conceptual frame, within which we can correlate and make sense of diverse events even as we use it as a convenient short-hand" (2008). It is comprised of four distinct features. First, it relates to the interactive design and function of Websites. Second, it relates to a business practice which data about users can be gathered and used in meaningful ways. Third, it relates to services that allow active participation of the user, or 'prouser', in the creation, maintenance and expansion of content. And, fourth, it is a "political statement of a kind of libertarian capitalism" (Allen, 2008). Again, the idea of interactivity is foundational.

Keeping these definitions in mind, it is interesting to reflect on traditional notions of political campaigning. Political campaigns have been described as "organized efforts to inform, persuade and mobilize" (Norris, 2001). An interactive element isn't immediately clear here. In elaborating this model of campaign communication, Norris (2001) states that political campaigns contain four elements: "the messages that the campaign organization is seeking to communicate, the channels of communication employed by these organizations, the impact of these messages on their targeted audience, and the feedback loop from the audience back to the organization." Here one might infer interactivity in the form of the feedback loop from the audience to the campaign. Indeed, this is really the only potential space for interactivity under this somewhat linear model of campaign communication. It does little to capture the more networked sense of sociality underpinning the concepts of social media or Web 2.0. Under such a communicative model, social media platforms would likely be rendered one of many channels of communication employed by campaigns. This implies that the technology be used more to 'push' information from campaigns to the public. Thinking of social media in this way causes one to overlook its nuances and the characteristics that make it unique; namely, its potential for interactivity and its highly networked nature.

Rather than invoking the term social media campaign simply because of the presence of social media as one channel of communication, we need to think about what it means and how it differs from other, more traditional channels and campaign strategies. If we are to think about the linear model outlined by Norris and how it might be changed in light of the development of social networking platforms, we might emphasize the third feature of Web 2.0 outlined by Allen (2008) above which details the active participation of users in the creation, maintenance and expansion of content. Such participation can be reinforced with the notion of interactivity offered by Boyd which underpins our various understandings of the concepts of social and sociality. Thinking about the social media campaign in this non-linear way, it begins to resemble more of a networked model of sociality which is dynamic, chaotic, and unstable at times, but which is interactive with a high potential for participation and sharing. Here we can borrow from Wittel's conceptualization of network sociality as one where "social relations are not 'narrational' but informational; they are not based on mutual experience or common history.....Network sociality consists of fleeting and transient, yet iterative social relations" (Wittel, 2001, p. 51). This, Wittel (2001), is careful to distinguish, differs from concepts of community sociality as the idea of "Community entails stability, coherence, embeddedness and belonging. It involves strong and long-lasting ties, proximity and a common history or narrative of the collective" (p. 51). Network sociality, on the other hand, bares characteristics that are not dissimilar from the attributes of the network society described by scholars such as Manual Castells (1998) and Darin Barney (2004). Here, the network form of organization is dominant and informational. Politically, those whose access to media is non-interactive and limited to "passive consumption of commodified content" are disenfranchised (Barney, 2004, p. 122).

Drawing on these understandings of sociality, networked sociality, social networking and Web 2.0, and thinking of them in the context of political campaigning, we can say that a social media campaign should have three main characteristics. First, and really quite obviously, it needs to have a social media presence. Increasingly, this would mean presence on a variety of the platforms described by Boyd and Allen given the rapidly changing nature of the social media sphere. Second, it requires interactivity. This is the crux of social media and the idea of sociality more generally. Third, it needs to be networked. Keeping these characteristics in mind, we can now start to address the chapter's second question: does the term social media campaign adequately capture or describe recent election campaigns which are commonly referred to as social?

RISE OF THE SOCIAL MEDIA CAMPAIGN

Barak Obama's 2008 presidential campaign is largely thought of as the archetypical social media campaign. According to Joe Rospars, Obama's Head of New Media, "the Obama campaign prioritized the Web because it provided a conduit to the very heart of the organization: the ordinary people" (2010). The iconic status of Obama's campaign and the 2008 presidential election begs the question: what about this particular election made people perceive it as a successful social media campaign? On one level the answer to this question is simple. The 2008 presidential election was the first high profile election in the era of new media. There was a novelty factor. Most social networking sites didn't come on the scene until 2005. Facebook, for example, wasn't made available to the general public until 2006. Twitter emerged the same year. YouTube started a year earlier, but hadn't yet gained widespread popularity. As the first presidential election to engage with these technologies, it, in some ways, was dubbed a social media election simply because the technology was used by the campaigns involved. There was an interest and excitement around this use because it was different. But the simple presence of social media tells us little about its impact or why the 2008 election continues to be described as a good example - the example other campaigns seek to emulate - of a social media campaign?

While Obama's use of social media has gained particular notoriety, in part due to his successful bid for presidential office, it should be noted that the technology was used by other campaigns during that particular election. Barak Obama and John McCain both engaged with Facebook, MySpace, Twitter and YouTube. Those interested in the campaigns carefully followed metrics, such as the number of friends or followers each candidate had and how many videos each posted in the case of YouTube (Towner & Dulio, 2012). This information is interesting, but tells us little about the how those friends, or followers, engaged with the campaigns. The numbers in themselves tell us little about interactivity, which, as was established above is a defining feature of social media and a key measure of a social media campaign.

Smith and Rainie's 2008 study of the election lends a bit more detail into how the technology was used. According to the study, 25% of Obama supporters engaged politically in an online social network, 21% shared photos, video or audio, 18% signed up for election updates, 15% donated money online, 11% volunteered online and 12% signed up for email alerts (Smith & Rainie, 2008, p.11). Comparatively, John McCain lagged in all categories. Given the nascent state of the technology, the significance of such statistics cannot be overlooked, but they do prompt one to again question whether the campaigns should be called social media campaigns. At best, 25% of supporters engaged politically. And, many of the activities outlined by Smith and Rainie are not particularly social. Signing up for email alerts and election updates, for example, aren't particularly interactive activities. Indeed they are reminiscent of traditional push or broadcast styles of communication more than indicators of a new form of networked, social communication.

Beyond the more popular social networking platforms, such as Facebook, Twitter or YouTube, the trend to label the campaigns as social media campaigns might come from the creation of social networking sites that were built specifically for the election. Obama's campaign team, aided by Chris Hughes who cofounded Facebook, created its own social networking platform called MyBO. McCain's campaign followed suit with McCainSpace. As Towner and Dulio (2012) state, both social networking sites "allowed individuals to create their own profiles, interact with others and donate funds, among other things" (p. 99). Effectively, the ability to engage with the technology in these ways satisfies Boyd's (2007) defining criteria for social networking. At first blush the development of MyBO and MCCainSpace would seem logical and solid grounds for deeming the election a social media election. However, there is an argument to be made that the sites, while certainly innovative and potentially useful to their respective campaigns, in some ways ran counter to the spirit of social networking and, as such, couldn't have fostered the sense of sociality required of a truly social campaign. Membership or inclusion on the sites was primarily meant for campaign supporters. They served as means by which to bring together groups of like-minded persons rather than the public at large. This is not a criticism. Innovative means of mobilizing supporters might be seen as an extremely smart campaign strategy. In Obama's case, MyBO proved an effective way to organize supporters and have them engage in 'real world', more traditional campaign activities, such as canvassing. However, the narrow user group of the sites does again prompt one to question their potential for sociality. Indeed, the sites remind us more of the characteristics of a community outlined by Wittel (2001), where users have a common history or narrative of the collective. MyBO and McCainSpace give the sense that they are about coherence, belonging and building a stable base of supporters. Again, this might constitute a sort of community sociality and may be valuable from a strategic perspective, but may not be representative of the sort of networked sociality that we draw from social networking sites that would therefore be reminiscent of a social media campaign.

Where we see more concrete evidence of sociality is with the intersection between the online and offline environments. Those involved with MyBO organized over 200,000 offline events and coordinated volunteers to reach out and engage with the broader community through activities such as canvassing (Vargas, 2008). Here we might say that social media was used as a tool to foster sociality in the real world. Organizationally such use of social media was invaluable and successful. We can identify interaction not only between those using MyBO, but also between those on MyBO and those who may have chosen not to engage with the site, or even with the election.

It has been suggested that while social networking and Internet use more generally, added an element of novelty in 2008, the campaigns were still oriented toward more traditional goals, such as fundraising (Towner & Dulio, 2012), advertising and gathering contact information of potential supporters (Kaye, 2009). It is relatively easy to gauge success when it comes to such goals. And, there is no question that Obama's campaign was successful. His campaign used the Internet to raise half a billion dollars (Vargas, 2008). It spent $16 million on Internet advertising (Towner & Dulio, 2012, p. 97). In addition, the campaign used every opportunity to collect email addresses and cell phone numbers in an effort to build its database of contacts. In total it is estimated that the campaign's database included over 13 million email addresses and a million phone numbers (Vargas, 2008). The database was used to push messages regarding campaign updates and fundraising goals to potential supporters. There is little doubt that the campaign's innovative use of the Internet in these ways contributed to Obama's successful bid for the presidency. However, the degree of sociality associated with such activities is questionable. In spite of this, these are the indicators that are often used as measures of a successful social media campaign.

It is also interesting to consider the role of those outside of the professionally run campaigns. People did engage with the campaign, and the election in general, via the Internet. According to Smith and Rainie "voters in 2008 were not just followers of the political process. They also used a wide range of digital tools and technologies to get involved in the race, to harness their creativity in support of their chosen candidate, and to join forces with others who shared their same political goals and interests" (2008, p.21). While the type of involvement discussed by Smith and Rainie is not specifically nor solely related to social media, they do raise an important point. Citizens were using social media as a mechanism to disseminate content they produced and to share information to a wider audience. The popular 'Obama Girl' videos on YouTube serve as one example among many. Here we see indicators of a social media campaign, but lack evidence regarding the extent of sociality, or the reach of the network. Moreover, citizen led efforts often appeared to be running parallel to the official campaigns. In this case we might characterize an election as consisting of social media campaigns led and sustained by citizens, and perhaps media which reported on their efforts. However, the parallel nature of citizen led campaigns does not automatically point to social media campaigns run by parties or candidates.

Much in the same way that we can question the sociality of the 2008 presidential campaign, we can unpack and scrutinize Canada's first social media campaign, the 2011 federal election. Again, the novelty factor comes into play. However, it is interesting that 2011 was dubbed Canada's first social media election in spite of the fact that it was the country's second federal election in the era of social media. The fact that it wasn't used as widely in the previous, 2008, general election suggests, to some extent, that title of social media election was bestowed in 2011 simply because of increased presence. Much of what we actually know about the use of social media during the recent election is numerical. In the same way that people paid close attention to things such as the number of candidates' friends and followers during the US election, so did those in Canada. The media tracked popularity, number of tweets in the case of Twitter, and number of candidates with accounts on an array of social networking platforms (Canadian Press, 2011a). Such numbers are interesting trivia, but again, they tell very little about use and interactivity, key measures of a social media campaign as defined here. A closer inspection of every candidate's Facebook page for example, showed that while some might host a page, that page was little more than a shell with only bits of information and no opportunity for interactivity. Some simply contained Wikipedia entries, including Gilles Duceppe's, the leader of the Bloc Quebecois (Francoli, Greenberg, & Waddell, 2011).

Another common measure of social media use during the election was number of tweets sent by candidates and parties as well as number of tweets circulating that related to the election. It was estimated that over 99,000 election-related tweets were sent the first week of the campaign alone (Canadian Press, 2011b). Such data might provide more insight into use than counts of Facebook friends, but is still slightly problematic in that it only captures data using specific election related hashtags, determined by the researchers, and tells little of the number of unique users or the content of the messages.

While not all parties followed in the footsteps of Obama or McCain to create their own indigenous social networking sites, it was a tactic emulated by the Conservative Party in the form of ToryNation.ca. As one blogger writes, ToryNation is "a 24/7 virtual campaign office. Apparently if you sign in, you get full access to your own online action centre to help: Spread the Conservative message, Find Events nearby, Raise Money, Connect with other Conservatives, and Recruit Volunteers" (Hamilton, 2011). ToryNation led Hamilton (2011) to declare that Stephen Harper, leader of the Conservative Party of Canada, was "out-Obama-ing" Michael Ignatieff, leader of the Liberal Party. The description of features offered on ToryNation raise the same kinds of question about sociality as MyBO and McCainSpace. It was a tool for supporters, not geared toward engaging the public at large in the campaign. And, unlike MyBO, ToryNation emphasized things such as fundraising over the organization of activities in the offline environment.

The Canadian Press in conjunction with public affairs strategist Mark Blevis, attempted to study social media beyond individual candidates and parties to see whether it was being used for conversation. Their focus was specifically on Twitter. As they note, such a strategy has its limitations: "The methodology is not scientific; searches are being tailored to try to capture material that is clearly linked to the campaign by using a set of 10 hashtags for Twitter and specific sets of keywords for other media or issues" (Canadian Press, 2011b). Francoli, Greenberg and Waddell (2011) engage in a similar undertaking. They use an analytic tool called *ViralHeat* to gauge influence and reach of each of the leaders and their respective parties in the social media sphere. The analysis encompasses a wider range of social networking tools, beyond Twitter, but it suffers similar limitations as that carried out by The Canadian Press and Mark Blevis. The researchers had to determine what terms to follow and then had to train the software to exclude similar terms that might skew the results. CPC for example, refers not only to the Conservative Party of Canada, but also to a host of other organizations including the Canadian Police College. Accuracy of the findings depends on the researchers' ability to effectively screen for and minimize false or misleading results. While there was definite "chatter" in the social media sphere around the election and the different campaigns, these studies found that the "participants were small in number overall and were most likely already committed partisans or voters who would have been more likely to cast ballots whether the technology existed or not (Francoli, Greenberg, & Waddell, 2011, pp. 241-242). Given this, it was concluded that it might be more accurate to refer to the 2011 general election as Canada's first experimental social media election. The sentiment behind the play on phrase first social media election used by media is one of hesitation and reluctance given the lack of evidence of networked sociality and interactivity.

FINDINGS AND DISCUSSION

Reflecting on the meaning of sociality as it relates to a political social media campaign, and the two elections described above, it is useful to return to the original two questions posed in this chapter. First, what makes a political campaign social? Second, is the term social media campaign an adequate term to describe recent campaign practices?

What Makes a Political Campaign Social?

Drawing on traditional understandings of sociality and common definitions of social media and Web 2.0, this chapter has identified three key and interrelated characteristics of a political social media campaign: technology, interactivity and networks. To be considered a social media campaign, a campaign must engage with technology by incorporating social media tools. As was described by Boyd (2007) and Allen (2008), these are tools that allow users to construct and manage a public profile, to maintain a list of connections, to view the connections made by others, and to allow active participation of users and their connections. Here, indicators such as the quantifying of tweets and friends or followers on social networking sites serve as a good starting point for determining the social media presence of a campaign, but presence alone is not sufficient.

In addition to setting up social media profiles, campaigns must use the technology in an interactive manner. While social media by design allows for interactivity, users have significant control over the way that interactive features are, or are not as the case may be, incorporated. Facebook, for example, allows for features such as discussion boards, polls, video and real time chat. However, it also allows for the most basic of profiles which simply broadcasts information about an individual or group. While this sort of informational, unidirectional use of a social media platform may serve as a sort of electronic campaign pamphlet and as such may have some value, it does not engaging with the technology's interactive or social potential. Rather, it is reminiscent of older, more linear and non-networked forms of campaign communication.

A social media campaign must be networked. Networked sociality, as was discussed by Wittel (2001), is somewhat chaotic and can be unstable. It is informational and stems from the ability to harness the interactive features of social media. It flows from a campaign's willingness to step out of the traditional, linear model of campaign communication and to afford people the freedom to create, maintain and expand content, to draw on Allen's (2008) understanding of Web 2.0. Here, such activities don't simply take place outside of traditional campaign activities and communication; rather they are integrated with campaigns.

Keeping these three criteria in mind while reflecting on the American 2008 presidential campaign, which has been seen as the archetypical social media campaign, and the 2011 Canadian federal election campaign, we can turn to the second question posed in this chapter.

Is the Term 'Social Media Campaign' an Adequate Term to Describe Recent Campaign Practices?

While the campaigns involved in the two elections discussed here fulfilled the first criteria of a social media election by having a presence on a range of social media platforms, evidence of interactivity and network are not quite as clear. In these cases evidence of sociality is somewhat limited. We can speculate that such lack of evidence might be attributed to two phenomena: the failure of campaigns to be interactive and lack of knowledge about sociality. Campaigns may not have used social media to its full potential. Instead of embracing interactivity and the idea of a network, which is chaotic and difficult to control, they may have clung to traditional ideas of campaign communication where feedback and involvement of those outside of the campaign is largely uni-directional and highly controlled. Here, email lists and text alert systems come to mind. Michael Turk, a founder of CRAFT|Media/Digital makes this point arguing that campaigns are "not engaging people. They're still trying to use *social media* as a one-way, top-down message dissemination vehicle" (quoted in Towner and Rainie, 2012, p. 104). The desire to control the message and campaign are likely not the only factors contributing to the lack of interactivity and network. Resources also come into play. Determining how to open lines of communication and continually contribute and respond to the network draws on resources that may not be readily available to all campaigns.

However, it is interesting to think of what we know about campaigns in another way and to consider an alternate possibility: that the campaigns may well be much more social than researchers and those analyzing campaigns realize. The dynamism of networked sociality and election campaigns as they are carried out in social media, render them difficult to understand. Networked sociality is, by its nature, not only interactive, but also chaotic and unstable. This is certainly true of social media. Numbers of friends and followers change with regularity. Users control their own privacy settings and therefore the flow of information on their profiles. This makes it difficult for people to understand the reach and impact of social media. For example, a campaign cannot assume that all of the friends of its followers on a platform such as Facebook, will see messages from the campaign in their newsfeeds. Some may have accounts set so such messages do not appear effectively limiting their reach. This problem is intimately related to questions of methodology.

FUTURE RESEARCH DIRECTIONS

Researchers and those interested in campaigns are struggling to determine what methods to use to capture what it means to be social and to break away from the linear model of campaign communication offered by those such as Norris (2001). The dynamism and nature of networked sociality makes measurement very difficult. As was discussed, the more popular measures of success in the campaigns discussed above were indicators such as numbers of friends or followers, number of tweets sent on Twitter, dollars raised, etc. Such data is easily quantifiable, but again, it tells little of interactivity. If technology has contributed to the complexity of the network, making social media campaigns difficult to understand, it may also serve as the solution to this confusion. Experimenting with technology that helps us to measure the social aspect of election campaigns will be increasingly important as campaign further embrace technology.

Given that social media and its use in political campaigns is still a relatively recent practice, it would not be unfair to suggest that we are witnesses both of the above factors come into play. Campaigns have used social media in interesting ways, particularly to support traditional campaign goals, but have not fully or seamlessly incorporated the technology rendering our recognition of sociality somewhat limited. The Canadian and American elections do show technology being used in innovative ways and in ways that, as was seen with Obama's campaign, contributed to great success when it comes to goals such as fundraising, advertising and building a network of contacts. However, these objectives rely more on communication between individuals and the campaign and really do not tell us much about interactivity or activities among those outside of the campaign. On the other hand, higher levels of networked sociality may exist, but may not have been well captured.

Those studying what have been dubbed social media elections have been, and need to continue to, find new ways to measure sociality. Such an expanded understanding of interactivity would provide a much fuller understanding of a social media campaign and networked sociality. This, in turn, will further inform claims about e-democracy and e-participation which explore the impact of digital media on democracy and citizen engagement. With the incomplete understanding we have of interactivity we may want to reconsider the appropriateness of the term 'social media campaign.' Instead, we might apply other labels that more effectively capture our current state of knowledge. Again, debate over such terms is more than semantics. Different terms evoke a range of realities and carry with them differing assumptions. Naming and defining a practice, such as a social media campaign, provides us with a point of departure for future analyses that can capture deviation and change. While the primary purpose of this chapter is simply to raise question about the definition and appropriateness of the term 'social media campaign', and not to detail to pros and cons of alternative language, two suggestions are offered as starting points for discussion: Internet campaign and social campaign. The first, an older concept, is much more general than social media campaign. It relates to a range of activities that take place in the online environment. While some of these activities may contain potential for sociality, not all do, and indeed the term Internet campaign makes no claim of sociality. This more general term allows us to recognize innovative campaign activities that may not be based on social media. It also fits well with existing knowledge of online campaigning which has focused on data that is easy to identify and quantify.

Alternatively, the term 'social campaign' does lay claims of sociality, but does not limit them to the social media sphere. This allows for greater flexibility to recognize interaction in the real world environment. As discussed above, activities and engagement in the offline world was where sociality can be seen. This was effectively brought about by social media sites such as MyBO or ToryNation, but evidence of interactivity and sociality within the sites themselves was somewhat limited. All terms will have pros and cons and will appeal to some or none. However, as this chapter has argued, it is useful to give the term 'social media campaign' further thought in the future.

REFERENCES

Allen, M. (2008). Web 2.0: An argument against convergence. *First Monday*, *13*(3). doi:10.5210/fm.v13i3.2139

Arthur, C. (2010, May 3). 2010: The first social media election: This is the first British general election in the social media age, but what difference has it made? *The Guardian*. Retrieved January 6, 2012 from http://www.guardian.co.uk/media/2010/apr/30/social-media-election-2010

Barney, D. (2004). *The network society*. Cambridge, UK: Polity.

Bboyd, D. (2007). Social network sites: Definition, history, and scholarship. *Journal of Computer-Mediated Communication, 13*(1).

Bourdieu, P. (1977). *Outline of a theory of practice*. Cambridge, UK: Cambridge University Press. doi:10.1017/CBO9780511812507

Canadian Press. (2011a). *The social media battleground of the 2011 federal election*. Retrieved May 3, 2012 from http://www.marketingmag.ca/news/media-news/the-social-media-battleground-of-the-2011-federal-election-25038

Canadian Press. (2011b). *Social media takes off in first week of campaign*. Retrieved May 3, 2012 from http://www.ctv.ca/servlet/ArticleNews/story/CTVNews/20110402/social-media-election-110402/20110402?s_name=election2011

Castells, M. (1998). *End of millennium*. Oxford, UK: Blackwell.

Curry, B. (2011, March 27). Canada's first social media election is on, but will people vote? *Globe and Mail*. Retrieved January 6, 2012 from http://www.theglobeandmail.com/news/politics/canadas-first-social-media-election-is-on-butwill-people-vote/article1959166/

Dolwick, J. (2009). The social and beyond: Introducing actor-network theory. *J Mari Arch, 4*, 21–49. doi:10.1007/s11457-009-9044-3

Durkheim, E. (1895). *The rules of the sociological method*. New York: The Free Press.

Francoli, M., Greenberg, J., & Waddell, C. (2011). The campaign in digital media. In *The Canadian federal election of 2011*. Toronto: Dundurn.

Goffman, E. (1959). *The presentation of self in everyday life*. New York: Doubleday and Anchor Books.

Hamilton, A. (2011). *How Stephen Harper is out-Obama-ing Michael Ignatieff*. Retrieved May 3, 2012 from http://www.aranhamilton.com/post/4350146223/how-stephen-harper-is-out-obama-ing-michael-ignatieff

Kaye, K. (2009). *Campaign '08: A turning point for digital media*. CreateSpace.

Metzgar, E., & Maruggi, A. (2009). Social media and the 2008 U.S. presidential election. *Journal of New Communications Research, 4*(1), 141–165.

Norris, P. (2001). *Do campaign communications matter for civic engagement? American elections from Eisenhower to G.W. Bush*. Retrieved May 1, 2012 from http://www.hks.harvard.edu/fs/pnorris/Acrobat/Farrell&Schmitt-Beck%20Chapter%209.pdf

O'Reilly. (2005). *What is web 2.0: Design patterns and business models for the next generation of software*. Retrieved January 6, 2012 from oreilly.com/pub/a/Web2/archive/what-is-Web-20.html

Rospars, J. (2010). *Election 2010: New digital battlefield, same old politics none of the parties have leveraged new media in this campaign to build support in the way Barack Obama did*. Retrieved January 10, 2012 from http://www.guardian.co.uk/commentisfree/2010/may/04/new-digital-battlefield-old-politics

Smith, A., & Rainie, L. (2008). *The internet and the 2008 election*. Pew Internet and American Life Project. Retrieved January 10, 2012 from http://www.pewInternet.org/~/media//Files/Reports/2008/PIP_2008_election.pdf.pdf

Towner, T., & Dulio, D. (2012). New media and political marketing in the United States: 2012 and beyond. *Journal of Political Marketing, 11*, 95–119. doi:10.1080/15377857.2012.642748

Vargas, J. (2008, November 20). Obama raised half a billion online. *The Washington Post*. Retrieved May 4, 2012 from http://voices.washingtonpost.com/44/2008/11/obama-raised-half-a-billion-on.html

Wittel, A. (2001). Toward a network sociality. *Theory, Culture & Society, 18*(6), 51–76. doi:10.1177/02632760122052048

KEY TERMS AND DEFINITIONS

e-Democracy: The use of information and communication technology to enhance democratic practice.

e-Participation: The use of information and communication technologies to consult and engage publics in decision making.

Networked Sociality: A model of sociality which is dynamic, chaotic, and unstable at times, but which is interactive with a high potential for participation and sharing.

Political Campaigning: Pippa Norris (2001) describes political campaigning as organized efforts to inform, persuade and mobilize.

Social Media Campaign: A campaign that has a social media presence, is interactive, and is networked.

Social Networking Sites: Digital platforms where users have a profile, a list of connections, and where they engage in content creation and sharing. Interactivity is a defining characteristic.

Sociality: A model of human relations which, among other things, is characterized by an interactive, or joint, activity.

Chapter 10
Can Digital Technologies Threaten Democracy by Creating Information Cocoons?

Cédric Gossart
Institut Mines-Télécom, France

ABSTRACT

This chapter examines the extent to which digital technologies can threaten democracy by creating "information cocoons," within which information is filtered and tailored to our tastes and prevailing opinions. Digital technologies allow us to filter information and contacts in a very efficient way, thereby creating a risk that we end up exchanging information only with like-minded people. Since humans' bounded rationality cannot cope with the amount of information available on the Internet, we are confronted with problems of cognitive dissonance that we attempt to solve by ignoring opinions and arguments that differ too much from our own. Recent political events in the Arab world suggest that digital technologies support democratisation. But there is also a risk that these technologies might impoverish democratic debates and reduce exchanges amongst the stakeholders of a given political arena while radicalising their points of views. This threat is serious and needs to be investigated. To do so, this chapter suggests a methodology to evaluate that risk, as well as ways to mitigate it. Various methods have been used to analyse the polarisation of opinions in human societies, such as the ones analysing the traces left by Internet users in blogs or hypertext links. The authors provide a review of these methods after having explained the main factor conducive to the creation of information closure.

INTRODUCTION

A public problem can be defined as "the transformation of some social fact into a public issue and/or state intervention (…) if it has been constructed by the voluntary action of various operators" (Neveu, 1999). All public problems follow a specific path, which can be divided into the four phases of the transformation of private difficulties into public problems, the flourishing of speeches describing prejudices and the formulation of claims, the institutionalisation or bureaucratisation of the public problem, and the publication and realisation of a programme of public action (Cefaï, 1996).

DOI: 10.4018/978-1-4666-6038-0.ch010

Copyright © 2014, IGI Global. Copying or distributing in print or electronic forms without written permission of IGI Global is prohibited.

This paper explores the role that information and communication technologies (ICTs) can play in the emergence of public problems. Indeed, if these technologies can support democratic claims, they can also hamper their expression. The transformation of a private claim into a public problem is a key step in the process leading to its integration in the political agenda.

Few studies have analysed the factors that can block this process of transformation (Pariser, 2011). In order to better understand how ICTs can impact the emergence of public problems, we will first introduce the theoretical framework of this analysis. We will then examine the various ways by which ICTs can influence this emergence, and suggest ways to identify them by analysing the case of information cocoons.

BACKGROUND

Human societies have always used some form of communication, even long before the development of language. Today, communicating involves the use of digital technologies, which are often equated with stronger and more transparent democracies. Indeed, they allow politicians to communicate in real time and to engage in more participatory policy-making. However, ICTs also have negative effects on democracies, which tend to be underestimated. Before examining one of them, this next section underlines the key role of the first stage of the construction of public policies.

Many sociologists of public problems such as Emerson and Messinger (1977), W. Felstiner et al. (1980 - 1981), Dewey (1991), or Cefaï (1996) have sought to understand the processes by which private issues are transformed into public problems (Chateauraynaud, 2011). For example, the carrying capacity of public arenas as well as the "degree of dramatisation" reached to capture public attention have a strong influence on the selection of public problems (Hilgartner & Bosk, 1988). In *L'État au concret*, J.G. Padioleau argued that a problem emerges when social actors perceive gaps between what could happen and what should happen. ICTs can indeed be used to widen this gap, e.g. by placing a greater emphasis on public problems, even if they are not a major concern for citizens.

The histories, trajectories, owners and places of emergence of public problems can be traced through the three stages of naming (identification of the public problem), Blaming (identification of who can be held responsible for it), and Claiming (what can be asked for compensation) (W. L. F. Felstiner et al., 1991). If one stage is missing or is too weak, the problem may not emerge as a public one. And some actors which are more powerful than others, such as the "moral entrepreneurs" (Becker, 1997), have a stronger capacity to alter the development of these phases; starting with the first one during which public problems emerge. Nowadays, they are even more powerful if they master the art of communicating, which is making an increasing use of ICTs. Indeed, power consists in the capacity to match one's own definition of a problem with the definition of what needs to be done (Etzioni, 1976).

The media play a critical role in this process, since they can offer efficient channels of communication to name, blame, or claim. S. Cohen has underlined their influence in the transformation of mere rockers gangs' fights into a major national security problem (Cohen 2002). Today, digital technologies are a very important tool to diffuse and manage information. This has led to a profusion of information that has forced end-users into using multiple filters to access (some of) it. Such a surfeit of information can be detrimental to the emergence of public problems. Despite this important democratic issue, as underlined in the next section the role of digital technologies in the construction of public policies has seldom been analysed (Greffet, 2011).

THE CONSTRUCTION OF PUBLIC POLICIES

A public policy is a programme of action specific to one or to several public or governmental authorities (Thoenig, 1985). It can also be seen as what governments do and do not do (Dye, 1981). Understanding why some issues are not tackled by governments can help bring out the factors underlying the non emergence of public problems. This can be done by looking at all the phases of the construction of a public policy, which according to the sequential approach (Kübler & Maillard, 2009) can be described by a series of successful steps presented in Figure 1.

Analysing the impact of ICTs on the construction of public policies can be done by examining each of the aforementioned phases. In this paper, we shall focus on the first one during which private issues are transformed into public problems. This transformation happens in "public arenas" (Hilgartner & Bosk, 1988), where actors compete for the ownership of public problems following rules that are specific to each arena. For example, dominant actors in the climate change arena need to use science-based arguments, preferably the ones that are summarised by the IPCC. Alternatively, some of them get around the scientific debate by spreading falsified scientific arguments through the media, such as Claude Allègre in France or Patrick Michaels in the US. The structure of the arena comprises social networks, which allow actors to have a routinised access to public institutions and to media, information agencies, lobbies, rules defined by institutions, and other human, technological or financial resources. Dominant actors are labelled "owners of public problems" (Gusfield, 1980), which stresses that the ownership of a problem can change hands. The strength of these actors partly relies on tool boxes which are made of reserves of experiences and expressions capable of imposing their way of thinking (Cefaï, 1996). It is paramount for these owners to have a privileged access to institutions and media (Hall et al., 1993). Being able to impose one's own definition of a problem is also a key asset in a public arena, since it will strongly influence the policy that might be developed to address it. In a snowball effect, all the actors end up using your definition, not even remembering where it came from. ICTs can help impose such elements of language in public arenas. For example, in the

Figure 1. The phases of a public policy (Adapted from Howlett and Ramesh (1995), Bardach (1996), Anstead and Chadwick (2009)).

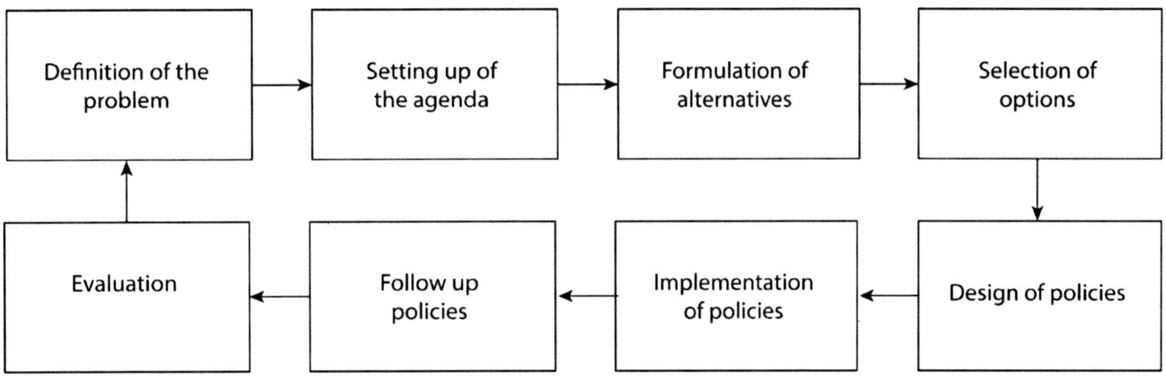

1970s the UK Ministry of Interior had used its monopoly on the collection and diffusion of criminal statistics to impose its definition of crime and to suppress all other interpretations of on-going urban riots (Hall et al., 1993).

But actors are also powerful because in addition to their definition of a public problem, their framing of an issue can also become dominant. The frame of a public problem is a shared social construction which incorporates a definition of the problem (Rhinard, 2008), a proposal to solve it, and a justification to take action. If one of these steps is too weak or missing, it would weaken the position of an actor in a public arena. For example, J. Gusfield has shown how conservative actors in the USA could change the frame used to explain traffic accidents from "accident-fatality" to "accident-crime"; the (drunk) driver eventually being pointed as the main factor of traffic casualties (Gusfield, 1980).

ATTENTION: INFORMATION CLOSURE!

ICTs are part of the tools that empower the actors of a public arena, their advantage being that they echo the claims of small or poor groups and raise up their voice in the arena. These technologies can trigger competition among public information sources (Schlesinger and Tumbler 1994), which sometimes release contradictory information off the record in order to weaken their competitors, and to keep or shift the ownership of public problems. But the generalised use of these digital technologies also raises dangers for democracies, notably by reducing the diversity of opinions in society. If ICTs are widely used to communicate and diffuse information, they can also contribute to deprive us of new information or contacts, thereby deterring the emergence of a new public problem. Because of ICTs or the way they are used, new information or contacts are kept out of our reach, in a process of "information closure" (Pledel, 2007). We explore in this section some of the key factors contributing to information closure.

The Capture of Attention

The attention of individuals and organisations are limited resources, which many actors are trying to exploit. Putting a topic on the political agenda requires capturing politicians' attention, but also the public's attention to get their support. But these attentions are subjected to intensive requests which tend to saturate them; and thus they might not be able to integrate new pieces of information or to be used to make new contacts in the arena. Public attention can be defined as a 'rare input' (Hilgartner & Bosk, 1988), whose allocation is regulated by competition in a system of public arenas. Therefore, actors are competing in order to impose the publicity of their public problems at the expense of other public problems (Cefaï, 1996). For example, B. Stiegler argues that merchants asphyxiate desire by capturing libidinous energy for marketing purposes (Stiegler, 2008b). The philosopher calls ICTs "technologies of the mind" upon which immaterial capitalism thrives (Petit et al., 2008). He even perceives a serious threat to our civilisation (Stiegler, 2008a), because these technologies are now targeting children. For example, because of intensive video-gaming some of them can suffer from hyperactivity and attention deficit disorder (Boullier, 2009).

Information Closure

The profusion of information on the Internet can cause information overload (Edmunds & Morris, 2000), which leads people to develop technological and psychological protection mechanisms. These mechanisms foster the creation of information cocoons (Sunstein, 2007) that threaten deliberative democracies. Psychological defences seek to avoid cognitive dissonance, by which prevailing beliefs or opinions clash with newly perceived ones. We will for example limit our information searches to certain areas in which we feel comfortable, which can be done very easily by using digital filters such as RSS feeds or bookmarks. This behaviour causes problems for the construction of public policies because citizens need to be receptive to changes in their environment in order to trigger and support new policies. For example, ICTs enable us to build a "Daily Me," our own personal newspaper tailored to our information needs of the day. As a New York Times columnist recently put it: "The danger is that this self-selected 'news' acts as a narcotic, lulling us into a self-confident stupor through which we will perceive in blacks and whites a world that typically unfolds in greys." This can result in locking us up in our individual spheres and lower our expectations and motivation to support the public unfolding of new issues that could become public problems. Some even argue that cognitive dissonance can explain why people get accustomed to risk: we do not want to see the risk, for example because it is too painful or costly to envisage its consequences, and thus we ignore it (Schoeneich & Busset-Henchoz, 1998).

But technology can also help us tailor information and contacts to our needs, especially ICTs. C. Sunstein argues that this can lead to lock us in comfortable information cocoons and generate inert people (Sunstein, 2007), which is the greatest danger for freedom in a democracy. In order to avoid that inertness, a diversity of viewpoint must be maintained, which is not obvious with ICTs. For example, the author notices that in many blogs such diversity is actually missing. Along similar lines, I. Pledel argues that "Technical and social environments (…) create norms and boundaries: the blogosphere is not homogeneous. Informational closure, especially cognitive and spatial closures, limits the deliberation" (Pledel, 2007). How can we identify such closures in order to suggest ways to avoid them?

ACCOUNTING FOR INFORMATION CLOSURE

Information closure corresponds to the "reduction of the capacity of the agent to search, locate, sort out, filter, and select information that might be useful and relevant for him/her" (Pledel, 2007). It is dangerous to the extent that it either isolates individuals or hinders their capacity to communicate. The author distinguishes between spatial and cognitive information closures.

Within blogs for example, spatial closure occurs if Internet links rely upon one another within a closed set. It is not intentional, but rather emerges as a side effect of individual practices (e.g. adding a hyperlink in a blog to signal interesting content, moderating comments, providing proofs by posting a link), or because of interpersonal browsing (Cardon, 2008). Thus, spatial closure emerges because of the very nature of digital technologies. For example, RSS feeds or bookmarks or tags are important sources of spatial closure, because once they are set the individual only accesses information that trickles down these pipelines. Within blogs, spatial closures can be measured by studying the following elements:

- The number of hypertext links (e.g. the ones posted in blogs),
- The range of blog rolls,
- The indexing of the blog in blog search engines,
- Self citation,
- Traffic rank,
- The number of links pointing to the blog (degree of openness).

On the Internet, maps of Website networks can be drawn in order to show the density of the links between the main Websites of a given arena, such as the French political blogosphere in 2012 presented in Figure 2.

Figure 2. The French politicosphere in 2012

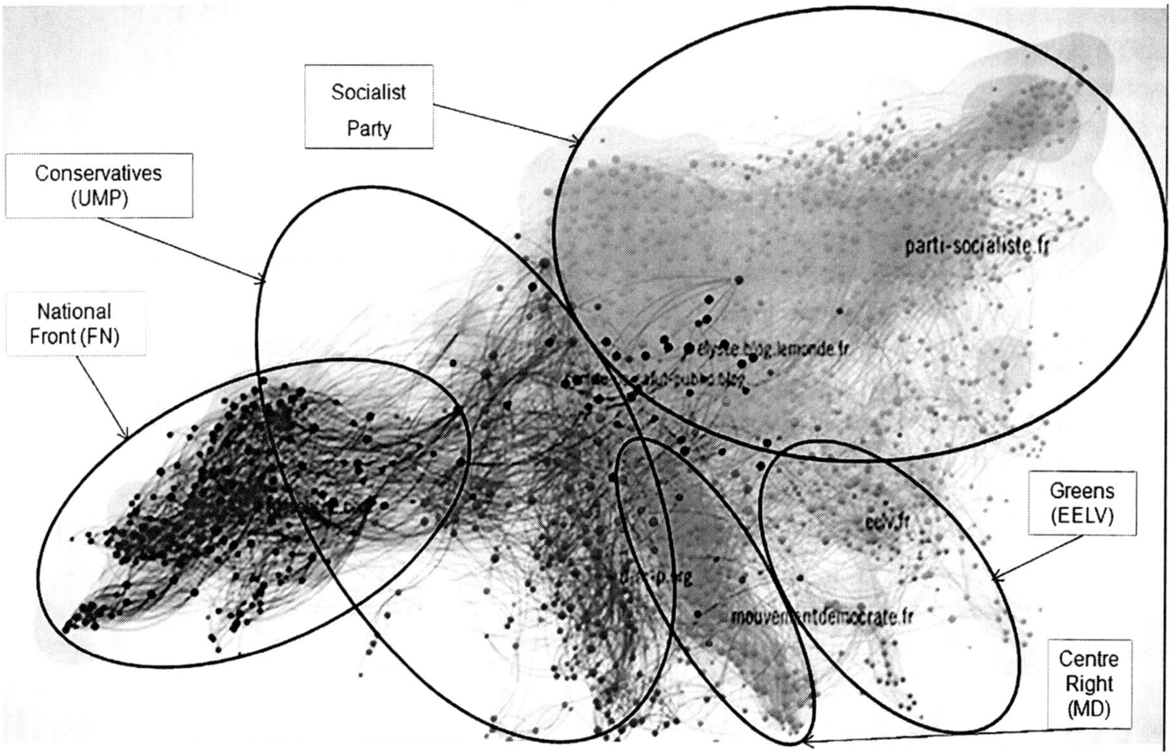

When looking at the blogosphere of militants, as evidenced in Figure 3, one can notice that is even more polarised.

Similar maps exist for other countries. As shown in Figure 4, they also highlight a similar polarisation.

While spatial closure is more related to the technological characteristics of digital technologies, cognitive closure is more idiosyncratic. It could be compared with open/narrow-mindedness, and thus can be intentional or not. For example, depending on their level of intelligence some individuals will have a higher capacity to process information and to integrate new ones. In the case of blogs, since they revolve around a specific theme it is likely that the community will be quite homogeneous. Within these communities there are rules that guide people's information autonomy, such as agreed communication rules, trial period before joining the community based on the quality of information provided or posted on other blogs, sharing of contacts, etc. Besides, within a blog people seek to acquire credibility, which implies to quote others' posts and to avoid contradiction. Studies confirm that some actors have a greater capacity to filter information up the blog ladder:

The unequal distribution of readership, combined with internal norms and linking practices allows interesting news and opinions to rise to the "top" of the blogosphere, and thus to the attention of elite actors, whose understanding of politics may be changed by frames adopted from the blogosphere. (Farrell & Drezner 2008)

Remaining within the boundaries of such closed communities is all the more comfortable since there are risks of exposing oneself to the outside world (comments, critics, insults, trolling). This cognitive closure is more difficult to

Figure 3. The blogosphere of French political militants

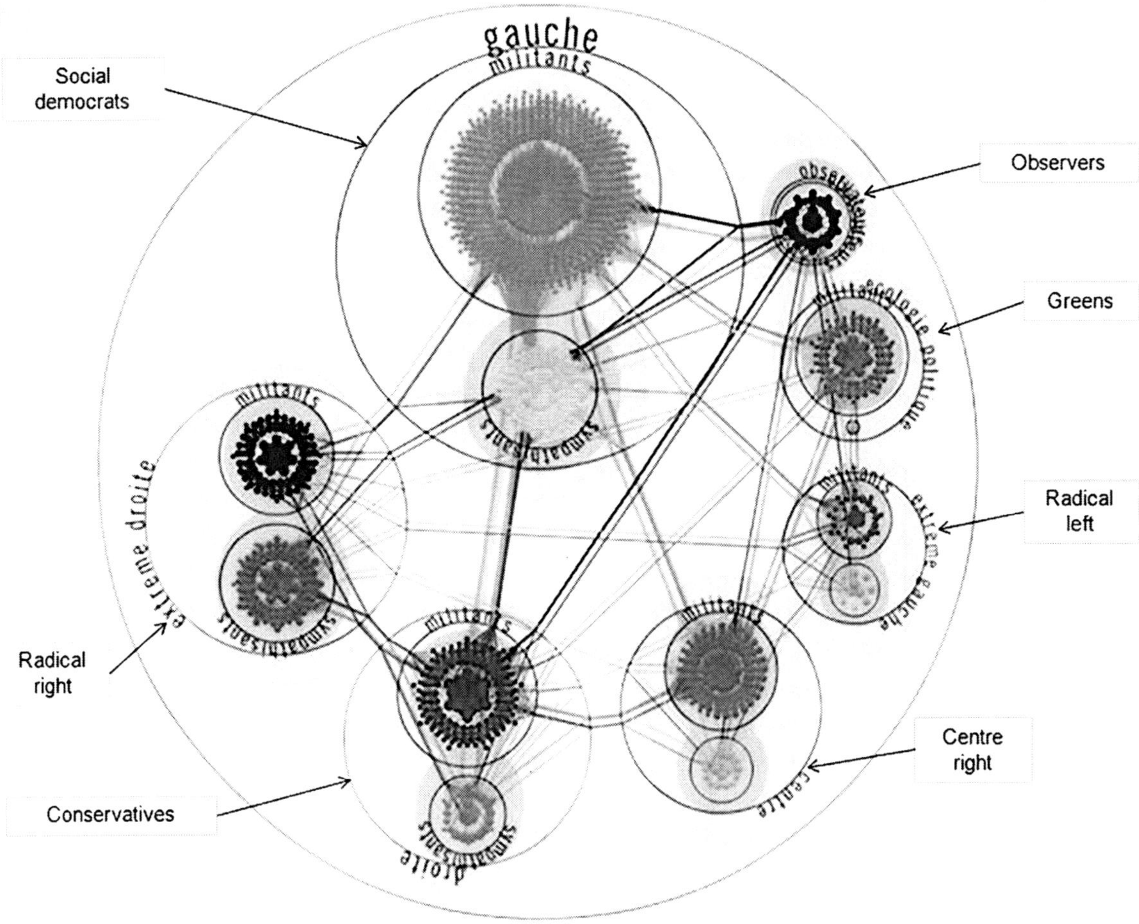

measure than the spatial one, since it requires more qualitative analyses. One can for example use the subjectivity index (e.g. by counting how many time "I" was employed) or the virulence index (number of contradicting comments and trolling), or analyse the marks of dissatisfaction or contradictory information and their impact on their author and other actors (e.g. did they change opinion following my post?).

According to I. Pledel, various reasons can explain why cognitive closure happens (Pledel, 2007). At first, the "Common cause" argument underlines that because participants need to gain credibility within the group, they adapt their style, tone, or even civil identity to facilitate their integration to the group. Second, the "Fear of others' judgement" can induce participants to support a point of view that will not clash with anybody's feelings or opinions. Finally, a process of "Intentional filtering of navigation" can create information cocoons, except if the system leaves room for serendipity or if the person is curious and fearless enough to escape from his/her cocoon.

CONCLUSION

In this article we have analysed the factors explaining why ICTs could be a threat to democracy. Intuitively, the opposite opinion prevails: didn't

Figure 4. The US politicosphere in 2009 (http://politicosphere.net/map, accessed 14 November 2012)

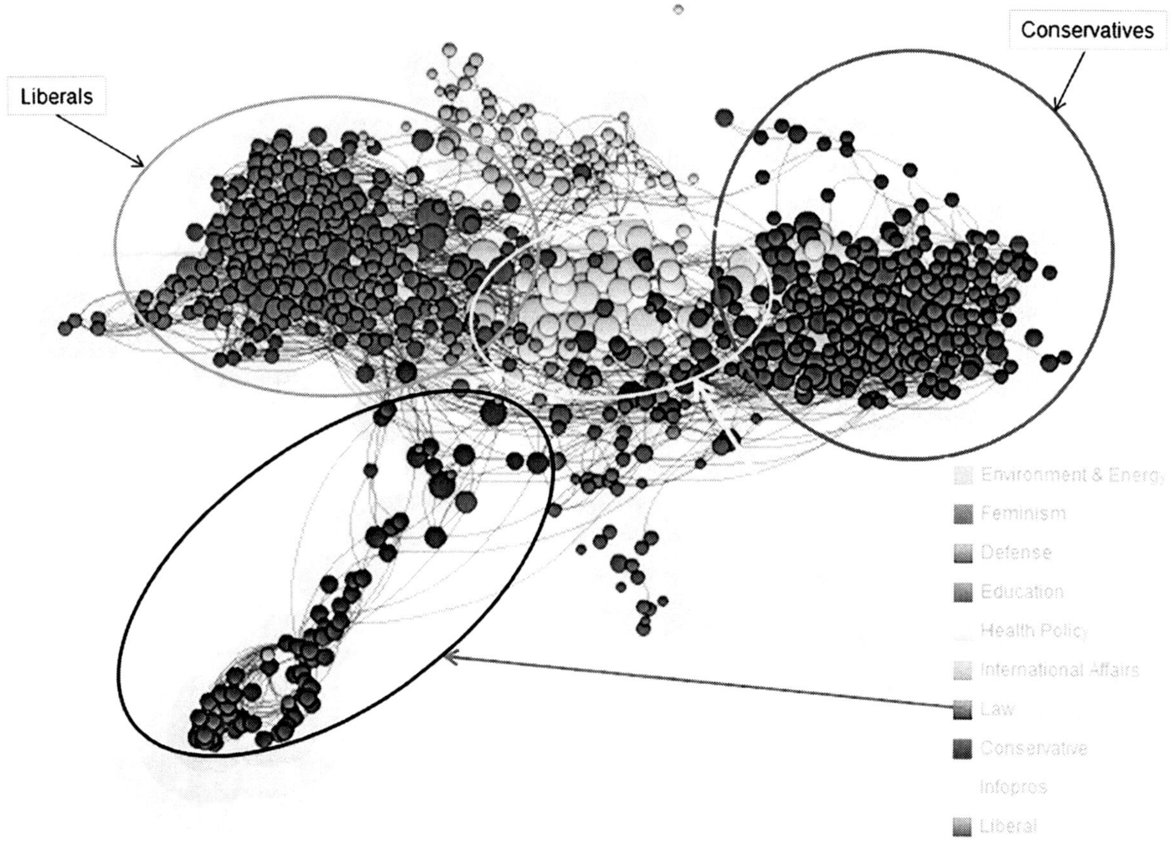

social networks, blogs and the Internet provide support to people fighting in the Arab revolutions, defending human rights in china,1 or representing suburban minorities in France (Zappi, 2010)? We have argued that ICTs can also contribute to create information cocoons that impoverish the diversity of information and the people we can get in touch with. As C. Sunstein put it, a diversity of opinions and exchanges is paramount to the very survival of deliberative democracies (Sunstein, 2007). If this diversity is too poor, there is a risk of 'balkanisation' within this society, as in the aftermath of the 2004 US elections (Adamic & Glance, 2005). It is therefore essential to analyse those risks and this paper has highlighted methods to do so. Future studies could for example enable us to further explore the possible balkanisation of the politicosphere, and to anticipate it by developing policies to protect the democratic space it deserves to be.

REFERENCES

Adamic, L., & Glance, N. (2005). The political blogosphere and the 2004 U.S. election: Divided they blog. In *Proceedings of the 3rd International Workshop on Link Discovery,* (pp. 36-43). ACM. doi:citeulike-article-id:1244437

Anstead, N., & Chadwick, A. (2009). Parties, election campaigning, and the internet: Toward a comparative institutional approach. In A. Chadwick, & P. Howard (Eds.), *Routledge handbook of internet politics* (pp. 56–71). London: Routledge.

Bardach, E. (1996). *The eight step path of policy analysis: A handbook for practice*. Berkeley, CA: Berkeley Academic Press.

Becker, H. S. (1997). Outsiders: Studies in the sociology of deviance (New ed.). New York: Free Press.

Boullier, D. (2009). Les industries de l'attention: Au-delà de la fidélisation et de l'opinion. *Reseaux*, (154): 232–246.

Cardon, D. (2008). *Le design de la visibilité: Un essai de typologie du web 2.0*. Retrieved from http://www.Internetactu.net/2008/02/01/le-design-de-la-visibilite-un-essai-de-typologie-du-Web-20

Cefaï, D. (1996). La construction des problèmes publics: Définitions de situations dans des arènes publiques. *Reseaux*, *14*(75), 43–66.

Chateauraynaud, F. (2011). *Argumenter dans un champ de forces: Essai de balistique sociologique*. Paris: Pétra.

Cohen, S. (2002). *Folk devils and moral panics: The creation of the mods and rockers* (3rd ed.). Abingdon, UK: Routledge.

Dewey, J. (1991). *The public and its problems*. Athens, OH: Ohio University Press.

Dye, T. R. (1981). *Understanding public policy*. Upper Saddle River, NJ: Prentice-Hall.

Edmunds, A., & Morris, A. (2000). The problem of information overload in business organisations: A review of the literature. *International Journal of Information Management*, *20*(1), 17–28. doi:10.1016/S0268-4012(99)00051-1

Emerson, R. M., & Messinger, S. L. (1977). The micro-politics of trouble. *Social Problems*, *25*(2), 121–134. doi:10.2307/800289

Etzioni, A. (1976). *Social problems*. Upper Saddle River, NJ: Prentice-Hall.

Farrell, H., & Drezner, D. (2008). The power and politics of blogs. *Public Choice*, *134*(1), 15–30. doi: doi:10.1007/s11127-007-9198-1

Felstiner, W., Abel, R., & Sarat, A. (1980 - 1981). The emergence and transformation of disputes: Naming, blaming, claiming. *Law & Society Review*, *15*(3/4), 631-654. doi:citeulike-article-id:511899

Felstiner, W. L. F., Abel, R. L., & Sarat, A. (1991). L'émergence et la transformation des litiges: Réaliser, reprocher, réclamer. *Politix*, *16*, 41–54. doi:10.3406/polix.1991.1477

Greffet, F. (2011). *Continuerlalutte.com: Les partis politiques sur le web*. Paris: Presses de Sciences Po.

Gusfield, J. R. (1980). *The culture of public problems: Drinking-driving and the symbolic order*. Chicago: The University of Chicago Press.

Hall, S., Critcher, C., Jefferson, T., Clarke, J. N., & Roberts, B. (1993). *Policing the crisis: Mugging, the state and law and order*. London: Macmillan.

Hilgartner, S., & Bosk, C. L. (1988). The rise and fall of social problems: A public arenas model. *American Journal of Sociology*, *94*(1), 53–78. doi:10.1086/228951

Howlett, M., & Ramesh, M. (1995). *Studying public policy: Policy cycles and policy subsystems*. Oxford, UK: Oxford University Press.

Kübler, D., & Maillard, J. (2009). *Analyser les politiques publiques*. Grenoble: Presses universitaires de Grenoble.

Neveu, E. (1999). L'approche constructiviste des problèmes publics. *Etudes de Communication*, *22*, 41–57. doi:10.4000/edc.2342

Pariser, E. (2011). *The filter bubble: What the internet is hiding from you*. New York: Penguin.

Petit, P., Bontems, V., & Stiegler, B. (2008). *Economie de l'hypermatériel et psychopouvoir (entretiens avec Bernard Stiegler)*. Paris: Mille et une nuits.

Pledel, I. (2007). Le blog face à la clôture informationnelle: La délibération au service de l'apprentissage. *Distances et Savoirs*, *5*(2), 275–288. doi:10.3166/ds.5.275-288

Rhinard, M. (2008). Le cadrage de la politique antiterroriste de l'UE. In *La construction des problèmes publics en Europe*. Strasbourg: Presses Universitaires de Strasbourg.

Schlesinger, P., & Tumbler, H. (1994). *Reporting crime: The media politics of criminal justice*. Oxford, UK: Clarendon.

Schoeneich, P., & Busset-Henchoz, M.-C. (1998). La dissonance cognitive: Facteur explicatif de l'accoutumance au risque. *Revue de Geographie Alpine*, 53–62. doi:10.3406/rga.1998.2878

Stiegler, B. (2008a). *La télécratie contre la démocratie: Lettre ouverte aux représentants politiques*. Paris: Flammarion.

Stiegler, B. (2008b). Le désir asphyxié, ou comment l'industrie culturelle détruit l'individu. *Manière de Voir, La Fabrique du Conformisme*, (96), 10-15.

Sunstein, C. R. (2007). *Republic 2.0*. Princeton, NJ: Princeton University Press.

Thoenig, J. C. (1985). *Traité de science politique: Les politiques publiques* (Vol. 4). Paris: PUF.

Zappi, S. (2010). Un caillou dans la chaussure de la presse française: Retour sur l'expérience bondy blog. *Mouvements*, *1*(61), 140–142. doi:10.3917/mouv.061.0140

KEY TERMS AND DEFINITIONS

Information Closure: Information closure corresponds to the reduction of the capacity of the agent to search, locate, sort out, filter, and select information that might be useful and relevant for them.

Information Cocoons: Information cocoons exist as a result of information is filtered and tailored to our tastes and prevailing opinions. Digital technologies allow us to filter information and contacts in a very efficient way, thereby creating a risk that we end up exchanging information only with like-minded people.

Public Attention: A 'rare input' whose allocation is regulated by competition in a system of public arenas where actors are competing in order to impose the publicity of their public problems at the expense of other public problems.

Public Problem: The transformation of some social fact into a public issue and/or state intervention if it has been constructed by the voluntary action of various operators.

Self-Selected News: Self-selected news acts as a narcotic, lulling us into a self-confident stupor through which we will perceive in blacks and whites a world that typically unfolds in greys.

Chapter 11

Trolling for the Lulz?
Using Media Theory to Understand Transgressive Humour and Other Internet Trolling in Online Communities

Jonathan Bishop
Centre for Research into Online Communities and E-Learning Systems, Belgium

ABSTRACT

Internet trolling as a term has changed in meaning since it first entered mainstream use on the Internet in the 1990s. In the 2010s, it has come to refer to the posting of provocative or offensive messages on the Internet to harm others. This change in usage of the term opens up new challenges for understanding the phenomenon, especially as some are still resistant to taking it beyond its original meaning. This chapter tries to distinguish the 1990s kind from the 2010s kind by referring to the former as classical trolling and the latter as anonymous trolling. Taking part in the former is considered to be "trolling for the Lolz" (i.e. positive) and the second to mean "trolling for the Lulz" (i.e. negative). Through using document and genre analysis, this chapter finds that there are common ways in which anonymous trolling manifests differently on different platforms. The chapter concludes by presenting a model for understanding which genres of online community are at risk for particular types of trolling.

INTRODUCTION

Internet trolling is a term that has changed with use over the last twenty years. In the 1990s Internet trolling was a term referring to the practice of posting provocative messages that were so obviously intended to be inflammatory that the resulting barrage of abusive posts that followed, called a 'flame war,' made regular members of online community feel entertained. In the 2000s the use of the term as being distinct from 'flaming' was challenged (Herring, Job-Sluder, Scheckler, & Barab, 2002) and by the 2010s the term had changed again to that the two were almost inseparable (Bishop, 2014; Hardaker, 2010). Internet trolling has now come to mean the posting of messages via a public communications network that are either provocative or offensive. Distinctions have been drawn between the two, with the 1990s variety being called 'classical trolling' and

DOI: 10.4018/978-1-4666-6038-0.ch011

Copyright © 2014, IGI Global. Copying or distributing in print or electronic forms without written permission of IGI Global is prohibited.

the 2010s variety being called 'Anonymous trolling' (Bishop, 2013a). The reasons for the first are self-evident, but in the case of 'Anonymous trolling,' which should always have a capital 'A,' more explanation is necessary. The word, 'Anonymous,' is named after a group of self-described Internet users who attempt to create organised abuse of others or disruption to services, such as through distributed denial of service attacks.

Terms like, 'Trolling for the Lulz' and 'Trolling for the Lolz' can be better understood with these classes of trolling. The former, which is where people post offensive messages for their own entertainment can be seen to resemble Anonymous trolling. The latter, which is the posting of messages for others' entertainment as well as one's own, can be seen to resemble classical trolling. The terms, 'troll' and 'trolling,' as latched onto by the mass media, could be considered to be the latest term used to describe abuse via technology, with the earlier term being cyberbullying. Some researchers have tried to make distinctions between abusive types of trolling as being 'flame trolling' and 'cyber-bullying' and the more positive sort being 'kudos trolling' and 'cyber-kindness' (Bishop, 2012b; Cassidy, Brown, & Jackson, 2013). Whichever terms are used it is clear that there are positive types of trolling and negative kinds, and it is possible to accommodate both the traditionalists and the more modern uses of the terms.

BACKGROUND

The change in meaning of Internet trolling has created a divide between the traditionalists who want it to have the classical meaning, and those who want it to have the Anonymous meaning. The character theory in Table 1 by Bishop (2012b, 2013c, 2014) could provide a means to resolve this dispute. When spoken about in terms of classical trolling, those who troll could be called, 'Trolls' (with the capital 'T') and those who take part in Anonymous trolling could be called, 'trolls' as is commonly done by the media. Trolls are not the only type of Internet users who take part in trolling, as there are many others, as can be seen from Table 1. Online community users, which include Trolls, are known collectively as trollers (Bishop, 2012b; Bishop, 2014; Herring et al., 2002).

As can be seen from Table 1, the Big Man is someone who does trolling by posting something to others in order to support their own worldview, even if it does not support others' collective opinions and ends up offending them. The type of troller most people in fact mean when they call someone a 'troll' is in fact the Snert. A Snert takes part in trolling to harm others for their own sick entertainment. The more pleasant trollers include the Flirt, who take part in trolling to help others be sociable, including through light 'teasing'. There is also the MHBFY Jenny, a troller who takes part in trolling to help people see the lighter side of life and to help them come to terms with their concerns. One of the most creative trollers is the Wizard, who does trolling through making-up and sharing content that has a humorous effect or promotes positive use and understanding. On a darker note, the E-Venger type of troller does trolling in order to trip someone up so that their 'true colours' are revealed. They may also, in the moment, fiercely attack someone who offended them in order to 'fight flames with flames'. A high profile example of this was with Liam Stacey, a student from Swansea, who posted a string of abuse to Twitter following being rebuked for posting an offensive comment about a footballer who suffered a cardiac arrest (Bishop, 2013a; Bishop, 2014; Cleland, 2013; Edwards, 2012; Fisher, 2013; Hall, Hanna, & Huey, 2013). Another type of troller – the Iconoclast – takes part in trolling to help others discover 'the truth', often by telling them things completely factual, but which may drive them into a state of consternation. They may post links to content that contradicts the worldview of their target, for instance. A slippery type of troller is the Chatroom Bob, who takes

Table 1. A character theory of trollers

Troller Character Type	Description
E-Venger	Driven by 'Vengeance' forces. An E-Venger does trolling in order to trip someone up so that their 'true colours' are revealed. An E-Venger is a type of 'Hater,' because they target those who 'wronged' them.
Iconoclast	Driven by 'Destructive' forces. An Iconoclast takes part in trolling to help others discover 'the truth', often by telling them things completely factual, but which may drive them into a state of consternation. They may post links to content that contradicts the worldview of their target. An Iconoclast is a type of 'Hater,' because they can make others aggressive when they challenge that person's worldview.
Snert	Driven by 'Anti-social' forces. A Snert takes part in trolling to harm others for their own sick entertainment. A Snert is a type of 'Hater,' because they try to harm others as a result of their warped morality that leads them to want to 'put others straight' for their own satisfaction.
Big Man	Driven by 'Order' forces. A Big Man does trolling by posting something they think is pleasing to others in order to support their own worldview, which often offends that person and turns them against the Big Man. A Big Man is a type of 'Lolcow,' because whilst trying to be an unwanted arbitrator others unite against them and this continues while they are a member of a specific online community.
Ripper	Driven by 'Thanatotic' forces. A Ripper takes part in self-deprecating trolling in order to build a false sense of empathy from others. A Ripper is a type of 'Lolcow' because others get satisfaction out of mocking them.
Chatroom Bob	Driven by 'Existential' forces. A chatroom bob takes part in trolling to gain the trust of others members in order to exploit them. Chatroom Bobs are a type of 'Lolcow,' because they are targeted by others who can see through their games.
MHBFY Jenny	Driven by 'Forgiveness forces'. A MHBFY Jenny takes part in trolling to help people see the lighter side of life and to help others come to terms with their concerns. A MHBFY Jenny is a 'Bzzzter,' because they will try to be helpful when in reality they do not understand the other person's situation.
Wizard	Driven by 'Creative' forces. A Wizard does trolling through making up and sharing content that has a humorous effect. A Wizard is a type of 'Bzzzter', because they may post content for the sake of it even if they know it is not accurate or reliable.
Flirt	Driven by 'Social' forces. A Flirt takes part in trolling to help others be sociable, including through light 'teasing.' A Flirt is a type of 'Bzzzter', because they post anecdotes which may not be relevant to the specific situation.
Lurker	Driven by 'Surveillance' forces. Lurkers make silent calls by accident, etc., clicking on adverts or 'like' buttons, using 'referrer spoofers', reporting posts, modifying opinion polls or user kudos scores. Lurkers are a type of 'Eyeballer,' because they will observe what others are saying and rarely see the need or have the willingness to participate.
Troll	Driven by 'Chaos' forces. A Troll takes part in trolling to entertain others, bringing some fun and mischief to an online community. A Troll is a type of 'Eyeballer,' because they will wait for the opportune moment to disrupt the community's equilibrium.
Elder	Driven by 'Escape' forces. An Elder is an outbound member of the community, often engaging in "trolling for newbies," where they wind up the newer members often without questioning from other members. An Elder is a type of 'Eyeballer,' because they will look out for unsuspecting members to target for entertainment, such as playing devil's advocate.

part in trolling to gain the trust of other members in order to exploit them (Bishop, 2012d; Bishop, 2013b; Jansen & James, 1995; Jansen & James, 2002). Their close cousin – the Ripper – takes part in self-deprecating trolling in order to build a false sense of empathy from others.

Finally there are two less dominant Trollers that can be seen in Table 1 – the Lurker and the Elder. Lurkers, who lack a visible presence in the community for the reason that they are often on the periphery, are like their Elder cousins, who are outbound and also on the periphery (Bishop,

2007; Kimball, Stables, & Green, 2001). Lurkers troll using silent calls by accident, etc., clicking on adverts or 'like' buttons, using 'referrer spoofers', modifying opinion polls or user kudos scores. An Elder on the other hand trolls through engaging in 'trolling for newbies', where they wind up the newer members often without questioning of their actions from other members. So as can be seen from Table 1, far from the Troll being the only type of Troller, there are 11 other kinds and in fact the Troll, who wants to entertain others, is far removed from the Snert, who wants to harm others.

AN INVESTIGATION INTO THE DIFFERENT TYPES OF TROLLING IN DIFFERENT GENRES OF WEB-BASED COMMUNITY

Websites or other platforms such as 'viral email' are dedicated to humour by creating large dynamic archives of material that had been circulated by being 'passed along' or using 'viral' methods (Shifman, Coleman, & Ward, 2007). While at the start of the millennium only minor amounts of viral transfer of transgressive humour occurred via Websites, since then it has become a major part of the proliferation of flame trolling across the Web and beyond emails and newsgroups. Viral humour can play a part in meta-communication, such as where extended threads on online communities like 4chan can result in discursive construction of communication action patterns that could be better utilised as part of information systems that support communication and cooperation in virtual intercultural communities (Yetim, 2001). Such narratives can form part of the signalling mechanism for the formation of sub-cultures, particularly ones that instigate Internet trolling or lurking (Bishop, 2012a). Table 2 presents a list and description of online community genres on which social networking platforms can be built to enable these types of communication.

Original genres like the personal homepage have now been transposed into social networking services as 'profile pages' and individual-controlled 'groups,' which are linked together more often than not through the circle of friends social networking technology. Message Boards are also a common type of online community, composed of threads of discussions that can often be started by any member of the community. Email lists and newsletters are flexible online communities that people can easily join, leave and participate in using only their email account. Chat groups can take many forms and usually allow the instant sending of a message for others to respond to immediately. Virtual worlds also allow for fluid interactions and users can often fashion a particular character for themselves. Weblogs and directories have a particular structure that makes then distinct from other online community genres. Finally Wikis and Hypertext fiction are unique in that it is often possible for someone to create a new page to add to the existing ones and in the case of Wikis it is often possible for others to edit these pages, even if they have been posted by others.

Whilst the advantages and disadvantages of these Web-based communities are clear, the differences between them in terms of how trolling is manifested is less clear. It is therefore a goal of this paper to understand the differences between the different genres.

Methodology

The methodological approach taken in this study is document analysis. Document analysis is done to analyse entire forms, such as intelligent form analysis and table detection, or to describe the layout and structure of a document (Kleber, Diem, & Sablatnig, 2010). In the case of this study it will be the latter. One new problem in Web document analysis is the rich variety of data formats (Lopresti & Zhou, 1998). This paper attempts to show how through understanding online communities as genres can help aid the understanding of new knowledge around Internet trolling.

Table 2. Genres of Web-based community

Genre	Advantages/Disadvantages
Personal Homepage	Advantages: Regularly updated, allows people to connect with those that they know through leaving messages and joining circle of friends. Disadvantage: Members often need to re-register for each site and cannot usually take their 'Circle of Friends' with them.
Message Boards	Advantages: Posts can be accessed at any time. Easy to ignore undesirable content. Disadvantages: Threads can become very long and reading through the messages is time consuming.
Email Lists and Newsletters	Advantages: Allows a user to receive a message as soon as it is sent. Disadvantages: Cannot always access an archive of messages.
Chat Groups and Instant Messagng	Advantages: Synchronous. Users can communicate in real-time. Disadvantages: Posts can be sent simultaneously and the user can become lost in the conversation.
Virtual Worlds	Advantages: 3D metaphors allow a user to get more involved in the community. Disadvantages: Requires certain hardware and software that not all users have.
Weblogs and Directories	Advantages: Easily updated, regular content. Disadvantages: Members cannot start topics, only respond to them.
Wikis and Hypertext Fiction	Advantages: Can allow for collaborative work on literary projects. Disadvantages: Can bring out the worst in people, such as their destructive natures.

Documents

The documents that were chosen to be analysed for this study were from the social media platforms that were commonly used. For the personal homepage this was Facebook. Whilst this may not seem obvious for some, Facebook can be seen as a social networking service that is made up of lots of independent online communities. In other words, a Facebook Profile or Page is a personal homepage according to the definition in Bishop (2009). In terms of Weblogs and Directories, Yahoo!Answers was chosen. Using the definition in Bishop (2009) it can be seen that as this Website involves a specific user making an opening post and inviting comments, with this post being listed among other posts, then it fits into this genre. Yahoo!Answers is known to be notorious for trolling. For the Wikis and Hypertext Fiction category Wikipedia was chosen. Whilst wikis like Encyclopaedia Dramatica are dedicated to Anonymous trolling, as Wikipedia is more mainstream it would provide a more authentic and like-for-like comparison to the other genres investigated. In terms of Chat Groups and Instant Messaging, Twitter was chosen. Whilst to most people, academics included, Twitter is a micro-blogging platform, if one applies Bishop (2009) today, as opposed to when it was published this makes more sense. Messages on Twitter are exchanged between users synchronously in that anyone can create a new post directed at anyone. It can therefore be seen that Twitter resembles a chatroom more than a blog, which in the case of the latter is asynchronous and posts can only be initiated by the blog owner. The Website, 4chan, was chosen for analysis for the Message Board genre. Whilst this is used by the Anonymous group to troll for the Lulz, it was originally set-up as an American alternative to the Japanese Futaba Channel, 2chan, both intended as Manga 'imageboards'. Google Groups was the document source selected for 'Email Lists and Newsletters.' Whilst others were available, this platform was chosen because it was based around the Usenet platform, which existed since the 1990s.

Results

The results of the study showed that the differences identified between genres of online community exists, but the ways in which others were abused was almost the same, even though the posts manifested differently in keeping with the genre style.

Personal Homepage (Facebook)

The social networking service Facebook was at the time of writing one of the most popular Websites of its kind. Facebook, like MySpace, is based around using buddy-lists to join personal homepages (i.e. profiles) together. The difference between these three platforms is quite simple. Facebook allows users to add anyone who confirms the friendship request, and the user can group their friends into 'Circles,' something later adopted by Google+. MySpace allowed people to add anyone they chosen, but was limited in how users could group their friends. One can see a collection of self-authored Facebook pages as being no different to a GeoCities Website, except it requires little skill for users to set up a personal home page and link it to their friends on Facebook. Even Facebook's innovative 'Facebook Apps' platform is little different from what CGI scripts and Java applets were in the day of Geocities. The Wall is also little different from a Guestbook. Even so, its ease of use led it to become the most popular hosts of online communities of its time. It also became a platform among those that were most open to subjecting users to flame trolling. Whilst abuses of memorial pages came to prominence with Natasha MacBryde and Georgia Varley, both from England, the country of Wales has had its fair share of abuse on the platform. One of the most notable examples was the mocking of Phillip Hill, 45, Charles Breslin, 62, David Powell, 50, and Garry Jenkins, 39, who were miners who died tragically in the Gleision Colliery near Swansea. These men were working in a deep pit mine which flooded, eventually killing them. Following the death, memorial Webpages were set up to mark their tragic deaths, which were set upon by flame trollers, probably because of the genuine outpour of public sympathy by people in Wales for their countrymen, which they felt misplaced (Walter, Hourizi, Moncur, & Pitsillides, 2011). The Member of Parliament for Neath Peter Hain tweeted: "Some people are just sick. Hope police hunt down those responsible and ensure they feel full force of the law."

The personal homepage on Facebook, unlike earlier platforms one might argue, includes not only profile pages for users, but the more feature-rich Facebook Pages for promoting organisations, and in many cases today, for 'memorial Websites' where family members and others can remember those loved ones who have passed away. High profile cases of flame trolling on Facebook include the bullying of Natasha MacBryde by Sean Duffy, or the harassment of Georgia Varley's family on Facebook.

Weblogs and Directories (Yahoo!Answers)

As discussed in the previous section, a Weblog is defined by having a single or small group of people who can initiate a discussion for others to comment on. This is similar to directories, such as e-commerce Websites, where the e-tailer lists products they are offering and invites other to comment on them. YouTube could be considered a Weblog as people post a video for others to comment on, and it could also be a directory, because the videos are presented categorically or through recommendations in some cases. This shows this genre proposed by Bishop (2009) to be solidly founded.

The Weblog and directory considered in this section is Yahoo!Answers. This social networking platform allows people to ask and answer questions on any topic for those other users of the Website to answer. As can be seen from the image on the left of Figure 1 the questions asked about Wales are often typical of the stereotype of it being a coal mining country which had a troubled relationship with the Prime Minister Margaret Thatcher.

Equally users of Yahoo!Answers take to more direct forms of transgressive humour, such as making offensive jokes about Welsh people and asking others to join in with suggestions, as can be seen from the image in Figure 2. References to "shagging sheep" and the all too common abuse of Welsh people surface often as a normal course of activity. Few complaints are ever made, perhaps legitimising transgressive humour like this.

As one can see from Figure 3, a discussion on teenage suicides in Bridgend involves the responder confirming to the questioner that the cases are being whipped up by the media to cause a moral panic. The answerer then makes a transgressive jibe about the area by saying there must be a virus in the air that is making teens suicidal. In Wales the media often present groups of youths as 'gangs', describing how they can exploit mobile phones and Internet chat rooms to pass fight details to interested groups. Trollers, or 'trolls' are presented little differently.

Wikis and Hypertext Fiction (Wikipedia)

Wikipedia is a social media Website where theoretically anyone can participate. In reality it is mainly a close group of people who control specific pages, locking out anyone with a different opinion to them. On Wikipedia it is possible to control content if one is able to amass enough supporters. This happened in the case of Ryan Giggs, a Welsh footballer whose page was ransacked following allegations that he got a super-injunction against another Welsh person called Imogen Thomas. As can be seen from Figure 4, Giggs Wikipedia page had edits which made this claim and users left comments in the notes section which had to be deleted by the Wikipedia management in order to avoid charges of contempt of court.

The whole incident shows the vulnerability of public figures to social media services. For instance it is part of Wikipedia's rules to stop people with 'conflicts of interests' in an article from editing them, which means strictly speaking it is difficult for people who have articles about them on Wikipedia to protect themselves from abuse.

Chat Groups and Instant Messaging (Twitter)

On Twitter it is possible for anyone to start a conversation with anyone, simply by typing their user name prefixed with an '@', such as @Imogen_Thomas. It makes sense therefore to extend 'Chat Groups' in Bishop (2009) to be called 'Chat Groups and Instant Messaging.'

This lack of control one would normally see on blogging platforms is one of Twitter's weaknesses and in fact Imogen Thomas has been a major victim of this following her associations with Ryan Giggs and the saga around the case that she allegedly slept with him. Thomas has over 330,000 followers on Twitter. The Snerts/Hater Trollers said "vile" things to Thomas for their own sick entertainment, making it a clear cause of transgressive humour. Thomas posted: "Can the haters stop writing [to] me? Don't you think I have suffered enough?" which did nothing to help, leading to her following it up with "I actually think I'm having a little breakdown - crazy. One minute I'm feeling okay, as ok as can be, the next I'm so low, depressed. Need my mum."

Thomas told the Wales on Sunday newspaper about her experiences of flame trolling, "I don't want to have to face it every single day. Some days I can just cope with it fine, but other days it can

Figure 1. Transgressive humour about Welsh coal miners on Yahoo!Answers

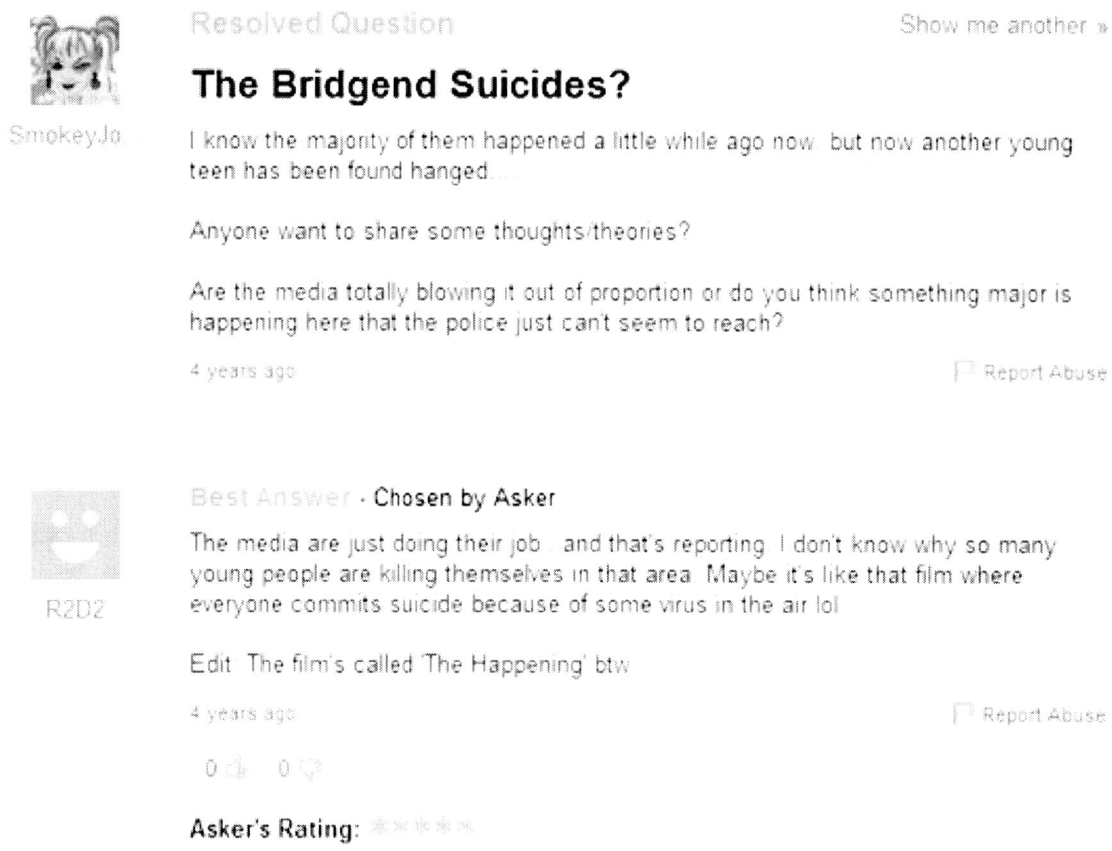

really catch me on a bad day. It's just not fair. I shouldn't be having that much stick - I think I've suffered enough. I just want them to let me get on with my life but some people are reluctant to let me do it."

It is not uncommon for people in Wales to attack their fellow compatriots if they become successful. While this was made light of in books like The Xenophobe's Guide to the Welsh (Winterson-Richards, 2008), it is a serious problem for anyone with aspirations to make it in their homeland. One may link it to the "politics of envy" where local socialist parties get elected among the more disadvantaged through adopting rhetoric that all capitalists are privileged and greedy, which resonates with people unable to take advantage of the free market to get out of poverty, or be attacked if they try. The aforementioned book (Winterson-Richards, 2008) makes it clear, even humourously that those from Wales most likely to be successful and thinking favourably about Wales and its people are those Welsh people who do not live there.

Figure 2. Transgressive humour about Wales in relation to 'sheep' on Yahoo!Answers

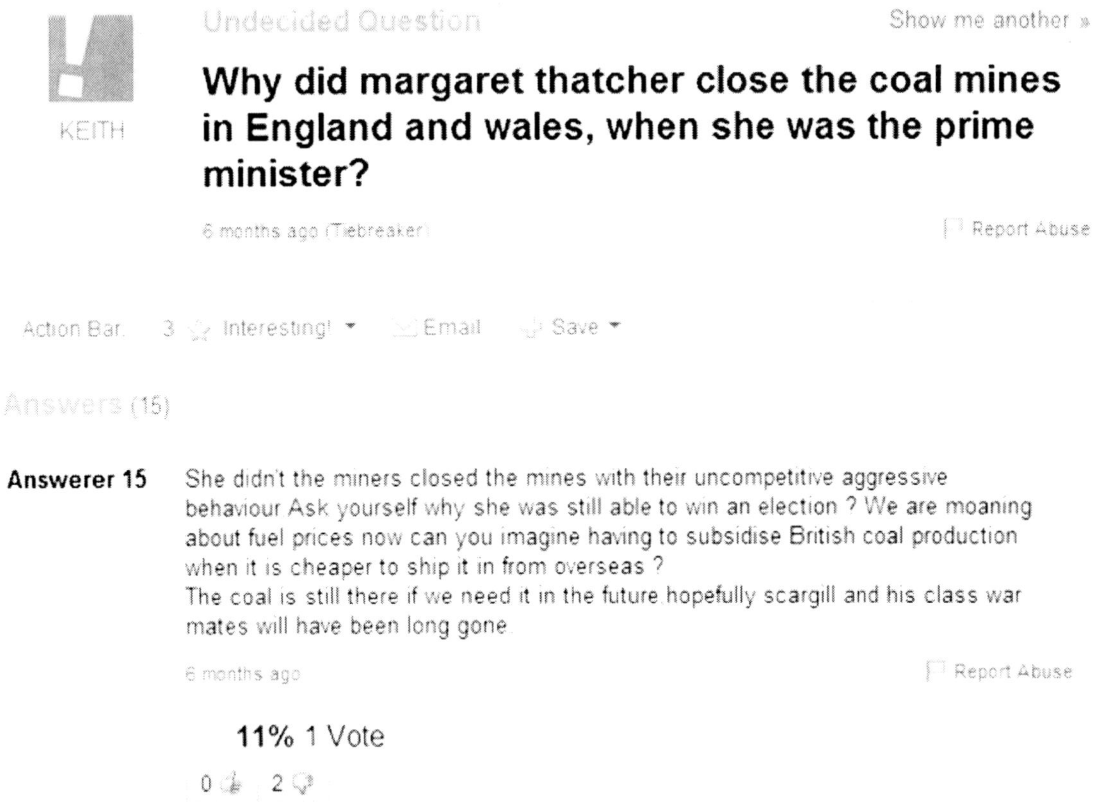

Message Boards (4chan)

The Website 4chan (www.4chan.org) is built around a message board format where users are asked to anonymously submit abusive images and others for comment by others as a kind of anti-social empathy platform. Known as a 'clubhouse', where its users conduct and then post their flame trolling abuses, they produced some of their worst following the death of pop star Michael Jackson, where emotional discussions were the norm on the Website (Schweitzer & Garcia, 2010). In terms of coal mining and people from Wales in general, many of the posts were derogatory. As can be seen from Figure 5, the reactions to the Bridgend suicides discussed in the last section could be considered insensitive at least.

The newspaper coverage following these suicides created a sense that society was damaged and the community where they occurred, Bridgend, was portrayed in a sinister way (as Figure 3). For instance in one edition of the Wales on Sunday, it was described as a "dark and frightening place associated with a spate of teenage suicides." Mass panic emerged in the media and stories emerged with parents calling for social networking Websites to be shut down because they encourage suicide, such as a mother from Swansea called Claire Jones, according to an edition of the South Wales Evening Post. With these two presentations of the Bridgend suicides it can be seen that the shock and awe around the suicide is replicated in the current representations of Internet trolling, where it is seen as a social ill that someone must

Figure 3. Transgressive humour about Welsh suicide victims on Yahoo!Answers

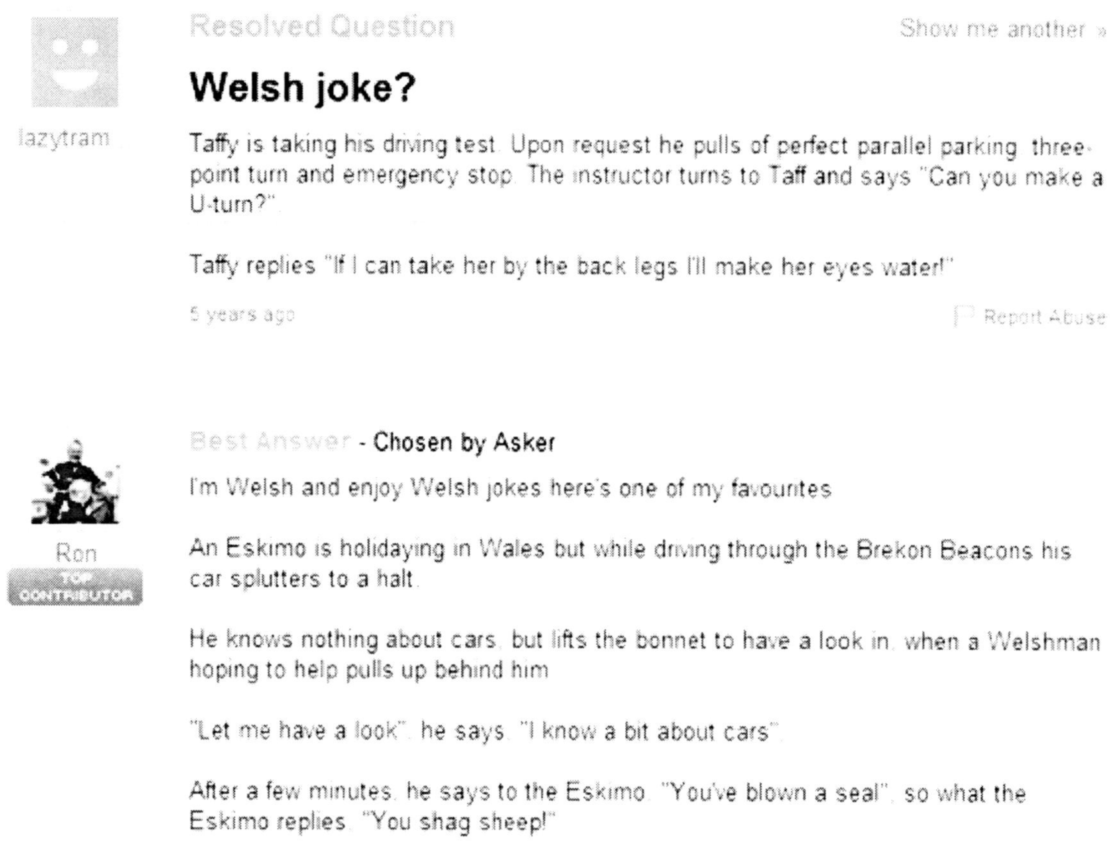

be responsible for. In other instances on 4chan those countries reliant on coal or formerly reliant on coal like Wales were portrayed as being 'backwards' and Welsh people were treated less favourably. This one thread shown in Figure 6 continued the constant discrimination against the Welsh who are often told by others, "Taffy was a Welshman, Taffy was a thief" (Thomas, 1997).

Transgressive humour like this often causes public controversies, and such recurring events in media democracies, play out social divides through a dramatisation of moral and political rifts (Kuipers, 2011). The example in Figure 6 is a perfect depiction of what is called 'meta-communication' and serves as a way to force the creation of sub-cultures where some users of a Website may feel like an outcast. It is presented as a kudos troll that complements a group, in this case saying that Welsh people are the best, whilst actually being a flame trolling presented 'good' Welsh people as criminals. It can therefore be seen that flame trolling can be subtle enough to convey the positive messages in signalling theory whilst actually having a more disingenuous outcome (Connelly, Certo, Ireland, & Reutzel, 2011).

Trollers rooted deep in meta-communicative signalling are often what are known as 'Poe trollers' and 'Concern trollers'. Concern trolling post kudos in support of the opinion of the mainstream whilst having concerns that support their actual point of view (Goode, 2010). Trolling of this kind, particularly if it is entertaining is difficult to identify as transgressive humour due to it looking more like those messages seen in signalling

Figure 4. 'Vandalism' of Ryan Giggs's page on Wikipedia

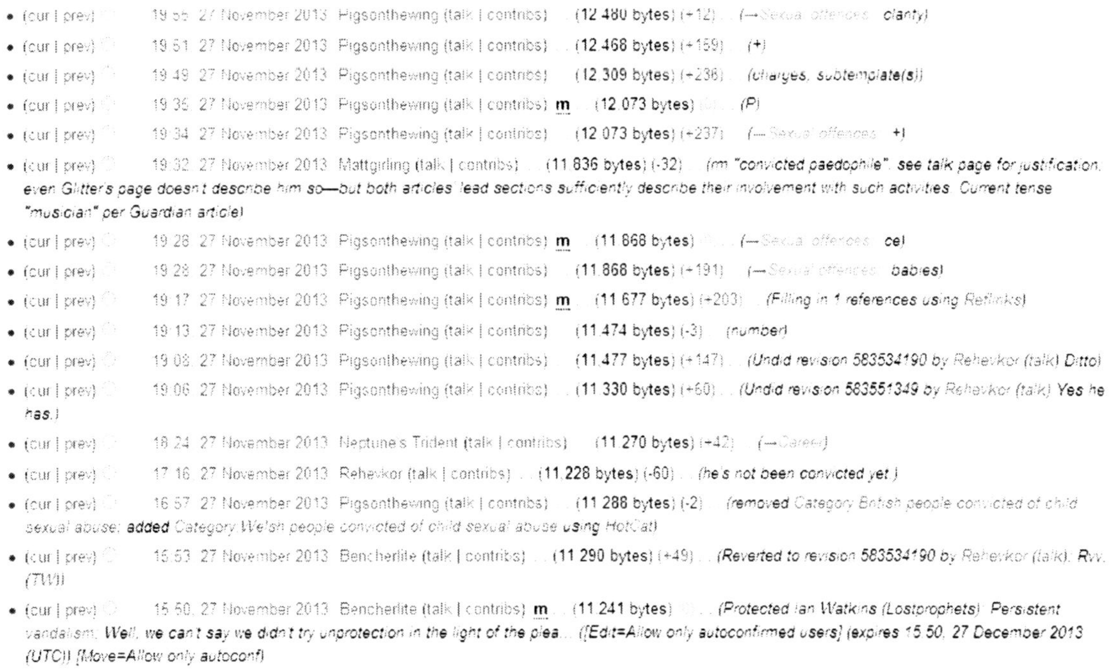

theory. Equally, Poe Trollers take on the persona of someone whose point of view they disagree with and argue it in such a way to discredit it. They are so named after Nathan Poe who created 'Poe's law' which says that one cannot tell the difference between a genuine supporter of a religious point of view who is extreme and these figures of parody without the use of 'emoticons' to let people know they are trolling.

Newsletters and Discussion Lists (Google Groups)

Newsletters and Discussion Lists are quite similar and have a shared background. Once it was very common for Websites to keep users up-to-date with what was going on in the online community by sending them emails with summaries of activities. Because of how the email was once popular,

Figure 5. 4chan's reaction to Bridgend suicides

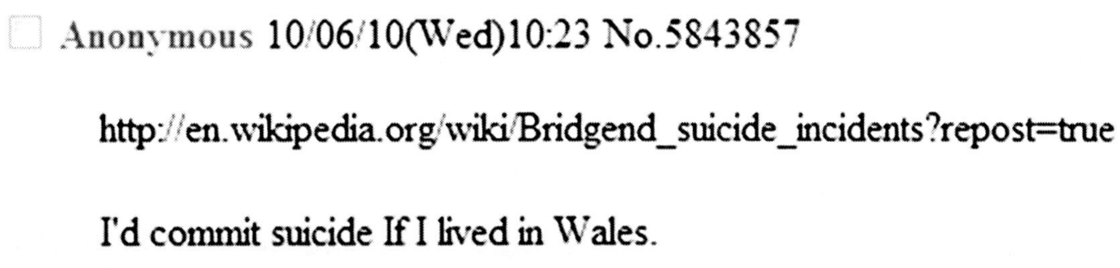

Figure 6. A criminal portrayal of Wales by 4chan

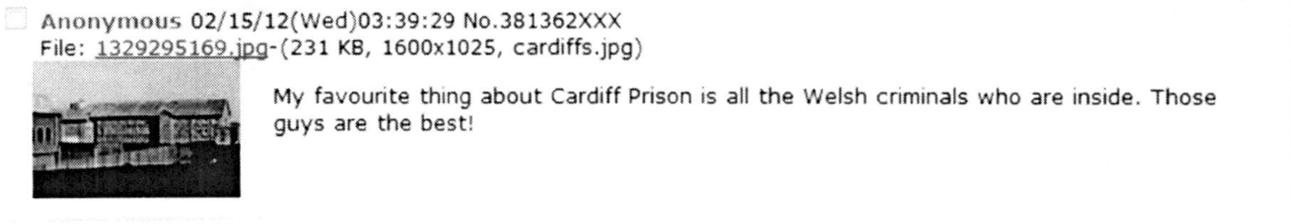

discussion lists came about where people would send emails to an email address which then sends that email out to a number of other email addresses registered on the server. Both these have spawned a degree of flame trolling where with the immediacy of email, people can post abusive replies as soon as as they receive it. The most popular was at one point Usenet, but with the advent of the Web-based eGroups, later taken over by Yahoo! the accessibility of this platform improved.

Today it is possible to access these Usenet groups from Google, and this section will now look at some of the representations of Wales in them. As can be seen in Figure 7, the flame troller on this thread is trying to make light of the fact that many Welsh people are on low wages and are having to work hard to obtain them. This type of transgressive humour can cause self-esteem issues, as people are likely to feel a lack of worth and importance essential to motivation (Brown, Jackson, & Cassidy, 2006).

In the picture in Figure 8 it is possible to see that on Usenet especially, not all narratives are of an abusive nature, especially to the Welsh. The poster in this cases identifies with the plight of the miners who died at Gleision Colliery after their memorial pages were ransacked by flame trollers. This is an emerging response to transgressive humour, where users of the Internet do not always see it as a justifiable form of participation but seek fair and responsible interactions.

TOWARDS A TROLLING MAGNITUDE SCALE FOR UNDERSTANDING INTERNET TROLLING

It has been found that it is possible to classify trolling into different severities based on the amount of effort it takes to enact a particular form of trolling (Bishop, 2012c). This uses classifications of Internet trolling from established literature (Jansen & James, 1995; Jansen & James, 2002). A modification of this framework from Bishop (2012c) is presented in Table 2. Added to it are two additional elements – trolling magnitude and at-risk-genres. The former is a rating system that uses the severity of trolling as a numerical value between 1 and 4. A trolling incident that happens in the moment will be around a trolling magnitude (TM) of 1 and an incident that requires a lot of planning and creation will have a TM of around 4.

As can be seen from Table 3, these severities are linked to the specific genres discussed earlier. Chat Groups and Instant Messaging are more likely to be at risk of Playtime trolling (between 1 and 1.99) where the immediacy of the situation takes over due to low involvement and medium to high flow. Weblogs and Directories are most at risk of Tactical trolling (between 2 and 2.99) where users will need to put some thought into writing an extensive article, sometimes up to 500 words. People wanting to comment may be required to register to post, reducing the immediacy of their

Figure 7. Post about Wales in Google Groups (Usenet)

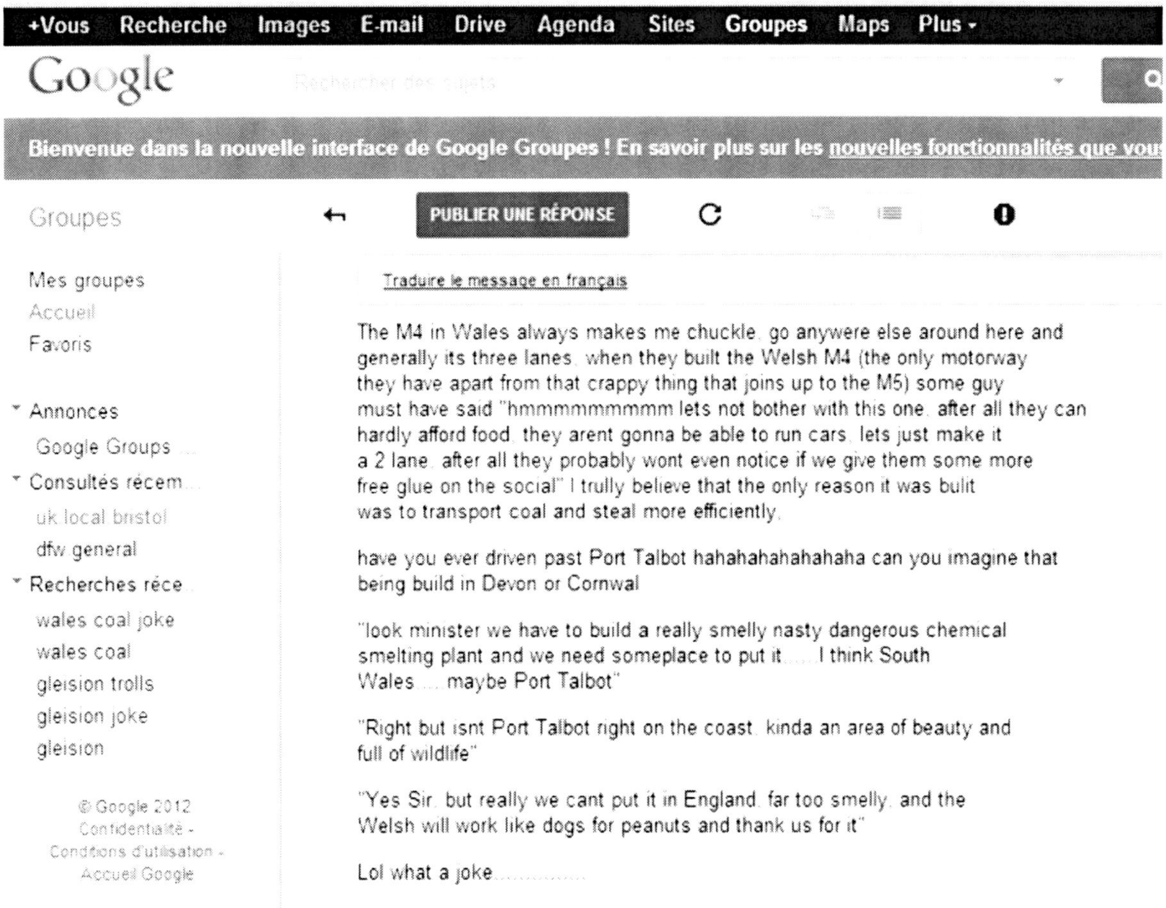

posts. Blogging can be seen as a 'thought dump' for ideas, and platforms like Yahoo!Answers allow people to give their non-expert opinion for the person asking the question to decide the merits of it, even if it is not accurate. Such platforms may offend Big Men and Iconoclasts, but be very welcoming to Flirts and MHBFY Jennies.

Wikis and Hypertext Fiction are most likely to attract Strategic trolling (between 3 and 3.99), where the user has to make an effort to get the content onto the Website, meaning they will have to scheme to get offensive content adopted without others noticing, or by teaming up with others of the same worldview. This can include involving others in 'owning' a page on Wikipedia so only the content one wants on there is permitted by those who edit it and monitor it. If someone tries to change it, then by being part of a team with others one can ensure the page is not changed. The people most adept at this are the E-Vengers who are motivated to get back at someone, the Big Men who will go to great lengths to 'enforce' their opinion, and the Iconoclasts who will try to ensure a particular worldview is not represented.

Finally, Personal homepages are most likely to be used for Domination trolling (between 4.0 and 4.99), where users have to go to huge efforts to make their abusive content available. Whether this involves setting up a Facebook Group using a fake account linked to a fake email, or using a dedicated Website to target a particular person, one needs to go out of one's way to do this type

Figure 8. Post about Wales in Google Groups (Usenet)

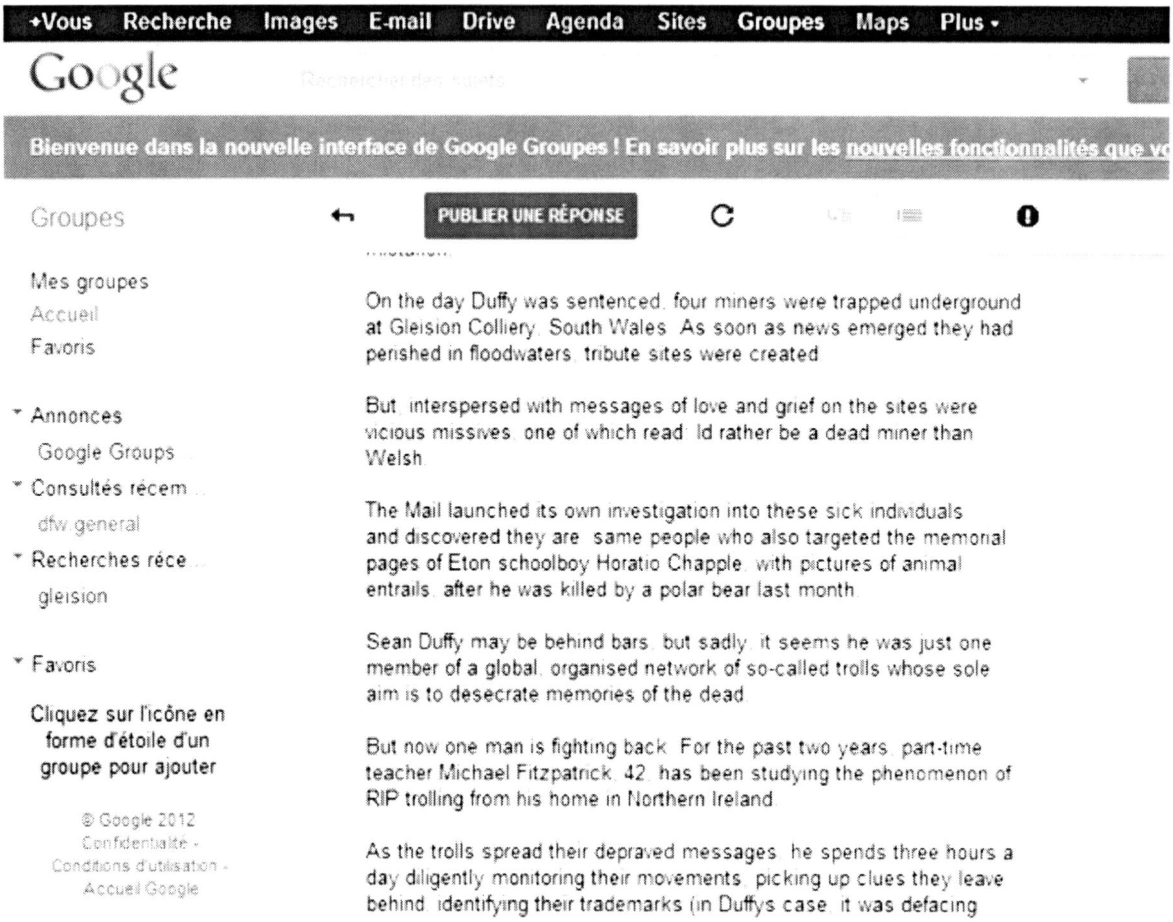

of trolling. Most notoriously, Sean Duffy created a video called 'Tasha the Tank Engine' to mock the death of teenager Natasha MacBryde, who died in a railway tragedy. This type of trolling is suited to E-Vengers, Chatroom bobs and Snerts, who will make the effort as part of a long term campaign against their target, who need not have wronged them other than by being more successful than them.

IMPLICATIONS AND FUTURE RESEARCH DIRECTIONS

Media Studies as a discipline has a lot to offer the study of new media cultures and societies. Concepts such as genre and character theories, as has been shown in this chapter, can go some way to explain what appears to be new phenomena, when in fact traditional understandings of media-text can apply. Multimedia Studies as a discipline, therefore, needs to extend the use of media theory to capture the online world with frameworks as applicable to new media, as they were with old media. The genre and character theories used in this chapter have shown that Internet trolling has some common features, but also raises new questions. These include whether the nature of trolling requires that new types of Web-based community need to be developed, which are not prone to trolling. From this the question will be asked whether such a platform is a new genre, or falls within pre-existing ones.

Table 3. A Framework for identifying severities of trolling using Trolling Magnitude (TM)

TM	Trolling type	Severity	Flow/Involvement	At Risk Genres
1.0-1.49	Playtime	Minor	High Flow/Low Involvement	Chat Groups and Instant Messaging, Email lists and Newsletters
1.5-1.99		Major	Med Flow/Low Involvement	
2.0-2.49	Tactical	Minor	Med Flow/High Involvement	Weblogs and Directories, Message Boards
2.5-2.99		Major	High Flow / High Involvement	
3-3.49	Strategic	Minor	High Flow, Med involvement	Wikis and Hypertext Fiction
3.5-3.99		Major	High Flow, Med Involvement	
4.0-4.49	Domination	Minor	Low Flow, Med Involvement	Personal Homepages, Virtual Worlds
4.5-4.99		Major	Low Flow, High Involvement	

DISCUSSION

While 'trolling' has existed as a term since the 1990s to reflect provocative messages, there has been an exponential increase in the term being used to describe abusive behaviour online in the 2010s. Trolling has therefore come to mean anything from the intentional bullying of others, to the posting of transgressive media for humourous effect, often with the hope it will 'go viral'.

The paper looked at the different representations of transgressive humour in different genres of online communities, by focusing on depictions of people in Wales and their heritage of coal mining. The types of troller that use these different genres were also assessed. The paper found that much humour replicates that in the real world, such as references to sheep, 'Taffy the Thief' and low skilled jobs. References to tragic deaths of Welsh people were mixed, with Websites like 4chan mocking Welsh people who died, while Usenet groups were being more sympathetic.

The paper reassessed the description of Twitter as a microblogging platform, as unlike Weblogs anyone can start a topic on anything directed at anyone. This suggests that Twitter now fits into the chat group and instant messaging genre more than microblogging. The implications of social media for celebrities such as Welsh footballer Ryan Giggs, and another Welsh celebrity, Imogen Thomas, who it was alleged slept with him, is that it is going to be hard to escape into a secure place of privacy as in the past, as they will be hit by flame trollers from all angles.

In the media, including the media in Wales, it is often the case that trolling and so-called "trolls" are often presented in the same light as the moral panics around the tragedies they are focusing on. For instance the Bridgend teenage suicide catastrophes were presented as a sign of a failing society. The same theme of a society out of control was used for the trollers who reported to either encourage suicide or posted jibes about the victims and Welsh people in general. Moral panics, like that seen around trolling and teenage suicides seem to be inevitable, whatever time we live in, whatever 'social ill' is most common at the time.

Finally, the paper presents a 'trolling magnitude scale' for assessing the severity of trolling so that following the demise of the moral panic around 'trolls,' it will be possible to fairly assess which acts of flame trolling are most harmful and which are not. By combining the online community genre theory with research on flow and involvement, a framework is constructed so that it is possible to see which online community platforms are most at risk of certain types and severities of trolling.

REFERENCES

Bishop, J. (2007). Increasing participation in online communities: A framework for human–computer interaction. *Computers in Human Behavior*, *23*(4), 1881–1893. doi:10.1016/j.chb.2005.11.004

Bishop, J. (2009). Enhancing the understanding of genres of web-based communities: The role of the ecological cognition framework. *International Journal of Web Based Communities*, *5*(1), 4–17. doi:10.1504/IJWBC.2009.021558

Bishop, J. (2012a). The psychology of trolling and lurking: The role of defriending and gamification for increasing participation in online communities using seductive narratives. In H. Li (Ed.), *Virtual community participation and motivation: Cross-disciplinary theories* (pp. 160–176). Hershey, PA: IGI Global.

Bishop, J. (2012b). Scope and limitations in the government of wales act 2006 for tackling Internet abuses in the form of 'flame trolling'. *Statute Law Review*, *33*(2), 207–216. doi:10.1093/slr/hms016

Bishop, J. (2012c). Tackling internet abuse in great Britain: Towards a framework for classifying severities of 'flame trolling'. In *Proceedings of the 11th International Conference on Security and Management (SAM'12)*. SAM.

Bishop, J. (2012d). Taming the chatroom bob: The role of brain-computer interfaces that manipulate prefrontal cortex optimization for increasing participation of victims of traumatic sex and other abuse online. In *Proceedings of the 13th International Conference on Bioinformatics and Computational Biology (BIOCOMP'12)*. BIOCOMP.

Bishop, J. (2013a). The effect of deindividuation of the internet troller on criminal procedure implementation: An interview with a hater. *International Journal of Cyber Criminology*, *7*(1), 28–48.

Bishop, J. (2013b). Increasing capital revenue in social networking communities: Building social and economic relationships through avatars and characters. In J. Bishop (Ed.), *Examining the concepts, issues, and implications of Internet trolling* (pp. 44–61). Hershey, PA: IGI Global. doi:10.4018/978-1-4666-2803-8.ch005

Bishop, J. (2013c). The psychology of trolling and lurking: The role of defriending and gamification for increasing participation in online communities using seductive narratives. In J. Bishop (Ed.), *Examining the concepts, issues and implications of Internet trolling* (pp. 106–123). Hershey, PA: IGI Global. doi:10.4018/978-1-4666-2803-8.ch009

Bishop, J. (2014). Representations of 'trolls' in mass media communication: A review of media-texts and moral panics relating to 'internet trolling'. *International Journal of Web Based Communities*, *10*(1), 7–24. doi:10.1504/IJWBC.2014.058384

Brown, K., Jackson, M., & Cassidy, W. (2006). Cyber-bullying: Developing policy to direct responses that are equitable and effective in addressing this special form of bullying. *Canadian Journal of Educational Administration and Policy*, *57*(1), 1–36.

Cassidy, W., Brown, K., & Jackson, M. (2013). Moving from cyber-bullying to cyber-kindness: What do students, educators and parents say? In J. Bishop (Ed.), *Examining the concepts, issues and implications of internet trolling* (pp. 62–83). Hershey, PA: IGI Global. doi:10.4018/978-1-4666-2803-8.ch006

Cleland, J. (2013). Racism, football fans, and online message boards: How social media has added a new dimension to racist discourse in english football. *Journal of Sport and Social Issues*. doi:10.1177/0193723513499922

Connelly, B. L., Certo, S. T., Ireland, R. D., & Reutzel, C. R. (2011). Signaling theory: A review and assessment. *Journal of Management*, *37*(1), 39–67. doi:10.1177/0149206310388419

Edwards, L. (2012). Section 127 of the communications act 2003: Threat or menace?. *SCL Journal, 23*(4).

Fisher, E. J. (2013). From cyber bullying to cyber coping: The misuse of mobile technology and social media and their effects on people's lives. *Business and Economic Review*, *3*(2), 127–145. doi:10.5296/ber.v3i2.4176

Goode, S. D. (2010). *Understanding and addressing adult sexual attraction to children: A study of pedophiles in contemporary society*. Abingdon, UK: Routledge.

Hall, M., Hanna, L., & Huey, G. (2013). Use and views on social networking sites of pharmacy students in the United Kingdom. *American Journal of Pharmaceutical Education*, *77*(1). doi:10.5688/ajpe7719 PMID:23459621

Hardaker, C. (2010). Trolling in asynchronous computer-mediated communication: From user discussions to academic definitions. *Journal of Politeness Research.Language, Behaviour. Culture (Canadian Ethnology Society)*, *6*(2), 215–242.

Herring, S., Job-Sluder, K., Scheckler, R., & Barab, S. (2002). Searching for safety online: Managing trolling in a feminist forum. *The Information Society*, *18*(5), 371–384. doi:10.1080/01972240290108186

Jansen, E., & James, V. (1995). *NetLingo: The internet dictionary*. Oxnard, CA: Netlingo Inc.

Jansen, E., & James, V. (2002). *NetLingo: The internet dictionary*. Oxnard, CA: Netlingo Inc.

Kimball, R., Stables, K., & Green, R. (2001). The nature and purpose of design and technology. In G. Owen-Jackson (Ed.), *Teaching design and technology in secondary schools: A reader*. London: Routledge.

Kleber, F., Diem, M., & Sablatnig, R. (2010). *Document reconstruction by layout analysis of snippets*. Paper presented at the IS&T/SPIE Electronic Imaging. New York, NY.

Kuipers, G. (2011). The politics of humour in the public sphere: Cartoons, power and modernity in the first transnational humour scandal. *European Journal of Cultural Studies*, *14*(1), 63–80. doi:10.1177/1367549410370072

Lopresti, D., & Zhou, J. (1998). Document analysis and the world wide web. *Series in Machine Perception and Artificial Intelligence*, *29*, 479–502. doi:10.1142/9789812797704_0025

Schweitzer, F., & Garcia, D. (2010). An agent-based model of collective emotions in online communities. *The European Physical Journal B-Condensed Matter and Complex Systems*, *77*(4), 533–545. doi:10.1140/epjb/e2010-00292-1

Shifman, L., Coleman, S., & Ward, S. (2007). Only joking? Online humour in the 2005 UK general election. *Information Communication and Society*, *10*(4), 465–487. doi:10.1080/13691180701559947

Thomas, J. (1997). 'Taffy was a welshman, taffy was a thief': Anti-Welshness, the press and neil kinnock. *LLAFUR-CARDIFF*, *7*, 95–108.

Walter, T., Hourizi, R., Moncur, W., & Pitsillides, S. (2011). Does the Internet change how we die and mourn? An overview. *Omega*, *64*(4), 12. doi:10.2190/OM.64.4.a PMID:22530294

Winterson-Richards, J. (2008). *The xenophobe's guide to the Welsh*. London: Oval Books.

Yetim, F. (2001). A meta-communication model for structuring intercultural communication action patterns. *ACM SIGGROUP Bulletin*, *22*(2), 16–20.

KEY TERMS AND DEFINITIONS

Genre: A media studies concept that involves the systematic analysis of a media-text to explain its properties so that it is possible to distinguish it from other media texts.

Lurker: A user of an online community that does not participate in the posting of content to that Website.

Online Community: A type of virtual community that is enabled through Internet technologies.

Trolling: The posting of content to the Internet, such as online communities or Web-based communities, which is intended to be provocative or offensive.

Virtual Community: A community where those that form part of it exist in different localities (i.e. virtual communities).

Web-Based Community: A particular genre of online community that is based around a hypertext approach to the Internet.

Section 4

E-Government, E-Voting, and E-Democracy

Chapter 12
Internet Voting:
Situation, Questions, and Trends

Chantal Enguehard
Université de Nantes, France

ABSTRACT

In the Internet age, the increasing prevalence of online voting regularly sparks controversy regarding security. This chapter addresses the topic of Internet voting by describing the characteristics of a democratic election and placing this new mode of voting within the context of the entire family of electronic voting systems. The link between transparency of the electoral system, voter confidence, and legitimacy is then reiterated, and the components of reliability and safety requirements of security are detailed. This analysis and the overview of several real implementations of Internet voting systems in this chapter show that transparency vanishes due to the combination of anonymity and virtualization of the votes while absolute security seems out of reach. Finally, it appears that the search for procedures for verifying the proper operation of the procedures should be accompanied by a strong evolution of the electorate legal rules.

INTRODUCTION

Internet voting has become an issue requiring serious consideration in a world where e-commerce, social networking and the exchange of emails have already transformed our habits. It may be claimed that this new way of voting could increase voter turnout by providing another voting channel, would cost less and would deliver voting results reliably and more quickly (European Commission for democracy through law, 2004). Although it is little used in the political world, this method of voting is becoming increasingly popular in the professional world, in associations and in universities. There remain, however, difficulties regarding compliance with the criteria that characterize a democratic election.

The scope of a study on the elections could include preparation of voter lists, campaign for candidates or the announcement of results. Here I restrict focus to the voting period between the preparation of electoral material equipment up the count of votes. I take into account different points of view: from political professionals, office holders and voters.

DOI: 10.4018/978-1-4666-6038-0.ch012

Copyright © 2014, IGI Global. Copying or distributing in print or electronic forms without written permission of IGI Global is prohibited.

The first part provides the background of the subject. Internet voting is defined and its main stages are presented; it is then placed in context with other types of electronic voting. A review of available literature presents some previous research regarding Internet voting focusing on some specific features: the question of the ritual of voting, usability of Internet voting, digital divide, etc. The main challenges are explained. The second part is entirely dedicated to the examination of the balance between security and transparency. The main characteristics of a democratic election and the links between transparency, confidence and legitimacy of representatives are stated and security is defined. I then examine these concepts with regard to Internet voting: I demonstrate that Internet voting is not a transparent mode of voting and detail the security problem that could occur during an Internet election. Finally I analyze to what extent the promise of security would be able to compensate for the loss of direct transparency. The third part presents Internet voting deployments that concern political elections or official referenda. The last part attempts to give an idea of the possible future of online elections. It briefly presents the inherent limit of free software and of the "end-to-end verifiable and auditable voting systems" (E2E) approaches and outlines the problem where election results may be undermined by loss of confidence in the integrity of the voting software.

BACKGROUND

Internet voting belongs both to the fields of political elections and computer science. I present some areas that are addressed by these two disciplines so that the reader is able to understand what difficulties surround the implementation of Internet voting.

Internet Voting

Terms

Internet voting is also understood by the interchangeable terms: "online voting" and "i-voting."

Definition

Internet voting allows voters to cast votes from any computer connected to the Web and equipped with a browser compatible with the voting Web application running on a server (see Figure 1). That computer could be either at home, at work, in a public place like a library, in a university, in an Internet cafe, etc. Voters must identify themselves before casting their vote. A server collects and stores the votes until the polls close. It finally tallies votes and produces the results.

Stages of Internet Voting

Internet voting, as occurs in uncontrolled environments, is considered as a remote voting system and follows the same stages as the other remote voting systems: the organizers of the vote prepare electoral material (B1), and its transmission (B2). The electoral material travels through the transmission channel (C1) and is received by the voter (E1). Voters express their choice (E2) and then prepare to send their vote (E3). The ballot is transmitted (C2). The polling station receives ballots (B3) and then performs the necessary counts (B4) (Enguehard & Lehn, 2009).

But the inner organization of the stages is different through the different remote voting systems. The preparation of the voting material (B1, B2) and the its transmission to the voters (C1) until reception (E1) include the definition of the list of voters and imply the sending of the voting materials by mail. However, the nature of the sent material

Figure 1. Internet voting

differs: for instance, the procedure of postal voting requests a ballot while Internet voting requires the communication of a username and a password or a Personal Identification Number (PIN)i. Some stages become fully computerized when coming to Internet voting: expression of the voter's choice is processed by interacting with the interface of the voting server (E2) (this step requires extensive information exchanges between the voting server and the computer used by the voter); usually there is an encryption of the vote and voter identification (E3), then follow the transmission of information via the Internet to the voting server (C2), the decryption after receipt and the updating the list of signing sheet (B3), and finally the counting of the cast votes (B4) (see Figure 2).

Internet Voting and the Other Types of Electronic Voting

I discuss Internet voting within the general context of electronic voting systems.

Figure 2. Stages of a remote voting

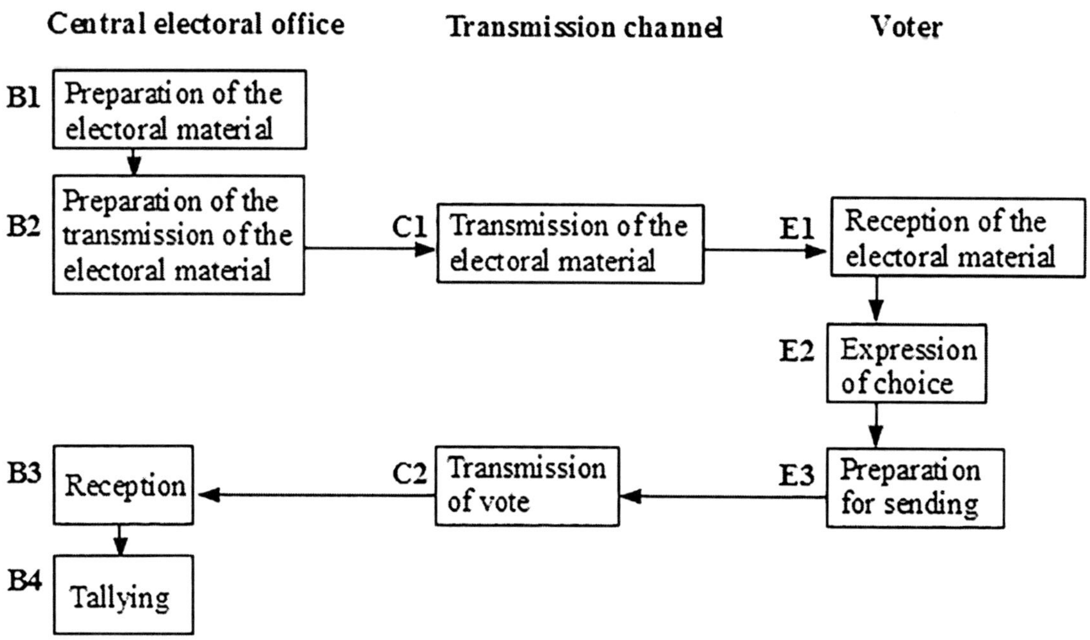

Table 1. Classification of electronic voting systems according to three characteristics

	Environment		**Ballots**		**Management of a Signing Sheet**	
	Controlled	**Uncontrolled**	**Materialized**	**Dematerialized**	**Yes**	**No**
DREs Voting Machines	X			X		X
Voting Boxes	X			X		X
Voting Kiosks	X			X	X	
Digital Pens	X		X			X
Optical Mark Recognition Scanners	X		X			X
Voting Computer with VVAT	X		X			X
Telephone		X		X	X	
SMS		X		X	X	
Internet		X		X	X	
Hybrid Voting		X	X		X	

Electronic voting includes all forms of voting involving an electronic system to cast ballots or tally votes. Because there is a lack of organizational, legal and technological models, defined by international standards, it is difficult to precisely describe the voting procedures associated with each system. It is common that slight variations distinguish the models. I present a general pattern, however, so that the reader can imagine the diversity of existing systems (see Table 1).

Optical mark recognition scanners were used for the first time in 1962 in Kern City, California (Jones, 2003). They are the oldest form of electronic voting. Voters tick the boxes of their choice on their ballot as usual, and then cast their votes that are kept in an urn. At the end of voting period, the ballots fed an optical mark recognition scanner that tallies votes.

Direct Recording Electronic (DREs) voting machines appeared in 1975 in the Netherlands and spread in India, Brazil, Belgium, United States, etc. To express their choice voters interact directly with the device via hardware buttons, touch screen, or a numeric keypad. The votes are recorded directly in an electronic memory[1]. At the end of the voting period, the device provides election results by showing them on screen or printing them on a ticket. Some computers also send their voting results to the central electoral office.

The concept of *voting computers with a Voter Verified Audit Trail (VVAT)* emerges with the new millennium (Mercuri, 2002) to compensate for the inability to verify the accuracy of the results issued of DREs voting machines: when the voter has confirmed the choice she cast, the computer prints a ticket, with the expressed choice. This bulletin, which the voter can verify the accuracy is then directed to a ballot box for any recounts of results.

Digital pens must be used with specially adapted ballots. These devices are equipped with a miniature camera that can store trips made during the filling of the ballot. The data recorded in the pen are then processed by software to provide election results.

Voting Kiosks are terminals connected to a central computer (the server). They are located in the polls. The device collects the votes and is responsible for managing the signing sheets of voters. A voter can vote using any kiosk in any polling station. After the phases of identification and authentication, the vote takes place as with a DRE voting machine.

The *voting boxes* are only used at restricted meetings. Each voter has a box equipped with a numeric keypad and expresses his choice by pressing keys; there are no signing sheets. A centralized computer received and expressed the results.

The *telephone* can be used in a voting situation. The voter dials a number specially dedicated to the election, the individual gives her identity, proves it by a numeric password (sent in advance by mail), and then expressed her choice by using the keys on her phone. A centralized system collects votes and gives the results at the end of the voting period.

This procedure can be adapted for *Short Message Service (SMS)*. The voter receives a first code to prove her identify and a list of numbers to express her choice. During the voting period she casts her vote by sending a SMS containing the code number corresponding to her choice.

Postal remote voting moved to a *hybrid voting system*: each voter expresses her choice by ticking boxes on a voting card with an identifier (bar code or number). These cards are referred to the central electoral office, by open or closed letter. On the day of counting, the cards are read by a scanner that maintains the register of signing sheet and tallies votes.

This set of electronic voting systems can be structured according to three characteristics:

Controlled/Uncontrolled Environment

The quality of the environment has a direct impact on privacy. When the environment is controlled by official pollsters, it is possible to enforce guidelines to protect voters against coercion (as, for example, the use of the booth). On the contrary, with remote voting procedure, the environment is uncontrolled (people vote from home, work, etc.) and voters are not protected against coercion.

Physical/Virtual Ballots

According to the voting systems, voters indicate their choices using physical ballots, usually made of paper, or by interacting with an electronic system registering their choices directly to an electronic memory. When the votes are physical, it is possible to envisage a counting process that is independent from the automatic count. This option is no more feasible when the ballots are virtualized. In addition virtual ballots are less stable than physical ones: a large amount of digital information can be modified in a moment while it would be labor intensive to perform the same operation on printed ballots.

Management of Signing Sheet

Holding the signing sheet allows to control that each voter is registered, and that she votes only once. The management of signing sheet by a single electronic system that also registers cast votes poses the problem of the respect for the anonymity (see Figure 3).

Expected Benefits

The idea to vote via the Internet became really popular with the new millennium, especially among political professionals and office holders; many voters also had the impression that it would be very convenient to vote from everywhere, even if living abroad, being in vacation or traveling for business.

Many potential advantages were and are still associated with this new mode of voting:

Increasing Voter Turnout

The most often cited advantage is the possibility to cast ballots from any place connected to the Internet from abroad or work, etc., and especially from home: the first Internet voting in the work that took place in Arizona in 2000 was associated with the idea of voting "*in your pajamas*" (Mohen and

Figure 3. Cartography of electronic voting systems

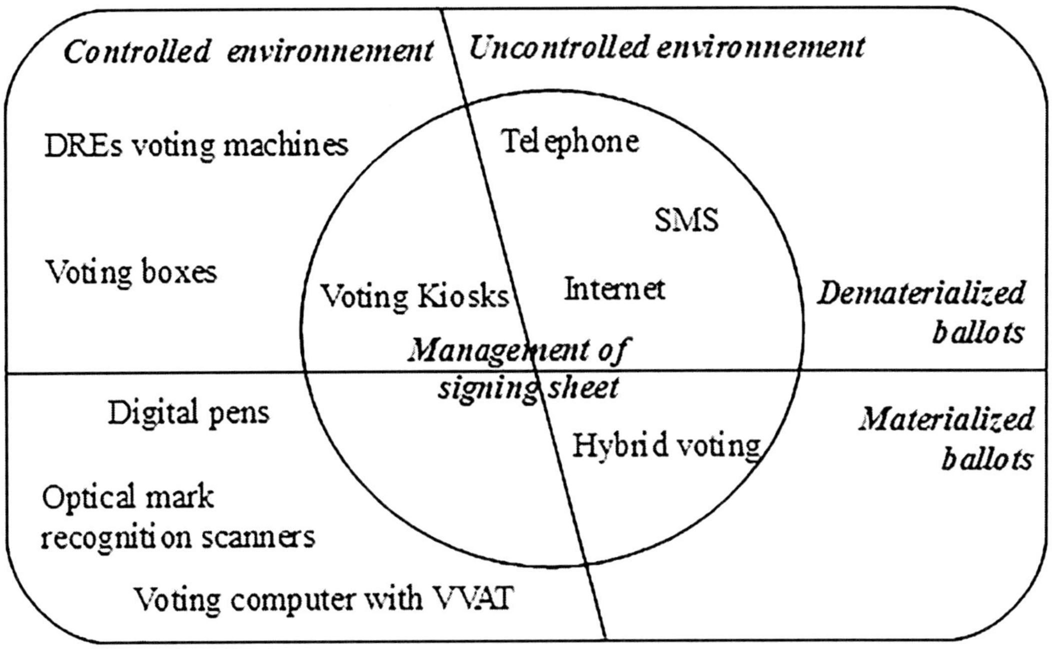

Glidden, 2001). This convenience to vote should bring more people to cast ballots, and so increase voter turnout (National French Assembly, 2005).

Flexible Ballot Presentation

Being a computerized application, Internet voting systems could be designed to allow the voters to change font size or language on demand, the presentation of candidates' names could be randomize but this possibility could also create difficulty for users who have pre-planned their voting (Bederson et al., 2003).

More Direct Form of Democracy

With Internet voting it would be possible to consult people more often and on various subjects (Oostveen & van der Besselaar, 2004).

Reducing Costs

For officials, reducing costs of elections is a strong motivation to introduce Internet voting (Oostveen & van der Besselaar, 2004; Gharadaghy & Volkamer, 2010).

Reducing Fraud

Officials in charge of elections worry about fraud. They believe that the level of expertise required to commit fraud on electronic systems is much greater than for not electronic voting systems, and consequently that fewer people could commit a fraud on an Internet voting system (National Academy of Sciences, 2005).

Reducing Human Errors

When a voter tries to cast her ballot, its validity can be controlled so that errors (like selecting too much candidates in a race) could be immediately detected. The voting application could then signal the errors to the voters and ask her to correct it (Gharadaghy and Volkamer, 2010). In addition, counting votes automatically may reduce the incidence of human error and improve the accuracy of the tallying (Oostveen & van der Besselaar, 2006).

Reducing Work

According to officials, organizing an election is a hard and thankless work. The use of an Internet voting system is a transfer of a part of the burden to a private society.

Literature Review

Electronic voting became a subject after the 2000 U.S. presidential election when many researchers address problems with voting systems. One difficulty is that analyzing electronic voting systems requires multidisciplinary research: for instance, the procedural issue about voter authentication or electoral litigation deals with legal questions that may influence voters or candidates; social aspects must be investigated when analyzing the voter turnout; computer sciences are at the heart of the security and accuracy issues, etc. (Alvarez & Antonsson, 2007). As Internet voting is one of the multiple existing electronic voting, most of the research that deal with electronic voting in general can be considered when focusing on Internet voting. These researches address many different themes. I present briefly the questions of the ritual of voting, usability, digital divide, confidentiality, anonymity and evaluation of the accuracy of voting systems. The security and transparency themes are developed in depth further in this chapter.

Ritual of Voting

As voting and elections can be presented as the *DNA of democracy*, voting constitutes an important skill, and often the only direct one, that allows a person to participate as a citizen. Voting at the poll station is an occasion to meet some people, at least the officials, and to show her will to participate to the political life: the vote is secret but the participation is public. Internet voting, when used to cast votes, changes deeply the traditional ritual of voting that are familiar to voters: it is not required to go to the poll station, to fill a ballot and to cast it in a ballot box, and there is no more public tally of the ballots. On the contrary, with Internet voting it is possible to vote from any computer connected to the Internet network: the voting act becomes individualist. Some pollsters think that these modifications could affect the feeling of citizenry, enlarge the gap between people and politics, and finally make the voter turnout decrease. This change of the voting context could also have some consequences of the expressed choice; being alone, the voter might less perceive himself as a part of the people. For instance, meeting a disabled person, or somebody from a minority, on the way to the poll station, or at the poll station, could help the voter to take these persons in account when voting (Coleman, 2005; Hoff, 1999; Oostveen & Van den Besselaar, 2006).

Usability

Every citizen who possesses the right to vote should be able to cast a ballot as intended. Actually, some part of the population are not capable to use electronic voting systems easily: for instance, selecting an option with an electronic mouse or on a touch-screen can be difficult for elderly people (with trembling hands); uneducated, illiterate and those with poor Information Technology (IT) skills can have experience difficulties when using unfamiliar and unusual software. These persons, who may represent a significant proportion of the community, may be deprived of their right to vote. According to (Newell and Gregor, 1997), 10% to 20% of the population from occidental countries suffers from disability; the last United Nations study on World Population Ageing measures that 21% of the population of the most developed countries is 60 or older, and makes a prediction of 33% in 2050 (United Nations, 2005).

Building the interface of voting systems that are usable for the whole citizens is particularly difficult: people vote rarely, thus there is little or no training; to comply with the secret vote principle, they must vote alone without any direct assistance. In addition the task of voting can be complicated by the number of races or the need to correct mistakes during the voting process. Even the design of the ballot (wording and placement of instructions for instance) can help or embarrass voters to express successfully their choices (Laskowski, 2006). Some analysis of electronic voting machines revealed that some voters do not feel comfortable with the system they had to use (Bederson et al. 2003) and that 2% to 3% did not vote as intended (Herrnson et al., 2006). This rate is high enough to change the outcome of close elections. This feeling about their (un) ability to vote could influence their confidence in the results. Finally, "usability is as important as security and reliability in providing a successful experience to voters." (Laskowski, 2006).

Digital Divide

The Digital divide is usually defined as the lack of availability of access to the Internet. This access varies depending on "race," gender, regions and socio-economic situation. For instance, in the United States, 30% of the population lacks broadband access (Powell et al. 2010). In addition, there is a more subtle divide in relation with the skills required to use a computer (installing the software and hardware, learning, finding information from social networks or forum, possessing advanced or older types of computers, etc.) (Oostveen & van den Besselaar, 2006). The "digitally included" part of the population would be more likely to vote by Internet, and, consequently, to be represented by elected; on the other side, the "digitally excluded" who are not advanced Internet users would be more excluded from the political life (Birdsall, 2005; Powell et al. 2010). It appears that the access to this new mode of voting is not equally distributed. This situation may be more understandable when translated into the real world: this unequal access would then begin the creation of new poll stations in urban and rich areas and the diminution of their numbers in rural and poor areas.

Voters perceived this breach in the equal principle: all factors being equal, the chances that a graduate supports Internet voting are nearly twice as much as those of a person with a lower degree (Caporusso, 2010). Consequently, Internet elections may be even less representative than traditional ones (Oostveen & van der Besselaar, 2004).

Confidentiality, Anonymity, and Evaluation of the Accuracy of Internet Voting Systems

I present these three concepts together because they are intimately linked.

A poll station is a controlled environment where officials control that legal rules are respected. Confidentiality is then protected by the mandatory isolation in a voting booth when a voter expresses her choice. When vote is remote, the environment is uncontrolled, each voter choices and casts her vote outside poll stations, without any official to ensure that she votes alone. Internet voting being a remote voting method, it is not suitable to protect any voter against vote-buying or selling, bribery or intimidation by family members, colleagues, teachers, churches, union bosses, employers etc. who may try to influence or control the voter's decision (Green, 2000; Oostveen & van der Besselaar, 2004; 2006; Phillips & von Spakovsky, 2001).

Financial transactions that take place on Internet are always followed by the reception of a receipt which lists the date and exact time of the transaction, the nature and the amount of the exchange and the names of the persons or societies that are involved. With Internet voting, the identity of the voter should not be stored within its cast vote in order to protect the secrecy of the vote, and the voter cannot receive any detailed receipt that would allow her to sell her vote, or may expose her to coercion (Oostveen & van der Besselaar, 2004). It is also difficult to prove to voters that their anonymity is respected and that their vote will stay secret for everybody, including the technical staff, and for always. This doubt may lead some voters to change their choices (Enguehard & Lehn, 2009).

It is easy to check the accuracy of an Internet transaction (financial or commercial, for instance) and to find any discrepancy because these transactions are traceable. When it is question of vote, the need to protect the voter's right to a secret ballot does not allow this kind of procedure. (Mercuri, 2002) defines the concept of verifiability for electronic voting systems that can print the ballots (each ballot should be reviewed by the voter; all the ballots are deposited in an urn to make a recount possible) but such procedure is not suitable for an Internet election. Thus, it is not possible to audit a vote performed with an Internet voting system or to measure its accuracy by following this concept.

The Voting Technology Project (VTP) research group created a new metric suitable for U.S. Elections when electronic voting systems that do not produce any ballot paper are used by voters: the "residual vote." It is defined as the "percentage of ballots cast in an election jurisdiction that did not produce a valid vote in a specific race, most importantly in the top-of-the-ballot race, usually for president or governor" (Voting Technology Project, 2001). The main problem to use this metric is its statistical nature: it is necessary to collect some large amount of consistent data. Working on technologies used in poll station (Alvarez & Antonsson, 2007) found that it is not rare that states report inconsistent data. Collecting such data on Internet voting is even more difficult because Internet voting is used by different countries and to elect representatives at local, regional or national political elections, or for private elections (unions, universities, organization, companies, etc.). Finally, it appears that there is a lack of investigations on the evaluation of the accuracy of Internet voting technologies and that more research should be developed in this area.

Main Challenges

Many years after the first use of Internet voting in the USA for the presidential preference primary of the Arizona Democratic Party (Mohen & Glidden, 2001), most of the promised benefits have not been delivered. Because of the digital divide and the problem of usability, the convenience of Internet voting is not equally distributed and disfavors the weak. Because of a lack of technical abilities, some people do not manage to vote as they intend and, sometimes, are unaware of their failure. Several studies show that Internet voting is mainly used by people who would have voted anyway using another voting method, and that there is no noticeable effect on voter turnout, as with previous attempts to address the problem of decreasing voter participation with technical measures such as mail-in ballots (Bochsler, 2009; Caporusso, 2010; Christin & Trechsel, 2004; Oostveen & van der Besselaar, 2004; Phillips & von Spakovsky, 2001). There is no evidence about costs reduction because Internet voting is almost always another voting channel added to more traditional ones and the (partly hidden) costs of complex technologies are generally high. In addition cost of online voting would vary enormously (Coleman, 2002)[2]. With Internet voting, a fraud can be perpetrated on a large scale by one person alone whereas a large fraud with a not electronic system would be labor intensive (National Academy of Sciences, 2005) and, being completely electronic, without any materiel evidence, such a fraud could remain unseen.

There is a tremendous amount of research on verifiable Internet voting systems. Cryptographers try to produce bold proposals to enable each voter to verify if her cast vote have not been changed (individual verifiability) and if the tabulation of votes is fair (universal verifiability), while preserving the secrecy of the vote (unconditional secrecy) and still being able to unveil the results of their audit to a third party (Adida et al. 2009). Such systems are said "end-to-end verifiable and auditable voting systems" (E2E). But it remains several drawbacks to this day. First, these innovations are incomprehensible to those without specialist knowledge in computer science and mathematics (and thus the electoral courts), then encryption can allow encoding of additional information (could be the identity of the voter, or reveal the vote even though it is encrypted) and the anonymity of the votes still depends on the destruction of files (which is a nontrivial operation) and on the non-disclosure of encryption keys (Jones, 2009). In addition, cryptographers readily admit that if they try to establish theoretically sure protocols, their implementation and use can reveal not foreseen vulnerabilities, particularly in interactions with the environment: hardware, software, voters, election managers (Anderson, 1993; Ryan & Peacok, 2005).

Finally, it appears that it is still, until now, impossible to build an Internet voting system that fully respect the unconditional secrecy and unconditional verifiability (Gharadaghy & Volkamer, 2010).

THE RIGHT QUESTION

I examine the characteristics of a democratic election as defined by international organizations and make two observations: 1 - security is not explicitly cited; 2 - transparency appears as a key concept. Nevertheless, many discussions on Internet voting are focused on the question of security (a recurring theme in computer sciences) while the missing of transparency is rarely questioned.

Thus I choose to examine very precisely this strange situation. For this purpose, I define the two notions of security and transparency and develop how these issues relate to Internet voting. Then, I analyze if the research of a better security could compensate the disappearance of transparency.

From a methodological point of view I will compare Internet voting with postal voting because both are remote, one is electronic, and the other is not (Enguehard & Lehn, 2009).

Political Domain of Internet Voting

As stated in its etymology, democracy[3] is a political system in which the power belongs to the people; it is famously defined in article 2 of the Constitution of the French Republic: "Government of the people, by the people and for the people."

However, it must be noted that no system of direct democracy (in which the people exercises directly the power) has existed, perhaps because of the practical difficulties of organization. Also most of the democracies are representative: the people exercise its sovereignty by interposed representatives, these representatives being chosen through elections. The people, holding the power, therefore agree to place it in the representatives' hands. At each election, I can therefore consider that the power comes back into the hands of people who appoint again its representatives.

I notice that the people are the core of this delegation granted: it has power and is active in the choice of its representatives. This basic concept should not be confused with an opposite and wrong perspective in which the representatives are in power and consult the people for their renewal.

The nomination process is manifested in elections that must obey to several basic principles to be considered as democratic and universal, these principles are expressed by international organizations, for examples:

The United Nations, in the article 21 of the Universal Declaration of Human Rights:

The will of the people shall be the basis of the authority of government; this will shall be expressed in periodic and genuine elections which shall be by universal and equal suffrage and shall be held by secret vote or by equivalent free voting procedures. (United Nations, 1948)

The Organization for Security and Co-operation in Europe, in its Election Observation Book:

A genuine election is a political competition that takes place in an environment characterized by confidence, transparency, and accountability and that provides voters with an informed choice between distinct political alternatives. (Organization for Security and Co-operation in Europe, 2005)

These statements focus on several key (but not sufficient) principles that democratic elections must adhere to. These principles (fair elections, universal suffrage, freedom of voting, transparency, etc.) can be expressed more clearly as concepts. Five of them caught our attention:

- **Transparency:** The stages of the election can be observed and controlled;
- **Unicity:** The "one elector, one vote" principle;
- **Confidentiality:** Each voter expresses her choice alone[4];
- **Anonymity:** It is impossible to link a ballot to the voter who cast it;
- **Sincerity:** The results of the election reflect faithfully the will of the voters; for instance, the candidate that won the most votes is declared the winner;
- **Equality:** There is no discrimination between voters among gender, ethnicity, etc.

Adherence to these principles depends on the organization of elections that is therefore observed.

Among these characteristics, transparency appears as the most important one because this is the essential condition to observe if some of the other principles are not respected: some voters cast several ballots; the procedure let possible the linking between voter and ballots; the tallying of the ballots is erroneous and change the issue of the vote; the places to vote are not equally distributed amongst the population; etc. In addition to observation, transparency must also allow to collect some material proofs of discrepancies in order to complain before the election court. The election court could then examine the presented evidence to determine how the results must be modified or if the election should be canceled. According to the Organization for Security and Cooperation in Europe, post-election-day complaints and appeals are an important component of an election process (Organization for Security and Co-operation in Europe, 2005).

Definitions

Transparency, Confidence, and Legitimacy of Representatives

Transparency is a "*cornerstone of the election*" (Organization for Security and Co-operation in Europe, 2008) because it affects the confidence of voters in the electoral system. Being able to assess compliance with unicity, anonymity and confidentiality allows to ensure that voters do not suffer from coercion, that there was no ballot stuffing: the electoral process of collecting votes can be examined. The possibility to participate in the vote tallying and check the centralization of the results will test the sincerity of the election. Transparency reveals differences with the normal procedure, and particularly fraud, to make them known to the competent court in proceedings of electoral disputes.

Confidence is even more pronounced when voters have a legal capacity (having the right) and technical capacity (low-level technical skills) to observe directly the election, without relying on a mandatory intermediate.

In turn, voter confidence in the electoral system based the legitimacy of representatives (Hall &

Loeber, 2010). The American constitution emphasizes this direct link between the people and elected persons: the word "citizen" appears several times, and the right to vote is explicitly mentioned in four of the 27 amendments (15, 19, 24 and 26).

If the confidence in the electoral system is high, supporters of the losing side acknowledge the defeat of their candidate and accept that the newly representative exercise its new powers. Conversely, when voters are skeptical that the official election results reflect the urns content, representatives see their legitimacy being challenged and cannot perform their duties calmly, the situation may degenerate into riots affecting the stability of the country. Examples of such excesses are legion: election of Ali Bongo in Cameroon in September 2009, election of Mahmoud Ahmadinejad in Iran in June 2009, parliamentary elections in Mongolia in June 2008, election of Mwai Kibaki in Kenya in December 2007, etc.

Security

Security is the conjunction of safety and reliability. *Safety* encompasses all material, human, organizational ways to prevent or counteract any malicious attack. The level of safety is total if no attack can succeed. *Reliability* refers to the ability of a system to function without error and without fail. The level of reliability is total if no failures, no malfunction can happen. *Total security* is a situation when no attack can succeed, no malfunction can happen.

Internet Voting and the Question of Transparency

Comparison between Internet Voting and Postal Voting on Transparency

The procedure for postal voting has many areas of opacity due to its asynchronous development (there are several days between the moment voters cast ballots and the moment of the tally) and in multiple locations, characteristics which make observation difficult. In France, postal voting has also been banned for political elections by the law of 31 December 1975 as a result of massive fraud.

The Internet voting dematerializes ballots and procedures for counting and managing signing sheets. It replaces the real objects (ballots, signing sheets) by a representation of them in an electronic format.

This transfer of real objects into their virtual representations has several important consequences:

1. The physical nature of objects being changed, their properties have also undergone profound changes. The distinction between a real object and its representation is essential. It was brilliantly illustrated by Rene Magritte in his work, aptly titled "The Treason of Images." The realistic representation of a pipe is captioned by the sentence "Ceci n'est pas une pipe" ("This is not a pipe"). Indeed, it is impossible to put tobacco in the represented pipe, to put the light on and to draw a few puffs. However, it is possible to get this painting, to remove the frame and roll it, that would not stand a wooden pipe. The properties of a pipe are, in essence, different from those of a representation of a pipe. Thus, the counting of the ballots of postal voting requires the opening of envelopes, the update of signing sheets, the extraction of ballots, cancellation of non-conforming votes and counting votes. The amendment by fraud or mistake of a large number of votes can hardly go unnoticed because of the presence of witnesses and the amount of paper to move. However the revision of a substantial amount of digital data can be achieved instantly and invisibly.
2. While real objects are characterized by their macroscopic nature, the virtual objects are represented by a series of binary digit (bit) of infinitesimal nature. Their observation is possible only through software and technical objects. Direct observations are impossible.
3. Real objects are characterized by their permanence in time: this is the same ballot

mailed by a voter which will be counted when tallying the votes. Virtual objects are subjected to a series of transformations: a voter casts his choice by a click of mouse; this mechanical force of a few joules is converted into an electrical impulse itself converted into binary-coded information that may encounters some other treatments (encryption, encapsulation in a message, decryption, etc.).

4. Check the success of software treatments can be done only through the examination of time-stamped trace of all events recorded in a logbook. Consulting this log to track the progress of programs, step by step from beginning to end (since the choice of the voter, until the final count) would inevitably lead to know the choices and the identities of voters, in contradiction with the principle of anonymity. Restricting the ability to observe some steps asked about the relevance of such truncated observations. In addition the neutrality and objectivity of parts of programs that write in the logbook should be questioned.

It appears then that Internet voting is less transparent than postal voting.

Supervise and Monitor Elections

Because of the deployment of electronic voting in general and Internet voting in particular, international organizations are trying to adapt their text corpus and to change the observations procedures on which they rely.

The European Commission for Democracy through Law (Venice Commission) has produced two recommendations to advise the States in their implementation of elections.

The Commission openly evokes the risk of fraud occurring in a context of electronic voting in the 2002 recommendation and calls for measures to make the statement but they have little technical consistency. Thus, "enabling the vote to check his or her vote" does not allow the voter to detect a change in her vote because of the virtualization: a voting system can submit a piece of information to the voter while recording another one. Other recommendations seem unrealistic, for instance, "Electronic voting methods must be secure and reliable." Finally, in his effort to adapt to electronic voting, the Committee defines the notion of transparency: "Furthermore, the system's transparency must be guaranteed in the sense that it must be possible to check that it is functioning properly." suggesting erroneously that it would be possible to verify the proper functioning of a complex computer system during an election (European Commission for democracy through law, 2002).

The 2004 recommendations is all about electronic voting, and explicitly takes into account Internet voting but some recommendations suggest a distance from the technological reality of Internet voting. For example, recommendation 23 on transparency "Any observers, to the extent permitted by law, shall be able to be present to observe and comment on the e-elections, including the establishing of the results." does not take into account the consequences of the virtualization of objects of the vote. Thus, it assumes that observers could be able to observe the count in recommendation 56 "When counting the votes, representatives of the competent electoral authority shall be able to participate in, and any observers able to observe, the count" (European Commission for democracy through law, 2004).

Throughout these recommendations, the Venice Commission devotes *in fine* that direct transparency has disappeared: only a few experts, with their rights limited by the technical reality and the laws in force, are able to attempt to observe the system voting.

One year later, the Office for Democratic Institutions and Human Rights of the Organization for Security and Co-operation in Europe class cautiously in the "Possible problems to be aware of: Electronic voting systems with no voter-verified auditable paper trail or other manual audit capacity." (Organization for Security and Co-operation in Europe, 2005).

This organization added:

It is questionable whether electronic voting should be introduced where there exists a significant level of distrust or dissatisfaction with the election administration. Introduction of an electronic voting system, which by its nature is more difficult to observe, may only reinforce existing distrust and further diminish public confidence in elections. (Organization for Security and Co-operation in Europe, 2008)

Internet Voting and Security[5]

Before addressing the security of Internet voting, it is necessary to explain why such an application cannot be compared to commercial Web applications. Then, the two features of security, reliability and safety, could be detailed considering Internet voting.

A Special Computer Application

The result of commercial Web application is fully predictable because there is no secrecy between the seller and the buyer about the amount of money to transfer. On the contrary, it is impossible to predict the outcome of an election before it is held, and therefore to know whether the stated results are consistent with the choices that voters had intended to cast. Indeed, relying on the results of previous elections would deny the possibility of alternation, and gauge the accuracy of results based on their compliance with polls (carried out before or during the election) would lead ultimately to disappearance of the elections in favor of the polls. This characteristic particularity distinguishes voting from other Internet applications that populate the Web because all of which have visible and predictable results, whether buying, publishing a comment or sending a message.

In addition, multiple tests are not a sufficient to ensure that a complex computer application works as expected because it is not possible to simulate the unfolding of a true election involving thousands of people whose interactions with the voting system are potentially infinitely varied, with all the hazards that can happen. Testing an application with success does not predict with certainty its behavior at another use.

Reliability

The reliability problems are due to hardware errors (e-cards, microprocessors) or software errors located on the voting server or on computers used by voters whose maintenance is of variable quality. As an error may lead to changes cast votes and, as in the absence of such an prediction of the results, an error may stay invisible the National Institute of Standards and Technology (2007) recommends to the Election Assistance Commission that every voting system should be software-independent (i.e. "Software independence means that an undetected error or fault in the voting system's software is not capable of causing an undetectable change in election results"). Therefore, the control of the results of an electronic voting system should not be processed by a software application that, too, may experience malfunctions. These results were confirmed by numerous academic studies on dematerialized voting (Dill & Doherty, 2004; Jefferson et al. 2004; Mercuri, 2002; Simons, 2004), the Irish independent commission on electronic voting (Commission on Electronic Voting, 2004, 2006) and the OSCE (Organization for Security and Co-operation in Europe, 2004).

Currently, the only approach to write a program devoid of error is to write precise specifications of software, then perform a systematic construction of programs by mathematical operators, without manual intervention. Theoretically, this approach is rarely followed from beginning to end because of the difficulty of writing sufficiently precise specifications and because of the cost of the process for large projects. In practice, independent modules are produced in this manner, while human programmers still write some programs. In this case, cross-review of the manually written programs must be provided by involving several specialists. The formal specification should also be cross-reviewed.

The cost of a project designed along these lines are very high, and the development of Internet voting programs is far from following such standards, especially since added a further difficulty with the programs that operate in an outside environment not concerned with such rigorous approach: computers used by voters. Furthermore, although rigorous and restrictive, these methods cannot guarantee that the risk of fraud is completely annihilated: a portion of malicious code (malware) could be hidden in the compiler or interpreter of code.

Safety

Internet voting, like any other application unfolding on the Web, is vulnerable to many attacks whose perpetrators can be located in any country (external attacks).

The denial of service attack is to bombard the voting server with requests in order to prevent legitimate voters from voting. The server is saturated, cannot respond to all requests and may even fall down. This attack is very simple to conduct, its effects are visible.

The man-in-the-middle attack is to impersonate the server for the computer of the voter, and to impersonate the voter for the server, the fraudster may well change the cast vote. Encryption offers good protection against this attack if the public key encryption sent to the voter has not been intercepted by the fraudster. It must therefore be sent in a secure mail, such as voting material. By cons it is not necessary to know the encryption key to capture and destroy the ballot, depriving the voter of his right to vote. It is easy to send her a message to make her believe that her vote was correctly recorded. This intervention, although somewhat technical, is accessible to any motivated person with the technical skills since dates of elections are known well in advance and the same voting applications will be used over several elections (for reasons of profitability). It is therefore possible to observe its interface in detail and to imitate its operation with enough talent to deceive an elector who has only very partial knowledge (Rubin, 2001).

The use of viruses and worms6 is far more formidable. As anti-virus software can only detect already known viruses, new viruses are not detectable before taking action. For example, in 2001 the Code Red worm has infected 360,000 computers in just fourteen hours before being detected and that an anti-virus could act. The latest viruses are more virulent and capable to spread using multiple methods, they are able to pass firewalls and other defenses, and are difficult to analyze (Moore et al. 2003; Schneier, 1999). Attackers can create new viruses, or modify existing ones to avoid detection (construction kits can be found on Internet). The attackers have the advantage of testing their creations by using anti-virus commonly distributed and used by their potential victims.

A virus can easily infect a large number of computers without being detected and remain dormant until Election Day: most of the voters' computers are less protected than the election site computers and are never scrutinized by officials. A virus is likely to make different types of actions, unbeknownst to the voter and the election organizers, like capturing the information needed to connect before it is sent to the server and communicate it to a third party, or change the cast vote before encryption.

Voters may also be victims of pharming attack and interact with a site mimicking the official voting Web site, being not capable to uncover the theft because of a falsified safety certificate that has been accepted during the days preceding the vote, thus preventing the outbreak of a security alert.

The external threats of fraud can be quantified in terms of increased cyber-attacks (cyber war), the professionalization of the attackers and the upward trend of recorded Internet payment frauds (Banque de France, 2012).

Those responsible for the design and / or functioning of an Internet voting application may themselves be the perpetrators of attacks (internal fraud). It may be a programmer, a technician responsible for maintenance and updates, or any person with a physical or logical access to the server. According to the opportunities, such a person can, for example, affect the results, or violate the privacy by making copies of data transmitted on the server. These attacks are very serious because they are easy to carry, they may involve a great number of votes, far more important than with external attacks, and still remain completely invisible. Thus the procedures prior to the elections with the objective to check the voting system by using a test ballot box in which members of the electoral commission cast votes to issue control purposes, has no value. This situation is unprecedented and meets, to date, no satisfactory solution as reminds Ken Thompson, co-designer of the UNIX system.

You can't trust code that you did not totally create yourself. (Especially code from companies that employ people like me.) No amount of source-level verification or scrutiny will protect you from using untrusted code. (...) As the level of program gets lower, these bugs will be harder and harder to detect. A well installed microcode bug will be almost impossible to detect. (Thompson, 1984)

The great danger is that an Internet election can be conducted without problem, and that apparently seems to demonstrate that the system is reliable, robust and secure, and would push to extend this mode of election more broadly. But the fact that no attack has been detected does not prove that there was no (Madise & Martens, 2006; Oppliger, 2002). Most of the attacks, if carried out with finesse, would be extremely difficult to detect, even if they had changed the outcome of major elections.

Analysis

Discussions about the Internet voting are mostly on the issue of security, leading to the idea that this voting method will be widely used when security issues would be resolved. I analyze to what extent the promise of security would be able to compensate for the loss of direct transparency (see Table 2).

I detail the different situations corresponding to the valences of both security and transparency settings.

For this demonstration, I assume that security can be total, although this possibility is theoretical: the total security would be achieved if it were certain that the voting system could not meet any crash, any technical failure and that not a fraud could be committed successfully. This objective is speculative and beyond the reach of the computer industry in the state of knowledge.

Transparency can be direct (without human or software media) or indirect (exercised through an intermediary). For this last case, the term "transparency," although widely used in such context, is inadequate: if voters do not have the possibility to observe the election process (because of legal or technical limitations), the process is opaque.

In both cases the security is deemed total. However, if transparency is not direct (case 3) it is impossible to provide guarantees that the total security is effective, the electoral system is then unable to create confidence among voters.

In both cases transparency is direct. Even when security is not deemed complete (case 2), voters can exercise control and assert their right to electoral disputes.

Table 2. Four cases

	Total Security	Non Total Security
Direct Transparency	Case 1: The transparency allows voters to see the smooth running of elections.	Case 2: The voting procedure is likely to fail, because of error or fraud. The exercise of transparency reveals significant damage to the sincerity of the vote. The findings, brought before the competent court, permit the practice of law.
Opacity	Case 3: The lack of transparency prevents voters to see the smooth running of the election day and ground their confidence. This situation is conducive to the emergence and spread of unfounded rumors.	Case 4: The lack of direct transparency prevents voters to make a finding of fraud or malfunctions even if infringement of the sincerity of the vote. Without evidence, the courts cannot exercise the right.

I infer that the promise of security is not able to compensate for the loss of direct transparency.

About Internet voting, I have shown previously that the total security is far from being achieved and that direct transparency totally disappeared. Internet voting appears then as a voting process that can not inspire confidence. Voters seem to rely on the same analysis: in the USA, the 2008 CCES survey conducted by Polimetrix, asking to 32,800 individuals if they would "allow absentee voting over the Internet." measured that 46.9% oppose this reform. In the Netherlands, 47,1% appear to have very little or little confidence in Internet voting (Hall & Loeber, 2010).

DEPLOYMENT OF INTERNET VOTING

I present the Internet voting deployments that concern political elections or official referenda. Only four countries open this possibility to some of their voters: Estonia, Switzerland, France and Holland. I ordered them according to the development of such new mode of vote, beginning with the most engaged country. The level of detail of these presentations depends on the amount of information that could be collected.

Estonia

Estonia is a young democracy born is 1991. This is the only country to have authorized all of its voters to vote by Internet, but without making the mandatory use (Madise & Martens, 2006). Since then, five elections were held: local in 2005 and 2009, parliamentary in 2007 and 2011, European parliamentary in 2009 (Vabariigi Valimiskomisjon, 2013).

The voting system, developed by the National Election Committee (NEC) which is in charge of the elections, follows the general pattern described above, except as regards the identification process conducted through the electronic identity card which equipped almost the entire population. When voting, the card, swiped through a reader, plays the identifier role while the authentication is performed by entering a four digit code. Entering a second four-digit code allows the card to sign off electronically the cast vote. By consequence, there is no communication of voting material by mail. The legislation allows multiple voting: a voter can vote multiple times, each cast vote replacing the previous one. It may proceed via the Internet, or at the ballot box, a few days before the official day of elections (voting by Internet is then closed).

The 2007 elections were observed by a mission of the Organization for Security and Cooperation in Europe (Organization for Security and Co-operation in Europe, 2007). Regarding transparency, the mission noted that any direct observation of the process of vote counting done by the server is impossible. The opportunities to review the voting system appeared unrealistic: although many parties, associations and organizations have been able to attend all operations of the vote, see the documentation and source code, none has exercised this right by default skills and lack of funding to appoint experts. The voting system is therefore remained completely opaque. In addition, several security holes have been mentioned. Thus, the National Election Committee (NEC) has acknowledged its inability to secure computers of voters, particularly against viruses that could interfere with the voting process.

But many other faults, underestimated by the NEC, have been identified by the OSCE-ODIHR experts. For example, the computer doing the reading of CD (Compact Disc) containing the results remained connected to Internet while the counting process was launched. Furthermore, this computer does not seem secure, which can be an input for an external attack targeting the server. As the legal texts do not specify the prerequisites or requirements for certification and testing that the voting system must comply with, these steps have been taken informally and the results are not public. An audit has been conducted with the procedures followed to the letter, but they seem inadequate to detect differences between the observations and the ultimate goals of the system. The voting system can accommodate errors that were not detected. The identity of the voting program on the server is verified using a checksum calculation, which is an inadequate procedure: this calculation is used to detect errors but not voluntary modifications. Even if the server room is constantly filmed, and guarded by a police officer, there is no procedure to verify that there has been no unauthorized access by Internet. The program has been implemented without the various tasks are formally divided between the programmers. It therefore appears that the program can be surreptitiously changed without this change is detected.

The Estonian voting system has the peculiarity to allow multiple voting to promote respect for privacy (each vote annulling the previous one). This procedure records the dates and times of cast votes in the event logs which are then accessible to observers and parties. It is therefore possible to know whether a person has decided to vote again. This information may help the coercion on voters on preventing them to modify a vote cast in situation of coercion.

Regarding external attacks, it should be noted that dozens of Estonian government sites were shut down by nearly 150 coordinated attacks in May 2007, two months after elections.

The proportion of voters who chose to vote by Internet, grew from less than 2% in 2005 to 24% in 2011. In 2009, the duration of Internet voting grew from three days to seven days. Between the two Parliamentary elections of 2007 and 2011, the number of voters using Internet was multiplied by 4.6, while the turnout progression was de 1.5 points (around 62%) (Vabariigi Valiskomisjon, 2013).

The Estonian voting system, deployed in a country of young democratic tradition, appears to be particularly opaque (Maaten & Hall, 2008). Moreover it seems that the introduction of this new channel of voting would encourage to vote... persons who vote regularly (Bochsler, 2009).

Switzerland

Since 2003, Internet voting is allowed for non-political elections (only for referenda) and for a portion of the population in three Swiss cantons: Geneva, Neuchâtel and Zurich (where the SMS can also be used to vote) and, in 2010, it was used for the first time by some Swiss living abroad. It is gradually deployed, the number of people being allowed to use this new method of voting varies between votes, slowly increasing.

The canton of *Geneva* owns the electronic voting system that was developed by the cantonal computational service (Centre des Technologies de l'Information de l'Etat - CTI) in collaboration with the private companies Hewlett Packard Switzerland (hardware and software), Wisekey (encryption technology) and Blue-Infinity (security). Before the first Internet voting utilization, several studies has been devoted to security (Wenger, 2002; Oppliger, 2002) and noted the impossibility to perform comprehensive audits because of the complexity of software layers. Despite these recommendations, there are no experts at work during the polls, the only controls being carried out by representatives of the parties originally set up for postal voting. At least nine votes have taken place since the first use of the application to vote in 2003, the number of potential users varies from a thousand to nearly 90,000 persons. After an initial surge to 27% maybe due to the novelty, the rate of people who use Internet voting felt down to 11% in 2010 (the Swiss from abroad registered in the canton were authorized to vote by Internet).

The voting application of *Neuchâtel* is a part of a project developed by the companies Computer Associates and Lanexpert. At least eleven votes have taken place since September 2005, extending the opportunity to vote via the Internet from 1700 to 6800 people. The rate of Internet voting are significantly higher than in the canton of Geneva but follows the same process of erosion, decreasing steadily from 68% to 28% in 2010 (with the Swiss from abroad registered in the canton).

In the canton of *Zurich*, remote electronic voting can be done via the Internet but also by sending SMS messages. Again, the voter turnout tends to decline steadily. While with the first experiment in Blach had seen more than one third of the 4,000 votes cast by Internet, this proportion has fallen about 8% then 5% when the vote was extended to about 17,000 voters. With the last vote opened to 80,000 new voters (with the Swiss from abroad registered in the town of Zurich), the turn-out was 15%.

According to (Conseil Fédéral Suisse, 2002; Leuenberger and Huber-Hotz, 2006) there are numerous potentially invisible vulnerabilities that are difficult to reduce (Trojans, internal fraud, viruses) in the three Internet voting systems.

France

In France Internet voting has been allowed since 2003: French citizens living abroad have the possibility to use this new mode of vote to elect members of the Assembly of French Citizens Abroad (renewed by half every three years). It is the only political election that can be conducted remotely in this country. Internet voting has been proposed to the French living in the United States in June 2003 and was subsequently generalized in June 2006 to all French voters established in foreign countries. Voters receive their username and password by mail and had to download the interface.

In 2006, three security experts, including two that were appointed by candidates, issued reports highlighting the severe lack of transparency, inadequate testing, the difficulty in verifying the authenticity of the program, the possible consequences of computer errors and security flaws in the voting system (Appel, 2006; Lang, 2006).

The rate of voters that chose Internet to cast their ballots decreased from 64% in 2003 to 16% in 2006 and 6% in 2009.

In France, many Internet elections were held outside the political elections, mainly in the context of professional elections or insurance companies' elections. In all cases, the reports of experts who audited the voting systems are not discoverable to voters.

Holland

In the Netherlands, during the parliamentary elections of 22 November 2006, nearly 20,000 expatriates voted with the system of Internet voting Rijnland Internet Election System (RIES), developed by the company TTPI in collaboration with the elections office of the district Rijnland. This system has a feature to allow voters to verify their vote, even the aggregation of all the votes, by the calculation of different keys. Unfortunately offering this possibility implies to sacrifice the secrecy of the vote because the secrecy of vote is preserved only if each voter destroyed her keys and if the company responsible for managing the voting application also destroyed his keys. Moreover, it was found that the audit process is too complicated for ordinary voters, most of them have not been able to use it. And the verification of the aggregation of votes is a process more complex. In addition the system also appears very vulnerable to virus attacks on the voters' computers (Hubbers et al. 2005). On the one hand the developers themselves have found that it could not fit the entire population, on the other hand, the observers of the OSCE noted that transparency is still inadequate to respond to skepticism voters (Organization for Security and Co-operation in Europe, 2007).

WHAT FUTURE FOR ONLINE ELECTIONS?

It is now accepted that Internet voting is inherently opaque and that there is no real possibility of progress towards direct transparency. In particular, many reasons have invalidated the idea of restoring transparency by making public the software programs composing the voting: the detection of a security hole in a large program is virtually impossible, to prove the identity two systems is a complex task not solved so far, and most voters do not have the necessary skills, etc.

The research on E2E systems that give the possibility to voters to check if their votes are well counted may also collide against an operational problem, never considered by computer scientists because at the conjunction of technical and legal fields. Performing the individual verifiability to check if one's vote was not modified is a complex task, and there are probably few voters who would do this effort, and the number of these stubborn citizens would probably decrease with time. For computer scientists, it is clear that if one unique voter detects an error the system was not reliable and that results of the system may be false, including in significant proportions. An electoral court facing the same situation would simply consider that there is an error relating to one unit and would consider that the results of candidates must be considered with more or less one voice, which is rarely able to swing an election. The conclusion would be that the elections went smoothly and that the candidate who won the most votes is elected.

It is clear that the deployment of E2E electronic voting systems thus requires a major overhaul of the electoral law which should take into account the specificities of these systems.

A recent election in Austria demonstrates a new risk that was underestimated by previous studies: the propagation of unfounded rumors. In 2009, i-voting was an additional voting channel in the Austrian federation of students' elections. During the voting period, fake videos of vote flipping happened (Ehringfeld et al., 2010). This story illustrates the case of our previous analysis: the disappearance of transparency favors the apparition of rumors.

With Internet voting, electors are obliged to take matters of security, legitimacy and accuracy on trust. As shown above, there are many possible different attacks against an Internet voting system. There is no need for expensive and sophisticated weapons, it is not risky, and people educated with the necessary technical skills are numerous, including terrorists. The potential consequences of such a threat must be analyzed bearing in mind the situation of US citizens serving in the military. Any suspicion that the integrity of ballots is being compromised could introduce doubt between the soldiers and the military hierarchy. This doubt which strikes at the foundation of citizenship could affect all levels of the hierarchy and call into question the social and moral contract between each soldier and the country he or she serves: patriotism. In fact, such a destabilization could be brought about even without a real attack. It would be enough to spread a rumor pretending that some ballots have been tampered with. The introduction of the doubt into a soldier's mind to the effect that they are being betrayed by their country has the potential to affect their general level of confidence and obedience, with obvious consequences for the security of the nation.

CONCLUSION

This chapter has presented some democratic issues of Internet voting by demonstrating that the Internet voting is an opaque system of vote and that the promise of security cannot replace the loss of transparency. This has resulted in the inability to find anomalies and to submit appeals to the courts of electoral law. Internet Voting appears finally as an act dictated by trust and not by confidence.

In addition, after many uses during ten years, many announced benefits (diminution of costs, better accessibility, better accuracy, voter turnout increase, etc.) appears as false promises. I can retain that online voting is usually faster than postal voting and that the burden of organizing elections that weigh on office holders is lighten by the fact that online election are always completely or partly organized by private companies.

But Internet voting continues to expand, slowly in the political field where results in terms of voter turnout are not up to expectations, fast in the field of workplace elections where it appears easier to entrust the organization of elections to a service provider.

Far from the warnings of scientists, companies exploiting this new market, do not hesitate to promise the impossible to organizers of elections, seduced by the image of modernity that they can benefit and by the savings made in case of generalization (fewer traditional polling stations), not hesitating to sacrifice transparency in passing, and thus the confidence of voters.

The clear consensus of computer-science experts around the world who have studied these issues is that Internet elections cannot be trusted, for all the reasons that I have explained: the voters and political parties cannot audit the operation of the software and hardware that serves as the real bureau de vote. Therefore it is not clear to me how the assesseurs can sign anything but a surrealist image of a true procès-verbal. (Appel, 2006)

Finally, it appears that Internet voting is foremost a need to develop new market and a fertile ground for boasting of hypothetical developments regarding the security of banking transactions such as the confession of the previous chancellor Township of Geneva, Hensler who "*said he was confident the system would be secure and pave the way for others, such as banks, who place great value on protecting critical data.*"[7].

Nevertheless, Internet offers a great, but not used, opportunity to enhance transparency of not electronic elections that still widely take place: the results registered in all poll stations could be published with all the details, giving a real opportunity to the voters to know the results, verify their totalization, easing the collection of data by researchers that observe the difficulty or impossibility to access such information (Alvarez & Antonsson, 2007). Democracy would be enhanced by such general detailed publication of the data. Organizing this general publication of election results on Internet is technically simple and cheap: the official minute of each poll could, for example, be scanned and the obtained images presented on an official Web site.

ACKNOWLEDGMENT

I specially thank my friend John Johnson who kindly reviewed this article.

REFERENCES

Adida, B., de Marneffe, O., Pereira, O., & Quisquater, J.-J. (2009). *Electing a university president using open-audit voting*. Paper presented at the 3rd Int. Workshop on Security and Electronic Voting. Grenoble, France.

Alvarez, R.M., & Antonsson, E.K. (2007, Summer). Bridging science, technology, and politics. *The Bridge Linking Engineering and Society, Voting Technologies*, 6-10.

Anderson, R. (1993). Why cryptosystems fail. In *Proceedings of Conference on Computer and Communications Security*. ACM. Retrieved on August, 9, 2008, from http://www.cl.cam.ac.uk/~rja14/Papers/wcf.pdf

Appel, A. W. (2006, June). *Ceci n'est pas une urne: On the internet vote for the Assemblée des Français de l'étranger.* Retrieved on July, 12, 2006, from http://www.cs.princeton.edu/~appel/papers/urne.pdf

Bederson, B. B., Lee, B., Sherman, R., Herrnson, P. S., & Niemi, R. G. (2003). Electronic voting system usability issues. CHI Letters, 5(1), 145–152.

Bignon, J. (2003, March 25). *Rapport de l'assemblée nationale n° 721 tendant à autoriser le vote par correspondance électronique des Français établis hors de France pour les élections du Conseil supérieur des Français de l'étranger.*

Birdsall, S. (2005, October). The democratic divide. *First Monday, 10*(10). Retrieved on August, 31, 2013, from http://www.firstmonday.org/issues/issue10_4/birdsall/index.html

Bochsler, D. (2009). Can the internet increase political participation? An analysis of remote electronic voting's effect on turnout. *Potsdam ECPR Panels on Internet & Politics*. Retrieved on October, 4, 2010, from http://papers.ssrn.com/sol3/papers.cfm?abstract_id=1456827

Caporusso, L. (2010). The role of trust, participation and identity in the propensity to e- and i-vote. In *Proceedings of Electronic Voting 2010, 4th International Conference Electronic Voting (EVOTE 2010).* Bregenz, Austria: EVOTE.

Christin, T., & Trechsel, A. H. (2004). *Qui vote par internet? Rapport, Université de Genève.* Retrieved on August, 5, 2007, from http://www.geneve.ch/evoting/doc/rapports/200409_rapport_carouge_meyrin.pdf

Coleman, S. (2002). Elections in the 21st century: From paper ballot to e-voting. Om The independent commission on alternative voting methods. London: Electoral Reform Society.

Coleman, S. (2005). Internet voting and democratic politics in an age of crisis. In The European Union and e-voting: Addressing The European Parliament's internet voting challenge. London: Routledge.

Commission on Electronic Voting. (2004, December). Secrecy, accuracy and testing of the chosen electronic system. *First Report.* Retrieved on May, 13, 2006, from http://www.cev.ie/htm/report/first_report.htm

Commission on Electronic Voting. (2006, July). Secrecy, accuracy and testing of the chosen electronic voting system. *Second Report.* Retrieved on September, 1, 2006, from http://www.cev.ie/htm/report/download_second.htm

Conseil Fédéral Suisse. (2002, January 9). Rapport sur le vote électronique chances, risques et faisabilité. *Rapport n°02.009.* Retrieved on August, 31, 2013, from http://www.admin.ch/ch/f/ff/2002/612.pdf

Consulat Général de France à Washington. (2010). *Elections AFE 2010.* Retrieved on October, 30, 2010, from http://www.consulfrance-washington.org/spip.php?article567#4-Comment-comptez-vous-remedier de France, B. Observatoire de la Sécurité des Cartes de Paiement. (2012). *Rapport annuel, statistiques de fraude pour 2012*. Retrieved on August, 31, 2013, from http://www.banque-france.fr/observatoire/telechar/2013/Rapport-annuel-2012.pdf

des Français de l'Etranger, A. (2008, March). 10 propositions pour améliorer la participation électorale des Français de l'étranger. *Rapport de la commission temporaire de la participation électorale des français établis hors de France, avant-projet*. Retrieved on August, 23, 2009, from http://www.francais-du-monde.org/wp-content/uploads/2008/10/2008-10-propositionsrev.pdf

Dill, D., & Doherty, W. (2004, November 22). Electronic voting systems. *Report for the National Research Council*. Retrieved on August, 31, 2013, from http://www.openvotingconsortium.org/files/project_evoting_vvf.pdf

Ehringfeld, A., Naber, L., Grechenig, T., Krimmer, R., Traxl, M., & Fischer, G. (2010). Analysis of recommendation rec(2004)11 based on the experiences of specific attacks against the first legally binding implementation of e-voting in Austria. In *Proceedings of Electronic Voting 2010, 4th International Conference Electronic Voting (EVOTE 2010)*, (pp. 225-237). Bregenz, Austria: EVOTE.

Enguehard, C., & Lehn, R. (2009, July 13). *Vulnerability analysis of three remote voting methods*. Paper presented at the XXI IPSA World Congress of Political Science, RC10 Electronic Democracy - Dilemmas of Change? Santiago, Chile.

European Commission for Democracy through Law. (2002, July). *Guidelines on elections*. Retrieved on February, 23, 2008, from http://www.venice.coe.int/docs/2002/CDL-AD(2002)013-e.asp

European Commission for Democracy through Law. (2004, September). *Legal, operational and technical standards for e-voting* (Recommendation Rec(2004)11). Retrieved on August, 31, 2013, from https://wcd.coe.int/ViewDoc.jsp?id=778189

Gharadaghy, R., & Volkamer, M. (2010). Verifiability in electronic voting explanations for non security experts. In *Proceedings of Electronic Voting 2010, 4th International Conference Electronic Voting (EVOTE 2010)*, (pp. 151-162). Bregenz, Austria: EVOTE.

Green, P. (2000, October 5). The politics of the future: The internet and democracy in Australia. *ACT Electoral Commission, to the Australian Political Science Association's Politics of the Future Seminar at the Australian National University*. Retrieved on September, 1, 2007, from http://www.elections.act.gov.au/adobe/PolFut.pdf

Hall, T., & Loeber, L. (2010). Electronic elections in a politicized polity. In *Proceedings of 4th International Conference Electronic Voting (EVOTE 2010)*, (pp. 193-212). Bregenz, Austria: EVOTE.

Herrnson, P. S., Niemi, R. G., Hanmer, M. J., Bederson, B. B., Conrad, F. G., & Traugott, M. (2006, August 1). The importance of usability testing of voting systems. In *Proceedings of Electronic Voting Technology Workshop*. Vancouver, Canada: Academic Press. Retrieved on November, 27, 2006, from http://www.usenix.org/events/evt06/tech/full_papers/herrnson/herrnson.pdf

Hoff, J. (1999). Towards a theory of democracy for the information age (Discussion paper for the Democracy Platform UK-Nordic Meeting). London, UK.

Hubbers, E., Jacobs, B., & Pieters, W. (2005). RIES - Internet voting in action. In *Proceedings of the 29th Annual International Computer Software and Applications Conference,* (pp. 417-424). IEEE Computer Society.

Jefferson, D. R., Rubin, A. D., Simon, B., & Wagner, D. (2004). Analyzing internet voting security. Communications of the ACM, 47(10), 59–64. doi:10.1145/1022594.1022624 doi:10.1145/1022594.1022624

Jones, D. W. (2003). A brief illustrated history of voting. *Tutorial.* Retrieved on August, 18, 2006, from http://www.cs.uiowa.edu/~jones/voting/

Jones, D. W. (2009). *Some problems with end-to-end voting.* Paper presented at the End-to-End Voting Systems Workshop. Washington, DC.

Lang, B. (2006, June 23). *Rapport sur l'usage du vote électronique par l'Internet pour les élections à l'Assemblée des Français de l'Étranger de juin 2006.* Retrieved on July, 12, 2006, from http://traitdunion.info/ELECTIONS-AFE-2006/COMMPRESS/index.htm

Laskowski, S. J. (2006, August 1). *Making ballot language understandable to voters.* Paper presented at the Electronic Voting Technology Workshop. Vancouver, Canada.

Leuenberger, M., & Huber-Hotz, A. (2006, May 31). *Rapport sur les projets pilotes en matière de vote électronique* (Conseil Fédéral Suisse, Rapport n°06.056). Retrieved on May, 31, 2006, from http://www.admin.ch/ch/f/ff/2006/5205.pdf

Maaten, E., & Hall, T. (2008). Improving the transparency of remote e-voting: The Estonian experience. *EVOTE08.* Retrieved on August, 5, 2008, from http://www.e-voting.cc/static/evoting/files/maaten_hall_improving-transparency_31-43.pdf

Madise, Ü., & Martens, T. (2006). E-voting in Estonia 2005: The first practice of country-wide binding internet voting in the world. In *Proceedings of Electronic Voting 2006, 2nd International Workshop,* (pp. 15-26). Bregenz, Austria: Academic Press.

Mercuri, M. (2002). A better ballot box? IEEE Spectrum Online, 39(10), 46–50. doi:10.1109/MSPEC.2002.1038569doi:10.1109/MSPEC.2002.1038569

Mohen, J., & Glidden, J. (2001). The case for internet voting. Communications of the ACM, 44(1), 72–85. doi:10.1145/357489.357511 doi:10.1145/357489.357511

Moore, D., Paxson, V., Savage, S., Shannon, C., Staniford, S., & Weaver, N. (2003). Inside the slammer worm. *IEEE Security and Privacy.* Retrieved on August, 31, 2013, from http://www.cs.ucsd.edu/~savage/papers/IEEESP03.pdf

National Academy of Sciences. (2005). *Asking the right questions about electronic voting* (Free Executive Summary). National Research Council (NRC). Retrieved on August, 31, 2013, from http://www.nap.edu/catalog/11449.html

National French Assembly. (2005, July 12). Compte-rendu, première séance du mardi 12 juillet 2005. *14e Séance de la Session Extraordinaire 2004-2005.* Retrieved on August, 31, 2013, from http://www.assemblee-nationale.fr/12/cri/2004-2005-extra/20051014.asp

National Institute of Standards and Technology. (2007, August 31). *Voluntary voting system guidelines recommendations to the election assistance commission.* Retrieved on October, 12, 2008, from http://vote.nist.gov/VVSG-0807/Final-TGDC-VVSG-08312007.pdf

Newell, A. F., & Gregor, P. (1997). Human computer interfaces for people with disabilities. In Handbook of human-computer interaction (2nd ed.). Academic Press. doi:10.1016/B978-044481862-1.50101-1 doi:10.1016/B978-044481862-1.50101-1

Oostveen, A.-M., & van der Besselaar, P. (2004). Internet voting technologies and civic participation: The users' perspective. The Public, 11(1), 61–78.

Oostveen, A.-M., & van der Besselaar, P. (2006). Non-technical risks of remote electronic voting. In The encyclopedia of digital government. Hershey, PA: IGI Global. doi:10.4018/978-1-59140-789-8.ch190 doi:10.4018/978-1-59140-789-8.ch190

Oppliger, R. (2002, May 3). *Traitement du problème de la sécurité des plates-formes pour le vote par internet à Genève*. Retrieved on August, 31, 2013, from http://www.geneve.ch/evoting/doc/rapports/rapport_oppliger_fr.pdf

Organization for Security and Co-Operation in Europe-Office for Democratic Institutions and Human Rights. (2005). *Election observation book* (5th ed.). Retrieved on November, 17, 2006, from http://www.osce.org/publications/odihr/2005/04/14004_240_en.pdf

Organization for Security and Co-Operation in Europe-Office for Democratic Institutions and Human Rights. (2004, September 28). *USA 2 November 2004 elections: OSCE/ODIHR needs assessment mission report - 7-10 September 2004*. Retrieved on October, 14, 2006, from http://www.osce.org/documents/odihr/2004/09/3655_en.pdf

Organization for Security and Co-Operation in Europe-Office for Democratic Institutions and Human Rights. (2007a, March 12). *The Netherlands parliamentary elections 22 November 2006* (OSCE/ODIHR Election Assessment Mission Report). OSCE/ODIHR.

Organization for Security and Co-Operation in Europe-Office for Democratic Institutions and Human Rights. (2007b, June 28). *Republic of Estonia parliamentary elections 4 March 2007*. OSCE/ODIHR Election Assessment Mission Report.

Organization for Security and Co-Operation in Europe-Office for Democratic Institutions and Human Rights. (2008, October 28). *Discussion paper in preparation of guidelines for the observation of electronic voting*. Retrieved on October, 24, 2008, from http://www.osce.org/documents/odihr/2008/10/34647_en.pdf

Phillips, D. M., & von Spakovsky, H. A. (2001). Gauging the risks of internet elections. Communications of the ACM, 44(1), 72–85. doi:10.1145/357489.357512 doi:10.1145/357489.357512

Powell, A., Bryne, A., & Dailey, D. (2010). The essential internet: Digital exclusion in low-income American communities. *Policy & Internet, 2*(2).

Rubin, A. D. (2001). Security considerations for remote electronic voting over the internet. The Magazine of Usenix & Sage, 26(1), 20–28.

Ryan, P. Y. A., & Peacok, T. (2005, September 20). *Prêt à voter: Systems perspective* (Technical report CS-TR-929). Academic Press.

Schneier, B. (1999). The Trojan horse race. Communications of the ACM, 42(9). PubMed doi:10.1145/315762.315785 doi:10.1145/315762.315785 PMID:11543550

Simons, B. (2004). Electronic voting systems: The good, the bad, and the stupid. ACM Queue; Tomorrow's Computing Today, 2(7). doi:10.1145/1035594.1035606 doi:10.1145/1035594.1035606

Thompson, K. (1984). Reflections on trusting trust. Communications of the ACM, 27(8), 761–763. doi:10.1145/358198.358210 doi:10.1145/358198.358210

United Nations. (1948). The universal declaration of human rights. New York: Author.

United Nations. (2005). World population ageing. New York: Author.

Valimiskomisjon, V. (2013). *Internet voting in Estonia*. Retrieved on August, 31, 2013, from http://www.vvk.ee/index.php?id=11178

Voting Technology Project. (2001). *Voting: What is, what could be*. Retrieved on August, 31, 2013, from http://www.vote.caltech.edu/drupal/node/10

Wenger, M. (2002, January 28). *Rapport du comité de sécurité sur l'application du vote par internet*. Retrieved on August, 5, 2007, from http://www.ge.ch/evoting/doc/rapports/rapport_version_Internet.pdf

KEY TERMS AND DEFINITIONS

Anonymity: Impossibility to link a ballot to the voter who cast it.

Coercion: Vote selling or buying; intimidation by family members, colleagues, teachers, churches, union bosses, employers etc.

Confidentiality: Each voter expresses her choice alone; there is no more person that can see what is the choice of the voter when she expresses it. Physical isolation of the voter, for example in a voting booth, is the only sure answer.

Controlled Environment: The environment is said to be "controlled" when the voting process takes place in an identified poll in the presence of officials detaining the authority to maintain order and uphold the principles of ensuring the secrecy of voting and unicity.

Equality: There is no discrimination between voters among gender, ethnicity, etc.

Internet Voting: Mode of vote that allows voters to cast votes from any computer connected to the Web and equipped with a browser compatible with the voting Web application running on a server.

Remote Voting: The remote voting elections take place in uncontrolled environments, outside of any poll, without any officials.

Sincerity: The results of the election reflect faithfully the will of the voters; the candidate that won the most votes is declared the winner.

Transparency: The stages of the election, including the counting of the ballots, can be observed and controlled.

Uncontrolled Environment: The environment is said to be "uncontrolled" when the voting process takes place outside of a controlled poll and beyond the supervision of officials.

Unicity: Each eligible voter can vote ounce.

Voter Turnout: Percentage of eligible voters who cast a ballot in an election.

ENDNOTES

1 However, there are some exemptions; for instance, in Belgium, every vote is recorded on a magnetic card. The counting is done by the reading the magnetic cards by a counting device.

2 For instance, the organization of Internet voting for the French election of the members "Assemblée des Français de l'Etranger" cost 61,000 Euros in 2003 for 5354 cast votes, 2,000,000 Euros in 2006 for 10,193 cast votes and 200,000 Euros in 2009 for 6026 cast votes (Bignon, 2003; Assemblée de Français de l'Etranger, 2008; Consulat général de France à Washington, 2010).

3 "Democracy" literally means power (kratein = order) of the people (demos).

4 With remote voting (postal or Internet voting), confidentiality cannot be guaranteed.

5 (Enguehard et Lehn, 2009) details the vulnerabilities of three remote voting systems for comparison: postal voting, Internet voting and hybrid voting.

6 A worm is a virus that has the ability to spread by itself, using the network.

7 The Sydney Morning Herald, "Swiss to use encryption voting method," 13 October 2007.

Chapter 13
What Does E- add to Democracy?
Designing an Agenda for Democracy Theory in the Information Age

Patricia Mindus
Uppsala University, Sweden

ABSTRACT

Technologies carry politics since they embed values. It is therefore surprising that mainstream political and legal theory have taken the issue so lightly. Compared to what has been going on over the past few decades in the other branches of practical thought, namely ethics, economics, and the law, political theory lags behind. Yet the current emphasis on Internet politics that polarizes the apologists holding the Web to overcome the one-to-many architecture of opinion building in traditional representative democracy, and the critics who warn that cyber-optimism entails authoritarian technocracy has acted as a wake up call. This chapter sets the problem, "What is it about ICTs, as opposed to previous technical devices, that impact on politics and determine uncertainty about democratic matters?," into the broad context of practical philosophy by offering a conceptual map of clusters of micro-problems and concrete examples relating to "e-democracy." The point is to highlight when and why the hyphen of e-democracy has a conjunctive or a disjunctive function in respect to stocktaking from past experiences and settled democratic theories. The chapter's claim is that there is considerable scope to analyse how and why online politics fail or succeed. The field needs both further empirical and theoretical work.

INTRODUCTION

The democratization of communications, the theory goes, will bring about the democratization of the world. It is noteworthy that the praise of the political consequences of the massive use of ICTs is occurring just as a wave of pessimism is sweeping across many sectors of the digitally sensible world of culture. As an example of the growing unease with the general celebratory mood, *The Edge*'s special 2010 issue should be mentioned, where John Markoff affirmed that, from Arpanet to the Internet, we are in the midst of a "post-industrial dystopia" in which the Web

DOI: 10.4018/978-1-4666-6038-0.ch013

Copyright © 2014, IGI Global. Copying or distributing in print or electronic forms without written permission of IGI Global is prohibited.

is opening Pandora's box. A closer look at "liberation technologies" (Diamond, 2010) and the political use of new media and ICTs (Chadwich & Howard, 2009) suggest a more complicated reality: technological advances are no substitute for human wisdom. Many observe how "the tools of modern communications satisfy as wide a range of ambitions and appetites as their 20th century ancestors did, and many of these ambitions and appetites do not have anything to do with democracy" (Bremmer, 2010, p. 86), according to a reading still focused on the alleged neutrality of technology. Yet, taking a broader outlook on the interaction of technology and human evolution, "sometimes, we may forget how much we owe to flakes and wheels, to sparks and ploughs and to engines and satellites. We are reminded of such deep technological debt when we divide human life into prehistory and history. The significant threshold is there to acknowledge that it was the invention and development of information and communication technologies (ICTs) that made all the difference between who we were and who we are" (Floridi, 2012). Our times might thus be more than just an age of information; perhaps we are entering what Luciano Floridi calls hyperhistory; if this is true, then, regardless of what the outcomes will be, the stakes are high indeed.

My aim here is neither to fuel the enthusiasm of those who see a new form of democracy burgeoning, nor to take the conservative stance that see nothing new occurring. Rather, this chapter outlines possible ways to address the problem *in what does Internet change the paradigm for democracy studies?* The goal is to distinguish areas of transformation from revolutionary thrusts and thus offer the political scholar a broad theoretical setting that takes stock on developments in ethics and legal science as well as settled democratic theories. The chapter provides a conceptual map of clusters of micro-problems in order to further empirical work.

I will start by stressing that for digital democracy to be an interesting problem for enquiry it needs to constitute a problem *(i)* rich in consequences, *(ii)* clearly defined and/or definable, *(iii)* accessible, in the meaning easy to understand but hard to solve, *(iv)* intrinsically open, leaving disagreement as a viable option. This chapter shall evidently not transform the topic, which is still something of a moving target, into such a well-defined issue since such a task would go well beyond the purposes of this chapter. What I shall attempt to do is to draw a conceptual map of questions that need to be addressed – or better, of clusters of micro-problems – and that cannot be easily articulated unless we take the "e" added to democracy seriously. This should show why the issue does respond (at least) to the requirements *(i)*, *(iii)* ad *(iv)* listed above.

BACKGROUND

First, a word on democracy as a form of government is needed. It has over the ages been associated with a variety of adjectives: direct, representative, procedural, formal, substantial, social, liberal, constitutional, epistemic, deliberative, participative… and last but not least "real." The conceptual typologies of democratic regimes (parliamentary/presidential, bi- and multipartisan, coalescent, consociated, concordant, populist, plebiscitarian, polyarchic etc.) also span over a vast amount of different organisations, just like the broad variety of historical experiences associated with it, does. Some even go as far as to claim that we are dealing with an "essentially contested concept" (Crick, 2002). There is, however, reason to believe this is not so, and the 20th century tradition of though in theory of democracy offers some evidence in that direction (Kelsen, 1929-2000; Dahl, 1956; Bobbio, 1984-1987; Sartori, 1987).

For our present purposes I shall keep the broad connotations in the background and keep the constraints to a minimum (that some will surely feel are embarrassingly low), i.e. conceiving democracy quite generically to be a method for taking collective decisions, that historically relates to a set of values (e.g. peaceful resolution of conflicts) and that has a set of social conditions (e.g. formal citizenship status) as well as a set of legally guaranteed preconditions (e.g. freedom of speech). I am aware of the imperfect nature of the characterisation but it leaves us, in tackling digital democracy, with a sufficiently open texture definition to take in most practices, experiences, and ideas associated with the (often equally unspecified) term "e-democracy" (Zittel, 2008).

A reason for adopting this generic conception is that, like in many other practical fields of enquiry, methodological holism keeps together the various problematic aspects raised by a topic so as to avoid creating an epistemic level of analysis that misses out on important observables; in our case, such observables are connected to e-democracy even though not equal to its institutional manifestations (e.g. E-parliament, E-government etc.), e.g. an accessible, non-censured and neutral Web.

Let us now stress two observations that do not seem to have been properly connected hitherto: the first concerns technology and the second politics.

The first observation is nicely presented with a quote by the father of cybernetics, Norbert Weiner: "It has long been clear to me that the modern ultra-rapid computing machine was in principle an ideal central nervous system to an apparatus for automatic control [...]. Long before Nagasaki and the public awareness of the atomic bomb, it had occurred to me that we were here in the presence of another social potentiality of unheard-of importance for good and evil" (Weiner, 1948, pp. 27-28). ICT is now the fastest growing technology in history, "playing a cultural role far more influential than that of mills in the Middle Ages, mechanical clocks in the 17th century, and the loom or the steam engine in the age of the industrial revolution" (Floridi, 2011, p. 5) and this has led to the appearance of the infosphere, i.e. the environment in which millions of people spend their time nowadays. Only blind thoughtlessness could suppose that this has no impact on the relationships among people and the stewardship of our communities.

The second observation concerns the general silence of standard political and legal theory on the impact of technology on politics and law. Just to mark the point: for instance if one turns to John Rawls, an often acclaimed giant of contemporary political philosophy, he does not have much to say on the issue: in *Political liberalism* (1996) he feels it is sufficient to stress that the rules of evidence are different in a scientific society from those of democratic politics. Many democratic theorists agree on this point. It is therefore not surprising that, even as the neologism was emerging, Seymour Lipset's The Encyclopedia of Democracy from 1995 has no entry for e-democracy. A quick look around in mainstream political theory shows an embarrassing void when it comes to making sense of what is going in the infosphere. Conversely, among the fields of research that are more conversant with e-democracy, such as theory of social communication and science and technology studies, seem largely unaware of the body of work that has been steadily growing in legal and political theory concerning the concept, limits and preconditions of democracy.

A similar point can be made for legal theory: An example is the fact that legal theorists often view technology in traditional terms of law being (merely) a system of social control through the determination of sanctions. This tendency can be found among traditional positive lawyers as well as among critical theorists that build on the Foucaultian notion of regulation as understood prevailingly in juridical terms. However, it should be clear by now that technology inscribes and constitutes as much as it prescribes. The lack of determinate and separate institutions of enforcement does not necessarily invalidate the idea of technological regulation: "Rather than relying on sanctions imposed after the fact to enforce its rules, [software] simply prevents the forbidden behaviour from occurring" (Grimmelmann, 2005, p. 1723). This is the key idea behind the aggressive digital technologies developed by some corporations in the entertainment business that forbear the "final user" from making "free use" of the product that has been purchased, with the aim to hinder file-sharing or mash up: the aim of TPM (*technological protection measures*) or DRM (*digital rights management*) is to technologically prevent the very possibility of copyright infringement.

What then is hindering political and legal theorists from making the connection between democracy theory and philosophy of information and technology studies? It is possible to advance the claim that the lack of transversal interest is due to the ideal of the *neutrality* of technology that is pervasive in political theory. Less so, perhaps, in legal theory, where theorists realized that there is a dialectical relationship between the law's content (substantial law) and its form (procedural law). In fact, it is noteworthy that the claim that (information) technology is neutral continues to pervade the debate on the political dimension of the digital revolution. The claim is usually made by pointing to the use made of a determinate technology by groups that are ascribed to different ends of the political spectrum, as if the traditional political spectrum right/left would be the ultimate orientation points in any possible discussion of the political use of technology. An example is the statement that Brazilian ecologists use *GoogleMaps* for showing the effects of deforestation, but *GoogleMaps* is also being used by the Russian extreme right movement against illegal immigration for determining the location of ethnic minorities in big cities (Postel-Vinay, 2010, p. 22).

To rephrase it, technological information has a semantic dimension, involving "giving and making sense" of "reality." Information as semantic content can be seen as the upper level of the technological complex that marks our age (Benkler, 2006). Epistemologically, "information" however does not mean "belief" nor "knowledge," yet it is distinguishable from mere data, the uninterpreted differences of symbols or signs. Ontologically, "information is information, not matter or energy" (Weiner, 1948, p. 12). For our present purposes, let us adopt Floridi's terms: "semantic information is well-formed, meaningful and truthful data" (Floridi, 2011, p. 31). This semantic dimension of technology should keep us from falling flatly into the widespread belief that technology is a means to the service of human ends, a form of passive universe of "objects" whose functions and purposes are shaped by the pursuits of humans in the contexts where they occur. Artefacts *qua* means are never neutral. They make some things possible and exclude others. Technology is best grasp in terms of "constraining affordances" (Durante, 2011). "Artefacts embody values or 'have politics' [...]. Technology is not exogenous to human agency, as the contrast of humans to machines may initially suggest. Technology does not constitute a force that simply has to be used, resisted, bypassed or altogether avoided" (Kallinikos, 2010, p. 3). Today, there is of course a burgeoning contemporary literature on e-democracy but it can be distinguished from previous strains of research because, most of the time, it uses, at some level of analysis, the idea that the technology we are dealing with should be understood and grasped in terms of "information," not mere tools. Our starting point, thus, is that "the modern alliance between *sophia* and *techne* has reached a new level of synergy with the computer revolution" (Floridi, 2011, p. 27). But exactly how *new* is this synergy?

WHAT IS NEW AND WHAT IS NOT?

In mapping the problems implied by e-democracy in today's debate, I shall try to spell out the relations of political thinking with its "cousins," the other branches of practical thought, foremost ethics and the law. A cascade of issues, associated with digital democracy in its broadly construed meaning, will be stressed and assigned to respective levels of change. Some are partially convergent, yet most

Figure 1. Continuity reading and the digital revolution

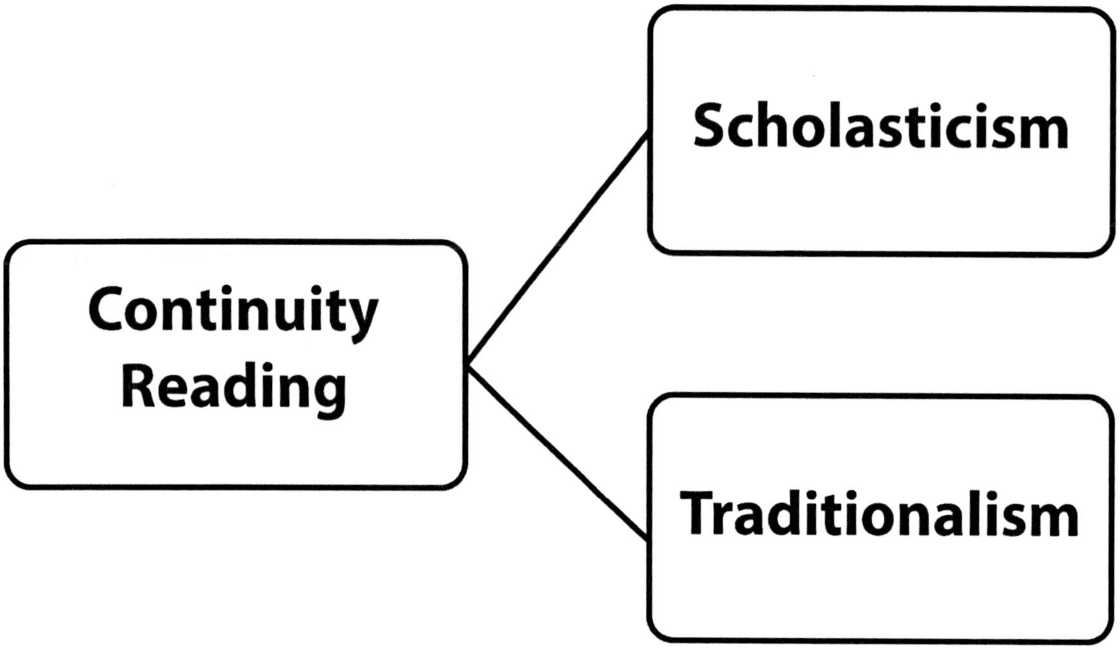

dissimilar. All push for reconsideration of the contemporary dialectic between means and ends.

The first crossroad on our map is the basic distinction (a) which features and characteristics appear to be in *continuity* with past experiences, conferring on the hyphen of e-democracy a conjunctive function and (b) what features and characteristics appear to be in *discontinuity* with past experiences, turning the same hyphen into a disjunctive sign.

If we first look at the continuity reading, we should distinguish between (a1) outlooks that do not account for the digital revolution and therefore are not equipped to operate with, or even notice, the current changes, and (a2) theories that uphold that we are witnessing new versions of old problems, yet refuse to consider these issues as offering unique features. I shall call the first outlook scholastic and the second traditionalist. Figure 1 scheme sums up the distinction:

Scholasticism here stands for what socio-linguists call "internal discourse," i.e. meta-theoretically acritical (or pedantic) attachment to a theoretical setting that ignores new data in the sense that it does not make use of a level of abstraction that turns the infosphere, and what is happening within it, into an observable of the system. Most political doctrines that are currently ignoring the informational turn have high probability of performing well in this category, with the consequent risk of ending up on the Hegelian dump of history. Perhaps a strict realist approach to political relationships that centres on the idea of power for power's sake, and hence does not take into account the declared values of those who engage in the digitally shaped political practice could be ascribed to (a1) since such a stance fails to perceive the ubiquity and pervasiveness of digitally re-wired collective endeavours (e.g. Ushahidi): it is just blind to the new environment.

The same goes for political theories that do not account for the huge impact on policy-making the Internet and the Web has had over the last decades. But also among approaches that have been investigating the political scene after the advent of the Internet often rely on comfortable convictions of "politics as usual": cyberspace "will be moulded by the everyday struggle for wealth and power" (Margolis & Resnick, 2000; Hafez, 2008) so that current political relationships and power distributions will ultimately be replicated online, opposing the view that the ICTs offer potential for radical redistribution of power. Similarly, Matthew Hindman, in *The Myth of Digital Democracy*, after tracking nearly three million Web pages, contends "that the beliefs that the Internet is democratizing politics are simply wrong" (2009, p. 3) and labels "Googlearchy" the current state of the Internet that would have done little to broaden political discourse but in fact empowers a small set of elites – some new, but most familiar. This is a perspective perfectly adaptable to Schumpeterian elitist theories of democracy (Schumpeter, 1942).

Now, a series of issues can be raised in relation to how new Internet politics are on the backdrop of scholasticism and traditionalism: are political theories, and theories of democracy in particular, that uphold the claim of the neutrality of technology to be ascribed to (a1) or (a2)? There is a vast portion of scholarly attention being directed to the "crisis of democracy" that had been growing steadily over the years: does this stream of research offer outlooks that should be placed under (a1) or (a2)? Political theory deals with underlying basic concepts such as obedience, legitimacy, order, justice that have transcended the passing of ages – from the classical age to the modern age – as well as the passing of forms of government, from monarchy, oligarchy/aristocracy to democracy. A fundamental question for political theory in this new setting would be to investigate the question of "diffusion of power": is there such a thing? In other words, is "power" more or less "powerful" when distributed? Are distributed power structures necessarily decentralized? Should we abandon the idea of a necessary link between force and power? If power is not exercised only through coercion, but also through the construction of meaning, does greater pluralism in semantic appliances imply a different configuration of the techno-social "relational capacity to influence asymmetrically the decisions of other social actor(s)," pursuant to one definition of power in the networked society (Castells, 2009, p. 10)?

Moreover, do such fundamental political categories, that seem well suited for being positioned under (a1) really fit there, or should we add a new category or modify existing ones? For instance, how is the notion of "consent" to be understood in a setting where "informed consent" is increasingly complex to grasp and offers little resemblance to past forms? How many of you actually read the juridical contracts before you click "accept"? Another example of calling into question fundamental categories of political thinking concerns a major assumption of existing theories of political organisation, i.e. that a political community implies *borders* (including cosmopolitanism that does not, contrarily to what it might seem at a first glance, exclude internal federal settings): Does the trans-border effects of cyberspace call for a problematisation of such an assumption? Many contemporary theories of the so-called "global civil society," like many McLuhan-inspired "global village"-theories, seem to engage in such a direction, whether implicitly or explicitly. Does cyberspace call for a rethinking of what has been called the "democratic boundary problem" (Whelan, 1983)? The Internet is a medium that does not obey a geographical fractioning of the kind we have been used to in political gerrymandering – IP addresses are logical not geographical places –, how does this affect how we determine the "sphere of law" over a determinate community? The underlying idea of "space" relevant for political purposes perhaps needs recasting.

Before being raised in relation to politics, the outlook offered by (a2) was raised in relation to other realms of practical knowledge such as ethics and law. Already in 1985, ethicists were engaging in what came to be known as the "uniqueness debate": on the one hand, Moor (1985) suggested that we think of the ethical questions surrounding ICT technology as policy vacuums, while Deborah Johnson (1985) defended the traditionalist account, based on the principle of analogy, according to which existing moral norms and principles can be applied to the new situations. In the field of legal science, while David Post (2002) stressed the discontinuity-reading, Jack Goldsmith (1998) embraced such a traditionalist account where the new "crimes" emerging with the Internet would have been subsumed into already existing categories. Is it warranted to suspect that a similar traditionalist outlook informs many of today's e-democracy sceptics? "Traditionalist" here does not have any politically loaded meaning since it merely indicates the cognitive and epistemological ability of a theory already in use to account for upcoming facts. This implies that the key difference between traditionalists and scholastics lies in the fact that the first accept the challenge of the information age but believe to have the answers, while the second does not accept the challenge. Traditionalist accounts can be important both as descriptive and as normative accounts. Descriptively traditionalist outlooks often correctly grasp the ways in which policy decisions are made in practice as people are getting used to new technology (early stages descriptivism), and, normatively, such accounts appropriately recommends stocktaking on past experiences. Yet the inherent risk with such outlooks is that they may overstretch the principle of analogy, suggesting a mechanical process of extending knowledge and thus obscuring important decisions that are being taken in the design of new technologies that will be used in operating within the "politically loaded" world of experience.

Let us now turn to the *discontinuity* readings (b). We should keep separate two positions that share – contrarily to continuity readings – the idea that computers have such an impact on the political relationships of human beings so as to warrant independent investigation of the "uniqueness" of political cyberspace and democracy in the digital age. Those who call for such independent investigation, nevertheless, develop different perspectives: the first (b1) focuses on the "transformation" brought on by digitalisation while the second (b2) concentrates on the "revolution" going on. Just as the information age of the "interconnected estate" has impacted on other branches of practical thought, such as ethics, economics and the law, the outlook under (b1) holds that we are witnessing new versions of old problems, and the novelty does not only consist in re-contextualization but in the fact that the issue raises unprecedented or unique features. This can be summed up in Figure 2.

The difference between positions under (a2) and (b1) can thus be spelled out: whereas (a2) claims that we are witnessing new versions of old problems, yet refuses to treat these problems as offering unique features, (b1) claims that not only are we confronted with novel questions but we could not correctly understand and respond to these challenges if we do not take into account the specificities of information technology (such as its malleability, ubiquity, easily scalable networks, the "long tail," the emergence of collective intelligence, velocity of transformation or "Moore's law" etc.). This means, in other words, that if we want to understand a position as being related to (a2) or (b1) we should ask "What is it about information technology, as opposed to firearms, or washing machines or light bulbs, that creates political issues and uncertainty about democratic matters?" Are current problems affecting democracy in the digital age really different in the sense that they require development of a "new form of democracy"? Or are ICT-related political issues simply old political problems in a new guise?

Figure 2. Transformation and revolution in discontinuity reading

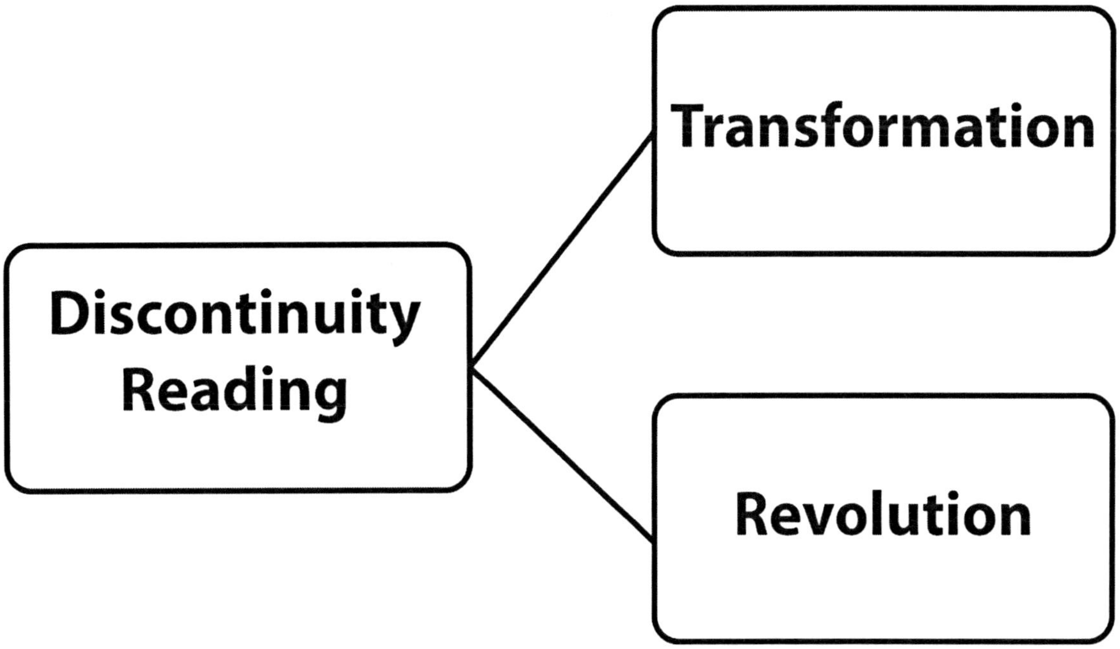

In order to better illustrate the difference between the transformative potential (b1) of Internet politics and its revolutionary thrust (b2), a quick comparative look at the other branches of practical philosophy is useful. Probably the first realm of practical knowledge that took the computer technology seriously was ethics: since the 80ies computer ethics has been addressing issues such as: Is it ethical for a Website to place a cookie on the hard drive of those who visit the site? Is data mining morally acceptable? Are Internet domain names being distributed in a fair way? Should surgery be performed remotely with medical imaging technology? Should computer graphical recreations of incidents, such as automobile accidents, be allowed to be used in courtrooms? Is it right for an individual to reproduce and alter an artistic image electronically that was originally created by someone else?

Economists took up the challenge with the new economy turn: post-industrialism became evident for the larger public with the dot-bubble in the early 2000s. The transformative aspects of the Internet emerged in economics as its ability to reduce internal administration costs, speed up communication, reduce costs of transmitting data: all aspects that meant the reduction of the number of middle-hands between original providers of goods and services and the final consumer. The futuristically minded understood that the disintermediation would challenge traditional economic functions of wholesalers and retailers, implying fewer big malls, offices, publishers etc. This spotlight on renewed economic functions is a good example of the outlook focusing on "transformation": It does not yet imply anything revolutionary, but it means that "business as usual" has to take into account the new setting.

On the political side, this trend was picked up by the transition to e-government in public administrations (e.g. electronic service delivery, the development of standardized management tools for legal documentation and information retrieval, such as XML standards; ZTTs in surveillance and congestion management; smart cards in public transport such as the London Oystercard): "the advent of the digital era is now the most general, pervasive, and structurally distinctive influence on how governance arrangements are changing in advanced industrialized states" (Margetts, 2009, p. 120). E-government streamlines, standardizes, and modifies public administrations but does not pretend to create e-democracy *ex novo*.

The transformative potential of the Internet also hit lawyers, prompted by the appearance of new "computer crimes" and the avalanche of law-making from the mid-90ies onwards concerning the regulation of the new technology (e.g. 1998 *Digital Millennium Copyright Act* that set the irresponsibility regime for ISPs without which much of the Web 2.0 could not have developed, with Del.icio.us, Essembly, FB, Flickr, Gather, MySpace, Partybuilder, YouTube, Ning, Metacafe, Revver, Blip.tv, CHBN, vSocial, Tagworld, Collectivex, Bebo, Care2, Hi5, Xanga...). All this can readily be understood in the framework of (b1): the transformative potential of the digital age was firmly grasped and new ways of tackling the updated versions of traditional ethical, economic and legal issues quickly developed.

HOW HAS THE TRANSFORMATION HIT THE POLITICAL REALM?

Today the transformative potential of information technology appears when we consider problems of how we should best update realms of political theory with lengthy histories, such as fundamental rights, institutionalized power, foremost that of the State; political participation, including parties, movements etc.; citizen education, including socialization practices of political relevance (e.g. consent-formation, political identification practices, and *net-etiquette*). All have, at some level of abstraction, a connection to (e)-democracy. "One of the weaknesses of Internet studies is a failure to link research to existing literatures or place it within current political contexts" (Ward & Gibson, 2009, p. 37). This implies that both futuristic optimists and realist normalizers fail to highlight that, under the present circumstances, *some* political institutions might benefit while other might not, *some* communicational settings may act as a catalyst for integrating *some* ICTs into participation and some may not. Scales of grey matter nonetheless. Here I shall briefly highlight some of the questions that can be raised in relation to fundamental rights and participation. The choice of focus is motivated by the relevance of the topics to the ideal of government most so-called settled democracies are projected against, i.e. liberal or constitutional democracy. This is summed up in Figure 3.

Get the Balance Right

In relation to fundamental rights, the digital age has changed profoundly the ways in which we balance relative fundamental rights against each other: Think about freedom of speech and privacy. It is becoming all the more evident that, once we enter the infosphere, the traditional *habeas corpus*, to be able to offer the guarantees, safeguards and liberties we expect from it, needs to be understood (in addition and beyond the traditional approach) in terms of *habeas data* (Rodotà, 2006). In other words, in a world where 35 hours of video is uploaded on YouTube every minute, Twitter registers 750 twits a second, 235 Websites created every 90 seconds, and 30 billion pieces of content posted on FB a month, the balancing of freedom of speech and privacy has changed substantially: in accordance with (a2), privacy has not ceased to be the "right to be let alone" in the meaning of the right to non-intromission (e.g. secrecy of correspondence and of one's home), but it has *also* assumed a previously unknown meaning of a *right to control over the treatment of personal data*. Think for example of the recent German protests

Figure 3. Transformation in the context of rights and participation

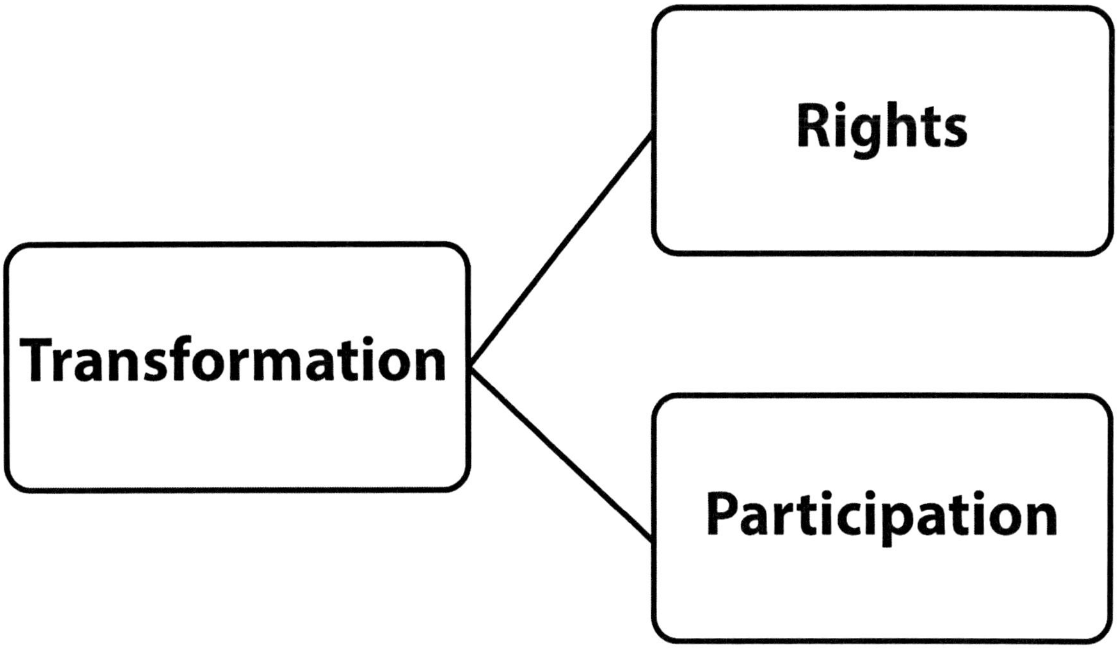

about *Google Streetview* violating people's privacy by filming homes, streets, cars etc. Perhaps the most emblematic case of the new forms of tensions in balancing fundamental rights such as privacy and freedom of speech is offered by sns such as FB: is the user overexposed? If so is it due to the quality and type of data left online or should we understand it to be the user's "intention"? How much intentionality can be legitimately read into "like"-ing? How does the notion of "informed consent" change in such a setting? Such issues have become urgent with the use of data mining techniques that enable sns to "treat" such quantities of data as to allow statistical retrieval of unreleased information: "non-sensible data" such as your zip code for instance may "tell" if you are more likely to purchase wine or beer. To what extent should these practices be allowed? What kind of supervision should data mining be subjected? Today Europe's independent authorities on privacy are charged with the supervision in *Workgroup ex art.29*. Should such controlling bodies be held accountable to voters? Do they differ from other kinds of independent agencies? If privacy encompasses control over personal data, does it encompass or entail a "right to be forgotten" in the infosphere? If so, would it be justified to strike the balance between privacy and free speech as in the *2012 Proposal for the EU General Data Protection Regulation* where in art. 17 free speech appears as derogation from the rule having a right to oblivion?

An over-inclusive conception of privacy, on the other hand, raises issues of yet another kind: could not privacy then be used as a pretext for non-proportionate limitations on information lawful to spread? Yet another aspect of the *habeas data* protection is how to balance the right to safeguard one's reputation and honour without impinging on other's freedom of speech. Many, including the UN in a recent report from July 2011, believe that defamation should be decriminalized in the new informational environment. This has an evident political consequence in democratic regimes since building trust in the public domain is strictly linked to ability of public authorities to maintain a good reputation in a free speech environment. Should these rights be balanced differently when a party belongs to the political arena? Another problem of balancing digitally informed fundamental rights is that of freedom of speech and "decency": many (liberal) states limit freedom of speech in the name of morality and common decency. However, common decency is a sensible and highly variable threshold in plural and multicultural societies: when should it trump freedom of speech? In addition, governments often put pressure on ISPs to adopt more restrictive policies, including filtering online content. Such a case was the removal of photos of breastfeeding mothers by FB. Are such measures justified? The fight against child pornography has repeatedly turned out to be a "trojan horse" suitable for concealing various repressive measures that had nothing to do with fighting pornography: e.g. entire IP addresses have been obscured deleting lawful material as well. Can such a throwing out the baby with the bathwater be motivated? A similar problem of balancing rights is offered by the case of confidential information: the principle of publicity would require there to be no "state secrets" but since there are, the tension between freedom of speech, mirrored in the right to information, clash with protection of confidentiality. How should the balance be struck? This raises the question of protecting whistleblowers, those who take risks in order to disclose confidential information to the benefit of the community (e.g. Wikileaks poses a similar problem: cf. Benkler, 2011). Chapter IV of the recent UN report on Free speech highlighted this transformative dimension of this core fundamental right, essential to liberal democratic society, by outlining some of the ways in which States are increasingly censoring information online, namely through: arbitrary blocking or filtering of content; criminalization of legitimate expression; imposition of intermediary liability; disconnecting users from Internet access, including on the basis of intellectual property rights law; cyber-attacks; and inadequate protection of the right to privacy and data protection; unclear responsibilities for ISPs (Pagallo, 2011).

Let us stress why there is room for analysis belonging to (b1) here and not only re-editions of settings under (a2): For instance, to show why the analogy with traditional media is insufficient and/or misleading for regulating the current blogosphere emphasis should be laid on the fact that, even though bloggers often have journalistic statuses, gaining access to political events and press conferences, they are fairly different from traditional journalists as far as editing issues are concerned. Another, yet interconnected aspect is the status of e-participation movements: the US netroots movement *MoveOn* is a 527 group and thus legally defined as non-partisan: how should such advocacy groups be legally framed in the new environment? Conversely, the problem of non e-commerce protected ISPs such as YouTube that in Europe is not covered by the ISP immunity given to e-com is connected to free speech.

To give a practical example of why the analogy with traditional media is misleading, let us consider the recently discussed Italian proposal of "transposing" existing freedom of speech norms to new media (cf. *Disegno di legge sulle intercettazioni*, from 2009). This example shows why it is urgent to distinguish classical features under (a) and unprecedented features under (b). The proposed bill suggested to apply to bloggers the same rules that are applied to newspapers and TV-editors: the Italian legal system confer upon traditional media an obligation to grant the person who considers herself to have had her reputation soiled a "right to reply" within 48 hours. Non-compliance would entail fines for individual bloggers up to 12500 euros. It does not make sense to apply such a norm to Websites and blogs since the Internet is a medium that does not follow the parcelling out by the hours that traditional media work with (indeed, new media have an a-synchronic and highly variable organisation such as *real time*, *on demand*…): it is not hard to understand that such an analogous extension of previously existing norms such as the traditionally conceived (one-to-many) "right to reply" would kill off the blogosphere since bloggers would need to renounce to any other activity or continue their activity as potential legal infringers – a risk few would take. Italy's lawmakers have also suggested in 2009 a requirement of a ministerial authorization for all streaming videos: another proposal that is incompatible with freedom of speech in the digital world, too cumbersome for individual prosumers, i.e. that are both con*sumers* and *pro*ducers at the same time.

Since fundamental rights of this kind (that guarantee so-called first-wave liberties or negative liberties) are essential preconditions for democracy, we must understand e-democracy to be involved with questions arising in this field as well, and here political theory has to develop frameworks in pace with the technological developments because it is currently underequipped to provide answers on how to balance rights in this new environment. To what extent does liberal theories of rights accommodate for the Internet Bill of Rights-movement?

Transformations to Participation and Its Prerequisites

In relation to (c3) – political participation and processes of formation of consent and dissent through parties and movements – we need to rethink basic aspects of mobilization, informational pluralism, dynamics of public opinion, structure of the public sphere etc. Empirical work on e-participation still disagrees on the benefic vs. malefic impacts of ICTs: on the one hand some see participation increasing and deliberation potentially improve decisions (Habermas, 2006), others warn that it might be dangerous (Sunstein, 2001; Putnam, 2000).

As social theory was discovering that being virtual is an extension of time-space distanciation, whereby relations between social actors are increasingly disembedded – i.e. one of the most conspicuous characteristics of late modernity that gives rise to a range of highly significant social reconfigurations – we still ignore how ICTs are impacting the political side of this virtuality. In the only entry dedicated to the digital age of Marc Bevir's recent *Encyclopedia of Political Theory*, namely "Virtual," Stephen Coleman (2010) stresses that "it is unwise to think of virtuality in a politically deterministic way. That is to say, being virtual neither empowers nor weakens citizens; it neither broadens nor constrains public spheres. […] In some situations, it allows people to engage in more meaningful communications that strengthen opportunities for consequential collective action; in other situations virtual interaction might be a poor substitute for physical intercourse. It is equally unwise to think of the virtual as being wholly decoupled from the real or physical; in most cases, acting virtually— such as sending an e-mail, taking a photograph, or joining a global movement—leads to social activities in the real world. Although some virtual experiences (such as online gaming) are fairly self-contained, most are not" (Coleman, 2010, p. 1404).

This ambiguity of uses imply that, among the transformative thrusts, we find other – perhaps unsuspected – challenges facing representative democracy today, primarily in relation to public opinion: are outsider, oppositional or fringe organizations likely to benefit (disproportionately?) from the rise of ICTs, potentially posing a challenge to mainstream politics? How should we understand this phenomenon dubbed the "Zapatista effect" (Hafez, 2008, p. 103)? This might not only be due to equalization, i.e. the fact that all bits are equal on the net making extremists positions no less available than mainstream opinions, but also to the deliberative effect on the Web 2.0: «when people talk what happens? Do group members compromise? Do they move towards the middle

[...]? The answer is now clear and it is not what intuition would suggest: groups go to extremes. More precisely, members of a deliberating group usually end up in a more extreme position [...]. Group polarization is a typical phenomenon in deliberating groups» (Sunstein, 2009a). An interesting case study here would perhaps be Finland: can the hyper-connectivity of the country that first constitutionalized access to broad band be correlated to polarization in politics, with the recent nationalistic upswing in the last elections?

A part from polarization, cocooning is another issue, i.e. the fact that people entrench into closed circles of political information where citizens can easily filter out news of certain kinds, an inclination due foremost to preference for avoiding "cognitive dissonance": it is not *per se* a new problem but ICTs enhance the effect by picking and choosing sources of information more freely in a panorama of more fragmented media where "trust" is bound to become a central epistemic value (Origgi, 2004) and perhaps also key to understanding political orientation. In a world where more than 50% of the world's population has access to some combination of ICTs (5 billion cell-phone users, around 2 billion Internet users, some 6,7% of the world's population having private access to the Web) another problem for public opinion is the long-term effects of unrestrained gossip on the democratic system that tend to make false rumours go viral (Sunstein, 2009b).

Another connected worry is the "mediocratisation of knowledge" (Duguid & Seely, 2002), i.e. the phenomenon of mistrust in experts that is often associated with the faith in crowed-sourced wisdom (Surowiecki, 2004). The open source pioneer Eric Raymond, for instance, has raised concerns about Wikipedia being "disastrous" from such a standpoint: According to Raymond, open source is not applicable to an encyclopaedia, as highlighted by the introduction of Wiki's 5 robots protecting entries against the obscenities and mass deletion of wikitrolls, the semi-closure of certain entries such as God, Al Gore, Galileo and Chopin, notwithstanding the "success story" that *Nature* published in 2005 finding a 4:3 error ratio between Wikipedia and the British encyclopaedia.

Linked to potential changes in the structure and dynamics of public opinion we find the changes in the *public sphere* that ICTs induce and that social and political theory is currently tracking: the Internet is often presented as a potential public sphere. Building on John B. Thompson's theoretical account of mediatisation as a process whereby "the exchange of symbolic forms is no longer restricted primarily to the contexts of face-to-face interaction, but is extensively and increasingly mediated by the institutions and mechanisms of mass communication" (1990, p. 15), some scholars have argued that social membership is increasingly taking a virtual form, for example, in online social movements and communities, and enabled relationships between governments and citizens. This was the ground for the rise of the "Netizen" in the 90ies as a "virtual citizen." It is noteworthy that unlike "virtual representation" in traditional political theory, which sought to justify the absence of people from power by characterizing them as virtually spoken *for*, Internet-related virtuality tend to be employed as a way of enhancing participation, by characterizing citizens as virtually spoken *with*.

The changes in the public sphere call for better understanding: at the same time public opinion appears to be divided (polarized, segmented, fragmented etc.) and empowered. One transformative (and understudied) aspect of participation is the increased support from expat communities ("virtual overseas party branches"), a direct impact of global diasporas using ICTs. Another challenge at this level of analysis (c.3) is to design mobilization procedures adapted to inforgs. It is often stressed that online donors tend to be "middle-class, fairly well educated and politically active" (Chadwick & Howard, 2009, p. 18): How do you design mobilization procedures adapted to politically inactive inforgs? In the early 2000's it was often stressed that online campaigning would only attract the least participative age group: How is it when the digital natives grow older? "Across Europe to date [we face a] reinforcement rather than a mobilization story" (Ward & Gibson, 2009, p. 29). There is considerable scope to analyse how and why online recruitment fails or succeeds.

Last but not least, a politically relevant aspect of the digital age and its specific forms of interaction is how the repertoire of civil disobedience is changing. The non-violent movement has developed alternative strategies to violence even since it first appeared (e.g. boycotts, sit-ins etc.) but the Internet has made the flourishing of non-violent new forms of opposition gain momentum. These include electronic civil disobedience and hacktivism where online activists have targeted governments and corporations through the defacing of Websites, publishing of private information, through swarming and denial of service attacks (DDoS) that tie up Websites and networks. Besides criticism coming from targets, there is criticism also from the very activists: is online activism a shallow form of participation that distracts from real-world activities? Does it promote isolated activists?

WHERE LIES THE REVOLUTIONARY THRUST?

Let us now go back to the cousins of political philosophy so as to better grasp what in the current state-of-the-art concerning e-democracy really signals novelty. As the transformative dimension pushes for a still on-going process of updating, a further step is being taken in many fields of practical relevance. I shall refer to this shift of perspective, or awakening to the uniqueness of the technology impacting our world, as the "revolutionary" thrust. The idea is that information technology leaves some things as they were, and changes others to such an extent that previously received wisdom is of little practical use in developing plausible answerers to the upcoming challenges, but ICTs also increasingly entail a list of unheard-of problems that we are not culturally and scientifically prepared to address and that therefore are, indeed, "revolutionary" in their novelty. So as to stress what distinguishes this category of phenomena from those listed under (b2), a quote is useful: Walter Maner wrote, back in 1996, that "for all of these issues, there was an essential involvement of computing technology. Except for this technology, these issues would not have arisen, or would not have arisen in their highly altered form. The failure to find satisfactory non-computer analogies testifies to the uniqueness of these issues. [...] Lack of an effective analogy forces us to discover new [...] values, formulate new [...] principles, develop new policies, and find new ways to think about the issues presented to us" (Maner, 1996, p. 152; Moor, 1985).

So as to illustrate the revolutionary thrust in adjacent fields of study, we can point to the rise of information ethics that goes beyond computer ethics in its earlier formulation since the fundamental subject of ethics is no longer held to be the human being, but subject to ethics is also informational entities. Like other realms of normative ethics abandoned the anthropocentrism of traditional ethics (e.g. Peter Singer and animal rights, Arne Naess and the deep ecology movement), in informative ethics anthropocentrism is substituted with ontocentrism (Floridi, 2011). Richard Stallman's four freedoms essential to software development in the GNU Manifesto (freedom to run a program for any purpose, freedom to study the mechanics of the program and modify it, freedom to redistribute copies, and freedom to improve and change modified versions for public use) could be read within such a development of ethics. The rights are not seldom presented as those of the software, not of traditional agents. This leaves room for plenty of debates but it clearly changes our moral toolkit drastically.

In economics, the "revolutionary" aspect of ICTs appeared in relation to the *long tail*, i.e. the retailing strategy of selling a large number of rarely required items in relatively small quantities – usually in addition to selling fewer popular items in large quantities. To Anderson (2004), examples of such long tails include *Amazon* and *Netflix*. We could add *iTunes* etc. Because of the negligible stocking, inventory and distribution costs of digital copies, such business models realize significant profit out of selling small volumes of hard-to-find items to many customers instead of only selling large volumes of a reduced number of popular items. Given enough choice, customers change their selection and buying patterns so as to result in the demand across products having a power law distribution or Pareto distribution. One innovatory consequence is the radically different capitalization processes (Benkler, 2006). Moreover, economics discovered the "revolutionary" implications of ICTs with the emergence of de-centralized non-market based transitional framework that compete with traditional forms of exchange; e.g. new forms of competition include the P2P collaboration groups that produce open-source software or create wikis, but also the crowdsourcing model, in which a company outsources work to a large group of market players using a collaborative online platform, and more generally work performed by individuals in commons-like networks that enable a "system of production, distribution, and consumption of information goods characterized by decentralized individual action carried out through widely distributed, nonmarket means that do not depend on market strategies" (Benkler, 2006). This economic dimension, it should not be forgotten, is strictly linked to the emergence of the Web 2.0 (O'Reilly, 2007) that is today at the center of the discussions on e-democracy.

Yet, the analysis of the specifically political dimension of the impact of this technology is still largely unexplored, which might seem all the more surprising since the Internet has a structure that *per se* promotes informative pluralism since it enjoys a "variable geometry" (to use a fashionable expression in EU studies): contrarily to one-to-many or point-to-point media as traditional broadcast and publishing, the Internet enables many-to-many communication (e.g. FB), one-to-one communication (e.g. e-agenda), many-to-one (e.g. mail). It also has an interactive capability unlike traditional "passivity-promoting" media. Add to this the lowering of entry costs into the discussion that stimulated the rise of UGC (User generated content). Finally, it is a decentralized or a-cephalous media, contrarily to traditional media: conceived an as anarchical space, there is no hierarchy among flows – every bit has the same "value" on the net. This is an aspect that is often referred to being intrinsically "democratic," even thought "egalitarian" is perhaps a better label.

These characteristics are raising some unprecedented problematic dimensions. Here I shall list, on the one hand, some unique general challenges and, on the other hand, some novelties specifically related to democratic ways of governing, foremost parliamentary rule. To orientate, the scheme in Figure 4 is useful.

General Challenges

Among the unprecedented general challenges that the Internet is raising we find the threats of cyber-terrorism (e.g. Russia's attack on Estonia in 2007) that seems to draw the broad brushstrokes of a new setting for International relations (Colarik, 2006; Janczewski 2008), as well as the digital divide separating the information haves and have-nots (Katz & Rice, 2002; Neumann, 1991; Bimber, 2003): the total bandwidth of the Internet in Africa is equal to that of the Brazilian city of Sao Paulo, and the total bandwidth of the Internet in Latin America is equal to that of Seoul, Korea. It is not only a matter of income, but it is multidimensional problem, involving availability of technology and physical infrastructure, as well as digital literacy. This means the divide cuts new boundaries within and across communities and cannot be subsumed into, or presupposed to be overlapping with, already existing categories of

Figure 4. General and particular challenges to revolution and parliamentarianism

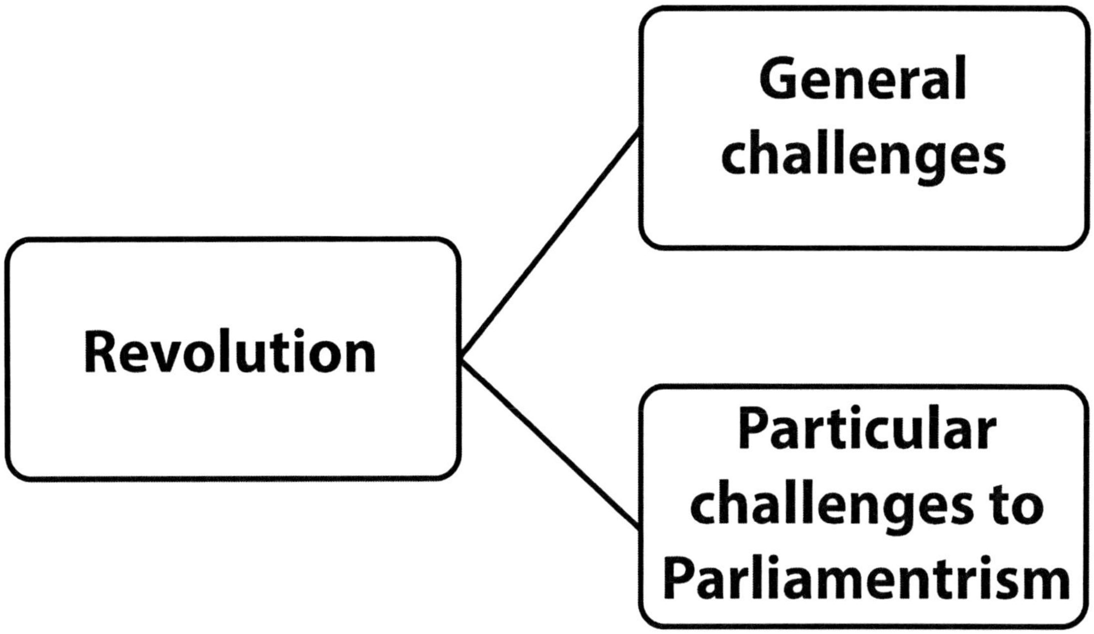

cognitive marginalization and subaltern groupings (it might replicate some, but it also develops others).

Another unprecedented challenge concerns the issue of recognizing and protecting what Hillary Clinton calls "the freedom to connect." Finland was the first country in the world to constitutionalize access to broadband. How should such a right be understood against the backdrop of modern constitutionalism? The right to connect should also be viewed in relation to the battle over Net neutrality. Such a right is linked to the digital divide as an instance of fighting informational inequality that we know has negative feedbacks on empowerment. In the background, we find the broader cultural struggle against the commodification of information and its increased propertization (Lessig, 2001, 2004) with its negative impact on creativity and innovation. How is such a right to access to be understood on the ground of conventional theories of rights? Is it part of a new cascade of collective claims that amount to a "new wave of rights" or can it be subsumed under previously recognized types of rights, such as the right of freedom of expression and the right to share information as they appear in the 1948 UN Declaration of Human Rights (art 19, art 27 §1)? Is the right to connect mirrored in an obligation to provide connectivity? Conferred to whom? Can it be coherently framed into traditional negative liberties? Part of the freedom to connect is clearly of negative quality – prohibiting the state and the market from hindering or creating illegitimate impediments to access –, yet it is also associated with major investment in infrastructural development that traditionally are linked to positive liberties. Is it therefore a right structurally more similar to the right to education than to free speech? Should it be compared to a right that grants freedom *from* intromission in communication or to the right *to* information? Just like other traditional rights of Man, strategies have to be developed to protect it against contrasting forces. How can such strategies best be adjusted to the type of right we are concerned with?

If we look at some of the challenges that Internet is facing today, we see that it is under siege by both the state and the market. While in relation to the state, it can be claimed that both direct intervention (such as arresting hacktivists and jailing bloggers) and indirect intervention (censure of contents, e.g. China blocking Websites containing key terms such as "democracy" and "human rights" as denounced by Reporters without borders, or states shutting down the Internet, e.g. Iran 2009, Egypt 2010) are reminiscent of traditional forms; yet what is unprecedented is that mechanisms used to censor information on the Internet are increasingly sophisticated, with multi-layered controls that are often hidden from the public. In relation to the market, some threats to the Internet might seem reminiscent of "old" problems such as for instance oligopolistic concentrations of ISPs (e.g. dominant positions of some players like Google, Microsoft, Apple, Facebook), yet others are new: The type of problem that are raised by the last mile or Net neutrality. Some companies that are guaranteeing the access to the Internet (often telecom-companies) are thinking of realizing a Net of fast-tracks, shortcuts etc. so as to maximize profits. Should this be allowed? Under what circumstances? How would an alternatively designed architecture alter the access to the right to connect?

Specific Challenges to Parliamentary Rule

Among the more specific challenges to democratic stiles of government, foremost in relation to parliamentary rule, ICTs are currently creating new ways for (d1) the transfer of information between different actors in the political arena and this makes (d2) citizens, political parties and civil society organizations acquire possibilities of more intense interaction; a perspective that can lead to (d.3) new ways of participating in the democratic process, such as (d.3.1.) through e-voting forms or (d.3.2.) innovative ways of analyzing public opinion.

For the information transfer between different institutionally codified actors in the political arena a viable option, differences in national systems have to be overcome. This is the goal of the promotion of parliamentary standardization: the *Global Centre for ICT in Parliament* organizes a conference (*World e-Parliament Conference*) designed as a forum for the sharing of best practices and laying down future guidelines. This standardization effort continues with *e-Parliament Framework 2010 – 2020*. Much work on standardization is being done through systems such as MetaLex that focuses on sharing documents in Extensible Markup Language (XML format), creating common metadata, facilitate citations and cross-references between different documents of different parliamentary systems, or on the determination of abstract classes of models that can serve as to identify similar structures despite varying appellatives (an article is logically invariable even though it might be called something else in some legal systems). Such an example is the *Akoma Ntoso* project. The standardization enables sharing of information between parliaments in a innovative way and to an unprecedented extent that is susceptible of laying the basis for greater bi- and multilateral parliamentary cooperation – quite surely a prerequisite for high-quality law-making in a world of increasing cross-border consequences and formerly reserved for operations within the executive branch. Of course, as in all phenomena of convergence, a risk of exaggerated streamlining and loss of pluralism might be present. The rapid growth of ICTs has changed the environment within which parliaments operate. Rather than being mere witnesses to these changes, they can choose to strengthen the legislative processes and participatory political engagement.

In the current phase, E-parliamentarization is essentially characterized by the digitization and sharing of documents, the focus is still on the individual act. However, the move that is occurring is a shift of focus from the output of legislation (i.e. acts) to promoting visibility and accessibility of the entire legislative process. The use of information technology opens up new prospects for cooperation, participation and sharing information and knowledge which makes it necessary to shift attention from the single final output (the law) to a more comprehensive approach to law-making, taking into consideration previously unavailable or marginalized information in the process such as amendments, reports, draft laws, the role of committees, legislative inquiries etc.). In other words, the new forms might stress previously hidden dissent.

This approach aims to improve the quality of legal drafting, making these documents clearer, less ambiguous etc. where the presupposition is that more eyes with contrasting interests and preferences examining a text will increase the probability of singling out and pinpointing potential loopholes and equivocality. The type of drafting is also changing: drafting can now be done in layers. A single piece of legislation thus appears as a normative chain of text versions: texts that modify existing documents, and those that are being modified by it, can be mapped and followed through time (versioning); the logical structure of norms is being captured through languages such as RuleML, and documents are being indexed based on conceptual analysis (ontologies) of its legal domains, and meta-information has been incorporated in documents, including constitutional court decisions or ECJ rulings etc. It is reasonable to assume that such changes will impact on the type, quality, and systematic character of interpretative practices. A challenge here is to assess the rule of law-promoting capacity such procedures may entail.

In the legislation process, citizens rarely have access to the content of legislation until it is in its final stages and can only know about the haggling and negotiating of representatives through the reporting of journalists – this is perhaps about to change. The E-parliament approach that is currently being implemented in many countries also intends to highlight discussions that were not previously available to citizen scrutiny. This does not merely imply increased availability of information but more radically it also shifts emphasis onto previously concealed dissent. In practice this means that accessible documents will not include only the final legislative output as published by official sources, but also other kinds of documentation that is relevant for the formation of the law, yet that has been traditionally kept at the margins of the process with the effect of occulting dissent: think of mark-ups in drafting processes, amendment tracking, parliamentary reports, *travaux préparatoires* etc. An example of how the digitalization of parliamentary workings is changing practical politics is the role of the motion to amend: often used in parliamentary proceedings to water down a motion into a form that is more likely to be accepted or to convert it into a form that is more likely to be rejected, it can now be used to block the legislative process: the European Parliament enabled its members to submit amendments to bills directly on the Web: the amendments are sometimes so many that a blockage of the entire legislative process occurs. Whether for the good or for the bad, it is beyond doubt that ICTs are modifying some parts of the internal workings of representative democracy.

Traditionally, citizens hardly ever look directly at the content of legislation, more often relying on the recycled analysis of pundits who very likely did not read the legislation either. This is another aspect that is liable to change. E-parliament tools also provide for the appearance of prosumers in the political information field: *TheyWorkForYou* for instance enable prosumers to mash parliamentary data from the official British *Hansard* to remixed it in such a way that lay audiences can profitably follow the course of an issue: it allows users to track a particular issue or MP, comment on parliamentary proceedings, register for updates on specific issues etc. An example of such an institutionally designed application is the *citizen's mail* making it possible to send email the European parliament. An example of civil society generated devise is *Issue Crawler* that searches the Web to establish where issues are being discussed and how those discussions are linked, making it easier to map the communicative landscape and sense how a debate is developing.

The innovative aspect of such possibilities lies in the fact that "the theoretical debate between direct, inclusive democracy and indirect, constitutionally balanced representation [...] totally ignores the possibility of options in between [...]. The public has generally been spoken *at*, rather than *with* [...]. Digital ICTs could play a vital role in changing the terms of that relationship" (Coleman, 2009, p. 96).

Another revolutionary impact of ICTs on parliamentarism is the possibility that is now opening up to devise workable inter-parliamentary dialogue, a possibility that until yesterday remained highly impracticable. The cooperation between parliaments arises from the possibility of sharing knowledge and information. It is currently being promoted by the *Global Centre for ICT in Parliament*, a joint initiative of the United Nations, the Inter-Parliamentary Union and a group of national and regional parliaments (European Parliament, the Pan African Parliament, the Chamber of Deputies of the Italian Parliament, national Assembly of Hungary, the People's Assembly of Egypt, National Assembly of South Africa) that was launched in November 2005 during the world Summit on the Information Society (WSIS). A potential impact could be the possibility, acknowledged in the Lisbon Treaty, of half of Europe's national parliaments working together to block a proposal of the Commission. Such possibilities might reinvigorate the tension between governments and parliaments around Europe. Similarly the *Ipex* seeks to expand the information base available to national parliaments with regard to specific EU documents.

Add to this the deliberative, participative and direct democratic practices that use ICTs, such as online discussions, online polls, e-petitions, e-consultations on issues and e-consultations on bills. ICTs seem to have an impact foremost on "direct democracy institutions" (e.g. citizen initiatives, referendum...), and especially on forms of candidate recruitment (e.g. primaries): "In the United States most of the Internet campaigning innovations [...] have occurred during primaries" (Anstead & Chadwick, 2009, p. 65).

In particular, we should stress that the most challenging forms of ICTs in politics are those that intend to apply crowdsourcing and wikis for legislative purposes, to attempt to circumvent strong interest groups or corporations. Recently, Brazil suggested a rather sophisticated "Wikislation" Website, *e-democracia*, as a method of creating Web content that could be applied to the legislative process. The idea is to create more direct participation by citizens and more transparency in the work done by legislators, by relying on the "wisdom of the crowd." Such forms of wikilation are very different from institutions such as the referendum that can hardly be considered "participation in policy making" since it leaves the citizenry with only a veto possibility through a Yes/No vote on a pre-established draft. It remains to see what results such ICT-enhanced procedures can yield in legislation. Yet what is sure is that they open an array of other issues, that go beyond the problems we have already highlighted: what is the role of the technical translators in the drafting process? Can such wikilations-architectures be structured though distributed participatory design or is top-down systematization necessary? Are such changes promoting legislation of higher quality? Should we conceive such co-legislation as alternative or composite to ordinary legislative measures? Can such mechanisms pose challenges also for the realms of decrees? Can such measures promote infra-party democratization? How do we design and enforce the access to participation by those belonging to a determinate constituency? How should such constituencies be determined?

IMPLICATIONS AND FUTURE RESEARCH DIRECTIONS

Technologies embed choices that are politically salient, yet mainstream political theory has taken the issue rather lightly. Compared to what has been going on over the past few decades in the other branches of practical thought, namely ethics, economics and the law, political theory lags behind in understanding the current technological revolution and its impact, potentialities and risks. Yet the current emphasis on Internet politics that polarizes the apologists that hold the Web to overcome the one-to-many architecture of opinion-building in traditional representative democracy, and the critics that warn cyber-optimism entails authoritarian technocracy has acted as a wake up call. This chapter has taken a first step in outlining a comprehensive research agenda on the problem "what is it about ICTs, as opposed to previous technical devices, that impact on politics and determine uncertainty about democratic matters?." This non-exhaustive yet hopefully indicative conceptual map of issues, with concrete examples relating to e-democracy, has been presented and can be summarized as in Figure 5.

There is considerable scope to analyse how and why online politics fails or succeeds, and how and why it deserves the label "democratic."

DISCUSSION

Technologies carry politics since they embed values. It is therefore surprising that mainstream political and legal theory have taken the issue so lightly. Compared to what has been going on over the past few decades in the other branches of practical thought, namely ethics, economics and the law, political theory lags behind. Traditionally, citizens hardly ever look directly at the content of legislation, more often relying on the recycled analysis of pundits who very likely did not read the legislation either. This is another aspect that

Figure 5. A schema of factors affecting digital democracies

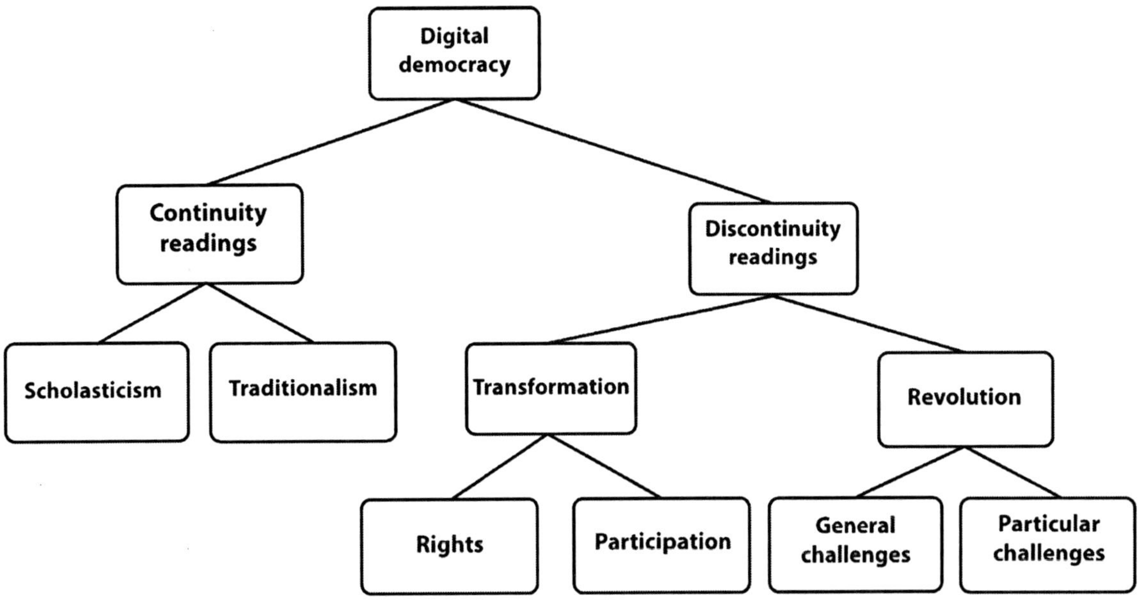

is liable to change. Even so, the current emphasis on Internet politics that polarizes the apologists holding the Web to overcome the one-to-many architecture of opinion-building in traditional representative democracy, and the critics that warn cyber-optimism entails authoritarian technocracy has acted as a wake up call. This chapter set out to ask the question "What is it about ICTs, as opposed to previous technical devices, that impact on politics and determine uncertainty about democratic matters?" In the broad context of practical philosophy, by offering a conceptual map of clusters of micro-problems and concrete examples relating to "e-democracy." The point is to highlight when and why the hyphen of e-democracy has a conjunctive or a disjunctive function, in respect to stocktaking from past experiences and settled democratic theories. Increasingly it is becoming evident that a politically relevant aspect of the digital age – and its specific forms of interaction – is how the repertoire of civil disobedience is changing. The non-violent movement has developed alternative strategies to violence even since it first appeared (e.g. boycotts, sit-ins etc.) but the Internet has made the flourishing of non-violent new forms of opposition gain momentum. Our conclusion is that there is considerable scope to analyse how and why online politics fails or succeeds. The field needs both further empirical and theoretical work.

REFERENCES

Anderson, C. (2004). *The long tail: Why the future of business is selling less of more*. New York, NY: Hyperion.

Anstead, N., & Chadwick, A. (2009). Parties, election campaigning, and the Internet: Toward a comparative institutional approach. In A. Chadwick, & P. Howard (Eds.), *Routledge handbook of internet politics* (pp. 56–71). London, UK: Routledge.

Benkler, Y. (2006). *The wealth of networks: How social production transforms market and freedom*. New Haven, CT: Yale University Press.

Benkler, Y. (2011). A free irresponsible press: Wikileaks and the battle over the soul of the networked estate. *Harvard Civil Rights-Civil Liberties Law Review*, *46*, 311–398.

Bimber, B. (2003). *Information and American democracy: Technology in the evolution of political power*. Cambridge, UK: Cambridge University Press. doi:10.1017/CBO9780511615573

Bobbio, N. (1987). *The future of democracy*. London, UK: Polity Press.

Bremmer, I. (2010, November-December). Democracy in cyberspace: What information technology can and cannot do. *Foreign Affairs*, 86–92.

Castells, M. (2009). *Communication power*. Oxford, UK: Oxford University Press.

Chadwick, A., & Howard, P. (Eds.). (2009). *Routledge handbook of internet politics*. London, UK: Routledge.

Clarke, R. (2006). *Introduction to dataveillance and information privacy, and definitions of terms*. Retrieved May 17, 2012, from http://www.rogerclarke.com/DV/Intro.html#DV

Colarik, A. (2006). *Cyber terrorism: Political and economic implications*. Hershey, PA: IGI Global. doi:10.4018/978-1-59904-021-9

Coleman, S. (2009). Making parliamentary democracy visible. In A. Chadwick, & P. Howard (Eds.), *Routledge handbook of internet politics* (pp. 86–98). London, UK: Routledge.

Coleman, S. (2010). Virtual (s.v.). In M. Bevir (Ed.), *Encylopedia of political theory*. London, UK: Sage. doi:10.4135/9781412958660.n464

Crick, B. (2002). *Democracy: A very short introduction*. Oxford, UK: Oxford University Press.

Dahl, R. (1956). *A preface to democratic theory*. Chicago, IL: Chicago University Press.

Diamond, L. (2010). Liberation technology. *Journal of Democracy*, *3*, 69–83. doi:10.1353/jod.0.0190

Duguid, P., & Seely, J. (20022). *The social life of information*. Boston, MA: Harvard Business School Press.

Durante, M. (2011). Normativity, constructionism, and constraining affordances. *Etica & Politica*, *13*(2), 180–200.

Edge. (2010). Retrieved May 17, 2012, from http://www.edge.org/3rd_culture/gelernter09/gelernter09_index.html

Floridi, L. (2011). *The philosophy of information*. Oxford, UK: Oxford University Press. doi:10.1093/acprof:oso/9780199232383.001.0001

Floridi, L. (2012). Hyperhistory and the philosophy of information policies. *Philosophy and Technology*, *25*(2), 129–131. doi:10.1007/s13347-012-0077-4

Goldsmith, J. (1998). Against cyberanarchy. *The University of Chicago Law Review. University of Chicago. Law School*, *68*, 1199–1250. doi:10.2307/1600262

Grimmelmann, J. (2005). Regulation by software. *The Yale Law Journal*, *114*, 1719–1758.

Habermas, J. (2006). Political communication in media society: Does democracy still enjoy an epistemic dimension? The impact of normative theory on empirical research. *Communication Theory*, *16*, 411–426. doi:10.1111/j.1468-2885.2006.00280.x

Hafez, K. (2008). The myth of media globalization. (A. Skinner, Trans.). *Arab Studies Quartely*, *30*(1).

Heidegger, M. (1977). *The question concerning technology and other essays*. New York City, NY: Harper & Row.

Hindman, M. (2009). *The myth of digital democracy*. Princeton, NJ: Princeton University Press.

Janczewski, L. (2008). *Cyber warfare and cyber terrorism*. Hershey, PA: IGI Global.

Johnson, D. (1985). *Computer ethics*. Upper Saddle River, NJ: Prentice Hall.

Kallinikos, J. (2010). *Governing through technology: Information artefacts and social practice*. Basingstoke, UK: Palgrave Macmillan. doi:10.1057/9780230295148

Katz, J. E., & Rice, R. E. (2002). *Social consequences of internet use: Access, involvement and expression*. Cambridge, MA: MIT Press.

Kelsen, H. (2000). On the essence and value of democracy. In A. Jacobson, & B. Schlink (Eds.), *Weimar: A jurisprudence of crisis*. Los Angeles, CA: University of California Press.

Lessig, L. (2001). *The future of ideas: The fate of the commons in a connected world*. New York, NY: Random House.

Lessig, L. (2004). *Free culture: How big media uses technology and the law to lock down culture and control creativity*. New York, NY: Penguin.

Maner, W. (1996). Unique ethical problems in information technology. *Science and Engineering Ethics*, *2*(2), 137–154. doi:10.1007/BF02583549

Margetts, H. (2009). Public management change and e-government. In A. Chadwick, & P. Howard (Eds.), *Routledge handbook of internet politics* (pp. 114–127). London, UK: Routledge.

Margolis, M., & Resnick, D. (2000). *Politics as usual: The cyberspace revolution*. Thousand Oaks, CA: Sage Publications.

Moor, J. H. (1985). What is computer ethics? *Metaphilosophy*, *16*(4) ,263–275.

Neuman, R. W. (1991). *The future of mass audience*. Cambridge, UK: Cambridge University Press.

O'Reilly, T. (2007). What is web 2.0? Design patterns and business models for the next generation of software on line. *Communications & Strategies, 1*(1).

Origgi, G. (2004). Is trust an epistemic notion? *Episteme*, *1*(1), 61–72. doi:10.3366/epi.2004.1.1.61

Pagallo, U. (2011, May). ISPs & rowdy web sites before the law: Should we change today's safe harbour clauses?. *Philosophy and Technology*, 335-34.

Post, D. (2002). Against against cyberspace. *Berkeley Technology Law Journal*, *17*, 1365–1383.

Postel-Vinay O. (2010, April). *Pour en finir avec le cyberoptimisme*, Books, April (dossier 12), 19-33.

Putnam, R. D. (2000). *Bowling alone: The collapse and revival of American community*. New York, NY: Simon and Schuster. doi:10.1145/358916.361990

Rawls, J. (1996). *Political liberalism*. New York, NY: Columbia University Press.

Rodotà, S. (2006). The retention of electronic commmunication traffic data. *Revista d'Internet, Dret I Política, 3*, 53-60.

Sartori, G. (1987). *The theory of democracy revisited*. Chatham, NJ: Chatham House.

Schumpeter, J. (1942). *Capitalism, socialism and democracy*. London, UK: Routledge.

Sunstein, C. (2001). *Republic.com*. Princeton, NJ: Princeton University Press.

Sunstein, C. (2009a). *Going to extremes: How like minds unite and divide*. Oxford, UK: Oxford University Press.

Sunstein, C. (2009b). *On rumours: How falsehoods spread, why we believe them, what can be done*. London, UK: Allen Lane.

Surowiecki, J. (n.d.). The wisdom of crowds: Why the many are smarter than the few and how collective wisdom shapes business, economies, societies and nations. New York, NY: Doubleday.

Thompson, J. B. (1990). *The media and modernity: A social theory of the media*. London, UK: Polity Press.

Van den Hoven, J. (2005). E-democracy, e-contestation and the monitorial citizen. *Ethics and Information Technology*, *7*, 51–59. doi:10.1007/s10676-005-4581-4

Ward, S., & Gibson, R. (2009). European political organizations and the internet. In A. Chadwick, & P. Howard (Eds.), *Routledge handbook of internet politics* (pp. 25–39). London, UK: Routledge.

Weiner, N. (1948). *Cybernetics or control and communication in the animal and the machine*. Cambridge, MA: MIT Press.

Whelan, F. G. (1983). Democratic theory and the boundary problem. In J. R. Pennock, & J. W. Chapman (Eds.), *Liberal democracy*. New York, NY: New York University Press.

Zittel, T. (2008). Parliaments and the internet: A perspective on the state of research. In *Parliaments in the digital age*. Oxford Internet Institute.

KEY TERMS AND DEFINITIONS

Democracy: Form of government based on the participation of the people to collective decision-making, often through election of representatives. The spread of the Internet is considered by several authors as impacting on representative democracy.

Globalization: Process of international integration, especially of culture and economics, resulting in "the compression of the world" (Robertson); "all those processes by which the peoples of the world are incorporated into a single world society" (Albrow). The spread of the Internet is often conceived as an accelerating element of globalization process.

Internet: Global computer network providing a variety of information and communication facilities, consisting of interconnected networks using standardized communication protocols.

Political Theory: Branch of practical philosophy that involves analysis on political phenomena and political systems.

Technology: Umbrella term that refers to technologies that provide real-time access to information through telecommunications. It includes any communication device or application, foremost the Internet, encompassing radio, television, cellular phones, computer and network hardware and software, satellite systems and so on, as well as the various services and applications associated with.

Chapter 14
Blackout in the Name of Sunshine:
When Open Government Law Stifles Civic Social Media

William R. Sherman
Seattle University, USA

ABSTRACT

Local governments, and particularly local public officials, have adopted online social networking tools en masse in an effort to communicate with constituents. As this chapter shows, the resulting information flow consists of communication from the public official to constituents, from constituents to the public official, and among constituents, but in the context of the public official's social network. This environment constitutes a "civic social network," which operates as the new public square. Many local governments, however, are attempting to bar officials' use of civic social networks because they risk violation of open government laws, such as open meeting and open records laws. This effort to stifle valuable civic communication harms norms of transparency and accountability – the very values that open government laws should promote. These laws should be revised or reinterpreted to allow civic social networks to fulfill their promise as the new public square.

INTRODUCTION

Local public officials, like businesses and individuals, are scrambling to use social media. It should come as no surprise that people whose lives center on constituent contact want to adopt tools that let them reach large numbers of people at little cost. But this phenomenon, which started with the use of formal, government-created Websites with press releases, updates, and photos, has gone much further. Today there is hardly a mayor or city councilmember in a major American city without a Facebook page, a Twitter account, and a blog. It is common for major policy announcements to occur by tweet and entire town hall meetings to happen in chat rooms. But most interestingly, civic social media have created a three-way information flow: from official to constituent; from constituent to official; and among constituents in the context of the public official's network.[1]

DOI: 10.4018/978-1-4666-6038-0.ch014

Copyright © 2014, IGI Global. Copying or distributing in print or electronic forms without written permission of IGI Global is prohibited.

This three-dimensional communication network is more than just an application of new; empirical evidence suggests that online discourse has become the new public square. (Mossberger et al., 2007; Brehm & Rahn, 1997; Jennings & Stoker, 2004). Local public officials and their constituents are flocking to social networking tools, and even government agencies that recently resisted have succumbed (Smith, 2010; Sherman, 2011).

But idealists hoping that social networks would enable a high-minded process of deliberative democracy have reason to be disappointed; study after study has demonstrated that online political discourse is factually unreliable, consists of opinion rather than objective information, creates "echo chambers" in which people only talk to or hear from those who already agree with them, and therefore reinforce polarization in politics (Dutton & Peltu, 2007). Nevertheless, social media have successfully enabled low-threshold civic engagement by citizens and public officials. A 2010 study showed that nearly one-third (31 percent) of online adults use platforms such as blogs, social networking sites, email, online video, or text messaging to get government information, and 13 percent of Internet users read a government agency or official's blog. Taken together, nearly a quarter of Internet users have posted comments or interacted with others online around government policies or public issues (Smith, 2010). Like it or not, civic social media are the new public square.

BACKGROUND

For all the enthusiasm by public officials and constituents, the rapid adoption of social networking tools has caught some local governments flat-footed. Those governments worry that public officials' use of civic social media may run afoul of laws mandating open meetings, freedom of information, ethics, and campaign finance limits. In many cases, local governments have either attempted to flat-out ban government use of social media or proposed restrictions that, for all intents and purposes, ban public officials from using social media in their official capacity.

Because few (if any) laws deal specifically with social media, policymakers have had to extrapolate from existing law. The results have been varied, as demonstrated by the following examples: (1) The City of Redondo Beach was advised to avoid all use of social networks for any purposes; (2) The City of Seattle was advised to adopt regulations that would bar City Council members from "friending" each other on social media, for fear of allowing inadvertent online meetings in violation of the Open Public Meetings Act, and bar any links that would lead to third-party content that is commercial (like advertisements) or political (like a comment from a constituent in support of a campaign); (3) Attorneys for a Florida municipal planning board told the board that, as a general matter, it should not have a social network profile "under any circumstances"; (4) Attorneys for a collection of Washington cities advised city council members to avoid posting any content regarding policy or city-related issues; and (5) counsel for the City of Fort Lauderdale discouraged any City participation on Facebook or "any similar interactive communication technology" (Sherman, 2011).

Agencies, legal counsel, and public officials have grappled with at least three types of potential statutory violations that apply to communications among public officials and constituents using social media.

Freedom of Information or Public Records Acts

Public officials' use of social media can create public records that are inaccessible to many members of the public in their original location, and may not be retained or cataloged in the same way as email or written correspondence. Consider the following scenario: Councilmember Jones posts on Twitter that he opposes Mayor Smith's proposal to fund city parks: "We cannot afford @MayorSmith's Cadillac #parkslevy. Time to get #backtobasics!" The post would be published online and anyone who had a Twitter account who had signed up to follow Councilmember Jones would instantly receive the message (as would anyone signed up to follow Mayor Smith and anyone searching for the hash tags #parkslevy or #backtobasics). In addition, those who do not have Twitter accounts may view the post for a certain period of time, but would not receive a notification when it was posted.

This raises two questions: First, is Councilmember Jones's tweet a public record? And second, if so, how would it be found, retained, and produced by the City in response to a public records or Freedom of Information Act request?

All fifty states have public records statutes, many modeled after the Federal Freedom of Information Act (FOIA) (Solove, 2001). These laws were a cornerstone of the "sunshine laws" movement that began in the 1950s and flourished in the post-Watergate era, opening government records to public access on the theory that sunshine is the best disinfectant—that is, public scrutiny exposes, and therefore hampers or remedies, corruption.

Briefly, these statutes require the government to provide public records upon request (with certain enumerated exceptions, such as confidential financial information, personnel files, and draft documents). Public records are usually defined as any writing or other record containing information relating to the conduct of government prepared, owned, used, or retained by any part of the government.

The key legal questions are well-settled; a public official's writings, regardless whether they are on a government Website or not, are public records, as long as the post is pertinent to city business. The harder question, then, is not the legal but the practical one: how best can the government retain a record of officials' posts on social media so that they can be produced upon request under FOIA?

Seen as a collection of written exchanges, the retention and production of social network posts is not conceptually difficult—they are not distinguishable from email. As O'Connor and Baratz note, "An ordinary email is nothing more than a piece of written correspondence transmitted through an efficient and inexpensive means. . . . [T]he public's interest in overseeing the workings of local government is protected in the same way that it is for call other types of written correspondence—the public may review such correspondence by making a records request under the open records provision of state law" (O'Connor & Baratz, 2004).

A trickier problem arises due to the ethereal nature of social network posts, which can be deleted at any time. Consider this scenario: An elected port commissioner criticizes a city councilmember's policy proposal in a post on Facebook; the councilmember responds by posting something on the port commissioner's Facebook page. For some reason (perhaps the official regrets his tone, or decides that this disagreement need not be public, or realizes he was wrong), the commissioner removes the original Facebook post, and deletes the response posted by the city councilmember.

It may be good for the tone of public discourse, and maybe even for policy, for these officials to be able to turn back the clock to the moment before they hit the "post" or "share" button. But there is no doubt that the entire exchange is, or should be, retained and produced as an accessible public record, and it is certainly in the public interest for voters to have access to the writings of their elected officials on policy matters.

Difficult as these questions are, they are essentially technical problems. The right retention tools can ensure that all of these writings, wise and unwise, are available for production in response to FOIA requests. Inexpensive solutions exist that would allow a public official (or her staff) save a weekly log of Facebook, Twitter, and blog posts (Sherman, 2011).

Open Public Meetings

Open meetings laws, however, present more difficult conceptual and practical problems. Because public officials can read each others' tweets, blog posts, and Facebook updates in real time and respond to them instantaneously, they may engage in communication that is more similar to a meeting than it is to ordinary correspondence. Consider a slight twist on the hypothetical Twitter post above: City Councilmember Jones posts his opposition to the mayor's parks levy on Facebook. Among the various comments to it are the following: Councilmember Nguyen clicks the "like" button on the post—signaling to all readers that he agrees with Councilmember Jones; Councilmember Diaz comments that she thinks the mayor's levy does not go far enough; Councilmember Rogers writes that he disagrees with Councilmember Jones but is open to persuasion; and Councilmember O'Connor links to Councilmember Jones's post on her own Facebook page and comments that the entire question is moot because voters won't pass the levy anyway. Did a city council meeting just take place on Facebook?

Probably. Open meeting statutes have existed in every state and the District of Columbia for over thirty years (Pupillo, 1993). These laws require that most meetings of city or county councils (as well as those of government-authorized boards, committees, and commissions) be held with notice to and access for the public. The laws can have quite powerful enforcement mechanisms; commonly, the remedies for violation include individual penalties for the officials, municipal liability for any costs and fees, and reversal of any government action taken at the improper meeting.

Open meeting statutes have been interpreted to cover not only in-person, face-to-face meetings but also so-called "serial" meetings and meetings at which communication is done in writing or by telephone. More recently, comparable communication by email—when it is interactive or deliberative in nature, occurs close in time and involves a quorum of the relevant government body—has been held to violate open meeting laws.

Although few, if any, court decisions apply open meeting laws to social networking, local governments have perceived social media as a particular risk because their structure is designed to facilitate casual interaction. For example, posts from "friends" or contacts automatically appear on an official's profile and it takes only a single click to interact with the author. Thus, if open meeting laws were applied to civic social media, a "meeting" might occur without any single official intending it. After all, these sites were developed, in part, to create virtual space in which users could interact with a minimum of effort.

The first state supreme court to address the applicability of open meeting laws to email focused its analysis on whether the email exchange had "indicia of simultaneity" that indicate government deliberation occurring in real time, but virtual space. Some other courts do not appear to find significant the differences between written communication and in-person deliberations. Generally, however, state courts agree that electronic communications like conference calls and email exchanges can constitute a meeting under certain circumstances.

In some significant ways, however, an exchange between officials on a civic social network such as Facebook or Twitter is different from an email exchange. For example, a communication in the comments to a blog post on Facebook or Twitter is available for anyone to see or join at any time, whereas there may not be a "feasible way for any and all interested members of the public to 'attend' an email communication" (O'Connor & Baratz, 2004). In fact, the transparency of the exchange and its openness to public participation is arguably as great or greater than most traditional public meetings. And, as a general matter, the overlapping purposes of FOIA laws (ensuring that government records, including correspondence, is available to the public) and open meetings laws (ensuring that deliberation is public and that constituents can engage in the deliberation) are fully accomplished in the social networking context in a way that they are not in an email exchange, which usually is only accessible if specifically requested (Schaeffer, 2004).

Under the current interpretations of open meeting laws, exchanges like the one at the outset of this section would likely be prohibited. But rather than seek an alternative interpretation of the law, or even merely train members to avoid a violation, social media skeptics are throwing the baby out with the bathwater. The City of Seattle, for example, has considered a policy that would "strongly discourage[]" city council members from "friending" each other at all—a solution akin to preventing email exchanges or telephone calls between members (Sherman, 2011). Other governments are advising officials to stay off social media altogether.

Misuse of Public Resources and Political Content

Policymakers are particularly concerned about the potential for government links to social media that contain political, non-government, or advertising content. Although the media platforms are not owned by the government, if the government's Website has a direct link to the social network, then government resources can be interpreted as supporting the content of the social media. This creates a risk of the illegal use of government resources (Sherman, 2011).

State laws universally bar the use of government resources to support a private individual or enterprise, or a political campaign. Because government Websites are maintained with public funds, a link from a government Website to a social media platform can run afoul of this prohibition—depending on the content of the media.

Consider this scenario: Mayor Smith has an official Web page at his city's main Website. On that page, there is a sidebar encouraging readers to follow the mayor on his blog, Twitter, Facebook, and Flickr, with links to those sites.

For the purpose of our analysis, assume that the mayor's blog, Twitter feed, Facebook page, and Flickr account are not managed using government funds but by the mayor himself or a volunteer. Further, assume that the blog is on Tumblr, Blogger or a similar third-party site. May the mayor endorse a candidate for office on his Twitter feed? May he post a photo of himself at a political rally on Flickr? These examples seem pretty straightforward; he may not, because doing so would result in city resources directly supporting campaign content.

But civic social media, by design, invite participation from the public, not just dispatches from officials, and are supported by advertising revenues. If the main city Website includes a direct link to the mayor's Facebook page, is it permissible for the Facebook page to feature commercial advertisements? What if a constituent posted a campaign-related message on the mayor's Facebook page, or tagged the mayor in a campaign-related Twitter post or photo on Flickr?

The problems raised by local governments can be illustrated by the following scenarios: (A) A city's official Web page includes links to Twitter handles maintained by public officials or city agencies. Twitter, as a private company, is enjoying the benefit of any user traffic driven to its site; (B) A city's official Web page includes links to a Twitter account maintained by a public official or city agency. The Twitter feed includes posts "promoted" by Twitter as paid advertising, and therefore is assisting certain businesses; and (C) A city councilmember's official Web page includes a link to his or her Twitter account. The councilmember is fastidious about avoiding posting any campaign-related content on his Twitter account. But, without the consent of the councilmember, Twitter displays "promoted" messages by various candidates in the Twitter feed, and constituents of the councilmember post material on the promoting certain candidates. For each of these scenarios, does the city's link constitute an improper use of government resources?

Enforcers tend to view scenarios A and B as permissible. Any support of the social media platform or advertiser is de minimis and unintentional. Furthermore, any support is a byproduct of an allowable government activity or a government purpose (in this case, the purpose would be public outreach and communication). From a practical standpoint, this makes sense—if a government link to a corporate Website or a Website containing advertising was prohibited, then a county could never link to an online newspaper article.

The third scenario, however, is problematic because support of a political campaign can never be a permissible government purpose. The difficulty of this scenario lies in the fact that the political content can appear on the public official's social network without being posted or approved by the public official. Moreover, depending on the social network's specific features, the public official may not even be able to remove the material from the social network.

Enforcers indicate that their preferred solution would require public officials to moderate the content on their social network pages to prevent political content from appearing. This assumes, first, that the public official has some control over the content—which he may not—and second, imposes on the public official the need to police the social media for inappropriate material. Thus, a public official would be prohibited from using any civic social network that could allow *other users* to post political material.

Why the Solutions Offered by Local Governments Do not Work

Barring social network use, prohibiting council members from "friending" each other, or holding public officials responsible for third-party content are impractical solutions. Regulators seem to have addressed social media by applying existing law to a new problem, and attempting to extrapolate a solution based on previous applications of the law to email, conference calls, and conference rooms in government buildings.

These solutions are also often internally inconsistent. For example, Seattle's draft policy encourages city council members to use social media that can record the identity of a commenter and restrict users' ability to comment, most often done by requiring registration (i.e., Blogger/Google's registration requirement). Yet the policy, mere lines later, states that, "[s]ites requiring membership or subscription should be avoided" (Sherman, 2011). This not only contradicts the desire for control that can only come with registration, but also rules out the majority of popular social networking sites, such as Facebook or Twitter.

The failure of open meeting and campaign laws to address social media stems from these local laws' approach: they deal with social media as if they are mere tools with which officials act in ways similar to the tools available in 1976. Consequently, it is a mistake to assume that existing rules will apply to social media with a couple of tweaks. Scenario C described above (dealing with the regulation of third-party content) demonstrates that the existing rules fail to address much of the most problematic, and hardest to police, behavior. I suggest that the challenge is not to develop micro-rules that would prevent this behavior, but instead to step back and take a systemic look at the behavioral norms and pressures that are developing around this institution. These behaviors have become so pronounced that they have begun to take the shape of a new unstructured institution—not an organization, but rather a set of interrelated strategic behaviors that, in turn, affects the behavior around it.

Social Networks Are a New Institutional Environment

Strikingly, the behaviors on all sides of the social media communication matrix—that is, among both officials and constituents—already have recognizable patterns and norms of such consistency that they constitute an emerging unstructured institution.

Why Do Public Officials Want to Use Social Media?

Traditionally, scholars who examine social networking by public officials sometimes view the dynamic between the government and the public as a relationship between supply of information (by public officials) and demand (by constituents) (Chadwick, 2009). Although that framework may help describe certain ways that the government and public interact on the Internet, it bears little resemblance to the social networking environment, which features much more give-and-take on both sides. In fact, any analysis of social media that fails to recognize the demand by officials of others in the network will miss the ways that officials' behavior helps solve many of the collective action problems that may otherwise stymie widespread use by the public.

Social science theory traditionally takes a rather cynical view of the motivations of public officials. Generally, elected officials are portrayed as valuing re-election above all else; for appointed officials, the expansion of budget and power is paramount (Niskanen, 1971). Political scientists have long since debunked, explained, and expanded this view of the motivations of public officials. Theoretical and empirical work concludes that re-election, budget, and power are all important goals of public officials, but that such a view oversimplifies a very complex and layered collection of values (Fenno, 1973; Fenno, 1976). Surely it is not difficult to identify behavior of public officials that appears to satisfy these goals, whether cynical or civic in nature. But what specifically does a public official value that might prompt him or her to use social media and affect how he or she might use them?

Clearly, officials value the ability to distribute information to a large number of people. There are specific qualities or types of mass communication that carry greater value; for example, public officials value in particular the ability to send a desired message; the ability to send it to a specific group of people (supporters, persuadable voters, people in a particular geographic area); and the ability to get the recipients to actually read/view/hear the message. Closely related is the effectiveness of the message—in other words, the ability to get the recipient to act in the manner intended.

But all of these examples deal with *outbound* connections, or the broadcast from the public official to constituents. But public officials value more than merely outbound messages, no matter how targeted and effective; they also value *inbound* connections. First, an inbound connection has value for the information that the content conveys—for example, support or opposition on a particular issue, or substantive information about a matter that may come before the official for a decision. Second, it has value for the information conveyed by the sender's identity; public officials want to know who, specifically, is in contact with their office and why. Third, the inbound connection may have secondary power that the receipt of such messages gives the public official (that is, a public official may value the ability to claim he has received a number of inquiries or communications on a subject). Fourth, the connection may be valuable because of the opinion or information it delivers. And fifth, the inbound connection carries significance as an indicator of a much stronger relationship between the constituent and the public official.

So we should expect to see public officials use social media only to the extent that: (a) they can free ride on others' efforts, thus avoiding a collective action problem; (b) they can capture the fruits of others' labor, therefore making any remaining effort or expenditure lesser than the projected benefit; or (c) the remaining potential benefits still outweigh the costs of full individual efforts. And public officials do so, but in very specific ways and for specific reasons.

First, public officials have adopted social media for outbound connections and communications—by which one transmits information in a one-way manner to constituents. More complex are the combinations of outbound and inbound connections that really distinguish social media from traditional junk mail. As described above, public officials attach significant value to inbound connections. The reason is easy to identify—it is that an outbound connection includes information about *identity*, but an inbound connection suggests the existence of a *relationship* (Grimmelmann, 2009). Most commonly, public officials use inbound connections to establish relationships with constituents, and carry on those relationships in an exchange of comments and posts on the public official's profile (whether on Facebook, Twitter, or a blog). Although it is clear that the dialogue between public officials and constituents establishes and strengthens relationships, public officials have been reluctant to incorporate online discourse into their formal decision-making process. (Chadwick, 2009). In addition, public officials appear interested in using social media to inform and motivate constituents around specific issues—in other words, to generate the sense of community that draws value from the cross-constituent relationships.

Public officials benefit from the concentration (or concentrated availability) of information about and generated by constituents that appears in social networks. Specifically, public officials capture rents from the concentration of individuals volunteering information about themselves. But the capture is non-exclusive; public officials merely get more out of this information than your average member of the public. And once the structure has been established, individual users sign up without incremental cost, and each additional user adds value to the network at large (value accruing to both the elected official and the other users—the elected official gets information from more sources and distributes more information to more sources, while the individual user enjoys a larger community of like-minded individuals) (Shepsle, 2006).

Public officials then create certain dynamics that affect other users within the system. For example, public officials can be expected to have more inbound than outbound connections, placing a strain on the officials' attention and driving them to use higher-efficiency tools to maintain an online presence. In addition, many of the benefits of social networks (such as access to others' personal information or access to their attention) are concentrated in public officials in much the same way they are concentrated in other "nodes."

The activity patterns of public officials also create incentives for other users. A public official who encourages constituents to interact (whether by explicitly asking them to or implicitly, by engaging with them when they do) is expressing a demand that often provokes its own supply. Similarly, a public official who cultivates a large collection of constituents online may create a community of easily organized users who may overcome other collective action problems.

Public officials who initiate the use of social media are "political entrepreneurs" or leaders that offer their constituencies an opportunity to overcome collective action problems by engaging in the civic social network. These dynamics encourage a pattern of behavior in which, in Shepsle's words, "particular individuals may make unusually large contributions of time and energy and financial and (especially) logistical resources not (only) because they care passionately about the group's objective but (also) because they see an opportunity to parlay this investment into something personally (read: selectively) rewarding" (Shepsle, 2006).

Why Do Constituents Interact with Public Officials in Civic Social Media?

Why do constituents use social media to interact with public officials? People apparently take time away from playing games, tagging photos, watching piano-playing-cat videos, and stalking former significant others to read and respond to a tweet from their city councilmember. The fact that this occurs is puzzling in that the probability that an individual will have influence on actual policy is minute. Further exacerbating the situation is the tendency of rational voters to free ride on the efforts of others: if two voters want the same policy, each would do best to let the other do the work of getting the policy adopted. At the same time that public choice theory posits that rational voters will refrain from low-threshold, low-reward political activity, it predicts that constituents (or groups or corporations) will seek to capture benefits created by others, especially where benefits can be concentrated and costs distributed.

A self-interested user will value anything that allows her to craft her identity specifically and increases the power of her individual voice relative to others. What makes this interesting from a public choice perspective is that this narcissism creates public goods because certain self-expressive (or self-indulgent) behaviors have an identifiable connection to civic engagement: the exercise of speech, self-governance, and associational liberty. Papacharissi, drawing upon Inglehart and Welzel, wrote of a "civically motivated narcissism," based on the idea that "self-expression values are connected to the desire to control one's environment, a stronger desire for autonomy, and the need to question authority" and that "self-expression values are not uncivic" (Papacharissi, 2008). Consequently, the exercise of purely self-interested or narcissistic behavior can create public goods.

Second, constituents value the creation of relationships with public officials and with other users (Grimmelmann, 2009). The act of adding someone as a contact (or friend, or followee) can have layers of significance: it can mean that the two users are actually friends; that they are merely acquaintances; that one is a "connector" or hub to many other users; a potential business contact; or a fan or supporter.

Third, constituents value the community that arises from the creation of relationships in civic social networks. For the purposes of this analysis, the most salient characteristic of community as developed by civic social networks is that they reduce the costs of organizing among individuals in the network to the vanishing point. The opportunity to create affinity or advocacy groups with hardly any identifiable costs has led to an explosion of lasting and temporary groups. Although there is evidence that those participating in political activities online are no different than those doing so offline, the availability of impulsive or casual group formation is quite different than what can take place offline (Feezell et al., 2009).

Finally, constituents value information. Much of this information stems from the other aspects of social networking—the awareness of who is in a particular public official's network, or what issues are significant to another constituent. Significantly, access to information is not a secretive or private benefit in the context of civic social media; because a connection between two users must include a certain level of access to information posted by each user, information is integrated into every relationship in the network. Users may enjoy being the first to discover or post information, but the value comes from the distribution of the information, not from possessing it to the exclusion of others. In this way, the things that public choice theorists might consider costs (becoming informed about public issues, organizing groups) are actually benefits that citizens enjoy when they act politically, and things that public choice theorists might consider valuable only if managed as a private good or rent, in fact, gain value when treated as a public good.

The values and activity patterns of constituents in civic social media create pressures and demands on other actors in the network. Most prominently, the presence of millions of constituents (and potential voters) on social networks, and the interest or willingness of a substantial subset of those constituents to engage with public officials online, creates a very strong incentive for public officials to join the networks.

Once the official is in the network, however, the behavior of constituents puts severe demands on public officials. The ease with which constituents or organizations may access a public official's attention using a social network leads to a very high demand on the public official's attention and time; consequently, officials themselves will seek to offer authenticity and relationship-strengthening interaction only at a level that is worth the time and effort. This behavior, in turn, reduces the value of the interaction; just as public officials discount the value of form emails, constituents discount the value of inauthentic or impersonal communications by public officials (Chadwick, 2009).

The desire of constituents for transparency, information, and accountability can also put severe demands on public officials and agencies that either cannot or would prefer not to put all communications and documents online for use by the network. Constituents will value highly all disclosure. Indeed, they will resist efforts by public officials to shield information from public view.

The use of civic social media by constituents creates a strong temptation for public officials to use the media for campaign activity as well. Constituents may not recognize the distinction between official activity and political activity, but, as discussed above, the distinction is critical for the prevention of corruption. There is no internal check on such activity—neither public officials nor constituents will punish or disincentivize campaign activity using a social network account connected to a government link—and therefore such behavior can only be prevented or punished by external enforcement.

Social Media Represent an Emerging Institutional Environment

Even though civic social networks have developed rapidly, they have settled into strong patterns of behavior by both constituents and public officials in those networks. Those patterns indicate that the media are not just a tool, like email or the telephone, but instead resemble an unstructured institution like the press or lobbyists.

Public choice theory has developed at least two major ways to think about institutions (often discussed under the subject "rational choice institutionalism"). Under the first, institutions are the set of rules and regulations constraining individuals', groups', and firms' activities; the focus of inquiry is how players choose to act under certain rules (Shepsle, 2006). The second approach does not assume the institutions as a given at all—instead, the rules are agreed upon by the players themselves and can be changed based on their pressures, preferences, and biases (Schelling, 1960). The first view describes a more specific, formal, structured institution, like a government agency, a nonprofit organization, or a body of law. The second describes a conceptual, unstructured institution, such as the press or the aggregated efforts of advocacy organizations.

Unstructured institutions are not "established" in any formal sense; they emerge when parties' behavior is affected or channeled by others' behavior and the demands and pressures that the behavior creates. Under this theory, institutions are changeable sets of norms that all or most people involved agree upon; there are no rules per se, but actors behave as if there are because they act strategically in response to their expectations of others' behavior and other factors in the environment. When expectations of behavior become particularly clear and become less temporary, then this behavior starts to look like an institution. This sort of institution is a sort of equilibrium of behavior which, although subject to change, is an identifiable pattern (Calvert, 1995; Schotter, 1981).

The behavior patterns and pressures indicate that civic social media constitute an emerging unstructured institution because they describe not just the use of a new communication tool, but a set of strategic behaviors and pressures. Those behaviors and pressures are critical to understand for local governments attempting to regulate public officials' use of civic social media.

There will always be a strong incentive for a public official to join social networks because of the interdependent strategic behaviors of public officials and constituents. That incentive, though, will lag behind constituent adoption of the social media platform unless the public official takes on the burden of the political entrepreneur. Similarly, there will be strong incentives for public officials to engage in some actual interactive behavior on the network, lest constituents ignore the public official the same way they ignore junk mail and unsolicited bulk email (or spam). To the extent public officials engage in interactive communication, the overwhelming incentive is for the public official to display the communication to other users so that the maximum exposure is achieved for the spent effort. Similarly, constituents engaged in civic social media experience low-threshold group formation and organizational tools, as well as a certain incentive for acquiring information and sharing it with other users.

Institutions behave differently than mere tools because these bargains or strategic behaviors by public officials and constituents tend to funnel activity in certain directions. In the case of civic social media, it indicates that transparency and accountability will be highly incentivized.

Transparency and Accountability in the New Public Square

The metaphor of civic social media as the "new public square" has as its defining feature an open space in full view of the public for anyone who wants it. If one chooses to enter the public square, one exposes oneself to anything else there—music, commerce, speech, governance, politics. And in particular, those public officials who enter the public square do so with much at stake: reputation, familiarity, ridicule, re-election. By entering the public square, a public official is engaging in her job, which under even a jaded vision of informed democracy involves some combination of tránsparency and accountability. In civic social media, public officials hear from and speak to constituents in full view of the online world. Constituents can deliver information, opinions, support, and opposition to those officials, and constituents can interact with each other, forming groups to advance shared interests. The ease with which communications from and interactions with public officials are available to the public demonstrates that, in this environment, the contours of the institution itself make FOIA requests obsolete, and includes constituents in the deliberative process at a much deeper level than notice of or attendance at a formal meeting would.

It is particularly perverse, then, that objections to public officials' use of civic social media are based on the fear of violating open meeting and public records laws. Prohibitions or certain limits on the use of civic social media—that is, ejecting public officials from the new public square—would result in less public deliberation, fewer publicly accessible records, and elimination of valuable tools to hold public officials accountable for their actions.

Open meeting, public records, and misuse of government resource laws exist in every state, and with good reason. The statutes work on two levels. Their immediate goals are to make information about what the government does and considers accessible, and to ensure that government funds are not misused. But those goals also advance other important aims; making information accessible is important, but the information only takes on meaning when it is used to hold public officials accountable, or to prevent a monopoly on inside information that would give some citizens an exclusive advantage other others. Similarly, the restrictions on the use of government resources for private or political gain have, at one level, a fiscally prudent purpose (that is, barring spending that does not advance a legitimate purpose of government). However, the more important consideration is preventing an environment where a private corporation or a campaign can enjoy a limited benefit to the exclusion of others.

Civic social networks advance all of these primary and secondary goals. Communications that would go unrecorded outside of the new public square (such as a face-to-face discussion or a telephone conversation) are not only documented but instantly accessible to the public when they occur in a civic social network. Attempts to get a public official's attention to hold her accountable are easily accessible, and the threshold expense to organize a group of constituents is virtually zero. In short, civic social media substantially improve public access to deliberative discussion and the records created by it.

The use of civic social media by public officials also helps reduce moral hazard associated with hidden action. This hazard appears where a strategic agent—the public official—takes action that isn't observable by the principal—the constituency. Civic social media cannot, of course, eliminate the many ways that public officials can hide actions or statements (for example, in a private conversation), but to the extent that communications in the network are available to the public, the opportunity for constituents to investigate officials' actions and statements is greatly improved.

Policymakers should adopt interpretations of open government statutes (or amend the statutes themselves) to make clear what aspects of written communication constitute a "meeting." The purposes of open meeting and public record statutes overlap significantly and raise interesting questions about when the availability of records is sufficient, and when actual presence at an exchange of those records is necessary. The doctrinal question also involves what we mean by "deliberation" and what types of government action trigger meeting requirements. But policymakers should ensure that when city council members interact with each other or the public in full view of an open civic social network, but no votes are taken or collective decisions are made, the purposes of the open meeting statutes are fulfilled to a greater extent than they would be if that interaction was barred.

FUTURE RESEARCH DIRECTIONS

The success of local government engagement with the public through civic social networks will depend on the modernization of open government law. That process will require additional scrutiny of the sources and purposes of those statutes, with some attention to doctrinal inconsistencies, such as the dual valence of "deliberation," which triggers secrecy in open records laws like FOIA, but requires openness in public meeting laws. Additionally, state and local governments would benefit greatly from further analysis of their engagement with the public on campaign issues that originate with government agencies, such as tax levies or bond issues; the rules of engagement for such activities forbid agencies to campaign for or against ballot measures, but the very nature of their development involves a certain amount of government advocacy. With the advent of civic social networks, that advocacy will be more difficult to track and the rules more difficult to enforce.

CONCLUSION

Civic social networks are the new public square, but many local governments fear that they present a threat to open government laws. The effort to use open meeting and open record laws to stifle valuable civic communication does violence to a new unstructured institution with a high degree of transparency and accountability – the very values that open government laws should promote. These laws should be revised or reinterpreted to allow civic social networks – and the laws themselves - to fulfill their promise.

REFERENCES

Brehm, J., & Rahn, W. (1997). Individual-level evidence for the causes and consequences of social capital. *American Journal of Political Science*, *41*, 999. doi:10.2307/2111684

Calvert, R. L. (1995). Rational actors, equilibrium, and social institutions. In *Explaining social institutions*. Academic Press.

Chadwick, A. (2009). Web 2.0: New Challenges for the study of e-democracy in an era of informational exuberance. *I/S. Journal of Law and Policy for the Information Society*, *5*, 9.

Dutton, W. H., & Peltu, M. (2007). Reconfiguring government-public engagements: Enhancing the communicative power of citizens. *Oxford Internet Institute*. Retrieved from http://www.oii.ox.ac.uk/research/publications/FD9.pdf

Feezell, J. T., et al. (2009). *Facebook is... fostering political investment: A study of online social networking groups and offline participation*. APSA Toronto Meeting Paper. Retrieved from http://ssrn.com/abstract=1451456

Fenno, R. F. Jr. (1973). *Congressmen in committees*. Academic Press.

Fenno, R. F. Jr. (1978). *Home style: House members in their districts*. Academic Press.

Grimmelmann, J. (2009). Saving facebook. *Iowa Law Review*, *94*, 1137.

Jennings, M. K., & Stoker, L. (2004). Social trust and civic engagement across time and generations. *Acta Politica*, *39*, 342. doi:10.1057/palgrave.ap.5500077

Mossberger, K. et al. (2007). *Digital citizenship: The internet, society, and participation*. Academic Press.

Niskanen, W. A. Jr. (1971). *Bureaucracy and representative government*. Academic Press.

O'Connor, J. F., & Baratz, M. J. (2004). Some assembly required: The application of state open meeting laws to email correspondence. *George Mason Law Review*, *12*, 722.

Papacharissi, Z. (2008). The virtual sphere 2.0: The internet, the public sphere and beyond. In *The handbook of internet politics* (pp. 236–239). Academic Press.

Pupillo, T. D. (1993). The changing weather forecast: Government in the sunshine in the 1990s—An analysis of state sunshine laws. *Washington University Law Quarterly*, *71*, 1167.

Schaeffer, S. (2004). Sunshine in cyberspace? Electronic deliberation and the reach of open meeting laws. *Saint Louis University Law Journal*, *48*, 778.

Schelling, T. (1960). *The strategy of conflict*. Academic Press.

Schotter, A. (1981). *The economic theory of social institutions*. Academic Press. doi:10.1017/CBO9780511983863

Shepsle, K. A. (2006). Rational choice institutionalism. In *The Oxford handbook of political institutions* (pp. 23–38). Oxford, UK: Oxford University Press.

Sherman, B. (2011). Your mayor, your friend: Public officials, social networking, and the unmapped new public square. *Pace Law Review*, *31*, 95.

Smith, A. (2010). Government online: The internet gives citizens new paths to government services and information. *Pew Internet*. Retrieved from http://pewInternet.org/~/media//Files/Reports/2010/PIP_Government_Online_2010_with_topline.pdf

Solove, D. J. (2002). Access and aggregation: Public records, privacy and the constitution. *Minnesota Law Review*, *86*, 1161.

KEY TERMS AND DEFINITIONS

Administrative Law: The body of law that governs the activities of administrative agencies of government, including rulemaking, adjudication, or the pursuit of a specific regulatory agenda.

Civic Social Network: A social network focused on politics, policy, or government.

FOIA: Acronym for Freedom of Information Act, a statute guaranteeing public access to certain government records.

Local Government: Government at the municipal, county, or similar level.

Open Government: A legal doctrine that holds that citizens have the right to access the documents and proceedings of the government to allow for effective public oversight.

Political Law: A field of study or legal practice area encompassing the intersection of politics and law.

Social Network: As defined by Danah Boyd, a Web-based service that allows individuals to (1) construct a public or semi-public profile within a bounded system, (2) articulate a list of other users with whom they share a connection, and (3) view and traverse their list of connections and those made by others within the system.

ENDNOTES

1 This chapter is revised and adapted from Sherman, B. (2011). Your Mayor, Your "Friend": Public Officials, Social Networking, and the Unmapped New Public Square. *Pace Law Review, 31,* 95.

Chapter 15
Who Cares for Identity Information in Government 2.0?
An Empirical Study

Bert-Jaap Koops
Tilburg University, The Netherlands

Bibi van den Berg
Leiden University, The Netherlands

ABSTRACT

This chapter presents the results of an empirical study on the effects of identity information on government-citizen interaction in government 2.0 applications. It triangulates findings from a survey among government 2.0 users and quantitative and qualitative analyses of Dutch government 2.0 Websites. This reveals the identity information Web 2.0 users want to have of other participants and are willing to provide about themselves, the importance of role information of civil servants, and the relationship of identity information with the interaction level on government 2.0 applications. The results show that, contrary to what the literature suggests, there is no significant correlation between identity information and interaction levels on government 2.0 discussion forums. The findings suggest that government 2.0 initiatives should be designed with a flexible and liberal approach to identity information.

1 INTRODUCTION

1.1 Background and Research Question

Web 2.0, also called social media, is an umbrella term for technologies and applications that facilitate user interactions and user-generated content, leading to new forms of social networks. Government 2.0 can be seen as the use of Web 2.0 by governments, more specifically – in the sense that we are interested in in this paper – to facilitate government-citizen interactions. Many discussion platforms are being set up where government and citizens can meet, but not all of these are successful. Several factors affect the potential for success of government 2.0 (Meijer, Koops, Pieterson, Overman, & Ten Tije, 2012). One possible factor that we want to explore in this paper, which has significant implications for the

DOI: 10.4018/978-1-4666-6038-0.ch015

Copyright © 2014, IGI Global. Copying or distributing in print or electronic forms without written permission of IGI Global is prohibited.

design of government 2.0 Websites, is the amount of identity information that users have to give when participating in government 2.0.

The reason we focus on identity information is that the literature suggests this to be a key enabler of trust, and mutual trust is a necessary condition for these government-citizen relationships to be successful. Particularly in online interactions, trust can never be taken for granted; it has to be established. Since online interactions involve communications at a distance, traditional trust-enhancing factors that we rely on in face-to-face interactions may not necessarily apply (Pettit, 2004). For the purposes of this paper, we focus on the context of virtual relationships, for which Haenni *et al.* (2009, p. 40ff) describe trust as a subjective, context-dependent characteristic of one party (the trustor) in relation to another party (the trustee) in a relevant context. Trust has many aspects; in this paper, we are interested in preconditional aspects or enablers for trust to be possible in the first place: availability (is the trustee available when needed?) and identity (is the identity of the trustee established?) (Cofta, 2007).

Closely related to these enablers of trust in the trustee are enablers of confidence in the reliability of the trustee's statements. In government 2.0 applications, the latter are perhaps even more important: do governments and citizens trust the *content* of their Web 2.0 interactions? Content reliability can be gauged from two types of criteria: content criteria, related to the content itself, for example consistency, coherence, and accuracy; and pedigree criteria, related to the information source, for example whether information comes from a source that is authoritative or that proved reliable in the past (Vedder & Wachbroit, 2003). In online contexts (as in many offline contexts), people find it hard to apply content criteria and usually rely on pedigree criteria (Vedder & Wachbroit, 2003). In other words, trust in the Web 2.0 content often boils down to trust in the content's source, that is, in the counter-party who contributes content. Since many pedigree criteria are connected to the information's source, knowing who the source is becomes important. This underpins the importance of identity as a preconditional dimension of trust: it is a facilitating enabler for the other enablers of trust.

1.1.1 Background

What, then, is identity? Given our focus on online interactions, we focus on the three aspects of identity most relevant in online environments. First, identity knowledge, i.e., the knowledge of identity information available about someone, for instance on the Internet. Gary T. Marx (2006) distinguishes five types of identity knowledge that can be placed on a continuum, ranging from identity information very close and specific to the individual (core identification and unique identification) through identity information specific to the type of individual (sensitive information and private information) to any identity information that can be attached to a person (individual information). These five types can be thought of as concentric circles, with core identification as the inner, most limited category, and individual information as the outer, most comprehensive category. It is useful to distinguish between these types of identity information, precisely because identification seems such a key element in government-citizen relationships.

A central policy question is how much and what kind of identity information is necessary in various contexts. In particular, whether identification of a unique person is appropriate and, if so, what form it should take (Marx, 2006). For government 2.0 applications, one can hypothesize that, based on identity being a key facilitating enabler for trust, people's willingness to participate in government 2.0 initiatives will be proportional to the availability of identity information. In particular, one can hypothesize that participation increases as identity information comes closer to the core of the identity circles.

The second aspect of identity relevant for online interactions, and closely related to the first, is that of numerical identity. This refers to the notion that something is identical to itself by being a unique object that may resemble other objects yet has some properties that set it apart from all others (Parfit, 1984). This is the main reason why we can identify objects or people as the unique beings they are. Numerical identity is relevant for online interactions, since the identities individuals express online consist of a collection of attributes that together uniquely identify an individual within a relevant group in a particular context (Pfitzmann & Hansen, 2010, p. 30).

The third aspect of identity relevant for this study is the notion of narrative identity (Ricœur, 1992), viz., the fact that individuals express and experience their identities to others and to themselves by telling stories about who they (think they) are. In online interactions, especially in environments that are designed to invoke identity expressions, users actively engage in building such stories about themselves, thereby constantly balancing between their self-conceptions and ideas of what they believe others would like to hear of them. At the same time, the actual stories that others tell about them are also relevant in Web 2.0 environments.

This brings us to a downside to high levels of identity knowledge, which risks *diminishing* people's willingness to participate in government 2.0, especially on the citizen side. The fact that identity information often relates to personal information implies a significant potential of privacy infringement of Web 2.0 participants. The information becomes more sensitive if it comes closer to the centre of Marx's circles of identity knowledge. From an informational-privacy perspective, the amount of personal data disclosed and processed should be kept to the minimum of what is necessary for the purpose at hand. A central data-protection principle, enshrined in the Council of Europe Convention 108 and the European Union's 1995 Data Protection Directive, is that personal data should not be excessive in relation to the purposes for which they are collected, stored, or processed. This data minimization or purpose-binding principle points in exactly the opposite direction from the hypothetical conclusion above that government 2.0 applications should incorporate as much identity knowledge as possible.

Privacy concerns are compounded in the context of Web 2.0, particularly with social media where traditional social contexts blur. Individuals always play roles in social life, e.g., husband, employee, fire brigade volunteer, clarinet player, etc., presenting themselves to their audiences in different ways (Goffman, 1959). These contexts are governed by norms and social practices particular to the context, for example related to the questions you are expected or allowed to ask (Nissenbaum, 2010). In today's social media, audience segregation is difficult to manage, resulting in 'friends' from various contexts seeing information they would not acquire in offline contexts (Van den Berg & Leenes, 2011). This infringement of 'contextual integrity' is one of the crucial current threats to privacy (Nissenbaum, 2010).

Although privacy is traditionally seen as a citizens' concern vis-à-vis the state, Web 2.0 introduces a complicating factor: state officials can take dual roles on the same media, as officials and as citizens. The networks in new media do not contain straightforward distinctions between 'the state' and 'the citizen', making the issue of 'contextual integrity' salient for all parties involved. Guidelines for civil servant participation in social media tend to stress role specification, for example in Britain: 'Wherever possible, disclose your position as a representative of your department or agency' (Cabinet Office, 2008). At the same time, most guidelines warn against giving too much (personal) information, because of the Internet's everlasting memory and the potential for abuse of information. Civil servants are allowed or stimulated to participate in Web 2.0 as private persons under a separate account, but warned that citizens can find them through search engines using identity information to combine their public-function and private profiles; hence, they should be careful which information they provide, both as a civil servant and as a citizen (Birza, Frank, & Klok, 2010). Providing more identity information, then, also poses risks on the government side of Web 2.0.

From this literature overview, we hypothesise that identity information is a major factor in people's willingness to participate in online applications, but that it is a double-edged sword. Having more identity knowledge of counter-parties will enhance people's participation, but having to provide identity knowledge to counter-parties risks diminishing people's participation in a context where risks to privacy arise. This paradox implies that applications must run the gauntlet of stimulating the exchange of identity information without forcing people to disclose more identity information than they feel comfortable in providing in the particular context of the application.

No research has been conducted yet on how users – both citizens and officials – deal with this ostensible paradox. Very little empirical evidence is available of the importance of identity information in government 2.0 applications. To fill this gap, we aim at answering the question: how does identity information impact on the interaction of governments and citizens in government 2.0 applications? To answer this question, we have conducted empirical research about the identity information Web 2.0 that users want to have of other participants, the identity information they are willing in practice to provide about themselves, and the importance of role information of civil servants, in the context of government 2.0 interactions.

The relevance of this research for politics and policy in the information age is that the use of social media in government-citizen interactions is increasing, but many initiatives are not altogether successful in terms of enhancing interactive participation of citizens in politics and policy-making. Our results may help in designing government 2.0 platforms in such a way that the identity information requested of users is in line with what citizens and civil servants are actually comfortable with to engage them in online interaction. This will give government 2.0 initiatives a better chance of success.

1.2 Methodology

We assume that the interaction in government 2.0 correlates with identity information. Interaction can be measured quantitatively – the number of discussions on a platform, the number of reactions to a posting – or qualitatively – the type and depth of responses. We therefore set out to study both quantitatively and qualitatively how identity information relates to the level of interaction on government 2.0 applications. We have studied this for Dutch government 2.0 Websites, using the eParticipation Dashboard[1] as our starting point, as this provides an almost comprehensive list of over 600 Dutch government 2.0 initiatives.

Our quantitative analysis consisted of three parts. First, we performed a quickscan of initiatives, looking at a random sample of around 50 interactive Websites. To create this sample, for each letter of the alphabet, we chose the first and last initiatives until we had sufficient interactive Websites. Since many Websites on the eParticipation Dashboard turned out not to be really interactive – they were either unidirectional (e.g., municipalities' YouTube channels or a Website requesting citizens to e-mail ideas) or they were no longer in use – we looked at 197 initiatives overall, of which 54 initiatives had some sort of active discussion platform. In this subset, we looked at how much identity information people had to provide in order to participate; we counted the number of profiles of platform participants, how many discussion lines the platform had, and how many postings each discussion line had (i.e., the initial posting plus the number of reactions).

We performed various analyses to find correlations between the amount of identity information and the number of discussion lines or reactions.

Since many of the initiatives in the quickscan had relatively little interaction, making overall statistical analysis difficult, from the more active platforms we subsequently generated a larger data set of around 500 discussion lines, consisting of identity information of the initiator of a discussion line (i.e., the one making the initial posting) and the number of reactions. We then analysed the possible correlations between the amount of identity information of the discussion initiator and the number of reactions.

Third, we zoomed in on one particular initiative that had a high level of interaction. We chose a random sample of a 100 user profiles and categorised these into profiles with a low, intermediate or high level of identity information. We then analysed whether the level of identity information correlated with the number of connections users have or the number of reactions (similar to Facebook's wall postings) that other people post on their personal profile.

Since the quantitative analysis turned out not to yield any insight into role information (in almost all cases it could not be determined from the postings which role the initiator of a posting played), we subsequently performed a survey of how people perceive the use of identification information on Web 2.0, including how they perceive roles and role markers of civil servants. We opted for an online survey, which yielded 72 completed responses. Although this is a limited number of respondents, and there is the issue of self-selection that applies to all online surveys, the respondents fit well in our target group of Web 2.0 users. Hence, the results are indicative, yielding some interesting insights for further research. Since the survey also covered opinions about the role of identity information in Web 2.0 in general, we present these results first in the next section, before the results of our quantitative study.

Finally, since the quantitative study only measured the number of reactions as an indicator of the interaction level on government 2.0 Websites, but not the content or quality of the reactions, we also conducted a qualitative study. We chose Websites from the e-Participation Dashboard that had a substantial amount of interaction, clear visibility of government representatives participating, and sufficient variation in identity information. Very few Websites fit this profile. We found two Websites, one in the legislative (Wageningen council) and one in the executive (Smallingerland municipality) branches of government, which we studied by looking at the content of discussions and the identity information in profiles, postings and reactions. We operationalised the quality of the interaction in terms of elementary criteria for good discussions, i.e., the *process* and the *product* but not the *procedure* of an argument (Wenzel, 1992). The process of an argument refers the idea that individuals use techniques to increase their chances of convincing the other, while the product refers to the content of that which is argued, and whether or not it is convincing and aligns with the ongoing debate (Wenzel, 1992). We have translated this into the following qualitative assessments: does a contribution to the discussion make sense in itself; does it address the topic of discussion; and does it argue on the basis of content arguments (instead of, e.g., ad hominem arguments)? We operationalised identity information in terms of (for Wageningen) discussants using a first name, a first and last name, or a nickname or (for Drachten) how many personal characteristics (age, profession, relationship status, personal interests, personal favourites) the users included in their profile. Both authors analysed separately, on the basis of these operationalisations, whether the presence or absence of identity information correlated to the quality of the discussion.

2 FINDINGS

2.1 User Survey

We performed a survey of how people perceive the use of identification information on Web 2.0. We opted for an online survey, which we advertised particularly on Ambtenaar 2.0, the major Dutch platform for civil servants. 106 people responded, of which 72 people completed the survey; we analysed the results of the completed surveys. Because the same of respondents is small, our findings yield only indicative results (N=72, unless specified otherwise), yet these point in interesting directions that seem to contradict established ideas in the literature.

Of the 72 respondents, 38 were male and 34 female. They were between 25 and 63 years old; the average age was 42. The respondent group was highly educated: 86% had a Bachelor's or Master's degree. The majority (64%) worked as civil servants, the rest were citizens. They were very experienced Internet users (average 4.29 on a scale of 1-5) and they say they trust the Internet for serious applications (average 4.43 on a scale of 1-5). Respondents frequently used Web 2.0 applications, notably Twitter, LinkedIn, YouTube, and Facebook. Less popular were blogs, Flickr, and Hyves, a Dutch variant of Facebook. From these background characteristics, the respondent group seemed to consist largely of skilled professionals well-versed in using social media. Although this is not representative for the Dutch population, it does fit our target group of Web 2.0 users, but because of the self-selecting response, we cannot say whether the results are representative for this target group.

Of the 26 citizens, less than half use Web 2.0 frequently or often to communicate with or about the government; they largely do so to obtain information (46%), to discuss government matters with others (46%), and also to ask questions (35%), voice their opinion (38%) or to discuss with the government about their policy (31%). The 46 civil servants use government 2.0 applications primarily for sharing information with colleagues (63% frequent users); fewer officials use it to discuss public policy with colleagues (24% frequent users). They also use government 2.0 for voicing their opinion about government policy (30% frequent users) and for providing information to citizens (30% frequent users). Government 2.0 is rarely used by civil servants to engage in discussions with citizens (17% frequent users) or to answer questions about government services (9% frequent users).

Citizens' responses are in line with our hypothesis that they prefer having identity information of others in Web 2.0 platforms: they like knowing exactly who the discussion participants are (58% (totally) agree, while 12% (totally) disagree), and they reject the statement that it does not matter *who* says something, but it matters *what* they say (58% (totally) disagree, while 23% (totally) agree). 77% frequently look at other people's profiles on Web 2.0 platforms. Still, 38% of the citizens do not hesitate to respond to anonymous contributions, just as many as those who do not respond to anonymous postings.

Both civil servants and citizens tend to attach weight to knowing the (real) name of discussion participants; 58% find this (very) important. This contrasts with a majority (57%) who find it not (at all) important that postings include a picture of discussants. When asked which types of identity information people like to have of other Web 2.0 participants, they are particularly interested in the name and profession. Age, address, and personal interests are less important (see Table 1).

We found no differences between civil servants and citizens in relation to the importance they attach to knowing others' identity information. There is some suggestion that people who frequently or often use LinkedIn tend more to find it (very) important to know other people's last name than people who do not, or only now and then, use LinkedIn (χ^2=3.6, *df*=1, *p*=.056), but

Table 1. Types of identity information and respondents' attitudes

Type	Important to Know about Others 1 = Not at All Important 5 = Very Important	Willingness to Provide when Joining a Website 1 = Very Little Willing 5 = Very Willing
First Name	3.4	3.8
Last Name	3.1	3.2
Employer	3.2	3.1
Profession	3.1	3.0
Photo	2.7	2.7
Personal Interests	2.5	2.7
Age	2.5	3.0
Email Address	2.3	2.3
Place of Residence	2.3	2.3

this does not apply to other identity information types (such as photo, profession or employer). Nor is there such a suggestion for other frequent Web 2.0 users; frequent Facebook users, for example, are no different from non- or occasional Facebook users in terms of wanting to know other people's last name.

Among the 46 civil servants, those who frequently use Web 2.0 to provide citizens with information, attach significantly more importance to knowing the last name of people participating in discussion platforms, compared to civil servants who do not, or only seldom, use Web 2.0 to inform citizens (χ^2=9.07, *df*=1, *p*=.003); no such association was found in relation to other types of identity information.[2] There is a weaker suggestion that civil servants who frequently use Web 2.0 to voice their opinion about public policy or services attach more importance to knowing the employer of other discussants on a site (χ^2=3.55, *df*=1, *p*=.06).

Among the 26 citizens, a significant difference was found between people who say they do not respond to anonymous contributions and people who do not mind responding to anonymous contributions; the former find it more important to know other discussants' last name (χ^2=6.83, *df*=1, *p*=.009) and employer (χ^2=4.47, *df*=1, *p*=.03). No such difference was found for other identity attributes, such as profession (χ^2=1.53, *df*=1, *p*=.22), age (χ^2=.08, *df*=1, p=.78), or a photo (χ^2=.44, *df*=1, *p*=.5). Among all respondents, 58% find it (very) important that Web 2.0 discussants mention their (real) name, and this group attaches more importance to knowing discussants' last name (χ^2=23.7, *df*=1, *p*<.001) but also to knowing other discussants' age (χ^2=6.58, *df*=1, *p*=.01), photo (χ^2=6.17, *df*=1, *p*=.01), employer (χ^2=6.12, *df*=1, *p*=.01), and profession (χ^2=3.98, *df*=1, *p*=.05).

When asked which types of identity information people are willing to provide about themselves when they register at a discussion platform or site, they tend to be willing to provide the same types of information they find important to know of others (see Table 1). For example, people who are (very) willing to provide their last name tend to find it more important to have a photo of other discussants, as opposed to people who are less willing to provide their last name (χ^2=8.2, *df*=1, *p*<=.01). Frequent users of LinkedIn are more willing to give their last name when registering on discussion platforms than non-users or sporadic users of LinkedIn (χ^2=4.2, *df*=1, *p*=.04); this does not apply to frequent users of Facebook (χ^2=0.5, *df*=1, *p*=.5). We did not find a correlation, however, between frequent LinkedIn users and willingness to provide a photo of oneself (χ^2=1.7, *df*=1,*p*=.2): while 61% of frequent LinkedIn users are (very) willing to provide their last name, only 39% are willing to provide a photo on a discussion platform or site.

People who say they think it (very) important that other discussants know who they are (63%) are also more willing to provide identity information of themselves, in particular their last name (χ^2=13.9, *df*=1, *p*<=.001) and employer (χ^2=7.86, *df*=1, *p*<=.01), and also a photo (χ^2=5.0, *df*=1, p=.03) and their profession (χ^2=4.40, *df*=1, *p*=.04); no such association was found for email address, age or residence.

One issue we were particularly interested in for government 2.0 applications, is the role(s) that civil servants have when discussing on Web 2.0 platforms. Do they speak in their professional role as government representatives or do or can they voice their personal opinion? And should they signpost in which capacity they speak? Our results suggest that government 2.0 participants appreciate civil servants participating in Web 2.0 discussions, and they also tend to find that civil servants can voice their personal opinion when participating in government-citizen discussions (47% (totally) agree, 21% neutral, 32% (totally) disagree). However, they overwhelmingly want the role in which government people speak signposted: someone from the government should always be clear whether s/he speaks on behalf of the government or voices a personal opinion (see Table 2).

We did not find significant differences between civil servants and citizens on the first three statements. On the fourth statement, civil servants seem to attach even more weight to clarifying the role in which they speak than citizens do; civil servants are more inclined to totally agree than to merely agree with the fourth statement, while citizens tend to agree rather than totally agree (N=66, χ^2=7.3, *df*=1, *p*=.01).

2.2 Quick Scan of Dutch Government 2.0 Initiatives

Of all 616 initiatives available on the eParticipation Dashboard[3] in March 2011, we looked at 197 initiatives. Of these 197 initiatives, 53% were established by the government and 45%

Table 2. Opinions about role information

Opinion (N=72) Statement	Totally Disagree	Disagree	Neutral	Agree	Totally Agree	Mean (Scale 1-5)
If citizens discuss with each other on a website, the government is allowed to participate in the discussion.	0%	1.4%	11.1%	72.2%	15.3%	4.0 (sd=.6)
A civil servant can participate in discussions among government and citizens, also if he voices his personal opinion.	9.7%	22.2%	20.8%	40.3%	6.9%	3.1 (sd=1.1)
A civil servant always speaks on behalf of his/her municipality or ministry.	8.3%	40.3%	19.4%	20.8%	11.1%	2.9 (sd=1.2)
Someone from the government should always make clear whether he or she speaks on behalf of the government or voices a personal opinion.	0%	5.6%	2.8%	37.5%	54.2%	4.4 (sd=.8)

were established by citizens, as classified by the eParticipation Dashboard Website. Of these 197, only 54 (27%) were suitable for further examination, i.e., had some kind of discussion forum on their Website on which citizens and government representatives engaged in discussions.

2.2.1 General

Of the 54 initiatives included in the quick scan,[4] 37% were political in character, followed by 28% local/cultural and 28% related to transportation; 22% were related to environment, 22% to public order, 20% to education, 15% to health, 9% to a specific age group, 7% to law, 6% to agriculture, and 2% was related to defence.

Over 85% of the Websites provide the opportunity for a personal profile and more than a third (37%) are linked to an existing social network site, particularly Hyves and Facebook. If the Website included the possibility to make a personal profile, users typically had to fill in their first (80%) and last name (74%). Other information, such as a profile picture (37%), age (51%) and gender (51%) was asked for less frequently. Additionally, people were usually not required to fill in their street name (10%) or city (32%).

The platforms we surveyed ranged in size, but the majority had more than a 100 profiles: 33% had more than 1000 profiles, 26% had between 100 and 1000 profiles, 28% had between 10 and 100 profiles, and 11% had less than 10 profile pages. Of the initiatives, 74% were active when we performed the quick scan; about a third had been active 1 and 2 days prior to the quick scan, and a third had been active more than 2 weeks before. Around 30% had only had 1 or 2 contributions in the past month, 26% had between 3 and 5 contributions, 13% had 6-10 contributions, while 19% had over 10 contributions in the past month.

A chi-square test did not reveal a significant difference between the government or citizens as the platform initiator in terms of how many profiles, discussions or reactions within discussions the platform had.

For some initiatives, it was clear that both citizens and representatives of the government had made a personal profile and/or engaged in the discussions, whereas for most others this was unclear. Since this information could only be extracted with certainty from very few Websites, we cannot make any statements about the number of citizens and the number of government representatives with profiles and discussion contributions.

2.2.2 Amount of Identity Information in Profiles and Interaction Level

In order to explore whether having to provide much identity information inhibits people to participate, we looked at the information people are asked to provide when making a personal profile and the number of personal profiles on a Website. Of the 45 Websites for which information was available about the type of personal information people are asked to provide when creating a profile, 27% requested only people's name, which we classified as little personal information; the remaining 73% requested more than the name, which we classified as more personal information. Of the 45 Websites, 89% included information about the number of profiles; 63% had less than 500 users with a personal profile as compared to 37% with more than 500 profiles. A chi-square test did not reveal a significant difference between initiatives with less than 500 profiles and those with more than 500 profiles with regard to how much personal information is required for a profile.

We also found no significant relation between whether or not people were asked to provide a photo and the number of profiles (χ^2=.11, df=1, p=.74) or reactions (χ^2=0, df=1, p=1) on the discussion platforms. In addition, there was no significant relation between whether or not the majority of users had provided their (last) name and the number of reactions (χ^2=0, df=1, p=.99), nor between whether or not the majority of users had provided a photo and the number of discussions (χ^2=0, *df*=1, *p*=1) or reactions (χ^2=.46, *df*=1, *p*=.5).

Next, we analysed whether having to provide little or more identity information inhibited people to participate in discussions. A chi-square test did not reveal a significant difference between initiatives having few (i.e., up to 10) discussions on their discussion platform and those with more than 10 discussions, in relation to how much personal information users had to provide (χ^2=.96, *df*=1, *p*=.33). Neither did we find a significant difference in relation to the identity information people had to provide, between platforms that had on average less than 5 postings within each discussion and those with on average more than 5 postings within discussions (χ^2=.00, *df*=1, *p*=1). The amount of identity information people are asked to provide was also not related to the average number of people participating within a discussion, classified as 1 or 2 discussants versus 3 or more discussants.

2.3 Detailed Study of Discussion Lines

Twenty initiatives were explored in more detail. These initiatives used Hyves discussion platforms, which offer a convenient way to analyse the identity information of someone initiating a discussion and the number of responses to such an initial posting. The identity information consists of a name (categorised as: first name, first and last name, and/or nickname), a photograph (categorised as: non-real (e.g., a cartoon or a picture of an object), real (a picture of a recognisable person, but with the face not clearly visible), or face (a clear picture of someone's face)), and the name-on-mouseover, which indicates the name in the Hyves profile that appears when you move the mouse over the discussant's name or photo.

From the Websites, we inventoried 543 discussion lines in total. Of these, 502 were initiated by an individual; we excluded from further analysis the 41 that were initiated by someone posting on behalf of a company, action group, or other organization.

82% discussion initiators indicated their first name, 5% their first and last name, and 24% used a nickname.[5] 34% had indicated a last name in their Hyves profile, and hence in the name-on-mouseover, while 12% used a nickname there. In combination, 31% had indicated their first and/or last name on the discussion platform and their last name in the mouseover; 10% had indicated a nickname on the discussion platform as well as in the mouseover; and 3% did not use a real name on the platform but had used their last name in the mouseover.

Of all discussion initiators, 10% did not provide a picture, 26% used a non-real picture, 26% used a real picture but without a clearly recognisable face, while 38% used a clear face picture. Of the individuals using a nickname on the platform, 38% had a personal picture (17% face, 83% non-face). Of the people using their first and last name on the platform, 65% had a personal picture (88% face, 12% non-face).

The mean number of reactions to a posting was 3.8 (sd=14.3). The number of reactions is highly skewed due to the fact that half of the postings received no reaction, while very few had very many reactions. Therefore, this variable was re-coded into a categorical variable with 50% discussions having no reaction, 16% having 1 reaction, 14% having 2-3 reactions, 13% having 4-10 reactions and 8% having more than 10 reactions.

No significant relation was found between the number of reactions in a discussion and whether or not the individual who initiated the discussion had indicated his first name (χ^2=6.7, *df*=4, *p*=.15) or a nickname (χ^2=1.21, *df*=4, *p*=.88). In addition, no significant relation was found between the number of reactions to a posting and whether or not the last name was indicated in the mouseover (χ^2=5.93, *df*=4, *p*=.2). Likewise, no significant relation was found between the number of reactions to a posting and whether or not the discussion initiator had provided a personal picture (χ^2=4.32, *df*=4, *p*=.37) or a face picture (χ^2=7.37, *df*=4, *p*=.12).

In order to explore the overall relation between the degree of personal information people provided and the number of reactions, we classified discussion initiators into three categories depending on whether they used a first name, last name, last name in mouseover, and a clear face picture. 19% were categorized as high degree of personal information, i.e., with three or all four of these attributes; 33% had a medium degree of personal information, i.e., with two of the four attributes; 34% had a low degree of personal information, i.e., only one attribute, and 14% had no personal information at all. A chi-square test did not reach significance, although it might suggest some tendency that the degree of personal information is linked to the number of reactions, with people providing much personal information receiving more reactions (χ^2=19.7, *df*=12, *p*=.07).

Next, we compared individuals who provided 'false' information (i.e. a nickname, a nickname in the mouseover and/or a non-personal picture) (N=56) with individuals who provided 'real' personal information (i.e. real-looking first and/or last name, last name in the mouseover and/or a personal picture) (N=274).[6] There was no significant relation between the number of reactions in a discussion and whether or not the discussion initiator had used 'false' or 'real' information (χ^2=1.72, *df*=4, *p*=.79).[7]

As an aside, our results showed that people on the Christian-right political platform (Christian Union) provided significantly more personal information than people on left/progressive platforms (Socialist Party, Party for the Animals, GreenLeft, Democrats '66). And political platforms showed more discussion, with significantly higher numbers of reactions, than environmental discussion platforms. However, since there was no signification relation between identity information and the number of reactions in terms of political orientation or of politics/environment topic of the platform, we do not detail these findings further.

2.4 Study of User Profiles on a Local Platform

To tease out more the interaction between members of a single government 2.0 initiative, we analysed the profiles on a local discussion platform called 'Drachtenwiljemeemaken' or DWJM for short.[8] (This platform was also chosen for a qualitative analysis; see section 2.5.2 *infra* for more details.) DWJM is one of the rare examples we encountered of a government-initiated Web 2.0 environment that has a high level of interaction. In October 2011 the site had almost 2000 members, which is significant for a small town such as Drachten (45,000 inhabitants)[9]. These members had made over 17,000 connections, so each profile page had an average of 9 connections. Moreover, 65,833 so-called 'reactions' had been added to profile pages (comparable to Facebook's wall postings), an average of 34 responses per page. Also, 845 polls had been conducted.

When members create a profile on this platform they are asked to fill out several fields: first and last name and/or company, age, gender, city, relationship status (married, single etc.), professional and educational background, interests and hobbies, personal motto, favourite films, series and music, and 'How do you contribute to Drachten?' None of these fields are mandatory. Users can restrict access to their profile to platform members only, but the majority of profiles is accessible to anyone visiting the platform. When users post information on the platform outside their own profile (e.g., a comment in a discussion, a poll, posting an event), a link to their profile page is used. This way, readers can always find out who is 'behind' the posting.

We randomly chose 100 profiles and stored the following details:

1. **Name:** Did the user supply a full name, nickname, first name, company name, or a combination of one of these?

2. **Picture:** Did the user provide a recognisable profile picture?
3. **Rich or Limited Identity Information:** Did the user provide many details regarding his identity or not? Whether or not information was deemed 'limited' or 'rich' was based on the number of fields filled on the profile page, the amount of words used to fill those fields, and whether or not other personal information was available (pictures, video, Weblogs etc.).
4. **Number of Connections:** How many connections did a user have?
5. **Number of Responses:** How many people have responded to the user's page?

In our sample of 100 profiles, 62% had a full name, while 7% used a full name and a company name. Of these 69 profiles, 20% did not provide a (recognisable) picture; 80% used a profile picture in which they were recognisably depicted. Roughly half of the profiles that use a full name had detailed information on the user's identity; the other half provided only some or very few details.

8% of the profiles used only a first name, or a first name combined with (presumably) the first letter of the last name. A further 4% of users provided a first name together with a company name. Of these users, 75% provided a profile picture, suggesting that choosing only a first name was probably not intended as a means of remaining anonymous. Indeed, over half of these users provide rich identity information on their profile page.

13% of the users offered a nickname instead of their full or first name, and 1% combined a nickname with a company name. Almost half of these users provided a recognisable profile picture. Again, remaining anonymous cannot have been an important motivation here.

Finally, 5% of the pages in our sample was owned by a company, without an individual's name or photo. We discarded these from the data set, and then analysed the remaining 95 profiles for their identity information and interaction levels.

Following our hypothesis that more identity information on a profile triggers more responses from others, we expected that DWJM users with more identity information have more connections and more responses on their profile page. This hypothesis was confirmed. When we grouped together our 95 users into three groups, there were:

- 28 users with a relatively low level of identity information (i.e., no identity information at all, or a first name or nickname with a photo but an information-poor profile, or a last name but no photo and an information-poor profile);
- 28 users with a medium level of identity information (i.e., a last name and a photo but an information-poor profile, or a first or last name and an information-rich profile but no photo);
- 39 users with a high level of identity information (i.e., a last name, a photo, and an information-rich profile).

We grouped the number of connections into three groups: few (0-5), intermediate (6-15) and many (16-384). We also grouped the number of reactions into three more or less equally sized groups: no reaction, some reactions (1-10) and many reactions (more than 11).

A chi-square test revealed a relation between users' level of identity information and the number of connections they have, with people providing much identity information having many connections ($\chi^2=25.4$, $df=4$, $p<=.001$). In addition, people with a low level of identity information have significantly fewer reactions than people providing intermediate or high levels of identity information ($\chi^2=20.7$, $df=4$, $p<=.001$). These results are presented in Table 3.

Table 3. Correlation between level of identity information in profile and interaction level on DWJM

ID Info Interaction	Low	Middle	High	Total
Low 0-5 Connections 0 Reactions	21 17	9 5	6 5	36 27
Middle 6-15 Connections 1-10 Reactions	4 6	8 14	14 19	26 39
High 16-384 Connections 11-1363 Reactions	3 5	11 9	19 15	33 29
Total	28	28	39	95

2.5 Qualitative Study of Two Initiatives

Since the quantitative study only measured the number of discussions, reactions and connections as an indicator of the interaction level of government 2.0 Websites, but not the content or quality of the reactions, we also conducted a qualitative study. We selected two Websites from the e-Participation Dashboard, one in the legislative and one in the executive branches of government, that had a substantial amount of interaction, clear visibility of government representatives participating, and sufficient variation in identity information.

2.5.1 Case 1: Praat met de Raad! (Wageningen)

For the legislative branch, we studied the initiative 'Praat met de Raad!' ('Talk with the council!') of Wageningen municipality, a small-to-medium-sized town in the Netherlands best known for its life sciences university. 'Talk with the council!' is part of the municipality Website, where nine of the 25 council members keep a blog.[10] Some council members have only a few postings, while others keep a more active blog. The public can respond to blog postings, and the council members and others can respond to the reactions in turn. We analysed the blog postings of all members in the past two years (June 2009 through June 2011) that had at least four reactions (to ensure sufficient variety in discussants' identity information), which yielded around 35 interactions in total.[11]

The blog functions partly as a discussion platform with citizens, but partly also as a platform for political discussions among council members and political parties themselves; regularly, council members respond to and engage in discussions regarding each others' blogs. Citizens also engage in discussions among themselves besides having discussions with, and sometimes requesting information from, council members. Judging from the discussions we read, the blog can be considered a success: there is lively interaction between council members and the public, with many discussions on the content of municipal policy issues. Discussants also refer to how parties in the council voted on certain issues, and citizens sometimes refer to upcoming elections – a sign that the discussions on the blog are taken seriously politically by both council members and the public.

Most citizens tend to use their first name, some also use their last name; only a few use a nickname. Often, we encountered the same people in the discussions, which creates the impression of a relatively small community where people tend to know one another, in virtual space if not also in real life. This implies that even citizens who use nicknames, initials, or only first names (such as DulacV, TeVe, and Bastiaan), tend to be familiar to the discussants, even if their real-life identity is not necessarily known.

We found that council members generally tend to respond to citizens regardless of the amount of identity information citizens provide. For example, council member No. 5 responds to both Bolleke (a nickname meaning something like 'small head') and 'un Woageninger' ('a citizen of Wageningen', spelled in dialect) with 'Dear Bolleke' and 'Dear Woageninger'. Also council member No. 6 responds to Bolleke and Guus in a discussion on half-pay for politicians; initially, she does not respond to citizen Guido van V[...] who uses his last name, but later on, she does respond to another comment of his. Council member No. 4 responds both to Henk and to mark van der V[...]. To a positive reaction by 'Wageningse zorgenmaker' ('worrier from Wageningen'), he politely responds with 'Thank you for your trust'. Overall, we could not see differences in the way that council members responded, in terms of elementary criteria for good discussions, whether they responded to citizens using a first name, a first and last name, or a nickname.

An exception is perhaps council member No. 3, who responds mainly to other council members, but often not to citizens' reactions. When he does, it often is to someone using a first and last name, while postings by citizens using only a first name or a nickname, such as Vrije Burger ('Free Citizen'), do not always get a response. An illustrative example is at the end of a long discussion about opening shops on Sundays, where council member No. 3 does not respond to short, well-formulated arguments by Henk and Jacco, while he does respond to a longer but sloppily typed and awkwardly formulated posting by mark van der v[...]. Nevertheless, earlier in this discussion thread the council member did respond to Frans and TeVe, so the pattern is not consistent, and council member No. 3 does not really alter our overall impression.

It was interesting to notice that sometimes the blog discussion focused on anonymous or pseudonymous discussants. When council member No. 8 blogged on diminishing rules for cutting trees, a lively discussion ensued among three discussants, Bastiaan M[...] (VVD) (providing his right-wing political affiliation in brackets), Joris T[...], and 'De Politiek-Geleuter-Vigilant' or PGV ('The Vigilant of Political Piffle'). The latter responded to the former two: 'First of all: I am NOT going to make myself known. Would you have appreciated my opinions differently if I had been called Jacco, Bastiaan, Marc, Jan, Robin, or Joris? Even more so: I think you will listen better to the content of my argument, if you don't know from which angle it comes...' Following a suggestion by 'rpgv' (presumably short for a 'vigilant of right-wing political piffle', or anti-PGV) that 'I think pgv is martin from the cinema', 'De Politiek-Geleuter-Vigilant' called himself 'just an ordinary, hard-working, middle-class citizen paying too much realty tax' while denying he was Martin from the cinema. Subsequently, another politician (associated with but not an official member of the council) invited PGV to come to the council meeting in person to really influence public policy, ending with the challenge: 'A disadvantage for you is that you then lose your anonymity...' Perhaps significantly, council member No. 8 did not enter into this discussion about anonymity between citizens at all.

Another aspect we looked at was whether and how discussants refer to their roles. Obviously, the council members publish blog posts in their function as council members, but in subsequent discussions, and in their reactions on other members' blogs, it need not always be clear whether they provide a private opinion, a personal political opinion, or a party opinion. We did not see explicit or even implicit references to the roles of government participants, nor instances where private and political opinions are explicitly separated. Only one council member, No. 5, states at one point that 'Personally, I support the second variant', but the use of 'personally' seems to be used here more for rhetorical emphasis than as a flag for distinguishing personal from professional or political opinions. Similarly, citizens provide few references to their roles, although they sometimes provide information about their profession or background when it is relevant for the discussion. One citizen, Sander-Jan, positions himself in a discussion with the statement 'I am an academic, not a politician', which also has more of a rhetorical than a role-identifying function.

From this government 2.0 initiative, it can be concluded that, although identity information is being discussed by participants in relation to pseudonymous postings, with a substantial part of discussants expecting people to provide their real names (at least a first name), identity information does not have a significant effect on the level or quality of discussions. Council members and other citizens generally respond to postings in similar ways regardless whether a citizen provides a first name, a first and last name, or a nickname. Role information is absent in the discussions; council members do not use any signposts as to whether they voice private, political, or party positions.

2.5.2 Case 2: Drachtenwiljemeemaken

For the executive branch, we analysed a local discussion platform called 'Drachtenwiljemeemaken',[12] a Web 2.0 platform that was initiated by the local government of Smallingerland, a municipality in the Netherlands of which Drachten, with 45,000 inhabitants, is the major town. The platform name is well chosen: in translation it can mean either 'You want to co-create Drachten', 'You want to be a part of Drachten', 'You want to experience Drachten', or even 'Drachten wants to be a part of you'. Drachtenwiljemeemaken (or DWJM for short) was launched in March 2009 as part of a citywide campaign to involve citizens in local politics and governance and to strengthen social cohesion. The leading slogan was 'Wat doe jij eigenlijk voor Drachten?' ('How are you actually contributing to Drachten?').

DWJM has a number of features that facilitate interaction between citizens, similar to those of social network sites such as Hyves and Facebook. Individuals can create a profile page, on which they can present themselves to others (using text, images, video, Weblogs etc.), and through which they can connect with others ('friending'). At the same time, local government uses this platform as a means to inform the public of many topics relating to the city, and to respond to citizens' questions or comments. Finally, the platform incorporates polling features: platform members can create polls on topics they find interesting and important, and others can respond. Only part of these polls are related to municipal issues, but obviously this functionality may be an important source of information to local government as an easy and direct way to discover what 'moves' Drachten citizens.

A quantitative analysis of the interaction on user profiles on DWJM has been discussed above in section 2.4. For our qualitative analysis of the relationship between identity information and interaction level on DWJM, the following procedure was followed:

1. We began by loosely surfing the network to get an overview of its functionality, activities and key players. Data were stored in a document of notes, including snapshots of user profiles, and highlights from conversations. We searched the platform using specific keywords, such as 'identity', 'anonymity' and 'local government'. Findings again were stored in notes.
2. We began a draft of hypotheses on the basis of these first surfing sessions, and formulated tentative overall findings, which were to be validated in the next step of the research.
3. In the second round of research, which was informed by the hypotheses we had formu-

lated, we looked more closely at the content of a selection of the data stored in the first round, focusing especially on government-citizen interactions on profile pages and in polls.

Before presenting the findings, it is important to make two remarks. First, among DWJM members, a relatively small set are very active, responding to (each) other's blog posts, contributing to discussions, initiating and filling out polls, posting events, and adding comments to other's profile pages. In many cases it is obvious that members also know these individuals in real life. Many are citizens in 'visible' positions and apparently well-known in the community, e.g., the presenter of a local radio show, a political activist, and a welfare worker.

Second, related to the first point, a complicating issue is the fact that platform members share an important offline characteristic, viz. their geographical location. This may imply that providing less identifying information (e.g., no profile picture, only a first name) does not necessarily mean that the person is not known. As we conducted the analysis, we noticed that for some individuals DWJM replicates their offline visibility and connectedness, rather than generating a new space for connection.

DWJM as an Information Channel for Local Government

DWJM is more than a social network site for citizens alone. It was initiated and developed by local government, and as such is also used as a channel for government/city information by local government. The 'news' section of the platform is used for this purpose. Here, one can find information on renovation plans for the city centre, traffic issues, the local government's budget plans, and cultural issues. Each news item has a possibility to leave feedback or ask questions, and several items indeed invoked some, or sometimes quite a few, citizen responses. Interestingly, sometimes citizens also respond to each other's comments, and the government's officials sometimes also join the discussion. This results in a real discussion of the government's plans and ideas. But DWJM is more than merely a news channel *from* government *to* citizens. The polling functionality, which enables any platform member to poll all other members on any topic, provides local government with another source about what citizens find important and interesting. Many polls are unrelated to city/governance/political matters (e.g., 'Who will win X factor?', 'Should pictures of the dead Osama bin Laden be released to the public?', 'Is Job Cohen [the former social-democrat leader] the right man to lead his party?'), but a significant number also relate to local policy, e.g., annoyance over dog poo in the streets, whether organising festivals improves city life, a smoking ban at bus stops, or whether Drachten is a city or a village. Interestingly, the three polls with most responses all deal with topics regarding municipal life: 'which supermarket in Drachten is the best?', 'what is Drachten's nicest area?' and 'who will you vote for in the local elections?'

DWJM as a Means of Communication between Citizens and Local Government

Local government uses a functional profile page to interact with citizens, under the name 'Gemeente Smallingerland', which is used by the municipality's communication department. Sometimes, when citizens raise a question or express an opinion on government issues, the government enters the discussion to provide an answer. For example, in a blog post someone called Anton P[...] asks a question about a decision made by the city council regarding a fund for the local shop-holder organisation. The communications department responds by providing the council-meeting minutes with the argumentation for the decision. Anton P[...] says he is grateful for the information.

From the postings we studied, citizens do not seem to care that the government uses a functional profile, instead of civil servants' profiles with real names, when responding to their questions or suggestions. Since the functional profile page has the municipality's logo as its profile picture, it is always clear to users that a representative of the government is speaking in their professional role. We found no negative responses in this respect to the use of a 'pseudonymous' government profile.

The fact that government officials separate their roles in this way – using the functional municipality profile when speaking on behalf of the government and personal profiles when speaking in a personal capacity – may not be sufficient, however. As we were scanning the discussions on this platform, we came across a blog post by a man named 'Paul' who works for the communications department of the municipality, and who, in this role, had responded to many citizen suggestions, comments and questions using the municipality's function profile. He had, however, also used a personal profile to participate in DWJM to communicate his personal interests and opinions. In this blog post, Paul writes that he will end his personal account on DWJM:

recently, I increasingly note that I cannot say something on DWJM as a person. There are individuals who always interpret my opinions as those of the communications department of the municipality, the organisation that initiated this site. And this happens especially whenever I criticise the dominant point of view in discussions. This makes me vulnerable. Too vulnerable I'm afraid. This saddens me deeply: after all, DWJM was kind of my baby. But children grow up and find their own way. This is the natural course of things. [authors' translation]

This blog post reveals that for the public, it is apparently difficult to separate the two roles of a civil servant on this platform, despite the fact that this user has a separate personal profile page and a professional profile page (i.e., the 'Gemeente Smallingerland' profile). It seems that citizens tend to ascribe an official status also to statements by civil servants who participate in a government 2.0 platform with a personal account.

We need to add, however, that two weeks after this blog post, this same user created a new profile on the platform, under the name of Paul L[...], blogging why he was back:

It's simple: I don't want to be silenced. It just happens that I have an opinion about all kinds of things and can hardly keep that to myself. So I will again participate in discussions with some frequency. Just to be clear: my contributions to this Website are personal. They are the opinions, ideas, misconceptions, big talk and silly jokes of the person Paul L[...]. The official Paul L[...] will respond on this Website from the account 'communication' [i.e., the municipality's account].

Although the confusion of roles may therefore not have been as dramatic as Paul's leaving the platform initially suggested, it still provides an interesting illustration of the difficulty of separating roles for public officials.

3 DISCUSSION

Before we discuss our findings about identity information and interaction, we can make a general observation about government 2.0. In our research, we looked at almost a third of over 600 initiatives listed on the eParticipation Dashboard, a Website that says it provides 'a current overview of all eParticipation initiatives in the Netherlands. eParticipation denotes the use of ICT to involve citizens more in the improvement of public service, public administration, and social cohesion.'[13] Many of these initiatives, however, are not (inter) active. Almost three quarters of our sample of 197 initiatives was one-way traffic (e.g., a municipality's or ministry's YouTube channel, or a Website requesting citizens to send in ideas but without displaying the contributions), was a still-born initiative with no activity, or had been used only for a brief, often pilot, period but was no longer active. Government 2.0 is not necessarily booming, at least in the sense of Web 2.0 applications that effectively enhance the interaction – which implies bidirectional exchanges – among government and citizens. This underlines the necessity of researching what makes government 2.0 initiatives a success or a failure. Is identity information or role confusion perhaps an inhibiting factor for government 2.0 to have successful interaction?

3.1 Identity Information

We started our research with a twofold hypothesis on the relationship between identity information and interaction on government 2.0 applications. One the one hand, having more identity knowledge of counter-parties will enhance people's participation in government 2.0, but on the other, having to provide identity knowledge to counter-parties risks diminishing people's participation in a context where risks to privacy arise.

The indicative results of our survey are in line with this hypothesis, in the sense that a majority of Web 2.0 users say they think it important to know the (real) name of discussion participants. People who say they find it important to know who other Web 2.0 participants are, are also more willing to provide personal information about themselves. This also applies the other way around: people who do not attach importance to knowing the identity of others, are also more hesitant to provide information about themselves. This could suggest that rather than an identity paradox (providing identity information on Web 2.0 is a two-edged sword), there are two types of Web 2.0 users: there is a group who find identity information important (both to know and to provide), and a group who find identity information unimportant (to know and to provide).

When we look at our empirical results, it is hard to find evidence of the link between identity information and the level of interaction on government 2.0 initiatives that we hypothesised. We conducted five interrelated studies to answer the research question, three quantitative and two qualitative. In four of these five studies, we found no correlation between the amount of identity information of users and the level of interaction. Platforms asking users to fill in much identity information do not have more or less profiles than platforms asking users only to provide their name; nor is there a difference in the number of discussions taking place on these platforms. This suggests that having to provide much identity information about oneself is not an inhibiting factor to participating in government 2.0.

A posting does not receive more or less reactions depending on whether the person initiating the discussion uses a last name or only a first name or a nickname, nor whether she uses a clear face picture or a fake picture. We found only a weak correlation (significant at a level of $p<.1$) between the degree of personal information and the number of reactions, with people providing much personal information receiving somewhat more reactions. In terms of the quality of interaction (i.e., does a contribution to the discussion make sense in itself, does it address the topic of discussion, and does it argue on the basis of content arguments instead of ad hominem arguments?) we could not find a difference in the Wageningen or Drachten discussions in terms of whether citizens provide much or little identity information. Representatives from the government seem to respond in a similar manner to citizens using pseudonyms or first names as they do to citizens using their full name.

In contrast to these results, however, the profile pages on Drachtenwiljemeemaken do show a very strong correlation between the level of identity information users provide in their profile and the number of connections they have as well as the number of reactions they get on their profile page.

How should we explain the difference in these partial findings? If we look closely at what we measured in each study, we conclude that the DWJM case concerned *profile pages* whereas the other studies looked at discussions taking place at *discussion platforms*. These are different functions of government 2.0 applications. The DWJM profile pages function like a social-networking site such as Facebook, allowing people to make online friends and to chat on each others' pages, thus strengthening the cohesion among the online community. This differs from discussions taking place on a platform 'in public', which is the case with the Hyves discussion groups and the Wageningen blog. Indeed, on the parts of DWJM where the citizens and municipality interact, we did not find substantial differences in the way that people responded to contributions.

Therefore, we conclude that overall our empirical research showed no correlation between identity information and interaction level in government 2.0 discussions. How should we interpret this finding, in light of our hypothesis and our survey's suggestion that a majority of people find it important to know other participants' identities? One explanation could be that we studied small communities, in which people often also interact offline. The people most active on the Wageningen and Drachten sites are rather likely to know each other offline, and hence, only a small amount of identity information – even only a first name – could be sufficient to identify people and establish sufficient trust to interact online. However, in our quickscan of 54 initiatives and in our study of discussions on 20 initiatives, many platforms were not local communities but topic-based communities at a national level. On such platforms, it is unlikely that little identity information is sufficient for other users to establish someone's offline identity, and hence users can only go by the identity information provided online to know 'who someone is'. Given that 48% of discussion initiators, in our study of 502 discussion lines, used little or no identity information, and yet received overall not significantly fewer reactions than people providing average or much identity information (at least not at a significance level of $p<.05$), we do not think that small communities having offline interactions as well as online ones can entirely explain the fact that we found no overall correlation between identity and interaction.

Taking into account the variety of sources we studied and the fact that both our quantitative and our qualitative analysis revealed no significant correlation between identity information and interaction levels on discussion forums (hence leaving aside the social networking taking place on profile pages) in government 2.0 initiatives, the conclusion is warranted that we have to reject our hypothesis. Knowing more identity information about other participants does not lead to more interaction in government 2.0, nor is the provision of identity information of oneself an inhibiting factor to participate in government 2.0. Apparently, people care less for identity information in government 2.0 than the literature suggests, at least in terms of willingness to participate in online interactions.

3.2 Role Information

The second part of our research interest was role information in government 2.0. How important is it for civil servants to make explicit in which role – as an official or as a private person – they make specific contributions in government 2.0 discussions? Does confusion about roles impact negatively on the interaction in government 2.0? While our survey was small-scale and not representative, the outcome is very strong, with 54% totally agreeing and 38% agreeing that civil servants' role should be explicitated. Hence, we feel safe to conclude that both citizens and civil servants participating in government 2.0 discussions consider it important that civil servants clarify whether they speak in a personal or in an official capacity.

It was difficult to test empirically the influence of (a lack of) role explicitation on the interaction level in government 2.0 initiatives. On most sites we studied, it was hard to recognise government representatives among the participants in discussions; either they hardly participated in discussions, or they did not participate visibly in an official capacity. On some Websites, such as the Wageningen blog, it was very clear who were the officials, as the council members blogged in their capacity as a council member. Sometimes, their contributions seemed to have a more personal rather than an official touch, although most often the discussions were professional in nature. They never used signposts as to whether they voiced private, political, or party positions, and we found no indication that this confused citizens or inhibited the level of interaction. The Drachten case was an interesting illustration of a clear role specification, as civil servants speaking in an official capacity used a functional profile of the municipality, while they used personal profiles when speaking in a private capacity. Perhaps surprisingly, there was still confusion, since a civil servant felt he was unjustly being seen by citizens as voicing official statements when he used his personal profile, leading him to – temporarily – withdraw his personal profile from the community. This could suggest that more role explicitation is needed than simply using two different profiles, perhaps by interspersing personal opinions, particularly when they concern controversial subjects, with clear signposts ("this is my personal opinion") in each contribution. However, we encountered hardly any such signposts anywhere in our research, while we also did not find any other suggestion that lack of role specification led to confusion or inhibited the interaction between government and citizens.

We therefore conclude that role specification, although it is perceived as a very important element of government 2.0, does not seem to be a real issue (yet) in practice. Perhaps this is because it is by and large clear to participants from the context whether or not someone is speaking in an official capacity.

4 IMPLICATIONS AND FUTURE RESEARCH DIRECTIONS

Our study was one of the first to research empirically the role of identity information in government 2.0 initiatives. Follow-up research could refine our quantitative study by looking at more dimensions than just the number of discussions or reactions to a posting. It would also be interesting to compare our findings with studies of government 2.0 in other countries. What could also be expanded in further research is which types of identity information are most important to ask from users; our survey suggests that first name, last name, employer, profession and perhaps a photo are the most relevant types. It would be interesting to research whether differences exist in desirable types of identity information for different user groups, in different countries, or in different types of government 2.0 platforms. Finally, the importance of role specification by government representatives participating in government 2.0 discussions is an urgent topic. While government 2.0 users seem to find it highly important that roles are explicitated, we did not see many examples of role demarcations in practice, nor of a possible confusion or a worse interaction because of the lack of role demarcation in contributions. This begs for further research to be conducted on how important role specification actually is in government 2.0, and what this implies for the way that government representatives could contribute to what many see as an important contribution of Web 2.0 to governance: increasing the interaction of government and citizens by using the new tools that social media are bringing us.

5 CONCLUSION

In this paper, we studied the relationship between identity information and interaction in government 2.0, hypothesising that people will want to have sufficient identity information of other users in order to participate, while they will be hesitant to provide much identity information of themselves in contexts – including government 2.0 platforms – where risks to privacy arise. This aligns with Marx's conception of circles of identity information, ranging from individual to truly identifying information. Based on our quantitative and qualitative empirical studies we reject this hypothesis. Knowing more identity information about other participants does not lead to more interaction in government 2.0, nor is having to provide identity information of oneself an inhibiting factor to participate in government 2.0.

What does this finding imply for the design of government 2.0 initiatives? We suggest that developers of government 2.0 platforms should not make it mandatory for participants to provide much identity information – just a name, and allowing the option of using a pseudonym – could suffice to trigger discussions. Such systems would rely on Marx's outermost circle of individual information to provide a minimum basis for numerical identity in the user group. At the same time, since many users are willing to provide information about themselves – understandable in light of individuals' striving for narrative identity – and such information is appreciated by others, developers would do well to include an optional possibility for users to provide more identity information than just their name, such as their employer, profession, and a photo, adopting Marx's middle circles of identity information. If discussion platforms in government 2.0 are combined with a social, community-building function – which will often be the case in multifunctional initiatives such as local government platforms – incorporating information-rich user profiles – still on a voluntary basis – seems a good idea, as the success of Drachtenwiljemeemaken suggests. Having an option for users to provide a wider range of identity information (closer to the inner circles of identity information, allowing users to express their narrative identities), while also allowing users to participate anonymously or on a first-name basis only, is a good way to cater for the two distinct groups that we encountered in our survey: those who find identity information important (both to know and to provide), and those who find identity information unimportant (to know and to provide).

ACKNOWLEDGMENT

This research was co-funded by the Alliantie Vitaal Bestuur (AVB), a partnership between several Dutch ministries and research institutes. The AVB provided helpful suggestions to broaden the research scope with a discussion of roles of public servants. The authors thank the AVB for their financial support.

We thank Laura Klaming for her assistance with data collection and analysis. We also thank Albert Verheij for his comments on an earlier version of this paper.

REFERENCES

Birza, L., Frank, P., & Klok, H. (2010). *Uitgangspunten online communicatie rijksambtenaren*. Den Haag: Ministerie van Algemene Zaken.

Cabinet Office. (2008). *Participation online: Guidance for civil servants*. London: UK Cabinet Office.

Cofta, P. (2007). Confidence, trust and identity. *BP Technology Journal*, *25*(2), 173–178. doi:10.1007/s10550-007-0042-4

Goffman, E. (1959). *The presentation of self in everyday life*. Garden City, NY: Doubleday.

Haenni, R., Jaquet-Chiffelle, D.-O., Anrig, B., & Benoist, E. (2009). Core concepts and definitions. In D.-O. Jaquet-Chiffelle, & H. Buitelaar (Eds.), *D17.4: Trust and identification in the light of virtual persons* (pp. 38–58). FIDIS Deliverable.

Marx, G. T. (2006). Varieties of personal information as influences on attitudes towards surveillance. In K. D. Haggerty, & R. V. Ericson (Eds.), *The new politics of surveillance and visibility* (pp. 79–110). Toronto: University of Toronto Press.

Meijer, A. J., Koops, B.-J., Pieterson, W., Overman, S., & Ten Tije, S. (2012). Government 2.0: Key challenges to its realization. *Electronic. Journal of E-Government*, *10*(1), 59–69.

Nissenbaum, H. (2010). *Privacy in context*. Stanford, CA: Stanford Law Books.

Parfit, D. (1984). *Reasons and persons*. Oxford, UK: Clarendon Press.

Pettit, P. (2004). Trust, reliance and the internet. *Analyse & Kritik*, *26*, 108–121.

Pfitzmann, A., & Hansen, M. (2010). *A terminology for talking about privacy by data minimization: Anonymity, unlinkability, undetectability, unobservability, pseudonymity, and identity management, version 0.33*. Academic Press.

Ricœur, P. (1992). *Oneself as another*. Chicago: University of Chicago Press.

Van den Berg, B., & Leenes, R. (2011). Keeping up appearances: Audience segregation in social network sites. In S. Gutwirth, Y. Poullet, P. De Hert, & R. Leenes (Eds.), *Computers, privacy and data protection: An element of choice* (pp. 211–233). Dordrecht, The Netherlands: Springer. doi:10.1007/978-94-007-0641-5_10

Vedder, A., & Wachbroit, R. (2003). Reliability of information on the internet: Some distinctions. *Ethics and Information Technology*, *5*, 211–215. doi:10.1023/B:ETIN.0000017738.60896.77

Wenzel, J. W. (1992). Perspectives on argument. In W. L. Benoit, D. Hample, & P. J. Benoit (Eds.), *Readings in argumentation* (pp. 121–145). Berlin: Walter de Gruyter & Co. doi:10.1515/9783110885651.121

KEY TERMS AND DEFINITIONS

Government 2.0: Government 2.0 can be seen as the use of Web 2.0 by governments to facilitate government-citizen interactions.

Identity Information: Identity information allows users to express their narrative identities while also allowing users to participate anonymously or on a first-name basis only.

Privacy: Privacy includes considerations as to the amount of personal data disclosed and processed under Data Protection Laws, including which should be kept to the minimum of what is necessary for the purpose at hand.

Social Media: Social media is where the traditional social contexts blur, as individuals always play roles in social life (e.g., husband, employee, fire brigade volunteer, clarinet player, etc.) thus presenting themselves to their audiences in different ways.

Web 2.0: Web 2.0 can be used to facilitate and improve government-citizen interactions.

ENDNOTES

1 http://eparticipatiemonitor.bendeburgers.nl/ (last accessed 2 May 2014).

2 A similar result was found for civil servants who frequently use Web 2.0 to discuss public policy or services with citizens, but since 2 cells had an expected count less than 5, no valid conclusions can be drawn about this.

3 Currently available at http://eparticipatiemonitor.bendeburgers.nl/ (last accessed 2 May 2014). At the time of research (2011), the eParticipation Dashboard was located at http://eparticipatiedashboard.burgerlink.nl/.

4 Some initiatives were related to more sectors.

5 There is some overlap between these categories, as some people combine a real-looking first name with a nickname, e.g., "Ron fruitcake."

6 172 people provided both 'false' information and 'real' information, e.g. a nickname and a personal picture.

7 1 cell had an expected count less than 5, so no valid conclusions can be drawn on the basis of this result.

8 http://www.drachtenwiljemeemaken.nl (llast accessed 2 May 2014).

9 http://nl.wikipedia.org/wiki/Drachten (last accessed 2 May 2014).

10 http://Weblog.wageningen.nl/ (last accessed 2 May 2014).

11 We present our findings mentioning the names of citizens as used on the blog, but abbreviated their last names for privacy reasons. The postings are in Dutch, which have been translated by us.

12 http://www.drachtenwiljemeemaken.nl (last accessed 2 May 2014).

13 http://tinyurl.com/oosyhy3 (our translation) (last accessed 2 May 2014).

Related References

To continue our tradition of advancing information science and technology research, we have compiled a list of recommended IGI Global readings. These references will provide additional information and guidance to further enrich your knowledge and assist you with your own research and future publications.

Adeyemo, O. (2013). The nationwide health information network: A biometric approach to prevent medical identity theft. In I. Management Association (Ed.), User-driven healthcare: Concepts, methodologies, tools, and applications (pp. 1636-1649). Hershey, PA: Medical Information Science Reference. doi: doi:10.4018/978-1-4666-2770-3.ch081

Adler, M., & Henman, P. (2009). Justice beyond the courts: The implications of computerisation for procedural justice in social security. In A. Martínez, & P. Abat (Eds.), *E-justice: Using information communication technologies in the court system* (pp. 65–86). Hershey, PA: Information Science Reference.

Aflalo, E., & Gabay, E. (2013). An information system for coping with student dropout. In L. Tomei (Ed.), *Learning tools and teaching approaches through ICT advancements* (pp. 176–187). Hershey, PA: Information Science Reference.

Ahmed, M. A., Janssen, M., & van den Hoven, J. (2012). Value sensitive transfer (VST) of systems among countries: Towards a framework. *International Journal of Electronic Government Research, 8*(1), 26–42. doi:10.4018/jegr.2012010102

Aikins, S. K. (2008). Issues and trends in internet-based citizen participation. In G. Garson, & M. Khosrow-Pour (Eds.), *Handbook of research on public information technology* (pp. 31–40). Hershey, PA: Information Science Reference. doi:10.4018/978-1-59904-857-4.ch004

Aikins, S. K. (2009). A comparative study of municipal adoption of internet-based citizen participation. In C. Reddick (Ed.), *Handbook of research on strategies for local e-government adoption and implementation: Comparative studies* (pp. 206–230). Hershey, PA: Information Science Reference. doi:10.4018/978-1-60566-282-4.ch011

Aikins, S. K. (2012). Improving e-government project management: Best practices and critical success factors. In I. Management Association (Ed.), Digital democracy: Concepts, methodologies, tools, and applications (pp. 1314-1332). Hershey, PA: Information Science Reference. doi: doi:10.4018/978-1-4666-1740-7.ch065

Akabawi, M. S. (2011). Ghabbour group ERP deployment: Learning from past technology failures. In E. Business Research and Case Center (Ed.), Cases on business and management in the MENA region: New trends and opportunities (pp. 177-203). Hershey, PA: Business Science Reference. doi: doi:10.4018/978-1-60960-583-4.ch012

Akabawi, M. S. (2013). Ghabbour group ERP deployment: Learning from past technology failures. In I. Management Association (Ed.), Industrial engineering: Concepts, methodologies, tools, and applications (pp. 933-958). Hershey, PA: Engineering Science Reference. doi: doi:10.4018/978-1-4666-1945-6.ch051

Akbulut, A. Y., & Motwani, J. (2008). Integration and information sharing in e-government. In G. Putnik, & M. Cruz-Cunha (Eds.), *Encyclopedia of networked and virtual organizations* (pp. 729–734). Hershey, PA: Information Science Reference. doi:10.4018/978-1-59904-885-7.ch096

Akers, E. J. (2008). Technology diffusion in public administration. In G. Garson, & M. Khosrow-Pour (Eds.), *Handbook of research on public information technology* (pp. 339–348). Hershey, PA: Information Science Reference. doi:10.4018/978-1-59904-857-4.ch033

Al-Shafi, S. (2008). Free wireless internet park services: An investigation of technology adoption in Qatar from a citizens' perspective. *Journal of Cases on Information Technology, 10*(3), 21–34. doi:10.4018/jcit.2008070103

Al-Shafi, S., & Weerakkody, V. (2009). Implementing free wi-fi in public parks: An empirical study in Qatar. *International Journal of Electronic Government Research, 5*(3), 21–35. doi:10.4018/jegr.2009070102

Aladwani, A. M. (2002). Organizational actions, computer attitudes and end-user satisfaction in public organizations: An empirical study. In C. Snodgrass, & E. Szewczak (Eds.), *Human factors in information systems* (pp. 153–168). Hershey, PA: IRM Press. doi:10.4018/joeuc.2002010104

Aladwani, A. M. (2002). Organizational actions, computer attitudes, and end-user satisfaction in public organizations: An empirical study. *Journal of Organizational and End User Computing, 14*(1), 42–49. doi:10.4018/joeuc.2002010104

Allen, B., Juillet, L., Paquet, G., & Roy, J. (2005). E-government and private-public partnerships: Relational challenges and strategic directions. In M. Khosrow-Pour (Ed.), *Practicing e-government: A global perspective* (pp. 364–382). Hershey, PA: Idea Group Publishing. doi:10.4018/978-1-59140-637-2.ch016

Alshawaf, A., & Knalil, O. E. (2008). IS success factors and IS organizational impact: Does ownership type matter in Kuwait? *International Journal of Enterprise Information Systems, 4*(2), 13–33. doi:10.4018/jeis.2008040102

Ambali, A. R. (2009). Digital divide and its implication on Malaysian e-government: Policy initiatives. In H. Rahman (Ed.), *Social and political implications of data mining: Knowledge management in e-government* (pp. 267–287). Hershey, PA: Information Science Reference. doi:10.4018/978-1-60566-230-5.ch016

Amoretti, F. (2007). Digital international governance. In A. Anttiroiko, & M. Malkia (Eds.), *Encyclopedia of digital government* (pp. 365–370). Hershey, PA: Information Science Reference.

Amoretti, F. (2008). Digital international governance. In A. Anttiroiko (Ed.), *Electronic government: Concepts, methodologies, tools, and applications* (pp. 688–696). Hershey, PA: Information Science Reference. doi:10.4018/978-1-59904-947-2.ch058

Amoretti, F. (2008). E-government at supranational level in the European Union. In A. Anttiroiko (Ed.), *Electronic government: Concepts, methodologies, tools, and applications* (pp. 1047–1055). Hershey, PA: Information Science Reference. doi:10.4018/978-1-59904-947-2.ch079

Amoretti, F. (2008). E-government regimes. In A. Anttiroiko (Ed.), *Electronic government: Concepts, methodologies, tools, and applications* (pp. 3846–3856). Hershey, PA: Information Science Reference. doi:10.4018/978-1-59904-947-2.ch280

Amoretti, F. (2009). Electronic constitution: A Braudelian perspective. In F. Amoretti (Ed.), *Electronic constitution: Social, cultural, and political implications* (pp. 1–19). Hershey, PA: Information Science Reference. doi:10.4018/978-1-60566-254-1.ch001

Amoretti, F., & Musella, F. (2009). Institutional isomorphism and new technologies. In M. Khosrow-Pour (Ed.), *Encyclopedia of information science and technology* (2nd ed., pp. 2066–2071). Hershey, PA: Information Science Reference.

Andersen, K. V., & Henriksen, H. Z. (2007). E-government research: Capabilities, interaction, orientation, and values. In D. Norris (Ed.), *Current issues and trends in e-government research* (pp. 269–288). Hershey, PA: CyberTech Publishing. doi:10.4018/978-1-59904-283-1.ch013

Anderson, K. V., & Henriksen, H. Z. (2005). The first leg of e-government research: domains and application areas 1998-2003. *International Journal of Electronic Government Research, 1*(4), 26–44. doi:10.4018/jegr.2005100102

Anttiroiko, A. (2009). Democratic e-governance. In M. Khosrow-Pour (Ed.), *Encyclopedia of information science and technology* (2nd ed., pp. 990–995). Hershey, PA: Information Science Reference.

Association, I. R. (2010). *Networking and telecommunications: Concepts, methodologies, tools and applications*. Hershey, PA: IGI Global. doi:10.4018/978-1-60566-986-1

Association, I. R. (2010). *Web-based education: Concepts, methodologies, tools and applications*. Hershey, PA: IGI Global. doi:10.4018/978-1-61520-963-7

Baker, P. M., Bell, A., & Moon, N. W. (2009). Accessibility issues in municipal wireless networks. In C. Reddick (Ed.), *Handbook of research on strategies for local e-government adoption and implementation: Comparative studies* (pp. 569–588). Hershey, PA: Information Science Reference. doi:10.4018/978-1-60566-282-4.ch030

Becker, S. A., Keimer, R., & Muth, T. (2010). A case on university and community collaboration: The sci-tech entrepreneurial training services (ETS) program. In S. Becker, & R. Niebuhr (Eds.), *Cases on technology innovation: Entrepreneurial successes and pitfalls* (pp. 68–90). Hershey, PA: Business Science Reference. doi:10.4018/978-1-61520-609-4.ch003

Becker, S. A., Keimer, R., & Muth, T. (2012). A case on university and community collaboration: The sci-tech entrepreneurial training services (ETS) program. In I. Management Association (Ed.), Regional development: Concepts, methodologies, tools, and applications (pp. 947-969). Hershey, PA: Information Science Reference. doi: doi:10.4018/978-1-4666-0882-5.ch507

Bernardi, R. (2012). Information technology and resistance to public sector reforms: A case study in Kenya. In T. Papadopoulos, & P. Kanellis (Eds.), *Public sector reform using information technologies: Transforming policy into practice* (pp. 59–78). Hershey, PA: Information Science Reference.

Bernardi, R. (2013). Information technology and resistance to public sector reforms: A case study in Kenya. In I. Management Association (Ed.), User-driven healthcare: Concepts, methodologies, tools, and applications (pp. 14-33). Hershey, PA: Medical Information Science Reference. doi: doi:10.4018/978-1-4666-2770-3.ch002

Bolívar, M. P., Pérez, M. D., & Hernández, A. M. (2012). Municipal e-government services in emerging economies: The Latin-American and Caribbean experiences. In Y. Chen, & P. Chu (Eds.), *Electronic governance and cross-boundary collaboration: Innovations and advancing tools* (pp. 198–226). Hershey, PA: Information Science Reference. doi:10.4018/978-1-4666-1740-7.ch025

Borycki, E. M., & Kushniruk, A. W. (2010). Use of clinical simulations to evaluate the impact of health information systems and ubiquitous computing devices upon health professional work. In S. Mohammed, & J. Fiaidhi (Eds.), *Ubiquitous health and medical informatics: The ubiquity 2.0 trend and beyond* (pp. 552–573). Hershey, PA: Medical Information Science Reference. doi:10.4018/978-1-61520-777-0.ch026

Borycki, E. M., & Kushniruk, A. W. (2011). Use of clinical simulations to evaluate the impact of health information systems and ubiquitous computing devices upon health professional work. In I. Management Association (Ed.), Clinical technologies: Concepts, methodologies, tools and applications (pp. 532-553). Hershey, PA: Medical Information Science Reference. doi: doi:10.4018/978-1-60960-561-2.ch220

Buchan, J. (2011). Developing a dynamic and responsive online learning environment: A case study of a large Australian university. In B. Czerkawski (Ed.), *Free and open source software for e-learning: Issues, successes and challenges* (pp. 92–109). Hershey, PA: Information Science Reference.

Buenger, A. W. (2008). Digital convergence and cybersecurity policy. In G. Garson, & M. Khosrow-Pour (Eds.), *Handbook of research on public information technology* (pp. 395–405). Hershey, PA: Information Science Reference. doi:10.4018/978-1-59904-857-4.ch038

Burn, J. M., & Loch, K. D. (2002). The societal impact of world wide web - Key challenges for the 21st century. In A. Salehnia (Ed.), *Ethical issues of information systems* (pp. 88–106). Hershey, PA: IRM Press. doi:10.4018/978-1-59140-062-2.ch002

Burn, J. M., & Loch, K. D. (2003). The societal impact of the world wide web-Key challenges for the 21st century. In M. Khosrow-Pour (Ed.), *Advanced topics in information resources management* (Vol. 2, pp. 32–51). Hershey, PA: Idea Group Publishing. doi:10.4018/978-1-59140-062-2.ch002

Bwalya, K. J., Du Plessis, T., & Rensleigh, C. (2012). The "quicksilver initiatives" as a framework for e-government strategy design in developing economies. In K. Bwalya, & S. Zulu (Eds.), *Handbook of research on e-government in emerging economies: Adoption, e-participation, and legal frameworks* (pp. 605–623). Hershey, PA: Information Science Reference. doi:10.4018/978-1-4666-0324-0.ch031

Cabotaje, C. E., & Alampay, E. A. (2013). Social media and citizen engagement: Two cases from the Philippines. In S. Saeed, & C. Reddick (Eds.), *Human-centered system design for electronic governance* (pp. 225–238). Hershey, PA: Information Science Reference. doi:10.4018/978-1-4666-3640-8.ch013

Camillo, A., Di Pietro, L., Di Virgilio, F., & Franco, M. (2013). Work-groups conflict at PetroTech-Italy, S.R.L.: The influence of culture on conflict dynamics. In B. Christiansen, E. Turkina, & N. Williams (Eds.), *Cultural and technological influences on global business* (pp. 272–289). Hershey, PA: Business Science Reference. doi:10.4018/978-1-4666-3966-9.ch015

Capra, E., Francalanci, C., & Marinoni, C. (2008). Soft success factors for m-government. In A. Anttiroiko (Ed.), *Electronic government: Concepts, methodologies, tools, and applications* (pp. 1213–1233). Hershey, PA: Information Science Reference. doi:10.4018/978-1-59904-947-2.ch089

Cartelli, A. (2009). The implementation of practices with ICT as a new teaching-learning paradigm. In A. Cartelli, & M. Palma (Eds.), *Encyclopedia of information communication technology* (pp. 413–417). Hershey, PA: Information Science Reference.

Charalabidis, Y., Lampathaki, F., & Askounis, D. (2010). Investigating the landscape in national interoperability frameworks. *International Journal of E-Services and Mobile Applications*, *2*(4), 28–41. doi:10.4018/jesma.2010100103

Charalabidis, Y., Lampathaki, F., & Askounis, D. (2012). Investigating the landscape in national interoperability frameworks. In A. Scupola (Ed.), *Innovative mobile platform developments for electronic services design and delivery* (pp. 218–231). Hershey, PA: Business Science Reference. doi:10.4018/978-1-4666-1568-7.ch013

Chen, I. (2005). Distance education associations. In C. Howard, J. Boettcher, L. Justice, K. Schenk, P. Rogers, & G. Berg (Eds.), *Encyclopedia of distance learning* (pp. 599–612). Hershey, PA: Information Science Reference. doi:10.4018/978-1-59140-555-9.ch087

Chen, I. (2008). Distance education associations. In L. Tomei (Ed.), *Online and distance learning: Concepts, methodologies, tools, and applications* (pp. 562–579). Hershey, PA: Information Science Reference.

Chen, Y. (2008). Managing IT outsourcing for digital government. In A. Anttiroiko (Ed.), *Electronic government: Concepts, methodologies, tools, and applications* (pp. 3107–3114). Hershey, PA: Information Science Reference. doi:10.4018/978-1-59904-947-2.ch229

Chen, Y., & Dimitrova, D. V. (2006). Electronic government and online engagement: Citizen interaction with government via web portals. *International Journal of Electronic Government Research*, *2*(1), 54–76. doi:10.4018/jegr.2006010104

Chen, Y., & Knepper, R. (2005). Digital government development strategies: Lessons for policy makers from a comparative perspective. In W. Huang, K. Siau, & K. Wei (Eds.), *Electronic government strategies and implementation* (pp. 394–420). Hershey, PA: Idea Group Publishing.

Chen, Y., & Knepper, R. (2008). Digital government development strategies: Lessons for policy makers from a comparative perspective. In H. Rahman (Ed.), *Developing successful ICT strategies: Competitive advantages in a global knowledge-driven society* (pp. 334–356). Hershey, PA: Information Science Reference.

Cherian, E. J., & Ryan, T. W. (2014). Incongruent needs: Why differences in the iron-triangle of priorities make health information technology adoption and use difficult. In C. El Morr (Ed.), *Research perspectives on the role of informatics in health policy and management* (pp. 209–221). Hershey, PA: Medical Information Science Reference.

Cho, H. J., & Hwang, S. (2010). Government 2.0 in Korea: Focusing on e-participation services. In C. Reddick (Ed.), *Politics, democracy and e-government: Participation and service delivery* (pp. 94–114). Hershey, PA: Information Science Reference. doi:10.4018/978-1-61520-933-0.ch006

Chorus, C., & Timmermans, H. (2010). Ubiquitous travel environments and travel control strategies: Prospects and challenges. In M. Wachowicz (Ed.), *Movement-aware applications for sustainable mobility: Technologies and approaches* (pp. 30–51). Hershey, PA: Information Science Reference. doi:10.4018/978-1-61520-769-5.ch003

Chuanshen, R. (2007). E-government construction and China's administrative litigation act. In A. Anttiroiko, & M. Malkia (Eds.), *Encyclopedia of digital government* (pp. 507–510). Hershey, PA: Information Science Reference.

Ciaghi, A., & Villafiorita, A. (2012). Law modeling and BPR for public administration improvement. In K. Bwalya, & S. Zulu (Eds.), *Handbook of research on e-government in emerging economies: Adoption, e-participation, and legal frameworks* (pp. 391–410). Hershey, PA: Information Science Reference. doi:10.4018/978-1-4666-0324-0.ch019

Ciaramitaro, B. L., & Skrocki, M. (2012). mHealth: Mobile healthcare. In B. Ciaramitaro (Ed.), Mobile technology consumption: Opportunities and challenges (pp. 99-109). Hershey, PA: Information Science Reference. doi: doi:10.4018/978-1-61350-150-4.ch007

Comite, U. (2012). Innovative processes and managerial effectiveness of e-procurement in healthcare. In A. Manoharan, & M. Holzer (Eds.), *Active citizen participation in e-government: A global perspective* (pp. 206–229). Hershey, PA: Information Science Reference. doi:10.4018/978-1-4666-0116-1.ch011

Cordella, A. (2013). E-government success: How to account for ICT, administrative rationalization, and institutional change. In J. Gil-Garcia (Ed.), *E-government success factors and measures: Theories, concepts, and methodologies* (pp. 40–51). Hershey, PA: Information Science Reference. doi:10.4018/978-1-4666-4058-0.ch003

Cropf, R. A. (2009). ICT and e-democracy. In M. Khosrow-Pour (Ed.), *Encyclopedia of information science and technology* (2nd ed., pp. 1789–1793). Hershey, PA: Information Science Reference.

Cropf, R. A. (2009). The virtual public sphere. In M. Pagani (Ed.), *Encyclopedia of multimedia technology and networking* (2nd ed., pp. 1525–1530). Hershey, PA: Information Science Reference.

D'Abundo, M. L. (2013). Electronic health record implementation in the United States healthcare industry: Making the process of change manageable. In V. Wang (Ed.), *Handbook of research on technologies for improving the 21st century workforce: Tools for lifelong learning* (pp. 272–286). Hershey, PA: Information Science Publishing.

Damurski, L. (2012). E-participation in urban planning: Online tools for citizen engagement in Poland and in Germany. *International Journal of E-Planning Research*, *1*(3), 40–67. doi:10.4018/ijepr.2012070103

de Almeida, M. O. (2007). E-government strategy in Brazil: Increasing transparency and efficiency through e-government procurement. In M. Gascó-Hernandez (Ed.), *Latin America online: Cases, successes and pitfalls* (pp. 34–82). Hershey, PA: IRM Press. doi:10.4018/978-1-59140-974-8.ch002

de Juana Espinosa, S. (2008). Empirical study of the municipalitites' motivations for adopting online presence. In A. Anttiroiko (Ed.), *Electronic government: Concepts, methodologies, tools, and applications* (pp. 3593–3608). Hershey, PA: Information Science Reference. doi:10.4018/978-1-59904-947-2.ch262

de Souza Dias, D. (2002). Motivation for using information technology. In C. Snodgrass, & E. Szewczak (Eds.), *Human factors in information systems* (pp. 55–60). Hershey, PA: IRM Press.

Demediuk, P. (2006). Government procurement ICT's impact on the sustainability of SMEs and regional communities. In S. Marshall, W. Taylor, & X. Yu (Eds.), *Encyclopedia of developing regional communities with information and communication technology* (pp. 321–324). Hershey, PA: Information Science Reference. doi:10.4018/978-1-59140-575-7.ch056

Devonshire, E., Forsyth, H., Reid, S., & Simpson, J. M. (2013). The challenges and opportunities of online postgraduate coursework programs in a traditional university context. In B. Tynan, J. Willems, & R. James (Eds.), *Outlooks and opportunities in blended and distance learning* (pp. 353–368). Hershey, PA: Information Science Reference.

Di Cerbo, F., Scotto, M., Sillitti, A., Succi, G., & Vernazza, T. (2007). Toward a GNU/Linux distribution for corporate environments. In S. Sowe, I. Stamelos, & I. Samoladas (Eds.), *Emerging free and open source software practices* (pp. 215–236). Hershey, PA: Idea Group Publishing. doi:10.4018/978-1-59904-210-7.ch010

Diesner, J., & Carley, K. M. (2005). Revealing social structure from texts: Meta-matrix text analysis as a novel method for network text analysis. In V. Narayanan, & D. Armstrong (Eds.), *Causal mapping for research in information technology* (pp. 81–108). Hershey, PA: Idea Group Publishing.

Dologite, D. G., Mockler, R. J., Bai, Q., & Viszhanyo, P. F. (2006). IS change agents in practice in a US-Chinese joint venture. In M. Hunter, & F. Tan (Eds.), *Advanced topics in global information management* (Vol. 5, pp. 331–352). Hershey, PA: Idea Group Publishing. doi:10.4018/978-1-59140-923-6.ch015

Drnevich, P., Brush, T. H., & Luckock, G. T. (2011). Process and structural implications for IT-enabled outsourcing. *International Journal of Strategic Information Technology and Applications*, *2*(4), 30–43. doi:10.4018/jsita.2011100103

Dwivedi, A. N. (2009). *Handbook of research on information technology management and clinical data administration in healthcare*. Hershey, PA: IGI Global. doi:10.4018/978-1-60566-356-2

Elbeltagi, I., McBride, N., & Hardaker, G. (2006). Evaluating the factors affecting DSS usage by senior managers in local authorities in Egypt. In M. Hunter, & F. Tan (Eds.), *Advanced topics in global information management* (Vol. 5, pp. 283–307). Hershey, PA: Idea Group Publishing. doi:10.4018/978-1-59140-923-6.ch013

Eom, S., & Fountain, J. E. (2013). Enhancing information services through public-private partnerships: Information technology knowledge transfer underlying structures to develop shared services in the U.S. and Korea. In J. Gil-Garcia (Ed.), *E-government success around the world: Cases, empirical studies, and practical recommendations* (pp. 15–40). Hershey, PA: Information Science Reference. doi:10.4018/978-1-4666-4173-0.ch002

Esteves, T., Leuenberger, D., & Van Leuven, N. (2012). Reaching citizen 2.0: How government uses social media to send public messages during times of calm and times of crisis. In K. Kloby, & M. D'Agostino (Eds.), *Citizen 2.0: Public and governmental interaction through web 2.0 technologies* (pp. 250–268). Hershey, PA: Information Science Reference. doi:10.4018/978-1-4666-0318-9.ch013

Estevez, E., Fillottrani, P., Janowski, T., & Ojo, A. (2012). Government information sharing: A framework for policy formulation. In Y. Chen, & P. Chu (Eds.), *Electronic governance and cross-boundary collaboration: Innovations and advancing tools* (pp. 23–55). Hershey, PA: Information Science Reference.

Ezz, I. E. (2008). E-governement emerging trends: Organizational challenges. In A. Anttiroiko (Ed.), *Electronic government: Concepts, methodologies, tools, and applications* (pp. 3721–3737). Hershey, PA: Information Science Reference. doi:10.4018/978-1-59904-947-2.ch269

Fabri, M. (2009). The Italian style of e-justice in a comparative perspective. In A. Martínez, & P. Abat (Eds.), *E-justice: Using information communication technologies in the court system* (pp. 1–19). Hershey, PA: Information Science Reference.

Fagbe, T., & Adekola, O. D. (2010). Workplace safety and personnel well-being: The impact of information technology. *International Journal of Green Computing*, *1*(1), 28–33. doi:10.4018/jgc.2010010103

Fagbe, T., & Adekola, O. D. (2011). Workplace safety and personnel well-being: The impact of information technology. In I. Management Association (Ed.), Global business: Concepts, methodologies, tools and applications (pp. 1438-1444). Hershey, PA: Business Science Reference. doi: doi:10.4018/978-1-60960-587-2.ch509

Farmer, L. (2008). Affective collaborative instruction with librarians. In S. Kelsey, & K. St.Amant (Eds.), *Handbook of research on computer mediated communication* (pp. 15–24). Hershey, PA: Information Science Reference. doi:10.4018/978-1-59904-863-5.ch002

Favier, L., & Mekhantar, J. (2007). Use of OSS by local e-administration: The French situation. In K. St.Amant, & B. Still (Eds.), *Handbook of research on open source software: Technological, economic, and social perspectives* (pp. 428–444). Hershey, PA: Information Science Reference. doi:10.4018/978-1-59140-999-1.ch033

Fernando, S. (2009). Issues of e-learning in third world countries. In M. Khosrow-Pour (Ed.), *Encyclopedia of information science and technology* (2nd ed., pp. 2273–2277). Hershey, PA: Information Science Reference.

Filho, J. R., & dos Santos Junior, J. R. (2009). Local e-government in Brazil: Poor interaction and local politics as usual. In C. Reddick (Ed.), *Handbook of research on strategies for local e-government adoption and implementation: Comparative studies* (pp. 863–878). Hershey, PA: Information Science Reference. doi:10.4018/978-1-60566-282-4.ch045

Fletcher, P. D. (2004). Portals and policy: Implications of electronic access to U.S. federal government information services. In A. Pavlichev, & G. Garson (Eds.), *Digital government: Principles and best practices* (pp. 52–62). Hershey, PA: Idea Group Publishing.

Fletcher, P. D. (2008). Portals and policy: Implications of electronic access to U.S. federal government information services. In A. Anttiroiko (Ed.), *Electronic government: Concepts, methodologies, tools, and applications* (pp. 3970–3979). Hershey, PA: Information Science Reference. doi:10.4018/978-1-59904-947-2.ch289

Forlano, L. (2004). The emergence of digital government: International perspectives. In A. Pavlichev, & G. Garson (Eds.), *Digital government: Principles and best practices* (pp. 34–51). Hershey, PA: Idea Group Publishing.

Franzel, J. M., & Coursey, D. H. (2004). Government web portals: Management issues and the approaches of five states. In A. Pavlichev, & G. Garson (Eds.), *Digital government: Principles and best practices* (pp. 63–77). Hershey, PA: Idea Group Publishing.

Gaivéo, J. M. (2013). Security of ICTs supporting healthcare activities. In M. Cruz-Cunha, I. Miranda, & P. Gonçalves (Eds.), *Handbook of research on ICTs for human-centered healthcare and social care services* (pp. 208–228). Hershey, PA: Medical Information Science Reference. doi:10.4018/978-1-4666-3986-7.ch011

Garson, G. D. (1999). *Information technology and computer applications in public administration: Issues and trends*. Hershey, PA: IGI Global. doi:10.4018/978-1-87828-952-0

Garson, G. D. (2003). Toward an information technology research agenda for public administration. In G. Garson (Ed.), *Public information technology: Policy and management issues* (pp. 331–357). Hershey, PA: Idea Group Publishing.

Garson, G. D. (2004). The promise of digital government. In A. Pavlichev, & G. Garson (Eds.), *Digital government: Principles and best practices* (pp. 2–15). Hershey, PA: Idea Group Publishing.

Garson, G. D. (2007). An information technology research agenda for public administration. In G. Garson (Ed.), *Modern public information technology systems: Issues and challenges* (pp. 365–392). Hershey, PA: Idea Group Publishing. doi:10.4018/978-1-59904-051-6.ch018

Gasco, M. (2007). Civil servants' resistance towards e-government development. In A. Anttiroiko, & M. Malkia (Eds.), *Encyclopedia of digital government* (pp. 190–195). Hershey, PA: Information Science Reference.

Gasco, M. (2008). Civil servants' resistance towards e-government development. In A. Anttiroiko (Ed.), *Electronic government: Concepts, methodologies, tools, and applications* (pp. 2580–2588). Hershey, PA: Information Science Reference. doi:10.4018/978-1-59904-947-2.ch190

Ghere, R. K. (2010). Accountability and information technology enactment: Implications for social empowerment. In E. Ferro, Y. Dwivedi, J. Gil-Garcia, & M. Williams (Eds.), *Handbook of research on overcoming digital divides: Constructing an equitable and competitive information society* (pp. 515–532). Hershey, PA: Information Science Reference.

Gibson, I. W. (2012). Simulation modeling of healthcare delivery. In A. Kolker, & P. Story (Eds.), *Management engineering for effective healthcare delivery: Principles and applications* (pp. 69–89). Hershey, PA: Medical Information Science Reference.

Gil-Garcia, J. R. (2007). Exploring e-government benefits and success factors. In A. Anttiroiko, & M. Malkia (Eds.), *Encyclopedia of digital government* (pp. 803–811). Hershey, PA: Information Science Reference.

Gil-Garcia, J. R., & González Miranda, F. (2010). E-government and opportunities for participation: The case of the Mexican state web portals. In C. Reddick (Ed.), *Politics, democracy and e-government: Participation and service delivery* (pp. 56–74). Hershey, PA: Information Science Reference. doi:10.4018/978-1-61520-933-0.ch004

Goldfinch, S. (2012). Public trust in government, trust in e-government, and use of e-government. In Z. Yan (Ed.), *Encyclopedia of cyber behavior* (pp. 987–995). Hershey, PA: Information Science Reference. doi:10.4018/978-1-4666-0315-8.ch081

Goodyear, M. (2012). Organizational change contributions to e-government project transitions. In S. Aikins (Ed.), *Managing e-government projects: Concepts, issues, and best practices* (pp. 1–21). Hershey, PA: Information Science Reference. doi:10.4018/978-1-4666-0086-7.ch001

Gordon, S., & Mulligan, P. (2003). Strategic models for the delivery of personal financial services: The role of infocracy. In S. Gordon (Ed.), *Computing information technology: The human side* (pp. 220–232). Hershey, PA: IRM Press.

Gordon, T. F. (2007). Legal knowledge systems. In A. Anttiroiko, & M. Malkia (Eds.), *Encyclopedia of digital government* (pp. 1161–1166). Hershey, PA: Information Science Reference.

Graham, J. E., & Semich, G. W. (2008). Integrating technology to transform pedagogy: Revisiting the progress of the three phase TUI model for faculty development. In L. Tomei (Ed.), *Adapting information and communication technologies for effective education* (pp. 1–12). Hershey, PA: Information Science Reference.

Grandinetti, L., & Pisacane, O. (2012). Web services for healthcare management. In D. Prakash Vidyarthi (Ed.), *Technologies and protocols for the future of internet design: Reinventing the web* (pp. 60–94). Hershey, PA: Information Science Reference. doi:10.4018/978-1-4666-0203-8.ch004

Groenewegen, P., & Wagenaar, F. P. (2008). VO as an alternative to hierarchy in the Dutch police sector. In G. Putnik, & M. Cruz-Cunha (Eds.), *Encyclopedia of networked and virtual organizations* (pp. 1851–1857). Hershey, PA: Information Science Reference. doi:10.4018/978-1-59904-885-7.ch245

Gronlund, A. (2001). Building an infrastructure to manage electronic services. In S. Dasgupta (Ed.), *Managing internet and intranet technologies in organizations: Challenges and opportunities* (pp. 71–103). Hershey, PA: Idea Group Publishing. doi:10.4018/978-1-878289-95-7.ch006

Gronlund, A. (2002). Introduction to electronic government: Design, applications and management. In Å. Grönlund (Ed.), *Electronic government: Design, applications and management* (pp. 1–21). Hershey, PA: Idea Group Publishing.

Gupta, A., Woosley, R., Crk, I., & Sarnikar, S. (2009). An information technology architecture for drug effectiveness reporting and post-marketing surveillance. In J. Tan (Ed.), *Medical informatics: Concepts, methodologies, tools, and applications* (pp. 631–646). Hershey, PA: Medical Information Science Reference.

Hallin, A., & Lundevall, K. (2007). mCity: User focused development of mobile services within the city of Stockholm. In I. Kushchu (Ed.), Mobile government: An emerging direction in e-government (pp. 12-29). Hershey, PA: Idea Group Publishing. doi: doi:10.4018/978-1-59140-884-0.ch002

Hallin, A., & Lundevall, K. (2009). mCity: User focused development of mobile services within the city of Stockholm. In S. Clarke (Ed.), Evolutionary concepts in end user productivity and performance: Applications for organizational progress (pp. 268-280). Hershey, PA: Information Science Reference. doi: doi:10.4018/978-1-60566-136-0.ch017

Hallin, A., & Lundevall, K. (2009). mCity: User focused development of mobile services within the city of Stockholm. In D. Taniar (Ed.), Mobile computing: Concepts, methodologies, tools, and applications (pp. 3455-3467). Hershey, PA: Information Science Reference. doi: doi:10.4018/978-1-60566-054-7.ch253

Hanson, A. (2005). Overcoming barriers in the planning of a virtual library. In M. Khosrow-Pour (Ed.), *Encyclopedia of information science and technology* (pp. 2255–2259). Hershey, PA: Information Science Reference. doi:10.4018/978-1-59140-553-5.ch397

Haque, A. (2008). Information technology and surveillance: Implications for public administration in a new word order. In T. Loendorf, & G. Garson (Eds.), *Patriotic information systems* (pp. 177–185). Hershey, PA: IGI Publishing.

Hauck, R. V., Thatcher, S. M., & Weisband, S. P. (2012). Temporal aspects of information technology use: Increasing shift work effectiveness. In J. Wang (Ed.), *Advancing the service sector with evolving technologies: Techniques and principles* (pp. 87–104). Hershey, PA: Business Science Reference. doi:10.4018/978-1-4666-0044-7.ch006

Hawk, S., & Witt, T. (2006). Telecommunications courses in information systems programs. *International Journal of Information and Communication Technology Education, 2*(1), 79–92. doi:10.4018/jicte.2006010107

Helms, M. M., Moore, R., & Ahmadi, M. (2009). Information technology (IT) and the healthcare industry: A SWOT analysis. In J. Tan (Ed.), *Medical informatics: Concepts, methodologies, tools, and applications* (pp. 134–152). Hershey, PA: Medical Information Science Reference.

Hendrickson, S. M., & Young, M. E. (2014). Electronic records management at a federally funded research and development center. In J. Krueger (Ed.), *Cases on electronic records and resource management implementation in diverse environments* (pp. 334–350). Hershey, PA: Information Science Reference.

Henman, P. (2010). Social policy and information communication technologies. In J. Martin, & L. Hawkins (Eds.), *Information communication technologies for human services education and delivery: Concepts and cases* (pp. 215–229). Hershey, PA: Information Science Reference.

Hismanoglu, M. (2011). Important issues in online education: E-pedagogy and marketing. In U. Demiray, & S. Sever (Eds.), *Marketing online education programs: Frameworks for promotion and communication* (pp. 184–209). Hershey, PA: Information Science Reference. doi:10.4018/978-1-60960-074-7.ch012

Ho, K. K. (2008). The e-government development, IT strategies, and portals of the Hong Kong SAR government. In A. Anttiroiko (Ed.), *Electronic government: Concepts, methodologies, tools, and applications* (pp. 715–733). Hershey, PA: Information Science Reference. doi:10.4018/978-1-59904-947-2.ch060

Holden, S. H. (2003). The evolution of information technology management at the federal level: Implications for public administration. In G. Garson (Ed.), *Public information technology: Policy and management issues* (pp. 53–73). Hershey, PA: Idea Group Publishing.

Holden, S. H. (2007). The evolution of federal information technology management literature: Does IT finally matter? In G. Garson (Ed.), *Modern public information technology systems: Issues and challenges* (pp. 17–34). Hershey, PA: Idea Group Publishing. doi:10.4018/978-1-59904-051-6.ch002

Holland, J. W. (2009). Automation of American criminal justice. In M. Khosrow-Pour (Ed.), *Encyclopedia of information science and technology* (2nd ed., pp. 300–302). Hershey, PA: Information Science Reference.

Holloway, K. (2013). Fair use, copyright, and academic integrity in an online academic environment. In I. Association (Ed.), *Digital rights management: Concepts, methodologies, tools, and applications* (pp. 917–928). Hershey, PA: Information Science Reference.

Horiuchi, C. (2005). E-government databases. In L. Rivero, J. Doorn, & V. Ferraggine (Eds.), *Encyclopedia of database technologies and applications* (pp. 206–210). Hershey, PA: Information Science Reference. doi:10.4018/978-1-59140-560-3.ch035

Horiuchi, C. (2006). Creating IS quality in government settings. In E. Duggan, & J. Reichgelt (Eds.), *Measuring information systems delivery quality* (pp. 311–327). Hershey, PA: Idea Group Publishing. doi:10.4018/978-1-59140-857-4.ch014

Hsiao, N., Chu, P., & Lee, C. (2012). Impact of e-governance on businesses: Model development and case study. In I. Management Association (Ed.), Digital democracy: Concepts, methodologies, tools, and applications (pp. 1407-1425). Hershey, PA: Information Science Reference. doi: doi:10.4018/978-1-4666-1740-7.ch070

Huang, T., & Lee, C. (2010). Evaluating the impact of e-government on citizens: Cost-benefit analysis. In C. Reddick (Ed.), *Citizens and e-government: Evaluating policy and management* (pp. 37–52). Hershey, PA: Information Science Reference. doi:10.4018/978-1-61520-931-6.ch003

Hunter, M. G., Diochon, M., Pugsley, D., & Wright, B. (2002). Unique challenges for small business adoption of information technology: The case of the Nova Scotia ten. In S. Burgess (Ed.), *Managing information technology in small business: Challenges and solutions* (pp. 98–117). Hershey, PA: Idea Group Publishing.

Hurskainen, J. (2003). Integration of business systems and applications in merger and alliance: Case metso automation. In T. Reponen (Ed.), *Information technology enabled global customer service* (pp. 207–225). Hershey, PA: Idea Group Publishing. doi:10.4018/978-1-59140-048-6.ch012

Iazzolino, G., & Pietrantonio, R. (2011). The soveria.it project: A best practice of e-government in southern Italy. In D. Piaggesi, K. Sund, & W. Castelnovo (Eds.), *Global strategy and practice of e-governance: Examples from around the world* (pp. 34–56). Hershey, PA: Information Science Reference. doi:10.4018/978-1-60960-489-9.ch003

Imran, A., & Gregor, S. (2012). A process model for successful e-government adoption in the least developed countries: A case of Bangladesh. In F. Tan (Ed.), *International comparisons of information communication technologies: Advancing applications* (pp. 321–350). Hershey, PA: Information Science Reference. doi:10.4018/978-1-4666-1740-7.ch018

Inoue, Y., & Bell, S. T. (2005). Electronic/digital government innovation, and publishing trends with IT. In M. Khosrow-Pour (Ed.), *Encyclopedia of information science and technology* (pp. 1018–1023). Hershey, PA: Information Science Reference. doi:10.4018/978-1-59140-553-5.ch180

Islam, M. M., & Ehsan, M. (2013). Understanding e-governance: A theoretical approach. In M. Islam, & M. Ehsan (Eds.), *From government to e-governance: Public administration in the digital age* (pp. 38–49). Hershey, PA: Information Science Reference.

Jaeger, B. (2009). E-government and e-democracy in the making. In M. Khosrow-Pour (Ed.), *Encyclopedia of information science and technology* (2nd ed., pp. 1318–1322). Hershey, PA: Information Science Reference.

Jain, R. B. (2007). Revamping the administrative structure and processes in India for online diplomacy. In A. Anttiroiko, & M. Malkia (Eds.), *Encyclopedia of digital government* (pp. 1418–1423). Hershey, PA: Information Science Reference.

Jain, R. B. (2008). Revamping the administrative structure and processes in India for online diplomacy. In A. Anttiroiko (Ed.), *Electronic government: Concepts, methodologies, tools, and applications* (pp. 3142–3149). Hershey, PA: Information Science Reference. doi:10.4018/978-1-59904-947-2.ch233

Jauhiainen, J. S., & Inkinen, T. (2009). E-governance and the information society in periphery. In C. Reddick (Ed.), *Handbook of research on strategies for local e-government adoption and implementation: Comparative studies* (pp. 497–514). Hershey, PA: Information Science Reference. doi:10.4018/978-1-60566-282-4.ch026

Jensen, M. J. (2009). Electronic democracy and citizen influence in government. In C. Reddick (Ed.), *Handbook of research on strategies for local e-government adoption and implementation: Comparative studies* (pp. 288–305). Hershey, PA: Information Science Reference. doi:10.4018/978-1-60566-282-4.ch015

Jiao, Y., Hurson, A. R., Potok, T. E., & Beckerman, B. G. (2009). Integrating mobile-based systems with healthcare databases. In J. Erickson (Ed.), *Database technologies: Concepts, methodologies, tools, and applications* (pp. 484–504). Hershey, PA: Information Science Reference. doi:10.4018/978-1-60566-058-5.ch031

Joia, L. A. (2002). A systematic model to integrate information technology into metabusinesses: A case study in the engineering realms. In F. Tan (Ed.), *Advanced topics in global information management* (Vol. 1, pp. 250–267). Hershey, PA: Idea Group Publishing. doi:10.4018/978-1-930708-43-3.ch016

Jones, T. H., & Song, I. (2000). Binary equivalents of ternary relationships in entity-relationship modeling: A logical decomposition approach. *Journal of Database Management, 11*(2), 12–19. doi:10.4018/jdm.2000040102

Juana-Espinosa, S. D. (2007). Empirical study of the municipalitites' motivations for adopting online presence. In L. Al-Hakim (Ed.), *Global e-government: Theory, applications and benchmarking* (pp. 261–279). Hershey, PA: Idea Group Publishing.

Jun, K., & Weare, C. (2012). Bridging from e-government practice to e-government research: Past trends and future directions. In K. Bwalya, & S. Zulu (Eds.), *Handbook of research on e-government in emerging economies: Adoption, e-participation, and legal frameworks* (pp. 263–289). Hershey, PA: Information Science Reference. doi:10.4018/978-1-4666-0324-0.ch013

Junqueira, A., Diniz, E. H., & Fernandez, M. (2010). Electronic government implementation projects with multiple agencies: Analysis of the electronic invoice project under PMBOK framework. In J. Cordoba-Pachon, & A. Ochoa-Arias (Eds.), *Systems thinking and e-participation: ICT in the governance of society* (pp. 135–153). Hershey, PA: Information Science Reference.

Juntunen, A. (2009). Joint service development with the local authorities. In C. Reddick (Ed.), *Handbook of research on strategies for local e-government adoption and implementation: Comparative studies* (pp. 902–920). Hershey, PA: Information Science Reference. doi:10.4018/978-1-60566-282-4.ch047

Kamel, S. (2001). *Using DSS for crisis management.* Hershey, PA: IGI Global.

Kamel, S. (2006). DSS for strategic decision making. In M. Khosrow-Pour (Ed.), *Cases on information technology and organizational politics & culture* (pp. 230–246). Hershey, PA: Idea Group Publishing. doi:10.4018/978-1-59904-411-8.ch015

Kamel, S. (2009). The software industry in Egypt as a potential contributor to economic growth. In M. Khosrow-Pour (Ed.), *Encyclopedia of information science and technology* (2nd ed., pp. 3531–3537). Hershey, PA: Information Science Reference.

Kamel, S., & Hussein, M. (2008). Xceed: Pioneering the contact center industry in Egypt. *Journal of Cases on Information Technology*, *10*(1), 67–91. doi:10.4018/jcit.2008010105

Kamel, S., & Wahba, K. (2003). The use of a hybrid model in web-based education: "The Global campus project. In A. Aggarwal (Ed.), *Web-based education: Learning from experience* (pp. 331–346). Hershey, PA: Information Science Publishing. doi:10.4018/978-1-59140-102-5.ch020

Kardaras, D. K., & Papathanassiou, E. A. (2008). An exploratory study of the e-government services in Greece. In G. Garson, & M. Khosrow-Pour (Eds.), *Handbook of research on public information technology* (pp. 162–174). Hershey, PA: Information Science Reference. doi:10.4018/978-1-59904-857-4.ch016

Kassahun, A. E., Molla, A., & Sarkar, P. (2012). Government process reengineering: What we know and what we need to know. In I. Management Association (Ed.), Digital democracy: Concepts, methodologies, tools, and applications (pp. 1730-1752). Hershey, PA: Information Science Reference. doi: doi:10.4018/978-1-4666-1740-7.ch086

Khan, B. (2005). Technological issues. In B. Khan (Ed.), *Managing e-learning strategies: Design, delivery, implementation and evaluation* (pp. 154–180). Hershey, PA: Information Science Publishing. doi:10.4018/978-1-59140-634-1.ch004

Khasawneh, A., Bsoul, M., Obeidat, I., & Al Azzam, I. (2012). Technology fears: A study of e-commerce loyalty perception by Jordanian customers. In J. Wang (Ed.), *Advancing the service sector with evolving technologies: Techniques and principles* (pp. 158–165). Hershey, PA: Business Science Reference. doi:10.4018/978-1-4666-0044-7.ch010

Khatibi, V., & Montazer, G. A. (2012). E-research methodology. In A. Juan, T. Daradoumis, M. Roca, S. Grasman, & J. Faulin (Eds.), *Collaborative and distributed e-research: Innovations in technologies, strategies and applications* (pp. 62–81). Hershey, PA: Information Science Reference. doi:10.4018/978-1-4666-0125-3.ch003

Kidd, T. (2011). The dragon in the school's backyard: A review of literature on the uses of technology in urban schools. In L. Tomei (Ed.), *Online courses and ICT in education: Emerging practices and applications* (pp. 242–257). Hershey, PA: Information Science Reference.

Kidd, T. T. (2010). My experience tells the story: Exploring technology adoption from a qualitative perspective - A pilot study. In H. Song, & T. Kidd (Eds.), *Handbook of research on human performance and instructional technology* (pp. 247–262). Hershey, PA: Information Science Reference.

Kieley, B., Lane, G., Paquet, G., & Roy, J. (2002). e-Government in Canada: Services online or public service renewal? In Å. Grönlund (Ed.), Electronic government: Design, applications and management (pp. 340-355). Hershey, PA: Idea Group Publishing. doi: doi:10.4018/978-1-930708-19-8.ch016

Kim, P. (2012). "Stay out of the way! My kid is video blogging through a phone!": A lesson learned from math tutoring social media for children in underserved communities. In I. Management Association (Ed.), Wireless technologies: Concepts, methodologies, tools and applications (pp. 1415-1428). Hershey, PA: Information Science Reference. doi: doi:10.4018/978-1-61350-101-6.ch517

Kirlidog, M. (2010). Financial aspects of national ICT strategies. In S. Kamel (Ed.), *E-strategies for technological diffusion and adoption: National ICT approaches for socioeconomic development* (pp. 277–292). Hershey, PA: Information Science Reference. doi:10.4018/978-1-60566-388-3.ch016

Kisielnicki, J. (2006). Transfer of information and knowledge in the project management. In E. Coakes, & S. Clarke (Eds.), *Encyclopedia of communities of practice in information and knowledge management* (pp. 544–551). Hershey, PA: Information Science Reference. doi:10.4018/978-1-59140-556-6.ch091

Kittner, M., & Van Slyke, C. (2006). Reorganizing information technology services in an academic environment. In M. Khosrow-Pour (Ed.), *Cases on the human side of information technology* (pp. 49–66). Hershey, PA: Idea Group Publishing. doi:10.4018/978-1-59904-405-7.ch004

Knoell, H. D. (2008). Semi virtual workplaces in German financial service enterprises. In P. Zemliansky, & K. St.Amant (Eds.), *Handbook of research on virtual workplaces and the new nature of business practices* (pp. 570–581). Hershey, PA: Information Science Reference. doi:10.4018/978-1-59904-893-2.ch041

Koh, S. L., & Maguire, S. (2009). Competing in the age of information technology in a developing economy: Experiences of an Indian bank. In S. Koh, & S. Maguire (Eds.), *Information and communication technologies management in turbulent business environments* (pp. 326–350). Hershey, PA: Information Science Reference. doi:10.4018/978-1-60566-424-8.ch018

Kollmann, T., & Häsel, M. (2009). Competence of information technology professionals in internet-based ventures. In I. Lee (Ed.), *Electronic business: Concepts, methodologies, tools, and applications* (pp. 1905–1919). Hershey, PA: Information Science Reference.

Kollmann, T., & Häsel, M. (2009). Competence of information technology professionals in internet-based ventures. In A. Cater-Steel (Ed.), *Information technology governance and service management: Frameworks and adaptations* (pp. 239–253). Hershey, PA: Information Science Reference.

Kollmann, T., & Häsel, M. (2010). Competence of information technology professionals in internet-based ventures. In I. Management Association (Ed.), Electronic services: Concepts, methodologies, tools and applications (pp. 1551-1565). Hershey, PA: Information Science Reference. doi: doi:10.4018/978-1-61520-967-5.ch094

Kraemer, K., & King, J. L. (2006). Information technology and administrative reform: Will e-government be different? *International Journal of Electronic Government Research, 2*(1), 1–20. doi:10.4018/jegr.2006010101

Kraemer, K., & King, J. L. (2008). Information technology and administrative reform: Will e-government be different? In D. Norris (Ed.), *E-government research: Policy and management* (pp. 1–20). Hershey, PA: IGI Publishing.

Lampathaki, F., Tsiakaliaris, C., Stasis, A., & Charalabidis, Y. (2011). National interoperability frameworks: The way forward. In Y. Charalabidis (Ed.), *Interoperability in digital public services and administration: Bridging e-government and e-business* (pp. 1–24). Hershey, PA: Information Science Reference.

Lan, Z., & Scott, C. R. (1996). The relative importance of computer-mediated information versus conventional non-computer-mediated information in public managerial decision making. *Information Resources Management Journal, 9*(1), 27–0. doi: doi:10.4018/irmj.1996010103

Law, W. (2004). *Public sector data management in a developing economy*. Hershey, PA: IGI Global.

Law, W. K. (2005). Information resources development challenges in a cross-cultural environment. In M. Khosrow-Pour (Ed.), *Encyclopedia of information science and technology* (pp. 1476–1481). Hershey, PA: Information Science Reference. doi:10.4018/978-1-59140-553-5.ch259

Law, W. K. (2009). Cross-cultural challenges for information resources management. In M. Khosrow-Pour (Ed.), *Encyclopedia of information science and technology* (2nd ed., pp. 840–846). Hershey, PA: Information Science Reference.

Law, W. K. (2011). Cross-cultural challenges for information resources management. In I. Management Association (Ed.), Global business: Concepts, methodologies, tools and applications (pp. 1924-1932). Hershey, PA: Business Science Reference. doi: doi:10.4018/978-1-60960-587-2.ch704

Malkia, M., & Savolainen, R. (2004). eTransformation in government, politics and society: Conceptual framework and introduction. In M. Malkia, A. Anttiroiko, & R. Savolainen (Eds.), eTransformation in governance: New directions in government and politics (pp. 1-21). Hershey, PA: Idea Group Publishing. doi: doi:10.4018/978-1-59140-130-8.ch001

Management Association. I. (2010). Information resources management: Concepts, methodologies, tools and applications (4 Volumes). Hershey, PA: IGI Global. doi: doi:10.4018/978-1-61520-965-1

Management Association. I. (2010). Electronic services: Concepts, methodologies, tools and applications (3 Volumes). Hershey, PA: IGI Global. doi: doi:10.4018/978-1-61520-967-5

Mandujano, S. (2011). Network manageability security. In D. Kar, & M. Syed (Eds.), *Network security, administration and management: Advancing technology and practice* (pp. 158–181). Hershey, PA: Information Science Reference. doi:10.4018/978-1-60960-777-7.ch009

Marich, M. J., Schooley, B. L., & Horan, T. A. (2012). A normative enterprise architecture for guiding end-to-end emergency response decision support. In M. Jennex (Ed.), *Managing crises and disasters with emerging technologies: Advancements* (pp. 71–87). Hershey, PA: Information Science Reference. doi:10.4018/978-1-4666-0167-3.ch006

Markov, R., & Okujava, S. (2008). Costs, benefits, and risks of e-government portals. In G. Putnik, & M. Cruz-Cunha (Eds.), *Encyclopedia of networked and virtual organizations* (pp. 354–363). Hershey, PA: Information Science Reference. doi:10.4018/978-1-59904-885-7.ch047

Martin, N., & Rice, J. (2013). Evaluating and designing electronic government for the future: Observations and insights from Australia. In V. Weerakkody (Ed.), *E-government services design, adoption, and evaluation* (pp. 238–258). Hershey, PA: Information Science Reference.

i. Martinez, A. C. (2008). Accessing administration's information via internet in Spain. In F. Tan (Ed.), *Global information technologies: Concepts, methodologies, tools, and applications* (pp. 2558–2573). Hershey, PA: Information Science Reference.

Mbarika, V. W., Meso, P. N., & Musa, P. F. (2006). A disconnect in stakeholders' perceptions from emerging realities of teledensity growth in Africa's least developed countries. In M. Hunter, & F. Tan (Eds.), *Advanced topics in global information management* (Vol. 5, pp. 263–282). Hershey, PA: Idea Group Publishing. doi:10.4018/978-1-59140-923-6.ch012

Mbarika, V. W., Meso, P. N., & Musa, P. F. (2008). A disconnect in stakeholders' perceptions from emerging realities of teledensity growth in Africa's least developed countries. In F. Tan (Ed.), *Global information technologies: Concepts, methodologies, tools, and applications* (pp. 2948–2962). Hershey, PA: Information Science Reference.

Means, T., Olson, E., & Spooner, J. (2013). Discovering ways that don't work on the road to success: Strengths and weaknesses revealed by an active learning studio classroom project. In A. Benson, J. Moore, & S. Williams van Rooij (Eds.), *Cases on educational technology planning, design, and implementation: A project management perspective* (pp. 94–113). Hershey, PA: Information Science Reference. doi:10.4018/978-1-4666-4237-9.ch006

Melitski, J., Holzer, M., Kim, S., Kim, C., & Rho, S. (2008). Digital government worldwide: An e-government assessment of municipal web sites. In G. Garson, & M. Khosrow-Pour (Eds.), *Handbook of research on public information technology* (pp. 790–804). Hershey, PA: Information Science Reference. doi:10.4018/978-1-59904-857-4.ch069

Memmola, M., Palumbo, G., & Rossini, M. (2009). Web & RFID technology: New frontiers in costing and process management for rehabilitation medicine. In L. Al-Hakim, & M. Memmola (Eds.), *Business web strategy: Design, alignment, and application* (pp. 145–169). Hershey, PA: Information Science Reference. doi:10.4018/978-1-60566-960-1.ch039

Meng, Z., Fahong, Z., & Lei, L. (2008). Information technology and environment. In Y. Kurihara, S. Takaya, H. Harui, & H. Kamae (Eds.), *Information technology and economic development* (pp. 201–212). Hershey, PA: Information Science Reference.

Mentzingen de Moraes, A. J., Ferneda, E., Costa, I., & Spinola, M. D. (2011). Practical approach for implementation of governance process in IT: Information technology areas. In N. Shi, & G. Silvius (Eds.), *Enterprise IT governance, business value and performance measurement* (pp. 19–40). Hershey, PA: Information Science Reference.

Merwin, G. A. Jr, McDonald, J. S., & Odera, L. C. (2008). Economic development: Government's cutting edge in IT. In M. Raisinghani (Ed.), *Handbook of research on global information technology management in the digital economy* (pp. 1–37). Hershey, PA: Information Science Reference. doi:10.4018/978-1-59904-875-8.ch001

Meso, P., & Duncan, N. (2002). Can national information infrastructures enhance social development in the least developed countries? An empirical investigation. In M. Dadashzadeh (Ed.), *Information technology management in developing countries* (pp. 23–51). Hershey, PA: IRM Press. doi:10.4018/978-1-931777-03-2.ch002

Meso, P. N., & Duncan, N. B. (2002). Can national information infrastructures enhance social development in the least developed countries? In F. Tan (Ed.), *Advanced topics in global information management* (Vol. 1, pp. 207–226). Hershey, PA: Idea Group Publishing. doi:10.4018/978-1-930708-43-3.ch014

Middleton, M. (2008). Evaluation of e-government web sites. In G. Garson, & M. Khosrow-Pour (Eds.), *Handbook of research on public information technology* (pp. 699–710). Hershey, PA: Information Science Reference. doi:10.4018/978-1-59904-857-4.ch063

Mingers, J. (2010). Pluralism, realism, and truth: The keys to knowledge in information systems research. In D. Paradice (Ed.), *Emerging systems approaches in information technologies: Concepts, theories, and applications* (pp. 86–98). Hershey, PA: Information Science Reference.

Mital, K. M. (2012). ICT, unique identity and inclusive growth: An Indian perspective. In A. Manoharan, & M. Holzer (Eds.), *E-governance and civic engagement: Factors and determinants of e-democracy* (pp. 584–612). Hershey, PA: Information Science Reference.

Mizell, A. P. (2008). Helping close the digital divide for financially disadvantaged seniors. In F. Tan (Ed.), *Global information technologies: Concepts, methodologies, tools, and applications* (pp. 2396–2402). Hershey, PA: Information Science Reference.

Molinari, F., Wills, C., Koumpis, A., & Moumtzi, V. (2011). A citizen-centric platform to support networking in the area of e-democracy. In H. Rahman (Ed.), *Cases on adoption, diffusion and evaluation of global e-governance systems: Impact at the grass roots* (pp. 282–302). Hershey, PA: Information Science Reference.

Molinari, F., Wills, C., Koumpis, A., & Moumtzi, V. (2013). A citizen-centric platform to support networking in the area of e-democracy. In H. Rahman (Ed.), *Cases on progressions and challenges in ICT utilization for citizen-centric governance* (pp. 265–297). Hershey, PA: Information Science Reference.

Monteverde, F. (2010). The process of e-government public policy inclusion in the governmental agenda: A framework for assessment and case study. In J. Cordoba-Pachon, & A. Ochoa-Arias (Eds.), *Systems thinking and e-participation: ICT in the governance of society* (pp. 233–245). Hershey, PA: Information Science Reference.

Moodley, S. (2008). Deconstructing the South African government's ICT for development discourse. In A. Anttiroiko (Ed.), *Electronic government: Concepts, methodologies, tools, and applications* (pp. 622–631). Hershey, PA: Information Science Reference. doi:10.4018/978-1-59904-947-2.ch053

Moodley, S. (2008). Deconstructing the South African government's ICT for development discourse. In C. Van Slyke (Ed.), *Information communication technologies: Concepts, methodologies, tools, and applications* (pp. 816–825). Hershey, PA: Information Science Reference. doi:10.4018/978-1-59904-949-6.ch052

Mora, M., Cervantes-Perez, F., Gelman-Muravchik, O., Forgionne, G. A., & Mejia-Olvera, M. (2003). DMSS implementation research: A conceptual analysis of the contributions and limitations of the factor-based and stage-based streams. In G. Forgionne, J. Gupta, & M. Mora (Eds.), *Decision-making support systems: Achievements and challenges for the new decade* (pp. 331–356). Hershey, PA: Idea Group Publishing. doi:10.4018/978-1-59140-045-5.ch020

Mörtberg, C., & Elovaara, P. (2010). Attaching people and technology: Between e and government. In S. Booth, S. Goodman, & G. Kirkup (Eds.), *Gender issues in learning and working with information technology: Social constructs and cultural contexts* (pp. 83–98). Hershey, PA: Information Science Reference. doi:10.4018/978-1-61520-813-5.ch005

Murphy, J., Harper, E., Devine, E. C., Burke, L. J., & Hook, M. L. (2011). Case study: Lessons learned when embedding evidence-based knowledge in a nurse care planning and documentation system. In A. Cashin, & R. Cook (Eds.), *Evidence-based practice in nursing informatics: Concepts and applications* (pp. 174–190). Hershey, PA: Medical Information Science Reference.

Mutula, S. M. (2013). E-government's role in poverty alleviation: Case study of South Africa. In H. Rahman (Ed.), *Cases on progressions and challenges in ICT utilization for citizen-centric governance* (pp. 44–68). Hershey, PA: Information Science Reference.

Nath, R., & Angeles, R. (2005). Relationships between supply characteristics and buyer-supplier coupling in e-procurement: An empirical analysis. [IJEBR]. *International Journal of E-Business Research, 1*(2), 40–55. doi:10.4018/jebr.2005040103

Nissen, M. E. (2006). Application cases in government. In M. Nissen (Ed.), *Harnessing knowledge dynamics: Principled organizational knowing & learning* (pp. 152–181). Hershey, PA: IRM Press.

Norris, D. F. (2003). Leading-edge information technologies and American local governments. In G. Garson (Ed.), *Public information technology: Policy and management issues* (pp. 139–169). Hershey, PA: Idea Group Publishing.

Norris, D. F. (2008). Information technology among U.S. local governments. In G. Garson, & M. Khosrow-Pour (Eds.), *Handbook of research on public information technology* (pp. 132–144). Hershey, PA: Information Science Reference. doi:10.4018/978-1-59904-857-4.ch013

Northrop, A. (1999). The challenge of teaching information technology in public administration graduate programs. In G. Garson (Ed.), *Information technology and computer applications in public administration: Issues and trends* (pp. 1–22). Hershey, PA: Information Science Reference. doi:10.4018/978-1-87828-952-0.ch001

Northrop, A. (2003). Information technology and public administration: The view from the profession. In G. Garson (Ed.), *Public information technology: Policy and management issues* (pp. 1–19). Hershey, PA: Idea Group Publishing.

Northrop, A. (2007). Lip service? How PA journals and textbooks view information technology. In G. Garson (Ed.), *Modern public information technology systems: Issues and challenges* (pp. 1–16). Hershey, PA: Idea Group Publishing. doi:10.4018/978-1-59904-051-6.ch001

Null, E. (2013). Legal and political barriers to municipal networks in the United States. In A. Abdelaal (Ed.), *Social and economic effects of community wireless networks and infrastructures* (pp. 27–56). Hershey, PA: Information Science Reference. doi:10.4018/978-1-4666-2997-4.ch003

Okunoye, A., Frolick, M., & Crable, E. (2006). ERP implementation in higher education: An account of pre-implementation and implementation phases. *Journal of Cases on Information Technology*, *8*(2), 110–132. doi:10.4018/jcit.2006040106

Olasina, G. (2012). A review of egovernment services in Nigeria. In A. Tella, & A. Issa (Eds.), *Library and information science in developing countries: Contemporary issues* (pp. 205–221). Hershey, PA: Information Science Reference.

Orgeron, C. P. (2008). A model for reengineering IT job classes in state government. In G. Garson, & M. Khosrow-Pour (Eds.), *Handbook of research on public information technology* (pp. 735–746). Hershey, PA: Information Science Reference. doi:10.4018/978-1-59904-857-4.ch066

Owsinski, J. W., & Pielak, A. M. (2011). Local authority websites in rural areas: Measuring quality and functionality, and assessing the role. In Z. Andreopoulou, B. Manos, N. Polman, & D. Viaggi (Eds.), *Agricultural and environmental informatics, governance and management: Emerging research applications* (pp. 39–60). Hershey, PA: Information Science Reference. doi:10.4018/978-1-60960-621-3.ch003

Owsiński, J. W., Pielak, A. M., Sęp, K., & Stańczak, J. (2014). Local web-based networks in rural municipalities: Extension, density, and meaning. In Z. Andreopoulou, V. Samathrakis, S. Louca, & M. Vlachopoulou (Eds.), *E-innovation for sustainable development of rural resources during global economic crisis* (pp. 126–151). Hershey, PA: Business Science Reference.

Pagani, M., & Pasinetti, C. (2008). Technical and functional quality in the development of t-government services. In A. Anttiroiko (Ed.), *Electronic government: Concepts, methodologies, tools, and applications* (pp. 2943–2965). Hershey, PA: Information Science Reference. doi:10.4018/978-1-59904-947-2.ch220

Pani, A. K., & Agrahari, A. (2005). On e-markets in emerging economy: An Indian experience. In M. Khosrow-Pour (Ed.), *Advanced topics in electronic commerce* (Vol. 1, pp. 287–299). Hershey, PA: Idea Group Publishing. doi:10.4018/978-1-59140-819-2.ch015

Papadopoulos, T., Angelopoulos, S., & Kitsios, F. (2011). A strategic approach to e-health interoperability using e-government frameworks. In A. Lazakidou, K. Siassiakos, & K. Ioannou (Eds.), *Wireless technologies for ambient assisted living and healthcare: Systems and applications* (pp. 213–229). Hershey, PA: Medical Information Science Reference.

Papadopoulos, T., Angelopoulos, S., & Kitsios, F. (2013). A strategic approach to e-health interoperability using e-government frameworks. In I. Management Association (Ed.), User-driven healthcare: Concepts, methodologies, tools, and applications (pp. 791-807). Hershey, PA: Medical Information Science Reference. doi: doi:10.4018/978-1-4666-2770-3.ch039

Papaleo, G., Chiarella, D., Aiello, M., & Caviglione, L. (2012). Analysis, development and deployment of statistical anomaly detection techniques for real e-mail traffic. In T. Chou (Ed.), *Information assurance and security technologies for risk assessment and threat management: Advances* (pp. 47–71). Hershey, PA: Information Science Reference.

Papp, R. (2003). Information technology & FDA compliance in the pharmaceutical industry. In M. Khosrow-Pour (Ed.), *Annals of cases on information technology* (Vol. 5, pp. 262–273). Hershey, PA: Information Science Reference. doi:10.4018/978-1-59140-061-5.ch017

Parsons, T. W. (2007). Developing a knowledge management portal. In A. Tatnall (Ed.), *Encyclopedia of portal technologies and applications* (pp. 223–227). Hershey, PA: Information Science Reference. doi:10.4018/978-1-59140-989-2.ch039

Passaris, C. E. (2007). Immigration and digital government. In A. Anttiroiko, & M. Malkia (Eds.), *Encyclopedia of digital government* (pp. 988–994). Hershey, PA: Information Science Reference.

Pavlichev, A. (2004). The e-government challenge for public administration. In A. Pavlichev, & G. Garson (Eds.), *Digital government: Principles and best practices* (pp. 276–290). Hershey, PA: Idea Group Publishing.

Penrod, J. I., & Harbor, A. F. (2000). Designing and implementing a learning organization-oriented information technology planning and management process. In L. Petrides (Ed.), *Case studies on information technology in higher education: Implications for policy and practice* (pp. 7–19). Hershey, PA: Idea Group Publishing. doi:10.4018/978-1-878289-74-2.ch001

Planas-Silva, M. D., & Joseph, R. C. (2011). Perspectives on the adoption of electronic resources for use in clinical trials. In M. Guah (Ed.), *Healthcare delivery reform and new technologies: Organizational initiatives* (pp. 19–28). Hershey, PA: Information Science Reference.

Pomazalová, N., & Rejman, S. (2013). The rationale behind implementation of new electronic tools for electronic public procurement. In N. Pomazalová (Ed.), *Public sector transformation processes and internet public procurement: Decision support systems* (pp. 85–117). Hershey, PA: Engineering Science Reference.

Postorino, M. N. (2012). City competitiveness and airport: Information science perspective. In M. Bulu (Ed.), *City competitiveness and improving urban subsystems: Technologies and applications* (pp. 61–83). Hershey, PA: Information Science Reference.

Poupa, C. (2002). Electronic government in Switzerland: Priorities for 2001-2005 - Electronic voting and federal portal. In Å. Grönlund (Ed.), *Electronic government: Design, applications and management* (pp. 356–369). Hershey, PA: Idea Group Publishing.

Powell, S. R. (2010). Interdisciplinarity in telecommunications and networking. In I. Association (Ed.), *Networking and telecommunications: Concepts, methodologies, tools and applications* (pp. 33–40). Hershey, PA: Information Science Reference. doi:10.4018/978-1-60566-986-1.ch004

Priya, P. S., & Mathiyalagan, N. (2011). A study of the implementation status of two e-governance projects in land revenue administration in India. In M. Shareef, V. Kumar, U. Kumar, & Y. Dwivedi (Eds.), *Stakeholder adoption of e-government services: Driving and resisting factors* (pp. 214–230). Hershey, PA: Information Science Reference. doi:10.4018/978-1-60960-601-5.ch011

Prysby, C., & Prysby, N. (2000). Electronic mail, employee privacy and the workplace. In L. Janczewski (Ed.), *Internet and intranet security management: Risks and solutions* (pp. 251–270). Hershey, PA: Idea Group Publishing. doi:10.4018/978-1-878289-71-1.ch009

Prysby, C. L., & Prysby, N. D. (2003). Electronic mail in the public workplace: Issues of privacy and public disclosure. In G. Garson (Ed.), *Public information technology: Policy and management issues* (pp. 271–298). Hershey, PA: Idea Group Publishing.

Prysby, C. L., & Prysby, N. D. (2007). You have mail, but who is reading it? Issues of e-mail in the public workplace. In G. Garson (Ed.), *Modern public information technology systems: Issues and challenges* (pp. 312–336). Hershey, PA: Idea Group Publishing. doi:10.4018/978-1-59904-051-6.ch016

Radl, A., & Chen, Y. (2005). Computer security in electronic government: A state-local education information system. *International Journal of Electronic Government Research, 1*(1), 79–99. doi:10.4018/jegr.2005010105

Rahman, H. (2008). Information dynamics in developing countries. In C. Van Slyke (Ed.), *Information communication technologies: Concepts, methodologies, tools, and applications* (pp. 104–114). Hershey, PA: Information Science Reference. doi:10.4018/978-1-59904-949-6.ch008

Ramanathan, J. (2009). Adaptive IT architecture as a catalyst for network capability in government. In P. Saha (Ed.), *Advances in government enterprise architecture* (pp. 149–172). Hershey, PA: Information Science Reference.

Ramos, I., & Berry, D. M. (2006). Social construction of information technology supporting work. In M. Khosrow-Pour (Ed.), *Cases on information technology: Lessons learned* (Vol. 7, pp. 36–52). Hershey, PA: Idea Group Publishing. doi:10.4018/978-1-59140-673-0.ch003

Ray, D., Gulla, U., Gupta, M. P., & Dash, S. S. (2009). Interoperability and constituents of interoperable systems in public sector. In V. Weerakkody, M. Janssen, & Y. Dwivedi (Eds.), *Handbook of research on ICT-enabled transformational government: A global perspective* (pp. 175–195). Hershey, PA: Information Science Reference. doi:10.4018/978-1-60566-390-6.ch010

Reddick, C. G. (2007). E-government and creating a citizen-centric government: A study of federal government CIOs. In G. Garson (Ed.), *Modern public information technology systems: Issues and challenges* (pp. 143–165). Hershey, PA: Idea Group Publishing. doi:10.4018/978-1-59904-051-6.ch008

Reddick, C. G. (2010). Citizen-centric e-government. In C. Reddick (Ed.), *Homeland security preparedness and information systems: Strategies for managing public policy* (pp. 45–75). Hershey, PA: Information Science Reference.

Reddick, C. G. (2010). E-government and creating a citizen-centric government: A study of federal government CIOs. In C. Reddick (Ed.), *Homeland security preparedness and information systems: Strategies for managing public policy* (pp. 230–250). Hershey, PA: Information Science Reference.

Reddick, C. G. (2010). Perceived effectiveness of e-government and its usage in city governments: Survey evidence from information technology directors. In C. Reddick (Ed.), *Homeland security preparedness and information systems: Strategies for managing public policy* (pp. 213–229). Hershey, PA: Information Science Reference.

Reddick, C. G. (2012). Customer relationship management adoption in local governments in the United States. In S. Chhabra, & M. Kumar (Eds.), *Strategic enterprise resource planning models for e-government: Applications and methodologies* (pp. 111–124). Hershey, PA: Information Science Reference. doi:10.4018/978-1-4666-1740-7.ch066

Reeder, F. S., & Pandy, S. M. (2008). Identifying effective funding models for e-government. In A. Anttiroiko (Ed.), *Electronic government: Concepts, methodologies, tools, and applications* (pp. 1108–1138). Hershey, PA: Information Science Reference. doi:10.4018/978-1-59904-947-2.ch083

Riesco, D., Acosta, E., & Montejano, G. (2003). An extension to a UML activity graph from workflow. In L. Favre (Ed.), *UML and the unified process* (pp. 294–314). Hershey, PA: IRM Press.

Ritzhaupt, A. D., & Gill, T. G. (2008). A hybrid and novel approach to teaching computer programming in MIS curriculum. In S. Negash, M. Whitman, A. Woszczynski, K. Hoganson, & H. Mattord (Eds.), *Handbook of distance learning for real-time and asynchronous information technology education* (pp. 259–281). Hershey, PA: Information Science Reference. doi:10.4018/978-1-59904-964-9.ch014

Roche, E. M. (1993). International computing and the international regime. *Journal of Global Information Management, 1*(2), 33–44. doi: doi:10.4018/jgim.1993040103

Rocheleau, B. (2007). Politics, accountability, and information management. In G. Garson (Ed.), *Modern public information technology systems: Issues and challenges* (pp. 35–71). Hershey, PA: Idea Group Publishing. doi:10.4018/978-1-59904-051-6.ch003

Rodrigues Filho, J. (2010). E-government in Brazil: Reinforcing dominant institutions or reducing citizenship? In C. Reddick (Ed.), *Politics, democracy and e-government: Participation and service delivery* (pp. 347–362). Hershey, PA: Information Science Reference. doi:10.4018/978-1-61520-933-0.ch021

Rodriguez, S. R., & Thorp, D. A. (2013). eLearning for industry: A case study of the project management process. In A. Benson, J. Moore, & S. Williams van Rooij (Eds.), Cases on educational technology planning, design, and implementation: A project management perspective (pp. 319-342). Hershey, PA: Information Science Reference. doi: doi:10.4018/978-1-4666-4237-9.ch017

Roman, A. V. (2013). Delineating three dimensions of e-government success: Security, functionality, and transformation. In J. Gil-Garcia (Ed.), *E-government success factors and measures: Theories, concepts, and methodologies* (pp. 171–192). Hershey, PA: Information Science Reference. doi:10.4018/978-1-4666-4058-0.ch010

Ross, S. C., Tyran, C. K., & Auer, D. J. (2008). Up in smoke: Rebuilding after an IT disaster. In H. Nemati (Ed.), *Information security and ethics: Concepts, methodologies, tools, and applications* (pp. 3659–3675). Hershey, PA: Information Science Reference.

Ross, S. C., Tyran, C. K., Auer, D. J., Junell, J. M., & Williams, T. G. (2005). Up in smoke: Rebuilding after an IT disaster. *Journal of Cases on Information Technology*, *7*(2), 31–49. doi:10.4018/jcit.2005040103

Roy, J. (2008). Security, sovereignty, and continental interoperability: Canada's elusive balance. In T. Loendorf, & G. Garson (Eds.), *Patriotic information systems* (pp. 153–176). Hershey, PA: IGI Publishing.

Rubeck, R. F., & Miller, G. A. (2009). vGOV: Remote video access to government services. In A. Scupola (Ed.), Cases on managing e-services (pp. 253-268). Hershey, PA: Information Science Reference. doi: doi:10.4018/978-1-60566-064-6.ch017

Saekow, A., & Boonmee, C. (2011). The challenges of implementing e-government interoperability in Thailand: Case of official electronic correspondence letters exchange across government departments. In Y. Charalabidis (Ed.), *Interoperability in digital public services and administration: Bridging e-government and e-business* (pp. 40–61). Hershey, PA: Information Science Reference.

Saekow, A., & Boonmee, C. (2012). The challenges of implementing e-government interoperability in Thailand: Case of official electronic correspondence letters exchange across government departments. In I. Management Association (Ed.), Digital democracy: Concepts, methodologies, tools, and applications (pp. 1883-1905). Hershey, PA: Information Science Reference. doi: doi:10.4018/978-1-4666-1740-7.ch094

Sagsan, M., & Medeni, T. (2012). Understanding "knowledge management (KM) paradigms" from social media perspective: An empirical study on discussion group for KM at professional networking site. In M. Cruz-Cunha, P. Gonçalves, N. Lopes, E. Miranda, & G. Putnik (Eds.), *Handbook of research on business social networking: Organizational, managerial, and technological dimensions* (pp. 738–755). Hershey, PA: Business Science Reference.

Sahi, G., & Madan, S. (2013). Information security threats in ERP enabled e-governance: Challenges and solutions. In I. Association (Ed.), *Enterprise resource planning: Concepts, methodologies, tools, and applications* (pp. 825–837). Hershey, PA: Business Science Reference. doi:10.4018/978-1-4666-4153-2.ch048

Sanford, C., & Bhattacherjee, A. (2008). IT implementation in a developing country municipality: A sociocognitive analysis. *International Journal of Technology and Human Interaction*, *4*(3), 68–93. doi:10.4018/jthi.2008070104

Schelin, S. H. (2003). E-government: An overview. In G. Garson (Ed.), *Public information technology: Policy and management issues* (pp. 120–138). Hershey, PA: Idea Group Publishing.

Schelin, S. H. (2004). Training for digital government. In A. Pavlichev, & G. Garson (Eds.), *Digital government: Principles and best practices* (pp. 263–275). Hershey, PA: Idea Group Publishing.

Schelin, S. H. (2007). E-government: An overview. In G. Garson (Ed.), *Modern public information technology systems: Issues and challenges* (pp. 110–126). Hershey, PA: Idea Group Publishing. doi:10.4018/978-1-59904-051-6.ch006

Schelin, S. H., & Garson, G. (2004). Theoretical justification of critical success factors. In G. Garson, & S. Schelin (Eds.), *IT solutions series: Humanizing information technology: Advice from experts* (pp. 4–15). Hershey, PA: CyberTech Publishing. doi:10.4018/978-1-59140-245-9.ch002

Scime, A. (2002). Information systems and computer science model curricula: A comparative look. In M. Dadashzadeh, A. Saber, & S. Saber (Eds.), *Information technology education in the new millennium* (pp. 146–158). Hershey, PA: IRM Press.

Scime, A. (2009). Computing curriculum analysis and development. In M. Khosrow-Pour (Ed.), *Encyclopedia of information science and technology* (2nd ed., pp. 667–671). Hershey, PA: Information Science Reference.

Scime, A., & Wania, C. (2008). Computing curricula: A comparison of models. In C. Van Slyke (Ed.), *Information communication technologies: Concepts, methodologies, tools, and applications* (pp. 1270–1283). Hershey, PA: Information Science Reference. doi:10.4018/978-1-59904-949-6.ch088

Seidman, S. B. (2009). An international perspective on professional software engineering credentials. In H. Ellis, S. Demurjian, & J. Naveda (Eds.), *Software engineering: Effective teaching and learning approaches and practices* (pp. 351–361). Hershey, PA: Information Science Reference.

Seifert, J. W. (2007). E-government act of 2002 in the United States. In A. Anttiroiko, & M. Malkia (Eds.), *Encyclopedia of digital government* (pp. 476–481). Hershey, PA: Information Science Reference.

Seifert, J. W., & Relyea, H. C. (2008). E-government act of 2002 in the United States. In A. Anttiroiko (Ed.), *Electronic government: Concepts, methodologies, tools, and applications* (pp. 154–161). Hershey, PA: Information Science Reference. doi:10.4018/978-1-59904-947-2.ch013

Seufert, S. (2002). E-learning business models: Framework and best practice examples. In M. Raisinghani (Ed.), *Cases on worldwide e-commerce: Theory in action* (pp. 70–94). Hershey, PA: Idea Group Publishing. doi:10.4018/978-1-930708-27-3.ch004

Shareef, M. A., & Archer, N. (2012). E-government service development. In M. Shareef, N. Archer, & S. Dutta (Eds.), *E-government service maturity and development: Cultural, organizational and technological perspectives* (pp. 1–14). Hershey, PA: Information Science Reference.

Shareef, M. A., & Archer, N. (2012). E-government initiatives: Review studies on different countries. In M. Shareef, N. Archer, & S. Dutta (Eds.), *E-government service maturity and development: Cultural, organizational and technological perspectives* (pp. 40–76). Hershey, PA: Information Science Reference.

Shareef, M. A., Kumar, U., & Kumar, V. (2011). E-government development: Performance evaluation parameters. In M. Shareef, V. Kumar, U. Kumar, & Y. Dwivedi (Eds.), *Stakeholder adoption of e-government services: Driving and resisting factors* (pp. 197–213). Hershey, PA: Information Science Reference. doi:10.4018/978-1-60960-601-5.ch010

Shareef, M. A., Kumar, U., Kumar, V., & Niktash, M. (2012). Electronic-government vision: Case studies for objectives, strategies, and initiatives. In M. Shareef, N. Archer, & S. Dutta (Eds.), *E-government service maturity and development: Cultural, organizational and technological perspectives* (pp. 15–39). Hershey, PA: Information Science Reference.

Shukla, P., Kumar, A., & Anu Kumar, P. B. (2013). Impact of national culture on business continuity management system implementation. *International Journal of Risk and Contingency Management, 2*(3), 23–36. doi:10.4018/ijrcm.2013070102

Shulman, S. W. (2007). The federal docket management system and the prospect for digital democracy in U S rule-making. In G. Garson (Ed.), *Modern public information technology systems: Issues and challenges* (pp. 166–184). Hershey, PA: Idea Group Publishing. doi:10.4018/978-1-59904-051-6.ch009

Simonovic, S. (2007). Problems of offline government in e-Serbia. In A. Anttiroiko, & M. Malkia (Eds.), *Encyclopedia of digital government* (pp. 1342–1351). Hershey, PA: Information Science Reference.

Simonovic, S. (2008). Problems of offline government in e-Serbia. In A. Anttiroiko (Ed.), *Electronic government: Concepts, methodologies, tools, and applications* (pp. 2929–2942). Hershey, PA: Information Science Reference. doi:10.4018/978-1-59904-947-2.ch219

Singh, A. M. (2005). Information systems and technology in South Africa. In M. Khosrow-Pour (Ed.), *Encyclopedia of information science and technology* (pp. 1497–1502). Hershey, PA: Information Science Reference. doi:10.4018/978-1-59140-553-5.ch263

Singh, S., & Naidoo, G. (2005). Towards an e-government solution: A South African perspective. In W. Huang, K. Siau, & K. Wei (Eds.), *Electronic government strategies and implementation* (pp. 325–353). Hershey, PA: Idea Group Publishing.

Snoke, R., & Underwood, A. (2002). Generic attributes of IS graduates: An analysis of Australian views. In F. Tan (Ed.), *Advanced topics in global information management* (Vol. 1, pp. 370–384). Hershey, PA: Idea Group Publishing. doi:10.4018/978-1-930708-43-3.ch023

Sommer, L. (2006). Revealing unseen organizations in higher education: A study framework and application example. In A. Metcalfe (Ed.), *Knowledge management and higher education: A critical analysis* (pp. 115–146). Hershey, PA: Information Science Publishing. doi:10.4018/978-1-59140-509-2.ch007

Song, H., Kidd, T., & Owens, E. (2011). Examining technological disparities and instructional practices in English language arts classroom: Implications for school leadership and teacher training. In L. Tomei (Ed.), *Online courses and ICT in education: Emerging practices and applications* (pp. 258–274). Hershey, PA: Information Science Reference.

Speaker, P. J., & Kleist, V. F. (2003). Using information technology to meet electronic commerce and MIS education demands. In A. Aggarwal (Ed.), *Web-based education: Learning from experience* (pp. 280–291). Hershey, PA: Information Science Publishing. doi:10.4018/978-1-59140-102-5.ch017

Spitler, V. K. (2007). Learning to use IT in the workplace: Mechanisms and masters. In M. Mahmood (Ed.), *Contemporary issues in end user computing* (pp. 292–323). Hershey, PA: Idea Group Publishing.

Stellefson, M. (2011). Considerations for marketing distance education courses in health education: Five important questions to examine before development. In U. Demiray, & S. Sever (Eds.), *Marketing online education programs: Frameworks for promotion and communication* (pp. 222–234). Hershey, PA: Information Science Reference. doi:10.4018/978-1-60960-074-7.ch014

Straub, D. W., & Loch, K. D. (2006). Creating and developing a program of global research. *Journal of Global Information Management, 14*(2), 1–28. doi:10.4018/jgim.2006040101

Straub, D. W., Loch, K. D., & Hill, C. E. (2002). Transfer of information technology to the Arab world: A test of cultural influence modeling. In M. Dadashzadeh (Ed.), *Information technology management in developing countries* (pp. 92–134). Hershey, PA: IRM Press. doi:10.4018/978-1-931777-03-2.ch005

Straub, D. W., Loch, K. D., & Hill, C. E. (2003). Transfer of information technology to the Arab world: A test of cultural influence modeling. In F. Tan (Ed.), *Advanced topics in global information management* (Vol. 2, pp. 141–172). Hershey, PA: Idea Group Publishing. doi:10.4018/978-1-59140-064-6.ch009

Suki, N. M., Ramayah, T., Ming, M. K., & Suki, N. M. (2013). Factors enhancing employed job seekers intentions to use social networking sites as a job search tool. In A. Mesquita (Ed.), *User perception and influencing factors of technology in everyday life* (pp. 265–281). Hershey, PA: Information Science Reference.

Suomi, R. (2006). Introducing electronic patient records to hospitals: Innovation adoption paths. In T. Spil, & R. Schuring (Eds.), *E-health systems diffusion and use: The innovation, the user and the use IT model* (pp. 128–146). Hershey, PA: Idea Group Publishing.

Swim, J., & Barker, L. (2012). Pathways into a gendered occupation: Brazilian women in IT. *International Journal of Social and Organizational Dynamics in IT, 2*(4), 34–51. doi:10.4018/ijsodit.2012100103

Tarafdar, M., & Vaidya, S. D. (2006). Adoption and implementation of IT in developing nations: Experiences from two public sector enterprises in India. In M. Khosrow-Pour (Ed.), *Cases on information technology planning, design and implementation* (pp. 208–233). Hershey, PA: Idea Group Publishing. doi:10.4018/978-1-59904-408-8.ch013

Tarafdar, M., & Vaidya, S. D. (2008). Adoption and implementation of IT in developing nations: Experiences from two public sector enterprises in India. In G. Garson, & M. Khosrow-Pour (Eds.), *Handbook of research on public information technology* (pp. 905–924). Hershey, PA: Information Science Reference. doi:10.4018/978-1-59904-857-4.ch076

Thesing, Z. (2007). Zarina thesing, pumpkin patch. In M. Hunter (Ed.), *Contemporary chief information officers: Management experiences* (pp. 83–94). Hershey, PA: IGI Publishing. doi:10.4018/978-1-59904-078-3.ch007

Thomas, J. C. (2004). Public involvement in public administration in the information age: Speculations on the effects of technology. In M. Malkia, A. Anttiroiko, & R. Savolainen (Eds.), *eTransformation in governance: New directions in government and politics* (pp. 67–84). Hershey, PA: Idea Group Publishing.

Treiblmaier, H., & Chong, S. (2013). Trust and perceived risk of personal information as antecedents of online information disclosure: Results from three countries. In F. Tan (Ed.), *Global diffusion and adoption of technologies for knowledge and information sharing* (pp. 341–361). Hershey, PA: Information Science Reference.

van Grembergen, W., & de Haes, S. (2008). IT governance in practice: Six case studies. In W. van Grembergen, & S. De Haes (Eds.), *Implementing information technology governance: Models, practices and cases* (pp. 125–237). Hershey, PA: IGI Publishing.

van Os, G., Homburg, V., & Bekkers, V. (2013). Contingencies and convergence in European social security: ICT coordination in the back office of the welfare state. In M. Cruz-Cunha, I. Miranda, & P. Gonçalves (Eds.), *Handbook of research on ICTs and management systems for improving efficiency in healthcare and social care* (pp. 268–287). Hershey, PA: Medical Information Science Reference. doi:10.4018/978-1-4666-3990-4.ch013

Velloso, A. B., Gassenferth, W., & Machado, M. A. (2012). Evaluating IBMEC-RJ's intranet usability using fuzzy logic. In M. Cruz-Cunha, P. Gonçalves, N. Lopes, E. Miranda, & G. Putnik (Eds.), *Handbook of research on business social networking: Organizational, managerial, and technological dimensions* (pp. 185–205). Hershey, PA: Business Science Reference.

Villablanca, A. C., Baxi, H., & Anderson, K. (2009). Novel data interface for evaluating cardiovascular outcomes in women. In A. Dwivedi (Ed.), *Handbook of research on information technology management and clinical data administration in healthcare* (pp. 34–53). Hershey, PA: Medical Information Science Reference. doi:10.4018/978-1-60566-356-2.ch003

Villablanca, A. C., Baxi, H., & Anderson, K. (2011). Novel data interface for evaluating cardiovascular outcomes in women. In I. Management Association (Ed.), Clinical technologies: Concepts, methodologies, tools and applications (pp. 2094-2113). Hershey, PA: Medical Information Science Reference. doi: doi:10.4018/978-1-60960-561-2.ch806

Virkar, S. (2011). Information and communication technologies in administrative reform for development: Exploring the case of property tax systems in Karnataka, India. In J. Steyn, J. Van Belle, & E. Mansilla (Eds.), *ICTs for global development and sustainability: Practice and applications* (pp. 127–149). Hershey, PA: Information Science Reference.

Virkar, S. (2013). Designing and implementing e-government projects: Actors, influences, and fields of play. In S. Saeed, & C. Reddick (Eds.), *Human-centered system design for electronic governance* (pp. 88–110). Hershey, PA: Information Science Reference. doi:10.4018/978-1-4666-3640-8.ch007

Wallace, A. (2009). E-justice: An Australian perspective. In A. Martínez, & P. Abat (Eds.), *E-justice: Using information communication technologies in the court system* (pp. 204–228). Hershey, PA: Information Science Reference.

Wang, G. (2012). E-democratic administration and bureaucratic responsiveness: A primary study of bureaucrats' perceptions of the civil service e-mail box in Taiwan. In K. Kloby, & M. D'Agostino (Eds.), *Citizen 2.0: Public and governmental interaction through web 2.0 technologies* (pp. 146–173). Hershey, PA: Information Science Reference. doi:10.4018/978-1-4666-0318-9.ch009

Wangpipatwong, S., Chutimaskul, W., & Papasratorn, B. (2011). Quality enhancing the continued use of e-government web sites: Evidence from e-citizens of Thailand. In V. Weerakkody (Ed.), *Applied technology integration in governmental organizations: New e-government research* (pp. 20–36). Hershey, PA: Information Science Reference.

Wedemeijer, L. (2006). Long-term evolution of a conceptual schema at a life insurance company. In M. Khosrow-Pour (Ed.), *Cases on database technologies and applications* (pp. 202–226). Hershey, PA: Idea Group Publishing. doi:10.4018/978-1-59904-399-9.ch012

Whybrow, E. (2008). Digital access, ICT fluency, and the economically disadvantages: Approaches to minimize the digital divide. In F. Tan (Ed.), *Global information technologies: Concepts, methodologies, tools, and applications* (pp. 1409–1422). Hershey, PA: Information Science Reference. doi:10.4018/978-1-59904-949-6.ch049

Whybrow, E. (2008). Digital access, ICT fluency, and the economically disadvantages: Approaches to minimize the digital divide. In C. Van Slyke (Ed.), *Information communication technologies: Concepts, methodologies, tools, and applications* (pp. 764–777). Hershey, PA: Information Science Reference. doi:10.4018/978-1-59904-949-6.ch049

Wickramasinghe, N., & Geisler, E. (2010). Key considerations for the adoption and implementation of knowledge management in healthcare operations. In M. Saito, N. Wickramasinghe, M. Fuji, & E. Geisler (Eds.), *Redesigning innovative healthcare operation and the role of knowledge management* (pp. 125–142). Hershey, PA: Medical Information Science Reference.

Wickramasinghe, N., & Geisler, E. (2012). Key considerations for the adoption and implementation of knowledge management in healthcare operations. In I. Management Association (Ed.), Organizational learning and knowledge: Concepts, methodologies, tools and applications (pp. 1316-1328). Hershey, PA: Business Science Reference. doi: doi:10.4018/978-1-60960-783-8.ch405

Wickramasinghe, N., & Goldberg, S. (2007). A framework for delivering m-health excellence. In L. Al-Hakim (Ed.), *Web mobile-based applications for healthcare management* (pp. 36–61). Hershey, PA: IRM Press. doi:10.4018/978-1-59140-658-7.ch002

Wickramasinghe, N., & Goldberg, S. (2008). Critical success factors for delivering m-health excellence. In N. Wickramasinghe, & E. Geisler (Eds.), *Encyclopedia of healthcare information systems* (pp. 339–351). Hershey, PA: Medical Information Science Reference. doi:10.4018/978-1-59904-889-5.ch045

Wyld, D. (2009). Radio frequency identification (RFID) technology. In J. Symonds, J. Ayoade, & D. Parry (Eds.), *Auto-identification and ubiquitous computing applications* (pp. 279–293). Hershey, PA: Information Science Reference. doi:10.4018/978-1-60566-298-5.ch017

Yaghmaei, F. (2010). Understanding computerised information systems usage in community health. In J. Rodrigues (Ed.), *Health information systems: Concepts, methodologies, tools, and applications* (pp. 1388–1399). Hershey, PA: Medical Information Science Reference.

Yee, G., El-Khatib, K., Korba, L., Patrick, A. S., Song, R., & Xu, Y. (2005). Privacy and trust in e-government. In W. Huang, K. Siau, & K. Wei (Eds.), *Electronic government strategies and implementation* (pp. 145–190). Hershey, PA: Idea Group Publishing.

Yeh, S., & Chu, P. (2010). Evaluation of e-government services: A citizen-centric approach to citizen e-complaint services. In C. Reddick (Ed.), *Citizens and e-government: Evaluating policy and management* (pp. 400–417). Hershey, PA: Information Science Reference. doi:10.4018/978-1-61520-931-6.ch022

Young-Jin, S., & Seang-tae, K. (2008). E-government concepts, measures, and best practices. In A. Anttiroiko (Ed.), *Electronic government: Concepts, methodologies, tools, and applications* (pp. 32–57). Hershey, PA: Information Science Reference. doi:10.4018/978-1-59904-947-2.ch004

Yun, H. J., & Opheim, C. (2012). New technology communication in American state governments: The impact on citizen participation. In K. Bwalya, & S. Zulu (Eds.), *Handbook of research on e-government in emerging economies: Adoption, e-participation, and legal frameworks* (pp. 573–590). Hershey, PA: Information Science Reference. doi:10.4018/978-1-4666-0324-0.ch029

Zhang, N., Guo, X., Chen, G., & Chau, P. Y. (2011). User evaluation of e-government systems: A Chinese cultural perspective. In F. Tan (Ed.), *International enterprises and global information technologies: Advancing management practices* (pp. 63–84). Hershey, PA: Information Science Reference. doi:10.4018/978-1-60960-605-3.ch004

Zuo, Y., & Hu, W. (2011). Trust-based information risk management in a supply chain network. In J. Wang (Ed.), *Supply chain optimization, management and integration: Emerging applications* (pp. 181–196). Hershey, PA: Business Science Reference.

Compilation of References

Adamic, L., & Glance, N. (2005). The political blogosphere and the 2004 U.S. election: Divided they blog. In *Proceedings of the 3rd International Workshop on Link Discovery*, (pp. 36-43). ACM. doi:citeulike-article-id:1244437

Adida, B., de Marneffe, O., Pereira, O., & Quisquater, J.-J. (2009). *Electing a university president using open-audit voting*. Paper presented at the 3rd Int. Workshop on Security and Electronic Voting. Grenoble, France.

Agre, P. (2003). Peer-to-peer and the promise of internet equality. *Communications of the ACM*, *46*(2), 39–42. doi:10.1145/606272.606298

Aldridge, A., & Levine, K. (2001). *Surveying the social world: Principles and practice in survey research*. Buckingham, UK: Open University Press.

Allen, C., Yaeckel, B., & Kania, D. (1998). *Internet world guide to one-to-one web marketing*. Hoboken, NJ: John Wiley & Sons, Inc.

Allen, M. (2008). Web 2.0: An argument against convergence. *First Monday*, *13*(3). doi:10.5210/fm.v13i3.2139

Altena, M., & Ngwenya, N. (2012). Sites that cope, cure and commemorate: Weblogs of terminally ill. *The Presence of the Dead in our Lives, 82*, 55.

Althaus, S. L., & Tewksbury, D. (2000). Patterns of internet and traditional news media use in a networked community. *Political Communication*, *17*, 21–45. doi:10.1080/105846000198495

Alvarez, R.M., & Antonsson, E.K. (2007, Summer). Bridging science, technology, and politics. *The Bridge Linking Engineering and Society, Voting Technologies*, 6-10.

Anderson, R. (1993). Why cryptosystems fail. In *Proceedings of Conference on Computer and Communications Security*. ACM. Retrieved on August, 9, 2008, from http://www.cl.cam.ac.uk/~rja14/Papers/wcf.pdf

Anderson, C. (2004). *The long tail: Why the future of business is selling less of more*. New York, NY: Hyperion.

Anstead, N., & Chadwick, A. (2009). Parties, election campaigning, and the Internet: Toward a comparative institutional approach. In A. Chadwick, & P. Howard (Eds.), *Routledge handbook of internet politics* (pp. 56–71). London, UK: Routledge.

Antunovic, D., & Hardin, M. (2013). Women bloggers: Identity and the conceptualization of sports. *New Media & Society*. doi:10.1177/1461444812472323

Appel, A. W. (2006, June). *Ceci n'est pas une urne: On the internet vote for the Assemblée des Français de l'étranger.* Retrieved on July, 12, 2006, from http://www.cs.princeton.edu/~appel/papers/urne.pdf

Arthur, C. (2010, May 3). 2010: The first social media election: This is the first British general election in the social media age, but what difference has it made? *The Guardian*. Retrieved January 6, 2012 from http://www.guardian.co.uk/media/2010/apr/30/social-media-election-2010

Atiyah, P. S. (1958). Public benefit in charities. *The Modern Law Review*, *21*(2), 138–154. doi:10.1111/j.1468-2230.1958.tb00465.x

Atton, C. (1999). A reassessment of the alternative press. *Media Culture & Society*, *21*(1), 51–76. doi:10.1177/016344399021001003

Atton, C. (2002). News cultures and new social movements: Radical journalism and the mainstream media. *Journalism Studies*, *3*(4), 491–505. doi:10.1080/1461670022000019209

Atton, C. (2003). What is 'alternative' journalism? *Journalism*, *4*, 267–272. doi:10.1177/14648849030043001

Badouard, R. (2010). Pathways and obstacles to e-participation at the European level. *Journal of eDemocracy and Open Government*, *2*(2), 99-110.

Bardach, E. (1996). *The eight step path of policy analysis: A handbook for practice*. Berkeley, CA: Berkeley Academic Press.

Barnes, K., Marateo, R., & Ferris, S. P. (2007). Teaching and learning with the net generation. *Innovate Journal of Online Education*, *3*(4), 771–772.

Barney, D. (2004). *The network society*. Cambridge, UK: Polity.

Barry, A. (2001). *Political machines: Governing a technological society*. London: Athlone Press.

Bboyd, D. (2007). Social network sites: Definition, history, and scholarship. *Journal of Computer-Mediated Communication*, *13*(1).

Becker, H. S. (1997). Outsiders: Studies in the sociology of deviance (New ed.). New York: Free Press.

Bederson, B. B., Lee, B., Sherman, R., Herrnson, P. S., & Niemi, R. G. (2003). Electronic voting system usability issues. CHI Letters, 5(1), 145–152.

Benkler, Y. (2006). *The wealth of networks: How social production transforms market and freedom*. New Haven, CT: Yale University Press.

Benkler, Y. (2011). A free irresponsible press: Wikileaks and the battle over the soul of the networked estate. *Harvard Civil Rights-Civil Liberties Law Review*, *46*, 311–398.

Berners-Lee, T. (2010, November 22). Long live the web: A call for continued open standards and neutrality. *Scientific American*. Retrieved July 27, 2013, from http://www.scientificamerican.com/article.cfm?id=long-live-the-Web

Berryman, J. (2006). What defines 'enough' information? How policy workers make judgements and decisions during information seeking: Preliminary results from an exploratory study. *Information Research*, *11*(4), 11–14.

Biddix, J. P., & Park, H. W. (2008). Online networks of student protest: The case of the living wage campaign. *New Media & Society*, *10*(6), 871–891. doi:10.1177/1461444808096249

Bignon, J. (2003, March 25). *Rapport de l'assemblée nationale n° 721 tendant à autoriser le vote par correspondance électronique des Français établis hors de France pour les élections du Conseil supérieur des Français de l'étranger*.

Bimber, B. (2003). *Information and American democracy: Technology in the evolution of political power*. Cambridge, UK: Cambridge University Press. doi:10.1017/CBO9780511615573

Birdsall, S. (2005, October). The democratic divide. *First Monday*, *10*(10). Retrieved on August, 31, 2013, from http://www.firstmonday.org/issues/issue10_4/birdsall/index.html

Birza, L., Frank, P., & Klok, H. (2010). *Uitgangspunten online communicatie rijksambtenaren*. Den Haag: Ministerie van Algemene Zaken.

Bishop, J. (2004). *The potential of persuasive technology for educating heterogeneous user groups*. (Unpublished MSc Thesis). Univeristy of Glamorgan, Pontypridd, UK.

Bishop, J. (2005). The role of mediating artifacts in the design of persuasive e-learning systems. In *Proceedings of the First International Conferences on Internet Technologies and Applications*, (pp. 54-62). University of Wales.

Bishop, J. (2007). *An investigation into how the European Union affects the development and provision of e-learning services*. (Unpublished LLM Thesis). University of Glamorgan, Pontypridd, UK.

Bishop, J. (2007). Evaluation-centred design of e-learning communities: A case study and review. In V. Grout, D. Oram & R. Picking (Eds.), *Proceedings of the Second International Conference on Internet Technologies and Applications* (pp. 1-9). Wrexham, UK: University of Wales Press.

Bishop, J. (2011). *The equatrics of intergenerational knowledge transformation in techno-cultures: Towards a model for enhancing information management in virtual worlds.* (Unpublished MScEcon Thesis). Aberystwyth University, Aberystwyth, UK.

Bishop, J. (2011). Mum's the wordpress: A comparative analysis of political and mommy bloggers. In *Proceedings of the 2011 Internet Conference on Internet Computing (ICOMP'2011).* ICOMP.

Bishop, J. (2012). Tackling internet abuse in great Britain: Towards a framework for classifying severities of 'flame trolling'. In *Proceedings of the 11th International Conference on Security and Management (SAM'12).* SAM.

Bishop, J. (2012). Taming the chatroom bob: The role of brain-computer interfaces that manipulate prefrontal cortex optimization for increasing participation of victims of traumatic sex and other abuse online. In *Proceedings of the 13th International Conference on Bioinformatics and Computational Biology (BIOCOMP'12).* BIOCOMP.

Bishop, J. (2007). Ecological cognition: A new dynamic for human-computer interaction. In B. Wallace, A. Ross, J. Davies, & T. Anderson (Eds.), *The mind, the body and the world: Psychology after cognitivism* (pp. 327–345). Exeter, UK: Imprint Academic.

Bishop, J. (2007). Increasing participation in online communities: A framework for human–computer interaction. *Computers in Human Behavior, 23*(4), 1881–1893. doi:10.1016/j.chb.2005.11.004

Bishop, J. (2009). *Developing a holistic approach for investigating online communities: A critical evaluation of two research articles (No. BHM802).* Swansea, UK: The Crocels Press.

Bishop, J. (2009). Enhancing the understanding of genres of web-based communities: The role of the ecological cognition framework. *International Journal of Web Based Communities, 5*(1), 4–17. doi:10.1504/IJWBC.2009.021558

Bishop, J. (2009). The role of multi-agent social networking systems in ubiquitous education: Enhancing peer-supported reflective learning. In T. T. Goh (Ed.), *Multiplatform e-learning systems and technologies: Mobile devices for ubiquitous ICT-based education* (pp. 72–88). Hershey, PA: IGI Global. doi:10.4018/978-1-60566-703-4.ch005

Bishop, J. (2011). *An analysis and discussion of an investigation of online information seeking behaviour research: The case of 'information seeking on the web: An integrated model of browsing and searching' (No. DSM1810).* Swansea, UK: The Crocels Press.

Bishop, J. (2012). Scope and limitations in the government of wales act 2006 for tackling internet abuses in the form of 'flame trolling'. *Statute Law Review, 33*(2), 207–216. doi:10.1093/slr/hms016

Bishop, J. (2012). Co-operative e-learning in the multilingual and multicultural school: The role of 'classroom 2.0' for increasing participation in education. In P. M. Pumilia-Gnarini, E. Favaron, E. Pacetti, J. Bishop, & L. Guerra (Eds.), *Didactic strategies and technologies for education: Incorporating advancements* (pp. 137–150). Hershey, PA: IGI Global. doi:10.4018/978-1-4666-2122-0.ch013

Bishop, J. (2012). The psychology of trolling and lurking: The role of defriending and gamification for increasing participation in online communities using seductive narratives. In H. Li (Ed.), *Virtual community participation and motivation: Cross-disciplinary theories* (pp. 160–176). Hershey, PA: IGI Global.

Bishop, J. (2012). Lessons from the emotivate project for increasing take-up of big society and responsible capitalism initiatives. In P. M. Pumilia-Gnarini, E. Favaron, E. Pacetti, J. Bishop, & L. Guerra (Eds.), *Didactic strategies and technologies for education: Incorporating advancements* (pp. 208–217). Hershey, PA: IGI Global. doi:10.4018/978-1-4666-2122-0.ch019

Bishop, J. (2013). The effect of deindividuation of the internet troller on criminal procedure implementation: An interview with a hater. *International Journal of Cyber Criminology, 7*(1), 28–48.

Bishop, J. (2013). Increasing capital revenue in social networking communities: Building social and economic relationships through avatars and characters. In J. Bishop (Ed.), *Examining the concepts, issues, and implications of Internet trolling* (pp. 44–61). Hershey, PA: IGI Global. doi:10.4018/978-1-4666-2803-8.ch005

Bishop, J. (2013). The psychology of trolling and lurking: The role of defriending and gamification for increasing participation in online communities using seductive narratives. In J. Bishop (Ed.), *Examining the concepts, issues and implications of Internet trolling* (pp. 106–123). Hershey, PA: IGI Global. doi:10.4018/978-1-4666-2803-8.ch009

Bishop, J. (2014). Representations of 'trolls' in mass media communication: A review of media-texts and moral panics relating to 'internet trolling'. *International Journal of Web Based Communities*, *10*(1), 7–24. doi:10.1504/IJWBC.2014.058384

Blondiaux, L. (2008). *Le nouvel esprit de la démocratie: Actualité de la démocratie participative* [The New Spirit of Democracy: Update on Participative Democracy]. Paris: Le Seuil.

Blondiaux, L., & Fourniau, J.-M. (2011). Un bilan des recherches sur la participation du public en démocratie: beaucoup de bruit pour rien? [Review of Research on Public Participation in Democracy: Much Ado about Nothing?]. *Participations*, *1*, 10–35. doi:10.3917/parti.001.0008

Bobbio, N. (1987). *The future of democracy*. London, UK: Polity Press.

Bochsler, D. (2009). Can the internet increase political participation? An analysis of remote electronic voting's effect on turnout. *Potsdam ECPR Panels on Internet & Politics*. Retrieved on October, 4, 2010, from http://papers.ssrn.com/sol3/papers.cfm?abstract_id=1456827

Boullier, D. (2009). Les industries de l'attention: Au-delà de la fidélisation et de l'opinion. *Reseaux*, (154): 232–246.

Bouneau, C., Burigana, D., & Varsori, A. (2010). *Trends in technological innovation and the European construction*. New York: Peter Lang.

Bourcier, D. (2006). Comment s'accorder sur les normes ? Le droit et la gouvernance face à internet. [How to Agree on Norms? Law and Governance Take On the Internet]. *Lex Electronica, 10*(3).

Bourdieu, P. (1977). *Outline of a theory of practice*. Cambridge, UK: Cambridge University Press. doi:10.1017/CBO9780511812507

Bowman, L. (2008). Re-examining gatekeeping. *Journalism Practice*, *2*(1), 99–112. doi:10.1080/17512780701768550

Bradier, A. (2004). Le gouvernement électronique: Une priorité européenne. [E-Government: A European Priority]. *Revue Française d'Administration Publique*, *2*(110), 337–347. doi:10.3917/rfap.110.0337

Braman, S. (2011). Designing for instability: Internet architecture and constant change. In *Media in transition 7 (MIT7) unstable platforms: The promise and peril of transition*. Cambridge, MA: Academic Press.

Brandenburg, K. (1999). *MP3 and AAC explained*. Paper presented at the Audio Engineering Society Conference: 17th International Conference: High-Quality Audio Coding. New York, NY.

Branston, G., & Stafford, R. (2010). *The media student's book*. London: Routledge.

Brehm, J., & Rahn, W. (1997). Individual-level evidence for the causes and consequences of social capital. *American Journal of Political Science*, *41*, 999. doi:10.2307/2111684

Bremmer, I. (2010, November-December). Democracy in cyberspace: What information technology can and cannot do. *Foreign Affairs*, 86–92.

Bressler, S. E., & Grantham, C. (2000). *Communities of commerce: Building internet business communities to accelerate growth, minimize risk, and increase customer loyalty*. New York: McGraw-Hill Professional.

Brooks, C., Cooke, J., & Vassileva, J. (2003). Versioning of learning objects. In *Proceedings of the Advanced Learning Technologies,* (pp. 296-297). IEEE.

Brown, K., Jackson, M., & Cassidy, W. (2006). Cyberbullying: Developing policy to direct responses that are equitable and effective in addressing this special form of bullying. *Canadian Journal of Educational Administration and Policy*, *57*(1), 1–36.

Bruns, A. (2005). *Gatewatching: Collaborative online news production*. New York: Peter Lang.

Bruns, A. (2008). News blogs and citizen journalism: New directions for e-journalism. In *E-journalism: New directions in electronic news media*. New Delhi: BR Publishing.

Bruns, A. (2008). The active audience: Transforming journalism from gatekeeping to gatewatching. In *Making online news: The ethnography of new media production*. New York: Peter Lang.

Bryman, A., & Bell, E. (2003). *Business research methods*. Oxford, UK: Oxford University Press.

Brynjolfsson, E., & Urban, G. L. (2001). *Strategies for e-business success*. Hoboken, NJ: John Wiley & Sons, Inc.

Buchanan, R. (2000). Good design in the digital age. *AIGA Journal of Design for the Network Economy*, *1*(1), 1–5.

Burnett, R., & Marshall, P. D. (2003). *Web theory: An introduction*. New York: Routledge.

Bygrave, L., & Bing, J. (2009). *Internet governance: Infrastructure and institutions*. Oxford, UK: Oxford University Press. doi:10.1093/acprof:oso/9780199561131.001.0001

Cabinet Office. (2008). *Participation online: Guidance for civil servants*. London: UK Cabinet Office.

Callon, M. (1991). Techno-economic networks and irreversibility. In *A sociology of monsters: Essays on power, technology, and domination* (pp. 132–161). London: Routledge.

Calvert, R. L. (1995). Rational actors, equilibrium, and social institutions. In *Explaining social institutions*. Academic Press.

Cammaerts, B. (2006). Media and communication strategies of glocalized activists: Beyond media-centric thinking. In *Reclaiming the media: Communication rights and expanding democratic media roles*. Bristol, UK: Intellect.

Canadian Press. (2011). *The social media battleground of the 2011 federal election*. Retrieved May 3, 2012 from http://www.marketingmag.ca/news/media-news/the-social-media-battleground-of-the-2011-federal-election-25038

Canadian Press. (2011). *Social media takes off in first week of campaign*. Retrieved May 3, 2012 from http://www.ctv.ca/servlet/ArticleNews/story/CTVNews/20110402/social-media-election-110402/20110402?s_name=election2011

Caporusso, L. (2010). The role of trust, participation and identity in the propensity to e- and i-vote. In *Proceedings of Electronic Voting 2010, 4th International Conference Electronic Voting (EVOTE 2010)*. Bregenz, Austria: EVOTE.

Cardon, D. (2008). *Le design de la visibilité: Un essai de typologie du web 2.0*. Retrieved from http://www.Internetactu.net/2008/02/01/le-design-de-la-visibilite-un-essai-de-typologie-du-Web-20

Carr, P. (2012). National identity versus commerce: An analysis of opportunities and limitations within the Welsh music scene for composers and performing musicians. *Popular Music History*, *5*(3), 265–285. doi:10.1558/pomh.v5i3.265

Casany, M. J., Alier, M., Mayol, E., Conde, M. A., & García-Peñalvo, F. J. (2013). Mobile learning as an asset for development: Challenges and oportunities. In *Information systems, e-learning, and knowledge management research* (pp. 244–250). Berlin: Springer. doi:10.1007/978-3-642-35879-1_29

Cassidy, W., Brown, K., & Jackson, M. (2013). Moving from cyber-bullying to cyber-kindness: What do students, educators and parents say? In J. Bishop (Ed.), *Examining the concepts, issues and implications of Internet trolling* (pp. 62–83). Hershey, PA: IGI Global. doi:10.4018/978-1-4666-2803-8.ch006

Castells, M. (1998). *End of millennium*. Oxford, UK: Blackwell.

Castells, M. (2009). *Communication power*. Oxford, UK: Oxford University Press.

Cefaï, D. (1996). La construction des problèmes publics: Définitions de situations dans des arènes publiques. *Reseaux*, *14*(75), 43–66.

Chadwick, A. (2009). Web 2.0: New Challenges for the study of e-democracy in an era of informational exuberance. *I/S. Journal of Law and Policy for the Information Society*, *5*, 9.

Chadwick, A., & Howard, P. (Eds.). (2009). *Routledge handbook of internet politics*. London, UK: Routledge.

Chandler, J. A. (2001). *Local government today*. Manchester, UK: Manchester University Press.

Chateauraynaud, F. (2011). *Argumenter dans un champ de forces: Essai de balistique sociologique*. Paris: Pétra.

Choi, Y. S., & Ross, L. (2006). Policy and power: The impact of the internet on the younger generation in South Korea. *Social Policy and Society*, *5*(3), 421–429. doi:10.1017/S1474746406003095

Choo, C. W., Detlor, B., & Turnbull, D. (2000). Information seeking on the web: An integrated model of browsing and searching. *First Monday*, *5*, 2–7. doi:10.5210/fm.v5i2.729

Christin, T., & Trechsel, A. H. (2004). *Qui vote par internet? Rapport, Université de Genève*. Retrieved on August, 5, 2007, from http://www.geneve.ch/evoting/doc/rapports/200409_rapport_carouge_meyrin.pdf

Clark, D. (2007). Network neutrality: Words of power and 800-pound gorillas. *International Journal of Communication*, *1*, 701–708.

Clarke, R. (2006). *Introduction to dataveillance and information privacy, and definitions of terms*. Retrieved May 17, 2012, from http://www.rogerclarke.com/DV/Intro.html#DV

Cleland, J. (2013). Racism, football fans, and online message boards: How social media has added a new dimension to racist discourse in english football. *Journal of Sport and Social Issues*. doi:10.1177/0193723513499922

Cofta, P. (2007). Confidence, trust and identity. *BP Technology Journal*, *25*(2), 173–178. doi:10.1007/s10550-007-0042-4

Cohen, A. P. (1985). *The symbolic construction of community*. New York: Routledge. doi:10.4324/9780203323373

Cohen, L., Manion, L., & Morrison, K. (2000). *Research methods in education* (5th ed.). London: Routledge Falmer. doi:10.4324/9780203224342

Cohen, S. (2002). *Folk devils and moral panics: The creation of the mods and rockers* (3rd ed.). Abingdon, UK: Routledge.

Colarik, A. (2006). *Cyber terrorism: Political and economic implications*. Hershey, PA: IGI Global. doi:10.4018/978-1-59904-021-9

Coleman, S. (2002). Elections in the 21st century: From paper ballot to e-voting. Om The independent commission on alternative voting methods. London: Electoral Reform Society.

Coleman, S. (2005). Internet voting and democratic politics in an age of crisis. In The European Union and e-voting: Addressing The European Parliament's internet voting challenge. London: Routledge.

Coleman, S. (2008). Foundations of digital government. In *Digital government: E-government research, case studies, and implementation*. New York: Springer. doi:10.1007/978-0-387-71611-4_1

Coleman, S. (2009). Making parliamentary democracy visible. In A. Chadwick, & P. Howard (Eds.), *Routledge handbook of internet politics* (pp. 86–98). London, UK: Routledge.

Coleman, S. (2010). Virtual (s.v.). In M. Bevir (Ed.), *Encylopedia of political theory*. London, UK: Sage. doi:10.4135/9781412958660.n464

Commission on Electronic Voting. (2004, December). Secrecy, accuracy and testing of the chosen electronic system. *First Report*. Retrieved on May, 13, 2006, from http://www.cev.ie/htm/report/first_report.htm

Commission on Electronic Voting. (2006, July). Secrecy, accuracy and testing of the chosen electronic voting system. *Second Report*. Retrieved on September, 1, 2006, from http://www.cev.ie/htm/report/download_second.htm

Connaway, L. S., Radford, M. L., Dickey, T. J., De Angelis Williams, J., & Confer, P. (2008). Sense-making and synchronicity: Information-seeking behaviors of millennials and baby boomers. *Libri*, *58*(2), 123–135. doi:10.1515/libr.2008.014

Connelly, B. L., Certo, S. T., Ireland, R. D., & Reutzel, C. R. (2011). Signaling theory: A review and assessment. *Journal of Management*, *37*(1), 39–67. doi:10.1177/0149206310388419

Conseil Fédéral Suisse. (2002, January 9). Rapport sur le vote électronique chances, risques et faisabilité. *Rapport n°02.009*. Retrieved on August, 31, 2013, from http://www.admin.ch/ch/f/ff/2002/612.pdf

Consulat Général de France à Washington. (2010). *Elections AFE 2010*. Retrieved on October, 30, 2010, from http://www.consulfrance-washington.org/spip.php?article567#4-Comment-comptez-vous-remedier

Conway, J., & Lawrence, M. (2013). Competition between schools. In *Equality and diversity in education 1: Experiences of learning, teaching and managing schools*. Academic Press.

Crick, B. (2002). *Democracy: A very short introduction*. Oxford, UK: Oxford University Press.

Cunliffe, D. (2007). Minority languages and the internet: New threats, new opportunities. *Multilingual Matters, 138*, 133.

Curry, B. (2011, March 27). Canada's first social media election is on, but will people vote? *Globe and Mail*. Retrieved January 6, 2012 from http://www.theglobeandmail.com/news/politics/canadas-first-social-media-election-is-on-butwill-people-vote/article1959166/

Cutrell, E., & Guan, Z. (2007). What are you looking for? An eye-tracking study of information usage in web search. In *Proceedings of the SIGCHI Conference on Human Factors in Computing Systems*. ACM.

Dacheux, E. (2004). L'impossible défi: La politique de communication de l'Union Européenne. [An Impossible Challenge: The Communication Policy of the European Union]. Paris: CNRS Ed.s.

Dahl, R. (1956). *A preface to democratic theory*. Chicago, IL: Chicago University Press.

Damaschke, K. C., & Kommers, P. (2012). Motives and relevance of online friendships. *IJWBC, 8*(2), 266–280.

Davies, D. T. (2012). *Broadband services in Wales: First report of session 2012-13, report, together with formal minutes, oral and written evidence*. The Stationery Office.

Davies, H., & Bressan, B. (2010). *A history of international research networking*. Hoboken, NJ: Wiley-VCH. doi:10.1002/9783527629336

Dawes, S. (2008). The evolution and continuing challenges of e-governance. *Public Administration Review*, 86–102. doi:10.1111/j.1540-6210.2008.00981.x

de France, B. Observatoire de la Sécurité des Cartes de Paiement. (2012). *Rapport annuel, statistiques de fraude pour 2012*. Retrieved on August, 31, 2013, from http://www.banque-france.fr/observatoire/telechar/2013/Rapport-annuel-2012.pdf

de Souza, C. S., & Preece, J. (2004). A framework for analyzing and understanding online communities. *Interacting with Computers, 16*(3), 579–610. doi:10.1016/j.intcom.2003.12.006

DeNardis, L. (2009). *Protocol politics: The globalization of internet governance*. Cambridge, MA: The MIT Press. doi:10.7551/mitpress/9780262042574.001.0001

des Français de l'Etranger, A. (2008, March). 10 propositions pour améliorer la participation électorale des Français de l'étranger. *Rapport de la commission temporaire de la participation électorale des français établis hors de France, avant-projet*. Retrieved on August, 23, 2009, from http://www.francais-du-monde.org/wp-content/uploads/2008/10/2008-10-propositionsrev.pdf

Deuze, M. (2003). The web and its journalisms: Considering the consequences of different types of news-media online. *New Media & Society, 5*(2), 203–230. doi:10.1177/1461444803005002004

Dewey, J. (1991). *The public and its problems*. Athens, OH: Ohio University Press.

Diamond, L. (2010). Liberation technology. *Journal of Democracy, 3*, 69–83. doi:10.1353/jod.0.0190

Dill, D., & Doherty, W. (2004, November 22). Electronic voting systems. *Report for the National Research Council*. Retrieved on August, 31, 2013, from http://www.openvotingconsortium.org/files/project_evoting_vvf.pdf

Dimaggio, P., Hargittai, E., Neuman, W. R., & Ronbinson, J. (2001). Social implications of the internet. *Annual Review of Sociology, 27*, 307–336. doi:10.1146/annurev.soc.27.1.307

Dimitrova, D. V., Connolly-Ahern, C., Williams, A. P., Kaid, L. L., & Reid, A. (2003). Hyperlinking as gatekeeping: Online newspaper coverage of the execution of an American terrorist. *Journalism Studies*, *4*(3), 401–414. doi:10.1080/14616700306488

Dimmock, C. (2011). Diversifying schools and leveraging school improvement: A comparative analysis of the English radical, and Singapore conservative, specialist schools' policies. *British Journal of Educational Studies*, *59*(4), 439–458. doi:10.1080/00071005.2011.636732

Dolwick, J. (2009). The social and beyond: Introducing actor-network theory. *J Mari Arch*, *4*, 21–49. doi:10.1007/s11457-009-9044-3

Domingo, D., Quand, T., Heinonen, A., Paulussen, S., Singer, J. B., & Vujnovic, M. (2008). Participatory journalism practices in the media and beyond. *Journalism Practice*, *2*(3), 326–342. doi:10.1080/17512780802281065

Downing, J. (1984). *Radical media: The political experience of alternative communication*. Boston: South End Press.

Downing, J. (1988). The alternative public realm: The organization of the 1980s anti-nuclear press in West Germany and Britain. *Media Culture & Society*, *10*, 163–181. doi:10.1177/016344388010002003

Downing, J., Villarreal Ford, T., Gil, G., & Stein, L. (2001). *Radical media: Rebellious communication and social movements*. Thousand Oaks, CA: Sage.

Drowning, K. E., Nichols, D. P., & MacAdam, B. (1993). *Reaching a multicultural student community: A handbook for academic librarians*. Westport, CT: Greenwood Publishing Group, Inc.

Duguid, P., & Seely, J. (20022). *The social life of information*. Boston, MA: Harvard Business School Press.

Durante, M. (2011). Normativity, constructionism, and constraining affordances. *Etica & Politica*, *13*(2), 180–200.

Durkheim, E. (1895). *The rules of the sociological method*. New York: The Free Press.

Durkheim, E. (1997). *The division of labor in society* (L. A. Coser, Trans.). New York: Free Press.

Dutton, W. H., & Peltu, M. (2007). Reconfiguring government-public engagements: Enhancing the communicative power of citizens. *Oxford Internet Institute*. Retrieved from http://www.oii.ox.ac.uk/research/publications/FD9.pdf

Dye, T. R. (1981). *Understanding public policy*. Upper Saddle River, NJ: Prentice-Hall.

Ebeling, E. R. (1994). Building community through education. *Building a Community of Citizens: Civil Society in the 21st Century*, 119-132.

Edge. (2010). Retrieved May 17, 2012, from http://www.edge.org/3rd_culture/gelernter09/gelernter09_index.html

Edmunds, A., & Morris, A. (2000). The problem of information overload in business organisations: A review of the literature. *International Journal of Information Management*, *20*(1), 17–28. doi:10.1016/S0268-4012(99)00051-1

Edwards, L. (2012). Section 127 of the communications act 2003: Threat or menace?. *SCL Journal*, *23*(4).

Edwards, R. (2011). *Sarah Hill, 'Blewytirhwng?' The place of welsh pop music*. Burlington, VT: Ashgate.

Ehringfeld, A., Naber, L., Grechenig, T., Krimmer, R., Traxl, M., & Fischer, G. (2010). Analysis of recommendation rec(2004)11 based on the experiences of specific attacks against the first legally binding implementation of e-voting in Austria. In *Proceedings of Electronic Voting 2010, 4th International Conference Electronic Voting (EVOTE 2010)*, (pp. 225-237). Bregenz, Austria: EVOTE.

Elkin-Koren, N. (2006). Making technology visible: Liability of internet service providers for peer-to-peer traffic. *New York University Journal of Legislation and Public Policy*, *9*(15), 15–76.

Ellis, D., & Haugan, M. (1997). Modelling the information seeking patterns of engineers and research scientists in an industrial environment. *The Journal of Documentation*, *53*(4), 384–403. doi:10.1108/EUM0000000007204

Emerson, R. M., & Messinger, S. L. (1977). The micro-politics of trouble. *Social Problems*, *25*(2), 121–134. doi:10.2307/800289

Enguehard, C., & Lehn, R. (2009, July 13). *Vulnerability analysis of three remote voting methods*. Paper presented at the XXI IPSA World Congress of Political Science, RC10 Electronic Democracy - Dilemmas of Change? Santiago, Chile.

Ericson, R. V., Baranek, P. M., & Chan, J. B. L. (1989). *Negotiation control: A study of news sources*. Milton Keynes, UK: Open University Press.

Etzioni, A. (1976). *Social problems*. Upper Saddle River, NJ: Prentice-Hall.

Etzioni, A. (1993). *The spirit of community: Rights, responsibilities and the communitarian agenda*. New York: Crown.

European Commission for Democracy through Law. (2002, July). *Guidelines on elections*. Retrieved on February, 23, 2008, from http://www.venice.coe.int/docs/2002/CDL-AD(2002)013-e.asp

European Commission for Democracy through Law. (2004, September). *Legal, operational and technical standards for e-voting* (Recommendation Rec(2004)11). Retrieved on August, 31, 2013, from https://wcd.coe.int/ViewDoc.jsp?id=778189

Eveland, W. P., & Dunwoody, S. (2001). User control and structural isomorphism or disorientation and cognitive load? Learning from the web versus print. *Communication Research*, *28*, 48–78. doi:10.1177/009365001028001002

Farrell, H., & Drezner, D. (2008). The power and politics of blogs. *Public Choice*, *134*(1), 15–30. doi: doi:10.1007/s11127-007-9198-1

Faucilhon, J. (2010). *Rêveurs, marchands et pirates: Que reste-t-il du rêve de l'internet* [Dreamers, Merchants and Pirates: What remains of the Internet dream?]. Lekti.

Fawcett, N. (2000). Just what is innovation? *Technology Review*, (4): 1–7.

Faye, I. (2012). *Thank you hater*. MAR.

Feezell, J. T., et al. (2009). *Facebook is...fostering political investment: A study of online social networking groups and offline participation*. APSA Toronto Meeting Paper. Retrieved from http://ssrn.com/abstract=1451456

Felstiner, W., Abel, R., & Sarat, A. (1980 - 1981). The emergence and transformation of disputes: Naming, blaming, claiming. *Law & Society Review*, *15*(3/4), 631-654. doi:citeulike-article-id:511899

Felstiner, W. L. F., Abel, R. L., & Sarat, A. (1991). L'émergence et la transformation des litiges: Réaliser, reprocher, réclamer. *Politix*, *16*, 41–54. doi:10.3406/polix.1991.1477

Fenno, R. F. Jr. (1973). *Congressmen in committees*. Academic Press.

Fenno, R. F. Jr. (1978). *Home style: House members in their districts*. Academic Press.

Figallo, C. (1998). *Hosting web communities: Building relationships, increasing customer loyalty, and maintaining a competitive edge*. New York: John Wiley & Sons, Inc.

Fisher, E. J. (2013). From cyber bullying to cyber coping: The misuse of mobile technology and social media and their effects on people's lives. *Business and Economic Review*, *3*(2), 127–145. doi:10.5296/ber.v3i2.4176

Flichy, P. (2001). *L'imaginaire d'Internet* [The Internet Imaginaire]. Paris: La Découverte.

Floridi, L. (2011). *The philosophy of information*. Oxford, UK: Oxford University Press. doi:10.1093/acprof:oso/9780199232383.001.0001

Floridi, L. (2012). Hyperhistory and the philosophy of information policies. *Philosophy and Technology*, *25*(2), 129–131. doi:10.1007/s13347-012-0077-4

Fluckiger, F. (2000). Le réseau des chercheurs Européens. [The Network of European Researchers]. *La Recherche*, 328.

Forde, S., Foxwell, K., & Meadows, M. (2003). Through the lens of the local: Public arena journalism in the Australian community broadcasting sector. *Journalism*, *4*, 314–335. doi:10.1177/14648849030043004

Fox, G. (2001). Peer-to-peer networks. *Computing in Science & Engineering*, *3*(3), 75–77. doi:10.1109/5992.919270

Francoli, M., Greenberg, J., & Waddell, C. (2011). The campaign in digital media. In *The Canadian federal election of 2011*. Toronto: Dundurn.

French General Council on Industry. Energy and Technology (CGIET). (2010). *La neutralité dans le réseau internet*. [Neutrality in the Internet Network]. Retrieved July 27, 2013, from http://www.cgiet.org/documents/2010_05_31_2009_31_CGIET_Neutralite-rapportfinal.pdf

French National Assembly. (2011). *Rapport d'information sur la neutralité de l'internet et des réseaux.* [Information Report on the Neutrality of the Internet and of networks]. Retrieved July 27, 2013, from http://www.scribd.com/doc/52921570/Rapport-provisoire-de-la-mission-d-information-sur-la-neutralite-du-net.

Fuller, M. (Ed.). (2008). *Software studies: A lexicon.* Cambridge, MA: The MIT Press. doi:10.7551/mit-press/9780262062749.001.0001

Galtung, J., & Ruge, M. (1965). The structure of foreign news. *Journal of Peace Research, 1*, 64–90. doi:10.1177/002234336500200104

Gamson, W., & Wolfsfeld, G. (1993). Movements and media as interacting system. *The Annals of the American Academy of Political and Social Science, 582*, 114–125. doi:10.1177/0002716293528001009

Geessink, L. (2013). *Segmenting and targeting new charity donors. (Bachelor of Business AdministrationThesis).* Twente, The Netherlands: University of Twente.

Gewirtz, S., Ball, S. J., & Bowe, R. (1995). *Markets, choice, and equity in education.* Buckingham, UK: Open University.

Gharadaghy, R., & Volkamer, M. (2010). Verifiability in electronic voting explanations for non security experts. In *Proceedings of Electronic Voting 2010, 4th International Conference Electronic Voting (EVOTE 2010),* (pp. 151-162). Bregenz, Austria: EVOTE.

Gibton, D. (2001). Grounded theory method: The meaning of data analysis process and the theory building in qualitative research. In *Genres and traditions in qualitative research.* Tel-Aviv, Israel: Devir.

Girden, E. R. (2001). *Evaluating research articles from start to finish* (2nd ed.). Thousand Oaks, CA: Sage Publications, Inc.

Gitlin, T. (1980). *The whole world is watching- Media in the making and the unmaking of the new left.* Berkeley, CA: University of California Press.

Glaser, B., & Strauss, A. L. (1967). *The discovery of grounded theory.* Chicago: Aldine.

Goffman, E. (1959). *The presentation of self in everyday life.* New York: Doubleday and Anchor Books.

Goldsmith, J. (1998). Against cyberanarchy. *The University of Chicago Law Review. University of Chicago. Law School, 68*, 1199–1250. doi:10.2307/1600262

Goldsmith, J., & Wu, T. (2006). *Who controls the internet? Illusions of a borderless world.* Oxford, UK: Oxford University Press.

Goode, S. D. (2010). *Understanding and addressing adult sexual attraction to children: A study of pedophiles in contemporary society.* Abingdon, UK: Routledge.

Gorard, S., & Fitz, J. (1998). Under starters orders: The established market, the Cardiff study and the Smithfield project. *International Studies in Sociology of Education, 8*(3), 299–316. doi:10.1080/0962021980020030

Gordon, U. (2010). Against the wall: Anarchist mobilization in the Israeli–Palestinian conflict. *Peace and Change, 35*(3), 412–433. doi:10.1111/j.1468-0130.2010.00641.x

Gorman, P. (1998). Information seeking of primary care physicians: Conceptual models and empirical studies. In *Proceedings of the Second International Conference on Research in Information Needs, Seeking and use in Different Contexts.* Academic Press.

Green, P. (2000, October 5). The politics of the future: The internet and democracy in Australia. *ACT Electoral Commission, to the Australian Political Science Association's Politics of the Future Seminar at the Australian National University.* Retrieved on September, 1, 2007, from http://www.elections.act.gov.au/adobe/PolFut.pdf

Greffet, F. (2011). *Continuerlalutte.com: Les partis politiques sur le web.* Paris: Presses de Sciences Po.

Griffiths, A., & Wall, S. (2000). *Intermediate microeconomics: Theory and applications.* Reading, MA: Addison-Wesley Longman Ltd.

Grimes, T. R. (1990). Truth, content, and the hypothetico-deductive method. *Philosophy of Science, 57*(3), 514–522. doi:10.1086/289571

Grimmelmann, J. (2005). Regulation by software. *The Yale Law Journal, 114*, 1719–1758.

Grimmelmann, J. (2009). Saving facebook. *Iowa Law Review, 94*, 1137.

Gusfield, J. R. (1980). *The culture of public problems: Drinking-driving and the symbolic order*. Chicago: The University of Chicago Press.

Habermas, J. (2006). Political communication in media society: Does democracy still enjoy an epistemic dimension? The impact of normative theory on empirical research. *Communication Theory*, *16*, 411–426. doi:10.1111/j.1468-2885.2006.00280.x

Haenni, R., Jaquet-Chiffelle, D.-O., Anrig, B., & Benoist, E. (2009). Core concepts and definitions. In D.-O. Jaquet-Chiffelle, & H. Buitelaar (Eds.), *D17.4: Trust and identification in the light of virtual persons* (pp. 38–58). FIDIS Deliverable.

Hafez, K. (2008). The myth of media globalization. (A. Skinner, Trans.). *Arab Studies Quartely*, *30*(1).

Hagel, J., & Armstrong, A. (1997). *Net gain: Expanding markets through virtual communities*. Boston, MA: Harvard University Press.

Hall, T., & Loeber, L. (2010). Electronic elections in a politicized polity. In *Proceedings of 4th International Conference Electronic Voting (EVOTE 2010)*, (pp. 193-212). Bregenz, Austria: EVOTE.

Hall, M., Hanna, L., & Huey, G. (2013). Use and views on social networking sites of pharmacy students in the United Kingdom. *American Journal of Pharmaceutical Education*, *77*(1). doi:10.5688/ajpe7719 PMID:23459621

Hall, S., Critcher, C., Jefferson, T., Clarke, J. N., & Roberts, B. (1993). *Policing the crisis: Mugging, the state and law and order*. London: Macmillan.

Hamilton, A. (2011). *How Stephen Harper is out-Obama-ing Michael Ignatieff*. Retrieved May 3, 2012 from http://www.aranhamilton.com/post/4350146223/how-stephen-harper-is-out-obama-ing-michael-ignatieff

Hamilton, J., & Atton, C. (2001). Theorizing Anglo-American alternative media: Toward a contextual history and analysis of US and UK scholarship. *Media History*, *7*(2), 119–135. doi:10.1080/13688800120092200

Harcup, T. (2003). The unspoken – said: The journalism of alternative media. *Journalism*, *4*(3), 356–376. doi:10.1177/14648849030043006

Hardaker, C. (2010). Trolling in asynchronous computer-mediated communication: From user discussions to academic definitions. *Journal of Politeness Research. Language, Behaviour. Culture (Canadian Ethnology Society)*, *6*(2), 215–242.

Hartley, J. (1982). *Understanding news*. London: Routledge.

Harvey, J. A., & Busher, H. (1996). Marketing schools and consumer choice. *International Journal of Educational Management*, *10*(4), 26–32. doi:10.1108/09513549610122165

Harvey, L. J., & Myers, M. D. (1995). Scholarship and practice: The contribution of ethnographic research methods to bridging the gap. *Information Technology & People*, *8*(3), 13–27. doi:10.1108/09593849510098244

Harwood, E. M., & Hutchinson, E. (2009). Data collection methods series: Part 2: Select the most feasible data collection mode. *Journal of Wound, Ostomy, and Continence Nursing*, *36*(2), 129. doi:10.1097/01.WON.0000347654.49228.44 PMID:19287261

Hatcher, R. (2011). The conservative-liberal democrat coalition government's free schools in england. *Educational Review*, *63*(4), 485–503. doi:10.1080/00131911.2011.616635

Heath, A., Sullivan, A., Boliver, V., & Zimdars, A. (2013). Education under new labour, 1997–2010. *Oxford Review of Economic Policy*, *29*(1), 227–247. doi:10.1093/oxrep/grt003

Heidegger, M. (1977). *The question concerning technology and other essays*. New York City, NY: Harper & Row.

Helfrich, S., Kuhlen, R., Sachs, W., & Siefkes, C. (2009). *Gemeingüter – Wohlstand durch teilen* [Common Goods: Prosperity by Sharing]. Berlin: Heinrich Böll Stiftung.

Henn, M., Weinstein, M., & Foard, N. (2006). *Social research*. London: Sage Publications Ltd.

Henwood, K., & Pidgeon, N. (1993). *Qualitative research and psychological theorizing*. London, UK: Sage Publications.

Herring, S., Job-Sluder, K., Scheckler, R., & Barab, S. (2002). Searching for safety online: Managing trolling in a feminist forum. *The Information Society*, *18*(5), 371–384. doi:10.1080/01972240290108186

Herrnson, P. S., Niemi, R. G., Hanmer, M. J., Bederson, B. B., Conrad, F. G., & Traugott, M. (2006, August 1). The importance of usability testing of voting systems. In *Proceedings of Electronic Voting Technology Workshop*. Vancouver, Canada: Academic Press. Retrieved on November, 27, 2006, from http://www.usenix.org/events/evt06/tech/full_papers/herrnson/herrnson.pdf

Hertog, J.K., & MecLeod, D.M. (1995). Anarchists wreak havoc in downtown Minneapolis: A multi-level study of media coverage of radical protest. *Journalism & Mass Communication Monographs, 151*.

Hess, C., & Ostrom, E. (2006). *Understanding knowledge as a commons: From theory to practice*. Cambridge, MA: The MIT Press.

Hilgartner, S., & Bosk, C. L. (1988). The rise and fall of social problems: A public arenas model. *American Journal of Sociology*, *94*(1), 53–78. doi:10.1086/228951

Hindman, M. (2009). *The myth of digital democracy*. Princeton, NJ: Princeton University Press.

Hix, D., & Hartson, H. R. (1993). *Developing user interfaces: Ensuring usability through product & process*. New York: John Wiley & Sons, Inc.

Hoff, J. (1999). Towards a theory of democracy for the information age (Discussion paper for the Democracy Platform UK-Nordic Meeting). London, UK.

Holtom, D. (2007). 10 research note: What are the true costs of community-based learning? *Contemporary Wales*, *20*(1), 159–178.

Holzinger, A. (2005). Usability engineering methods for software developers. *Communications of the ACM*, *48*(1), 71–74. doi:10.1145/1039539.1039541

Honeycutt, C., & Cunliffe, D. (2010). The use of the welsh language on Facebook: An initial investigation. *Information Communication and Society*, *13*(2), 226–248. doi:10.1080/13691180902914628

Housley, W., Moles, K., & Smith, R. (2009). Identity, brand or citizenship? The case of post-devolution wales. *Contemporary Wales*, *22*(1), 196–210.

Howlett, M., & Ramesh, M. (1995). *Studying public policy: Policy cycles and policy subsystems*. Oxford, UK: Oxford University Press.

Hubbers, E., Jacobs, B., & Pieters, W. (2005). RIES - Internet voting in action. In *Proceedings of the 29th Annual International Computer Software and Applications Conference*, (pp. 417-424). IEEE Computer Society.

Humphreys, P. (2011). Personalised education and co-operation—Connections. *Journal of Cooperative Studies*, *44*(3), 52.

Huston, G. (2008). *The end of end to end?* The ISP Column.

Iwobi, A. (2009). Out with the old, in with the new: Religion, charitable status and the charities act 2006. *Legal Studies*, *29*(4), 619–650. doi:10.1111/j.1748-121X.2009.00129.x

Janczewski, L. (2008). *Cyber warfare and cyber terrorism*. Hershey, PA: IGI Global.

Jansen, E., & James, V. (2002). *NetLingo: The internet dictionary*. Oxnard, CA: Netlingo Inc.

Jaschinski, C., & Kommers, P. (2012). Does beauty matter? The role of friends' attractiveness and gender on social attractiveness ratings of individuals on Facebook. *IJWBC*, *8*(3), 389–401. doi:10.1504/IJWBC.2012.048060

Jefferson, D. R., Rubin, A. D., Simon, B., & Wagner, D. (2004). Analyzing internet voting security. Communications of the ACM, 47(10), 59–64. doi:10.1145/1022594.1022624 doi:10.1145/1022594.1022624

Jennings, M. K., & Stoker, L. (2004). Social trust and civic engagement across time and generations. *Acta Politica*, *39*, 342. doi:10.1057/palgrave.ap.5500077

Johnson, D. (1985). *Computer ethics*. Upper Saddle River, NJ: Prentice Hall.

Jones, D. W. (2003). A brief illustrated history of voting. *Tutorial*. Retrieved on August, 18, 2006, from http://www.cs.uiowa.edu/~jones/voting/

Jones, D. W. (2009). *Some problems with end-to-end voting*. Paper presented at the End-to-End Voting Systems Workshop. Washington, DC.

Jones, I. (1997). Mixing qualitative and quantitative methods in sports fan research. *Qualitative Report*, *3*(4), 1–6.

Jones, P., Packham, G., Beynon-Davies, P., & Pickernell, D. (2011). False promises: E-business deployment in Wales' SME community. *Journal of Systems and Information Technology*, *13*(2), 163–178. doi:10.1108/13287261111135990

Kallinikos, J. (2010). *Governing through technology: Information artefacts and social practice*. Basingstoke, UK: Palgrave Macmillan. doi:10.1057/9780230295148

Kampf, R. (1993). *The searching after the cracks in the wall: The attempts to promote feminist issues in the Israeli media*. (MA Thesis). Hebrew University, Jerusalem, Israel.

Kanamori, K., & Kobayashi, I. (2004). Mobile videophone and e-learning for students with physical impairments. In *Proceedings of the 2nd IEEE International Workshop on Wireless and Mobile Technologies in Education (WMTE'04)*, (pp. 203-204). IEEE.

Kassim, H., & Le Galès, P. (Eds.). (2010). Exploring governance in a multilevel polity: A policy instrument approach. *West European Politics*, *33*(1). doi:10.1080/01402380903354031

Katz, J. E., & Rice, R. E. (2002). *Social consequences of Internet use: Access, involvement and expression*. Cambridge, MA: MIT Press.

Kaye, K. (2009). *Campaign '08: A turning point for digital media*. CreateSpace.

Kelsen, H. (2000). On the essence and value of democracy. In A. Jacobson, & B. Schlink (Eds.), *Weimar: A jurisprudence of crisis*. Los Angeles, CA: University of California Press.

Kim, A. J. (2000). *Community building on the web: Secret strategies for successful online communities*. Berkeley, CA: Peachpit Press.

Kimball, R., Stables, K., & Green, R. (2001). The nature and purpose of design and technology. In G. Owen-Jackson (Ed.), *Teaching design and technology in secondary schools: A reader*. London: Routledge.

Kitto, S., Nordquist, J., Peller, J., Grant, R., & Reeves, S. (2013). The disconnections between space, place and learning in interprofessional education: An overview of key issues. *Journal of Interprofessional Care*, *27*(S2), 5–8. doi:10.3109/13561820.2013.801410 PMID:23930685

Kleber, F., Diem, M., & Sablatnig, R. (2010). *Document reconstruction by layout analysis of snippets*. Paper presented at the IS&T/SPIE Electronic Imaging. New York, NY.

Knuttila, L. (2011). User unknown: 4chan, anonymity and contingency. *First Monday*, *16*(10). doi:10.5210/fm.v16i10.3665

Koskela, T., Julkunen, J., Keranen, V., Kostamo, N., & Ylianttila, M. (2009). *User experiences on a community-based music voting service*. Paper presented at the Services-I. New York, NY.

Kovarick, B. (2002). *Web design for the mass media*. Boston: Allyn & Bacon.

Krzic, M., Strivelli, R. A., Holmes, E., Grand, S., Dyanatkar, S., & Lavkulich, L. M. et al. (2013). Virtual soil monoliths: Blending traditional and web-based educational approaches. *Journal of Natural Resources and Life Sciences Education*, *42*(1), 1–8.

Kübler, D., & Maillard, J. (2009). *Analyser les politiques publiques*. Grenoble: Presses universitaires de Grenoble.

Kuipers, G. (2011). The politics of humour in the public sphere: Cartoons, power and modernity in the first transnational humour scandal. *European Journal of Cultural Studies*, *14*(1), 63–80. doi:10.1177/1367549410370072

Kuniavsky, M. (2003). *Observing the user experience: A practitioner's guide to user research*. London: Morgan Kaufmann Publishers.

La Rue, F. (2011). *Report of the special rapporteur on the promotion and protection of the right to freedom of opinion and expression*. United Nations General Assembly. Retrieved July 27, 2013, from http://www.ohchr.org/Documents/HRBodies/HRCouncil/RegularSession/Session20/A-HRC-20-17_en.pdf

Lai-Yee Ma, M. (2005). *The internet as a social movement agent: A case study on the youth online forum.* Paper presented at the Digital Content and Technology Conference for the Graduate Students in Asia. Retrieved 28 December 2012 from http://www.docin.com/p-58500323.html

Lambert, S. (2007). To post or not to post: Gatekeeping effects of breaking news on internet newspaper websites. In *Proceedings of International Symposium on Online Journalism.* Retrieved 28 December 2012 from http://online.journalism.utexas.edu/2007/papers/Lambert.pdf

Lang, B. (2006, June 23). *Rapport sur l'usage du vote électronique par l'Internet pour les élections à l'Assemblée des Français de l'Étranger de juin 2006.* Retrieved on July, 12, 2006, from http://traitdunion.info/ELECTIONS-AFE-2006/COMMPRESS/index.htm

Laskowski, S. J. (2006, August 1). *Making ballot language understandable to voters.* Paper presented at the Electronic Voting Technology Workshop. Vancouver, Canada.

Le Crosnier, H. (2008). Tentative de définition du vectorialisme. [Attempting to Define Vectoralism]. In *Traitements et pratiques documentaires: vers un changement de paradigme? Actes de la deuxième conférence document numérique et société.* [Documentary Processing and Practices: Towards a Paradigm Shift? Second Conference on the Digital Document and Society]. ADBS, Sciences et techniques de l'information.

Lee, A. Y. (2013). Literacy and competencies required to participate in knowledge societies. *Conceptual Relationship of Information Literacy and Media Literacy in Knowledge Societies,* 3.

Lee, A., Lang, R., Davenport, K., Moore, M., Rispoli, M., & van der Meer, L. et al. (2013). Comparison of therapist implemented and iPad-assisted interventions for children with autism. *Developmental Neurorehabilitation,* (0): 1–7. doi:10.3109/17518423.2013.830231 PMID:23030702

Leedy, P. D., & Ormrod, J. E. (2009). *Practical research: Planning and design.* Academic Press.

Lehman-Wilzig, S. (2007). The end of the traditional printed newspaper: Factors of online journalism that threaten traditional printed journalism. In *Online newspapers in Israel.* Tel-Aviv, Israel: The Israel Democracy Institute and Burda Center for Innovative Communications.

Lenk, K. (2009). *Une théorie politique de l'eGovernment est-elle possible?* [Is a Political Theory of eGovernment Possible?]. Paris: CERSA.

Lessig, L. (2002). *The future of ideas: The fate of the commons in a connected world.* New York: Vintage.

Lessig, L. (2004). *Free culture: How big media uses technology and the law to lock down culture and control creativity.* New York, NY: Penguin.

Leuenberger, M., & Huber-Hotz, A. (2006, May 31). *Rapport sur les projets pilotes en matière de vote électronique* (Conseil Fédéral Suisse, Rapport n°06.056). Retrieved on May, 31, 2006, from http://www.admin.ch/ch/f/ff/2006/5205.pdf

Leung, L. (2003). Impacts of net-generation attributes, seductive properties of the internet, and gratifications-obtained on internet use. *Telematics and Informatics, 20*(2), 107–129. doi:10.1016/S0736-5853(02)00019-9

Lewis, C. (1982). Using the 'thinking-aloud' method in cognitive interface design (No. Research report RC9265). Yorktown Heights, NY: IBM T.J. Watson Research Centre.

Liebes, T. (1997). *Reporting the Arab Israeli conflict: How hegemony works.* London: Routledege. doi:10.4324/9780203180457

Liebes, T., & Kampf, Z. (2009). From black and white to shades of gray: Palestinians in the Israeli media during the second intifada. *The International Journal of Press/Politics, 14*(4), 434–453. doi:10.1177/1940161209336226

Lindstrom, M. (1999). *Brand building on the Internet.* London: Kogan Page Publishing.

Loader, B. D. (2004). *Cyberspace divide: Equality, agency and policy in the information society.* London: Routledge.

Lopresti, D., & Zhou, J. (1998). Document analysis and the world wide web. *Series in Machine Perception and Artificial Intelligence, 29,* 479–502. doi:10.1142/9789812797704_0025

Lutters, W. G., & Ackerman, M. S. (2003). Joining the backstage: Locality and centrality in an online community. *Information Technology & People, 16*(2), 157–182. doi:10.1108/09593840310478676

Maaten, E., & Hall, T. (2008). Improving the transparency of remote e-voting: The Estonian experience. *EVOTE08*. Retrieved on August, 5, 2008, from http://www.e-voting.cc/static/evoting/files/maaten_hall_improving-transparency_31-43.pdf

Macintosh, A. (2008). e-Democracy and e-Participation research in Europe. In Digital governement: E-government research, case studies, and implementation. New York: Springer.

MacKenzie, N., & Walsh, A. (2009). Enhancing the curriculum: Shareable multimedia learning objects. *Journal of Systems and Information Technology*, *11*(1), 71–83. doi:10.1108/13287260910932421

Madise, Ü., & Martens, T. (2006). E-voting in Estonia 2005: The first practice of country-wide binding internet voting in the world. In *Proceedings of Electronic Voting 2006, 2nd International Workshop*, (pp. 15-26). Bregenz, Austria: Academic Press.

Malcolm, J. (2008). *Multi-stakeholder governance and the internet governance forum*. Wembley, WA: Terminus Press.

Maner, W. (1996). Unique ethical problems in information technology. *Science and Engineering Ethics*, *2*(2), 137–154. doi:10.1007/BF02583549

Mann, C., & Stewart, F. (2000). *Internet communication and qualitative research: A handbook for research online*. London: Sage Publications.

Manning, P. (2001). *News and news sources: A critical introduction*. London: Sage.

Mansourian, Y., & Madden, A. D. (2007). Methodological approaches in web search research. *The Electronic Library*, *25*(1), 90–101. doi:10.1108/02640470710729146

Marczyk, G. R., DeMatteo, D., & Festinger, D. (2005). *Essentials of research design and methodology*. Hoboken, NJ: John Wiley & Sons.

Margetts, H. (2009). Public management change and e-government. In A. Chadwick, & P. Howard (Eds.), *Routledge handbook of internet politics* (pp. 114–127). London, UK: Routledge.

Margolis, M., & Resnick, D. (2000). *Politics as usual: The cyberspace revolution*. Thousand Oaks, CA: Sage Publications.

Martin, O. (2011). *The hidden prehistory of European research networking*. Retrieved July 27, 2013, from http://ictconsulting.ch/reports/EuropeanInternetHistory-draft-B.pdf

Martzoukou, K. (2004). A review of web information seeking research: Considerations of method and foci of interest. *Information Research*, *10*(2), 10–12.

Marx, G. T. (2006). Varieties of personal information as influences on attitudes towards surveillance. In K. D. Haggerty, & R. V. Ericson (Eds.), *The new politics of surveillance and visibility* (pp. 79–110). Toronto: University of Toronto Press.

Massit-Folléa, F., Méadel, C., & Monnoyer-Smith, L. (Eds.). (2012). *Normative experience in internet politics*. Paris: Presses de l'Ecole des Mines.

Mattelard, A. (2006). *Histoire de la société de l'information* [History of the Information Society]. Paris: La Découverte.

Maynard, A. (1975). *Experiment with choice in education*. London, UK: Institute of Economic Affairs.

McAdams, M., & Berger, S. (2001). Hypertext. *Journal of Electronic Publishing*, *6*(3). doi:10.3998/3336451.0006.301

McNiff, J., Lomax, P., & Whitehead, J. (2003). *You and your action research project*. London: Routledge.

McSporran, M., & Young, S. (2001). Does gender matter in online learning?. *Research in Learning Technology, 9*(2).

Mee, A. (2006). E-learning funding for schools: A policy paradox? *British Journal of Educational Technology*, *38*(1), 63–71. doi:10.1111/j.1467-8535.2006.00596.x

Meijer, A. J., Koops, B.-J., Pieterson, W., Overman, S., & Ten Tije, S. (2012). Government 2.0: Key challenges to its realization. *Electronic. Journal of E-Government*, *10*(1), 59–69.

Melucci, A. (1996). *Challenging codes: Collective action in the information age*. Cambridge, UK: Cambridge University Press. doi:10.1017/CBO9780511520891

Mercuri, M. (2002). A better ballot box? IEEE Spectrum Online, 39(10), 46–50. doi:10.1109/MSPEC.2002.1038569 doi:10.1109/MSPEC.2002.1038569

Metzgar, E., & Maruggi, A. (2009). Social media and the 2008 U.S. presidential election. *Journal of New Communications Research*, *4*(1), 141–165.

Minar, N., & Hedlund, P. (2001). A network of peers – Peer-to-peer models through the history of the Internet. In *Peer-to-peer: Harnessing the power of disruptive technologies*. Sebastopol, CA: O'Reilly.

Moglen, E. (2010). Freedom in the cloud: Software freedom, privacy and security for web 2.0 and cloud computing. In *Proceedings of ISOC Meeting*. New York: ISOC.

Mohen, J., & Glidden, J. (2001). The case for internet voting. Communications of the ACM, 44(1), 72–85. doi:10.1145/357489.357511 doi:10.1145/357489.357511

Moore, D., Paxson, V., Savage, S., Shannon, C., Staniford, S., & Weaver, N. (2003). Inside the slammer worm. *IEEE Security and Privacy*. Retrieved on August, 31, 2013, from http://www.cs.ucsd.edu/~savage/papers/IEEESP03.pdf

Moor, J. H. (1985). What is computer ethics? *Metaphilosophy*, *16*(4), 263–275.

Morris, D., Cunliffe, D., & Prys, C. (2012). Social networks and minority languages speakers: The use of social networking sites among young people. *Sociolinguistic Studies*, *6*(1), 1–20. doi:10.1558/sols.v6i1.1

Mossberger, K. et al. (2007). *Digital citizenship: The internet, society, and participation*. Academic Press.

Musiani, F. (2010). When social links are network links: The dawn of peer-to-peer social networks and its implications for privacy. *Observatorio*, *4*(3), 185–207.

National Academy of Sciences. (2005). *Asking the right questions about electronic voting* (Free Executive Summary). National Research Council (NRC). Retrieved on August, 31, 2013, from http://www.nap.edu/catalog/11449.html

National French Assembly. (2005, July 12). Compte-rendu, première séance du mardi 12 juillet 2005. *14e Séance de la Session Extraordinaire 2004-2005*. Retrieved on August, 31, 2013, from http://www.assemblee-nationale.fr/12/cri/2004-2005-extra/20051014.asp

National Institute of Standards and Technology. (2007, August 31). *Voluntary voting system guidelines recommendations to the election assistance commission*. Retrieved on October, 12, 2008, from http://vote.nist.gov/VVSG-0807/Final-TGDC-VVSG-08312007.pdf

Neuman, R. W. (1991). *The future of mass audience*. Cambridge, UK: Cambridge University Press.

Neven, F., & Duval, E. (2002). Reusable learning objects: A survey of LOM-based repositories. In *Proceedings of the Tenth ACM International Conference on Multimedia*, (pp. 291-294). ACM.

Neveu, E. (1999). L'approche constructiviste des problèmes publics. *Etudes de Communication*, *22*, 41–57. doi:10.4000/edc.2342

Newell, A. F., & Gregor, P. (1997). Human computer interfaces for people with disabilities. In Handbook of human-computer interaction (2nd ed.). Academic Press. doi:10.1016/B978-044481862-1.50101-1 doi:10.1016/B978-044481862-1.50101-1

Nielsen, J. (1993). *Usability engineering*. San Francisco, CA: Morgan Kaufman.

Nielsen, J. (2000). *Designing web usability*. New York, NY: New Riders.

Niskanen, W. A. Jr. (1971). *Bureaucracy and representative government*. Academic Press.

Nissenbaum, H. (2010). *Privacy in context*. Stanford, CA: Stanford Law Books.

Norris, P. (2001). *Do campaign communications matter for civic engagement? American elections from Eisenhower to G.W. Bush*. Retrieved May 1, 2012 from http://www.hks.harvard.edu/fs/pnorris/Acrobat/Farrell&Schmitt-Beck%20Chapter%209.pdf

Novo-Corti, I., Varela-Candamio, L., & García-Álvarez, M. T. (2013). Breaking the walls of social exclusion of women rural by means of ICTs: The case of 'digital divides' in galician. *Computers in Human Behavior*. PMID:24003265

O'Connor, J. F., & Baratz, M. J. (2004). Some assembly required: The application of state open meeting laws to email correspondence. *George Mason Law Review*, *12*, 722.

O'Reilly, T. (2007). What is web 2.0? Design patterns and business models for the next generation of software on line. *Communications & Strategies, 1*(1).

Oblinger, D. G. (2004). The next generation of educational engagement. *Journal of Interactive Media in Education*, 1.

O'Donnell, L., Carson, L., Forciea, M. A., Kinosian, B., Shea, J., & Yudin, J. et al. (2013). What students experienced: A narrative analysis of essays written by first-year medical students participating in a geriatrics home visit. *Journal of the American Geriatrics Society*. doi:10.1111/jgs.12405 PMID:23888907

O'Leary, Z. (2005). *The essential guide to doing research*. Thousand Oaks, CA: SAGE Publications Inc.

Oliver, B., & Goerke, V. (2007). Australian undergraduates' use and ownership of emerging technologies: Implications and opportunities for creating engaging learning experiences for the net generation. *Australasian Journal of Educational Technology*, *23*(2), 171.

O'Mahen, H. A., Woodford, J., McGinley, J., Warren, F. C., Richards, D. A., & Lynch, T. R. et al. (2013). Internet-based behavioral activation—Treatment for postnatal depression (netmums): A randomized controlled trial. *Journal of Affective Disorders*. doi:10.1016/j.jad.2013.03.005 PMID:23602514

Oostveen, A.-M., & van der Besselaar, P. (2004). Internet voting technologies and civic participation: The users' perspective. The Public, 11(1), 61–78.

Oostveen, A.-M., & van der Besselaar, P. (2006). Non-technical risks of remote electronic voting. In The encyclopedia of digital government. Hershey, PA: IGI Global. doi:10.4018/978-1-59140-789-8.ch190doi:10.4018/978-1-59140-789-8.ch190

Oppliger, R. (2002, May 3). *Traitement du problème de la sécurité des plates-formes pour le vote par internet à Genève*. Retrieved on August, 31, 2013, from http://www.geneve.ch/evoting/doc/rapports/rapport_oppliger_fr.pdf

O'Reilly. (2005). *What is web 2.0: Design patterns and business models for the next generation of software*. Retrieved January 6, 2012 from oreilly.com/pub/a/Web2/archive/what-is-Web-20.html

Organization for Security and Co-Operation in Europe-Office for Democratic Institutions and Human Rights. (2004, September 28). *USA 2 November 2004 elections: OSCE/ODIHR needs assessment mission report - 7-10 September 2004*. Retrieved on October, 14, 2006, from http://www.osce.org/documents/odihr/2004/09/3655_en.pdf

Origgi, G. (2004). Is trust an epistemic notion? *Episteme*, *1*(1), 61–72. doi:10.3366/epi.2004.1.1.61

Owens, L., & Palmer, L. K. (2003). Making the news: Anarchist counter-public relations on the world wide web. *Critical Studies in Media Communication*, *20*(4), 335–361. doi:10.1080/0739318032000142007

Pagallo, U. (2011, May). ISPs & rowdy web sites before the law: Should we change today's safe harbour clauses?. *Philosophy and Technology*, 335-34.

Paletz, D. L., & Entman, R. M. (1981). *Media power politics*. New York: Free Press.

Papacharissi, Z. (2008). The virtual sphere 2.0: The internet, the public sphere and beyond. In *The handbook of internet politics* (pp. 236–239). Academic Press.

Parfit, D. (1984). *Reasons and persons*. Oxford, UK: Clarendon Press.

Pariser, E. (2011). *The filter bubble: What the internet is hiding from you*. New York: Penguin.

Park, H. W., & Thelwall, M. (2003). Hyperlink analyses of the world wide web: A review. *Journal of Computer-Mediated Communication*, *8*(4).

Peng, F., Yeuh, T., Naphtali, I., & Xiaoming, H. (1999). Trends in online newspapers: A look at the U.S. web. *Newspaper Research Journal*, *20*(2), 52–64.

Peterson, A. (2001). *Contemporary political protester: Essays on political militancy*. Ashgate, UK: Hampshire.

PEW- Project for Excellence in Journalism. (2007). *The latest news headlines—Your vote counts*. Retrieved 28 December 2012 from http://www.journalism.org/sites/journalism.org/files/usernewspdf_0.pdf

Petit, P., Bontems, V., & Stiegler, B. (2008). *Economie de l'hypermatériel et psychopouvoir (entretiens avec Bernard Stiegler)*. Paris: Mille et une nuits.

Pettit, P. (2004). Trust, reliance and the internet. *Analyse & Kritik, 26*, 108–121.

Pfitzmann, A., & Hansen, M. (2010). *A terminology for talking about privacy by data minimization: Anonymity, unlinkability, undetectability, unobservability, pseudonymity, and identity management, version 0.33.* Academic Press.

Phillips, D. M., & von Spakovsky, H. A. (2001). Gauging the risks of internet elections. Communications of the ACM, 44(1), 72–85. doi:10.1145/357489.357512 doi:10.1145/357489.357512

Phillips, R., Lawton, D., Cairns, J., & Gardner, R. (2000). *Culture, community and curriculum in Wales: Citizenship education for the new democracy?* Education for Citizenship.

Phillips, W. (2011). LOLing at tragedy: Facebook trolls, memorial pages and resistance to grief online. *First Monday, 16*(12). doi:10.5210/fm.v16i12.3168

Pickard, V. (2006). Assessing the radical democracy of Indymedia: Discursive, technical, and institutional constructions. *Critical Studies in Media Communication, 23*(1), 19–38. doi:10.1080/07393180600570691

Pickerill, J. (2003). *Out in the open: Indymedia networks in Australia.* Paper presented at the Information, Communication and Society Symposium. Oxford, UK.

Pickerill, J. (2003). *Cyberprotest: Environmental activism online.* Manchester, UK: Manchester University Press.

Piela, A. (2013). *Claiming religious authority.* Academic Press.

Platon, S., & Deuze, M. (2003). Indymedia journalism a radical way of making, selecting and sharing news? *Journalism, 4*(3), 336–355. doi:10.1177/14648849030043005

Pledel, I. (2007). Le blog face à la clôture informationnelle: La délibération au service de l'apprentissage. *Distances et Savoirs, 5*(2), 275–288. doi:10.3166/ds.5.275-288

Post, D. (2002). Against against cyberspace. *Berkeley Technology Law Journal, 17*, 1365–1383.

Postel-Vinay O. (2010, April). *Pour en finir avec le cyberoptimisme*, Books, April (dossier 12), 19-33.

Powell, A., Bryne, A., & Dailey, D. (2010). The essential internet: Digital exclusion in low-income American communities. *Policy & Internet, 2*(2).

Powell, R. (2010). Good mothers, bad mothers and mommy bloggers: Rhetorical resistance and fluid subjectivities. *MP: An Online Feminist Journal,* 37-50.

Preece, J. (2000). *Online communities: Designing usability, supporting sociability.* Chichester, UK: John Wiley & Sons.

Preece, J., & Maloney-Krichmar, D. (2005). Online communities: Design, theory, and practice. *Journal of Computer-Mediated Communication, 10*(4).

Pupillo, T. D. (1993). The changing weather forecast: Government in the sunshine in the 1990s—An analysis of state sunshine laws. *Washington University Law Quarterly, 71*, 1167.

Putnam, R. D. (2000). *Bowling alone: The collapse and revival of American community.* New York, NY: Simon and Schuster. doi:10.1145/358916.361990

Raboy, M., Landry, M., & Shtern, J. (2010). *Digital solidarities, communication policy and multi-stakeholder global governance.* New York: Peter Lang.

Rawls, J. (1996). *Political liberalism.* New York, NY: Columbia University Press.

Reed, M. C. (2004). Why is mathematical biology so hard? *Notices of the American Mathematical Society, 51*(3), 338–342.

Reich, Z. (2008). How citizens create news stories: The ''news access'' problem reversed. *Journalism Studies, 9*(5), 739–758. doi:10.1080/14616700802207748

Rheingold, H. (2003). *Smart mobs: The next social revolution.* New York: Basic Books.

Rhinard, M. (2008). Le cadrage de la politique antiterroriste de l'UE. In *La construction des problèmes publics en Europe*. Strasbourg: Presses Universitaires de Strasbourg.

Ricœur, P. (1992). *Oneself as another.* Chicago: University of Chicago Press.

Rodotà, S. (2006). The retention of electronic commmunication traffic data. *Revista d'Internet, Dret I Política, 3*, 53-60.

Rodriguez, C. (2001). *Fissures in the mediascape: An international study of citizens' media*. Cresskill, NJ: Hampton.

Rogers, R. (2004). *Information politics on the web*. Cambridge, MA: MIT Press.

Rogers, R., & Ben-David, A. (2008). The Palestinian–Israeli peace process and transnational issue networks: The complicated place of the Israeli NGO. *New Media & Society*, *10*(3), 497–528. doi:10.1177/1461444807085321

Rogers, R., & Marres, N. N. (2000). Landscaping climate change: A mapping technique for understanding science and technology debates on the world wide web. *Public Understanding of Science (Bristol, England)*, *9*(2), 141–163. doi:10.1088/0963-6625/9/2/304

Rohwer, D., & Rohwer, M. (2012). How participants envision community music in Welsh men's choirs. *Research and Issues in Music Education, 10*(1).

Rospars, J. (2010). *Election 2010: New digital battlefield, same old politics none of the parties have leveraged new media in this campaign to build support in the way Barack Obama did.* Retrieved January 10, 2012 from http://www.guardian.co.uk/commentisfree/2010/may/04/new-digital-battlefield-old-politics

Ross, A. (1999). *No sweat*. New York: Verso.

Rowley, D. E. (1994). *Usability testing in the field: Bridging the laboratory to the user*. Boston, MA: Academic Press. doi:10.1145/259963.260374

Rubin, A. D. (2001). Security considerations for remote electronic voting over the internet. The Magazine of Usenix & Sage, 26(1), 20–28.

Rushby, N. J. (1979). *Computers in the teaching process*. New York: John Wiley & Sons, Inc.

Ryan, P. Y. A., & Peacok, T. (2005, September 20). *Prêt à voter: Systems perspective* (Technical report CS-TR-929). Academic Press.

Ryan, C. (1991). *Prime time activism: Media strategies for grassroots organizing*. Boston: South End Press.

Salter, L. (2003). Democracy, new social movements, and the internet: A Habermasian analysis. In *Cyberactivism: Online activism in theory and practices*. New York: Routledge.

Saltzer, J., Reed, D., & Clark, D. (1981). End-to-end arguments in system design. In *Proceedings of Second International Conference on Distributed Computing Systems* (pp. 509-512). Academic Press.

Sapsford, R. (2006). *Survey research*. Thousand Oaks, CA: Sage Publications Ltd.

Sarason, S. B. (1974). *The psychological sense of community: Prospects for a community psychology*. San Francisco: Jossey-Bass.

Sartori, G. (1987). *The theory of democracy revisited*. Chatham, NJ: Chatham House.

Saunders, B. J. (2007). From indymedia to indyjournalism– How indymedia is evolving. In *Proceedings of Our Media - the 6th International OURMedia Conference (OM6)*. Sydney, Australia. Retrieved 28 December 2012 from http://eprints.qut.edu.au/10902/1/10902.pdf

Saunders, M., Thornhill, A., & Lewis, P. (2009). *Research methods for business students*. New York: Financial Times/Prentice Hall.

Schaeffer, S. (2004). Sunshine in cyberspace? Electronic deliberation and the reach of open meeting laws. *Saint Louis University Law Journal*, *48*, 778.

Schafer, V. (2012). Internet, l'illusion démocratique: De la république des ingénieurs à la gouvernance (1968-2011). [Internet, the Democratic Illusion. From Engineers' Republic to Governance]. In Internet et politique. Paris: CNRS Ed.s/Les Essentiels d'Hermès.

Schafer, V., Le Crosnier, H., & Musiani, F. (Eds.). (2011). La neutralité de l'internet, un enjeu de communication. [Net Neutrality, an Issue of Communication]. CNRS Ed.s/Les Essentiels d'Hermès, Paris.

Schafer, V. (2012). *La France en réseaux, années 1960-1980* (Vol. 1). Paris: Cigref and Nuvis. [France in Networks, 1960-1980, Volume 1]

Schechter, S., Krishnan, M., & Smith, M. D. (1998). Using path profiles to predict HTTP requests. *Computer Networks and ISDN Systems, 30*(1-7), 457-467.

Schelling, T. (1960). *The strategy of conflict*. Academic Press.

Schipper, F., & Schot, J. (2009). Infrastructural Europeanism, or the project of building Europe on infrastructures. *History and Technology*, *27*(3), 245–264. doi:10.1080/07341512.2011.604166

Schlesinger, P., & Tumbler, H. (1994). *Reporting crime: The media politics of criminal justice*. Oxford, UK: Clarendon.

Schneier, B. (1999). The Trojan horse race. Communications of the ACM, 42(9). PubMeddoi:10.1145/315762.315785 doi:10.1145/315762.315785 PMID:11543550

Schoeneich, P., & Busset-Henchoz, M.-C. (1998). La dissonance cognitive: Facteur explicatif de l'accoutumance au risque. *Revue de Geographie Alpine*, 53–62. doi:10.3406/rga.1998.2878

Scholl, J. H. (2009). *Electronic government: A study domain beyond its infancy*. AMIS Volume on Electronic Government.

Schotter, A. (1981). *The economic theory of social institutions*. Academic Press. doi:10.1017/CBO9780511983863

Schumpeter, J. (1942). *Capitalism, socialism and democracy*. London, UK: Routledge.

Schweitzer, F., & Garcia, D. (2010). An agent-based model of collective emotions in online communities. *The European Physical Journal B-Condensed Matter and Complex Systems*, *77*(4), 533–545. doi:10.1140/epjb/e2010-00292-1

Secretary of State for Strategic Studies and the Development of the Digital Economy. (2010). *Consultation publique sur la 'neutralité du net', synthèse des réponses* [Public Consultation on 'Net Neutrality', Summary of Responses]. French Republic: Academic Press.

Selwyn, N. (2013). Researching the once-powerful in education: The value of retrospective elite interviewing in education policy research. *Journal of Education Policy*, *28*(3), 339–352. doi:10.1080/02680939.2012.728630

Seward, L., Harvey, V., & Carranza, J. (2009). Computer-mediated communication that brings learning into the present: Gender differences in status differentials and self-disclosure in online peer teaching. *International Journal of Information and Communication Technology Education*, *5*(2), 10–20. doi:10.4018/jicte.2009040102

Shepsle, K. A. (2006). Rational choice institutionalism. In *The Oxford handbook of political institutions* (pp. 23–38). Oxford, UK: Oxford University Press.

Sherman, B. (2011). Your mayor, your friend: Public officials, social networking, and the unmapped new public square. *Pace Law Review*, *31*, 95.

Shifman, L., Coleman, S., & Ward, S. (2007). Only joking? Online humour in the 2005 UK general election. *Information Communication and Society*, *10*(4), 465–487. doi:10.1080/13691180701559947

Shumate, M., & Dewitt, L. (2008). The north/south divide in NGO hyperlink networks. *Journal of Computer-Mediated Communication*, *13*, 405–428. doi:10.1111/j.1083-6101.2008.00402.x

Shumate, M., & Lipp, J. (2008). Connective collective action online: An examination of the hyperlink network structure of an NGO issue network. *Journal of Computer-Mediated Communication*, *14*, 178–201. doi:10.1111/j.1083-6101.2008.01436.x

Silverman, D. (2006). *Interpreting qualitative data: Methods for analyzing talk, text and interaction* (3rd ed.). London, UK: Sage Publications.

Simons, B. (2004). Electronic voting systems: The good, the bad, and the stupid. ACM Queue; Tomorrow's Computing Today, 2(7). doi:10.1145/1035594.1035606 doi:10.1145/1035594.1035606

Singer, J. B. (2005). The political J-blogger. *Journalism*, *6*(2), 173–198. doi:10.1177/1464884905051009

Smith, A. (2010). Government online: The internet gives citizens new paths to government services and information. *Pew Internet*. Retrieved from http://pewInternet.org/~/media//Files/Reports/2010/PIP_Government_Online_2010_with_topline.pdf

Smith, A., & Rainie, L. (2008). *The internet and the 2008 election*. Pew Internet and American Life Project. Retrieved January 10, 2012 from http://www.pewInternet.org/~/media//Files/Reports/2008/PIP_2008_election.pdf.pdf

Smith, S., & Dalakiouridou, E. (2009). Contextualising public (e)participation in the governance of the European Union. *European Journal of ePractice*, *7*, 1-11.

Smith, C. P. (2000). Content analysis and narrative analysis. In H. T. Reis, & C. M. Judd (Eds.), *Handbook of research methods in social and personal psychology*. Cambridge, UK: Cambridge University Press.

Solove, D. J. (2002). Access and aggregation: Public records, privacy and the constitution. *Minnesota Law Review*, *86*, 1161.

Star, S. L. (1999). The ethnography of infrastructure. *The American Behavioral Scientist*, *43*(3), 377–391. doi:10.1177/00027649921955326

Star, S. L., & Bowker, G. (2002). How to infrastructure. In *Handbook of new media* (pp. 151–162). London: Sage.

Steger, U. (2005). *Sustainable development and innovation in the energy sector*. London: Springer.

Stengrim, L. (2005). Negotiating postmodern democracy, political activism, and knowledge production: Indymedia's grassroots and e-savvy answer to media oligopoly. *Communication and Critical. Cultural Studies*, *2*(4), 281–304.

Stiegler, B. (2008). Le désir asphyxié, ou comment l'industrie culturelle détruit l'individu. *Manière de Voir, La Fabrique du Conformisme*, (96), 10-15.

Stiegler, B. (2008). *La télécratie contre la démocratie: Lettre ouverte aux représentants politiques*. Paris: Flammarion.

Sturman, L., Rowe, N., Sainsbury, M., Wheater, R., & Kerr, D. (2012). Citizens in transition in England, Wales and Scotland: Young citizens at 18-25. Academic Press.

Sunstein, C. (2001). *Republic.com*. Princeton, NJ: Princeton University Press.

Sunstein, C. (2009). *Going to extremes: How like minds unite and divide*. Oxford, UK: Oxford University Press.

Sunstein, C. (2009). *On rumours: How falsehoods spread, why we believe them, what can be done*. London, UK: Allen Lane.

Sunstein, C. R. (2007). *Republic 2.0*. Princeton, NJ: Princeton University Press.

Surowiecki, J. (n.d.). The wisdom of crowds: Why the many are smarter than the few and how collective wisdom shapes business, economies, societies and nations. New York, NY: Doubleday.

Tak, J. (2006). Political advertising in Japan, South Korea, and Taiwan. In *The SAGE handbook of political advertising*. Thousand Oaks, CA: Sage Publications, Incorporated. doi:10.4135/9781412973403.n17

Tapscott, D. (1998). *Growing up digital: The rise of the net generation*. London: McGraw-Hill.

Taylor, L. A. (2000). Home education regulations in europe and recent UK research. *Peabody Journal of Education*, *75*(1), 49–70. doi:10.1207/S15327930PJE751&2_5

Taylor, V., & Whittier, N. E. (1992). Collective identity in social movement communities: Lesbian feminist mobilization. In *Frontiers in social movement theory*. New Haven, CT: Yale University Press.

Thoenig, J. C. (1985). *Traité de science politique: Les politiques publiques* (Vol. 4). Paris: PUF.

Thomas, J. (2006). The regional and local media in Wales. *Local Journalism and Local Media: Making the Local News*.

Thomas, J. (1997). 'Taffy was a welshman, taffy was a thief': Anti-Welshness, the press and neil kinnock. *LLAFUR-CARDIFF*, *7*, 95–108.

Thompson, K. (1984). Reflections on trusting trust. Communications of the ACM, 27(8), 761–763. doi:10.1145/358198.358210doi:10.1145/358198.358210

Thompson, J. B. (1990). *The media and modernity: A social theory of the media*. London, UK: Polity Press.

Thorpe, J. (2011). Co-operative schools in the UK. *Journal of Co-Operative Studies*, *44*(3), 57–62.

Towner, T., & Dulio, D. (2012). New media and political marketing in the United States: 2012 and beyond. *Journal of Political Marketing*, *11*, 95–119. doi:10.1080/15377857.2012.642748

Twisk, J., de Boer, M., de Vente, W., & Heymans, M. (2013). Multiple imputation of missing values was not necessary before performing a longitudinal mixed-model analysis. *Journal of Clinical Epidemiology*. doi:10.1016/j.jclinepi.2013.03.017 PMID:23790725

United Nations. (1948). The universal declaration of human rights. New York: Author.

United Nations. (2005). World population ageing. New York: Author.

Valimiskomisjon, V. (2013). *Internet voting in Estonia*. Retrieved on August, 31, 2013, from http://www.vvk.ee/index.php?id=11178

van de Donk, W., Loader, B. D., Nixon, P. G., & Rucht, D. (2004). Introduction social movements and ICTs. In *Cyberprotest: New media, citizens and social movements*. London: Routledge.

Van den Berg, B., & Leenes, R. (2011). Keeping up appearances: Audience segregation in social network sites. In S. Gutwirth, Y. Poullet, P. De Hert, & R. Leenes (Eds.), *Computers, privacy and data protection: An element of choice* (pp. 211–233). Dordrecht, The Netherlands: Springer. doi:10.1007/978-94-007-0641-5_10

Van den Hoven, J. (2005). E-democracy, e-contestation and the monitorial citizen. *Ethics and Information Technology*, *7*, 51–59. doi:10.1007/s10676-005-4581-4

van Deursen, A., & van Dijk, J. (2011). Internet skills and the digital divide. *New Media & Society*, *13*(6), 893–911. doi:10.1177/1461444810386774

Van Dijk, J. A. G. M. (2005). *The network society: Social aspects of new media* (2nd ed.). London: Sage Publications Ltd.

Van Dijk, T. A. (1996). Power and news media. In *Political communication in action- states, institutions, movements, audiences*. Hampton Press.

Van Schewick, B. (2010). *Internet architecture and innovation*. Cambridge, MA: The MIT Press.

Van Zoonen, L. (1996). A dance of death: New social movements and mass media. In *Political communication in action- States, institutions, movements, audiences*. Hampton Press.

Vargas, J. (2008, November 20). Obama raised half a billion online. *The Washington Post*. Retrieved May 4, 2012 from http://voices.washingtonpost.com/44/2008/11/obama-raised-half-a-billion-on.html

Vedder, A., & Wachbroit, R. (2003). Reliability of information on the internet: Some distinctions. *Ethics and Information Technology*, *5*, 211–215. doi:10.1023/B:ETIN.0000017738.60896.77

Vedel, T. (1996). Les politiques des autoroutes de l'information dans les pays industrialisés: Une analyse comparative.[The Politics of Information Highways in Industrialised Countries: A Comparative Analysis]. *Reseaux*, *78*, 11–28.

Vedel, T. (2003). Political communication in the age of the internet. In *Political communication in the new era: A cross national prespective*. London: Routledge.

Voida, A., Mynatt, E. D., Erickson, T., & Kellogg, W. A. (2004). Interviewing over instant messaging. In *Proceedings of Conference on Human Factors in Computing Systems*, (pp. 1344-1347). Academic Press.

Voting Technology Project. (2001). *Voting: What is, what could be*. Retrieved on August, 31, 2013, from http://www.vote.caltech.edu/drupal/node/10

Walford, G. (2000). From city technology colleges to sponsored grant-maintained schools. *Oxford Review of Education*, *26*(2), 145–158. doi:10.1080/03054980050031363

Walliman, N. (2006). *Social research methods*. London: Sage Publicaitons Ltd. doi:10.4135/9781849209939

Walter, T., Hourizi, R., Moncur, W., & Pitsillides, S. (2011). Does the internet change how we die and mourn? An overview. *Omega*, *64*(4), 12. doi:10.2190/OM.64.4.a PMID:22530294

Ward, S., & Gibson, R. (2009). European political organizations and the internet. In A. Chadwick, & P. Howard (Eds.), *Routledge handbook of internet politics* (pp. 25–39). London, UK: Routledge.

Warusfel, B. (2000). La gestion de l'internet entre autorégulation et rivalités institutionnelles: Un phénomène mondial à la recherche de son modèle de gouvernance. [Internet Management between Self-Regulation and Institutional Rivalries: A Global Phenomenon in Search of a Governance Model]. *Annuaire Français de Relations Internationales*, *1*, 595–617.

Weiner, N. (1948). *Cybernetics or control and communication in the animal and the machine*. Cambridge, MA: MIT Press.

Wenger, M. (2002, January 28). *Rapport du comité de sécurité sur l'application du vote par internet*. Retrieved on August, 5, 2007, from http://www.ge.ch/evoting/doc/rapports/rapport_version_Internet.pdf

Wenzel, J. W. (1992). Perspectives on argument. In W. L. Benoit, D. Hample, & P. J. Benoit (Eds.), *Readings in argumentation* (pp. 121–145). Berlin: Walter de Gruyter & Co. doi:10.1515/9783110885651.121

Whelan, F. G. (1983). Democratic theory and the boundary problem. In J. R. Pennock, & J. W. Chapman (Eds.), *Liberal democracy*. New York, NY: New York University Press.

Williamson, K. (2002). *Research methods for students and professionals: Information management and systems*. Wagga Wagga, Australia: Centre for Information Studies, Charles Sturt University. doi:10.1533/9781780634203

Winterson-Richards, J. (2008). *The xenophobe's guide to the Welsh*. London: Oval Books.

Wittel, A. (2001). Toward a network sociality. *Theory, Culture & Society*, *18*(6), 51–76. doi:10.1177/02632760122052048

Wolfsfeld, G. (1991). Media, protest and political violence. *Journalism & Mass Communication Monographs, 127*.

Wolfsfeld, G., Frosh, P., & Awabdy, T. M. (2008). *Ethnocentric news of violent conflict: Journalistic mechanism for covering the second Intifada on Israeli, Plaestinian and Al-Jazeera television*. Paper presented at the Annual Meeting of the International Communication Association. New York, NY.

Wolfsfeld, G. (1997). *Media and political conflict: News from the Middle East*. Cambridge, UK: Academic Press.

Working Group on Internet Governance. (2005). *Report of the working group on internet governance at the world summit on the information society* (Document WSIS-II/PC-3/DOC/5-E). Retrieved July 27, 2013, from http://www.itu.int/wsis/docs2/pc3/off5.pdf

Wu, T. (2003). Network neutrality, broadband discrimination. *Journal on Telecommunications & High Technology Law*, *2*, 141.

Yang, C. L., & Chen-Burger, Y. H. (2012). On-line communities making scense: A hybrid micro-blogging platform community analysis framework. *Agent and Multi-Agent Systems.Technologies and Applications*, 134-143.

Yetim, F. (2001). A meta-communication model for structuring intercultural communication action patterns. *ACM SIGGROUP Bulletin*, *22*(2), 16–20.

Yoon, Y. (2005). Legitimacy, public relation, and media access: Proposing and testing a media access model. *Communication Research*, *32*(6), 762–793. doi:10.1177/0093650205281081

Young, M. (2011). The return to subjects: A sociological perspective on the UK coalition government's approach to the 14–19 curriculum. *Curriculum Journal*, *22*(2), 265–278. doi:10.1080/09585176.2011.574994

Zappi, S. (2010). Un caillou dans la chaussure de la presse française: Retour sur l'expérience bondy blog. *Mouvements*, *1*(61), 140–142. doi:10.3917/mouv.061.0140

Zittel, T. (2008). Parliaments and the internet: A perspective on the state of research. In *Parliaments in the digital age*. Oxford Internet Institute.

About the Contributors

Jonathan Bishop is an information technology executive, researcher, and writer. Jonathan has always been interested in blending his interests in politics with technology. He first became a councilor in 2003 during his MSc in E-Learning at the University of South Wales, and following gaining his LLM in European Union Law from USW, he became a town councilor between 2008 and 2012, during which time he also gained an MScEcon in Information Systems from Aberystwyth University. Jonathan is now the leader of a minor party in the UK called The Pluralist Party, which he has contested 4 elections, seeking to encourage inter-party dialogue and cooperation among those in politics with different ideologies. At the time of going to press, he had contested a total of 7 public elections to 4 different local councils. In 2005, Jonathan founded the Centre for Research into Online Communities and E-Learning Systems, which has led to a number of companies and initiatives, including Crocels CMG CYF, The Crocels Press Limited, and Crocels News, Inc. In his spare time, Jonathan enjoys swimming, listening to music, and chess.

* * *

Romain Badouard is an Assistant Professor at the University of Cergy-Pontoise (France). His research mainly addresses online political participation, open government and Internet governance, with a specific focus on the European context.

Mark Beech is an unemployed career politician nominally affiliated with the Official Monster Raving Loony Party and current Nominating Officer for The Pluralist Party. He has also represented the Labour Party and as an independent campaigner. Mark co-founded the social enterprise, Glamorgan Blended Learning Ltd (GBL) in 2006, through which he helped organise regeneration projects. He is the Chief Personnel, Strategy and Quality Officer of the Crocels Community Media Group of which GBL is a member under its new name of Crocels CMG CYF. In December 2010 Mark registered as an independent campaigner for the Welsh Assembly devolution referendum held on 3 March 2011 as part of the No campaign, which was described as fragmented by the press. In May 2010, Mark became the first member of his family to stand for the UK Parliament, in the seat of Cardiff Central.

Chantal Enguehard has been Assistant Professor in Computer Sciences at the University of Nantes (France) since 1994. She studied at the University of Technology of Compiègne (France), and graduated as an engineer in computer sciences (specializing in Artificial Intelligence) in 1988. She was awarded a PhD from the same university in 1992. Her research lies within natural language processing (on African languages), terminology processing and ethics and computer. On this last subject, she examines thoroughly the question of electronic voting. She favours a multidisciplinary approach, taking in account not only the pure computerization problems, but also their political, legal, economic and social features. She has been consulted on the subject of electronic voting by the French Ministry of Interior (which is in charge of organizing elections) in 2007 and the parliamentary commission on laws of the French Sénat in 2013.

Mary Francoli is an Assistant Professor and Undergraduate Supervisor at Carleton University's School of Journalism and Communication. She received her Ph.D. in political science from The University of Western Ontario.

Cédric Gossart obtained his PhD from the University of Sussex (SPRU-Science and Technology Policy Studies). He is currently an associate professor in the Institut Mines-Telecom (Telecom Business School). His is the co-animator of the research network "TIC & Environnement" of the Institut Mines-Télécom (RT8). He is a member of the research group KIND (Knowledge, Innovation and Network Dynamics). His interests include: Public policies and digital technologies, sustainable transitions, green ICTs, ecological footprint of ICTs, and waste of Electrical and Electronic Equipments (WEEE).

Bert-Jaap Koops is Professor of Regulation & Technology at the Tilburg Institute for Law, Technology, and Society (TILT), Tilburg University, The Netherlands. From 2005-2010, he was a member of De Jonge Akademie, a young-researcher branch of the Royal Netherlands Academy of Arts and Sciences. His main research fields are cybercrime, cyber-investigation, forensics, privacy, and data protection. He is also interested in topics such as identity, digital constitutional rights, "code as law," and regulatory implications of human enhancement, genetics, robotics, and neuroscience. Koops studied mathematics and general and comparative literature at Groningen University, and received his PhD in law at Tilburg University in 1999. He co-edited seven books in English on technology regulation, *Emerging Electronic Highways* (1996), *ICT Law and Internationalisation* (2000), *Starting Points for ICT Regulation* (2006), *Cybercrime and Jurisdiction: A Global Survey* (2006), *Constitutional Rights and New Technologies* (2008), *Dimensions of Technology Regulation* (2010), and *Engineering the Human* (2013).

Piet Kommers is Associate Professor in Media, Communication and Education at the University of Twente. He is executive editor of the International Journal for Web-based Communities and Co-Chair of the IADIS conferences in Societal Effects of ICT. His consultancy projects are in the fields of International Higher Education for national authorities in various countries. His advisory role for UNESCO gave him the title of Honorary Professor. He is working at European projects in the fields of Teaching in Nature, Open Governance, and Aging Society.

Hervé Le Crosnier is teaching Internet technologies and digital culture at University of Caen. Associated with the ISCC (Institut des Sciences de la Communication du CNRS), he published with Valérie Schafer an introductory book about Net Neutrality in 2012, and another one with Mélanie Dulong de Rosnay about intellectual proprerty facing globalisation in 2013.

Lisa Mannay is a twice graduate of the University of South Wales, gaining a HND in Multimedia and a BSc in Multimedia Studies. Lisa has been significantly involved in the performing arts, including acting and local music scenes. She has significant experience in marketing and uses social media to share auto-ethnographic experiences of sales environments.

Patricia Mindus is an Associate Professor in Practical Philosophy. Her areas of expertise include Political and Legal theory, Citizenship Studies, EU Studies. Before joining the Philosophy Department at Uppsala University, she worked as research fellow at the Department of Political Studies, University of Turin and as assistant professor in Political Theory, Theory of Human Rights, and History of Political Thought at the universities of Turin and Aosta (Italy). She currently co-directs the transdisciplinary research project KUSKO - Knowledge Societies: Organisation and Communication of Knowledge, and IVR special workshop on Legitimacy 2.0.

Ivan Mugabi is a professional lawyer. He holds a Bachelors Degree in law LLB (Hons) and three Masters degrees in law, including International Commercial law, Human Rights laws, and commercial laws. Ivan's enthusiasm for research stretches back to his second year of law school, when he embarked on his legal internship with the Law Chambers of Advocates. This exposed Ivan research skills meaning he gained in depth knowledge of both substantive and procedural nature more especially from the context of the administrative law perspective. Ivan embraced the research project towards his Masters degree at the University of South Wales, and has improved his knowledge and experience of law through involvement with Crocels.

Francesca Musiani has a PhD in the socio-economics of innovation and is currently a post-doctoral researcher at the Centre for the Sociology of Innovation, MINES ParisTech/CNRS. Recently, she was the 2012-13 Yahoo! Fellow in Residence at Georgetown University and an affiliate of the Berkman Center for Internet and Society at Harvard University. She is the author of *Nains Sans Géants: Architecture Décentralisée et Services Internet* (2013, Presses des Mines). Her research explores Internet governance in an interdisciplinary perspective.

Valérie Schafer is a researcher at the French National Center for Scientific Research (Institute for Communication Sciences, CNRS). She holds a PhD in technical history, and she specializes on packet switching networks and history of computing and telecommunications. Dr. Schafer's current research deals with the Internet history in France and Europe.

Keren Sereno graduated from her Master in Political Communication with honors (cum laude) from the Department of Communication and Journalism at The Hebrew University in Israel. Since 2008, Keren has been working as independent researcher and as teacher assistant in various academic institutions in Israel. Her research interests are the uses of the Internet by social movements and their implications on collective action.

William Sherman is a Visiting Assistant Professor at Seattle University School of Law, where he teaches Administrative Law, Criminal Procedure, Open Government Law, and Legal Writing. He also serves as Chair of the City of Seattle's Ethics and Elections Commission, which administers the City's campaign finance, elections, ethics, lobbying, and whistleblower codes. Professor Sherman practiced political and election law, commercial litigation, consumer protection, and local government law at the

Sherman Law Firm PLLC from 2008-2012. A 1999 graduate of the University of Michigan Law School, where he was Editor-in-Chief of the *Michigan Law Review*, he served as a law clerk in the United States District Court for the Western District of Washington and then for the Ninth Circuit Court of Appeals. His article, "Your Mayor, Your 'Friend': Public Officials, Social Networking, and the Unmapped New Public Square," was published in a symposium issue of the *Pace Law Review* in 2011. His book review essay, "A Pragmatic Republic, If You Can Keep It," will be published by the *Michigan Law Review* in 2014.

Bibi van den Berg (1975) has an MA in philosophy (with honours) from Erasmus University Rotterdam, with a specialisation in philosophy of technology and philosophical anthropology. She completed her PhD in philosophy, on the construction and expression of identities in a world of Ambient Intelligence, at the same university in 2009. From 2009 until 2012, she held a postdoc position at the Tilburg Institute for Law, Technology, and Society (TILT) of Tilburg University, where she conducted research in two areas: social, legal and ethical issues in the deployment of autonomous technologies, and questions relating to identity and privacy in online worlds. As of 2012, van den Berg is an assistant professor and research director at eLaw, the Centre for Law in the Information Society of Leiden University. At eLaw she teaches a course on Internet regulation, and conducts research into the philosophical foundations of techno-regulation.

Lucia Vesnic-Alujevic is a researcher in the field of digital communications and online politics. After obtaining her PhD from Ghent University in 2011, she worked as a Visiting Fellow at CES. She currently works as a postdoctoral researcher at the European Commission's Joint Research Centre. Her research interests include political communication, new technologies, online communication and political participation.

Index

CPSIA information can be obtained at www.ICGtesting.com
Printed in the USA
BVOW06*1508310514

354891BV00007B/72/P